IDEAS IN THE MAKING

A SOURCEBOOK FOR

WORLD INTELLECTUAL HISTORY TO 1300

READINGS FROM ANCIENT, CLASSICAL, AND POSTCLASSICAL TIMES

ILLUSTRATIVE EXTRACTS FROM
THE PRIMARY SOURCES
TRANSLATED INTO ENGLISH

SELECTED, ARRANGED, AND EDITED
BY
DAVID MIANO

EXECUTIVE DIRECTOR, *SCHOLA ANTIQUORUM*

SAN DIEGO
COGNELLA
2014

Bassim Hamadeh, CEO and Publisher
Michael Simpson, Vice President of Acquisitions
Jamie Giganti, Managing Editor
Jess Busch, Graphic Design Supervisor
Jessica Knott, Project Editor
Luiz Ferreira, Licensing Associate
Sean Adams, Associate Editor

First published in the United States of America in 2014 by Cognella, Inc.

Trademark Notice: Product or corporate names may be trademarks or registered trademarks, and are used only for identification and explanation without intent to infringe.

Cover image copyright© 2012 by Depositphotos Inc./Dmytro Sukharevskyy.

Printed in the United States of America

ISBN: 978-1-62131-508-7

www.cognella.com   800-200-3908

Contents

THE EARLY CLASSICAL PERIOD (500–200 BCE)   131

THE MIDDLE CLASSICAL PERIOD (200 BCE–200 CE)   221

Preface

This book is designed to set before the student a sufficient amount of documentation to illustrate the most important features of the world's intellectual history. In my own classes, I have observed that students find the study of history far more valuable to them on a personal level when they are given a chance to see how ideas were formulated over time and how those ideas impacted or influenced the future. They thus can perceive more clearly the origins of their own ideas. Specifically I have chosen readings that deal with questions of ethics, morality, justice, community, political philosophy, historiography, and the understanding of the self and of humanity. It is hoped that by examining how the ancients tackled questions related to these issues, students can get a true sense of how thoughts trigger events. They will also begin to see that there have been, and still are, many different ways to look at a particular issue.

This volume has been prepared for beginning students. It is not designed for "hard" study, but for *reading*. It is therefore stripped of the learned notes, citations, references, etc., which are rightly expected by the scholar. The introductions and footnotes serve merely to make the selections comprehensible to readers who have little experience in historical issues. I have chosen deliberately to keep my commentary brief, as I have found that students are inclined to rely heavily on such secondary information when answering questions rather than on what they read in the sources, and I wish to avoid this problem.

This sourcebook should make an excellent daily companion to any standard textbook in World History. Then again, it can stand all on its own. I am aware that some teachers hold the opinion that undergraduates merely need to get an overall picture of history and are not ready to engage critically with primary sources. However, I favor the view that even students who have no plan on becoming historians should begin learning the historical method right away. They need to see exactly how historians do their jobs—how sources fit together to shed light on the past and how those sources must be critically analyzed. In other words, an effective teaching plan will allow the student to *do* history, rather than simply to *hear* history, and one cannot *do* history without source documents. On a utilitarian level, historical exercises can provide the student with invaluable skills: how to find facts, how to evaluate testimony, how to differentiate good information from bad, and how to present a case in a coherent and persuasive way. Not only that, but reading primary sources immerses one in the times being studied. The student who gets ahold of this volume is sure to breathe in more of the atmosphere of the past than from any possible study of a conventional textbook.

In compiling a work of this kind, a great number of translations have been requisitioned from various sources. In order to keep the book affordable, most of these are from the public domain and therefore quite old, but care was taken to make sure that the translations are in step with current research and that they will be easily understood by a modern audience. In many cases I have made alterations to the wording after diligently comparing the translation with more recent ones. One notable series of changes that I have made is the updating of Chinese names from the old Wade-Giles transliteration system to that of the Pinyin, which is preferred today. The translations from the Bible are my own and were made especially for this book.

Because history does not unfold in an organized fashion, professors must impose some sort of artificial organization upon the material in their courses to assist their students in remembering and comprehending the past. However, no two professors are alike, so it would be impossible for me to present these readings in an order that would please everybody. I am aware that some sourcebooks out there are arranged topically, and others geographically. The problem with a topical arrangement is that it usually pleases the editor, but not many others, and it may force an instructor to follow a scheme that he or she is not otherwise inclined to follow. The problem with a geographical arrangement, in my opinion, is that it makes comparative study more difficult. I have chosen instead to run in strict chronological order, what I perceive to be the most neutral form of presentation. The readings can be assigned in whatever order the instructor prefers without doing any damage to the book's pedagogical system.

Some may be curious why I chose to end the book at the year 1300, considering that it is common for the first half of world history sequences at colleges and universities to end at 1500 or 1650. There are plenty of sourcebooks that end at 1500 or later, and I see little reason to add yet another to the list. The value of this text is in its *fuller coverage of earlier sources*. Like most ancient historians, I do not believe that 1500 is a fair dividing line between World History 1 and 2, much less 1650. Typically beginning around 3500 BCE, the first half of a world history sequence must survey 5,000 years of human history (if going to 1500), while the second half of world history need only cover one tenth of that time. This certainly does not do ancient history much justice. Sadly, that is why most sourcebooks for "World History 1" do not provide a sufficiently representative selection of readings from the ancient period. There simply is not enough room! This is a shame, because the roots of our modern culture extend much further back than a few hundred years. Profound influences on various aspects of our lives—social patterns, forms of government, philosophical ideas, law, art, architecture, entertainment—can be traced back not merely centuries, but millennia. If I had my druthers, World History 1 courses would end at 600 CE (the end of the ancient period), but alas, we ancient and medieval historians are outnumbered. A cutoff at 1300 is a compromise and works well in my classes. Speaking approximately, it falls at the end of the High Middle Ages in Europe (just before the Italian Renaissance), the end of the Crusades, the end of the Abbasid Caliphate in the Middle East, the end of the Mamluk dynasty in India, the end of the Mongol Empire across Asia, and the end of the Kamakura period in Japan.

The pedagogical features of this book include source analysis questions at the end of every reading, which can be assigned as homework, and essay questions, placed at the end of the book, for longer writing assignments. The questions have been developed to guide students in working through the sources and to help them cultivate critical analysis skills. Exposure to the sorts of questions historians might ask, and experience in answering them, will shake the students of any assumption that what is printed in a textbook is a series of proven facts. They will be able to see that historical investigation is limited to a weighing of probabilities about the past, rather than a quest for absolute truth.

If, while using this volume, you come across an error of fact in my commentary, or if you otherwise have a suggestion for improvement, please contact me and let me know your thoughts. My email address is dmiano@sdccd.edu.

Happy teaching!
David Miano

Introduction

As a student of history, it is necessary not only for you to learn history, but also to learn how history is learned. How exactly do historians arrive at their conclusions? As you might surmise, they do *not* do so by reading a textbook. History textbooks merely report, in summary form, what the current state of knowledge is. They generally do not tell you where the information came from, nor do they explain how that information has been interpreted. You can get a better sense of what a historian does by reading a scholarly book. What the present volume does, however, is allow you to go even further than that. It is designed to put you into a historian's shoes, to give you a feel for the techniques and guidelines used by historians by doing what they do.

Why is this book full of readings? It is because historical knowledge is built upon the knowledge of previous "knowers." Every historian must turn to the writings of persons from the past in order to gain information. We cannot travel into the past literally, but we can do so in spirit by reading documents from the times. These sources of information must then be evaluated, organized, and interpreted in accordance with a historical method.

Each reading in this book may be used as a *primary* source by a historian or student of history. Primary sources are, generally speaking, the most valuable of all sources, because they come directly from the time and place being studied and may even be written by witnesses of an event or series of events that today's historians wish to understand. Primary sources are to be distinguished from *secondary* sources, which are further removed from an event being studied, either by time or by circumstance. When reading one of the sources in this book, you must keep in mind that, in one sense, it could be functioning as a primary source and in another sense as a secondary source. Be able to discern when it is functioning as one or the other. Yes, it is possible for a source to be both primary *and* secondary. It all depends on the historical question being asked. Thus, for example, if I am reading Sima Qian's account of the reign of King Wu of the Zhou Dynasty, I would consider it a secondary source of information about King Wu, who lived many centuries before the account was written, but a primary source for the first century BCE, when Sima Qian wrote the account. Even though Sima Qian may not directly speak of his own times in his story of King Wu, he may reveal his own ideas and values in the way he tells the story.

A primary source does not interpret or analyze itself. That work is up to the historian, or under the present circumstances, up to you. The sad truth is, the writers of times past often adjust, skew, or even mutilate a story, intentionally or unintentionally, so if you want to find out what really happened, you can't simply take their words at face value. To assist you in analyzing each source, I have provided a brief introduction, which lets you know where and when the source was composed and who may have written it (if such information is available) and even more importantly, questions you can ask yourself about the source. These questions are the sort that a trained historian asks automatically, such as:

- Why was this source written? What is its purpose?
- What unspoken assumptions does the source contain?
- How does the author's gender and socioeconomic background compare to those about whom he or she is writing?

- What biases are detectable in the source?
- How do other sources compare with this one?

As you can see, when a historian reads, he or she is engaged in a kind of dialogue with the text. You also are encouraged to read actively, not passively, the sources provided you in this book. Understand the content, evaluate its usefulness, analyze its significance, and synthesize all that you have read into a coherent picture. Then it is hoped you will begin to appreciate what historians actually do.

The Early Bronze Age
(3300–2100 BCE)

Victory Stela of Naram Sin (Akkadian Empire)

The Early Bronze Age

B.C.E	3200	3100	3000	2900	2800	2700	2600	2500	2400	2300	2200	2100
South America				Norte Chico								
Northeast Africa			Proto-dynastic Period	Egyptian Early Dynastic Period				Egyptian Old Kingdom				
South Mesopotamia			Jemdet Nasr Period	Sumerian Early Dynastic Period							Akkadian Empire	Gutian Period
South Asia								Indus Valley (Harappan) Civilization				

1. The Instructions of Shuruppak

Translated by Jeremy A. Black

The Instructions of Shuruppak comes from the Early Dynastic Period in Mesopotamian history (c. 2900–2270 BCE) and is written in Sumerian by an anonymous author. It consists of sayings that are designed to impart wisdom and virtue and thus falls into the genre called "Instructions in Wisdom." Most works in this genre are presented as if a father is speaking to his son, and the present work is no exception. Here Shuruppak offers sage advice to his son Ziudsura. As far as we know, Shuruppak (translated in the following selection as Shuruppag) is a legendary figure from the ancient Sumerian city of the same name. Ziudsura, his son, is also a prominent character in Sumerian myth, as he is the one who is said to have survived the Great Flood by building a boat, in much the same way as the biblical Noah and the Babylonian Atrahasis/Utnapishtim. The following is a selection of some of the more interesting proverbs. The numbers on the side refer to the line numbers on the original tablets. Use them when citing this source. Ellipses (…) represent lacunae (gaps) in the text where a tablet is damaged.

1. In those days, in those far remote days,
2. in those nights, in those faraway nights,
3. in those years, in those far remote years,
4. at that time the wise one who knew how to speak in elaborate words lived in the Land;
5. Shuruppag, the wise one, who knew how to speak with elaborate words lived in the Land.
6. Shuruppag gave instructions to his son;
7. Shuruppag, the son of Ubara-Tutu
8. gave instructions to his son Ziudsura:
9. My son, let me give you instructions: you should pay attention!
10. Ziudsura, let me speak a word to you: you should pay attention!
11. Do not neglect my instructions!
12. Do not transgress the words I speak!
13. The instructions of an old man are precious; you should comply with them!
14. You should not buy a donkey which brays; it will split your midriff.
15. You should not locate a field on a road; …
16. You should not plough a field at a path; …
17. You should not make a well in your field: people will cause damage on it for you.
18. You should not place your house next to a public square: there is always a crowd there.

19. You should not vouch for someone: that man will have a hold on you;

20. and you yourself, you should not let somebody vouch for you.

21. You should not make an inspection on a man: the flood will give it back to you.

22. You should not loiter about where there is a quarrel;

23. you should not let the quarrel make you a witness.

24. You should not let yourself ... in a quarrel.

25. You should not cause a quarrel; ...

26. ... the gate of the palace ...

27. Stand aside from a quarrel, ... you should not take another road.

28. You should not steal anything; you should not ... yourself.

29. You should not break into a house; you should not wish for the money chest.

30. A thief is a lion, but after he has been caught, he will be a slave.

31. My son, you should not commit robbery; you should not cut yourself with an axe.

32. You should not make a young man best man. You should not ... yourself.

33. You should not play around with a married young woman: the slander could be serious.

34. My son, you should not sit alone in a chamber with a married woman.

35. You should not pick a quarrel; you should not disgrace yourself.

36. You should not ... lies; ...

37. You should not boast; then your words will be trusted.

38. You should not deliberate for too long; you cannot bear ... glances.

39. You should not eat stolen food with anyone.

40. You should not sink your hand into blood.

41. After you have apportioned the bones, you will be made to restore the ox, you will be made to restore the sheep.

42. You should not speak improperly;

43. later it will lay a trap for you.

44. You should not scatter your sheep into unknown pastures.

45. You should not hire someone's ox for an uncertain ...

46. A safe ... means a safe journey.

47. You should not travel during the night: it can hide both good and evil.

48. You should not buy an onager: it lasts only until the end of the day.

49. You should not have sex with your slave girl: she will chew you up.

50. You should not curse strongly: it rebounds on you.

51. You should not draw up water which you cannot reach: it will make you weak.

52. (line unclear)

53. You should not drive away a debtor: he will be hostile towards you.

54. You should not establish a home with an arrogant man:

55. he will make your life like that of a slave girl.

56. You will not be able to travel through any human dwelling

57. without being shouted at: "There you go! There you go!"

58. You should not undo the ... of the garden's reed fence;

59. "Restore it! Restore it!" they will say to you.

60. You should not provide a stranger with food; you should not wipe out a quarrel.

61. My son, you should not use violence; …
62. You should not commit rape on someone's daughter; the courtyard will learn of it.
63. You should not drive away a powerful man; you should not destroy the outer wall.
64. You should not drive away a young man; you should not make him turn against the city.
65. The eyes of the slanderer always move around as shiftily as a spindle.
66. You should never remain in his presence; his intentions should not be allowed to have an effect on you.
67. You should not boast in beer halls like a deceitful man.
68. Having reached the field of manhood, you should not jump with your hand.
69. The warrior is unique, he alone is the equal of many;
70. Utu is unique, he alone is the equal of many.
71. With your life you should always be on the side of the warrior;
72. with your life you should always be on the side of Utu.

124. You tell your son to come to your home;
125. you tell your daughter to go to her women's quarters.
126. You should not pass judgment when you drink beer.
127. You should not worry unduly about what leaves the house.
128. Heaven is far, earth is most precious,
129. but it is with heaven that you multiply your goods,
130. and all foreign lands breathe under it.
131. At harvest time, at the most priceless time,
132. collect like a slave girl, eat like a queen;
133. my son, to collect like a slave girl, to eat like a queen, this is how it should be.

153. You should not beat a farmer's son: he has constructed your embankments and ditches.
154. You should not buy a prostitute: she is a mouth that bites.
155. You should not buy a house-born slave: he is a herb that makes the stomach sick.
156. You should not buy a free man: he will always lean against the wall.
157. You should not buy a palace slave girl: she will always be the bottom of the barrel.
158. You should rather bring down a foreign slave from the mountains,
159. or you should bring somebody from a place where he is an alien;
160. my son,
161. then he will pour water for you where the sun rises and he will walk before you.
162. He does not belong to any family, so he does not want to go to his family;
163. he does not belong to any city, so he does not want to go to his city.
164. He will not … with you, he will not be presumptuous with you.
165. My son,
166. you should not travel alone eastwards.
167. Your acquaintance should not …
168. A name placed on another one … ;
169. you should not pile up a mountain on another one.
170. Fate is a wet bank;
171. it can make one slip.

172. The elder brother is indeed like a father; the elder sister is indeed like a mother.

173. Listen therefore to your elder brother,

174. and you should be obedient to your elder sister as if she were your mother.

175. You should not work using only your eyes;

176. you will not multiply your possessions using only your mouth.

177. The negligent one ruins his family.

178. The need for food makes some people ascend the mountains;

179. it also brings traitors and foreigners,

180. since the need for food brings down other people from the mountains.

181. A small city provides its king with a calf;

182. a huge city digs a house plot.

193. When you bring a slave girl from the hills,

194. she brings both good and evil with her.

195. The good is in the hands; the evil is in the heart.

196. The heart does not let go of the good;

197. but the heart cannot let go of the evil either.

198. As if it were a watery place, the heart does not abandon the good.

199. Evil is a store-room ...

202. A loving heart maintains a family;

203. a hateful heart destroys a family.

204. To have authority, to have possessions and to be steadfast are princely divine powers.

205. You should submit to the respected;

206. you should be humble before the powerful.

207. My son, you will then survive against the wicked.

208. You should not choose a wife during a festival.

209. Her inside is illusory; her outside is illusory.

210. The silver on her is borrowed; the lapis lazuli on her is borrowed.

211. The dress on her is borrowed; the linen garment on her is borrowed.

212. With ... nothing is comparable.

215. One appoints a reliable woman for a good household.

216. A woman with her own property ruins the house.

217. A drunkard will drown the harvest.

242. Nothing at all is to be valued, but life should be sweet.

243. You should not serve things; things should serve you.

246. You should not abuse a ewe; otherwise you will give birth to a daughter.

247. You should not throw a lump of earth into the money chest; otherwise you will give birth to a son.

248. You should not abduct a wife; you should not make her cry.

249. The place where the wife is abducted to ...

254. The wet-nurses in the women's quarters determine the fate of their lord.

255. You should not speak arrogantly to your mother; that causes hatred for you.

256. You should not question the words of your mother and your personal god.

257. The mother, like Utu, gives birth to the man;

258. the father, like a god, makes him bright.

259. The father is like a god: his words are reliable.

260. The instructions of the father should be complied with.

261. Without suburbs a city has no centre either.

262. My son, a field situated at the bottom of the embankments,

263. be it wet or dry, is nevertheless a source of income.

264. It is inconceivable that something is lost forever.

266. To get lost is bad for a dog; but terrible for a man.

267. On the unfamiliar way at the edge of the mountains,

268. the gods of the mountains are man-eaters.

269. They do not build houses there as men do; they do not build cities there as men do.

Think about it.

1. Considering that Shuruppak and Ziusudra weren't real persons, then what do you think the purpose of this document might be?
2. Which parts of these instructions surprise you the most and why?
3. What can we learn about ancient Mesopotamian values from these instructions?

---

c. 2200 BCE

2. The Precepts of Ptah-hotep

Translated by M. Philippe Virey

This work, known also as the Instruction of Ptahhotep and the Maxims of Ptahhotep, is a well-preserved Egyptian text of the "Instructions in Wisdom" genre (known as *sebayt* in Egyptian) containing ethical teachings. As with most texts from this genre, the "instructions" are presented by a father to his son. In this case the father purports to be Ptahhotep, a vizier who had worked under the pharaoh Isesi from the Fifth Dynasty in Egypt's Old Kingdom. It is more likely that it is pseudepigraphal

"The Precepts of Ptah-Hotep," *The Sacred Books and Early Literature of the East, Volume II: Egypt,* ed. Charles F. Horne, trans. M. Philippe Virey, pp. 62–78. Parke, Austin, and Lipscomb, Inc., 1917. Copyright in the Public Domain.

and was written in the Sixth Dynasty (c. 2325–2150 BCE), when the Instructions in Wisdom texts are more likely to have first appeared. It now exists in several versions with some slight differences between them. The oldest is in the Prisse Papyrus, which dates to the Twelfth Dynasty of the Middle Kingdom (c. 1991–1783 BCE). It is also the only complete surviving copy of the text. The Precepts are presented here in their entirety. Ellipses (...) represent lacunae (gaps) in the text where the papyrus is damaged.

Precepts of the prefect, the lord Ptah-hotep, under the Majesty of the King of the South and North, Assa, living eternally forever.

1.   The prefect, the feudal lord Ptah-hotep, says: O Ptah[1] with the two crocodiles, my lord, the progress of age changes into senility. Decay falls upon man and decline takes the place of youth. A vexation weighs upon him every day; sight fails, the ear becomes deaf; his strength dissolves without ceasing. The mouth is silent, speech fails him; the mind decays, remembering not the day before. The whole body suffers. That which is good becomes evil; taste completely disappears. Old age makes a man altogether miserable; the nose is stopped up, breathing no more from exhaustion. Standing or sitting there is here a condition of ... Who will cause me to have authority to speak, that I may declare to him the words of those who have heard the counsels of former days? And the counsels heard of the gods, who will give me authority to declare them? Cause that it be so and that evil be removed from those that are enlightened; send the double ... The majesty of this god says: Instruct him in the sayings of former days. It is this which constitutes the merit of the children of the great. All that which makes the soul equal penetrates him who hears it, and that which it says produces no satiety.

2.   Beginning of the arrangement of the good sayings, spoken by the noble lord, the divine father, beloved of Ptah, the son of the king, the first-born of his race, the prefect and feudal lord Ptah-hotep, so as to instruct the ignorant in the knowledge of the arguments of the good sayings. It is profitable for him who hears them, it is a loss to him who shall transgress them. He says to his son:

3.   Be not arrogant because of that which you know; deal with the ignorant as with the learned; for the barriers of art are not closed, no artist being in possession of the perfection to which he should aspire. But good words are more difficult to find than the emerald, for it is by slaves that that is discovered among the rocks of pegmatite.

4.   If you find a disputant while he is hot, and if he is superior to you in ability, lower the hands, bend the back, do not get into a passion with him. As he will not let you destroy his words, it is utterly wrong to interrupt him; that proclaims that you are incapable of keeping yourself calm, when you are contradicted. If then you have to do with a disputant while he is hot, imitate one who does not stir. You have the advantage over him if you keep silence when he is uttering evil words. "The better of the two is he who is impassive," say the bystanders, and you are right in the opinion of the great.

5.   If you find a disputant while he is hot, do not despise him because you are not of the same opinion. Be not angry against him when he is wrong; away with such a thing. He fights against himself; require him not further to flatter your feelings. Do not amuse yourself with the spectacle which you have before you; it is odious, it is mean, it is the part of a despicable soul so to do. As soon as you let yourself be moved by your feelings, combat this desire as a thing that is reproved by the great.

6.   If you have, as leader, to decide on the conduct of a great number of men, seek the most perfect manner of doing so that your own conduct may be without reproach. Justice is great, invariable, and assured; it has not been disturbed since the age

---

1   Egyptian craftsman god.

of Ptah. To throw obstacles in the way of the laws is to open the way before violence. Shall that which is below gain the upper hand, if the unjust does not attain to the place of justice? Even he who says: I take for myself, of my own free-will; but says not: I take by virtue of my authority. The limitations of justice are invariable; such is the instruction which every man receives from his father.

7. Inspire not men with fear, else Ptah will fight against you in the same manner. If any one asserts that he lives by such means, Ptah will take away the bread from his mouth; if any one asserts that he enriches himself thereby, Ptah says: I may take those riches to myself. If any one asserts that he beats others, Ptah will end by reducing him to impotence. Let no one inspire men with fear; this is the will of Ptah. Let one provide sustenance for them in the lap of peace; it will then be that they will freely give what has been torn from them by terror.

8. If you are among the persons seated at meat in the house of a greater man than yourself, take that which he gives you, bowing to the ground. Regard that which is placed before you, but point not at it; regard it not frequently; he is a blameworthy person who departs from this rule. Speak not to the great man more than he requires, for one knows not what may be displeasing to him. Speak when he invites you and your worth will be pleasing. As for the great man who has plenty of means of existence, his conduct is as he himself wishes. He does that which pleases him; if he desires to repose, he realizes his intention. The great man stretching forth his hand does that to which other men do not attain. But as the means of existence are under the will of Ptah, one can not rebel against it.

9. If you are one of those who bring the messages of one great man to another, conform yourself exactly to that wherewith he has charged you; perform for him the commission as he has enjoined you. Beware of altering in speaking the offensive words which one great person addresses to another; he who perverts the trustfulness of his way, in order to repeat only what produces pleasure in the words of every man, great or small, is a detestable person.

10. If you are a farmer, gather the crops in the field which the great Ptah has given you, do not boast in the house of your neighbors; it is better to make oneself dreaded by one's deeds. As for him who, master of his own way of acting, being all-powerful, seizes the goods of others like a crocodile in the midst even of watchment, his children are an object of malediction, of scorn, and of hatred on account of it, while his father is grievously distressed, and as for the mother who has borne him, happy is another rather than herself. But a man becomes a god when he is chief of a tribe which has confidence in following him.

11. If you abase yourself in obeying a superior, your conduct is entirely good before Ptah. Knowing who you ought to obey and who you ought to command, do not lift up your heart against him. As you know that in him is authority, be respectful toward him as belonging to him. Wealth comes only at Ptah's own good-will, and his caprice only is the law; as for him who ... Ptah, who has created his superiority, turns himself from him and he is overthrown.

12. Be active during the time of your existence, do no more than is commanded. Do not spoil the time of your activity; he is a blameworthy person who makes a bad use of his moments. Do not lose the daily opportunity of increasing that which your house possesses. Activity produces riches, and riches do not endure when it slackens.

13. If you are a wise man, bring up a son who shall be pleasing to Ptah. If he conforms his conduct to your way and occupies himself with your affairs as is right, do to him all the good you can; he is your son, a person attached to you whom your own self has begotten. Separate not your heart from him. ... But if he conducts himself ill and transgresses your wish, if he rejects all counsel, if his mouth goes according to the evil word, strike him on the mouth in return. Give orders without hesitation to those who do wrong, to him whose temper is turbulent; and

he will not deviate from the straight path, and there will be no obstacle to interrupt the way.

14. If you are employed in the larit, stand or sit rather than walk about. Lay down rules for yourself from the first: not to absent yourself even when weariness overtakes you. Keep an eye on him who enters announcing that what he asks is secret; what is entrusted to you is above appreciation, and all contrary argument is a matter to be rejected. He is a god who penetrates into a place where no relaxation of the rules is made for the privileged.

15. If you are with people who display for you an extreme affection, saying: "Aspiration of my heart, aspiration of my heart, where there is no remedy! That which is said in your heart, let it be realized by springing up spontaneously. Sovereign master, I give myself to your opinion. Your name is approved without speaking. Your body is full of vigor, your face is above your neighbors." If then you are accustomed to this excess of flattery, and there be an obstacle to you in your desires, then your impulse is to obey your passion. But he who ... according to his caprice, his soul is ... , his body is ... While the man who is master of his soul is superior to those whom Ptah has loaded with his gifts; the man who obeys his passion is under the power of his wife.

16. Declare your line of conduct without reticence; give your opinion in the council of your lord; while there are people who turn back upon their own words when they speak, so as not to offend him who has put forward a statement, and answer not in this fashion: "He is the great man who will recognize the error of another; and when he shall raise his voice to oppose the other about it he will keep silence after what I have said."

17. If you are a leader, setting forward your plans according to that which you decide, perform perfect actions which posterity may remember, without letting the words prevail with you which multiply flattery, which excite pride and produce vanity.

18. If you are a leader of peace, listen to the discourse of the petitioner. Be not abrupt with him; that would trouble him. Say not to him: "You have already recounted this." Indulgence will encourage him to accomplish the object of his coming. As for being abrupt with the complainant because he described what passed when the injury was done, instead of complaining of the injury itself let it not be! The way to obtain a clear explanation is to listen with kindness.

19. If you desire to excite respect within the house you enter, for example the house of a superior, a friend, or any person of consideration, in short everywhere where you enter, keep yourself from making advances to a woman, for there is nothing good in so doing. There is no prudence in taking part in it, and thousands of men destroy themselves in order to enjoy a moment, brief as a dream, while they gain death, so as to know it. It is a villainous intention, that of a man who thus excites himself; if he goes on to carry it out, his mind abandons him. For as for him who is without repugnance for such an act, there is no good sense at all in him.

20. If you desire that your conduct should be good and preserved from all evil, keep yourself from every attack of bad humor. It is a fatal malady which leads to discord, and there is no longer any existence for him who gives way to it. For it introduces discord between fathers and mothers, as well as between brothers and sisters; it causes the wife and the husband to hate each other; it contains all kinds of wickedness, it embodies all kinds of wrong. When a man has established his just equilibrium and walks in this path, there where he makes his dwelling, there is no room for bad humor.

21. Be not of an irritable temper as regards that which happens at your side; grumble not over your own affairs. Be not of an irritable temper in regard to your neighbors; better is a compliment to that which displeases than rudeness. It is wrong to get into a passion with one's neighbors, to be no longer master of one's words. When there is only a little irritation, one creates for oneself an affliction for the time when one will again be cool.

22. If you are wise, look after your house; love your wife without alloy. Fill her stomach, clothe her back; these are the cares to be bestowed on her person. Caress her, fulfil her desires during the time of her existence; it is a kindness which does honor to its possessor. Be not brutal; tact will influence her better than violence; her ... behold to what she aspires, at what she aims, what she regards. It is that which fixes her in your house; if you repel her, it is an abyss. Open your arms for her, respond to her arms; call her, display to her your love.

23. Treat your dependents well, in so far as it belongs to you to do so; and it belongs to those whom Ptah has favored. If any one fails in treating his dependents well it is said: "He is a person ..." As we do not know the events which may happen tomorrow, he is a wise person by whom one is well treated. When there comes the necessity of showing zeal, it will then be the dependents themselves who say: "Come on, come on," if good treatment has not quitted the place; if it has quitted it, the dependents are defaulters.

24. Do not repeat any extravagance of language; do not listen to it; it is a thing which has escaped from a hasty mouth. If it is repeated, look, without hearing it, toward the earth; say nothing in regard to it. Cause him who speaks to you to know what is just, even him who provokes to injustice; cause that which is just to be done, cause it to triumph. As for that which is hateful according to the law, condemn it by unveiling it.

25. If you are a wise man, sitting in the council of your lord, direct your thought toward that which is wise. Be silent rather than scatter your words. When you speak, know that which can be brought against you. To speak in the council is an art, and speech is criticized more than any other labor; it is contradiction which puts it to the proof.

26. If you are powerful, respect knowledge and calmness of language. Command only to direct; to be absolute is to run into evil. Let not your heart be haughty, neither let it be mean. Do not let your orders remain unsaid and cause your answers to penetrate; but speak without heat, assume a serious countenance. As for the vivacity of an ardent heart, temper it; the gentle man penetrates all obstacles. He who agitates himself all the day long has not a good moment; and he who amuses himself all the day long keeps not his fortune. Aim at fulness like pilots; once one is seated another works, and seeks to obey one's orders.

27. Disturb not a great man; weaken not the attention of him who is occupied. His care is to embrace his task, and he strips his person through the love which he puts into it. That transports men to Ptah, even the love for the work which they accomplish. Compose then your face even in trouble, that peace may be with you, when agitation is with ... These are the people who succeed in what they desire.

28. Teach others to render homage to a great man. If you gather the crop for him among men, cause it to return fully to its owner, at whose hands is your subsistence. But the gift of affection is worth more than the provisions with which your back is covered. For that which the great man receives from you will enable your house to live, without speaking of the maintenance you enjoy, which you desire to preserve; it is thereby that he extends a beneficent hand, and that in your home good things are added to good things. Let your love pass into the heart of those who love you; cause those about you to be loving and obedient.

29. If you are a son of the guardians deputed to watch over the public tranquillity, execute your commission without knowing its meaning, and speak with firmness. Substitute not for that which the instructor has said what you believe to be his intention; the great use words as it suits them. Your part is to transmit rather than to comment upon.

30. If you are annoyed at a thing, if you are tormented by someone who is acting within his right, get out of his sight, and remember him no more when he has ceased to address you.

31. If you have become great after having been little, if you have become rich after having been

poor, when you are at the head of the city, know how not to take advantage of the fact that you have reached the first rank, harden not your heart because of your elevation; you are become only the administrator, the prefect, of the provisions which belong to Ptah. Put not behind you the neighbor who is like you; be unto him as a companion.

32. Bend your back before your superior. You are attached to the palace of the king; your house is established in its fortune, and your profits are as is fitting. Yet a man is annoyed at having an authority above himself, and passes the period of life in being vexed thereat. Although that hurts not your ... Do not plunder the house of your neighbors, seize not by force the goods which are beside you. Exclaim not then against that which you hear, and do not feel humiliated. It is necessary to reflect when one is hindered by it that the pressure of authority is felt also by one's neighbor.

33. Do not make ... you know that there are obstacles to the water which comes to its hinder part, and that there is no trickling of that which is in its bosom. Let it not ... after having corrupted his heart.

34. If you aim at polished manners, call not him whom you accost. Converse with him especially in such a way as not to annoy him. Enter on a discussion with him only after having left him time to saturate his mind with the subject of the conversation. If he lets his ignorance display itself, and if he gives you all opportunity to disgrace him, treat him with courtesy rather; proceed not to drive him into a corner; do not ... the word to him; answer not in a crushing manner; crush him not; worry him not; in order that in his turn he may not return to the subject, but depart to the profit of your conversation.

35. Let your countenance be cheerful during the time of your existence. When we see one departing from the storehouse who has entered in order to bring his share of provision, with his face contracted, it shows that his stomach is empty and that authority is offensive to him. Let not that happen to you; it is ...

36. Know those who are faithful to you when you are in low estate. Your merit then is worth more than those who did you honor. His ... , behold that which a man possesses completely. That is of more importance than his high rank; for this is a matter which passes from one to another. The merit of one's son is advantageous to the father, and that which he really is, is worth more than the remembrance of his father's rank.

37. Distinguish the superintendent who directs from the workman, for manual labor is little elevated; the inaction of the hands is honorable. If a man is not in the evil way, that which places him there is the want of subordination to authority.

38. If you take a wife, do not ... Let her be more contented than any of her fellow-citizens. She will be attached to you doubly, if her chain is pleasant. Do not repel her; grant that which pleases her; it is to her contentment that she appreciates your work.

39. If you hear those things which I have said to you, your wisdom will be fully advanced. Although they are the means which are suitable for arriving at the maat, and it is that which makes them precious, their memory would recede from the mouth of men. But thanks to the beauty of their arrangement in rhythm all their words will now be carried without alteration over this earth eternally. That will create a canvass to be embellished, whereof the great will speak, in order to instruct men in its sayings. After having listened to them the pupil will become a master, even he who shall have properly listened to the sayings because he shall have heard them. Let him win success by placing himself in the first rank; that is for him a position perfect and durable, and he has nothing further to desire forever. By knowledge his path is assured, and he is made happy by it on the earth. The wise man is satiated by knowledge; he is a great man through his own merits. His tongue is in accord with his mind; just are his lips when he speaks, his eyes when he gazes, his ears when he hears. The advantage of his son is to do that which is just without deceiving himself.

40. To attend therefore profits the son of him who has attended. To attend is the result of the fact that one has attended. A teachable auditor is formed, because I have attended. Good when he has attended, good when he speaks, he who has attended has profited, and it is profitable to attend to him who has attended. To attend is worth more than anything else, for it produces love, the good thing that is twice good. The son who accepts the instruction of his father will grow old on that account. What Ptah loves is that one should attend; if one attends not, it is abhorrent to Ptah. The heart makes itself its own master when it attends and when it does not attend; but if it attends, then his heart is a beneficent master to a man. In attending to instruction, a man loves what he attends to, and to do that which is prescribed is pleasant. When a son attends to his father, it is a twofold joy for both; when wise things are prescribed to him, the son is gentle toward his master. Attending to him who has attended when such things have been prescribed to him, he engraves upon his heart that which is approved by his father; and the recollection of it is preserved in the mouth of the living who exist upon this earth.

41. When a son receives the instruction of his father there is no error in all his plans. Train your son to be a teachable man whose wisdom is agreeable to the great. Let him direct his mouth according to that which has been said to him; in the docility of a son is discovered his wisdom. His conduct is perfect while error carries away the unteachable. Tomorrow knowledge will support him, while the ignorant will be destroyed.

42. As for the man without experience who listens not, he effects nothing whatsoever. He sees knowledge in ignorance, profit in loss; he commits all kinds of error, always accordingly choosing the contrary of what is praiseworthy. He lives on that which is mortal, in this fashion. His food is evil words, whereat he is filled with astonishment. That which the great know to be mortal he lives upon every day, flying from that which would be profitable to him, because of the multitude of errors which present themselves before him every day.

43. A son who attends is like a follower of Horus; he is happy after having attended. He becomes great, he arrives at dignity, he gives the same lesson to his children. Let none innovate upon the precepts of his father; let the same precepts form his lessons to his children. "Verily," will his children say to him, "to accomplish what you say works marvels." Cause therefore that to flourish which is just, in order to nourish your children with it. If the teachers allow themselves to be led toward evil principles, verily the people who understand them not will speak accordingly, and that being said to those who are docile they will act accordingly. Then all the world considers them as masters and they inspire confidence in the public; but their glory endures not so long as would please them. Take not away then a word from the ancient teaching, and add not one; put not one thing in place of another; beware of uncovering the rebellious ideas which arise in you; but teach according to the words of the wise. Attend if you wish to dwell in the mouth of those who shall attend to your words, when you have entered upon the office of master, that your words may be upon our lips ... and that there may be a chair from which to deliver your arguments.

44. Let your thoughts be abundant, but let your mouth be under restraint, and you shall argue with the great. Put yourself in unison with the ways of your master; cause him to say: "He is my son," so that those who shall hear it shall say "Praise be to her who has borne him to him!" Apply yourself while you speak; speak only of perfect things; and let the great who shall hear you say: "Twice good is that which issues from his mouth!"

45. Do that which your master bids you. Twice good is the precept of his father, from whom he has issued, from his flesh. What he tells us, let it be fixed in our heart; to satisfy him greatly let us do for him more than he has prescribed. Verily a good son is one of the gifts of Ptah, a son who does even better than he has been told to do. For his master he

does what is satisfactory, putting himself with all his heart on the part of right. So I shall bring it about that your body shall be healthful, that the Pharaoh shall be satisfied with you in all circumstances and that you shall obtain years of life without default. It has caused me on earth to obtain one hundred and ten years of life, along with the gift of the favor of the Pharoah among the first of those whom their works have ennobled, satisfying the Pharoah in a place of dignity.

It is finished, from its beginning to its end, according to that which is found in writing.

Think about it.

1. According to the introduction, what are the sources of good instruction?
2. To what audience are these instructions directed—all Egyptians, or a certain class in particular?
3. What similarities do you see between this document and The Instructions of Shuruppak (reading #1)?

The Middle Bronze Age
(2100–1550 BCE)

Minoan Fresco: "Prince of the Lillies"

The Middle Bronze Age

B.C.E.	2000	1900	1800	1700	1600	1500
South America	Norte Chico					
Mediterranean		Minoan Civilization				
Northeast Africa	1st Intermediate	Egyptian Middle Kingdom				2nd Intermediate
South Mesopotamia	Ur III	Isin Dynasty	Old Babylonian Empire			Kassite Period
South Asia	Indus Valley Civilization				Early Vedic Period	
Central Asia	Oxus Civilization					
East Asia	Xia Dynasty					Shang Dynasty

3. The Code of Ur-Namma

Translated by Martha T. Roth

The Code of Ur-Namma is a legislative document from ancient Mesopotamia written in Sumerian. The text claims to be composed by Ur-Namma (known also as Ur-Nammu), the founder of the Third Dynasty of Ur, who united Sumer and Akkad for the second time in history and reigned circa 2112–2095 BCE. Some scholars suggest that it was published not by Ur-Namma, but by his son and successor Shulgi (c. 2094–2047 BCE), who was known for his administrative reforms. Although we have found three different tablets containing the code, all are damaged. Only the beginning of the text (a prologue and a bit fewer than forty laws) is preserved. What follows is a selection of some of the more interesting laws. Ellipses (...) represent lacunae (gaps) in the text where the tablet is damaged.

Laws

1 If a man commits a homicide, they shall kill that man.

2 If a man acts lawlessly, they shall kill him.

3 If a man detains (another), that man shall be imprisoned and he shall weigh and deliver 15 shekels of silver.

4 If a male slave marries a female slave, his beloved, and that male slave (later) is given his freedom, she (or: he?) will not leave (or: be evicted from?) the house.

5 If a male slave marries a native woman, she/he shall place one male child in the service of his master; the child who is placed in the service of his master, his paternal estate, ... the wall, the house, [...]; a child of the native woman will not be owned by the master, he will be pressed into slavery.

6 If a man violates the rights of another and deflowers the virgin wife of a young man, they shall kill that male.

7 If the wife of a young man, on her own initiative, approaches a man and initiates sexual relations with him, they shall kill that woman; that male shall be released.

8 If a man acts in violation of the rights of another and deflowers the virgin slave woman of a man, he shall weigh and deliver 5 shekels of silver.

9 If a man divorces his first-ranking wife, he shall weigh and deliver 60 shekels of silver.

10 If he divorces a widow, he shall weigh and deliver 30 shekels of silver.

11 If a man has sexual relations with the widow without a formal written contract, he will not weigh and deliver any silver (as a divorce settlement).

13 If a man accuses another man of [...], and he has him brought to the divine River Ordeal but the divine River Ordeal clears him, the one who had him brought (i.e., the accuser) [...] shall weigh and deliver 3 shekels of silver.

14 If a man accuses the wife of a young man of promiscuity but the River Ordeal clears her, the man who accused her shall weigh and deliver 20 shekels of silver.

15 If a son-in-law enters the household of his father-in-law but subsequently the father-in-law gives his wife to his (the son-in-law's) comrade, he (the father-in-law) shall weigh and deliver to him (the jilted son-in-law) twofold (the value of) the pr-estations which he (the son-in-law) brought (when he entered the house).

17 If a slave or a slave woman [...] ventures beyond the borders of (his or) her city and a man returns (him or) her, the slave's master shall weigh and deliver [x] shekels of silver to the man who returned (the slave).

18 If a man cuts off the foot of another man with [...], he shall weigh and deliver 10 shekels of silver.

19 If a man shatters the [...]-bone of another man with a club, he shall weigh and deliver 60 shekels of silver.

20 If a man cuts off the nose of another man with [...], he shall weigh and deliver 40 shekels of silver.

21 If a man cuts off the [...] of another man with [...], he shall weigh and deliver [x] shekels of silver.

22 If a man knocks out another man's tooth with [...], he shall weigh and deliver 2 shekels of silver.

24 If [...], he shall bring a slave woman; if he has no slave woman, he shall instead weigh and deliver 10 shekels of silver; if he has no silver, he shall give him whatever of value he has.

25 If a slave woman curses someone acting with the authority of her mistress, they shall scour her mouth with one sila of salt.

26 If a slave woman strikes someone acting with the authority of her mistress, [...].

28 If a man presents himself as a witness but is demonstrated to be a perjurer, he shall weigh and deliver 15 shekels of silver.

29 If a man presents himself as a witness but refuses to take the oath, he shall make compensation of whatever was the object of the case.

30 If a man violates the rights of another and cultivates the field of another man, and he sues (to secure the right to harvest the crop, claiming that) he (the owner) neglected (the field)—that man shall forfeit his expenses.

31 If a man floods another man's field, he shall measure and deliver 900 silas of grain per 100 sars of field.

32 If a man gives a field to another man to cul-tivate but he does not cultivate it and allows it to become wasteland, he shall measure out 900 silas of grain per 100 sars.

Think about it.

1. This text outlines improper behavior as readings #1 and #2 do, but how does it differ from the earlier readings?
2. How do the legal rights of free persons differ from those of slaves in this law code?
3. How are most crimes punished? What sort of punishments do you not see here?

4. The Cursing of Akkadê

Translated by Thorkild Jacobsen

This composition is a Sumerian poem that tells the story of fall of the Akkadian Empire. It was written by an anonymous author during the Third Dynasty of Ur (c. 2112–2004 BCE), not long after the events it describes were supposed to have happened. The purpose of the poem was apparently to serve as a warning to rulers about the consequences of disregarding the will of the gods. Strangely, while the poem provides a reason for Akkadê's demise, the story as presented in the poem does not appear to describe very accurately what took place. The genre of this poem is difficult to classify, as there are no clear comparable works of the type from the same general time period.

Enlil Gives Akkadê Dominion

When Enlil's frowning brow had killed Kishi,
as were it the bull of heaven,[1]
had felled the house of Uruk land down in the dust,
as one would a great ox,
and Enlil then and there had given Sargon, king of Akkadê,   5
lordship and kingship from south to north—
in those days holy Inanna was building
Akkadê's temple close to be her august home,
set up the throne in Ulmash,[2]

Inanna Organizes Her New Home

Like a young (married) man building a house for the first time,   10
like a young daughter setting up a home,
holy Inanna went without sleep to provision the storehouses with things,
furnish that city with dwellings and building plots,
feed its people superb food,

---

1 A mythological creature thought to be killed in the thunderstorms in the spring. Its bellowing, and the roar of a lion attacking it, were heard in thunder.
2 The main temple of Inanna in Akkadê.

give its people superb water to drink,   15
have the courtyard joyful with (celebrants with) rinsed heads,[3]
have the people sit down in festival grounds,
have acquaintances eat together
and outsiders circle around like strange birds in the sky,
have Marhashi put back in the rolls,[4]   20
have monkeys, huge elephants,
water buffaloes, beasts of faraway places,
jostle each other in the wide streets,
and dogs, panthers, mountain goats,
and *alum* sheep full of long wool.[5]   25

Riches Overflow

In those days she filled Akkadê's stores for emmer wheat with gold,
filled its stores for white emmer wheat with silver,
had copper, tin, and slabs of lapis lazuli regularly delivered into its barns for grain,
while she plastered its grain piles over with mud-plaster outside.[6]

Citizens Made Happy

She gave its old women (the gift of) counsel,   30
gave its old men (the gift of just) testimony,
to its maidens she gave playgrounds,
to its young men she gave arms (worthy) of weapons,
to its little ones she gave a merry heart.
Hand-holding nursing mothers, daughters of generals,   35
were dancing to the *algasurrû* lyre;
the heart of the city was (one) of *tigi*-harps,
its outskirts (of) reed pipes and tambourines,
its quay, where the boats moored,
was (resounding with) jocund shouts.   40

Peace And Prosperity. Lucrative Foreign Trade

All lands lay in safe pastures,
its (Akkadê's) people looked out over pleasant tracts,
its king, the shepherd Naram-Suen,
radiated light flamelike on Akkadê's holy throne dais.
Its city wall—like a great mountain range—abutted heaven,   45

---

3 Washing the hair was a necessity for being ritually clean for the festival.
4 This phrase, which is not altogether clear, probably means subjecting the faraway eastern country of Marhashi and imposing corvée service on it.
5 Signs of the city's far-flung trade.
6 The influx of precious metals and stones was so great that the storehouses for grains had to be used for them, the grain being stored outside in plastered-over piles.

in its city-gates—like unto the Tigris going to the sea—
Inanna opened up the gateways.
From Sumer's own stores barges were towed (upstream).
The Mardu bedouins of the highland, men who knew not grain,
were coming in to her with perfect bulls, perfect kids, 50
the Meluhhans, men of the black mountains,[7]
were bringing down strange goods to her from them,
the Elamites and Subareans[8],
were toting things to her as were they packasses.
All the city rulers, the heads of temples, 55
and the surveyors of the desert fringe,
were bringing in punctually their monthly and new year food offerings.
O how it caused vexation in Akkadê's city gate![9]
Holy Inanna (just) didn't know how to receive (all) those food portions,
but like the citizens she did not tire of the pleasure of finding 60
(store)houses and (storage) plots to keep up with them.

Rebuilding Of Ekur Denied

Upon this fell—as an ominous silence—
the matter of Ekur.[10]
Akkadê became to her fraught with shuddering,
fear befell her in Ulmash, 65
she took her seat out of the city.
Like a maiden who decides to abandon home,
Holy Inanna abandoned Akkadê's temple close,
like a warrior going up against armed might,
she brought (the forces for) fight and battle out of the city, 70
confronted with them murderous foes.

Akkadê Loses Its Kingship And Turns Aggressive

Not five days it was, not ten days it was
(before) Ninurta had the ornament of lordship,
the crown of kingship, the podium, (?) and the throne granted to kingship,
fetched into his (temple) Eshumesha.[11] 75
Utu took advisement away from the city,
Enki took away its wits.
Its halo, that abutted heaven,

---

7 Meluhha is generally believed to be the Indus River Valley Civilization.
8 Elam was the region around Susa in western Iran. Subartu was the area occupied by northern Iraq and eastern Syria.
9 The gate would be a bottleneck for traffic of such magnitude.
10 Denial of permission to build or rebuild a god's temple indicated lack of favor with him. Lack of favor with Enlil, the chief god of the country, the one who bestowed or took away kingship and generally controlled the country's political fortunes, was clearly terrifying.
11 I.e., removed them from Akkadé and took them to Nippur.

An drew up into heaven's inside.
Its holy mooring stakes,   80
that were (firmly) driven in,
Enki pulled (down) into the Apsu.
Its weapons Inanna had carried off.
Akkadê's temple close ended its life
as were it but a little carp in the deep.   85
The city's enemies appeared in front of it;
like a huge elephant it put the neck down,
like a huge bull it lifted the horns,
like a raging basilisk[12] it slithered the head (from side to side),
and, heavy-weight that it was,   90
it went pillaging instead of in combat.

Naram-Suen Has A Vision Of The Future

That Akkadê's royalty was not to occupy a good steady seat,
that nothing whatever that was in store for it was propitious,
that the house would be shaken,
the treasuries dispersed,   95
which Naram-Suen had seen in a dream vision,
he let (only) his heart know,
put it not on his tongue,
spoke of it with no man.

Naram-Suen Tries Penitence

Because of Ekur he dressed in mourning[13]   100
covered his chariot over with a cargo mat,
took down the cabin from his barge,
cut down on his royal requirements.
For all of seven years Naram-Suen persevered,
—who ever saw a king holding (his) head in (his) hands for all of seven years?   105

Loses Patience And Disregards The Omen And Begins Demolishing Ekur

When in (his) seeking an omen about the temple,
building the temple was not in the omen,
and a second time seeking an omen about the temple,
building the temple was not in the omen:
he, to change what had been entrusted to him,   110
denied, O Enlil! what had been told him,

---

12   The term thus translated denotes a much-feared, perhaps mythical, animal classed by the ancients with serpents.
13   This was the normal reaction if temple-building was denied. It was kept up until the omina turned favorable, which they did not do in this case.

scattered what had been put together for him.

He called up his troops and like a bruiser entering the main courtyard,

he balled the hands at Ekur;

like one having (strong) knees bending down to wrestle,   115

he counted the *gigunu*[14] worth but thirty shekel;

like a marauder raiding a town,

he set up big storm ladders against the house.

To dismantle Ekur as were it a great ship,

to remove earth (from it) like one mining a silver mountain,   120

to cleave it as were it a lapis lazuli range,

to make it collapse like a city Ishkur has flooded,

he had great copper axes cast for the temple.

Though (verily) it was not the cedar mountains,

both edges he sharpened on the *agasiliqqu* axes.   125

Cosmic Effects Of Demolition

To its socle he put copper mattocks,

—and the ground settled in the country's foundations.[15]

to its top he put copper axes,

—and with that the temple let the neck sink to the ground like a young man who is killed,

and with it the necks of all lands were let sink to the ground.   130

Its rain-gutters he peeled off,

—and the rains vanished in the sky.

Its doorsills he took down,

—and the decorum of the country changed.[16]

In its "gate in which the grain is not to be cut" he cut the grain,[17]   135

—and with that, grain was cut off from the country's lands.

Into its "gate of peace" he had pickaxes strike,

—and for ail lands their peace became hostility.

Destruction Of Holy Of Holies On Top

In the "grand arch,"[18] like a heavy spring flood,

he made Ekur's (wooden) posts (into splinters) like (fire)wood.   140

Into its holy of holies, the house knowing not daylight, looked the nation,

---

14   The *gigunu* was the temple on the stage tower. It was surrounded by trees.

15   Here and in the following lines the demolishing of the various parts of the temple is having effects—as if by sympathetic magic—on the country and on nature. Apparently the temple was thought of as, in its own right, a fetish for the nation.

16   The sills seem to symbolize restraint

17   Apparently the gate in question had a sacred patch of grain next to it. It may have had a special connection with Ninlil, who was a grain goddess.

18   The arch of the gate to the summit of the stage tower where the holy of holies was located.

and upon the gods' holy bath vessels looked (men of) Uri.[19]
Its *lahamu* (figures)[20] standing along the great supporting terrace and the house,
although they were not men who had committed sacrilege,[21]
Naram-Suen threw into the fire;   145
and for the cedars, cypresses, *supalus,* and boxwoods,
its trees of the *gigunu*[22] he cast lots.

Precious Metals To Akkadê
    Its gold he did up in crates,
    its silver he did up in leather packs,
    with its copper he filled the harbor quay like grain brought en masse.   150
    Its silver the silversmith was (re)shaping,
    its (precious) stones the jeweler was (re-)shaping,
    its copper the metal-caster was pounding (into scrap).
    Though it was not the goods of a sacked city,
    he had big boats moor at the quay by the house,   155
    he had big boats moor at the quay toward Enlil's temple,
    and the goods leave the city.
    As he made the goods leave the city Akkadê's sense left it.
    He was letting the boats pitch in taking off,
    and Akkadê's judgment wavered.   160

Enlil's Revenge: Barbarians Invade
    the roaring storm, hushing the people one and all,
    the risen floodstorm, having none that could oppose,
    Enlil, in (considering) what he would lay waste
    because his beloved Ekur had been laid waste,
    decided to lift his eyes unto the mountains of Gubin,[23]   165
    decided to bring down from it as one the wide(spread) foothill (tribes).
    No likes of the nation,
    not counted with the country,
    the Gutians, knowing no restraints,
    (of) human face, dogs' cunning, monkey's build,   170
    Enlil decided to bring out of the mountains.
    Numerous like locusts they came striding,
    stretched out their arms in the desert for him like gazelle and wild-ass snares,
    nothing escaped their arms,

---

19   The part of southern Mesopotamia north of Nippur. It was later called Akkad.
20   Mythical guardian beings. Here as pictured on metopes. Usually they are represented as naked heroes with the hair in distinctive side curls. Often they carry vessels with flowing water emblematic of rivers, at other times they support doorposts.
21   Burning will have been the typical manner of executing a person who had committed sacrilege.
22   See n. 14, above.
23   Not certainly identified. The homeland of the Gutians was the Iranian mountains northeast of the Diyala region.

nobody did their arms leave.   175
No envoy traveled the road.
No ambassador's boat was passing by on the river.
Enlil's yellow goats had been driven as spoil from the fold,
their herdsmen made to follow them.
The cows had been driven as spoil from their pen,   180
their cowherders made to follow them.
The watch was put in neck-stocks,[24]
footpads sat in ambush on the roads,
in the country's city gates the door leaves were stuck in the mud,
in all lands on the walls of their cities they were crying sore cries,   185
inside the city, not in the wide desert outside, they had the gardens.[25]

The Country Devastated
It being like the days when cities were (first) built,
the great fields carried no grain,
the flooded tracts carried no fish,
the gardens' irrigation beds carried no sirop and wine,   190
for long days rain rained not,
no underbrush grew up.

In those days oil for one (silver) shekel was half a quart,
barley for one shekel was half a quart,
wool for one shekel was half a mina,   195
fish for one shekel filled a ten-quart measure.
Thus they bought at the market rate of their cities.[26]
He who lay down (ill) on the roof died on the roof.
He who lay down (ill) in the house was not buried.
The people from their hunger were coming to blows among themselves.   200
At Kiur, Enlil's great place, dogs banded together;
in the silent streets, these dogs would devour men walking by twos,
dogs would devour men walking by threes,
numerous teeth were strewn about numerous heads tossed around,
teeth were strewn heads sown as seedcorn   205
decent heads were exchanged for crooked heads,
men lay on top of men,
crooks bled from above on blood of decent men.

---

24 I.e., the police were taken captive.
25 Partly for protection, partly because the deserted areas of the city offered room for them.
26 These are exorbitant prices, such as were charged only in times of dire famine.

Nippur Laments

In those days Enlil built out of (scraps) from his great sanctuaries a small reed sanctuary,

between sunrise and sunset its stores dwindled. 210

Old women who were left over from that day,

old men who were left over from that day,

and the chief elegist who was left over from that year,

set up, for seven days and seven nights,

seven harps toward him on the ground, 215

like the firm base of heaven,

and played within them (also) tambourine,

sistron and kettledrum for him (thunderously) like Ishkur.

The old women held not back (cries of): "Woe, my city!"

The old men held not back (cries of): "Woe, its men!" 220

The elegist held not back (cries of): "Woe, Ekur!"

Its maidens held not back (from) pulling out (their) hair,

its lads held not back the pointed knives (lacerating themselves).

Weeping, Enlil's ancestors were placing their supplications on Enlil's holy knees,

in Duku, laden with holy dread,[27] 225

and so Enlil entered the holy "holy of holies" and lay down eschewing food.[28]

The Great Gods Curse Akkadê

At that time Suen, Enki, Inanna, Ninurta,

Ishkur, Utu, Nusku, Nidaba,

and the great gods were trying to calm Enlil's heart,

were making pleas (saying:) 230

"Enlil, may the city that sacked your city be done to as your city was,

that defiled your *gigunu* be done to as Nippur was.

May the one who knew the city turn the head unto the clay-pit (left) of it,

and may the men who knew men (there) not find them in it,

may a brother not recognize his brother, 235

may its maiden be wickedly killed in her home,

may its father cry out bitterly in his house where the wife was killed,

may its doves mourn in their crannies,

may things be thrown at its sparrows in their hiding places,

may it be wary like a frightened dove!" 240

Second Curse

A second time Suen, Enki, Inanna, Ninurta,

Ishkur, Utu, Nusku, and heavenly Nidaba verily spoke,

---

27   Duku, "the holy mound," was a sacred locality. Originally and basically the term designated the plastered-over pile of harvested grain, but it was extended to underground storage generally. Enlil's ancestors—powers for fertility in the earth—were located in Duku.

28   Typical reaction to deep distress.

set their face toward the city,

and were bitterly cursing Akkadê (saying:)

"O city, you rushed at Ekur"   245

—O Enlil, may it come to be!—

"Akkadê, you rushed at Ekur"

—O Enlil, may it come to be!—

"May at your holy city wall, as high as it is,

laments be sent up,   250

may your *gigunus* be heaped up like dust,

may the standing *lahamus*[29] of the upper terrace pitch from it to earth,

like huge lads drunk with wine!

May your clay return to its Apsu,

be clay cursed by Enki!   255

May your grain return to its furrow,

be grain cursed by the grain goddess!

May your wood return to its forests,

be wood cursed by the carpenter god!

May the bull-butcher butcher the spouse!   260

May your sheep-slaughterer slaughter the son!

May the waters wash away your pauper as he finds children (to sell) for money![30]

May your harlot hang herself in the gate of her hostel!

May your hierodule who is a mother,

and your courtesan who is a mother,   265

stab the child!

May your gold have the purchasing power of silver,

May your silver be priced as … ,

May your copper be priced as lead!

Akkadê, may your strong one be cut off from his strength,   270

may he not (manage to) lift the provision sack onto his saddle,

may his arms not enjoy (controlling) your choice (chariot) donkeys,

may he lie (ill) into evening.

May that city die in famine,

may your patrician, who eats finest bread,   275

lie down hungry,

may your man who used to get up from firstfruits eat cutting (?) from his beams,

may he grind with his teeth,

the leather fittings of "the great door of the leather fittings" of his father's house,

into your palace built in joy of heart may anguish be cast,   300

may the "badman"[31] of the deserts of silent tracts howl, howl, and howl from it.

---

29 See above, n. 20.

30 At a guess: as he is looking for babies set adrift on the river by parents unable to feed them.

31 Apparently a term for a demon similar to a banshee.

"Over your consecrated grounds where ritual handwashings are established,

may the fox of the ruined mounds sweep its tail,

in your 'gate of the country' that was established may the sleeper-bird,

the bird (foreboder) of anguish place (its) nest.   305

In your city that, (celebrating) with *tigi*-harps, does not sleep,

that for merriness of heart lies not down,

may Nanna's bull Turesi[32] bellow as were it roaming a desert of silent tracts.

May long grass grow on your canal banks where the boats were hauled,

and may grass, lamentably, grow on your road laid down for chariots.   400

Moreover, may no man pass along your canal banks where boats are hauled,

places where (in future) water is to be drawn,

by splay-horned mouflons and fleet snakes of the mountains (only).

May your central plain growing fine grass grow reeds for lament.

Akkadê, may your waters pouring sweet pour (as) saline waters.   405

May one who has said: 'Let me settle in that city!'

not have pleasant residence there,

who has said: 'Let me lie down in Akkadê'

not have pleasant resting place there!"

Curses Take Effect

Presently under the sun of that day thus it verily came to be,   500

long grass grew up on its canal banks where the boats were hauled,

grass, lamentably, grew up on its road laid down for chariots,

moreover, no man passed along on its canal banks where boats were hauled,

places where water was (now) drawn by splay-horned mouflons and fleet snakes of the mountains (only).

Its central plain growing fine grass grew reeds of lament,   505

Akkadê's water flowing sweet flowed (as) saline waters.

For who had said: 'Let me settle in that city!'

residence was not pleasant,

for who had said: 'Let me lie down in Akkadê!'

the resting place was not pleasant,   600

Akkadê was destroyed!

A praise hymn for Inanna.

---

32   It is not clear just what the bull of Nanna, the moon god, refers to.

Think about it.

1.   According to this poem, why was Akkadê destroyed?
2.   What lesson is this poem trying to convey?
3.   According to this poem, what, in particular, do the gods expect of a ruler?

5. The Man Who Was Tired of Life

Translated by Raymond O. Faulkner

The following is a piece of an Egyptian work in the Wisdom Literature genre sometimes called "The Man Who Was Tired of Life" or "A Dispute between a Man and His Ba." It dates to the Middle Kingdom (c. 2040–1640 BCE) and exists in one surviving document, Papyrus Berlin #3024. The content is a conversation between an unhappy man and his *ba* (a term for one of the souls in a person representing the personality or character). Unfortunately, the beginning of the work is missing. What is preserved of the work is reproduced here in full. Ellipses (...) represent lacunae (gaps) in the text where the papyrus is damaged.

(1) [...] you in order to say [...] their [tongues] cannot question, for it will be crookedness [...] payments their tongues cannot question.

(2) I opened my mouth to my soul, that I might answer what it had said: This is too much for me today, that my soul does not argue with me; it is too great for exaggeration, it is as if one ignored me. Let my soul not depart, that it may attend to it for me [...] in my body like a net of cord, but it will not succeed in escaping the day of trouble. See, my soul misleads me, but I do not listen to it; draws me toward death ere I have come to it and casts me on the fire to burn me [...] it approaches me on the day of trouble and it stands on yonder side as does a [...]. Such is he who goes forth that he may bring himself for him. O my soul, too stupid to ease misery in life and yet holding me back from death ere I come to it, sweeten the West[1] for me. Is it (too much) trouble? Yet life is a transitory state, and even trees fall. Trample on wrong, for my misery endures. May Thoth[2] who

pacifies the gods judge me; may Khons[3] defend me, even he who writes truly; may Re[4] hear my plaint, even he who commands the solar bark; may Isdes[5] defend me in the Holy Chamber, because the needy one is weighed down with the burden which he has lifted up from me; it is pleasant that the gods should ward off the secret (thoughts) of my body.

(3) What my soul said to me: Are you not a man? Indeed you are alive, but what do you profit? Yet you yearn for life like a man of wealth.

(4) I said: I have not gone, (even though) that is on the ground. Indeed, you leap away, but you will not be cared for. Every prisoner says: "I will take you," but you are dead, though your name lives. Yonder is a resting place attractive to the heart; the West is a dwelling place, rowing [...] face. If my guiltless soul listens to me and its heart is in accord with me, it will be fortunate, for I will cause it to attain the West, like one who is in his pyramid, to whose burial a survivor attended. I will [...] over your corpse, so that you

---

1   The destination of the dead, beyond the desert where the sun sets.

2   The moon god, and god of scribes.

3   Another moon god similar to Thoth, used here in parallel.

4   The sun god.

5   A baboon associated with Thoth.

make another soul envious in weariness. I will [...], then you will not be cold, so that you make envious another soul which is hot. I will drink water at the eddy, I will raise up shade so that you make envious another soul which is hungry. If you hold me back from death in this manner, you will find nowhere you can rest in the West. Be so kind, my soul, my brother, as to become my heir who shall make offering and stand at the tomb on the day of burial, that he may prepare a bier for the necropolis.

(5) My soul opened its mouth to me that it might answer what I had said: If you think of burial, it is a sad matter; it is a bringer of weeping through making a man miserable; it is taking a man from his house, he being cast on the high ground, never again will you go up that you may see the sun. Those who built in granite and constructed halls in goodly pyramids with fine work, when the builders became gods their stelae were destroyed, like the weary ones who died on the riverbank through lack of a survivor, the flood having taken its toll and the sun likewise to whom talk the fishes of the banks of the water. Listen to me;

behold it is good for men to hear. Follow the happy day and forget care.

(6) A peasant ploughed his plot and loaded his harvest aboard a ship, towing it when his time of festival drew near. He saw the coming of the darkness of the norther, for he was vigilant in the boat when the sun set. He escaped with his wife and children, but came to grief on a lake infested by night with crocodiles. At last he sat down and broke silence, saying: I weep not for yonder mother, who has no more going forth from the West for another (term) upon earth; I sorrow rather for her children broken in the egg, who have looked in the face of the crocodile god ere they have lived. A peasant asked for a meal, and his wife said to him: There is [...] for supper. He went out to [...] for a moment and returned to his house (raging) as if he were an ape. His wife reasoned with him, but he would not listen to her, he [...] and the bystanders were helpless.

(7) I opened my mouth to my soul that I might answer what it had said:

Behold, my name is detested,
Behold, more than the smell of vultures
On a summer's day when the sky is hot.
Behold, my name is detested,
Behold, more than the smell of a catch of fish
On a day of catching when the sky is hot.
Behold, my name is detested,
Behold, more than the smell of ducks,
More than a covert of reeds full of waterfowl.
Behold, my name is detested,
Behold, more than the smell of fishermen,
More than the creeks of the marshes where they have fished.
Behold, my name is detested,
Behold, more than the smell of crocodiles,
More than sitting by sandbanks full of crocodiles.
Behold, my name is detested,
Behold, more than a woman
About whom lies are told to a man.

Behold, my name is detested,

Behold, more than a sturdy child

Of whom it is said: "he belongs to his rival."

Behold, my name is detested,

Behold, more than a town belonging to the monarch

Which mutters sedition when his back is turned.

To whom can I speak today?

Brothers are evil

And the friends of today unlovable.

To whom can I speak today?

Hearts are rapacious

And everyone takes his neighbor's goods.

To whom can I speak today?

Gentleness has perished

And the violent man has come down on everyone.

To whom can I speak today?

Men are contented with evil

And goodness is neglected everywhere.

To whom can I speak today?

He who should enrage a man by his ill deeds,

He makes everyone laugh by his wicked wrongdoing.

To whom can I speak today?

Men plunder

And every man robs his neighbor.

To whom can I speak today?

The wrongdoer is an intimate friend

And the brother with whom one used to act is become an enemy.

To whom can I speak today?

None remember the past,

And no one now helps him who used to do (good).

To whom can I speak today?

Brothers are evil,

And men have recourse to strangers for affection.

To whom can I speak today?

Faces are averted,

And every man looks askance at his brethren.

To whom can I speak today?

Hearts are rapacious

And there is no man's heart in which one can trust.

To whom can I speak today?

There are no just persons

And the land is left over to the doers of wrong.

To whom can I speak today?

There is a lack of an intimate friend

And men have recourse to someone unknown in order to complain to him.

To whom can I speak today?

There is no contented man,

And that person who once walked with him no longer exists.

To whom can I speak today?

I am heavy-laden with trouble

Through lack of an intimate friend.

To whom can I speak today?

The wrong which roams the earth,

There is no end to it.

Death is in my sight today

As when a sick man becomes well,

Like going out-of-doors after detention.

Death is in my sight today

Like the smell of myrrh,

Like sitting under an awning on a windy day.

Death is in my sight today

Like the perfume of lotuses,

Like sitting on the shore of the Land of Drunkenness.

Death is in my sight today

Like a trodden way,

As when a man returns home from an expedition.

Death is in my sight today

Like the clearing of the sky,

Like a man who [...] for something which he does not know.

Death is in my sight today.

As when a man desires to see home

When he has spent many years in captivity.

Verily, he who is yonder will be a living god,

Averting the ill of him who does it.

Verily, he who is yonder will be one who stands in the Bark of the Sun,

Causing choice things to be given therefrom for the temples.

Verily, he who is yonder will be a sage

Who will not be prevented from appealing to Re when he speaks.

(8) What my soul said to me: Cast complaint upon the peg, my comrade and brother; make offering on the brazier and cleave to life, according as I have said. Desire me here, thrust the West aside, but desire that you may attain the West when your body goes to earth, that I may alight after you are weary; then will we make an abode together.

It is finished from its beginning to its end, just as it was found in writing.

c. 1772 BCE

6. The Code of Hammurabi

Translated by Claude H. W. Johns

The law code enacted by Hammurabi (c. 1792–1750 BCE) of the Old Babylonian Empire in Mesopotamia was composed around 1772 BCE and contains 272 laws. Various copies of it have been found, but the most complete version is on a 7.4-foot-tall finger-shaped diorite stela now sitting in the Louvre. It is written in Akkadian and is the longest text we currently have from the Old Babylonian period. The fact that it was copied in later generations suggests that for some time it was used as a model for conceptions of justice.

Witchcraft and the ordeal by water

§ 1. If a man has accused another of laying a *nêrtu* (death spell?) upon him, but has not proved it, he shall be put to death.

§ 2. If a man has accused another of laying a *kišpu* (spell) upon him, but has not proved it, the accused shall go to the sacred river, he shall plunge into the sacred river, and if the sacred river shall conquer him, he that accused him shall take possession of his house. If the sacred river shall show his innocence and he is saved, his accuser shall be put to death. He that plunged into the sacred river shall appropriate the house of him that accused him.

False witness in capital suit

§ 3. If a man has borne false witness in a trial, or has not established the statement that he has made, if that case be a capital trial, that man shall be put to death.

In civil case

§ 4. If he has borne false witness in a civil law case, he shall pay the damages in that suit.

Judgment once given not to be altered

§ 5. If a judge has given a verdict, rendered a decision, granted a written judgment, and afterward has altered his judgment, that judge shall be prosecuted for altering the judgment he gave and shall pay twelvefold the penalty laid down in that judgment. Further, he shall be publicly expelled from his judgment-seat and shall not return nor take his seat with the judges at a trial.

Burglary and acceptance of stolen goods

§ 6. If a man has stolen goods from a temple, or house, he shall be put to death; and he that has received the stolen property front him shall be put to death.

Dealings with irresponsible persons

§ 7. If a man has bought or received on deposit from a minor or a slave, either silver, gold, male or female slave, ox, ass, or sheep, or anything else, except by consent of elders, or power of attorney, he shall be put to death for theft.

Theft

§ 8. If a patrician[1] has stolen ox, sheep, ass, pig, or ship, whether from a temple, or a house, he shall pay thirtyfold. If he be a plebeian[2], he shall return tenfold, be put to death.

Judgment by default

§ 13. If a man has not his witnesses at hand, the judge shall set him a fixed time not exceeding six months, and if within six months he has not produced his witnesses, the man has lied; he shall bear the penalty of the suit.

Kidnapping

§ 14. If a man has stolen a child, he shall be put to death.

Adduction of slave

§ 15. If a man has induced either a male or female slave from the house of a patrician, or plebeian, to leave the city, he shall be put to death.

Harboring a fugitive slave

§ 16. If a mail has harbored in his house a male or female slave from a patrician's or plebeian's house, and has not caused the fugitive to leave on the demand of the officer over the slaves condemned to public forced labor, that householder shall be put to death.

The capture of a fugitive slave

§ 17. If a man has caught either a male or female runaway slave in the open field and has brought him back to his owner, the owner of the slave shall give him two shekels of silver.

§ 18. If such a slave will not name his owner, his captor shall bring him to the palace, where he shall be examined as to his past and returned to his owner.

§ 19. If the captor has secreted that slave in his house and afterward that slave has been caught in his possession, he shall be put to death.

§ 20. If the slave has fled from the hands of his captor, the latter shall swear to the owner of the slave and he shall be free from blame.

Burglary

§ 21. If a man has broken into a house he shall be killed before the breach and buried there.

Highway robbery

§ 22. If a man has committed highway robbery and has been caught, that man shall be put to death.

§ 23. If the highwayman has not been caught, the man that has been robbed shall state on oath what he has lost and the city or district governor in whose territory or district the robbery took place shall restore to him what he has lost.

§ 24. If a life [has been lost], the city or district governor shall pay one mina of silver to the deceased's relatives.

---

1   A person of a high class.
2   A person of a low class.

Theft at a fire

§ 25. If a fire has broken out in a man's house and one who has come to put it out has coveted the property of the householder and appropriated any of it, that man shall be cast into the self-same fire.

Fraud in ordinary drink-traffic

§ 108. If the mistress of a beer-shop has not received corn as the drink-price of beer or has demanded silver on an excessive scale, and has made the measure of beer less than the measure of corn, that beer-seller shall be prosecuted and drowned.

Connivance at unlawful assemblages

§ 109. If the mistress of a beer-shop has assembled seditious slanderers in her house and those seditious persons have not been captured and have not been haled to the palace, that beer-seller shall be put to death.

Drink-traffic forbidden to votaries

§ 110. If a votary[3], who is not living in the convent, open a beer-shop, or enter a beer-shop for drink, that woman shall be put to death.

Slander of votary or married woman

§ 127. If a man has caused the finger to be pointed at a votary, or a man's wife, and has not justified himself, that man shall be brought before the judges, and have his forehead branded.

Marriage-bonds

§ 128. If a man has taken a wife and has not executed a marriage-contract, that woman is not a wife.

Punishment of flagrant adultery

§ 129. If a man's wife is caught lying with another, they shall be strangled and cast into the water. If the wife's husband would save his wife, the king can save his servant.

Rape of a betrothed virgin

§ 130. If a man has ravished another's betrothed wife, who is a virgin, while still living in her father's house, and has been caught in the act, that man shall be put to death; the woman shall go free.

Suspicion of adultery cleared by oath

§ 131. If a man's wife has been accused by her husband, and has not been caught lying with another, she shall swear her innocence, and return to her house.

Ordeal of water permissible to accused wife

§ 132. If a man's wife has the finger pointed at her on account of another, but has not been caught lying with him, for her husband's sake she shall plunge into the sacred river.

Rights and duties of the wives of those who have been taken captive in war

§ 133. If a man has been taken captive, and there was maintenance in his house, but his wife has left her house and entered into another man's house; because that woman has not preserved her body, and has entered into the house of another, that woman shall be prosecuted and shall be drowned.

§ 134. If a man has been taken captive, but there was not maintenance in his house, and his wife has entered into the house of another, that woman has no blame.

§ 135. If a man has been taken captive, but there was no maintenance in his house for his wife, and she has entered into the house of another, and has borne him children, if in the future her [first] husband shall return and regain his city, that woman shall return to her first husband, but the children shall follow their own father.

Right of a deserted wife to remarry

§ 136. If a man has left his city and fled, and, after he has gone, his wife to his wife has entered into the house of another; if the man return and seize his

---

3 A person in religious service, in this case female.

wife, the wife of the fugitive shall not return to her husband, because he hated his city and fled.

Rights of a divorced woman who has borne children

§ 137. If a man has determined to divorce a concubine who has borne him children, or a votary who has granted him children, he shall return to that woman her marriage-portion, and shall give her the usufruct of field, garden, and goods, to bring up her children. After her children have grown up, out of whatever is given to her children, they shall give her one son's share, and the husband of her choice shall marry her.

Rights of a divorced woman who is childless

§ 138. If a man has divorced his wife, who has not borne him children, he shall pay over to her as much money as was given for her bride-price and the marriage-portion which she brought from her father's house, and so shall divorce her.

§ 139. If there was no bride-price, he shall give her one mina of silver, as a price of divorce.

§ 140. If he be a plebeian, he shall give her one-third of a mina of silver.

Status of a worthless wife

§ 141. If a man's wife, living in her husband's house, has persisted in going out, has acted the fool, has wasted her house, has belittled her husband, he shall prosecute her. If her husband has said, "I divorce her," she shall go her way; he shall give her nothing as her price of divorce. If her husband has said, "I will not divorce her," he may take another woman to wife; the wife shall live as a slave in her husband's house.

Status of a wife who repudiates her husband

§ 142. If a woman has hated her husband and has said, "You shall not possess me," her past shall be inquired into, as to what she lacks. If she has been discreet, and has no vice, and her husband has gone out, and has greatly belittled her, that woman has no blame, she shall take her marriage-portion and go off to her father's house.

§ 143. If she has not been discreet, has gone out, ruined her house, belittled her husband, she shall be drowned.

Marriage with a votary

§ 144. If a man has married a votary, and that votary has given a maid to her husband, and so caused him to have children, and, if that man is inclined to marry a concubine, that man shall not be allowed to do so, he shall not marry a concubine.

§ 145. If a man has married a votary, and she has not granted him children, and he is determined to marry a concubine, that man shall marry the concubine, and bring her into his house, but the concubine shall not place herself on an equality with the votary.

A votary's rights against a maid assigned to her husband

§ 146. If a man has married a votary, and she has given a maid to her husband, and the maid has borne children, and if afterward that maid has placed herself on an equality with her mistress, because she has borne children, her mistress shall not sell her, she shall place a slave-mark upon her, and reckon her with the slave-girls.

§ 147. If she has not borne children, her mistress shall sell her.

Status of a wife afflicted with a disease

§ 148. If a man has married a wife and a disease has seized her, if he is determined to marry a second wife, he shall many her. He shall not divorce the wife whom the disease has seized. In the home they made together she shall dwell, and he shall maintain her as long as she lives.

§ 149. If that woman was not pleased to stay in her husband's house, he shall pay over to her the marriage-portion which she brought from her father's house, and she shall go away.

Wife's right to property deeded to her by her husband

§ 150. If a man has presented field, garden, house, or goods to his wife, has granted her a deed of gift, her children, after her husband's death, shall not dispute her right; the mother shall leave it after her death to that one of her children whom she loves best. She shall not leave it to her kindred.

Marital responsibility for ante-nuptial debts

§ 151. If a woman, who is living in a man's house, has persuaded her husband to bind himself, and grant her a deed to the effect that she shall not be held for debt by a creditor of her husband's; if that man had a debt upon him before he married that woman, his creditor shall not take his wife for it. Also, if that woman had a debt upon her before she entered that man's house, her creditor shall not take her husband for it.

§ 152. From the time that that woman entered into the man's house they together shall be liable for all debts subsequently incurred.

Connivance at husband's murder by a wife

§ 153. If a man's wife, for the sake of another, has caused her husband to be killed, that woman shall be impaled.

Incest with own daughter

§ 154. If a man has committed incest with his daughter, that man shall be banished from the city.

Incest with daughter-in-law

§ 155. If a man has betrothed a maiden to his son and his son has known her, and afterward the man has lain in her bosom, and been caught, that man shall be strangled and she shall be cast into the water.

§ 156. If a man has betrothed a maiden to his son, and his son has not known her, and that man has lain in her bosom, he shall pay her half a mina of silver, and shall pay over to her whatever she brought from her father's house, and the husband of her choice shall marry her.

Incest with mother

§ 157. If a man, after his father's death, has lain in the bosom of his mother, they shall both of them be burnt together.

Incest with step-mother

§ 158. If a man, after his father's death, be caught in the bosom of his step-mother, who has borne children, that man shall be cut off from his father's house.

Penalty for breach of promise

§ 159. If a man, who has presented a gift to the house of his prospective father-in-law and has given the bride-price, has afterward promise looked upon another woman and has said to his father-in-law, "I will not marry your daughter"; the father of the girl shall keep whatever he has brought as a present.

Rights of a rejected suitor

§ 160. If a man has presented a gift to the house of his prospective father-in-law, and has given the bride-price, bat the father of the girl has said, "I will not give you my daughter," the father shall return double all that was presented him.

Slandering rival not to profit by his calumny

§ 161. If a man has brought a gift to the house of his prospective father-in-law, and has given the bride-price, but his comrade has slandered him and his father-in-law has said to the suitor, "You shall not marry my daughter," [the father] shall return double all that was presented him. Further, the comrade shall not marry the girl.

Disposal of a wife's marriage portion

§ 162. If a man has married a wife, and she has borne him children, and that woman has gone to her fate, her father shall lay no claim to her marriage-portion. Her marriage-portion is her children's only,

§ 163. If a man has married a wife, and she has not borne him children, and that woman has gone to her fate; if his father-in-law has returned to him the bride-price, which that man brought into the house of his father-in-law, her husband shall have no claim on the marriage-portion of that woman. Her marriage-portion indeed belongs to her father's house.

§ 164. If the father-in-law has not returned the Id ride-price, the husband shall deduct the amount of her bride-price from her marriage-portion, and shall return her marriage-portion to her father's house.

Effect upon the inheritance of a father's gift to a favorite son

§ 165. If a man has presented field, garden, or house to his son, the first in his eyes, and has written him a deed of gift; after the father has gone to his fate, when the brothers share, he shall keep the present his father gave him, and over and above shall share equally with them in the goods of his father's estate.

Reservation of a bride-price for a young unmarried brother

§ 166. If a man has taken wives for the other sons he had, but has not taken a wife for his young son, after the father has gone to his fate, when the brothers share, they shall set aside from the goods of their father's estate money, as a bride-price, for their young brother, who has not married a wife, over and above his share, and they shall cause him to take a wife.

Inheritance of children in case of two fruitful marriages

§ 167. If a man has taken a wife, and she has borne him children and that woman has gone to her fate, and he has taken a second wife, and she also has borne children; after the father has gone to his fate, the sons shall not share according to mothers, but each family shall take the marriage-portion of its mother, and all shall share the goods of their father's estate equally.

Disinheritance of a son

§ 168. If a man has determined to disinherit his son and has declared before the judge, "I cut off my son," the judge shall inquire into the son's past, and, if the son has not committed a grave misdemeanor such as should cut him off from son ship, the father shall disinherit his son.

§ 169. If he has committed a grave crime against his father, which cuts off from sonship, for the first offence he shall pardon him. If he has committed a grave crime a second time, the father shall cut off his son from sonship.

Status of children by a slavewoman

§ 170. If a man has had children borne to him by his wife, and also by a maid, if the father in his lifetime has said, "My sons," to the children whom his maid bore him, and has reckoned them with the sons of his wife; then after the father has gone to his fate, the children of the wife and of the maid shall share equally. The children of the wife shall apportion the shares and make their own selections.

§ 171. And if the father, in his lifetime, has not said, "My sons," to the children whom the maid bore him, after the father has gone to his fate, the children of the maid shall not share with the children of the wife in the goods of their father's house. The maid and her children, however, shall obtain their freedom. The children of the wife have no claim for service on the children of the maid.

The rights of a widow in personal property

The wife shall take her marriage-portion, and any gift that her husband has given her and for which lie has written a deed of gift and she shall dwell in her husband's house; as long as she lives, she shall enjoy it, she shall not sell it. After her death it is indeed her children's.

§ 172. If her husband has not given her a gift, her marriage-portion shall be given her in full, and, from the goods of her husband's estate, she shall bike a share equal to that of one son.

Her rights in the home

If her children have persecuted her in order to have her leave the house, and the judge has inquired into her past, and laid the blame on the children, that woman shall not leave her husband's house. If that woman has determined to leave, she shall relinquish to her children the gift her husband gave her, she shall take the marriage-portion of her father's estate, and the husband of her choice may marry her.

§ 173. If that woman, where she has gone, has borne children to her later husband, after that woman has died, the children of both marriages shall share her marriage-portion.

§ 174. If she has not borne children to her later husband, the children of her first husband shall take her marriage-portion.

Property rights of the children of slave father and free mother

§ 175. If either a slave of a patrician, or of a plebeian, has married the daughter of a free man, and she has borne children, the owner of the slave shall have no claim for service on the children of a free woman. And if a slave, either of a patrician or of a plebeian, has married a free woman and when he married her she entered the slave's house with a marriage-portion from her father's estate, be he slave of a patrician or of a plebeian, and from the time that they started to keep house, they have acquired property; after the slave, whether of a patrician or of a plebeian, has gone to his fate, the free woman shall take her marriage-portion, and whatever her husband and she acquired, since they started house-keeping. She shall divide it into two portions. The master of the slave shall take one half, the other half the free woman shall take for her children.

§ 176. If the free woman had no marriage-portion, whatever her husband and she acquired since they started ho use-keeping he shall divide into two portions. The owner of the slave shall take one half, the other half the free woman shall bike for her children.

Property rights of the young children of a widow who remarries

§ 177. If a widow, whose children are young, has determined to many again, she shall not many without consent of the judge. When she is allowed to remarry, the judge shall inquire as to what remains of the property of her former husband, and shall intrust the property of her former husband to that woman and her second husband, He shall give them an inventory. They shall watch over the property, and bring up the children. Not a utensil shall they sell. A buyer of any utensil belonging to the widow's children shall lose his money and shall return the article to its owners.

The property rights of a votary

§ 178. If a female votary, or vowed woman, has had given her by her father a portion, as for marriage, and he has written her a deed, and in the deed which he has written her he has not written that she may leave it as she pleases, and has not granted her all her desire; after her father has gone to his fate, her brothers shall take her field, or garden, and, according to the value of her share, shall give her corn, oil, and wool, and shall content her heart. If they do not give her corn, oil, and wool, according to the value of her share, and do not satisfy her, she shall let her field and garden to a farmer, whom she chooses, and the farmer shall support her. The field, garden, or whatever her father gave her, she shall enjoy, as long as she lives. She shall not sell it, nor mortgage it. The reversion of her inheritance indeed belongs to her brothers.

Her right to convey property

§ 179. If a female votary, or vowed woman, has had a portion given her by her father, and he has written her a deed, and in the deed that he has written her has [declared] that she may give it as she pleases, and has granted her all her desire; after her father has gone to his fate, she shall leave it as she pleases; her brothers shall make no claim against her.

Her right of inheritance

§ 180. If the father has not given a portion to his daughter, who is a female votary, or vowed woman; after her father has gone to his fate, she shall share in the property of her father's house, like any other child. As long as she lives, she shall enjoy her share; after her, it indeed belongs to her brothers.

Her proportion of her father's property

§ 181. If a father has vowed his daughter to a god, as a temple maid, or a virgin, and has given her no portion; after the father has gone to his fate, she shall share in the property of her father's estate, taking one-third of a child's share. She shall enjoy her share, as long as she lives. After her, it belongs to her brothers.

Additional privileges of votary of Marduk of Babylon

§ 182. If a father has not given a portion, as for marriage, to his daughter, a votary of Marduk of Babylon, and has not written her a deed; after her father has gone to his fate, she shall share with her brothers from the goods of her father's estate, taking one-third of a child's share. She shall not be subject to duty. The votary of Marduk shall leave it after her to whom she pleases.

Rights of a daughter by a concubine, if provided for by father on marriage

§ 183. If a father has given a portion, as for marriage, to his daughter by a concubine, and has given her to a husband, and has written her a deed; after her father has gone to his fate, she shall not share in the goods of her father's house.

If not so provided for by father

§ 184. If a man has not given a portion, as for marriage, to his daughter by a concubine, and has not given her to a husband; after her father has gone to his fate, her brothers shall present her with a marriage-portion, according to the wealth of her father's estate, and shall give her to a husband.

Adoption of natural son

§ 185. If a man has taken a young child, a natural soil of his, to be his son, and has brought him up, no one shall make a claim against that foster child.

Adoption of child of living parents

§ 186. If a man has taken a young child to be his soil, and after he has taken him, the child discover his own parents, he shall return to his father's house.

§ 187. The son of a royal favorite, of one that stands in the palace, or the son of a votary shall not be reclaimed.

Responsibilities of a craftsman to his adopted child

§§ 188, 189. If a craftsman has taken a child to bring up and has taught him his handicraft, lie shall not be reclaimed. If he has not taught him his handicraft that foster child shall return to his fathers house.

Rights of inheritance of an adopted son

§ 190. If a man has brought lip the child, whom he has taken to be his son, but has not reckoned him with his sons, that foster child shall return to his father's house.

Obligations on discarding an adopted son

§ 191. If a man has brought up the child, whom he took to be his son, and then sets up a home, and after he has acquired children, decides to disinherit the foster child, that son shall not go his way [penniless]; the father that brought him up shall give him one-third of a son's share in his goods and he shall depart. He shall not give him field, garden, or house.

Punishment for the repudiation of adoptive parents

§ 192. If the son of a palace favorite or the son of avowed woman has said to the father that brought him up, "You are not my father," or to the mother that brought him up, "You are not my mother," his tongue shall be cut out.

§ 193. If the son of a palace favorite or the son of a vowed woman has come to know his father's house and has hated his father that brought him up, or his mother that brought him up, and shall go off' to his father's house, his eyes shall lie torn out.

Penalty for substituting one infant for another

§ 194. If a man has given his son to a wet-nurse to suckle, and that son has died in the hands of the nurse, and the nurse, without consent of the child's father or mother, has nursed another child, they shall prosecute her; because she has nursed another child, without consent of the father or mother, her breasts shall be cut off.

Assault on a father

§ 195. If a son has struck his father, his hands shall be cut off.

Graded penalties for assault and battery

§ 196. If a man has knocked out the eye of a patrician, his eye shall be knocked out.

§ 197. If he has broken the limb of a patrician, his limb shall be broken.

§ 198. If tie has knocked out the eye of a plebeian or has broken the limb of a plebeian, he shall pay one mina of silver.

§ 199. If he has knocked out the eye of a patrician's servant, or broken the limb of a patrician's servant, he shall pay half his value.

§ 200. If a patrician has knocked out the tooth of a man that is his equal, his tooth shall be knocked out.

§ 201. If he has knocked out the tooth of a plebeian, he shall pay one-third of a mina of silver.

Brutal assault

§ 202. If a man has smitten the privates of a man, higher in rank than he, he shall be scourged with sixty blows of an ox-hide scourge, in the assembly.

§ 203. If a man has smitten the privates of a patrician of his own rank, he shall pay one mina of silver.

§ 204. If a plebeian has smitten the privates of a plebeian, he shall pay ten shekels of silver.

§ 205. If the slave of anyone has smitten the privates of a free-born man, his ear shall be cut off.

Fatal assault

§ 206. If a man has struck another in a quarrel, and caused him a permanent injury, that man shall swear, "I struck him without malice," and shall pay the doctor.

§ 207. If he has died of his blows, [the man] shall swear [similarly], and pay one-half a mina of silver; or,

§ 208. If [the deceased] was a plebeian, he shall pay one-third of a mina of silver.

Assaults upon pregnant women

§ 209. If a man has struck a free woman with child, and has caused her to miscarry, he shall pay ten shekels for her miscarriage.

§ 210. If that woman die, his daughter shall lie killed.

§ 211. If it be the daughter of a plebeian, that has miscarried through his blows, he shall pay five shekels of silver.

§ 212. If that woman die, he shall pay half a mina of silver.

§ 213. If he has struck a man's maid and caused her to miscarry, he shall pay two shekels of silver.

§ 214. If that woman die, he shall pay one-third of a mina of silver.

Gradation of surgeon's fees

§ 215. If a surgeon has operated with the bronze lancet on a patrician for a serious injury, and has cured him, or has removed with a bronze lancet a cataract for a patrician, and has cured his eye, he shall take ten shekels of silver.

§ 216. If it be plebeian, he shall take five shekels of silver.

§ 217. If it be a man's slave, the owner of the slave shall give two shekels of silver to the surgeon.

Penalties for unskillful operations

§ 218. If a surgeon has operated with the bronze lancet on a patrician for a serious injury, and has caused his death, or has removed a cataract for a patrician, with the bronze lancet, and has made him lose his eye, his hands shall be cut off.

§ 219. If the surgeon has treated a serious injury of a plebeian's slave, with the bronze lancet, and has caused his death, he shall render slave for slave.

§ 220. If he has removed a cataract with the bronze lancet, and made the slave lose his eye, he shall pay half his value.

§ 221. If a surgeon has cured the limb of a patrician, or has doctored a diseased bowel, the patient shall pay five shekels of silver to the surgeon.

§ 222. If he be a plebeian, he shall pay three shekels of silver.

§ 223. If he lie a man's slave, the owner of the slave shall give two shekels of silver to the doctor. Fees for the treatment of the diseases of animals

§ 224. If a veterinary surgeon has treated an ox, or ail ass, for a severe injury, and cured it, the owner of the ox, or the ass, shall pay the surgeon one-sixth of a shekel of silver, as his fee.

§ 225. If he has treated an ox, or an ass, for a severe injury, and caused it to die, he shall pay one-quarter of its value to the owner of the ox, or the ass.

Brander's liabilities

§ 226. If a brander has cut out a mark on a slave, without the consent of his owner, that brander shall have his hands cut off,

§ 227. If someone has deceived the brander, and induced him to cut out a mark on a slave, that man shall be put to death and buried in his house; the brander shall swear, "I did not mark him knowingly," and shall go free.

Builder's fee and liabilities for bad workmanship

§ 228. If a builder has built a house for a man, and finished it, lie shall pay him a fee of two shekels of silver, for each *SAR* built on.

§ 229. If a builder has built a house for a man, and has not made his work sound, and the house be built has fallen, and caused the death of its owner, that builder shall be put to death.

§ 230. If it is the owner's son that is killed, the builder's son shall Ire put to death.

§ 231. If it is the slave of the owner that is killed, the builder shall give slave for slave to the owner of the house.

§ 232. If lie has caused the loss of goods, he shall render back whatever he has destroyed. Moreover, because he did not make sound the house he built, and it fell, at his own cost he shall rebuild the house that fell.

§ 233. If a builder has built a house tor a man, and has not keyed his work, and the wall has fallen, that builder shall make that wail firm at his own expense.

Compensation for defect discovered in a slave after sale

§ 278. If a mail has bought a male or female slave and the slave has not fulfilled his month, but the *bennu* disease has fallen upon him, he shall return the slave to the seller and the buyer shall take back the money he paid.

§ 279. If a man has bought a male or female slave and a claim has been raised, the seller shall answer the claim.

Manumission of native slaves taken captive and bought back by travelling merchant of foreign slaves

§ 280. If a man, in a foreign land, has bought a male, or female, slave of another, and if when lie has come home the owner of the male or female slave has recognized his slave, and if the slave be a native of the land, he shall grant him his liberty without money.

§ 281. If the slave was a native of another country, the buyer shall declare on oath the amount of money he paid, and the owner of the slave shall repay the merchant what he paid and keep his slave. Punishment for repudiating a master

§ 282. If a slave has said to his master, "You are not my master," he shall be brought to account as his slave, and his master shall cut off his ear.

c. 18th century BCE

7. The Epic of Gilgamesh

Translated by Alexander Heidel

Earlier Sumerian poems about Gilgamesh were eventually combined to form an Akkadian epic poem during the Old Babylonian period (c. 18th century BCE). Only a few fragments of it survive. At some time between 1300 and 1000 BCE, a priest by the name of Sîn-lēqi-unninni transcribed a revised version, of which we have found many copies (the best preserved of them from a library at Nineveh in Assyria dated to the 7th century BCE). Since we do not have very much of the earlier version, it is difficult to tell how much Sîn-lēqi-unninni's epic differs from it. What follows is a scene from the epic that takes place soon after Gilgamesh travels beyond the ocean, in search of immortality, to a mystical land where Utnapishtim (also known as Atrahasis) lives. Utnapishtim tells Gilgamesh the story of the Great Flood and how he gained immortality. Ellipses (…) represent lacunae (gaps) in the text where the tablet is damaged.

Tablet XI

Gilgamesh said to him, to Utnapishtim the Distant:
"I look upon thee, Utnapishtim,
Thine appearance is not different; thou art like unto me.
Yea, thou art not different; thou art like unto me.
My heart had pictured thee as one perfect for the doing of battle;
But thou liest (idly) on (thy) side, (or) on thy back.
Tell me, how didst thou enter into the company of the gods and obtain life (everlasting)?"
Utnapishtim said to him, to Gilgamesh:
"Gilgamesh, I will reveal unto thee a hidden thing,

Namely, a secret of the gods will I tell thee.

Shurippak[1]—a city which thou knowest,

And which is situated on the bank of the river Euphrates—

That city was (already) old, and the gods were in its midst.

(Now) their heart prompted the great gods to bring a deluge.

There was Anu,[2] their father;

Warlike Enlil,[3] their counselor;

Ninurta,[4] their representative;

Ennugi,[5] their vizier;

Ninigiku, (that is,) Ea,[6] also sat with them.

Their speech he repeated to a reed hut:[7]

'Heed hut, reed hut! Wall, wall!

Reed hut, hearken! Wall, consider!

Man of Shurippak,[8] son of Ubara-Tutu!

Tear down (thy) house, build a ship!

Abandon (thy) possessions, seek (to save) life!

Disregard (thy) goods, and save (thy) life!

Cause to go up into the ship the seed of all living creatures.

The ship which thou shalt build,

Its measurements shall be (accurately) measured;

Its width and its length shall be equal.

Cover it like the subterranean waters.'

When I understood this, I said to Ea, my lord:

'Behold, my lord, what thou hast thus commanded,

I will honor (and) carry out.

But what shall I answer the city, the people, and the elders?'

Ea opened his mouth and said,

Speaking to me, his servant:

'Thus shalt thou say to them:

I have learned that Enlil hates me,

That I may no (longer) dwell in your city,

Nor turn my face to the land of Enlil.

I will therefore go down to the *apsû*[9] and dwell with Ea, my lord.

---

1   Usually called Shuruppak.

2   The sky god.

3   The storm and weather god.

4   God of war and lord of the wells and irrigation works.

5   Attendant of Enlil.

6   The god of crafts, mischief, water, intelligence, and creation.

7   Probably the dwelling of Utnapishtim.

8   This expression, as shown by the following lines, refers to Utnapishtim.

9   The *apsû*, the place where Ea had his dwelling, was the subterranean sweet-water ocean, from which, e.g., the water of the rivers and marshes was thought to spring forth. But here, in view of all the things Utnapishtim takes along, the reference probably is to the marshy area at the northern shores of the Persian Gulf.

On you he will (then) rain down plenty;

[...] of birds, [...] of fishes.

[...] harvest-wealth.

In the evening the leader of the storm

Will cause a wheat-rain to rain down upon you.'[10]

As soon as the first shimmer of morning beamed forth,

The land was gathered about me.

(*lines 50-53 too fragmentary for translation*)

The child brought pitch,

(While) the strong brought whatever else was needful.

On the fifth day I laid its framework.

One *ikû*[11] was its floor space, one hundred and twenty cubits each was the height of its walls;

One hundred and twenty cubits measured each side of its deck.[12]

I 'laid the shape' of the outside (and) fashioned it.[13]

Six (lower) decks I built into it,

(Thus) dividing (it) into seven (stories).

Its ground plan I divided into nine (sections).[14]

I drove water-stoppers into it.[15]

I provided punting-poles and stored up a supply.[16]

Six *shar*[17] of pitch I poured into the furnace,

(And) three *shar* of asphalt I poured into it.

Three *shar* of oil the basket-carriers brought:

Besides a *shar* of oil which the saturation (of the water-stoppers) consumed,

Two *shar* of oil which the boatman stowed away.

Bullocks I slaughtered for the people;

Sheep I killed every day.

Must, red wine, oil, and white wine,

I gave the workmen to drink as if it were river water,

(So that) they made a feast as on New Year's Day.

I [...] ointment I put my hands.

[...] the ship was completed.

Difficult was the [...].

---

10   Here the original obviously has a play on words, the purpose of which is to deceive the inhabitants of Shurippak to the last moment. This line can also be translated: "He will cause a destructive rain (lit.: a rain of misfortune) to rain down upon you." This evidently is the real meaning of the passage. But Ea knew that the people of Shurippak would interpret these words differently.

11   About 3,600 square meters, or approximately an acre.

12   Placing the Babylonian cubit at about half a meter (see the article by Sachs referred to above), the deck had a surface of approximately 3,600 square meters, or one *ikû*. Utnapishtim's boat was an exact cube.

13   The ship. Utnapishtim now attached the planking to the framework.

14   Each of the seven stories was divided into nine sections, or compartments.

15   This line probably means that he drove wedge-shaped pieces of wood between the seams to help make the boat watertight.

16   *Or*: what was needful (cf. line 55).

17   *Var.*: three *shar*. One *shar* is 3,600. The measure is not given in these lines. Perhaps we have to supply *sûtu*; one *sûtu* was equal to a little over two gallons. Three *shar* would then correspond to about 24,000 gallons.

[...] above and below.

[...] its two-thirds.

Whatever I had I loaded aboard her.

Whatever I had of silver I loaded aboard her;

Whatever I had of gold I loaded aboard her;

Whatever I had of the seed of all living creatures I loaded aboard her.

After I had caused all my family and relations to go up into the ship,

I caused the game of the field, the beasts of the field, (and) all the craftsmen to go (into it),

Shamash[18] set for me a definite time:

'When the leader of the storm causes a destructive rain to rain down in the evening,

Enter the ship and close thy door.'

That definite time arrived:

In the evening the leader of the storm caused a destructive rain to rain down.

I viewed the appearance of the weather;

The weather was frightful to behold.

I entered the ship and closed my door.

For the navigation of the ship to the boatman Puzur-Amurri

I intrusted the mighty structure with its goods.

As soon as the first shimmer of morning beamed forth,

A black cloud came up from out the horizon,

Adad[19] thunders within it,

While Shullat and Ḥanish[20] go before,

Coming as heralds over hill and plain;

Irragal[21] pulls out the masts;

Ninurta comes along (and) causes the dikes to give way;

The Anunnaki[22] raised (their) torches,

Lighting up the land with their brightness;[23]

The raging of Adad reached unto heaven

(And) turned into darkness all that was light.

[...] the land he broke like a pot.

(For) one day the tempest blew,

Past it blew and [...].

Like a battle it came over the people.

No man could see his fellow.

The people could not be recognized from heaven.

(Even) the gods were terror-stricken at the deluge.

---

18   The sun god.
19   Another god of storm and rain.
20   Minor weather gods.
21   Another name for Nergal, the god of the underworld.
22   The judges in the underworld.
23   These two lines perhaps refer to sheet lightning on the horizon; forked lightning, which is accompanied by thunder peals, is attributed to Adad.

They fled (and) ascended to the heaven of Anu;

The gods cowered like dogs (and) crouched in distress.

Ishtar[24] cried out like a woman in travail;

The lovely-voiced Lady of the gods lamented:

'In truth, the olden time has turned to clay,

Because I commanded evil in the assembly of the gods!

How could I command (such) evil in the assembly of the gods?

(How) could I command war to destroy my people,

(For) it is I who bring forth[25] (these) my people

Like the spawn of fish they (now) fill the sea!'

The Anunnaki-gods wept with her;

The gods sat bowed (and) weeping.

Covered were their lips […]

Six days and six nights

The wind blew, the downpour, the tempest, (and) the flood overwhelmed the land.

When the seventh day arrived, the tempest, the flood,

Which had fought like an army, subsided in (its) onslaught.

The sea grew quiet, the storm abated, the flood ceased.

I opened a window, and light fell upon my face.

I looked upon the sea,[26] (all) was silence,

And all mankind had turned to clay;

The […] was as level as a (flat) roof.

I bowed, sat down, and wept,

My tears running down over my face.

I looked in (all) directions for the boundaries of the sea.

At (a distance of) twelve[27] (double-hours) there emerged a stretch of land.

On Mount Nisir[28] the ship landed.

Mount Nisir held the ship fast and did not let (it) move.

One day, a second day Mount Nisir held the ship fast and did not let (it) move.

A third day, a fourth day Mount Nisir held the ship fast and did not let (it) move.

A fifth day, a sixth day Mount Nisir held the ship fast and did not let (it) move.[29]

When the seventh day arrived,

I sent forth a dove and let (her) go.

The dove went away and came back to me;

There was no resting-place, and so she returned.

---

24   Goddess of fertility.

25   *Lit.*: give birth to.

26   *Var.*: at the weather.

27   *Var.*: fourteen.

28   This name could also be read Nimush.

29   In place of the words "held the ship fast and did not let (it) move," in lines 142–44, the original has the sign of reduplication or repetition, which means that the statement is to be completed on the basis of the preceding line. In this instance, the sign of reduplication could be rendered with "etc."

(Then) I sent forth a swallow and let (her) go.

The swallow went away and came back to me;

There was no resting-place, and so she returned.

(Then) I sent forth a raven and let (her) go.

The raven went away, and when she saw that the waters had abated,

She ate, she flew about, she cawed, (and) did not return.

(Then) I sent forth (everything) to the four winds and offered a sacrifice.

I poured out a libation on the peak of the mountain.

Seven and (yet) seven kettles I set up.

Under them I heaped up (sweet) cane, cedar, and myrtle.

The gods smelled the savor,

The gods smelled the sweet savor.

The gods gathered like flies over the sacrificer.

As soon as the great goddess[30] arrived,

She lifted up the great jewels which Anu had made according to her wish:

'O ye gods here present, as surely as I shall not forget the lapis lazuli on my neck,

I shall remember these days and shall not forget (them) ever!

Let the gods come near to the offering;

(But) Enlil shall not come near to the offering,

Because without reflection he brought on the deluge

And consigned my people to destruction!'

As soon as Enlil arrived

And saw the ship, Enlil was wroth;

He was filled with anger against the gods, the Igigi:[31]

'Has any of the mortals escaped? No man was to live through the destruction!'[1]

Ninurta Opened his mouth and said, speaking to warrior Enlil:

'Who can do things without Ea?

For Ea alone understands every matter.'

Ea opened his mouth and said, speaking to warrior Enlil:

'O warrior, thou wisest among the gods!

How, O how couldst thou without reflection bring on (this) deluge?

On the sinner lay his sin; on the transgressor lay his transgression!

Let loose, that he shall not be cut off; null tight, that he may not get (too) loose[32]

Instead of thy sending a deluge, would that a lion had come and diminished mankind!

(Or) instead of thy sending a deluge, would that a wolf had come and diminished mankind!

(Or) instead of thy sending a deluge, would that a famine had occurred and destroyed the land!

(Or) instead of thy sending a deluge, would that Irra[33] had come and smitten mankind!

(Moreover,) it was not I who revealed the secret of the great gods;

---

30   I.e., Ishtar.

31   The gods of heaven.

32   I.e., punish man, lest he get too wild; but do not be too severe, lest he perish.

33   The god of pestilence.

(But) to Atrahasis[34] I showed a dream, and so he learned the secret of the gods.

And now take counsel concerning him.'

Then Enlil went up into the ship.

He took my hand and caused me to go aboard.

He caused my wife to go aboard (and) to kneel down at my side

Standing between us, he touched our foreheads and blessed us:

'Hitherto Utnapishtim has been but a man;

But now Utnapishtim and his wife shall be like unto us gods.

In the distance, at the mouth of the rivers, Utnapishtim shall dwell!'

So they took me and caused me to dwell in the distance, at the mouth of the rivers."

---

34   This name—in reality a descriptive epithet meaning "the exceedingly wise"—is another designation for Utnapishtim.

Think about it.

1. How did Utnapishtim gain eternal life?
2. What was the reason for the Flood?
3. What does this story tell you about the way the ancient Mesopotamians viewed their gods?

---

c. 18th century BCE

8. Enuma Elish

Translated by Leonard W. King

The Enuma Elish ("When on high"), named after its opening words as was the custom in ancient times, is the Babylonian Epic of Creation. It was written in Akkadian most likely during the Old Babylonian period (c. 18th century BCE). Our oldest copies come from the library of the Assyrian king Ashurbanipal at Nineveh (7th century BCE). Parts of the poem are still missing, but we possess most of it. The hero of the poem is the storm god Marduk, chief deity of the city of Babylon. In the following excerpt, the council of the gods invests Marduk with supreme authority, so that he may wage war against their enemy Tiamat (goddess of the deep) and her allies.

Leonard W. King, *The Seven Tablets of Creation, or The Babylonian and Assyrian Legends Concerning the Creation of the World and of Mankind*. Luzac Oriental, 1902. Copyright in the Public Domain.

Then did they collect and go,

The great gods, all of them, who decree fate.

They entered in before Anšar,[1] they filled the Court of Assembly[2];

They kissed one another, in the assembly as they came together[3].

They made ready for the feast, at the banquet they sat;   5

They ate bread, they mixed sesame-wine.

The sweet drink, the mead dispelled their fears[4],

They were drunk with drinking, their bodies were filled.

They were wholly at ease, their spirit was exalted;

Then for Marduk, their avenger, did they decree the fate.   10

They prepared for him a lordly throne-dais[5],

Before his fathers as prince he took his place.

"Thou art chiefest among the great gods,

Thy fate is unequalled, thy word is Anu![6]

O Marduk, thou art chiefest among the great gods,   15

Thy fate is unequalled, thy word is Anu!

Henceforth not without avail shall be thy command,

In thy power shall it be to exalt and to abase.

Established shall be the word of thy mouth, irresistible shall be thy command;

None among the gods shall transgress thy boundary.   20

Abundance, the desire of the shrines of the gods,

Shall be established in thy sanctuary, even though they lack (offerings).

O Marduk, thou art our avenger!

We give thee sovereignty over the whole world.

Sit thou down in might, be exalted in thy command.   25

Thy weapon shall never lose its power, it shall crush thy foe.

O lord, spare the life of him that putteth his trust in thee,

But as for the god who began the rebellion, pour out his life."

Then set they in their midst a garment,

And unto Marduk their first-born they spake: 30

"May thy fate, O lord, be supreme among the gods,

To destroy and to create; speak thou the word, and (thy command) shall be fulfilled.

Command now and let the garment vanish;

And speak the word again and let the garment reappear!"

Then he spake with his mouth, and the garment vanished;   35

Again he commanded it, and the garment reappeared.

---

1   Sky god, father of Anu.

2   as per the translation of Alexander Heidel in *The Babylonian Genesis* (2nd ed., Chicago: University of Chicago Press, 1951), pp. 35-36.

3   Ibid.

4   Ibid.

5   Ibid.

6   Anu is the sky god and (up to this point) king of the gods. Now Marduk takes his place as king.

When the gods, his fathers, beheld (the fulfilment of) his word,
They rejoiced, and they did homage (unto him, saying), "Marduk is king!"
They bestowed upon him the sceptre, and the throne, and the ring,
They give him an invincible weapon, which overwhelmeth the foe.   40
"Go, and cut off the life of Tiamat,
And let the wind carry her blood into secret places."

Think about it.

1. How does Marduk gain his preeminence over the other gods?
2. What authority is he given?
3. Some say that the story is meant to be a metaphor for how the king of Babylon became preeminent over the other kings of southern Mesopotamia. If so, what would this tale tell you of the relationship that existed between the king of Babylon and the other kings?

The Late Bronze Age
(1550–1200 BCE)

Tudhaliya IV (Hittite New Kingdom)

The Late Bronze Age

B.C.E	1500	1400	1300	1200
Central America		Olmec Civilization		
Eastern Mediterrean	Mycenaean (Greek) Civilization			
	Hittite Old Kingdom	Hittite Middle Kingdom	Hittite New Kingdom	
Northeast Africa	2nd Intermediate	Egyptian New Kingdom		
North Mesopotamia		Mitanni		Assyrian Middle Kingdom
South Mesopotamia	Kassite Period			
South Asia	Early Vedic Period			
East Asia	Shang Dynasty			

9. Old Hittite Laws

Translated by Harry A. Hoffner, Jr.

This selection of laws is taken from tablets found at the Hittite capital city of Hattuša in Anatolia. They were first composed during the Hittite Old Kingdom period (c. 1650–1500 BCE) and were copied regularly through the Middle and New Kingdom periods (c. 1500–1180 BCE) with very few changes. We have copies from all three of these periods. There are 200 laws, and they were organized into two series of 100 laws each. They are written in "case law" format (if-then statements: "if a person does this, then this will happen"). Ellipses (...) represent lacunae (gaps) in the text where the tablet is damaged.

1. If anyone kills a man or a woman in a quarrel, he shall bring him for burial and shall give 4 persons, male or female respectively. He shall look to his house for it.

2. If anyone kills a male or female slave in a quarrel, he shall bring him for burial and shall give 2 persons (lit., heads), male or female respectively. He shall look to his house for it.

3. If anyone strikes a free man or woman so that he dies, but it is an accident, he shall bring him fof burial and shall give 2 persons. He shall look to his house for it.

4. If anyone strikes a male or female slave so that he dies, but it is an accident, he shall bring him for burial and shall give one person. He shall look to his house for it.

5. If anyone kills a merchant (in a foreign land), he shall pay 4,000 shekels of silver. He shall look to his house for it. If it is in the lands of Luwiya or Pala, he shall pay the 4,000 shekels of silver and also replace his goods. If it is in the land of Hatti, he shall also bring the merchant himself for burial.

6. If a person, man or woman, is killed in another city, the victim's heir shall deduct 12,000 square meters from the land of the person on whose property the person was killed and shall take it for himself.

7. If anyone blinds a free person or knocks out his tooth, they used to pay 40 shekels of silver. But now he shall pay 20 shekels of silver. He shall look to his house for it.

8. If anyone blinds a male or female slave or knocks out his tooth, he shall pay 10 shekels of silver. He shall look to his house for it.

9. If anyone injures a person's head, they used to pay 6 shekels of silver: the injured party took 3 shekels of silver, and they used to take 3 shekels of silver for the palace. But now the king has waived the palace share, so that only the injured party takes 3 shekels of silver.

10. If anyone injures a person and temporarily incapacitates him, he shall provide medical care for

Law Collections from Mesopotamia and Asia Minor, ed. Martha T. Roth, trans. Harry A. Hoffner, Jr., pp. 217–219, 221–222, 233–234, 236–237. Copyright © 1997 by Society of Biblical Literature. Reprinted with permission.

him. In his place he shall provide a person to work on his estate until he recovers. When he recovers, his assailant shall pay him 6 shekels of silver and shall pay the physician's fee as well.

11. If anyone breaks a free person's arm or leg, he shall pay him 20 shekels of silver. He shall look to his house for it.

12. If anyone breaks a male or female slave's arm or leg, he shall pay 10 shekels of silver. He shall look to his house for it.

13. If anyone bites off the nose of a free person, he shall pay 40 shekels of silver. He shall look to his house for it.

14. If anyone bites off the nose of a male or female slave, he shall pay 3 shekels of silver. He shall look to his house for it.

15. If anyone tears off the ear of a free person, he shall pay 12 shekels of silver. He shall look to his house for it.

16. If anyone tears off the ear of a male or female slave, he shall pay him 3 shekels of silver.

17. If anyone causes a free woman to miscarry, if it is her tenth month, he shall pay 10 shekels of silver, if it is her fifth month, he shall pay 5 shekels of silver. He shall look to his house for it.

****

28a. If a daughter has been promised to a man, but another man runs off with her, he who runs off with her shall give to the first man whatever he paid and shall compensate him. The father and mother (of the woman) shall not make compensation. 28b. If her father and mother give her to another man, the father and mother shall make compensation (to the first man). 28c. If the father and mother refuse to do so, they shall separate her from him.

29. If a daughter has been betrothed to a man, and he pays a brideprice for her, but afterwards the father and mother contest the agreement, they shall separate her from the man, but they shall restore the brideprice double.

30. But if before a man has taken the daughter in marriage he refuses her, he shall forfeit the brideprice which he has paid.

31. If a free man and a female slave are lovers and live together, and he takes her as his wife, and they make a house and children, but afterwards either they become estranged or they each find a new marriage partner, they shall divide the house equally, and the man shall take the children, with the woman taking one child.

32. If a male slave takes a free woman in marriage, and they make a home and children, when they divide their house, they shall divide their possessions equally, and the free woman shall take most of the children, with the male slave taking one child.

33. If a male slave takes a female slave in marriage, and they have children, when they divide their house, they shall divide their possessions equally. The slave woman shall take most of the children, with the male slave taking one child.

34. If a male slave pays a brideprice for a woman and takes her as his wife, no one shall free her from slavery.

35. If a herdsman takes a free woman in marriage, she will become a slave for (only) 3 years.

36. If a slave pays a brideprice for a free young man and acquires him as a son-in-law, no one shall free him from slavery.

37. If anyone elopes with a woman, and a group of supporters goes after them, if 3 or 2 men are killed, there shall be no compensation: "You (singular) have become a wolf."

38. If persons are engaged in a lawsuit, and some supporter goes to them, if a litigant becomes furious and strikes the supporter, so that he dies, there shall be no compensation.

****

163. If anyone's animals go crazy, and he performs a purification ritual upon them, and drives them back home, and he puts the mud (used in the ritual) on the mud pile, but doesn't tell his colleague, so that the colleague doesn't know, and drives his own animals there, and they die, there will be compensation.

164. If anyone goes to someone's house to impress something, starts a quarrel, and breaks either the sacrificial bread or the libation vessel,

165. he shall give one sheep, 10 loaves of bread, and one jug of ... beer, and reconsecrate his house. Until a year's time has passed he shall keep away from his house.

166. If anyone sows his own seed on top of another man's seed, his neck shall be placed upon a plow. They shall hitch up 2 teams of oxen: they shall turn the faces of one team one way and the other team the other. Both the offender and the oxen will be put to death, and the party who first sowed the field shall reap it for himself. This is the way they used to proceed.

167. But now they shall substitute one sheep for the man and 2 sheep for the oxen. He shall give 30 loaves of bread and 3 jugs of ... beer, and reconsecrate (the land?). And he who sowed the field first shall reap it.

****

170. If a free man kills a snake, and speaks another's name, he shall pay 40 shekels of silver. If it is a slave, he alone shall be put to death.

171. If a mother removes her son's garment, she is disinheriting her sons. If her son comes back into her house (i.e., is reinstated), he/she takes her door and removes it, he/she takes her ... and her ... and removes them, in this way she takes them (i.e., the sons) back; she makes her son her son again.

172. If anyone preserves a free man's life in a year of famine, the saved man shall give a substitute for himself. If it is a slave, he shall pay 10 shekels of silver.

173a. If anyone rejects a judgment of the king, his house will become a heap of ruins. If anyone rejects a judgment of a magistrate, they shall cut off his head.

173b. If a slave rebels against his owner, he shall go into a clay jar.

174. If men are hitting each other, and one of them dies, the other shall give one slave.

175. If either a shepherd or a foreman takes a free woman in marriage, she will become a slave after either two or four years. They shall ... her children, but no one shall seize their belts.

****

187. If a man has sexual relations with a cow, it is an unpermitted sexual pairing: he will be put to death. They shall conduct him to the king's court. Whether the king orders him killed or spares his life, he shall not appear before the king (lest he defile the royal person).

188. If a man has sexual relations with a sheep, it is an unpermitted sexual pairing: he will be put to death. They will conduct him to the king's court. The king may have him executed, or may spare his life. But he shall not appear before the king.

189. If a man has sexual relations with his own mother, it is an unpermitted sexual pairing. If a man has sexual relations with his daughter, it is an unpermitted sexual pairing. If a man has sexual relations with his son, it is an unpermitted sexual pairing.

190. If they ... with the dead—man, woman—it is not an offense. If a man has sexual relations with his stepmother, it is not an offense. But if his father is still living, it is an unpermitted sexual pairing.

191. If a free man sleeps with free sisters who have the same mother and with their mother—one in one country and the other in another, it is not an offense. But if it happens in the same location, and he knows the women are related, it is an unpermitted sexual pairing.

192. If a man's wife dies, he may take herj sister as his wife. It is not an offense.

193. If a man has a wife, and the man dies, his brother shall take his widow as wife. (If the brother dies,) his father shall take her. When afterwards his father dies, his (i.e., the father's) brother shall take the woman whom he had.

194. If a free man sleeps with slave women who have the same mother and with their mother, it is not an offense. If brothers sleep with a free woman, it is not an offense. If father and son sleep with the same female slave or prostitute, it is not an offense.

195a. If a man sleeps with his brother's wife, while his brother is alive, it is an unpermitted sexual pairing. 195b. If a free man has a free woman in marriage and approaches her daughter sexually, it is an unpermitted sexual pairing. 195c. If he has the daughter in marriage and approaches her mother or her sister sexually, it is an unpermitted sexual pairing.

196. If anyone's male and female slaves enter into unpermitted sexual pairings, they shall move them elsewhere: they shall settle one in one city and one in another. A sheep shall be offered in place of one and a sheep in place of the other.

197. If a man seizes a woman in the mountains (and rapes her), it is the man's offense, but if he seizes her in her house, it is the woman's offense: the woman shall die. If the woman's husband discovers them in the act, he may kill them without committing a crime.

198. If he brings them to the palace gate (i.e., the royal court) and says: "My wife shall not die," he can spare his wife's life, but he must also spare the lover and 'clothe his head.' If he says, "Both of them shall die," they shall 'roll the wheel.' The king may have them killed or he may spare them.

199. If anyone has sexual relations with a pig or a dog, he shall die. He shall bring him to the palace gate (i.e., the royal court). The king may have them (i.e., the human and the animal) killed or he may spare them, but the human shall not approach the king. If an ox leaps on a man (in sexual excitement), the ox shall die; the man shall not die. They shall substitute one sheep for the man and put it to death. If a pig leaps on a man (in sexual excitement), it is not an offense.

200a. If a man has sexual relations with either a horse or a mule, it is not an offense, but he shall not approach the king, nor shall he become a priest. If anyone sleeps with an *arnuwalaš*-woman,[1] and also sleeps with her mother, it is not an offense.

---

1   displaced person, deportee, forced alien resident.

Think about it.

1.   What similarities and differences do you see between these laws and those of Hammurabi?
2.   What might the differences tell you about the differences in values these cultures had?

10. The Kirta Epic

Translated by Edward L. Greenstein

The Epic of Kirta (also known as the Epic of Keret) is one of three epic texts found at the site of ancient Ugarit in northern Canaan. This long poem, written down by a scribe named Ilimilku in the middle of the 14th century BCE on clay tablets in a Semitic language we call Ugaritic (after the name of the city), tells the story of a royal hero named Kirta. Whether this Kirta was a real person is unknown, though it is interesting that his name is Hurrian, which would associate him with the state of Mitanni of which Ugarit was temporarily a part. There is no mention of the city of Ugarit in the poem (Kirta's hometown is an otherwise-unknown place called Khubur), which might suggest that the story is not of Ugaritic origin. However, many of the gods featured in the poem were those known to have been worshipped at Ugarit. Two excerpted scenes are reproduced below. In the first, the god Baal asks the god El to bless Kirta with children. After this, Kirta does have children, including an important firstborn son, Yassib. The second scene is the final one in the poem. It takes place after Kirta has become very ill and is close to death. Ellipses (…) represent lacunae (gaps) in the text where a tablet is damaged.

Second Tablet

Column II

11–12	Once the party of gods has arrived, Up speaks Almighty Baal:
13–14	"Do not, Kind El the Compassionate, depart!
14–16	Won't you bless the Noble Kirta? Prosper the Pleasant, Lad of El?"
16–18	El holds a cup in his hand,
	A chalice he holds in his right.
18–20	He blesses, yes, blesses his servant;
	El blesses Kirta the Noble,
	Prospers the Pleasant, Lad of El:
21–23	"The wife you have taken, O Kirta,
	The wife to your palace you've taken,
	The girl you've brought into your court,
23–25	Seven children to you she will bear,
	Eight, she will bear to you eight!
25	She will bear you the Lad, Yassib,
26–28	Who'll draw on the milk of Astarte,

Ugaritic Narrative Poetry, ed. Simon B. Parker, trans. Edward L. Greenstein, pp. 24–25, 38–42. Copyright © 1997 by Society of Biblical Literature. Reprinted with permission.

And suck at the breast of Maid Anath,
The wet-nurses of the gods."

Third Tablet

Column V

10–12	"Who of the gods removes illness? Who can dispel a disease?"
12–13	None of the gods will answer him.
13–14	He says it a second, a third time:
14–15	"Who of the gods removes illness? Who can dispel a disease?"
16	None of the gods will answer him.
16–17	He says it a fourth, and a fifth time:
17–18	"Who of the gods removes illness? Who can dispel a disease?"
19	None of the gods will answer him.
19–20	He says it a sixth, and a seventh time:
20–21	"Who of the gods removes illness? Who can dispel a disease?"
22	None of the gods will answer him.
23	So answers Kind El the Compassionate:
24–25	"Stay seated, my sons, on your seats, On your elevated thrones.
25–28	As for me, I'll use skills and create! I'll create a Remover of Illness, A Dispeller of Disease!"
28–29	He fills his hands with soil, With good soil fills his fingers.
29–30	He pinches off some clay.

Column VI Column VI

1–2	"Death, be shattered! Shataqat, triumphant!"
2–3	Shataqat then departs, The house of Kirta she enters.
4–5	(…) she penetrates and enters. (…) she enters, all the way in.
6–7	She swoops like a kite over villages, Swoops like a flyer over towns.
8–9	With a wand she unbinds the knot — And thus the disease from his head.
10	She returns and washes him clean of sweat.

11–12	She opens his throat up for eating,
	She opens his gullet to dine.
13–14	Death—is shattered,
	Shataqat, triumphant!
14–16	He gives a command, Noble Kirta,
	He raises his voice and proclaims:
16–17	"Listen, O Lady Huraya!
17–18	Prepare a lamb I might eat,
	Mutton, that I might dine."
19	Lady Huraya listens;
20–21	Prepares a lamb he might eat,
	Mutton, that he might dine.
21–22	It's only a day, and a second—
	And Kirta returns to his prime.
23–24	He sits on the throne of his kingship,
	Ensconced in the seat of his rule.
25–26	Yassib, too, sits in the palace;
	And his spirit instructs him this way:
27–29	"Go to your father, O Yassib,
	Go to your father and say,
	Declare to Kirta, your sire:
29–30	'Hearken, alert your ear!
30–31	In time of attack you take flight,
	And lie low in the mountains.
32	You've let your hand fall to vice.
33–34	You don't pursue the widow's case,
	You don't take up the wretched's claim.
35–36	Your sickbed is your consort,
	Your infirmity, your company.
37–38	Step down—and I'll be the king!
	From your rule—I'll sit on the throne!'"
39–40	Yassib the Young departs,
	He enters his father's presence.
40–41	He raises his voice and proclaims:
41–42	"Hear now, O Noble Kirta!
42	Hearken, alert your ear!
43–44	In time of attack you take flight,
	And lie low in the mountains.
44–45	You've let your hand fall to vice.
45–47	You don't pursue the widow's case,
	You don't take up the wretched's claim.
47–48	You don't expel the poor's oppressor.

48–50	You don't feed the orphan who faces you,
	Nor the widow who stands at your back.
50–52	Your sickbed is your consort,
	Your infirmity, your company.
52–54	Step down—and I'll be the king!
	From your rule—I'll sit on the throne!"
54	Noble Kirta answers:
54–57	"May Horon crack, my son,
	May Horon crack your head,
	Astarte-named-with-Baal, your skull!
57–58	May you fall at the peak of your years,
	Be subdued while you still make a fist!

Think about it.

1. What is considered a great blessing to Kirta according to this tale, and why might such a blessing have been important in those days, especially to kings?
2. What does Yassib do wrong, and what does he imply about the proper behavior of kings?
3. How is the ending ironic?

---

c. 1340 BCE

11. Great Hymn to the Aten

Translated by E. A. Wallis Budge

This hymn dedicated to the sun god Aten, reproduced here in full, is a product of the reign of the Egyptian New Kingdom pharaoh Akhenaten (c. 1352–1336 BCE), the religious reformer who supplanted traditional polytheism with a new monotheistic cult. The hymn has been found on the walls of several tombs of Akhenaten's capital city, Akhetaten, and is the longest of several Aten hymns that were written at the time. It may have been written by Akhenaten himself. The antiquated English of Budge's translation has been modernized to make for easier reading.

E. A. Wallis Budge, "Great Hymn to Aten," *Tutankhamen: Amenism, Atenism and Egyptian Monotheism*, pp. 122–135. Martin Hopkinson and Company Ltd, 1923. Copyright in the Public Domain.

1

A Hymn of praise of Horakhty, the living one exalted in the Eastern Horizon in his name of Shu who is in the Aten, who lives for ever and ever, the living and great Aten, he who is in the Sed-Festival, the lord of the Circle, the Lord of the Disk, the Lord of heaven, the Lord of earth, the lord of the House of the Aten in Akhetaten, of the King of the South and the North, who lives in Truth, lord of the Two Lands (i.e., Egypt), Nefer-kheperu-Ra Wa-en-Ra, the son of Ra, who lives in Truth, Lord of Crowns, Akhenaten, great in the period of his life, and of the great royal woman whom he loves, Lady of the Two Lands, Nefer-nefru-Aten Nefertiti, who lives in health and youth for ever and ever.

2

He says: Your rising is beautiful in the horizon of heaven, O Aten, ordainer of life. You shoot up in the horizon of the East, you fill every land with your beneficence. You are beautiful and great and sparkling, and exalted above every land. Your arrows (i.e., rays) envelop (i.e., penetrate) everywhere all the lands which you have made.

3

You are as Ra. You bring them according to their number, you subdue them for your beloved son. You yourself are afar off, but your beams are upon the earth; you are in their faces, they admire your go-ings. You set in the horizon of the west, the earth is in darkness, in the form of death. Men lie down in a booth wrapped up in cloths, one eye cannot see its fellow. If all their possessions, which are under their heads, be carried away they perceive it not.

4

Every lion emerges from his lair, all the creeping things bite, darkness is a warm retreat. The land is in silence. He who made them has set in his horizon. The earth becomes light, you shoot up in the hori-zon, shining in the Aten in the day, you scatter the darkness. You send out your arrows (i.e., rays), the Two Lands make festival, men wake up, stand upon their feet, it is you who raises them up. They wash their members, they take their apparel

5

and array themselves therein, their hands are stretched out in praise at your rising, throughout the land they do their works. Beasts and cattle of all kinds settle down upon the pastures, shrubs and vegetables flourish, the feathered fowl fly about over their marshes, their feathers praising your Ka (per-son). All the cattle rise up on their legs, creatures that fly and insects of all kinds

6

spring into life, when you rise up on them. The boats drop down and sail up the river, likewise every road opens (or shows itself) at your rising, the fish in the river swim towards your face, your beams are in the depths of the Great Green (i.e., the Mediterranean and Red Seas). You make offspring to take form in women, creating seed in men. You make the son to live in the womb of his mother, making him to be quiet that he cries not; you are a nurse

7

in the womb, giving breath to vivify that which he has made. When he drops from the womb ... on the day of his birth he opens his mouth in the ordi-nary manner, you provide his sustenance. The young bird in the egg speaks in the shell, you give breath to him inside it to make him to live. You make for him his mature form so that he can crack the shell being inside the egg. He comes forth from the egg, he chirps with all his might, when he has come forth from it (the egg), he walks on his two feet. O how many are the things which you have made! They are hidden from the face, O

8

One God, like whom there is no other. You did create the earth by your heart (or will), you alone ex-isting, men and women, cattle, beasts of every kind that are upon the earth, and that move upon feet (or legs), all the creatures that are in the sky and that fly with their wings, and the deserts of Syria and Kush (Nubia), and the Land of Egypt. You set every person in his place. You provide their daily food, every man having the portion allotted to him, you compute the duration of his life. Their tongues are different in speech, their characteristics (or forms), and

9

likewise their skins in colour, giving distinguishing marks to the dwellers in foreign lands. You make Hapi (the Nile) in the Tuat (Underworld), you bring it when you wish to make mortals to live, inasmuch as you have made them for yourself, their Lord who supports them to the uttermost, O Lord of every land, you shine upon them, O Aten of the day, great one of majesty. You make the life of all remote lands. You set a Nile in heaven, which comes down to them.

10

It makes a flood on the mountains like the Great Green Sea, it makes to be watered their fields in their villages. How beneficent are your plans, O Lord of Eternity! A Nile in heaven art you for the dwellers in the foreign lands (or deserts), and for all the beasts of the desert that go upon feet (or legs). Hapi (the Nile) comes from the Tuat for the land of Egypt. Your beams nourish every field; you rise up and they live, they germinate for you. You make the Seasons to develop everything that you have made:

11

The season of Pert (i.e., Nov. 16-March 16) so that they may refresh themselves, and the season Heh (i.e., March 16-Nov. 16) in order to taste you. You have made the heaven which is remote that you may shine therein and look upon everything that you have made. Your being is one, you shine (or, shoot up) among your creatures as the Living Aten, rising, shining, departing afar off, returning. You have made millions of creations (or, evolutions) from your one self (viz.) towns and cities, villages, fields, roads and river. Every eye (i.e., all men) beholds you confronting it. You are the Aten of the day at its zenith.

12

At your departure your eye ... you created their faces so that you might not see. ... one you made ... You are in my heart. There is no other who knows you except your son Nefer-kheperu-Ra Wa-en-Ra (Akhenaten). You have made him wise to understand your plans and your power. The earth came into being by your hand, even as you have created them (i.e., men). You rise, they live; you set, they die. As for you, there is duration of life in your members, life is in you. All eyes gaze upon

13

your beauties until you set, when all labours are relinquished. You set in the West, you rise, making to flourish ... for the King. Every man who stands on his foot, since you laid the foundation of the earth, you have raised up for your son who came forth from your body, the King of the South and the North, Living in Truth, Lord of Crowns, Akhenaten, great in the duration of his life and for the Royal Wife, great of majesty, Lady of the Two Lands, Nefer-nefru-Aten Nefertiti, living and young for ever and ever.

Think about it.

1. Why, according to the poem, does Aten deserve to be praised as the supreme deity?
2. What role does the pharaoh Akhenaten play in Aten's universe?

12. Middle Assyrian Laws

Translated by Godfrey R. Driver and John C. Miles

This selection of laws comes from a group of tablets found at the site of ancient Assur. They are written in the Assyrian dialect of Akkadian and appear to have been published during the reign of Tiglath-pileser I (c. 1115–1077 BCE). However, it is likely that they are copies of originals composed in the early part of the Middle Assyrian period (c. 1365–1208 BCE). The laws presented here are from Tablet A and concern crimes related to women. They provide us with an interesting glimpse of women's rights in ancient Assyria.

~ 1 If a woman, whether a married woman, or a lady by birth, has entered a temple and has stolen from the temple anything belonging to the sanctuary (and) it has been found in her hand, whether charge or proof has been brought against her, the stolen proof shall be taken and enquiry shall be made of the god; as he orders the woman to be treated, she shall be treated.

~ 2 If a woman, whether a married woman or a lady by birth, has uttered blasphemy or spoken sedition, that woman shall bear her liability; her husband (and) her sons (and) her daughters shall not be touched.

~ 3 If a man either is ill or has died (and) his wife has stolen anything from his house (and) delivered it either to a man or to a woman or to any other (free) person, the man's wife and also the receivers shall be put to death. And, if a married woman, whose husband is alive and well, has stolen anything from her husband's house (and) delivered (it) either to a man or to a woman or to any other (free) person, the man shall charge his wife and shall inflict a punishment, and the receiver who has received the stolen property from the hand of the man's wife shall give up the stolen property, and the same punishment as the man has inflicted on his wife shall be inflicted on the receiver.

~4 If either a slave or a slave-girl has received anything from the hand of a married woman, the nose and the ears of the slave or slave-girl shall be cut off, (and thereby) (the theft of) the stolen property shall be requited; the man shall cut off his wife's ears. Or, if the man has let his wife go free (and) has not cut off her ears, (the nose and ears) of the slave or the slave-girl shall not be cut off and (the theft of) the stolen property shall not be requited.

~5 If a married woman has stolen anything from any other man's house and has taken property exceeding the value of 5 manehs of lead, the owner of the stolen property shall swear, saying: 'On my oath! I did not let her take (it' and) saying: '(There has been) a theft from my house.' If her husband compounds, he shall give up the stolen property and ransom her, (and) he shall cut off her ears. If her husband does not compound for her ransom, the owner of the stolen property shall take her and shall cut off her nose.

~ 6 If a married woman has made a pawn away from home, the receiver shall be liable for (the theft of) the stolen property.

~ 7 If a woman has laid hand on a man (and) a charge has been brought against her, she shall pay 30 manehs of lead (and) shall be beaten 20 stripes with rods.

~ 8 If a woman has crushed a man's testicle in an affray, one of her fingers shall be cut off; and if, although a physician has bound it up, the second testicle is affected with it and becomes inflamed, or if she has crushed the second testicle in the affray, both her nipples shall be torn out.

~ 9 If a man has laid a hand upon a married woman and has treated her as a young child (and) charge (and) proof have been brought against him, one of his fingers shall be cut off. If he has kissed her, the edge of the blade of an axe shall be drawn along his lower lip (and) it shall be cut off.

~ 10 If either a man or a woman has entered a man's house and has killed either a man or a woman, the murderers shall be given up to the owner of the house; if he chooses, they shall be put to death, (or), if he chooses, he may make a composition (and) take any of their property. Or if the murderers have nothing to give in (their) house, either a son or a daughter ... in the house ... who ...

~ 12 If a married woman has passed along the (public) streets (and) a man has seized her (and) said to her: 'Let me lie with thee', (if) she does not consent (and) strenuously defends herself but by force he takes her (and) lies with her, whether he has been found upon the married woman or witnesses have brought a charge against him of having lain with the woman, the man shall be put to death; for the woman there is no punishment.

~ 13 If a married woman has come out of her house and gone to a man, where he is dwelling, (if) he has lain with her (and) knew that she was a married woman, the man and also the woman shall be put to death.

~ 14 If a man has lain with a married woman either in a temple brothel or in the (public) street (and) knew that she was a married woman, the man who lay with her shall be treated as the (married) man declares that his wife shall be treated. If the man who lay with her did not know that she was a married woman (and) has lain with her, he is quit; the (married) man shall charge his wife and shall treat her as he will.

~ 15 If a man has caught a man with his wife (and) charge (and) proof have been brought against him, both of them shall surely be put to death; there is no liability therefor. If he has taken and brought (him) either before the king or before the judges (and) charge (and) proof have been brought against him, if the woman's husband puts his wife to death, then he shall put the man to death; (but) if he has cut off his wife's nose, he shall make the man a eunuch and the whole of his face shall be mutilated. Or, if he has allowed his wife to go free, the man shall be allowed to go free.

~ 16 If a man has lain with a married woman, (having been deceived) by her crafty words, there is no punishment for the man; the (married) man shall inflict a punishment on his wife as he will. But if he (has gone further and) has lain with her by force (and) charge (and) proof have been brought against him, his punishment shall be as that of the married woman.

~ 17 If a man has spoken to a man, saying: 'Thy wife is behaving as a (common) whore', (and) there are no witnesses, they shall make a covenant (and) go to the (ordeal by) river.

~ 18 If a man has spoken to his neighbour either secretly or in a quarrel, saying: 'Thy wife has behaved as a (common) whore' (and) saying: 'I myself will charge her', (if) he cannot bring a (definite) charge against (her and therefore) has not charged (her), that man shall be beaten 40 blows with rods (and) shall do labour for the king for 1 full month; he shall be cut off and shall pay 1 talent of lead.

~ 19 If a man has secretly defamed his neighbour, saying: 'He is a (common) catamite', or has spoken to him in a quarrel in the presence of (other) people, saying: 'Thou art being used as a catamite' (and) saying: 'I myself will charge thee', (if) he cannot bring a (definite) charge against (him and therefore) has not charged (him), that man shall be beaten 50 blows with rods (and) shall do labour for the king for 1 full month; he shall be cut off and shall pay 1 talent of lead.

~ 20 If a man has defiled his neighbor (and) charge (and) proof have been brought against him, he shall be defiled (and) made a eunuch.

~ 21 If a man has struck a lady by birth and has caused her to cast the fruit of her womb (and) charge (and) proof have been brought against him, he shall pay 2 talents 30 manehs of lead; he shall be beaten 50 blows with rods (and) shall do labour for the king for 1 full month.

~ 22 If a man (who is) neither her father nor her brother nor her son but any other (man) has caused a married woman to take a (trading) journey and did not know that she was a married woman, he shall verily swear (to this), and he shall pay 2 talents of lead to the woman's husband. If he knew that she was a married woman, he shall pay (these) damages and shall swear, saying: 'On my oath! I have not lain with her'. But, if the married woman (then) has spoken, saying: 'He has lain with me', although the man has paid the damages to the (other) man, he shall go to the (ordeal by) river without any covenant; if he declines the (ordeal by) river, he himself shall be treated as the woman's husband has treated his wife.

~ 23 If a married woman has taken any (other) married woman into her house (and) has delivered her to a man for (the purpose of) adultery, and the man knew that she was a married woman, he shall be treated as one who has committed adultery with a married woman and the procuress shall be treated as the woman's husband has treated his adulterous wife. Or, if the woman's husband does no-thing to his adulterous wife, nothing shall be done to the adulterer or the procuress; they shall be allowed to go free. Or, if the married woman did not know (what was intended), but the (other) woman, who took her into her house, by threats brought a man to her and he has lain with her, if the woman, when she goes out of the house, has made complaint that she has been ravished, she shall be allowed to go free; she is quit. The adulterer and the procuress shall be put to death. But, if the woman has not made complaint, the (married) man shall inflict (such) punishment on his wife as he will; the adulterer and the procuress shall be put to death.

~ 24 If a married woman has run away from her husband (and) has entered an Assyrian('s) house, whether it is within that city (where her husband lives) or (in one) of the neighbouring cities where he has appointed a house for her, (and) she has stayed with the mistress of the house (and) has passed the night (there) three (or) four times, (and) the master of the house did not know that a married woman was staying in his house, (then, if) afterwards that woman is caught, the master of the house whose wife has run away from him shall mutilate his wife and take her (back). The married woman with whom his wife stayed shall have her ears cut off; if he pleases, her husband shall pay 3 talents 30 manehs of lead as the price for her or, if he pleases, she shall be taken (away). But, if the owner of the house knew that the married woman was staying in his house with his wife, he shall pay the 'third'. But, if he has denied (it and) says: 'I did not indeed know', they shall go to the (ordeal by) river; and if the man in whose house the married woman was staying has declined the (ordeal by) river, he shall pay the 'third'; (but) he goes quit (and) will (be deemed to) have fulfilled the whole (ordeal) of the river, if the man whose wife has run away from him has declined the (ordeal by) river. Or, if the man whose wife has run away from him has not mutilated his wife but takes (back) his wife, there is not any punishment (inflicted on either party).

~ 25 If a woman is still dwelling in her father's house and her husband is dead, (and) her husband's brothers have made no division (of the inheritance) and she has no son, her husband's brothers, having made no division, shall take any ornaments which her husband has bestowed on her (and which) are still in her possession. They shall have what remains passed before the gods (and) make a (formal) claim (and) take (what is theirs). They shall not be seized for (trial by ordeal by) the river-goddess or the oath.

~ 26 If a woman is still dwelling in her father's house and her husband is dead, (then,) if there are sons of her husband, they shall take any ornaments which her husband has bestowed on her; (but) if there are no sons of her husband, she indeed shall take (them).

~ 27 If a woman is still dwelling in her father's house (and) her husband has been visiting (her), any settled property which her husband has given her, he may take (back) as his own; he may not claim what comes from her father's house.

~ 28 If a widow has entered a man's house, carrying her infant son with her, (and) he has grown up in the house of her spouse and a deed of adoption is not drawn up, he shall take no portion of his stepfather's house (and) shall not be liable for his debts; she shall take a portion according to his share from the house of him who begot him.

~ 29 If a woman has entered her husband's house, her dowry or whatever she has brought from her father's house or what her father-in-law has given her on her entry are reserved for her sons; her father-in-law's sons shall not claim (it). But, if her husband survives her, 'he may give (it in) what (shares) he will to his sons.

~ 30 If a father has conveyed (or) brought the (customary) gift to the house of his son's father-in-law (and) the woman has not been given to his son, and another of his sons, whose wife is dwelling in her father's house, has died, he shall give his dead son's wife to be a spouse to his other son to whose father-in-law's house he has brought (the gift). If the owner of the girl, who has accepted the present, is not willing to give his daughter, the father who has brought the present, if he pleases, may take his daughter-in-law (and) give her to his son; or, if he pleases, he may surely take (back) so much as he has brought, lead, silver, gold, (or other things) not being edible, in full amount; he shall not claim the things which are edible.

~ 31 If a man has brought the (customary) present to his father-in-law's house and his wife has died, (and) his father-in-law has (other) daughters, if his father-in-law pleases, he may marry a daughter of his father-in-law in place of his dead wife; or, if he pleases, he may take (back) the money which he has given. Neither corn nor sheep nor any (other) thing which is edible shall be given (back) to him; he shall receive only the money.

~ 32 If a woman is still dwelling in her father's house and her settled property has been given (to her), whether she is taken or is not taken to her father-in-law's house, she shall bear (any) debts or liability or punishment of her husband.

~ 33 If a woman is still dwelling in her father's house (and) her husband is dead and she has sons, she shall dwell in a house belonging to them where she chooses. If she has no son, her father-in-law shall give her to whichever of his sons he likes. Or, if he pleases, he shall give her as a spouse to her father-in-law. If her husband and her father-in-law are indeed dead and she has no son, she becomes (in law) a widow; she shall go whither she pleases.

~ 34 If a man cohabits with a widow without having drawn up a marriage-contract (and) she dwells two years in his house, she (becomes) a wife; she shall not go forth.

~ 35 If a widow enters a man's house (to live with him), everything which she brings (with her becomes) all her husband 's; or, if the man enters into (the house of) the woman (to live with her), everything which he brings (with him becomes) all the woman's.

~ 36 If a woman is still dwelling in her father's house or if her husband has made her to dwell apart and her husband has gone to the field(s) (and) has left her neither oil nor wool nor clothing nor food nor anything else and has had no provision brought to her from the field(s), that woman shall remain faithful to her husband for five years (and) not go to dwell with an (other) husband. If she has sons (and) they hire themselves out and earn their own living, the woman shall respect her husband (and) shall not go to dwell with an(other) husband. If she has no sons, she shall respect her husband for five years; at the beginning of the sixth year she may go to dwell with the husband of her choice. Her husband on coming (back) shall not claim her; she is free for her later husband. If he has delayed beyond the term of five years (and) has not kept himself away of his own accord, (inasmuch as) either a brigand has seized him and he has disappeared, or he has been seized as (if he were) a robber and been delayed (in return-ing), on coming (back) he shall make a (formal) claim (and) give a woman equivalent to his wife; and (then) he shall take back his wife. Or, if the king has sent him to any other country (and) he has been delayed beyond the term of five years, his wife shall respect him and shall not go to dwell with an(other) husband. But, if she has gone to dwell with an(other) husband before the end of five years and has borne children, her husband on coming (back) shall take her herself and also her children, because she has not respected the marriage-contract but has been married (!).

~ 37 If a man divorces his wife, if (it is) his will, he shall give her something; if (it is) not his will, he shall not give her anything; she shall go forth empty.

~ 38 If a woman is still dwelling in her father's house and her husband divorces her, he may take the ornaments which he himself has bestowed on her; he shall not claim the bridal gift which he has brought; he (then) is quit in respect to the woman.

~ 39 If a man has given to a husband a girl who is not his daughter (but) whose father was formerly in debt (to him) and (who) has been made to dwell (with his creditor) as a pledge, (then) the former creditor, (if) he comes forward, shall obtain satisfaction for the price of the woman from the man who gave her (in marriage); if the man who gave her has nothing to give, the (other) man shall take him. But, if she is being treated with cruelty, she is quit in respect of the man who (so) treats her. And, if the woman's spouse, whether by being induced to sign a bond or by letting himself be held (otherwise) liable, gives satisfaction for the price of the woman, then the man who gave her is quit.

~ 40 Women, whether married or widows or Assyrians who go out into the (public) street must not have their heads uncovered. Ladies by birth … whether (it is) a veil or robe or mantle?, must be veiled; they must not have their heads uncovered. Whether … or … or … shall not be veiled but, when they go in the (public) street alone, they shall surely be veiled. A concubine (?), who goes with her mistress in the (public) streets, must be veiled. A hierodule, whom a husband has married, must be veiled in the (public) streets but one, whom a husband has not married, must have her head uncovered in a (public) street; she shall not be veiled. A harlot shall not be veiled; her head must be uncovered. He who sees a veiled harlot shall arrest her; he shall produce (free) men (as) witnesses (and bring her to the entrance of the residency. Her jewellery shall not be taken (from her, but) the man who has arrested her shall take her clothing; she shall be beaten 50 stripes with rods, (and) pitch shall be poured on her head. Or if a man has seen a veiled harlot and has let her go (and) has not brought her to the entrance of the residency, that man shall be beaten 50 stripes with rods; the informer against him shall take his clothing; his ears shall be pierced (and) a cord shall be passed through (them) and be tied behind him; he shall do labour for the king for 1 full month. Slave-girls shall not be veiled, and he who sees a veiled slave-girl shall arrest her (and) bring her to the entrance of the residency; her ears shall be cut off, (and) the man who has ar-rested her shall take her clothes. If a man has seen a veiled slave-girl and has let her go (and) has not arrested her (and) brought her to the entrance of the residency, (and) charge (and) proof have been brought against him, he shall be beaten 50 stripes with rods; his ears shall be pierced (and) a cord shall be passed through (them) and be tied behind him; the informer against him shall take his clothes; he shall do labour for the king for 1 full month.

~ 41 If a man will veil his concubine (?), he shall summon 5 (or) 6 of his neighbours to be present (and) veil her before them (and) shall speak, saying: 'She (is) my wife'; she (thus becomes) his wife. A concubine who has not been veiled before the men (and) whose husband has not spoken, saying: 'She (is) my wife', (is) not a wife but (still) a concubine (?). If a man has died (and) his veiled wife has no sons, the sons of concubines (become his) sons; they shall take a share (of his property).

~ 42 If a man on the day of anointing has poured oil on the head of a lady or has brought wedding-gifts to the feast (?), no return (of the gifts) shall be made.

~ 43 If the man has either poured oil on the (lady's) head or brought wedding-gifts (and) the son to whom he has assigned the wife has either died or disappeared, he may give her to whichever he pleases of the rest of his sons from the eldest to the youngest who is 10 years old. If the father is dead and the son to whom he assigned the wife is dead but the dead son has a son who is 10 years old, he shall marry her; but if the grandsons are younger than 10 years old, the girl's father, if he pleases, shall give his daughter (to one of them) or, if he pleases, shall make a return (of the gifts) on equal terms. If there is no son, he shall surely give (back) so much as he has received, precious stones and any (other) things not being edible, in full amount but shall not give back what is edible.

~ 44 If an Assyrian man, or if an Assyrian woman, who is dwelling in a man's house as a pledge for his value, has been taken (in discharge of the debt) up to the full value, he may flog (him), he may pluck out (his hair), he may bruise (and) bore his ears.

~ 45 If a woman has been given (in marriage) and the enemy has taken her husband (prisoner and) she has no father-in-law or son, she shall remain faithful to her husband for two years. During these two years, if she has nothing to eat, she shall come forward and make a declaration, (and) she becomes a dependent of the residency; her … shall provide her with food (and) she shall do work for him. If she is the wife of a sapper, she … shall provide her with food, (and) she shall do work for him. Or, if her husband held a field and a house as a fief in his city, she shall come forward and make a declaration to the judges, saying: 'I have nothing to eat'; the judges shall inquire of the mayor (and) the elders of the city (and), inasmuch as he held a field in that city as a fief, they shall acquire the field and the house for her support for two years and give (a lease of) them to her. She must dwell there, and they shall write her a tablet; she shall wait for two full years (and) she may (then) go to live with the husband of her choice, (and) they shall write her a tablet as (for) a widow. If afterwards her missing husband returns to the country, he shall take back his wife who has been married away (from him); he shall not claim the sons whom she has borne to her latter husband, but her latter husband shall take (them); (as for) the field and house which were leased away (from him) as her maintenance at the full price, if he has not (re-)entered the armed service of the king, he shall pay (on the same terms) as they were leased and take (them back). Or, if he does not return (but) has died in another country, the king shall grant his house and his field where he shall grant (them).

~ 46 If a woman whose husband is dead does not go forth from her house on her husband's death, (and) if her husband has assigned her nothing in writing, she shall dwell in a house belonging to her sons where she chooses; her husband's sons shall provide her with food; they shall enter into a covenant for her for (the provision of) her food and her drink as (for) a bride whom they love. If she is a second (wife and) she has no sons, she shall dwell with one (of her husband's sons and) they shall provide her with food in common; if she has sons (and) the sons of the former (wife) do not agree to provide her with food, she shall dwell in a house belonging to her own sons where she chooses, (and) her own sons too shall provide her with food and she shall do their work. But if indeed among her sons (there is one) who has taken her (as his spouse), he who takes her (as his spouse) shall surely provide her with food and her (own) sons shall not provide her with food.

~ 47 If either a man or a woman have made magical preparations and they have been seized in their hands (and) charge (and) proof have been brought against them, the maker of the magical preparations shall be put to death. The man who saw the making of the magical preparations (and) heard from the mouth of an eyewitness of the magical preparations who told him, (saying) 'I myself saw (it)', shall come forward (as) an ear-witness (and) tell the king; if what he has told the king is denied by the eye-witness, he shall make a statement in the presence of the Bull the son of the Sun-god, saying: 'On my oath, he said (it)'; (and then) he is quit. (As for) the eye-witness who told (it) and denied (it), the king shall interrogate him (in such way) as he thinks fit (and) shall read his inmost thoughts. The exorcist, when he is fetched, shall make the man speak, and the former shall speak, saying: From the adjuration, wherewith thou hast been adjured before the king and his son, they will not release thee; thou hast surely been adjured according to the words of the tablet wherewith thou hast been adjured before the king and his son.

~ 48 If a man, in whose house his debtor's daughter is dwelling as (security for) a debt, asks her fatherhe may give her to a husband; but, if her father does not agree, he shall not give her (to a husband). If her father is dead (and) he asks one of her brothers, then the latter shall speak to her (other) brothers; if a brother speaks, saying: 'I will redeem my sister within 1 full month', if he does not redeem her within 1 full month, the creditor, if he pleases, shall declare her quit (of all claims and) give her to an husband, or, if he pleases, he shall give her for money according to his tablet …

~ 50 If a man has struck a married woman and caused her to lose the fruit of her womb, the wife of the man who caused the (other) married woman to lose the fruit of her womb shall be treated as he has treated her; for the fruit of her womb he pays (on the principle of) a life (for a life). But, if that woman dies, the man shall be put to death; for the fruit of her womb, he pays (on the principle of) a life (for a life). Or if that woman's husband has no son (and) his wife has been struck and has cast the fruit of her womb, for the fruit of her womb the striker shall be put to death. If the fruit of the womb is a girl, he none the less, pays (on the principle of) a life (for a life).

~ 51 If a man has struck a married woman who does not rear her children and has caused her to cast the fruit of her womb, this punishment (shall be inflicted): he shall pay 2 talents of lead.

~ 52 If a man has struck a harlot and caused her to cast the fruit of her womb, blow for blow shall be laid upon him; (thus) he pays (on the principle of) a life (for a life).

~ 53 If a woman has cast the fruit of her womb by her own act (and) charge (and) proof have been brought against her, she shall be impaled (and) shall not be buried. If she has died in casting the fruit of her womb, she shall be impaled (and) shall not be buried. If that woman was concealed when she cast the fruit of her womb (and) it was not told to the king …

~ 55 If a man has taken by constraint and dishonoured a man's daughter (who is) a virgin, who is dwelling in her father's house (and) her father has not been asked for her (hand in marriage and) … has not been opened (and) she has not been married, and there has been no claim on her father's house, whether it was within the city or in the open country or at night in the (public) street or in a garner or at a festival of the city, the father of the virgin shall take the wife of the ravisher of the virgin (and) give her to be dishonoured; he shall not give her (back) to her husband (but) shall take her. The father shall give his daughter who has been ravished as a spouse to her ravisher. If the ravisher has no wife, he shall give 'the third' (in) silver the price of a virgin to her father, (and) her ravisher shall marry her; he shall not turn her away. If the father does not please, he shall receive 'the third' for the virgin (in) silver (and) give his daughter to whom he pleases.

~ 56 If a virgin has given herself to a man, the man shall swear (to this, and) his wife shall not be touched. The seducer shall give 'the third' the price of a virgin (in) silver (and) the father shall treat his daughter as he pleases.

~ 58 In all penalties involving either tearing out (the breasts) or cutting off (the nose or ears) of a married woman, so let the priest be informed and let him come; (let it be carried out) according to what is prescribed on the tablet.

~ 59 Apart from the penalties for a married woman which are prescribed on the tablet, a man may scourge his wife, pluck (her hair), may bruise and destroy her ears. There is no liability therefor.

Think about it.

1. What class distinctions are evident in these laws?
2. Compare the laws concerning women with earlier law codes you read. Were women treated better in Assyria? Why do you so answer?

---

c. 1700–1100 BCE

13. The Rig Veda

Translated by Ralph T. H. Griffith

The Rig Veda is a collection of hymns in archaic Sanskrit from ancient northwestern India. They were written down in the 7th century BCE at the earliest, but the antiquity of the language of the hymns suggests they were composed much earlier, likely during the Early Vedic Period (c. 1700–1100 BCE), memorized and passed down orally by the Brahmin priests before being committed to writing. It is organized into ten sections called *mandalas*, the oldest of these being Mandalas 2–7. It is believed their contents reveal historical information about the Early Vedic Period and the culture of the early Vedic peoples. The following is one hymn from the collection (Mandala 7, Hymn 18), which is one of three hymns that refer to a famous conflict called The Battle of the Ten Kings, in which King Sudas of the Tritsu tribe (part of the Bharata confederation) faced off against ten enemy kings of the Puru confederation.

1 All is with you, O Indra, all the treasures which erst our fathers won who sang your praises.

With you are milch cows good to milk, and horses: best winner are you of riches for the pious.

2 For like a King among his wives you dwell: with glories, as a Sage, surround and help us.

Make us, your servants, strong for wealth, and honor our songs with cows and steeds and decoration.

3 Here these our holy hymns, with joy and gladness in pious emulation, have approached you.

Hitherward may your path come that leads to riches: may we find shelter in your favor, Indra.

4 Vasiṣṭha has poured forth his prayers, desiring to milk you like a cow in goodly pasture.

All these my people call you Lord of cattle: may Indra come toward the prayer we offer.

5 What though the floods spread widely, Indra made them shallow and easy for Sudās to traverse.

He, worthy of our praises, caused the Simyu, foe of our hymn, to curse the rivers' fury.

6 Eager for spoil was Turvaśa Purodas, fain to win wealth, like fishes urged by hunger.

The Bhṛgus and the Druhyus quickly listened: friend rescued friend 'mid the two distant peoples.

7 Together came the Pakthas, the Bhalanas, the Alinas, the Sivas, the Visanins.

Yet to the Tṛtsus[1] came the Āryan's Comrade, through love of spoil and heroes' war, to lead them.

8 Fools, in their folly fain to waste her waters, they parted inexhaustible Paruṣṇī.[2]

Lord of the Earth, he with his might repressed them: still lay the herd and the affrighted herdsman.

9 As to their goal they sped to their destruction: they sought Paruṣṇī; e'en the swift returned not.

Indra abandoned, to Sudās the manly, the swiftly flying foes, unmanly babblers.

10 They went like cows unherded from the pasture, each clinging to a friend as chance directed.

They who drive spotted steeds, sent down by Pṛśni,[3] gave ear, the Warriors and the harnessed horses.

11 The King who scattered one-and-twenty people of both Vaikarna tribes through lust of glory-

As the skilled priest clips grass within the chamber, so has the Hero Indra wrought their downfall.

12 You, thunder-armed, o'erwhelmed in the waters famed ancient Kavasa and then the Druhyu.

Others here claiming friendship to their friendship, devoted to you, in you were joyful.

13 Indra at once with conquering might demolished all their strong places and their seven castles.

The goods of Anu's son he gave to Tṛtsu. May we in sacrifice conquer scorned Pūru.

14 The Anavas and Druhyus, seeking booty, have slept, the sixty hundred, yea, six thousand,

And six-and-sixty heroes. For the pious were all these mighty exploits done by Indra.

15 These Tṛtsus under Indra's careful guidance came speeding like loosed waters rushing downward.

The foemen, measuring exceeding closely, abandoned to Sudās all their provisions.

16 The hero's side who drank the dressed oblation, Indra's denier, far o'er earth he scattered.

Indra brought down the fierce destroyer's fury. He gave them various roads, the path's Controller.

17 E'en with the weak he wrought this matchless exploit: e'en with a goat he did to death a lion.

He pared the pillar's angles with a needle. Thus to Sudās Indra gave all provisions.

18 To you have all your enemies submitted: e'en the fierce Bheda have you made your subject.

Cast down your sharpened thunderbolt, O Indra, on him who harms the men who sing your praises.

19 Yamuna and the Tṛtsus aided Indra. There he stripped Bheda bare of all his treasures.

The Ajas and the Sigrus and the Yaksus brought in to him as tribute heads of horses.

20 Not to be scorned, but like dawns past and recent, O Indra, are your favors and your riches.

---

1   A tribe of the Bharatas.
2   The name of a river and the god associated with it.
3   A storm deity.

Devaka, Mānyamana's son, you slew, and smote Śambara from the lofty mountain.

21 They who, from home, have gladdened you, your servants Parasara, Vasiṣṭha, Satayatu,

Will not forget your friendship, liberal Giver. So shall the days dawn prosperous for the princes.

22 Priest-like, with praise, I move around the altar, earning Paijavana's[4] reward, O Agni,

Two hundred cows from Devavan's descendant, two chariots from Sudās with mares to draw them.

23 Gift of Paijavana, four horses bear me in foremost place, trained steeds with pearl to deck them.

Sudās's brown steeds, firmly-stepping, carry me and my son for progeny and glory.

24 Him whose fame spreads between wide earth and heaven, who, as dispenser, gives each chief his portion,

Seven flowing rivers glorify like Indra. He slew Yudhyamadhi in close encounter.

25 Attend on him O you heroic Maruts[5] as on Sudās's father Divodāsa.

Further Paijavana's desire with favor. Guard faithfully his lasting firm dominion.

---

4   Another name for Sudas.
5   Storm deities.

> ### *Think about it.*
>
> 1.   Using this poem as a historical source for the Battle of the Ten Kings, what conclusions can you draw about the battle?
> 2.   Does the author consider the victory miraculous? Who is given credit for the victory?

13ᵗʰ century BCE

---

14. The Legend of the Destruction of Mankind

Translated by E. A. Wallis Budge

The following text was found in the tomb of the Egyptian New Kingdom pharaoh Seti I (c. 1290–1279 BCE). It is a myth concerning the sun god Ra (Re) and how he came to be in heaven, having once resided on earth. The antiquated English of Budge's translation has been modernized to make for easier reading.

CHAPTER I.

1.   Here is the story of Ra, the god who was self-begotten and self-created, after he had assumed the sovereignty over men and women, and gods, and things, the one god. Now men and women were speaking words of complaint, saying:—"Behold, his Majesty (life, strength, and health to him!) has grown old, and his bones have become like silver, and his members have turned into gold and his hair is like real lapis-lazuli." His Majesty heard the words of complaint which men and women were uttering, and his Majesty (life, strength, and health to him!) said to those who were in his train:—"Cry out, and bring to me my Eye, and Shu, and Tefnut, and Seb, and Nut, and the father-gods, and the mother-gods who were with me, even when I was in Nu side by side with my god Nu. Let there be brought along with my Eye his ministers, and let them be led to me here secretly, so that men and women may not perceive them coming here, and may not therefore take to flight with their hearts. Come[1] with them to the Great House, and let them declare their plans (or, arrangements) fully, for I will go from Nu into the place wherein I brought about my own existence, and let those gods be brought to me there." Now the gods were drawn up on each side of Ra, and they bowed down before his Majesty until their heads touched the ground, and the maker of men and women, the king of those who have knowledge, spoke his words in the presence of the Father of the first-born gods. And the gods spoke in the presence of his Majesty, saying:—"Speak to us, for we are listening to them" (i.e., thy words). Then Ra spoke to Nu, saying:—"O first-born god from whom I came into being, O you gods of ancient time, my ancestors, take heed to what men and women are doing; for behold, those who were created by my Eye are uttering words of complaint against me. Tell me what you would do in the matter, and consider this thing for me, and seek out a plan for me, for I will not slay them until I have heard what you shall say to me concerning it."

2.   Then the Majesty of Nu, to son Ra, spoke, saying:—"You are the god who is greater than he who made you, you are the sovereign of those who were created with you, your throne is set, and the fear of you is great; let your Eye go against those who have uttered blasphemies against you." And the Majesty of Ra, said:—"Behold, they have betaken themselves to flight into the mountain lands, for their hearts are afraid because of the words which they have uttered." Then the gods spoke in the presence of his Majesty, saying:—"Let your Eye go forth and let it destroy for you those who revile you with words of evil, for there is no eye whatsoever that can go before it and resist you and it when it journeys in the form of Hathor." Thereupon this goddess went forth and slew the men and the women who were on the mountain (or, desert land).

3.   And the Majesty of this god said, "Come, come in peace, O Hathor, for the work is accomplished." Then this goddess said, "You have made me to live, for when I gained the mastery over men and women it was sweet to my heart;" and the Majesty of Ra said, "I myself will be master over them as their king, and I will destroy them." And it came to pass that Sekhet of the offerings waded about in the night season in their blood, beginning at Suten-henen.[2] Then the Majesty of Ra, spoke saying, "Cry out, and let there come to me swift and speedy messengers who shall be able to run like the wind . . . .;" and straightway messengers of this kind were brought to him. And the Majesty of this god spoke saying, "Let these messengers go to Abu,[3] and bring to me mandrakes in great numbers;" and when these mandrakes were brought to him the Majesty of this god gave them to Sekhet, the

---

1   The god here addressed appears to have been Nu.

2   Or, Henen-su, i.e., Herakleopolis, Magna.

3   i.e., Elephantine, or Syene, a place better known by the Arabic name ASWAN.

goddess who dwells in Annu (Heliopolis) to crush. And behold, when the maidservants were bruising the grain for making beer, these mandrakes were placed in the vessels which were to hold the beer, and some of the blood of the men and women who had been slain. Now they made seven thousand vessels of beer. Now when the Majesty of Ra, the King of the South and North, had come with the gods to look at the vessels of beer, and behold, the daylight had appeared after the slaughter of men and women by the goddess in their season as she sailed up the river, the Majesty of Ra said, "It is good, it is good, nevertheless I must protect men and women against her." And Ra, said, "Let them take up the vases and carry them to the place where the men and women were slaughtered by her." Then the Majesty of the King of the South and North in the three-fold beauty of the night caused to be poured out these vases of beer which make men to lie down (or, sleep), and the meadows of the Four Heavens[4] were filled with beer (or, water) by reason of the Souls of the Majesty of this god. And it came to pass that when this goddess arrived at the dawn of day, she found these Heavens flooded with beer, and she was pleased thereat; and she drank of the beer and blood, and her heart rejoiced, and she became drunk, and she gave no further attention to men and women. Then said the Majesty of Ra to this goddess, "Come in peace, come in peace, O Amit,"[5] and thereupon beautiful women came into being in the city of Amit (or, Amem). And the Majesty of Ra spoke concerning this goddess, saying, "Let there be made for her vessels of the beer which produces sleep at every holy time and season of the year, and they shall be in number according to the number of my hand-maidens;" and from that early time until now men have been accustomed to make on the occasions of the festival of Hathor vessels of the beer which make them to sleep in number according to the number of the handmaidens of Ra.

4. And the Majesty of Ra spoke to this goddess, saying, "I am smitten with the pain of the fire of sickness; from where comes to me this pain?" And the Majesty of Ra said, "I live, but my heart has become exceedingly weary[6] with existence with them (i.e., with men); I have slain some of them, but there is a remnant of worthless ones, for the destruction which I wrought among them was not as great as my power." Then the gods who were in his following said to him, "Be not overcome by your inactivity, for your might is in proportion to your will." And the Majesty of this god said to the Majesty of Nu, "My members are weak for (or, as at) the first time; I will not permit this to come upon me a second time." And the Majesty of the god Nu said, "O son Shu, be you the Eye for your father . . . . . and avenue him, and you goddess Nut, place him . . . . And the goddess Nut said, "How can this be then, O my father Nu? Hail," said Nut . . . . . to the god Nu, and the goddess straightway became a cow, and she set the Majesty of Ra upon her back . . . . . And when these things had been done, men and women saw the god Ra, upon the back of the cow. Then these men and women said, "Remain with us, and we will overthrow your enemies who speak words of blasphemy against you and destroy them." Then his Majesty Ra set out for the Great House, and the gods who were in the train of Ra remained with them (i.e., the men); during that time the earth was in darkness. And when the earth became light again and the morning had dawned, the men came forth with their bows and their weapons, and they set their arms in motion to shoot the enemies of Ra. Then said the Majesty of this god, "Your transgressions of violence are placed behind you, for the slaughtering of the enemies is above the slaughter of sacrifice;" thus came into being the slaughter of sacrifice.

---

4   i.e., the South, North, West, and East of the sky.
5   i.e., "the fair and gracious goddess."

---

6   Literally, "My heart hath stopped greatly."

5. And the Majesty of this god said to Nut, "I have placed myself upon your back in order to stretch myself out." What then is the meaning of this? It means that he united himself with Nut. Thus came into being . . . . . Then said the Majesty of this god, "I am departing from them (i.e., from men), and he must come after me who would see me;" thus came into being . . . . . Then the Majesty of this god looked forth from its interior, saying, "Gather together men for me, and make ready for me an abode for multitudes;" thus came into being . . . . And his Majesty (life, health, and strength be to him!) said, "Let a great field (*sekhet*) be produced (*hetep*);" thereupon Sekhet-hetep came into being. And the god said, "I will gather herbs (*aarat*) therein;" thereupon Sekhet-aaru came into being. And the god said, "I will make it to contain as dwellers things (*khet*) like stars of all sorts;" thereupon the stars (*akhekha*) came into being. Then the goddess Nut trembled because of the height. And the Majesty of Ra said, "I decree that supports be to bear the goddess up;" thereupon the props of heaven (*heh*) came into being. And the Majesty of Ra said, "O my son Shu, I pray you to set yourself under my daughter Nut, and guard you for me the supports (*heh*) of the millions (*heh*) which are there, and which live in darkness. Take you the goddess upon your head, and act as nurse for her;" thereupon came into being the custom of a son nursing a daughter, and the custom of a father carrying a son upon his head.

CHAPTER II.

[*describes a ritual done over the figure of a cow*]

CHAPTER III.

1. Then the majesty of this god spoke to Thoth, saying "Let a call go forth for me to the Majesty of the god Seb, saying, 'Come, with the utmost speed, at once.'" And when the Majesty of Seb had come, the Majesty of this god said to him, "Let war be made against your worms (or, serpents) which are in you; verily, they shall have fear of me as long as I have being; but you know their magical powers. Go to the place where my father Nu is, and say to him, 'Keep ward over the worms (or, serpents) which are in the earth and water.' And moreover, you shall make a writing for each of the nests of your serpents which are there, saying, 'Keep guard lest you cause injury to anything.' They shall know that I am removing myself from them, but indeed I shall shine upon them. Since, however, they indeed wish for a father, you shall be a father to them in this land for ever. Moreover, let good heed be taken to the men who have my words of power, and to those whose mouths have knowledge of such things; verily my own words of power are there, verily it shall not happen that any shall participate with me in my protection, by reason of the majesty which has come into being before me. I will decree them to your son Osiris, and their children shall be watched over, the hearts of their princes shall be obedient (or, ready) by reason of the magical powers of those who act according to their desire in all the earth through their words of power which are in their bodies."

CHAPTER IV.

1. And the majesty of this god said, "Call to me the god Thoth," and one brought the god to him forthwith. And the Majesty of this god said to Thoth, "Let us depart to a distance from heaven, from my place, because I would make light and the god of light (Khu) in the Tuat and in the Land of Caves. You shall write down the things which are in it, and you shall punish those who are in it, that is to say, the workers who have worked iniquity (or, rebellion). Through you I will keep away from the servants whom this heart of mine loathes. You shall be in my place (*ast*) Asti, and you shall therefore be called, O Thoth, the 'Asti of Ra.'

Moreover, I give you power to send (*hab*) forth . . . . .; thereupon shall come into being the Ibis (*habi*) bird of Thoth. I moreover give you power to lift up your hand before the two Companies of the gods who are greater than you, and what you do shall be fairer than the work of the god Khen; therefore shall the divine bird tekni of Thoth come into being. Moreover, I give you Power to embrace (*anh*) the two heavens with your beauties, and with your rays of light; therefore shall come into being the Moon-god (*Aah*) of Thoth. Moreover, I give you power to drive back (*anan*) the Ha-nebu;[7] therefore shall come into being the dog-headed Ape (*anan*) of Thoth, and he shall act as governor for me. Moreover, you are now in my place in the sight of all those who see you and who present offerings to you, and every being shall ascribe praise to you, O you who are God."

CHAPTER V.

1. [*Another ritual is described*] Then the Aged One himself (i.e., Ra) embraced the god Nu, and spoke to the gods who came forth in the east of the sky, "Ascribe praise to the god, the Aged One, from whom I have come into being. I am he who made the heavens, and I set in order the earth, and created the gods, and I was with them for an exceedingly long period; then was born the year and . . . . . . but my soul is older than it (i.e., time). It is the Soul of Shu, it is the Soul of Khnemu,[8] it is the Soul of Heh, it is the Soul of Kek and Kerh (i.e., Night and Darkness), it is the Soul of Nu and of Ra, it is the Soul of Osiris, the lord of Tettu, it is the Soul of the Sebak Crocodile-gods and of the Crocodiles, it is the Soul of every god who dwells in the divine Snakes, it is the Soul of Apep in Mount Bakhau (i.e., the Mount of Sunrise), and it is the Soul of Ra which pervades the whole world." *another ritual is described*

---

7   i.e., the "North-lords," that is to say, the peoples who lived in the extreme north of the Delta, and on its sea-coasts, and perhaps in the Islands of the Mediterranean.

---

8   There are mistakes in the text here.

Think about it.

1.   Why does Re want to destroy the humans?
2.   This story explains the origins of various things. What are they?
3.   Why does Re leave the earth?

The Iron Age (1200–500 BCE)

Tiglath-pileser III (Neo-Assyrian Empire)

The Iron Age

B.C.E.	1100	1000	900	800	700	600	500
Central America	Olmec Civilization						
South America				Chavin Culture			
Western Mediterranean					Roman Monarchy		
					Carthaginian Monarchy		
Eastern Mediterranean	Mycenaean Civilization	Greek Dark Age			Greek Archaic Period		
			Kingdom of Israel	Israel and Judah		Kingdom of Judah	Judahite Exile
Northeast Africa	Egyptian New Kingdom	3rd Intermediate Period				Egyptian Late Kingdom	
					Kingdom of Kush		Meroë
North Mesopotamia	Assyrian Middle Kingdom			Neo-Assyrian Empire			Neo-Babylonian Empire
South Mesopotamia	Babylonian Dynasties IV-IX						
Central Asia						Median Empire	
South Asia	Early Vedic Period	Later Vedic Period					
East Asia	Shang Dynasty		Zhou Dynasty				

15.   Early Israelite Victory Hymns

Translated by David Miano

These victory hymns are two of the earliest compositions now found in the Bible, both probably composed in the period 1150-1100 BCE. The Hebrew in which they are written is more ancient than the prose writing that surrounds the poems. The Song of the Sea (also known as the Song of Miriam) is set at a time when the Canaanites, Philistines, Edomites, and Moabites were all active in the land of Canaan. It celebrates a victory of the "people of Yahweh" (the name "Israel" is not used) over the Egyptians at the Suph Sea (traditionally understood to be the Red Sea today) and is the earliest version of the famous account of the salvation of the Israelites at the Red Sea. The mountain referred to has sometimes been assumed to be Mount Zion in Jerusalem, but the context suggests Mount Sinai or Horeb, the holy mountain in the traditional story to which the people fled soon after this event. The Song of Deborah (located in Chapter 5 of the book of Judges) does use the name Israel and recounts a military victory that the ten tribes of Israel scored over the Canaanites. The battle was fought at the River Taanach, near the city of Megiddo. The hymn gives us a rare glimpse into the culture of the early Israelites.

The Song of the Sea

^{15:1b}I will sing of Yahweh, for he acted most exaltedly!
Horse and its driver he pitched into the sea.
^{15:2}My strength and my power is Yah,
And he was salvation for me.
This is my god, and I glorify him,
My father's god, and I elevate him.
^{15:3}Yahweh is a warrior; Yahweh is his name.
^{15:4}Pharaoh's chariots and his army he cast into the sea,
And his elite officers sank in the Suph Sea.
^{15:5}The deep waters covered them;
They went down into the depths like a stone.
^{15:6}By your right hand, O Yahweh, resplendent in might,
By your right hand, O Yahweh, you shattered the enemy.
^{15:7}By your great superiority you threw down your antagonists;
You sent forth your anger, which devoured them like stubble;

^{15:8}By the blast of your nostrils the waters were heaped up,

The waves mounted as a bank,

The deep waters congealed in the heart of the sea.

^{15:9}Said the enemy, "I'll pursue; I'll overtake,

I'll seize the booty; my gullet will be filled with them;

I'll bare my sword; my hand will dispossess them."

^{15:10}You blew with your nostrils—the sea covered them;

They sank like lead in dreadful waters.

^{15:11}Who is like you among gods, O Yahweh?

Who is like you, dreadful in holiness,

Fearsome in splendors, O Worker of Wonder?

^{15:12}You stretched out your hand—earth swallowed them.

^{15:13}You led by your kindness the people whom you redeemed;

You guided them by your strength to the abode of your holiness.

^{15:14}Peoples heard; they shuddered.

Pangs seized the kings of Philistia.

^{15:15}Indeed, the sheiks of Edom were unnerved.

Shuddering gripped the chiefs of Moab.

The kings of Canaan collapsed completely.

^{15:16}Upon them fell fear and terror;

By your arm's greatness they were struck dumb like a stone.

Until your people passed through, O Yahweh,

Until the people you purchased passed through.

^{15:17}You brought them, and you planted them

In your hereditary mountain, the dais of your throne.

You made, O Yahweh, your sanctuary;

O Lord, your hands created it.

^{15:18}Yahweh, he will reign to time indefinite and beyond!

The Song of Deborah

^{5:2}When locks went loose in Israel,

When the people volunteered,

They blessed Yahweh.

^{5:3}Hear, you kings;

Listen, you princes,

I, to Yahweh; I will sing;

I will chant to Yahweh, the God of Israel.

^{5:4}O Yahweh, when you came out from Seir,

When you marched out of the fields of Edom,

The earth quaked,

The very skies dripped,

The very clouds dripped waters,
5:5The mountains shook,
Before Yahweh, the One of Sinai
Before Yahweh, the God of Israel.
5:6In the days of Shamgar, the son of Anat,
In the days of Jael, the routes were blocked,
And wayfarers took the roundabout routes,
5:7The villagers ceased in Israel, they ceased,
Until you rose up, O Deborah,
You rose up as a mother in Israel.
5:8They chose a new god,
Then war was at the gates.
Neither a shield nor a spear was seen
Among the forty contingents of Israel.
5:9My heart was with Israel's commanders,
The ones volunteering with the people.
They blessed Yahweh.
5:10You riders of tawny she-asses,
You sitters on saddle rugs,
And you travelers on the road,
5:11Declare it to the sound of cymbals,
Between the watering stations.
There may they recount the righteous act of Yahweh,
The righteous acts for his villagers in Israel.
Then Yahweh's people went down to the gates,
5:12"Awake, awake, O Deborah,
Awake, awake, sing a song!
Arise Barak, and take your prisoners,
O son of Abinoam!"
5:13At that time the remnant went down to the nobles,
Yahweh's people went down to him among the warriors.[1]
5:14From Ephraim, those whose root is in Amalek,
Behind you, Benjamin with your people,
From Machir, commanders came down,
From Zebulun, bearers of the leader's staff,
5:15And captains in Issachar with Deborah,
And Issachar was Barak's support;
Into the valley they were sent at his feet.
Among the divisions of Reuben were chieftains, resolved of heart,
5:16Why did you sit between the sheepfolds
To hear the bleatings of flocks?

---

1   Here follows a roll of the tribes in the alliance.

To the divisions of Reuben belong chieftains, faint of heart!
⁵:¹⁷Gilead tented beyond the Jordan,
And Dan, why did he linger in ships?
Asher sat at the seashore,
And tented by his harbors.
⁵:¹⁸Zebulun is a people that thought little of life to die,
And Naphtali too on the heights of the plain.
⁵:¹⁹Kings came, they fought;
At that time the kings of Canaan fought
In Taanach by Megiddo's waters.
They took no spoil of silver.
⁵:²⁰From the skies the stars fought;
From their courses they fought with Sisera.
⁵:²¹The torrent Qishon swept them away;
The torrent overwhelmed them, the torrent Qishon;
You trampled the souls of the mighty.
⁵:²²Then the hoofs of horses pounded,
From the galloping, galloping steeds.
⁵:²³"Curse Meroz," said Yahweh's messenger,
"Curse bitterly its inhabitants,
For they did not come to Yahweh's aid,
To Yahweh's aid among the warriors."
⁵:²⁴Most blessed among women is Jael,
The wife of Heber the Kenite,
Among tent-dwelling women most blessed.
⁵:²⁵He asked for water; she gave him milk;
In a princely bowl she brought him cream.
⁵:²⁶With her left hand she reached for a tent peg,
With her right hand for the workmen's hammer,
And she hammered Sisera; she smashed his head,
And she struck through and pierced his temple.
⁵:²⁷Between her feet he slumped, he fell down, he sprawled;
Between her feet he slumped, he fell down;
Where he slumped, there he fell down devastated.
⁵:²⁸Through the window she looked out and called out,
Sisera's mother through the lattice:
"Why does his chariot delay in coming?
 Why so late the clatter of his chariotry?"
⁵:²⁹The wisest of her ladies answered her;
Indeed, she returned her own words to her:
⁵:³⁰"Aren't they looting and dividing the spoil?
A damsel or two per man,
Spoil of dyed cloths for Sisera,

Spoil of dyed embroidered cloths,

Two dyed embroidered cloths round the neck of the spoiler."

5:31So may all your enemies perish, O Yahweh!

And may those loving him be as the sun rising in its might!

Think about it.

1. Using these poems as historical sources, what conclusions can you draw about each of the battles?
2. What similarities do you see between the two poems and between them and the poem from the Rig Veda?

---

c. 1000 BCE

16. The Gathas

Translated by Lawrence H. Mills

The Gathas are seventeen hymns of the Zoroastrian faith, written in Old Avestan, a language of the Indo-Iranian language family closely related to the archaic Sanskrit of the Rig Veda (reading #13). The hymns are believed to have been composed by Zarathustra (Zoroaster), an early Persian prophet who probably lived in the 11th or 10th century BCE. The Gathas were later compiled into a larger work called the Avesta and now comprise Yasna 28–34, 43–51, and 53 of that work. The following selection is Yasna 30, which is the earliest statement of Zoroastrian dualism that we possess. The point of the hymn is to show that God (Ahura Mazda) is not responsible for the existence of evil in the world. The antiquated English of Mills' translation has been modernized to make for easier reading.

1. And now I will proclaim, O you who are drawing near and seeking to be taught! those animadversions which appertain to Him who knows all things whatsoever; the praises which are for Ahura, and the sacrifices which spring from the Good Mind,[1] and likewise the benignant meditations inspired by Righteousness.[2] And I pray that propitious results may be seen in the lights.

2. Hear then with your ears; see the bright flames with the eyes of the Good Mind. It is for a decision

---

1   Vohu Manah, a moral state of mind personified. One of the Amesha Spentas (avatars of Ahura Mazda).

2   Asha, another one of the Amesha Spentas.

"Yasna XXX," *The Zend-Avesta, Part III, The Sacred Books of the East, Volume XXXI*, trans. Lawrence H. Mills, pp. 28–35. Oxford University Press, 1887. Copyright in the Public Domain.

as to religions, man and man, each individually for himself. Before the great effort of the cause, awake you all to our teaching!

3. Thus are the primeval spirits, who as a pair combining their opposite strivings, and yet each independent in his action, have been famed of old.[3] They are a better thing, they two, and a worse, as to thought, as to word, and as to deed. And between these two let the wisely acting choose aright. Choose not as the evil-doers!

Yes, when the two spirits came together at the first to make life, and life's absence, and to determine how the world at the last shall be ordered, for the wicked the worst life, for the holy the Best Mental State,[4]

5. (then when they had finished each his part in the deeds of creation, they chose distinctly each his separate realm). He who was the evil of them both chose the evil, thereby working the worst of possible results, but the more bounteous spirit chose the Divine Righteousness; yes, He so chose who clothes upon Himself the firm stones of heaven. And He chose likewise them who content Ahura with actions, which are performed really in accordance with the faith.

6. And between these two spirits the Demon-gods (and they who give them worship) can make no righteous choice, since we have beguiled them. As they were questioning and debating in their council, the Worst Mind[5] approached them that he might be chosen. (They made their fatal decision.) And thereupon they rushed together toward the Demon of Wrath,[6] that they might pollute the lives of mortals.

7. Upon this Aramaiti[7] approached, and with her came the Sovereign Power,[8] the Good Mind, and the Righteous Order.[9] And to the spiritual creations of good and of evil Aramaiti gave a body, she the abiding and ever strenuous. And for these (Your people) so let that body be at the last, O Mazda! as it was when You came first with creations!

8. And (when the great struggle shall have been fought out which began when the Daêvas[10] first seized the Demon of Wrath as their ally), and when the (just) vengeance shall have come upon these wretches, then, O Mazda! the Kingdom shall have been gained for You by Your Good Mind (within Your folk). For to those, O living Lord! does that Good Mind utter his command, who will deliver the Demon of the Lie into the two hands of the Righteous Order (as a captive to a destroyer).

9. And may we be such as those who bring on this great renovation, and make this world progressive, (till its perfection shall have been reached). As the Ahuras of Mazda even may we be; (yes, like Yourself), in helpful readiness to meet Your people, presenting benefits in union with the Righteous Order. For there will our thoughts be tending where true wisdom shall abide in her home.

10. (And when perfection shall have been attained) then shall the blow of destruction fall upon the Demon of Falsehood, (and her adherents shall perish with her), but swiftest in the happy abode of the Good Mind and of Ahura the righteous saints shall gather, they who proceed in their walk on earth in good repute and honour.

11. Wherefore, O you men! you are learning thus these religious incitations which Ahura gave in our happiness and our sorrow. (And you are also learning) what is the long wounding for the wicked, and the blessings which are in store for the righteous. And when these shall have begun their course, salvation shall be your portion!

---

3   That is, Ahura Mazda and Angra Mainyu (God and the Devil).
4   Haurvatat, another one of the Amesha Spentas, a personification of wholeness or perfection.
5   The opposite of Vohu Manah.
6   Angra Mainyu.
7   The personified piety or devotion of the saints; another one of the Amesha Spentas.
8   Khshathra, the personification of power or dominion, another Amesha Spenta.

---

9   Same as Righteousness above, Asha.
10 The demons.

1. According to the poem, how are the conditions of the present world the result of the interplay between the forces of good and evil?
2. When will evil be destroyed?

---

c. 10th–9th century BCE

17. The Shijing

Translated by James Legge

The Shijing (old spelling Shih-ching), known in English as the Classic of Poetry or Book of Odes, is a collection of 311 Chinese poems written between the 10th and 7th centuries BCE, during the period of China's Zhou Dynasty. The book later was greatly valued, especially by Confucianists, and quoted often. The poem presented here is no. 235 and known as "Wen Wang." It is from a group called the Major Court Hymns, usually dated to the 10th–9th centuries BCE, and celebrates the founding of the Zhou Dynasty by Wen and his son Wu. Technically Wen was never king; his son became the first king of the dynasty. Wen was given the title posthumously.

> King Wen is on high.
> Oh! bright is he in heaven.
> Although Zhou was an old country,
> The (favouring) appointment lighted on it recently
> Illustrious was the House of Zhou,   5
> And the appointment of God came at the proper season.
> King Wen ascends and descends
> On the left and the right of God
> Full of earnest activity was king Wen,
> And his fame is without end.   10
> The gifts (of God) to Zhou
> Extend to the descendants of king Wen,

James Legge, "Ode I: The Wăn Wang," *The Sacred Books of China: The Texts of Confucianism, The Sacred Books of the East, Vol. III.* Oxford University Press, 1879. Copyright in the Public Domain.

In the direct line and the collateral branches for a hundred generations
All the officers of Zhou
Shall (also) be illustrious from age to age.   15
They shall be illustrious from age to age,
Zealously and reverently pursuing their plans.
Admirable are the many officers,
Born in this royal kingdom.
The royal kingdom is able to produce them,   20
The supporters of (the House of) Zhou.
Numerous is the array of officers,
And by them king Wen enjoys his repose.
Profound was king Wen;
Oh! continuous and bright was his feeling of reverence.   25
Great is the appointment of Heaven!
There were the descendants of (the sovereigns of) Shang—
The descendants of the sovereigns of Shang
Were in number more than hundreds of thousands.
But when God gave the command,   30
They became subject to Zhou.
They became subject to Zhou,
(For) the appointment of Heaven is not unchangeable.
The officers of Yin[1], admirable and alert,
Assist at the libations in our capital   35
They assist at those libations,
Always wearing the hatchet-figures on their lower garments and their peculiar cap
O ye loyal ministers of the king,
Ever think of your ancestor!   40
Ever think of your ancestor,
Cultivating your virtue,
Always seeking to accord with the will (of Heaven):—
So shall you be seeking for much happiness,
Before Yin lost the multitudes,   45
(Its kings) were the correlates of God
Look to Yin as a beacon;
The great appointment is not easily preserved.
The appointment is not easily (preserved):—
Do not cause your own extinction.   50
Display and make bright your righteousness and fame,
And look at (the fate of) Yin in the light of Heaven.
The doings of high Heaven
Have neither sound nor smell

---

1   Yin is another name for the Shang.

Take your pattern from king Wen,
And the myriad regions will repose confidence in you.

Think about it.

1. According to the poem, what determines the rise and fall of dynasties?
2. What actions merit Heaven's approval?

---

c. 10th–8th century BCE

18. The Shujing

Translated by James Legge

The Shujing (old spelling Shu-ching), also commonly called the Shangshu, and in English the Classic of History or Book of Documents, is a compilation of speeches from the mouths of historical figures of Zhou period China, many with brief historical prologues. In the section of the book called "Documents of Zhou," there are five "announcements," which are written in archaic Chinese akin to bronze inscriptions from the early Western Zhou period (c. 1045–771 BCE) and thus are considered the oldest parts of the Shujing. One of them, the "Announcement of the Duke of Shao" (brother of King Wu, the founder of the Zhou dynasty), is presented here. In it the Duke of Shao, the Grand Guardian, as he was called, addresses his other brother, the Duke of Zhou, who was acting as regent of the kingdom during the boyhood of Wu's son and successor Cheng. Some scholars consider this piece to have been written in the 10th century BCE, shortly after the regency of the Duke of Zhou (c. 1042–1036). Others hold that it is to be dated later in the Western Zhou period (9th–8th century). Whatever the case, this is among the very earliest expositions of the Chinese political philosophy called the Mandate of Heaven.

THE BOOKS OF ZHOU

BOOK XII. THE ANNOUNCEMENT OF THE DUKE OF SHAO.

I. In the second month, on the day Yi-wei, six days after the full moon, the king early in the morning proceeded from Zhou, and came to Feng. Thence the Grand-guardian went before the duke of Zhou to inspect the localities, and in the third month, on the day Wu-shen, the third day after the first appearance of the new moon on Bing-wu, came in the morning to Lŏ. He consulted the tortoise

James Legge, *The Chinese Classics, Volume III, Part II*, pp. 420–433. Trübner & Company, 1865. Copyright in the Public Domain.

about the localities, and having obtained favourable indications, he set about laying out the plans. On Geng-xu, the third day after, he led the people of Yin to prepare the various sites on the north of the Luo; and this work was completed on the fifth day, Jia-yin. The day following, being the day Yi-mao, the duke of Zhou came in the morning to Lǒ, and thoroughly surveyed the plans for the new city. On Ding-si, the third day after, he offered two bulls as victims in the suburbs; and on the morrow, Wu-wu, at the altar to the spirit of the land in the new city, he sacrificed a bull, a goat, and a pig. After seven days, on Jia-zi, in the morning, from his written specifications he gave their several charges to the people of Yin, and to the chiefs of the States from the Hou, Dian, and Nan tenures. When the people of Yin had thus received their orders, they arose with vigour to do their work.

II. The Great-guardian then went out with the hereditary princes of the various States to bring their offerings; and when he entered again, he gave them to the duke of Zhou, saying, "With my head in my hands and bowed to the ground, I present these before the king and your Grace. Announcements for the instruction of the multitudes of Yin must come from you with whom is the management of affairs.

"Oh! God dwelling in the great heavens has changed his decree in favour of his eldest son, and this great dynasty of Yin. Our king has received that decree. Unbounded is the happiness connected with it, and unbounded is the anxiety:—Oh I how can he be other than reverent?

"When Heaven rejected and made an end of the decree in favour of the great State of Yin, there were many of the former intelligent kings of Yin in heaven. The king, however, who had succeeded to them, the last of their race, from the time of his entering into their appointment, proceeded in such a way as at last to keep the wise in obscurity and the vicious in office. The poor people in such a case, carrying their children and leading their wives, made their moan to Heaven. They even fled away, but were apprehended again. Oh! Heaven had compassion on the people of

the four quarters; its favouring decree lighted on our earnest founders. Let the king sedulously cultivate the virtue of reverence.

"Examining the men of antiquity, there was the founder of the Xia dynasty. Heaven guided his mind, allowed his descendants to succeed him, and protected them. He acquainted himself with Heaven, and was obedient.—But in process of time the decree in his favour fell to the ground. So also when we examine the case of Yin. Heaven guided its founder, so that he corrected the errors of Shang, and it protected his descendants. He also acquainted himself with Heaven, and was obedient.—But now the decadence in favour of him has fallen to the ground. Our king has now come to the throne in his youth:—let him not slight the aged and experienced, for it may be said of them that they have studied the virtuous conduct of our ancient worthies, and still more, that they have matured their plans in the light of Heaven.

"Oh! although the king is young, yet is he the eldest son of Heaven. Let him but effect a great harmony with the people, and that will be the blessing of the present time. Let not the king presume to be remiss in this, but continually regard and stand in awe of the perilousness of the people.

"Let the king come here as the vicegerent of God, and undertake himself the duties of government in the centre of the land. Tan said, 'Now that this great city has been built, from henceforth he may be the mate of great Heaven; from henceforth he may reverently sacrifice to the upper and lower spirits; from henceforth he may in this central spot administer successful government.' Thus shall the king enjoy the favouring regard of Heaven all complete, and the government of the people will now be prosperous.

"Let the king first bring under his influence the managers of affairs of Yin, associating them with the managers of affairs of our dynasty of Zhou. This will regulate their perverted natures, and they will make daily advancement.

"Let the King make reverence the resting-place of his mind. He may not but maintain the virtue of reverence.

"We should by all means survey the dynasties of Xia and Yin. I do not presume to know and say, 'The dynasty of Xia was to enjoy the favouring decree of Heaven for so many years,' nor do I presume to know and say, 'It could not continue longer.' The fact was simply that, for want of the virtue of reverence, the decree in it a favour prematurely fell to the ground. Similarly, I do not presume to know and say, 'The dynasty of Yin was to enjoy the favouring decree of Heaven for so many years,' nor do I presume to say: 'It could not continue longer.' The fact simply was that, for want of the virtues of reverence, the decree in its favour prematurely fell to the ground. The king has now inherited the decree,—the same decree, I consider, which belonged to those two dynasties. Let him seek to inherit the virtues of their meritorious sovereigns;—especially at this commencement of his duties.

"Oh I it is as on the birth of a son, when all depends on the training of his early life, through which he may secure his wisdom in the future, as if it were decreed to him. Now Heaven may have decreed wisdom to our king; it may have decreed good fortune or bad; it may have decreed a long course of years:—we only know that now is with him the commencement of his duties.

"Dwelling in the new city, let the king now sedulously cultivate the virtue of reverence. When he is all-devoted to this virtue, he may pray to Heaven for a long-abiding decree in his favour.

"In the position of king, let him not, because of the excesses of the people in violation of the laws, presume also to rule by the violent infliction of death. When the people are regulated gently, the merit of government is seen.

"It is for him who is in the position of king to overtop all with his virtue. In this case the people will imitate him throughout the whole empire, and the king will become more illustrious.

"Let the king and his ministers labour with a common anxiety, saying, 'We have received the decree of Heaven, and it shall be great as the long-continued years of Xia,—it shall not fail of the long-continued years of Yin.' I wish the king through the inferior people to receive the long-abiding decree of Heaven."

III. The duke of Shao then did obeisance with his head to his hands and bowed to the ground, and said, "I, a small minister, presume with the king's heretofore hostile people, with all his officers, and his loyal friendly people, to maintain and receive his majesty's dread command and brilliant virtue. That the king should finally obtain the decree all complete, and that he should become illustrious,—this I dare not to labour about. I only respectfully bring these offerings to present to his Majesty, to assist in his prayers to Heaven for its long-abiding decree.'"

Think about it.

1. Why, according to the Duke of Shao, is it impossible to predict how long a dynasty will last?
2. What sort of a ruler should a king be?

19. The Iliad

Translated by Richmond Lattimore

The Iliad is a Greek epic poem traditionally ascribed to the bard Homer. It was composed orally near the end of the Greek Dark Age (c. 9th–8th century BCE) and finally written down in the 8th century. The story is set in the final year of the Trojan War and features the warrior hero Achilles. The scene below takes place after Achilles has chosen to abandon the battle over a slight paid him by Agamemnon. Achilles is speaking to Odysseus, the king of Ithaca, who has been urging Achilles to return to the fight.

Then in answer to him spoke Achilleus of the swift feet:
"Son of Laërtes and seed of Zeus, resourceful Odysseus:
without consideration for you I must make my answer,
310   the way I think, and the way it will be accomplished, that you may not
come one after another, and sit by me, and speak softly.
For as I detest the doorways of Death, I detest that man, who
hides one thing in the depths of his heart, and speaks forth another.
But I will speak to you the way it seems best to me: neither
315   do I think the son of Atreus, Agamemnon, will persuade me,
nor the rest of the Danaäns, since there was no gratitude given
for fighting incessantly forever against your enemies.
Fate is the same for the man who holds back, the same if he fights hard.
We are all held in a single honor, the brave with the weaklings.
320   A man dies still if he has done nothing, as one who has done much.
Nothing is won for me, now that my heart has gone through its afflictions
in forever setting my life on the hazard of battle.
for as to her unwinged young ones the mother bird brings back
morsels, wherever she can find them, but as for herself it is suffering,
325   such was I, as I lay through all the many nights unsleeping,
such as I wore through the bloody days of the fighting,
striving with warriors for the sake of these men's women.
But I say that I have stormed from my ships twelve cities
of men, and by land eleven more through the generous Troad.
330   From all these we took forth treasures, goodly and numerous,

and we would bring them back, and give them to Agamemnon,
Atreus' son; while he, waiting back beside the swift ships,
would take them, and distribute them little by little, and keep many.
All the other prizes of honor he gave the great men and the princes
335   are held fast by them, but from me alone of all the Achaians
he has taken and keeps the bride of my heart. Let him lie beside her
and be happy. Yet why must the Argives fight with the Trojans?
And why was it the son of Atreus assembled and led here
these people? Was it not for the sake of lovely-haired Helen?
340   Are the sons of Atreus alone among mortal men the ones
who love their wives? Since any who is a good man, and careful,
loves her who is his own and cares for her, even as I now
loved this one from my heart, though it was my spear that won her.
Now that he has deceived me and taken from my hands my prize of honor,
345   let him try me no more. I know him well. He will not persuade me.
Let him take counsel with you, Odysseus, and the rest of the princes
how to fight the ravening fire away from his vessels.
Indeed, there has been much hard work done even without me;
he has built himself a wall and driven a ditch about it,
350   making it great and wide, and fixed the sharp stakes inside it.
Yet even so he cannot hold the strength of manslaughtering
Hektor; and yet when I was fighting among the Achaians
Hektor would not drive his attack beyond the wall's shelter
but would come forth only so far as the Skaian gates and the oak tree.
355   There once he endured me alone, and barely escaped my onslaught.
But, now I am unwilling to fight against brilliant Hektor;
tomorrow, when I have sacrificed to Zeus and to all gods,
and loaded well my ships, and rowed out onto the salt water,
you will see, if you have a mind to it and if it concerns you,
360   my ships in the dawn at sea on the Hellespont where the fish swarm
and my men manning them with good will to row. If the glorious
shaker of the earth should grant us a favoring passage
on the third day thereafter we might raise generous Phthia.
I have many possessions there that I left behind when I came here
365   on this desperate venture, and from here there is more gold, and red bronze,
and fair-girdled women, and gray iron I will take back;
all that was allotted to me. But my prize: he who gave it,
powerful Agamemnon, son of Atreus, has taken it back again
outrageously. Go back and proclaim to him all that I tell you,
370   openly, so other Achaians may turn against him in anger
if he hopes yet one more time to swindle some other Danaän,
wrapped as he is forever in shamelessness; yet he would not,
bold as a dog though he be, dare look in my face any longer.

I will join with him in no counsel, and in no action.

375 He cheated me and he did me hurt. Let him not beguile me

with words again. This is enough for him. Let him of his own will

be damned, since Zeus of the counsels has taken his wits away from him.

I hate his gifts. I hold him light as the strip of a splinter.

Not if he gave me ten times as much, and twenty times over

380 as he possesses now, not if more should come to him from elsewhere,

or gave all that is brought in to Orchomenos, all that is brought in

to Thebes of Egypt, where the greatest possessions lie up in the houses,

Thebes of the hundred gates, where through each of the gates two hundred

fighting men come forth to war with horses and chariots;

385 not if he gave me gifts as many as the sand or the dust is,

not even so would Agamemnon have his way with my spirit

until he had made good to me all this heartrending insolence.

Nor will I marry a daughter of Atreus' son, Agamemnon,

not if she challenged Aphrodite the golden for loveliness,

390 not if she matched the work of her hands with gray-eyed Athene;

not even so will I marry her; let him pick some other Achaian,

one who is to his liking and is kinglier than I am.

For if the gods will keep me alive, and I win homeward,

Peleus himself will presently arrange a wife for me.

395 There are many Achaian girls in the land of Hellas and Phthia,

daughters of great men who hold strong places in guard. And of these

any one that I please I might make my beloved lady.

And the great desire in my heart drives me rather in that place

to take a wedded wife in marriage, the bride of my fancy,

400 to enjoy with her the possessions won by aged Peleus. For not

worth the value of my life are all the possessions they fable

were won for Ilion, that strong-founded citadel, in the old days

when there was peace, before the coming of the sons of the Achaians;

not all that the stone doorsill of the Archer holds fast within it,

405 of Phoibos Apollo in Pytho of the rocks. Of possessions

cattle and fat sheep are things to be had for the lifting,

and tripods can be won, and the tawny high heads of horses,

but a man's life cannot come back again, it cannot be lifted

nor captured again by force, once it has crossed the teeth's barrier.

410 For my mother Thetis the goddess of the silver feet tells me

I carry two sorts of destiny toward the day of my death. Either,

if I stay here and fight beside the city of the Trojans,

my return home is gone, but my glory shall be everlasting;

but if I return home to the beloved land of my fathers,

415 the excellence of my glory is gone, but there will be a long life

left for me, and my end in death will not come to me quickly.

And this would be my counsel to others also, to sail back
home again, since no longer shall you find any term set
on the sheer city of Ilion, since Zeus of the wide brows has strongly
420   held his own hand over it, and its people are made bold.
Do you go back therefore to the great men of the Achaians,
and take them this message, since such is the privilege of the princes:
that they think out in their minds some other scheme that is better,
which might rescue their ships, and the people of the Achaians
425   who man the hollow ships, since this plan will not work for them
which they thought of by reason of my anger. Let Phoinix
remain here with us and sleep here, so that tomorrow
he may come with us in our ships to the beloved land of our fathers,
if he will; but I will never use force to hold him."

Think about it.

1.   What is Achilles' justification for not fighting?
2.   Why does home seem more appealing to him than fighting on the battlefield?

---

c. 700 BCE

20. Theogony, Works and Days

Translated by Daryl Hine

What follows are selections from two works composed by the Greek poet Hesiod, who lived in Boeotia in Greece at some time between 750 and 650 BCE. *The Theogony* tells the story of the origins of the cosmos and of the gods. *Works and Days* is an instructional manual (about morality and farming), which is addressed to Hesiod's brother Perses. Both works were probably performed publicly to music.

Theogony

There is no way of escaping from Zeus's implacable mind-set.
"Iapetus's son, over all of the others exceedingly smart and
Knowledgeable, old fellow, you haven't forgotten your cunning!"
Zeus, being angry, spoke thus, with a deathless intention in mind, and,
Ever recalling the trick that was played on him, would not entrust the

535   Fierce inexhaustible fire to the hands of men, who must perish,
Creatures engendered of ash trees, who dwell on the face of the earth.
But Prometheus, Iapetus's brave son, thoroughly fooled him,
For he stole inexhaustible fire, whose blaze can be seen from
Far, in a hollow cane, which offended profoundly the mind of

540   Zeus, who thunders aloft, and his fond heart grew very angry
Seeing the twinkle of fire from afar among men, who are mortal.
Straightaway, Zeus prepared for them evil in place of purloined fire.
Famous Hephaestus,[1] the lame god, molded of water and earth the
Shape of a modest maiden by Zeus's advice and divine will.

545   Then Athena, the gray-eyed goddess, clad her and dressed her
Up in a silvery garment. Over her head she draped a
Finely embroidered veil with her hands, a most marvelous sight; with
Lovely garlands of new-grown wildflowers, Pallas Athena
Crowned her. Also, a garland of gold she put on her head, which

550   Famous Hephaestus the lame one himself devised with his own hands,
Artfully fashioning it as a favor to fatherly Zeus.
On it was wrought much intricate workmanship, wonderful to be
Seen; of the monstrous creatures such as the sea and the dry land
Nourish, he put many on it—so radiant beauty and splendor

555   Shone from it—creatures so lifelike one might suppose they had voices.
So when Hephaestus had made this beautiful bane in exchange for
Good, he conducted her to that place where the humans and gods were,
All tricked out by the gray-eyed daughter of powerful Zeus.
Wonderment seized the immortal gods and men who are mortal

560   When they beheld such a sheer deception and hardship for mankind;
But from her are descended untold generations of women.
And from her you may trace the descent of the pestilent races of women;
Dwelling among mortal men, they occasion us plenty of trouble,
Bearing with us in prosperity, never in miserable hardship.

565   Likewise, in beetling beehives bees feed mischievous drones, for
Daily and all day long until sundown, while honeybees labor
Building the white wax honeycombs, drones on the other hand stay at
Home in the sheltering hive and gobble the labor of others.

---

1 Vulcan in Latin.

Similarly did Zeus, who thunders aloft, create women,
570   Bad for mankind, in cahoots in all manner of tiresome mischief.
And he provided another bad thing in exchange for a good thing.
If, to avoid getting wed and the vexing behavior of women,
One doesn't go in for marriage, he arrives at lamentable old age
Lacking somebody to tend to him when he is old, and though he lacks
575   Nothing to live on when he is alive, at his death his relations,
Heirs to a vacant estate, will apportion his substance among them.
Yet on the other hand, for one who chooses the chances of marriage,
To have and to hold a respectable wife in accord with his wishes
From the beginning and through all his days, good squabbles with bad; for
580   Any who finds his children unruly will certainly lead a
Life of incessant heartache: that's an incurable evil.
Thus it is possible neither to fool Zeus nor circumvent his
Wits, for not even Prometheus, Iapetus's son, although clever,
Could quite get himself out from the yoke of his heavy displeasure,
585   But necessarily, smart though he was, strong bondage repressed him.

Work and Days

Plainly the gods keep secret from humankind the means of survival;
Otherwise, you in a day could easily do enough work to
Last you a whole year long, and without any further exertion.
45   Soon, very soon you would hang up over the fireplace your rudder;
Then would be finished the labors of oxen and hard-working donkeys.
No, Zeus kept it a secret because in his heart he was angry,
Seeing how devious-minded Prometheus once had fooled him;
Therefore did almighty Zeus plot sorrows and troubles for mankind.
50   He hid fire, which, however, then Iapetus's great-hearted son, to
Benefit humankind, pilfered from Zeus, the purveyor of counsel,
Hid in a hollowed-out stalk to baffle the lover of thunder.
Then cloud-gathering Zeus to Prometheus said in his anger:
"Iapetus's brat, since you're so much smarter than anyone else, you're
55   Happy to outwit me, and rejoice in the fire you have stolen—
For yourself a calamity, also for men of the future.
For I shall give them a bad thing, too, in exchange for this fire, which
Heartily all may delight in, embracing a homegrown evil."
Speaking, the father of gods and of mankind exploded in laughter.
60   Then he commanded Hephaestus,[2] the world-famed craftsman, as soon as
Possible to mix water and earth, and infuse in it human

---

2 Vulcan in Latin, the god of workmanship.

Speech, also strength, and to make it look like a goddess, and give it
Likewise a girl-like form that was pretty and lovesome. Athena
Would instruct her in handwork and weaving of intricate fabrics;
65   Furthermore, gold Aphrodite[3] should drip charm over her head to
Cause heartsore longing, emotional anguish exhausting the body.
Zeus gave instructions to Hermes, the sure guide, slayer of Argus,[4]
To put in her the heart of a bitch and a devious nature.
Then did the famed lame god manufacture at once from the earth a
70   Fair simulacrum of one shy maiden, according to Zeus's will.
Next to her skin did the godlike Graces and gracious Persuasion
Carefully place gold necklaces; round her adorable head the
Hours who are gorgeously coiffed wove garlands of beautiful spring flowers.
Hermes, our sure guide, slayer of Argus, contrived in her breast
75   Lies and misleadingly false words joined to a devious nature,
At the behest of the deep-voiced thunderer, Zeus; and the herald
God of the gods then gave her a voice. And he called her Pandora,
Seeing how all who inhabit lofty Olympus had given
Something to pretty Pandora, that giant bane to industrious mankind.
80   When he had finished this downright desperate piece of deception,
To Epimetheus Zeus then dispatched the slayer of Argus,
Famed swift messenger of the immortals, with her as a present.
But Epimetheus had forgotten Prometheus's warning,
Not to accept anything from Olympian Zeus, but to send it
85   Back where it came from, lest it become a disaster for mortals.
Once he'd accepted it, he, possessing the bane, recognized it.
Formerly dwelt on earth all the various tribes of the human
Race, on their own and remote from evils and difficult labor
And from distressing diseases that bring doom closer to each one.
90   For in misfortune do humans age rapidly, quicker than ever.
Using her fingers, the maid pried open the lid of the great jar,
Sprinkling its contents; her purpose, to bring sad hardships to mankind.
Nothing but Hope stayed there in her stout, irrefrangible dwelling,
Under the lip of the jar, inside, and she never would venture
95   Outdoors, having the lid of the vessel itself to prevent her,
Willed there by Zeus, who arranges the storm clouds and carries the aegis.[5]
Otherwise, myriad miseries flit round miserable mortals;
Furthermore, full is the earth of much mischief, the deep sea also.
Illnesses visiting humans daily and nightly at all hours

---

3   Venus in Latin, the goddess of love.
4   A many-eyed monster, which Hermes killed. It became a peacock. We still say "argus-eyed."
5   Stock epithet whose meaning is obscure: "who carries the goatskin"? "Who follows the lapwing or snipe that presages a storm"? We say "under the aegis of."

100   All by themselves bring terrible troubles aplenty to mortals
Silently, seeing their power of speech was suppressed by all-wise Zeus.

Think about it.

1. According to Hesiod, why is the world full of evils?
2. What is Hesiod's view of women?

---

21. The Yahwist Legend

Translated by David Miano

In the Hebrew Bible, the current literary complex known as The Primary History (consisting of the books Genesis, Exodus, Leviticus, Numbers, Deuteronomy, Joshua, Judges, 1 Samuel, 2 Samuel, 1 Kings, and 2 Kings) is a combination of a number of earlier written sources. The Yahwist Legend (named for its anonymous author we call the Yahwist) is thought by many scholars to be the earliest of these. Though often referred to as a "history," this work, which tells the story of Israel's past, provides no dates for any of the events it describes. Since the legend concludes with the reign of King Solomon of Israel (c. 974–934 BCE) and there is evidence that it was edited by someone subscribing to Deuteronomic theology (which became prevalent in the 7th century BCE), its date must be placed between the 10th and 7th centuries BCE, but probably no earlier than the 8th, when writing prose narrative was first becoming customary in this part of the world. With its praise for the dynasty of David, the author probably lived in the kingdom of Judah. What follows are three passages from this work.

The Garden of Eden

²:⁵Before any shrub of the field had come on the land and before any grass of the field had sprouted, because Yahweh God had not yet made it rain on the land, and there was no human to cultivate the soil, ²:⁶a flow would well up from the land, and it would water the entire surface of the ground. ²:⁷And Yahweh God formed a human of dirt from the ground, and he blew into his nostrils the breath of life, and the human became a living soul.

²:⁸Then Yahweh God planted a garden in Eden in the east, and he put there the human that he had formed. ²:⁹And Yahweh God caused to grow from

the ground every tree pleasing to see and good to eat. The tree of life was in the middle of the garden, and the tree of the knowledge of good and bad....

²:¹⁵Yahweh God took the human and put him in the garden of Eden to cultivate it and tend it. ²:¹⁶Then Yahweh God commanded the human, saying, "From every tree of the garden you may certainly eat, ²:¹⁷but from the tree of the knowledge of good and bad you may not eat, because in the day of your eating from it, you shall certainly die."

²:¹⁸Then Yahweh God said, "It is not good for the human to be alone. I will make for him a helper to suit him." ²:¹⁹So Yahweh God formed from the land all the wild animals of the field and all the birds of the heavens, and he brought them to the human to see what he would call them; and whatever the human called them, each living soul, that was its name. ²:²⁰The human gave names to all the tame animals, to the birds of the heavens, and to all the wild animals, but for a human there was found no helper to suit him. ²:²¹So Yahweh caused the human to fall into a deep slumber, and as he slept, he took one of his ribs and then closed the flesh up over the spot. ²:²²Then Yahweh God fashioned the rib, which he had taken from the human, into a woman. When he brought her to the human, ²:²³the human said,

"This one, at last,
Is bone from my bones
And flesh from my flesh.
This one shall be called 'woman,'
For from a man she was taken."

²:²⁴This is why a man leaves his father and his mother and clings to his woman and they become one flesh. ²:²⁵The two of them were naked, the human and his woman, and they were not ashamed.

³:¹Now the snake was the cleverest of all the wild animals of the field that Yahweh God had made, and it said to the woman, "Did God really say that you are not allowed to eat from every tree of the garden?" ³:²The woman replied to the snake, "We may eat from the fruit of the trees of the garden, ³:³but from the fruit of the tree that is in the middle of the garden, God said, 'Do not eat from it, and do not touch it, or else you will die."

³:⁴And the serpent said to the woman, "You certainly will not die, ³:⁵because God knows that in the day you eat from it, your eyes will be opened, and you will be like gods knowing good and bad."

³:⁶Then the woman saw that the tree was good for eating and that it was delightful to the eyes, and the tree was desirable for making one wise, so she took from its fruit, and she ate; and she also gave to her man when he was with her, and he ate. ³:⁷Then the eyes of both of them became opened, and they knew that they were naked. So they sewed fig leaves together and made loincloths for themselves.

³:⁸Then they heard the sound of Yahweh God walking in the garden at the windy time of day, and the human and his woman hid from Yahweh God's face in the midst of the trees of the garden. ³:⁹And Yahweh God called to the human, and he said to him, "Where are you?"

³:¹⁰And he replied, "Your sound I heard in the garden, and I was afraid, because I was naked, so I hid."

³:¹¹And he said, "Who told you that you were naked? Have you eaten from the tree from which I commanded you not to eat?"

³:¹²And the human replied, "The woman whom you put at my side—she gave to me from the tree, and I ate."

³:¹³And Yahweh God said to the woman, "What is this that you've done?"

And the woman replied, "The snake—it tricked me, and I ate."

³:¹⁴Then Yahweh God said to the snake, "Because you have done this,

"More cursed are you
Than all the tame animals
And all the wild animals of the field.
Upon your belly you shall crawl,
And dirt you shall eat
All the days of your life.
³:¹⁵I will create hatred
Between you and the woman,

And between your offspring and hers.

He shall strike you on the head,

And you shall strike him on the heel."

3:16 And to the woman he said,

"Very severe I will make

Your pangs in childbearing.

In pain you shall bear children,

And for your man your urge shall be,

And he, he shall rule over you."

3:17 And to Adam[1] he said, "Because you have listened to the voice of your woman, and you have eaten from the tree from which I commanded you not to eat, saying, 'You shall not eat from it,'

"Cursed is the ground on your account.

In heavy labor you shall eat of it

All the days of your life,

3:18 And thorns and thistles it shall sprout for you,

And your food is the grass of the field.

3:19 By the sweat of your face

You shall eat food

Until you return to the ground,

For from it you were taken,

For dirt you are,

And to dirt you will return."

3:20 And the human named his woman Eve,[2] because she would become mother of all the living. 3:21 Then Yahweh God made garments of skins for Adam and his woman, and he clothed them.

3:22 Then Yahweh God said, "Here the human has become like one of us, knowing good and bad. So now, lest he put out his hand and take also from the tree of life and eat and live forever…," 3:23 and Yahweh God banished him from the garden of Eden to work the ground from which he had been taken. 3:24 He drove the human out, and east of the garden of Eden he stationed the cherubs[3] and the fiery ever-turning sword to guard the path to the tree of life.

The Flood

6:5 Yahweh saw that the human's[4] badness was great in the land and that every inclination of his heart's thoughts was only bad all day long. 6:6 And Yahweh was sorry that he had made the human in the land, and he was grieved to his heart. 6:7 So Yahweh said, "I will wipe the human whom I have created from the face of the ground—from human to tame animal to creeper, and even the bird of the sky, because I am sorry that I have made them."

6:8 Yet Noah found favor in Yahweh's sight. 7:1 So Yahweh said to Noah, "Go into the container,[5] you and your entire household, for I have seen that you alone are righteous before me in this generation. 7:2 Of every pure animal[6] take with you seven pairs, male and female, and of every animal that is not pure, just two, male and female; 7:3 also of the birds of the sky seven pairs, male and female, to keep their progeny alive on the face of all the land. 7:4 For in seven more days I will make rain on the land for forty days and forty nights, and I will wipe every living thing that I have made from the face of the ground."

7:5 And Noah did everything as Yahweh had commanded him, 7:7 and Noah and his sons and his wife and his sons' wives went into the container to escape the waters of the flood, 7:16b and Yahweh shut him in.

7:17 The flood lasted forty days upon the land, 7:18 and the waters grew mighty and increased greatly upon the land, and the container floated on the face of the waters. 7:19 The waters grew so exceedingly mighty upon the land that all the high mountains under the whole sky were covered. 7:23 And every living thing that was on the face of the ground was wiped out, from human to tame animal to creeper, and even the bird of the sky; yes they were wiped from the land. Only Noah was left, and those that were with him in the container.

---

1 The first time the human is named. In Hebrew it is simply "the human" without the definite article "the."

2 Meaning "life."

3 Human-headed winged lions.

4 The writer is now using the term "human" collectively to refer to all the humans.

5 The Hebrew word traditionally has been translated "ark," but it means a box, chest, or container. It does not mean boat.

6 Pure according to the Israelite sacrificial code.

8:6At the end of forty days it happened that Noah opened the window of the container that he had made, 8:8and he sent out the dove from him to see if the waters had receded from the face of the ground; 8:9but the dove found no place to set the sole of her foot, and she returned to him into the container, because the waters were on the face of the whole land. So he put out his hand and took her and brought her into the ark with him. 8:10Then he waited another seven days, and again he sent out the dove from the ark; 8:11and the dove came back to him at sunset, and there in her beak was a freshly plucked olive leaf; so Noah knew that the waters had receded from the land. 8:12Then he waited yet another seven days, and he sent out the dove; and she did not return to him any more.

8:13bThen Noah removed the cover of the container, and he looked and saw that the face of the ground had dried. 8:20So Noah built an altar to Yahweh, and took of every pure animal and of every pure bird, and he offered burnt offerings on the altar. 8:21And when Yahweh smelled the soothing smell, Yahweh said in his heart, "I will never again curse the ground because of the human, for the inclination of the human's heart is bad from his youth; nor will I ever again strike down every living thing as I have done.

8:22All the days the land endures,
Seedtime and harvest,
Cold and heat,
Summer and winter,
Day and night,
Will not cease."

The Ten Commandments (Early Version)

34:5Yahweh descended in the cloud and stood with [Moses] there, and he invoked the name Yahweh. 34:6And Yahweh passed in front of him, and Yahweh said, "Yahweh is a god merciful and benevolent, slow to anger, and abundant in steadfast love and faithfulness, 34:7keeping steadfast love to the thousandth generation, putting up with crime and transgression and sin, yet by no means acquitting the guilty, but reckoning the crime of the parents upon the children, and upon the children's children, and upon the third generation, and upon the fourth generation.

34:14For you must not bow down to another god, because Yahweh, whose name is Jealous, is a jealous god.

34:17You must not make cast idols.

34:18You must keep the Unleavened Bread Festival. Seven days you shall eat unleavened bread, which I commanded you [to keep] at the time of the month of Abib, because in the month of Abib you came out from Egypt.

34:19Everything that first loosens the womb is mine, and from all your livestock the male, the firstborn of cow and sheep. 34:20The firstborn of a donkey you must redeem with a sheep, and if you do not redeem it you shall break its neck. All the firstborn of your sons you must redeem, and they must not appear before me empty-handed.

34:21Six days you may work, but on the seventh day you must rest; even in plowing time and in harvest time you must rest.

34:22You must make for yourself the Festival of Weeks, the first fruits of wheat harvest, and the Festival of Ingathering at the turn of the year.

34:23Three times in the year all your males must appear before the Lord Yahweh, the God of Israel, 34:24for I will cast out nations before you and enlarge your borders. And no one shall covet your land when you go up to appear before Yahweh your God three times in the year.

34:25You must not slaughter my sacrificial blood on leavened food, and the sacrifice of the Passover festival must not be left until the morning.

34:26The choicest of the ground's firstfruits you must bring to the house of Yahweh your God.

You must not cook a kid in its mother's milk.

34:27And Yahweh said to Moses, "Write down these statements for yourself, because based on these statements I have cut a covenant with you and

with Israel. [34:28b]So he wrote on the tablets the statements of the covenant, the Ten Statements.[7]

---

7   The Hebrew word usually translated "commandments"
simply means "words" or "statements."

Think about it.

1.   The Garden of Eden story explains the origins of various things. What are they?
2.   What similarities do you see between the animosity between Yahweh and the snake in the Garden of
      Eden story and between Zeus and Prometheus in the Hesiod tale?
3.   What similarities do you see between this story and the one you read from The Epic of Gilgamesh
      (reading # 7)?

7th century BCE

---

22. The Brihadâranyaka Upanishad

Translated by F. Max Müller

The Brihadâranyaka Upanishad is one of the oldest texts in the Upanishad collection and was composed in Sanskrit probably
around the 7th century BCE as a commentary on a hymn from the Rig Veda called the *Purusha sukta*. Its authorship has been
ascribed to Yājñavalkya, a legendary Brahmin sage. The text reproduced here, called the *Purusha vidya brahmana*, relates the
story of creation and provides an early description of Brahman.

Purusha vidya Brahmana

1. In the beginning this was Self[1] alone, in the shape of a person.[2] He looking round saw nothing but
his Self. He first said, 'This is I;' therefore he became
I by name. Therefore even now, if a man is asked, he
first says, 'This is I,' and then pronounces the other

---

1   *Atman*, used here to refer to the universal Self (Brahman) and,
further down, to the individual self or soul (for which, in later
writings, it is used exclusively).

2   *Purusha*, a term frequently used to refer to the great cosmic
Self.

---

name which he may have. And because before all this, he (the Self) burnt down all evils, therefore he was a person. Verily he who knows this burns down everyone who tries to be before him.

2. He feared, and therefore anyone who is lonely fears. He thought, 'As there is nothing but myself, why should I fear?' Thence his fear passed away. For what should he have feared? Verily fear arises from a second only.

3. But he felt no delight. Therefore a man who is lonely feels no delight. He wished for a second. He was so large as man and wife together. He then made this his Self to fall in two, and thence arose husband and wife.[3] Therefore Yājñavalkya said: 'We two are thus (each of us) like half a shell.' Therefore the void which was there, is filled by the wife. He embraced her, and men were born.

4. She thought, 'How can he embrace me, after having produced me from himself? I shall hide myself.'

She then became a cow, the other became a bull and embraced her, and hence cows were born. The one became a mare, the other a stallion; the one a male ass, the other a female ass. He embraced her, and hence one-hoofed animals were born. The one became a she-goat, the other a he-goat; the one became a ewe, the other a ram. He embraced her, and hence goats and sheep were born. And thus he created everything that exists in pairs, down to the ants.

5. He knew, 'I indeed am this creation, for I created all this.' Hence he became the creation, and he who knows this lives in this his creation.

6. Next he thus produced fire by rubbing. From the mouth, as from the fire-hole, and from the hands he created fire. Therefore both the mouth and the hands are inside without hair, for the fire-hole is inside without hair.

And when they say, 'Sacrifice to this or sacrifice to that god,' each god is but his manifestation, for he is all gods.

Now, whatever there is moist, that he created from seed; this is Soma.[4] So far verily is this universe either food or eater. Soma indeed is food, Agni[5] eater. This is the highest creation of Brahman, when he created the gods from his better part, and when he, who was (then) mortal, created the immortals. Therefore it was the highest creation. And he who knows this, lives in this his highest creation.

7. Now all this was then undeveloped. It became developed by form and name, so that one could say, 'He, called so and so, is such a one.' Therefore at present also all this is developed by name and form, so that one can say, 'He, called so and so, is such a one.'

He (Brahman or the Self) entered thither, to the very tips of the finger-nails, as a razor might be fitted in a razor-case, or as fire in a fire-place.

He cannot be seen, for, in part only, when breathing, he is breath by name; when speaking, speech by name; when seeing, eye by name; when hearing, ear by name; when thinking, mind by name. All these are but the names of his acts. And he who worships (regards) him as the one or the other, does not know him, for he is apart from this (when qualified) by the one or the other (predicate). Let men worship him as Self, for in the Self all these are one. This Self is the footstep of everything, for through it one knows everything. And as one can find again by footsteps what was lost, thus he who knows this finds glory and praise.

8. This, which is nearer to us than anything, this Self, is dearer than a son, dearer than wealth, dearer than all else.

And if one were to say to one who declares another than the Self dear, that he will lose what is dear to him, very likely it would be so. Let him worship

---

3   The words for husband and wife (*pati* and *patnī*) are playing on the word for "two" (*pat*).

4   A Vedic ritual drink.
5   Fire personified, the god of sacrifices (because sacrifices were burned), and the divine model for sacrificial priests.

the Self alone as dear. He who worships the Self alone as dear, the object of his love will never perish.

9. Here they say: 'If men think that by knowledge of Brahman they will become everything, what then did that Brahman know, from whence all this sprang?'

10. Verily in the beginning this was Brahman, that Brahman knew (its) Self only, saying, 'I am Brahman.' From it all this sprang. Thus, whatever Deva[6] was awakened (so as to know Brahman), he indeed became that (Brahman); and the same with Rishis[7] and men. The Rishi Vâmadeva saw and understood it, singing, 'I was Manu (moon), I was the sun.' Therefore now also he who thus knows that he is Brahman, becomes all this, and even the Devas cannot prevent it, for he himself is their Self.

Now if a man worships another deity, thinking the deity is one and he another, he does not know. He is like a beast for the Devas. For verily, as many beasts nourish a man, thus does every man nourish the Devas. If only one beast is taken away, it is not pleasant; how much more when many are taken! Therefore it is not pleasant to the Devas that men should know this.

11. Verily in the beginning this was Brahman, one only. That being one, was not strong enough. It created still further the most excellent Kshatra,[8] viz. those Kshatras among the Devas—Indra, Varuna, Soma, Rudra, Parganya, Yama, Mrityu, Îsâna. Therefore there is nothing beyond the Kshatra, and therefore at the Râgasûya sacrifice the Brâhmana[9] sits down below the Kshatriya.[10] He confers that glory on the Kshatra alone. But Brahman is (nevertheless) the birth-place of the Kshatra. Therefore though a king is exalted, he sits down at the end (of the sacrifice) below the Brahman, as his birth-place.

He who injures him, injures his own birth-place. He becomes worse, because he has injured one better than himself.

12. He was not strong enough. He created the Vis,[11] the classes of Devas which in their different orders are called Vasus, Rudras, Âdityas, Visve-devas, Maruts.

13. He was not strong enough. He created the Shudra colour (caste),[12] as Pûshan.[13] This earth verily is Pûshan; for the earth nourishes all this whatsoever.

14. He was not strong enough. He created still further the most excellent Law (dharma). Law is the Kshatra of the Kshatra, therefore there is nothing higher than the Law. Thenceforth even a weak man rules a stronger with the help of the Law, as with the help of a king. Thus the Law is what is called the true. And if a man declares what is true, they say he declares the Law; and if he declares the Law, they say he declares what is true. Thus both are the same.

15. There are then this Brahman, Kshatra, Vis, and Shudra. Among the Devas that Brahman existed as Agni (fire) only, among men as Brâhmana, as Kshatriya through the (divine) Kshatriya, as Vaishya through the (divine) Vaishya, as Shudra through the (divine) Shudra. Therefore people wish for their future state among the Devas through Agni only;[14] and among men through the Brâhmana, for in these two forms did Brahman exist.

Now if a man departs this life without having seen his true future life (in the Self), then that Self, not being known, does not receive and bless him, as if the Veda had not been read, or as if a good work had not been done. Nay, even if one who does not know that (Self), should perform here on earth some great holy work, it will Perish for him in the end. Let a man worship the Self only as his true state. If a man

---

6   Deity.
7   Sages.
8   "Authority." The Kshatras are the high gods.
9   Or Brahmin (priest).
10   One among the ruling elite in the human realm.

11   The lesser gods.
12   The low gods.
13   Solar god, feeder of cattle.
14   In other words, they must offer sacrifices.

worships the Self only as his true state, his work does not Perish, for whatever he desires that he gets from that Self.

16. Now verily this Self (of the ignorant man) is the world of all creatures. In so far as man sacrifices and pours out libations, he is the world of the Devas; in so far as he repeats the hymns, etc., he is the world of the Rishis; in so far as he offers cakes to the Fathers and tries to obtain offspring, he is the world of the Fathers; in so far as he gives shelter and food to men, he is the world of men; in so far as he finds fodder and water for the animals, he is the world of the animals; in so far as quadrupeds, birds, and even ants live in his houses, he is their world. And as every one wishes his own world not to be injured, thus all beings wish that he who knows this should not be injured. Verily this is known and has been well reasoned.

17. In the beginning this was Self alone, one only. He desired, 'Let there be a wife for me that I may have offspring, and let there be wealth for me that I may offer sacrifices.' Verily this is the whole desire, and, even if wishing for more, he would not find it. Therefore now also a lonely person desires, 'Let there be a wife for me that I may have offspring, and let there be wealth for me that I may offer sacrifices.' And so long as he does not obtain either of these things, he thinks he is incomplete. Now his completeness (is made up as follows): mind is his self (the husband); speech the wife; breath the child; the eye all worldly wealth, for he finds it with the eye; the ear his divine wealth, for he hears it with the ear. The body is his work, for with the body he works. This is the fivefold sacrifice, for fivefold is the animal, fivefold man, fivefold all this whatsoever. He who knows this, obtains all this.

Think about it.

1. Where can one find Brahman?
2. What is the only thing one can know and worship, and why is this so?
3. What happens when a person leaves this life not knowing the Self?

---

c. 622 BCE

23. The Josianic Code

Translated by David Miano

The laws presented here come from a code believed to have been implemented during the reign of King Josiah of Judah (640–609 BCE). The Deuteronomic History (see intro to reading #24) claims that the core of this law was found in the Jerusalem temple during renovations in the 18th year of Josiah's reign (c. 622 BCE) and that the laws were written by Moses. However ancient their inspiration, the laws that were ultimately propounded by Josiah's administration are notable for some radical departures from previous customs, such as the centralization of Yahweh worship in Jerusalem and the outlawing of religious centers elsewhere in the country. I have selected what I think are some of the more interesting laws from the code.

Deut 12:13-20

Take care that you do not offer your burnt offerings in any place that you see, but only in the place that Yahweh will choose among one of your tribes. There you shall offer your burnt offerings, and there you shall do everything that I command you. Yet when your soul desires, you may slaughter and eat meat, according to Yahweh's blessing that he has given you, within any of your city gates. The pure and the impure may eat of it, as they would of gazelle and deer. Only the blood you may not eat; onto the ground you shall pour it out like water.

Deut 19:15

A single witness shall not be brought against a man for any crime or any transgression. For any transgression that he commits, on the testimony of two witnesses or on the testimony of three witnesses shall a charge be sustained.

Deut 20:10-18

When you approach a city to make war against it and offer it conditions of surrender, it shall be that if it surrenders and opens for you, then all the people who are found in it shall become forced laborers, and they shall serve you. But if it does not surrender to you and makes war against you, and you besiege it, and Yahweh delivers it into your hand, then you shall strike every male of it with the edge of the sword. Only the women, the children, the domestic animals, and everything else in the city—all its spoil—you shall seize for yourself. And you may consume the spoil of your enemies that Yahweh your God has given to you. Thus you shall do to all the cities that lie at a great distance from you, but of the cities of these people that Yahweh your God has given to you as an inheritance, you shall not keep alive anything that breathes. No, you shall completely annihilate them—the Hittites, the Amorites, the Canaanites, the Perizzites, the Hivites, the Jebusites—as Yahweh your God has commanded you, so that they may not teach you to do according to all their disgusting practices, which they have performed for their gods, and make you sin against Yahweh your God.

Deut 22:13-29

If a man takes a woman and cohabits with her, but then he hates her and makes shameful accusations against her and gives her a bad name by saying, "This woman I took, but when I came near to her, I did not find in her the evidence of virginity!" Then the young woman's father and her mother shall take and bring the evidence of the young woman's virginity to the elders of the city gate. And the young woman's father shall say to the elders, "My daughter I have given to this man to be his woman, but he hates her, and here he has made shameful accusations against her, saying, 'I have not found in your daughter the evidence of virginity.' And this is the evidence of my daughter's virginity." And they shall spread the cloth before the elders of the city. Then the elders of that city shall take the man and punish him; they shall fine him one hundred shekels of silver and give it to the young woman's father, because he has given a virgin of Israel a bad name. And she shall be his woman; he may not send her away all his days. But if this accusation is true—the evidence of virginity has not been found for the young woman—then they shall bring the young woman out to the door of her father's house, and the men of her city shall stone her with stones until she dies, because she has done a shameful act in Israel by prostituting herself in her father's house. So you shall cut off the evil from your midst.

If a man is found lying down with a woman married to a husband, they shall die—yes, both of them: the man who lied down with the woman and the woman. So you shall cut off the evil from Israel.

If there happens to be a young woman, a virgin betrothed to a man, and a man finds her in the city and lies down with her, then you shall bring them both out to the gate of that city and stone them with stones until they die—the young woman because she did not cry out in the city, and the man because he has defiled his neighbor's woman. So you shall cut off the evil from your midst. But if in the open country the man finds the betrothed young woman, and the man seizes her and lies down with her, then only the man who has lied down with her shall die, and to the young woman you shall do nothing. In the young woman's case there is not a transgression worthy of death, because, as in the case of a man who rises up against his neighbor and kills him, a living soul, the reasoning is the same: in the open country he found her; the betrothed young woman cried out, and no one rescued her.

If a man finds a young virgin woman who is not betrothed, and he seizes her and lies down with her, and they are caught, then the man who lied down with her shall give to the young woman's father fifty shekels of silver, and she shall become his woman. Because he has defiled her, he may not send her away all his days.

Deut 24:1-4

If a man has taken a woman and married her, and it happens that she finds no favor in his eyes, because he has found some indecency in her, and he writes out for her a paper of separation and puts it in her hand and sends her out of his house, and she leaves his house and goes and becomes another man's, and the latter man hates her and writes her a paper of separation and puts it in her hand and send her out of his house (or if the latter man, who took her to be his woman, dies), her first husband who sent her away may not again take her to be his woman after she has been defiled, because it is an abomination before Yahweh, and you shall not bring transgression into the land that Yahweh your God has given you as an inheritance.

Deut 24:16

Parents shall not be put to death on account of their children, and children shall not be put to death on account of their parents; each shall be put to death for his own transgression.

Deut 25:1-3, 5-11

If there is a dispute between men, and they enter into litigation and are judged, and the innocent one is declared innocent, and the wrongdoer is declared guilty, it shall be that if the wrongdoer is to be flogged, the judge shall make him lie down and be flogged in his presence with a number of lashes appropriate for his guilt. Forty times he may strike him; he may not add more, lest he beat him beyond this limit of beatings and your fellow be degraded before your eyes.

If brothers are dwelling together and one of them dies, and he has no son, the wife of the deceased shall not go outside to a strange man; her husband's brother shall go and take her as his own woman and perform the levirate's duty. And it shall be that the first son that she bears shall succeed to the name of the deceased brother, so that his name will not be blotted out from Israel. And if the man does not desire to take his brother's woman, then his brother's wife shall go up to the city gate, to the elders, and she shall say, "My husband's brother refuses to provide a successor to his brother's name in Israel. He is not willing to perform the levirate's duty for me." Then the elders of his city shall summon him and speak to him, and if he stands firm and says, "I do not desire to take her," then his brother's wife shall approach him in front of the elders, and she shall take his sandal from his foot, spit in his face, and say, "This is what is done to a man who will not build up his brother's house." And his name in Israel shall be, "the house of the one whose sandal was removed."

If men fight with one another, a man and his fellow, and the woman of one of them intervenes to rescue her man from the hand of his assailant, and she puts out her hand and grabs his genitals, then you shall cut off her hand; your eyes shall not have pity.

c. 610 BCE

24. The Deuteronomic History

Translated by David Miano

The theological ideas prevalent in Josiah's law code (see reading #23) are often called "Deuteronomic" by scholars today, because they are currently found in the Book of Deuteronomy in the Hebrew Bible. The Deuteronomic movement, which was quite active in Josiah's day (640–609 BCE), and government supported, also produced a new history of Israel and Judah, which judged past leaders by their adherence to Deuteronomic ideas. The Deuteronomic History, which was finished late in Josiah's reign, appears to have been either an expansion of the earlier Yahwist Legend or a sequel to it. A second edition with supplementary material was produced in the 6th century BCE.

The Davidic Covenant

7:1Now it came to pass that, when the king had taken up residence in his house and Yahweh had given him rest from (fighting) all his enemies round about, 7:2the king said to Nathan the prophet, "See now, I dwell in a house of cedar, but God's ark dwells amid the curtains."[1] 7:3And Nathan said to the king,

"Everything that is in your heart, go, do, for Yahweh is with you."

7:4But it so happened, on that same night, that Yahweh's word came to Nathan, saying, 7:5"Go and say to my servant, to David, 'This is what Yahweh has said, "Shall you yourself build me a house to dwell in? 7:6For I have not dwelt in a house since the day that I brought up the Israelites out of Egypt until

---

1   Referring to the temporary structure holding the ark at that time. The ark is the sacred chest containing the tablets on which the Ten Commandments are written.

today, and I am moving about in a tent and a tabernacle. ⁷:⁷In any place where I have travelled with all the Israelites, have I ever spoken a word to any of the chieftains of Israel, whom I commanded to shepherd my people Israel, saying, 'Why haven't you built me a house of cedar?'?'"

⁷:⁸Therefore this is what you shall say to my servant David: 'This is what Yahweh Sebaoth has said, "I myself have taken you from the pasture, from following the sheep, to be a prince over my people, over Israel. ⁷:⁹And I will be with you wherever you go, and I will cut off all of your enemies from before you, and I will make you a great name, like the names of all the great ones that are in the land. ⁷:¹⁰And I will assign a place to my people, to Israel, and establish them; and they will dwell in their own place and not be harassed anymore, and violent people will not afflict them continuously, as they did previously ⁷:¹¹and since the day that I commanded chieftains to be over my people Israel. Yes, I will give you rest from all your enemies.' And Yahweh has told you that Yahweh will make for you a house:² ⁷:¹²"For your days will be fulfilled, and you shall sleep with your fathers,³ and I will set up your offspring after you, who shall come forth from your lower body, and I will establish his kingdom. ⁷:¹³He himself will build a house for my name, and I will establish the throne of his kingdom indefinitely. ⁷:¹⁴I myself will be a father to him, and he himself will be a son to me, which (means) when he does wrong, I will correct him with a rod of men and with the blows of humans, ⁷:¹⁵but my mercy will not leave him, as I took it from Saul, whom I turned away before you. ⁷:¹⁶And your house and your kingdom shall be made firm indefinitely before you; your throne shall be established indefinitely.""

---

2   The word for "house" in Hebrew can mean both an actual dwelling place and also a family or dynasty, which is the way it is used here. There is an interesting play on words: David wants to build Yahweh a house (i.e., a temple), but Yahweh instead is going to build David a house (i.e., a dynasty).

3   In other words, be buried next to them.

⁷:¹⁷In accordance with all these words, and in accordance with this entire vision, so did Nathan speak to David.

Ahab and Jehoshaphat at Ramoth-Gilead

²²:¹Now three years Aram and Israel continued without war, ²²:²but in the third year Jehoshaphat the king of Judah paid a visit to the king of Israel. ²²:³And [Ahab] the king of Israel said to his servants, "Do you know that Ramoth-gilead is ours, and we show laziness by not taking it out of the hand of the king of Aram?" ²²:⁴Then he said to Jehoshaphat, "Will you go with me to battle at Ramoth-gilead?" And Jehoshaphat said to the king of Israel, "I am as you are; as my people are, so are your people; as my horses are, so are your horses."

²²:⁵But Jehoshaphat said to the king of Israel, "Inquire right now for the word of Yahweh." ²²:⁶So the king of Israel gathered the prophets, about four hundred men, and he said to them, "Shall I go against Ramoth-gilead in battle, or shall I refrain?" And they said, "Go up, for Yahweh will deliver it into the king's hand."

²²:⁷But Jehoshaphat said, "Is there not here another prophet of Yahweh of whom we may inquire?" ²²:⁸And the king of Israel said to Jehoshaphat, "One other man by whom we may inquire of Yahweh, but I hate him, because he never prophesies good things about me, but only bad. Micaiah the son of Imlah." And Jehoshaphat said, "May the king not say such a thing!" ²²:⁹So the king of Israel summoned one of his eunuchs, and he said, "Bring quickly Micaiah the son of Imlah."

²²:¹⁰And the king of Israel and Jehoshaphat the king of Judah were sitting on their thrones, dressed in their robes, at the threshing floor at Samaria's entrance gate, and all the prophets were prophesying before them, ²²:¹¹and Zedekiah the son of Chena'anah made for himself iron horns, and he said,

"This is what Yahweh has said, 'With these you shall gore the Arameans until you finish them!'" 2:12And all the prophets were prophesying similarly, saying, "Go up to Ramoth-gilead and be successful, and Yahweh will deliver into the king's hand." 22:13And the messenger who had gone to summon Micaiah said to him, "See? The words of the prophets are unanimously favorable to the king; may your word please be like the word of one of them, and speak favorably." 22:14And Micaiah said, "By Yahweh's life, whatever Yahweh says to me, that is what I will speak."

22:15And when he came to the king, the king said to him, "Micaiah, should we go to Ramoth-gilead to battle, or shall we refrain?" And he answered him, "Go up and be successful, and Yahweh will deliver it into the king's hand." 22:16But the king said to him, "How many times shall I put you under oath that you speak to me nothing except the truth in Yahweh's name?" 22:17So he said, "I have seen all Israel scattered upon the mountains, as sheep for which there is no shepherd, and Yahweh said, 'These have no master; let each return to his home in peace.'"

22:18And the king of Israel said to Jehoshaphat, "Didn't I tell you that he would not prophesy good things about me, but bad?" 22:19And [Micaiah] said, "That being the case, hear Yahweh's word: I saw Yahweh sitting on his throne, and all the forces of the heavens standing beside him at his right hand and at his left hand, 22:20and Yahweh said, 'Who will entice Ahab, so that he will go up and fall at Ramoth-gilead?' And one said one thing, and another said another. 22:21Then a spirit came forward and stood before Yahweh, and he said, 'I will entice him.' 22:22And Yahweh said to him, 'How so?' And he replied, 'I will go forth, and I will be a lying spirit in the mouth of all his prophets.' And he said, 'You shall entice him and also succeed; go forth and do so.' 22:23So now you see, Yahweh has put a lying spirit in the mouth of all these, your prophets; and Yahweh has spoken bad things about you."

22:24Then Zedekiah the son of Chena'anah came near and struck Micaiah on the cheek, and he said,

"How did Yahweh's spirit pass over me to speak to you?" 22:25And Micaiah replied, "Look, you will be seeing on that day when you go into an innermost room to hide yourself."

22:26And the king of Israel said, "Seize Micaiah, and take him back to Amon the city governor and to Joash the king's son 22:27and say, 'Thus says the king, "Put this one in the prison, and feed him scant bread and scant water until I come in peace."'" 22:28And Micaiah said, "If you return in peace, Yahweh has not spoken by me."

22:29So the king of Israel and Jehoshaphat the king of Judah went up to Ramoth-gilead. 22:30And the king of Israel said to Jehoshaphat, "I will disguise myself and go into battle, but you wear your robes." So the king of Israel disguised himself and went into battle.

22:31Now the king of Aram had commanded the captains of his chariotry—thirty-two under his command, "Fight with neither small nor great, but only with the king of Israel." 22:32And so it happened that when the captains of the chariots saw Jehoshaphat, they said, "Surely it is the king of Israel." And they turned toward him to fight, and Jehoshaphat cried out. 22:33And when the captains of the chariots saw that it was not the king of Israel, they turned away from him. 22:34But a man had drawn his bow innocently, and he struck the king of Israel between the joints of the armor. And he said to the chariot driver, "Turn about, and carry me out of the battle, because I am wounded." 22:35And the battle grew intense that day, and the king was propped up in his chariot facing the Arameans, and he died in the evening; and the blood of the wound flowed into the bottom of the chariot. 22:36And when the sun set a cry went through the army, "Each man to his city, and each man to his country!"

22:37So the king died, and he was brought to Samaria; and they buried the king in Samaria. 22:38And they washed the chariot by the pool of Samaria, and the dogs licked up his blood, and the prostitutes washed themselves in it, according to Yahweh's word that he had spoken.

--- 7th–6th century BCE ---

25. The King of Justice

Translated by Benjamin R. Foster

This excerpt from a fragmentary text comes from the Neo-Babylonian period in Mesopotamian history (626–539 BCE). It recounts the deeds of a king (whose name is not preserved) in an attempt to show his concern for justice and illustrates the sort of actions that were valued by kings in Babylon at that time.

II

(22) For the sake of due process he (the king) did not neglect truth and justice, nor did he rest day or night! He was always drawing up, with reasoned deliberation, cases and decisions pleasing to the great lord Marduk (and) framed for the benefit of all the people and the stability of Babylonia. He drew up improved regulations for the city, he rebuilt the law court. He drew up regulations ... his kingship is forever, *(one line gone).*

III

(2) The innocent man would take the ... . A man who returned to that law court (to reopen a case), such that, a tablet having been written and sealed, he was returning a second time for false and dishonest purposes, the king commanded the troops to cut off his head and paraded it through the land. The head ... cut off, he made a likeness of that man's head, and he had (the following) written upon that man's head and fastened forever after to the outer gate of that law court for all the people to see, "(This was) a man

whose case was judged, whose tablet of verdict was written and sealed, but who afterwards changed and came back for judgment. His head was cut off on this wise." Base and wicked men would see it, abscond, and never be heard of again.

(14) He put a stop to bribes and presents among the people, he gave the people satisfaction, he caused the land to dwell in tranquility, allowing none to do them any alarm. He pleased his lords Sin, Shamash and Ishtar—they being Lord and Lady—(and) Nabu who dwells in Esagila and Ezida, and who loves his kingship>. They (the gods) were reconciled in his reign on account of the regular offerings.

(21) A man charged a man with murder but did not prove it. They were brought before him (the king) and he ordered them (to be taken) above Sippar, to the bank of the Euphrates, before Ea, king of the depths, for trial. The troops of the guard, keeping both under close surveillance all night, lit a fire. At daybreak the prince, governor, and troops assembled as the king commanded, and took their places around them. Both went down (and) ... the river. Ea, king of the depths, in order to   his royal beloved (and) in order to see justice done, did what always had   ... The first ... he had jump in, he (the river god) brought him safely to the bank. The one who had charged him with murder sank in the water. From morning until noon no one saw him nor was aught heard of him. As for the troops of the guard, who had stood around them at the riverbank from evening until daybreak, their hearts sank and they set out to search ... "What shall we report? How shall we answer the king?" When the king heard, he was furious at the troops. A courier was coming and going, "Did you not watch over the man? Has he gotten across the river and lain down in the open country?" Since none saw him at any time, they could not answer. Anxious boat riders went along the river, bank to bank, checking the edge. When high noon came his corpse rose up from the river. He had been struck on the head, blood was running from the ears and nostrils. The top of his head was burned, as if with fire, his body was covered with sores. The people saw, and spoke (of it) in reverence; all the world was borne down with awe. The enemy, the wicked one, and the hostile betook themselves into hiding.

1. Oaths to Shamash could be sworn standing inside a magic circle.

Think about it.

1. What actions by the Babylonian king are used to demonstrate his commitment to truth and justice?
2. When the corpse of the man suspected of murder is found in the river, why do the people react as they do?

26. The Zadokite History

Translated by David Miano

Another writing that was incorporated into the Jewish Primary History (see intro to reading #21), and perhaps the easiest to distinguish, is a history of Israel composed by priests. Although there is a clear historical framework starting with the creation of the world and ending with the death of Moses, a large portion of the work is taken up by laws and procedural directions for priestly rituals. Its affinity with the Book of Ezekiel suggests a composition or compilation in Babylon in the early 6ᵗʰ century BCE, but there is still considerable debate among scholars over the dating of this source, and it appears to be the product of more than one author. The priests associated with this writing were supporters (and therefore probably members) of the priestly clan of Aaron and descendants of the high priest Zadok. Their group may have held some occasional power in the days of the Judahite monarchy but do not seem to have become dominant in Judah until after they returned from Babylon in the late 6ᵗʰ century BCE. What follows are two selections from this work.

The Flood

⁶:¹¹Now the earth was corrupt in God's presence, and the earth was filled with violence. ⁶:¹²And God saw the earth, and here it was corrupt, because all flesh had corrupted its ways upon the earth.

⁶:¹³And God said to Noah, "The end of all flesh has come before me, for the earth is filled with violence because of them; and now I am going to destroy them along with the earth. ⁶:¹⁴You shall make yourself a container of cypress wood; you shall make rooms in the container, and cover it inside and out with pitch. ⁶:¹⁵This is how you shall make it: the length of the container three hundred cubits, its width fifty cubits, and its height thirty cubits. ⁶:¹⁶You shall make a window for the container, and finish it to a cubit above; and the door of the container in its side. You shall make it with lower, second, and third levels. ⁶:¹⁷And as for me, here I am going to bring the flood, waters upon the earth, to destroy all flesh in which is the breath of life from under the skies; everything that is on the earth will expire. ⁶:¹⁸But I will establish my covenant with you; and you shall come into the container, you, your sons, your wife, and your sons' wives with you. ⁶:¹⁹And from every wild animal of all flesh, two of every kind you shall bring into the container to keep them alive with you; they shall be male and female. ⁶:²⁰From the birds according to their kinds, and from the tame animals according to their kinds, and from every creeper of the ground according to its kind, two of each shall come in to you to keep alive. ⁶:²¹And as for you, take for yourself whatever food that is eaten, and collect it for yourself; and it shall serve as food for you and

for them." [6:22]And Noah did everything that God commanded him; he did just so.

[7:6]Noah was six hundred years old when the flood came, waters upon the earth. [7:8]From pure animals, and from animals that are not pure, and from birds, and from everything that creeps on the ground, [7:9]two and two, male and female, they came into the container with Noah, as God had commanded Noah. [7:10]And after seven days passed, the waters of the flood came upon the earth. [7:11b]On that very day all the fountains of the great deep[1] burst forth, and the windows of the skies were opened, [7:12]and the rain was on the earth forty days and forty nights. [7:13]On this same day Noah and Shem, Ham, and Japheth, Noah's sons, and Noah's wife and the three wives of his sons, came into the container, [7:14]they and every wild animal of every kind, and every tame animal of every kind, and every creeper that creeps upon the earth, and every bird of every kind—every fowl, every winged creature. [7:15]And they came in to Noah into the container, two and two of all flesh in which there is the breath of life. [7:16]And those that entered, male and female of all flesh, came in as God had commanded him.

[7:17b]And the waters increased, and they raised up the container, and it was lifted above the earth. [7:20]And the waters grew so mighty that by fifteen cubits the mountains were covered. [7:21]And all flesh that moved upon the earth expired, including birds, tame animals, wild animals, every swarming thing that swarms upon the earth, and all humankind. [7:24]And the waters were mighty upon the earth for one hundred fifty days.

[8:1]But God remembered Noah and all the wild animals and all the tame animals that were with him in the container. And God made a wind blow over the earth, and the waters subsided; [8:2]and the fountains of the deep and the windows of the heavens were closed, and the rain from the skies was restrained. [8:3]And the waters receded from the earth more and

more, and by the end of one hundred fifty days the waters had disappeared.

[8:15]Then God said to Noah, [8:16]"Leave the container—you and your wife and your sons and your sons' wives with you. [8:17]Bring out with you every wild animal that is with you of all flesh, with birds and tame animals and every creeper that creeps on the earth, and let them swarm throughout the earth and be fruitful and multiply upon the earth." [8:18]So Noah went out, and his sons and his wife and his sons' wives with him. [8:19]Every wild animal, every creeper, and every bird—everything that crawls on the earth went out of the container by their families.

[9:1]And God blessed Noah and his sons, and he said to them, "Be fruitful and multiply and fill the earth. [9:2]And a fear of you, and a dread of you, shall be upon every wild animal of the earth, and every bird of the air—on everything that crawls on the ground and on all the fish of the sea. Into your hand they are delivered. [9:3]Every crawling thing that lives shall be food for you; just as I have given you green plants, I have given you everything. [9:4]Nevertheless, flesh with its life, its blood, you must not eat. [9:5]Surely your own life-blood I will seek. From the hand of the human—from the hand of each his brother—I will seek the life of the man. [9:6]Whoever sheds the blood of the human, by a human his blood shall be shed, for in God's image he made the human. [9:7]And as for you, be fruitful and multiply; swarm throughout the earth and multiply in it."

[9:8]Then God said to Noah and to his sons with him, [9:9]"And as for me, here I am establishing my covenant with you and your offspring after you, [9:10]and with every living creature that is with you—the birds, the tame animals, and every wild animal of the earth with you—from all that went out of the container to every animal of the earth. [9:11]And I have established my covenant with you that never again shall all flesh be cut off by the waters of the flood, and never again shall there be a flood to destroy the earth." [9:12]And God said, "This is the sign of the covenant that I am making between me and you and every living soul that is with you for generations

---

1   The waters under the earth.

everlasting: ⁹:¹³my bow I have set in the clouds, and it shall serve as a sign of a covenant between me and the earth. ⁹:¹⁴And it shall be that when I gather clouds over the earth and the bow is visible in the clouds, ⁹:¹⁵I will remember my covenant that is between me and you and every living soul of all flesh; and the waters shall never again become a flood to destroy all flesh. ⁹:¹⁶When the bow is in the clouds, I will see it to remember the everlasting covenant between God and every living soul of all flesh that is upon the earth." ⁹:¹⁷And God said to Noah, "This is the sign of the covenant that I have established between me and all flesh that is upon the earth."

The Instruction for Jealousies

⁵:¹²Speak to the children of Israel and say to them: If any man's woman goes astray and has been unfaithful to him, ⁵:¹³and if another man has lain with her, planting seed, but it has been hidden from the eyes of her man, so that she is undetected though she has been defiled, and there is no witness against her, and she was not caught in the act, ⁵:¹⁴and if a spirit of jealousy has comes over him, and he is jealous of his woman who has been defiled—or if a spirit of jealousy comes over him, and he is jealous of his woman, though she has not defiled herself— ⁵:¹⁵then the man shall bring his woman to the priest and shall bring her offering with her: one-tenth of an ephah of barley flour. He should not pour oil on it, nor put frankincense on it, for it is an offering of jealousies, a grain offering of remembrance, bringing a crime to remembrance.

⁵:¹⁶Then the priest will bring her near and stand her before Yahweh, ⁵:¹⁷and the priest will take holy water in a clay vessel, and some of the dirt that is on the floor of the tabernacle he will take and put it into the water. ⁵:¹⁸So the priest will stand the woman before Yahweh, and he will let down the woman's hair and place in her hands the offering of remembrance, which is an offering of jealousies. And in his hand the priest will have the bitter cursing water. ⁵:¹⁹Then the priest will make her take an oath, saying, "If a man has not lain with you, and if you have not gone astray to impurity while under your man's authority, be immune to the bitter cursing water. ⁵:²⁰But you, if you have gone astray while under your man's authority, and if you have been defiled, and if a man other than your man has lain with you," ⁵:²¹then the priest will make the woman swear the curse oath, and the priest will say to the woman, "May Yahweh make you an accursed oath-violater among your people, when Yahweh makes your thigh fall and your womb swell; ⁵:²²and this cursing water will enter your bowels and make your womb swell and your thigh fall!" And the woman shall say, "So be it. So be it." ⁵:²³Then the priest will write these curses in a scroll and rub them off into the bitter water, ⁵:²⁴and he will make the woman drink the bitter cursing water, and the cursing water will enter her and cause bitterness. ⁵:²⁵First the priest will take the offering of jealousies out of the woman's hand, and he will elevate the grain offering before Yahweh, and he will bring it to the altar. ⁵:²⁶And the priest will take a handful of the offering, a representative portion, and turn it into smoke on the altar. And afterward he will make the woman drink the water. ⁵:²⁷When he has had her drink the water, then it will happen that if she has been defiled and has been unfaithful to her husband, the cursing water will enter into her and cause bitterness, and her womb will swell and her thigh will fall, and the woman shall become accursed among her people. ⁵:²⁸But if the woman has not been defiled and is pure, then she will be immune and will conceive offspring.

⁵:²⁹This is the instruction for jealousies, when a woman, while under her man's authority, goes astray and is defiled, ⁵:³⁰or when a spirit of jealousy comes over a man, and he is jealous of his woman. And he shall stand the woman before Yahweh, and the priest shall apply this entire instruction to her. ⁵:³¹The man shall be clear of crime, but that woman shall bear her crime.

early 6th century BCE

27. Poems of Solon

Translated by John Porter

Solon (c. 638–558 BCE) was an Athenian aristocrat, who was elected eponymous archon (the titular head of state in Athens) around 594 BCE. He thereafter enacted a series of constitutional reforms, which among other things permitted non-noble, upper-income citizens of Athens to run for office for the first time. For this reason, he is sometimes considered one of the prime movers of Athenian democracy, which would be more fully developed later. Besides being a statesman and lawmaker, Solon also was a poet. His political, moral, and religious views can be seen in his poems, fragments of which are still in existence. Provided here are a few of these poetic fragments.

Fragment 4

Our city never will perish according to the decree of Zeus
or the will of the blessed gods immortal.
For such a great-spirited guard holds her hands protectingly above it,
Pallas Athena, she of the mighty father.
Rather, the townsmen themselves, in their folly, wish to destroy
our great city, persuaded by wealth,
and unjust is the mind of the leaders of the *demos:*[1] for them

---

1   the general populace; the common people.

Solon: Select Fragments, trans. John Porter. Copyright © 1995 by John Porter. Reprinted with permission.

many grievous sufferings are certain, the fruit of their great *hybris*.[2]
For they do not know how to suppress *koros*[3] or how to conduct the present
joys of their feasting in decorous fashion,
but instead they grow rich, putting their trust in unjust deeds.

* * * * * * * * * * * * * * *

... sparing not at all either the sacred possessions or those
of the *demos,* they plunder rapaciously, one here, one there,
nor do they beware the sacred ordinances of Dikê,[4]
who silently notes events as they happen, as well as those that came before,
and, in time, comes, surely, bringing retribution.
This ineluctable wound comes now against the entire city,
and she has come quickly into wretched slavery—
slavery, which rouses from their sleep internal strife and war—
war, which brings an end for the lovely youth of many.
For by its enemies this lovely city quickly is being
destroyed, amid the cabals dear to the unjust.
Such are the evils that roam among the *demos,* while, as regards the poor,
many have arrived in foreign lands
sold into slavery, bound in shameful fetters.

* * * * * * * * * * * * * * *

In this way does the misfortune of the *demos* come to each man's house:
doors no longer suffice to keep it out,
it leaps above the outer wall and finds a man in any case,
even if he, fleeing, should cower in the recesses of the inner chamber.
These things my spirit bids me teach the men of Athens:
that ill-governance brings evils a thousand-fold for the *polis,*
but Noble-governance [Eunomia] yields a city where all things are decorous and sound,
thickly enfolding in fetters those who are unjust:
it smoothes those things that are rough, it stops *koros* short, it sentences *hybris* to obscurity;
it causes the burgeoning flowers of *atê*[5] to whither,
and straightens crooked judgments; calms the
deeds of arrogance and stops the deeds of faction;
it stops the bilious anger of harsh strife and in its control
are all things proper and thoughtful among men.

---

2 a form of violent arrogance or aggression.
3 Satiety; an over-repletion of wealth and success.
4 Dikê is very much a retributive form of justice: transgressions against divine law lead inevitably to punishment.
5 a ruinous delusion; a state of mind in which one commits a foolish error that leads to disaster.

Fragment 13.1–32, 65–76

Glorious children of Memory and Olympian Zeus,
Pierian Muses, hear me as I pray:
grant me *olbos*[6] from the blessed gods, and from all
men a noble reputation always.
With these may I be sweet to my friends, bitter to my enemies,
an object of reverence to the former, to the latter a dreadful vision to see.
Indeed, I long to have wealth, but I do not wish to acquire it
unjustly: for Dikê is certain to come afterward.
Ploutos[7] which the gods grant stays beside a man
enduring and sound from its uttermost foundation to its pinnacle.
But that *ploutos* which men revere through *hybris* does not come
in decorous fashion but, persuaded by their unjust deeds,
it attends them against its will and quickly comes to be mingled with *atê.*
This latter grows from a small beginning, like a fire,
trivial at first, but a grievous evil in the end.
For the deeds of *hybris* do not prosper long for mortals:
rather, Zeus oversees the end of all things. Suddenly,
as the wind quickly scatters the clouds
in spring when it whips up the depths of the weariless
sea with its teaming waves and over the grain-bearing earth
it destroys the noble works of men, arriving at last at the lofty seat of the gods,
the heavens, and leaving behind a sparkling clear sky for all to see—
the might of the sun shines brightly over the good rich earth
and no trace of clouds is any longer to be seen:
in such fashion comes the punishment of Zeus. Nor does he indulge his wrath
at each transgression, as would a mortal man,
and yet never does it escape his eye forever just who possesses
a criminal spirit: such a one stands revealed altogether in the end.
But while some pay the penalty immediately, others do so later. And others still
themselves escape, nor does the allotted wrath of the gods come upon them,
yet it comes with dread certainty in later times: the innocent pay for their deeds,
either their children or the family line thereafter.

* * * * * * * * * * * * * * *

Indeed, there is danger involved in every undertaking, nor does one know,
at the time some project is being undertaken, how things will turn out for him.
Instead, one who attempts to act nobly and well with no warning

---

6 general prosperity, which includes health and well-being.
7 wealth, riches.

falls into great *atê*, grievous to bear,
yet to another who acts out of wickedness god gives good fortune
in all things, a lucky escape from his thoughtless folly.
Of *ploutos* no bound lies clearly marked for men:
those of us who now possess the richest livings
seek to double their goods. Who might satisfy them all?
The immortals have granted mortals means of profit,
but *atê* arises therefrom. The latter, when Zeus sends it as an agent
of punishment, besets now one man, now another.

Think about it.

1. What does Solon say is the cause of the city's problems?
2. How does Zeus bring justice upon evil men?

6th century BCE

28. Second Isaiah

Translated by David Miano

In the Book of Isaiah, as currently found in the Hebrew Bible, only the first 39 (or perhaps only 33) chapters, are considered by scholars to contain the prophecies of the 8th-century prophet Isaiah. Appended are prophecies of at least one, and perhaps two, anonymous prophets. Chapters 40–55 (or perhaps 34–55) are usually called "Second Isaiah," for lack of a more appropriate name. Here we find Hebrew poetry of the highest quality. The prophecies, which specifically name the Persian emperor Cyrus the Great (r. 559-530 BCE) as a hope for the Jews, can be dated confidently to the mid-6th century BCE.

45:1 This is what Yahweh has said to his anointed one:
To Cyrus whose right hand I have grasped
To subdue peoples before him,
 And loins of kings I will loosen,

To open doors before him,

And no gates shall be shut.

45:2I will go in front of you and level houses;

Bronze doors I will break apart,

And iron bars I will chop in two.

45:3I will give you treasures of the dark

And riches of secret places,

So that you may know that I am Yahweh,

The God of Israel who calls you by your name,

45:4For the sake of my servant Jacob,

And Israel, my chosen one.

And I call you by your name;

I address you, but you do not know me.

45:5I am Yahweh, and there is no one else;

Except for me there is no god.

I clothe you, but you do not know me,

45:6So that they may know from the sunrise and from the sunset

That there is none except me.

I am Yahweh, and there is no one else.

45:7I form light, and I create darkness;

I make peace, and I create evil.

I, Yahweh, am doing all these things.

45:8Pour down, O Skies, from above,

So that the clouds may rain down righteousness!

May Earth open and produce salvation,

And let it sprout righteousness too!

I, Yahweh, have created it.

Think about it.

1. What does this passage suggest about Yahweh and his relationship with foreign rulers?
2. What does it suggest about the gods of other countries?

29. The Deuteronomic History (additions)

Translated by David Miano

One interesting feature of the second edition of the Deuteronomic History (see intro to reading #24) is an updated version of the Ten Commandments (see reading #21 for the older version). The new Deuteronomic History extends its narrative to 560 BCE and was finished after that date, but probably before the return of the Jewish exiles from Babylon in 537 BCE.

Why Jerusalem Fell

[from the first edition]

²³:¹Then the king [Josiah] sent for all the elders of Judah and Jerusalem, and they were gathered to him. ²²:²And the king went up to the house of Yahweh, and with him all the men of Judah and all the inhabitants of Jerusalem, and the priests and the prophets—all the people, both small and great; and he read in their hearing all the words of the covenant scroll that had been found in the house of Yahweh. ²²:³And the king stood by the pillar and cut a covenant before Yahweh to walk after Yahweh and to keep his commandments and his testimonies and his statutes with all his heart and all his soul, to perform the words of this covenant that were written in this scroll; and all the people joined in the covenant.

²²:⁴Then the king commanded Hilkiah, the high priest, and the priests of the second order, and the keepers of the threshold, to bring out of the temple of Yahweh all the vessels made for Ba'al, for Asherah, and for all the forces of the heavens; and he burned them outside Jerusalem in the fields of Qidron, and he carried their ashes to Bethel.

²²:⁵And he deposed the idolatrous priests whom the kings of Judah had ordained to burn incense in the high places at the cities of Judah and round about Jerusalem, and those offering sacrifices to Ba'al, to the sun, and to the moon, and to the constellations, and to all the forces of the heavens.

²²:⁶And he brought the Asherah from the house of Yahweh outside Jerusalem to the brook of Qidron, and he burned it at the brook of Qidron and pounded it to dust, and he scattered the dust of it upon the graves of the common people. ²²:⁷And he tore down the cubicles of the male prostitutes that were in the house of Yahweh, cubicles of the Asherahs that the women had been weaving. ...

²²:²⁴And also the necromancers and the spirit-consulters, and the household images and the idols, and all the abominations that were seen in the land of Judah and in Jerusalem, Josiah burned so that he might establish the words of the instruction that were written in the scroll that Hilkiah the priest found in the house of Yahweh.

22:25 And before him there was no king like him, who turned to Yahweh with all his heart and with all his soul and with all his might, according to all the instruction of Moses; nor did any like him arise after him.

[an addition made in the second edition]

22:26 Nevertheless Yahweh did not turn back from the intensity of his great wrath, which burned against Judah on account of all the provocations with which Manasseh[1] had provoked him. **22:27**So Yahweh said, "I will remove also Judah out of my sight, just as I have removed Israel, and I will cast off this city that I have chosen, Jerusalem, and the house of which I said, 'My name shall be there.'" ...

24:1 In [Jehoiakim's][2] days Nebuchadnezzar the king of Babylon came up, and Jehoiakim became his vassal three years; and then he turned and rebelled against him. **24:2**And Yahweh sent against him the battalions of the Chaldeans, of the Arameans, of the Moabites, and of the Ammonites, and he sent them against Judah to destroy it,[3] according to Yahweh's word, which he had spoken through his servants the prophets. **24:3**Most assuredly at Yahweh's word this came upon Judah in order to remove them from his sight, for the sins of Manasseh, because of all that he had done, **22:4**and also for the innocent blood that he had shed, because he filled Jerusalem with innocent blood, and Yahweh was not willing to forgive.

The Ten Commandments (newer version)

5:6I am Yahweh your God, who freed you from the land of Egypt, from of the house of bondage.

5:7 You must not have any other gods in my presence.

5:8 You must not make for yourself a statue, or any image of anything that is in the skies above, or on the earth beneath, or in the waters under the earth; **5:9**you must not bow down to them or serve them, for I Yahweh your god am a jealous god, visiting the crime of fathers upon the children and upon the third generation and upon the fourth generation for those hating me, **5:10**but showing faithful love to the thousandth generation for those loving me and keeping my commandments.

5:11 You must not raise the name of Yahweh your God in vain, for Yahweh will not clear of guilt the one who raises his name in vain.

5:12 Remember the Sabbath day, to sanctify it, as Yahweh your God commanded you. **5:13**Six days you may labor and do all your work, **5:14**but the seventh day is a Sabbath to Yahweh your God; in it you must not do any work—you, or your son, or your daughter, or your manservant, or your maidservant, or your bull, or your ass, or any of your domestic animals, or the sojourner who is within your gates, so that your manservant and your maidservant may rest as you do. **5:15**You should remember that you were a slave in the land of Egypt, and Yahweh your God brought you out from there with a mighty hand and an outstretched arm; therefore Yahweh your God commanded you to keep the Sabbath day.

5:16 Honor your father and your mother, as Yahweh your God commanded you, so that your days may be prolonged, and that it may go well with you, on the soil that Yahweh your God is giving you.

5:17 You must not kill.

5:18 You must not commit adultery.

5:19 You must not steal.

5:20 You must not testify against your fellow as a false witness.

5:21 You must not covet your fellow's wife; and you must not covet your fellow's house, his field, or his manservant, or his maidservant, his ox, or his ass, or anything that belongs to your fellow.

---

1   An earlier king of Judah, Josiah's grandfather.

2   We skip ahead now to the reign of Josiah's son. Josiah has since died.

3   Jerusalem will finally be destroyed during the reign of Josiah's other son, Zedekiah.

1. What reason is given for the Babylonian conquest of Jerusalem? Why do you think this would be considered fair by the author?
2. In what ways do these Ten Commandments differ from the version you read in the Yahwist Legend? Why do you think these changes would have been appropriate after the people of Judah lost their kingdom?

The Early Classical Period
(500–200 BCE)

Socrates (Classical Greece)

Early Classical Period

B.C.E.	400	300	200
Central America	Olmec Civilization	Zapotec Civilization	
South America	Chavin Culture		
Western Mediterranean	Roman Republic		
	Carthaginian Republic		
Eastern Mediterranean	Classical Greece		Hellenistic Greece
Northeast Africa	Achaemenid Persian Empire		Kingdom of the Ptolemies
North Mesopotamia			
South Mesopotamia			Seleucid Empire
Central Asia			
East Africa	Meroë		
South Asia	Mahajanapandas		Mauryan Empire
East Asia	Warring States Period (late Zhou Dynasty)		Qin Empire

30. Enquiries

Translated by George Rawlinson

Istoriai, or Enquiries (often mistranslated "Histories"), is the earliest known Greek work of narrative history. It was written by Herodotus of Halicarnassus around 450 BCE. The subject of the work is the Greco-Persian Wars of the early 5th century BCE, but Herodotus covers all sorts of other historical topics to provide context for his subject. In the following excerpt, from Book I of his work, Herodotus explains how Pisistratus (who reigned between 546 and 527 BCE) was able to establish himself as tyrant of Athens.

59. On inquiring into the condition of these two nations, Croesus found that one, the Athenian, was in a state of grievous oppression and distraction under Pisistratus, the son of Hippocrates, who was at that time tyrant of Athens. Hippocrates, when he was a private citizen, is said to have gone once upon a time to Olympia to see the Games, when a wonderful prodigy happened to him. As he was employed in sacrificing, the cauldrons which stood near, full of water and of the flesh of the victims, began to boil without the help of fire, so that the water overflowed the pots. Chilon the Lacedaemonian, who happened to be there and to witness the prodigy, advised Hippocrates, if he were unmarried, never to take into his house a wife who could bear him a child; if he already had one, to send her back to her friends; if he had a son, to disown him. Chilon's advice did not at all please Hippocrates, who disregarded it, and some time after became the father of Pisistratus. This Pisistratus, at a time when there was civil contention in Attica between the party of the Sea-coast headed by Megacles the son of Alcmaeon, and that of the Plain headed by Lycurgus, one of the Aristolaids, formed the project of making himself tyrant, and with this view created a third party. Gathering together a band of partisans, and giving himself out for the protector of the Highlanders, he contrived the following stratagem. He wounded himself and his mules, and then drove his chariot into the market-place, professing to have just escaped an attack of his enemies, who had attempted his life as he was on his way into the country. He besought the people to assign him a guard to protect his person, reminding them of the glory which he had gained when he led the attack upon the Megarians, and took the town of Nisaea, at the same time performing many other exploits. The Athenians, deceived by his story, appointed him a band of citizens to serve as a guard, who were to carry clubs instead of spears, and to accompany him wherever he went. Thus strengthened, Pisistratus broke into revolt and seized the citadel. In this way he acquired the sovereignty of Athens, which he continued to hold without disturbing the previously existing offices or altering any of the laws. He administered the state according to

the established usages, and his arrangements were wise and salutary.

60. However, after a little time, the partisans of Megacles and those of Lycurgus agreed to forget their differences, and united to drive him out. So Pisistratus, having by the means described first made himself master of Athens, lost his power again before it had time to take root. No sooner, however, was he departed than the factions which had driven him out quarrelled anew, and at last Megacles, wearied with the struggle, sent a herald to Pisistratus, with an offer to re-establish him on the throne if he would marry his daughter. Pisistratus consented, and on these terms an agreement was concluded between the two, after which they proceeded to devise the mode of his restoration. And here the device on which they hit was the silliest that I find on record, more especially considering that the Greeks have been from very ancient times distinguished from the barbarians by superior sagacity and freedom from foolish simpleness, and remembering that the persons on whom this trick was played were not only Greeks but Athenians, who have the credit of surpassing all other Greeks in cleverness. There was in the Paeanian district a woman named Phya, whose height only fell short of four cubits by three fingers' breadth, and who was altogether comely to look upon. This woman they clothed in complete armour, and, instructing her as to the carriage which she was to maintain in order to beseem her part, they placed her in a chariot and drove to the city. Heralds had been sent forward to precede her, and to make proclamation to this effect: "Citizens of Athens, receive again Pisistratus with friendly minds. Minerva, who of all men honours him the most, herself conducts him back to her own citadel." This they proclaimed in all directions, and immediately the rumour spread throughout the country districts that Minerva was bringing back her favourite. They of the city also, fully persuaded that the woman was the veritable goddess, prostrated themselves before her, and received Pisistratus back.

61. Pisistratus, having thus recovered the sovereignty, married, according to agreement, the daughter of Megacles. As, however, he had already a family of grown up sons, and the Alcmaeonidae were supposed to be under a curse, he determined that there should be no issue of the marriage. His wife at first kept this matter to herself, but after a time, either her mother questioned her, or it may be that she told it of her own accord. At any rate, she informed her mother, and so it reached her father's ears. Megacles, indignant at receiving an affront from such a quarter, in his anger instantly made up his differences with the opposite faction, on which Pisistratus, aware of what was planning against him, took himself out of the country. Arrived at Eretria, he held a council with his children to decide what was to be done. The opinion of Hippias prevailed, and it was agreed to aim at regaining the sovereignty. The first step was to obtain advances of money from such states as were under obligations to them. By these means they collected large sums from several countries, especially from the Thebans, who gave them far more than any of the rest. To be brief, time passed, and all was at length got ready for their return. A band of Argos mercenaries arrived from the Peloponnese, and a certain Naxian named Lygdamis, who volunteered his services, was particularly zealous in the cause, supplying both men and money.

62. In the eleventh year of their exile the family of Pisistratus set sail from Eretria on their return home. They made the coast of Attica, near Marathon, where they encamped, and were joined by their partisans from the capital and by numbers from the country districts, who loved tyranny better than freedom. At Athens, while Pisistratus was obtaining funds, and even after he landed at Marathon, no one paid any attention to his proceedings. When, however, it became known that he had left Marathon, and was marching upon the city, preparations were made for resistance, the whole force of the state was levied, and led against the returning exiles. Meantime the army of Pisistratus, which had broken up from Marathon, meeting their adversaries near

the temple of the Pallenian Minerva, pitched their camp opposite them. Here a certain soothsayer, Amphilytus by name, an Acarnanian, moved by a divine impulse, came into the presence of Pisistratus, and approaching him uttered this prophecy in the hexameter measure:-

Now has the cast been made, the net is out-spread in the water,
Through the moonshiny night the tunnies will enter the meshes.

63. Such was the prophecy uttered under a divine inspiration. Pisistratus, apprehending its meaning, declared that he accepted the oracle, and instantly led on his army. The Athenians from the city had just finished their midday meal, after which they had betaken themselves, some to dice, others to sleep, when Pisistratus with his troops fell upon them and put them to the rout. As soon as the flight began, Pisistratus bethought himself of a most wise contrivance, whereby the might be induced to disperse and not unite in a body any more. He mounted his sons on horseback and sent them on in front to overtake the fugitives, and exhort them to be of good cheer, and return each man to his home. The Athenians took the advice, and Pisistratus became for the third time master of Athens.

64. Upon this he set himself to root his power more firmly, by the aid of a numerous body of mercenaries, and by keeping up a full exchequer, partly supplied from native sources, partly from the countries about the river Strymon. He also demanded hostages from many of the Athenians who had remained at home, and not left Athenians at his approach; and these he sent to Naxos, which he had conquered by force of arms, and given over into the charge of Lygdamis. Farther, he purified the island of Delos, according to the injunctions of an oracle, after the following fashion. All the dead bodies which had been interred within sight of the temple he dug up, and removed to another part of the isle. Thus was the tyranny of Pisistratus established at Athens, many of the Athenians having fallen in the battle, and many others having fled the country together with the son of Alcmaeon.

Think about it.

1. What does the account about Pisistratus tell you generally about the way in which men set themselves up as tyrants in aristocratic Greek societies?
2. How does Herodotus use references to prophecies in his tale? What purpose do they serve?

31. Antigone

Translated by David Grene

Sophocles (c. 497–406 BCE) was a playwright of Greek tragedy. In Athens, his home polis, he competed in over 30 drama competitions and won more than two-thirds of them, never being judged lower than second place. The following excerpts are from his play *Antigone* (produced c. 441 BCE), which is one of three tragedies he set in ancient Thebes of the pre-Trojan War period. It concerns a conflict between the city's ruler, Creon, and one of his subjects, Antigone, the daughter of Oedipus. Antigone wishes to give her brother Polynices a proper burial, but Creon has refused to grant permission, because of a law he created forbidding traitors to receive a burial. Here are pieces of two speeches Creon gives on the necessity of maintaining the law.

Creon
Gentlemen: as for our city's fortune,
the gods have shaken her, when the great waves broke,   180
but the gods have brought her through again to safety.
For yourselves, I chose you out of all and summoned you
to come to me, partly because I knew you
as always loyal to the throne—at first,
when Laius was king, and then again
when Oedipus saved our city and then again
when he died and you remained with steadfast truth
to their descendants,
until they met their double fate upon one day,
striking and stricken, defiled each by a brothers murder.   190
Now here I am, holding all authority
and the throne, in virtue of kinship with the dead.

It is impossible to know any man—
I mean his soul, intelligence, and judgment—
until he shows his skill in rule and law.
I think that a man supreme ruler of a whole city,
if he does not reach for the best counsel for her,

but through some fear, keeps his tongue under lock and key, 200
him I judge the worst of any;
I have always judged so; and anyone thinking
another man more a friend than his own country,
I rate him nowhere. For my part, God is my witness,
who sees all, always, I would not be silent
if I saw ruin, not safety, on the way
towards my fellow citizens. I would not count
any enemy of my country as a friend—
because of what I know, that she it is
which gives us our security. If she sails upright
and we sail on her, friends will be ours for the making.
In the light of rules like these, I will make her greater still. 210

In consonance with this, I here proclaim
to the citizens about Oedipus' sons.
For Eteocles, who died this city's champion,
showing his valor's supremacy everywhere,
he shall be buried in his grave with every rite
of sanctity given to heroes under earth.
However, his brother, Polyneices, a returned exile,
who sought to burn with fire from top to bottom
his native city, and the gods of his own people;
who sought to taste the blood he shared with us, 220
and lead the rest of us to slavery—
I here proclaim to the city that this man
shall no one honor with a grave and none shall mourn.
You shall leave him without burial; you shall watch him
chewed up by birds and dogs and violated.
Such is my mind in the matter; never by me
shall the wicked man have precedence in honor
over the just. But he that is loyal to the state
in death, in life alike, shall have my honor. 230

* * * * * * *

So let her cry if she will on the Zeus of kinship;
for if I rear those of my race and breeding
to be rebels, surely I will do so with those outside it.
For he who is in his household a good man
will be found a just man, too, in the city.
But he that breaches the law or does it violence
or thinks to dictate to those who govern him
shall never have my good word.

The man the city sets up in authority   720
must be obeyed in small things and in just
but also in their opposites.
I am confident such a man of whom I speak
will be a good ruler, and willing to be well ruled.
He will stand on his country's side, faithful and just,
in the storm of battle. There is nothing worse
than disobedience to authority.
It destroys cities, it demolishes homes;
it breaks and routs one's allies. Of successful lives   730
the most of them are saved by discipline.
So we must stand on the side of what is orderly;
we cannot give victory to a woman.
If we must accept defeat, let it be from a man;
we must not let people say that a woman beat us.

Think about it.

1. For Creon, why does the city take precedence over family and friends?
2. Why does Creon say that a ruler "must be obeyed in small things and in just, but also in their opposites"?

411 BCE

32. History of the Peloponnesian War

Translated by Richard Crawley

The *History of the Peloponnesian War* is a narrative account of the conflict that took place between the Greek states in the Delian League (led by Athens) and those in the Peloponnesian League (led by Sparta). It was written by Thucydides of Athens and completed around the year 411 BCE. Although the war ran from 431 to 404 BCE, the account concludes in 411, which has prompted historians to suggest that Thucydides died in that year. In the following excerpt, taken from the beginning of the account, Thucydides explains his approach to history.

Thucydides, *History of the Peloponnesian War*, trans. Richard Crawley, pp. 20–22. J.M. Dent & Sons Limited, 1910. Copyright in the Public Domain.

1. Thucydides, an Athenian, wrote the history of the war between the Peloponnesians and the Athenians, beginning at the moment that it broke out, and believing that it would be a great war and more worthy of relation than any that had preceded it. This belief was not without its grounds. The preparations of both the combatants were in every department in the last state of perfection; and he could see the rest of the Hellenic race taking sides in the quarrel; those who delayed doing so at once having it in contemplation. Indeed this was the greatest movement yet known in history, not only of the Hellenes, but of a large part of the barbarian world—I had almost said of mankind. For though the events of remote antiquity, and even those that more immediately preceded the war, could not from lapse of time be clearly ascertained, yet the evidences which an inquiry carried as far back as was practicable leads me to trust, all point to the conclusion that there was nothing on a great scale, either in war or in other matters.

2. Having now given the result of my inquiries into early times, I grant that there will be a difficulty in believing every particular detail. The way that most men deal with traditions, even traditions of their own country, is to receive them all alike as they are delivered, without applying any critical test whatever. The general Athenian public fancy that Hipparchus was tyrant when he fell by the hands of Harmodius and Aristogiton, not knowing that Hippias, the eldest of the sons of Pisistratus, was really supreme, and that Hipparchus and Thessalus were his brothers; and that Harmodius and Aristogiton suspecting, on the very day, nay at the very moment fixed on for the deed, that information had been conveyed to Hippias by their accomplices, concluded that he had been warned, and did not attack him, yet, not liking to be apprehended and risk their lives for nothing, fell upon Hipparchus near the temple of the daughters of Leos, and slew him as he was arranging the Panathenaic procession.

3. There are many other unfounded ideas current among the rest of the Hellenes, even on matters of contemporary history, which have not been obscured by time. For instance, there is the notion that the Lacedaemonian kings have two votes each, the fact being that they have only one; and that there is a company of Pitane, there being simply no such thing. So little pains do the vulgar take in the investigation of truth, accepting readily the first story that comes to hand. On the whole, however, the conclusions I have drawn from the proofs quoted may, I believe, safely be relied on. Assuredly they will not be disturbed either by the lays of a poet displaying the exaggeration of his craft, or by the compositions of the chroniclers that are attractive at truth's expense; the subjects they treat of being out of the reach of evidence, and time having robbed most of them of historical value by enthroning them in the region of legend. Turning from these, we can rest satisfied with having proceeded upon the clearest data, and having arrived at conclusions as exact as can be expected in matters of such antiquity. To come to this war: despite the known disposition of the actors in a struggle to overrate its importance, and when it is over to return to their admiration of earlier events, yet an examination of the facts will show that it was much greater than the wars which preceded it.

4. With reference to the speeches in this history, some were delivered before the war began, others while it was going on; some I heard myself, others I got from various quarters; it was in all cases difficult to carry them word for word in one's memory, so my habit has been to make the speakers say what was in my opinion demanded of them by the various occasions, of course adhering as closely as possible to the general sense of what they really said. And with reference to the narrative of events, far from permitting myself to derive it from the first source that came to hand, I did not even trust my own impressions, but it rests partly on what I saw myself, partly on what others saw for me, the accuracy of the report being always tried by the most severe and detailed tests possible. My conclusions have cost me some labour from the

want of coincidence between accounts of the same occurrences by different eye-witnesses, arising sometimes from imperfect memory, sometimes from undue partiality for one side or the other. The absence of romance in my history will, I fear, detract somewhat from its interest; but if it be judged useful by those inquirers who desire an exact knowledge of the past as an aid to the interpretation of the future, which in the course of human things must resemble if it does not reflect it, I shall be content. In fine, I have written my work, not as an essay which is to win the applause of the moment, but as a possession for all time.

Think about it.

1. What does Thucydides say is his approach to writing this history?
2. How does his approach differ from that of earlier historians you have read?

5th–4th century BCE

33. The Ramayana

Translated by Ralph T. H. Griffith

The Ramayana is an ancient Indian epic composed orally in Sanskrit by bards who used to recite it before kings and chiefs at sacrificial feasts. Its authorship is traditionally ascribed to the sage Valmiki, sometimes referred to as the first poet of India. Valmiki's historicity has not been confirmed. The story is set in the later Vedic period (c. 1200–600 BCE) and concerns Rama, the prince of Ayodhya, whose wife Sita is abducted by Ravana, the evil king of Lanka. The present version of the work is divided into seven books or *kāndas* and is a product of Brahmin editing during the early centuries CE. The Brahmins added the first and seventh books, which present Rama as an incarnation of the god Vishnu. The earliest written version goes back to the 5th or 4th century BCE. It was much shorter and featured a more human Rama. In the following scene from Book 2, Dasaratha, king of Ayodhya, is preparing to appoint Rama as his successor.

Book 2. Canto III. Dasaratha's Precepts.

The monarch with the prayer complied
Of suppliant hands, on every side
Uplifted like a lotus-bed:
And then these gracious words he said:
"Great joy and mighty fame are mine   5
Because your loving hearts incline,
In full assembly clearly shown

Selection from: "Book II, Canto III," *The Rámáyan of Válmíki*, trans. Ralph T. H. Griffith. Trübner & Company, 1870. Copyright in the Public Domain.

To place my Ráma on the throne."
Then to Vaśishṭha, standing near,
And Vámadeva loud and clear   10
The monarch spoke that all might hear:
"'Tis pure and lovely Chaitra[1] now
When flowers are sweet on every bough;
All needful things with haste prepare
That Ráma be appointed heir."   15
Then burst the people's rapture out
In loud acclaim and joyful shout;
And when the tumult slowly ceased
The king addressed the holy priest:
"Give order, Saint, with watchful heed   20
For what the coming rite will need.
This day let all things ready wait
Mine eldest son to consecrate."
Best of all men of second birth
Vaśishṭha heard the lord of earth,   25
And gave commandment to the bands
Of servitors with lifted hands
Who waited on their master's eye:
"Now by to-morrow's dawn supply
Rich gold and herbs and gems of price   30
And offerings for the sacrifice,
Wreaths of white flowers and roasted rice,
And oil and honey, separate;
New garments and a car of state,
An elephant with lucky signs,   35
A fourfold host in ordered lines,
The white umbrella, and a pair
Of chowries, and a banner fair;
A hundred vases, row on row,
To shine like fire in splendid glow,   40
A tiger's mighty skin, a bull
With gilded horns most beautiful.
All these, at dawn of coming day,
Around the royal shrine array,
Where burns the fire's undying ray.   45
Each palace door, each city gate
With wreaths of sandal decorate.
And with the garlands' fragrant scent

Let clouds of incense-smoke be blent.
Let food of noble kind and taste   50
Be for a hundred thousand placed;
Fresh curds with streams of milk bedewed
To feed the Bráhman[2] multitude.
With care be all their wants supplied.
And mid the twice-born chiefs divide   55
Rich largess, with the early morn,
And oil and curds and roasted corn.
Soon as the sun has shown his light
Pronounce the prayer to bless the rite,
And then be all the Bráhmans called   60
And in their ordered seats installed.
Let all musicians skilled to play,
And dancing-girls in bright array
Stand ready in the second ring
Within the palace of the king.   65
Each honoured tree, each holy shrine
With leaves and flowery wreaths entwine,
And here and there beneath the shade
Be food prepared and presents laid.
Then brightly clad, in warlike guise,   70
With long swords girt upon their thighs,
Let soldiers of the nobler sort
March to the monarch's splendid court."

Thus gave command the twice-born pair
To active servants stationed there.   75
Then hastened to the king and said
That all their task was duly sped,
The king to wise Sumantra spake:
"Now quick, my lord, thy chariot take,
And hither with thy swiftest speed   80
My son, my noble Ráma lead."

Sumantra, ere the word was given,
His chariot from the court had driven,
And Ráma, best of all who ride
In cars, came sitting by his side.   85
The lords of men had hastened forth

_____
1   Spring month.

2   More commonly spelled "Brahmin" today, referring to priests.
Not to be confused with "Brahman," the ultimate reality.

From east and west and south and north,
Áryan and stranger, those who dwell
In the wild wood and on the fell,
And as the Gods to Indra, they   90
Showed honour to the king that day.
Like Vásav, when his glorious form
Is circled by the Gods of storm,
Girt in his hall by kings he saw
His car-borne Ráma near him draw,   95
Like him who rules the minstrel band
Of heaven; whose valour filled the land,
Of mighty arm and stately pride
Like a wild elephant in stride,
As fair in face as that fair stone   100
Dear to the moon, of moonbeams grown,
With noble gifts and grace that took
The hearts of all, and chained each look,
World-cheering as the Lord of Rain
When floods relieve the parching plain. 105
The father, as the son came nigh,
Gazed with an ever-thirstier eye.
Sumantra helped the prince alight
From the good chariot passing bright,
And as to meet his sire he went   110
Followed behind him reverent.
Then Ráma clomb, the king to seek
That terrace like Kailása's peak,
And reached the presence of the king,
Sumantra closely following.   115
Before his father's face he came,
Raised suppliant hands and named his name,
And bowing lowly as is meet
Paid reverence to the monarch's feet.
But soon as Daśaratha viewed   120
The prince in humble attitude,
He raised him by the hand in haste
And his beloved son embraced,
Then signed him to a glorious throne,
Gem-decked and golden, near his own.   125
Then Ráma, best of Raghu's line,
Made the fair seat with lustre shine
As when the orient sun upsprings
And his pure beam on Meru flings.

The glory flashed on roof and wall,   130
And with strange sheen suffused the hall,
As when the moon's pure rays are sent
Through autumn's star-lit firmament.
Then swelled his breast with joy and pride
As his dear son the father eyed,   135
E'en as himself more fair arrayed
In some clear mirror's face displayed.
The aged monarch gazed awhile,
Then thus addressed him with a smile,
As Kaśyap, whom the worlds revere,   140
Speaks for the Lord of Gods to hear:
"O thou of all my sons most dear,
In virtue best, thy father's peer,
Child of my consort first in place,
Mine equal in her pride of race,   145
Because the people's hearts are bound
To thee by graces in thee found,
Be thou in Pushya's³ favouring hour
Made partner of my royal power.
I know that thou by nature's bent   150
Both modest art and excellent,
But though thy gifts no counsel need
My love suggests the friendly rede.
Mine own dear son, be modest still,
And rule each sense with earnest will.   155
Keep thou the evils far away
That spring from love and anger's sway.
Thy noble course alike pursue
In secret as in open view,
And every nerve, the love to gain   160
Of ministers and subjects, strain.
The happy prince who sees with pride
His thriving people satisfied;
Whose arsenals with arms are stored,
And treasury with golden hoard,—   165
His friends rejoice as joyed the Blest
When Amrit crowned their eager quest.
So well, my child, thy course maintain,
And from all ill thy soul refrain."

---

3   A lunar mansion in Hindu astronomy.

---

c. 8ᵗʰ century BCE – 4ᵗʰ century CE

34. The Mahabharata

Translated by Kâshinâth Trimbak Telang

At close to 100,000 verses, the Mahabharata is by far the longest epic from any culture. Written in Sanskrit and produced in India, it tells the story of the Kurukshetra War, a conflict between the Pandava brothers and their cousins, the Kauravas, over the throne of Hastinapura, which is estimated to have taken place in 950 BCE. Composed orally around the 9ᵗʰ or 8ᵗʰ century BCE, the Mahabharata was not put into written form until around 400 BCE. At that time it was simply called *Bharata* and consisted of only 24,000 verses. Additions were made to the epic over several centuries thereafter, and the present form is the product of the Gupta period (c. 320–550 CE). One of the most hallowed portions of the work is the Bhagavad Gita, which is often published separately. Here is a selection from the Bhagavad Gita. The piece is set just prior to the battle when Arjuna (Arguna in this translation), the commander of the Pandavas, is making preparations.

Book VI. Chapter 23.

Dhritarâshtra[1] said:

What did my (people) and the Pândavas do, O Sañgaya![2] when they assembled together on the holy field of Kurukshetra, desirous to do battle?

Sañgaya said:

Seeing the army of the Pândavas drawn up in battle-array, the prince Duryodhana[3] approached the preceptor, and spoke (these) words: 'O preceptor! observe this grand army of the sons of Pându, drawn up in battle-array by your talented pupil, the son of Drupada. In it are heroes (bearing) large bows, the equals of Bhîma and Arguna in battle—(namely), Yuyudhâna, Virâta, and Drupada, the master of a great car, and Dhrishtaketu, Kekitâna, and the

---

1 Blind king of Hastinapura, father of the Kauravas and uncle of the Pandavas.
2 Or Sanjaya. Dhritarashtra's advisor, who narrates the story of the battle for him.

---

3 Leader of the evil Kauravas.

The Bhagavadgîtâ, The Sacred Books of the East, Volume VIII, trans. Kâshinâth Trimbak Telang, pp. 37–52. Clarendon Press, 1882. Copyright in the Public Domain.

valiant king of Kâsî, Purugit and Kuntibhoga, and that eminent man Saibya; the heroic Yudhâmanyu, the valiant Uttamaugas, the son of Subhadrâ, and the sons of Draupadî—all masters of great cars. And now, O best of Brâhmanas! learn who are most distinguished among us, and are leaders of my army. I will name them to you, in order that you may know them well. Yourself, and Bhîshma, and Karna, and Kripa the victor of (many) battles; Asvatthâman, and Vikarna, and also the son of Somadatta, and many other brave men, who have given up their lives for me, who fight with various weapons, (and are) all dexterous in battle. Thus our army which is protected by Bhîshma is unlimited; while this army of theirs which is protected by Bhîma is very limited. And therefore do ye all, occupying respectively the positions assigned to you, protect Bhîshma only.'

Then his powerful grandsire, Bhîshma, the oldest of the Kauravas, roaring aloud like a lion, blew his conch, (thereby) affording delight to Duryodhana. And then all at once, conchs, and kettledrums, and tabors, and trumpets were played upon; and there was a tumultuous din. Then, too, Mâdhava and the son of Pându (Arguna), seated in a grand chariot to which white steeds were yoked, blew their heavenly conchs. Hrishîkesa blew the Pâñkaganya, and Dhanañgaya the Devadatta, and Bhîma, (the doer) of fearful deeds, blew the great conch Paundra. King Yudhishthira, the son of Kuntî, blew the Anantavigaya, and Nakula and Sahadeva (respectively) the Sughosha and Manipushpaka. And the king of Kâsî, too, who has an excellent bow, and Sikhandin, the master of a great car, and Dhrishtadyumna, Virâta, and the unconquered Sâtyaki, and Drupada, and the sons of Draupadî, and the son of Subhadrâ, of mighty arms, blew conchs severally from all sides, O king of the earth! That tumultuous din rent the hearts of all (the people) of Dhritarâshtra's (party), causing reverberations throughout heaven and earth. Then seeing (the people of) Dhritarâshtra's party regularly marshalled, the son of Pându, whose standard is the ape, raised his bow, after the discharge of missiles had commenced, and O king

of the earth! spake these words to Hrishîkesa[4]: 'O undegraded one! station my chariot between the two armies, while I observe those, who stand here desirous to engage in battle, and with whom, in the labours of this struggle, I must do battle. I will observe those who are assembled here and who are about to engage in battle, wishing to do service in battle to the evil-minded son of Dhritarâshtra.'

Sañgaya said:

Thus addressed by Gudâkesa, O descendant of Bharata! Hrishîkesa stationed that excellent chariot between the two armies, in front of Bhîshma and Drona and of all the kings of the earth, and said O son of Prithâ! look at these assembled Kauravas.' There the son of Prithâ saw in both armies, fathers and grandfathers, preceptors, maternal uncles, brothers, sons, grandsons, companions, fathers-in-law, as well as friends. And seeing all those kinsmen standing (there), the son of Kuntî was overcome by excessive pity, and spake thus despondingly.

Arguna said:

Seeing these kinsmen, O Krishna! standing (here) desirous to engage in battle, my limbs droop down; my mouth is quite dried up; a tremor comes on my body; and my hairs stand on end; the Gândîva (bow) slips from my hand; my skin burns intensely. I am unable, too, to stand up; my mind whirls round, as it were; O Kesava! I see adverse omens; and I do not perceive any good (to accrue) after killing (my) kinsmen in the battle. I do not wish for victory, O Krishna! nor sovereignty, nor pleasures: what is sovereignty to us, O Govinda! what enjoyments, and even life? Even those, for whose sake we desire sovereignty, enjoyments, and pleasures, are standing here for battle, abandoning life and wealth-preceptors, fathers, sons as well as grandfathers, maternal uncles, fathers-in-law, grandsons, brothers-in-law, as also (other) relatives. These I do not wish to kill, though they kill (me), O destroyer of Madhu! even for the sake

---

4 That is, Krishna. Hrishikesa ("Lord of Senses") is one of the many names of the god Vishnu. Krishna is considered to be an avatar of Vishnu.

of sovereignty over the three worlds, how much less then for this earth (alone)? What joy shall be ours, O Ganârdana! after killing Dhritarâshtra's sons? Killing these felons we shall only incur sin. Therefore it is not proper for us to kill our own kinsmen, the sons of Dhritarâshtra. For how, O Mâdhava! shall we be happy after killing our own relatives? Although having their consciences corrupted by avarice, they do not see the evils flowing from the extinction of a family, and the sin in treachery to friends, still, O Ganârdana! should not we, who do see the evils flowing from the extinction of a family, learn to refrain from that sin? On the extinction of a family, the eternal rites of families are destroyed. Those rites being destroyed, impiety predominates over the whole family. In consequence of the predominance of impiety, O Krishna! the women of the family become corrupt; and the women becoming corrupt, O descendant of Vrishni! intermingling of castes results; that intermingling necessarily leads the family and the destroyers of the family to hell; for when the ceremonies of (offering) the balls of food and water (to them) fail, their ancestors fall down (to hell). By these transgressions of the destroyers of families, which occasion interminglings of castes, the eternal rites of castes and rites, of families are subverted. And O Ganârdana! we have heard that men whose family-rites are subverted, must necessarily live in hell. Alas! we are engaged in committing a heinous sin, seeing that we are making efforts for killing our own kinsmen out of greed of the pleasures of sovereignty. If the sons of Dhritarâshtra, weapon in hand, should kill me in battle, me weaponless and not defending (myself), that would be better for me.

Sañgaya said:

Having spoken thus, Arguna cast aside his bow together with the arrows, on the battle-field, and sat down in (his) chariot, with a mind agitated by grief.

CHAPTER 24.

Sañgaya said:

To him, who was thus overcome with pity, and dejected, and whose eyes were full of tears and turbid, the destroyer of Madhu spoke these words.

The Deity said:

How (comes it that) this delusion, O Arguna! which is discarded by the good, which excludes from heaven, and occasions infamy, has overtaken you in this (place of) peril? Be not effeminate, O son of Prithâ! it is not worthy of you. Cast off this base weakness of heart, and arise, O terror of (your) foes!

Arguna said:

How, O destroyer of Madhu! shall I encounter with arrows in the battle Bhîshma and Drona—both, O destroyer of enemies! entitled to reverence? Not killing (my) preceptors—(men) of great glory—it is better to live even on alms in this world. But killing them, though they are avaricious of worldly goods, I should only enjoy blood-tainted enjoyments. Nor do we know which of the two is better for us-whether that we should vanquish them, or that they should vanquish us. Even those, whom having killed, we do not wish to live—even those sons of Dhritarâshtra stand (arrayed) against us. With a heart contaminated by the taint of helplessness, with a mind confounded about my duty, I ask you. Tell me what is assuredly good for me. I am your disciple; instruct me, who have thrown myself on your (indulgence). For I do not perceive what is to dispel that grief which will dry up my organs after I shall have obtained a prosperous kingdom on earth without a foe, or even the sovereignty of the gods.

Sañgaya said:

Having spoken thus to Hrishîkesa, O terror of (your) foes! Gudâkesa said to Govinda, 'I shall not engage in battle;' and verily remained silent. To him thus desponding between the two armies, O descendant of Bharata! Hrishîkesa spoke these words with a slight smile.

The Deity said:

You have grieved for those who deserve no grief, and you talk words of wisdom. Learned men grieve not for the living nor the dead. Never did I not exist, nor you, nor these rulers of men; nor will any one of us ever hereafter cease to be. As, in this body, infancy and youth and old age (come) to the embodied (self), so does the acquisition of another body; a sensible man is not deceived about that The contacts of the senses, O son of Kuntî! which produce cold and heat, pleasure and pain, are not permanent, they are ever coming and going. Bear them, O descendant of Bharata! For, O chief of men! that sensible man whom they (pain and pleasure being alike to him) afflict not, he merits immortality. There is no existence for that which is unreal; there is no non-existence for that which is real. And the (correct) conclusion about both is perceived by those who perceive the truth. Know that to be indestructible which pervades all this; the destruction of that inexhaustible (principle) none can bring about. These bodies appertaining to the embodied (self) which is eternal, indestructible, and indefinable, are said to be perishable; therefore do engage in battle, O descendant of Bharata! He who thinks it to be the killer and he who thinks it to be killed, both know nothing. It kills not, is not killed. It is not born, nor does it ever die, nor, having existed, does it exist no more. Unborn, everlasting, unchangeable, and primeval, it is not killed when the body is killed. O son of Prithâ! how can that man who knows it thus to be indestructible, everlasting, unborn, and inexhaustible, how and whom can he kill, whom can he cause to be killed? As a man, casting off old clothes, puts on others and new ones, so the embodied (self) casting off old bodies, goes to others and new ones. Weapons do not divide it (into pieces); fire does not burn it, waters do not moisten it; the wind does not dry it up. It is not divisible; it is not combustible; it is not to be moistened; it is not to be dried up. It is everlasting, all-pervading, stable, firm, and eternal. It is said to be unperceived, to be unthinkable, to be unchangeable. Therefore knowing it to be such, you ought not to grieve, But even if you think that it is constantly born, and constantly dies, still, O you of mighty arms! you ought not to grieve thus. For to one that is born, death is certain; and to one that dies, birth is certain. Therefore about (this) unavoidable thing, you ought not to grieve. The source of things, O descendant of Bharata! is unperceived; their middle state is perceived; and their end again is unperceived. What (occasion is there for any) lamentation regarding them? One looks upon it as a wonder; another similarly speaks of it as a wonder; another too hears of it as a wonder; and even after having heard of it, no one does really know it. This embodied (self), O descendant of Bharata! within every one's body is ever indestructible. Therefore you ought not to grieve for any being. Having regard to your own duty also, you ought not to falter, for there is nothing better for a Kshatriya than a righteous battle. Happy those Kshatriyas, O son of Prithâ! who can find such a battle (to fight)—come of itself—an open door to heaven! But if you will not fight this righteous battle, then you will have abandoned your own duty and your fame, and you will incur sin. All beings, too, will tell of your everlasting infamy; and to one who has been honoured, infamy is (a) greater (evil) than death. (Warriors who are) masters of great cars will think that you abstained from the battle through fear, and having been highly thought of by them, you will fall down to littleness. Your enemies, too, decrying your power, will speak much about you that should not be spoken. And what, indeed, more lamentable than that? Killed, you will obtain heaven; victorious, you will enjoy the earth. Therefore arise, O son of Kuntî! resolved to (engage in) battle. Looking alike on pleasure and pain, on gain and loss, on victory and defeat, then prepare for battle, and thus you will not incur sin. The knowledge here declared to you is that relating to the Sânkhya. Now hear that relating to the Yoga. Possessed of this knowledge, O son of Prithâ! you will cast off the bonds of action. In this (path to final emancipation) nothing that is commenced becomes abortive; no obstacles exist; and even a little of this (form of) piety protects one from great danger. There is here, O descendant of Kuru! but one state of mind consisting in firm understanding. But the states of mind of those who have no firm understanding are many-branched and endless. The state of mind consisting in firm understanding regarding steady contemplation does not belong to those, O son of Prithâ! who are strongly attached to (worldly) pleasures and power, and whose minds are drawn away by that flowery talk which is full of (ordinances of) specific acts for the attainment of (those) pleasures and (that) power, and which promises birth as the fruit of acts—(that flowery talk) which those unwise ones utter, who are enamoured of Vedic words, who say there is nothing else, who are full of desires, and whose goal is heaven. The Vedas (merely) relate to the effects of the three qualities; do you, O Arguna! rise above those effects of the three qualities, and be free from the pairs of opposites, always preserve courage, be free from anxiety for new acquisitions or protection of old acquisitions, and be self-controlled. To the instructed Brâhmana, there is in all the Vedas as much utility as in a reservoir of water into which waters flow from all sides. Your business is with action alone; not by any means with fruit. Let not the fruit of action be your motive (to action). Let not your attachment be (fixed) on inaction. Having recourse to devotion, O Dhanañgaya! perform actions, casting off (all) attachment, and being equable in success or ill-success; (such) equability is called devotion. Action, O Dhanañgaya! is far inferior to the devotion of the mind. In that devotion seek shelter. Wretched are those whose motive (to action) is the fruit (of action). He who has obtained devotion in this world casts off both merit and sin. Therefore apply yourself to devotion; devotion in (all) actions is wisdom. The wise who have obtained devotion cast off the fruit of action; and released from the shackles of (repeated) births, repair to that seat where there is no unhappiness. When your mind shall have crossed beyond the taint of delusion, then will you become indifferent to all that you have heard or will heard. When your mind, confounded by what you have heard, will stand firm and steady in contemplation, then will you acquire devotion.

Arguna said:

What are the characteristics, O Kesava! of one whose mind is steady, and who is intent on contemplation? How should one of steady mind speak, how sit, how move?

The Deity said:

When a man, O son of Prithâ! abandons all the desires of his heart, and is pleased in his self only and by his self, he is then called one of steady mind. He whose heart is not agitated in the midst of calamities, who has no longing for pleasures, and from whom (the feelings of) affection, fear, and wrath have departed, is called a sage of steady mind. His mind is steady, who, being without attachments anywhere, feels no exultation and no aversion on encountering the various agreeable and disagreeable (things of this world). A man's mind is steady, when he withdraws his senses from (all) objects of sense, as the tortoise (withdraws) its limbs from all sides. Objects of sense draw back from a person who is abstinent; not so the taste (for those objects). But even the taste departs from him, when he has seen the Supreme. The boisterous senses, O son of Kuntî! carry away by force the mind even of a wise man, who exerts himself (for final emancipation). Restraining them all, a man should remain engaged in devotion, making me his only resort. For his mind is steady whose senses are under his control. The man who ponders over objects of sense forms an attachment to them; from (that) attachment is produced desire; and from desire anger is produced; from anger results want of discrimination; from want of discrimination, confusion of the memory; from confusion of the memory, loss of reason; and in consequence of loss of reason. he is utterly ruined. But the self-restrained man who moves among objects with senses under the control of his own self, and free from affection and aversion, obtains tranquillity. When there is tranquillity, all his miseries are destroyed, for the mind of him whose heart is tranquil soon becomes steady. He who is not self-restrained has no steadiness of mind; nor has he who is not self-restrained perseverance in the pursuit of self-knowledge; there is no tranquillity for him who does not persevere in the pursuit of self-knowledge; and whence can there be happiness for one who is not tranquil? For the heart which follows the rambling senses leads away his judgment, as the wind leads a boat astray upon the waters. Therefore, O you of mighty arms! his mind is steady whose senses are restrained on all sides from objects of sense. The self-restrained man is awake, when it is night for all beings; and when all beings are awake, that is the night of the right-seeing sage. He into whom all objects of desire enter, as waters enter the ocean, which, (though) replenished, (still) keeps its position unmoved,-he only obtains tranquillity; not he who desires (those) objects of desire. The man who, casting off all desires, lives free from attachments, who is free from egoism, and from (the feeling that this or that is) mine, obtains tranquillity. This, O son of Prithâ! is the Brahmic state; attaining to this, one is never deluded; and remaining in it in (one's) last moments, one attains (brahma-nirvâna) the Brahmic bliss.

Think about it.

1. Why does Arjuna decide he does not wish to fight?
2. How does Krishna convince Arjuna that he grieves for nothing?
3. How might this sort of reasoning have had an effect on the way the Indians waged war?

5th–2nd centuries BCE

35. The Analects

Translated by James Legge

Written mostly within a century after the death of the Chinese philosopher Confucius (who died c. 479 BCE), the Analects (or *Lunyu*) is a collection of remembered sayings and ideas of Confucius assembled by his disciples. By the end of the Warring States Period (476–221 BCE), it existed in two versions, which were edited into a single version during the early Han dynasty (206 BCE–8 CE). What follows are some selections from that work.

James Legge, *The Chinese Classics, Volume I, Part I*. Trübner & Company, 1870. Copyright in the Public Domain.

Part 4

The Master said, "It is virtuous manners which constitute the excellence of a neighborhood. If a man in selecting a residence do not fix on one where such prevail, how can he be wise?"

The Master said, "Those who are without virtue cannot abide long either in a condition of poverty and hardship, or in a condition of enjoyment. The virtuous rest in virtue; the wise desire virtue."

The Master said, "It is only the truly virtuous man, who can love, or who can hate, others."

The Master said, "If the will be set on virtue, there will be no practice of wickedness."

The Master said, "Riches and honors are what men desire. If they cannot be obtained in the proper way, they should not be held. Poverty and meanness are what men dislike. If they cannot be avoided in the proper way, they should not be avoided.

"If a superior man abandon virtue, how can he fulfill the requirements of that name?

"The superior man does not, even for the space of a single meal, act contrary to virtue. In moments of haste, he cleaves to it. In seasons of danger, he cleaves to it."

The Master said, "I have not seen a person who loved virtue, or one who hated what was not virtuous. He who loved virtue, would esteem nothing above it. He who hated what is not virtuous, would practice virtue in such a way that he would not allow anything that is not virtuous to approach his person.

"Is any one able for one day to apply his strength to virtue? I have not seen the case in which his strength would be insufficient.

"Should there possibly be any such case, I have not seen it."

The Master said, "The faults of men are characteristic of the class to which they belong. By observing a man's faults, it may be known that he is virtuous."

The Master said, "If a man in the morning hear the right way, he may die in the evening hear regret."

The Master said, "A scholar, whose mind is set on truth, and who is ashamed of bad clothes and bad food, is not fit to be discoursed with."

The Master said, "The superior man, in the world, does not set his mind either for anything, or against anything; what is right he will follow."

The Master said, "The superior man thinks of virtue; the small man thinks of comfort. The superior man thinks of the sanctions of law; the small man thinks of favors which he may receive."

The Master said: "He who acts with a constant view to his own advantage will be much murmured against."

The Master said, "If a prince is able to govern his kingdom with the complaisance proper to the rules of propriety, what difficulty will he have? If he cannot govern it with that complaisance, what has he to do with the rules of propriety?"

The Master said, "A man should say, I am not concerned that I have no place, I am concerned how I may fit myself for one. I am not concerned that I am not known, I seek to be worthy to be known."

The Master said, "Shen, my doctrine is that of an all-pervading unity." The disciple Zeng replied, "Yes."

The Master went out, and the other disciples asked, saying, "What do his words mean?" Zeng said, "The doctrine of our master is to be true to the principles-of our nature and the benevolent exercise of them to others,-this and nothing more."

The Master said, "The mind of the superior man is conversant with righteousness; the mind of the mean man is conversant with gain."

The Master said, "When we see men of worth, we should think of equaling them; when we see men of a contrary character, we should turn inwards and examine ourselves."

The Master said, "In serving his parents, a son may remonstrate with them, but gently; when he sees that they do not incline to follow his advice, he shows an increased degree of reverence, but does not abandon his purpose; and should they punish him, he does not allow himself to murmur."

The Master said, "While his parents are alive, the son may not go abroad to a distance. If he does go abroad, he must have a fixed place to which he goes."

The Master said, "If the son for three years does not alter from the way of his father, he may be called filial."

The Master said, "The years of parents may by no means not be kept in the memory, as an occasion at once for joy and for fear."

The Master said, "The reason why the ancients did not readily give utterance to their words, was that they feared lest their actions should not come up to them."

The Master said, "The cautious seldom err." The Master said, "The superior man wishes to be slow in his speech and earnest in his conduct."

The Master said, "Virtue is not left to stand alone. He who practices it will have neighbors."

Zi You said, "In serving a prince, frequent remonstrances lead to disgrace. Between friends, frequent reproofs make the friendship distant."

Part 6

The Master said, "Where the solid qualities are in excess of accomplishments, we have rusticity; where the accomplishments are in excess of the solid qualities, we have the manners of a clerk. When the accomplishments and solid qualities are equally blended, we then have the man of virtue."

The Master said, "Man is born for uprightness. If a man lose his uprightness, and yet live, his escape from death is the effect of mere good fortune."

The Master said, "They who know the truth are not equal to those who love it, and they who love it are not equal to those who delight in it."

The Master said, "To those whose talents are above mediocrity, the highest subjects may be announced. To those who are below mediocrity, the highest subjects may not be announced."

Fan Chi asked what constituted wisdom. The Master said, "To give one's self earnestly to the duties due to men, and, while respecting spiritual beings, to keep aloof from them, may be called wisdom." He asked about perfect virtue. The Master said, "The man of virtue makes the difficulty to be overcome his first business, and success only a subsequent consideration;-this may be called perfect virtue."

The Master said, "The wise find pleasure in water; the virtuous find pleasure in hills. The wise are active; the virtuous are tranquil. The wise are joyful; the virtuous are long-lived."

[...]

Zai Wo asked, saying, "A benevolent man, though it be told him,-'There is a man in the well' will go in after him, I suppose." Confucius said, "Why should he do so?" A superior man may be made to go to the well, but he cannot be made to go down into it. He may be imposed upon, but he cannot be fooled."

The Master said, "The superior man, extensively studying all learning, and keeping himself under the restraint of the rules of propriety, may thus likewise not overstep what is right."

The Master having visited Nan Zi, Zi Lu was displeased, on which the Master swore, saying, "Wherein I have done improperly, may Heaven reject me, may Heaven reject me!"

The Master said, "Perfect is the virtue which is according to the Constant Mean! Rare for a long time has been its practice among the people."

Zi Gong said, "Suppose the case of a man extensively conferring benefits on the people, and able to assist all, what would you say of him? Might he be called perfectly virtuous?" The Master said, "Why speak only of virtue in connection with him? Must he not have the qualities of a sage? Even Yao and Shun were still solicitous about this.

"Now the man of perfect virtue, wishing to be established himself, seeks also to establish others; wishing to be enlarged himself, he seeks also to enlarge others.

"To be able to judge of others by what is nigh in ourselves;-this may be called the art of virtue."

Part 8

The Master said, "Tai Bo may be said to have reached the highest point of virtuous action. Thrice he declined the kingdom, and the people in ignorance of his motives could not express their approbation of his conduct."

The Master said, "Respectfulness, without the rules of propriety, becomes laborious bustle; carefulness, without the rules of propriety, becomes timidity; boldness, without the rules of propriety, becomes insubordination; straightforwardness, without the rules of propriety, becomes rudeness.

"When those who are in high stations perform well all their duties to their relations, the people are aroused to virtue. When old friends are not neglected by them, the people are preserved from meanness."

The philosopher Zeng being ill, he cared to him the disciples of his school, and said, "Uncover my feet, uncover my hands. It is said in the Book of Poetry, 'We should be apprehensive and cautious, as if on the brink of a deep gulf, as if treading on thin ice, I and so have I been. Now and hereafter, I know my escape from all injury to my person. O ye, my little children."

The philosopher Zeng being ill, Meng Jing went to ask how he was.

Zeng said to him, "When a bird is about to die, its notes are mournful; when a man is about to die, his words are good.

"There are three principles of conduct which the man of high rank should consider specially important:-that in his deportment and manner he keep from violence and heedlessness; that in regulating his countenance he keep near to sincerity; and that in his words and tones he keep far from lowness and impropriety. As to such matters as attending to the sacrificial vessels, there are the proper officers for them."

The philosopher Zeng said, "Gifted with ability, and yet putting questions to those who were not so; possessed of much, and yet putting questions to those possessed of little; having, as though he had not; full, and yet counting himself as empty; offended against, and yet entering into no altercation; formerly I had a friend who pursued this style of conduct."

The philosopher Zeng said, "Suppose that there is an individual who can be entrusted with the charge of a young orphan prince, and can be commissioned with authority over a state of a hundred li, and whom no emergency however great can drive from his principles:-is such a man a superior man? He is a superior man indeed."

The philosopher Zeng said, "The officer may not be without breadth of mind and vigorous endurance. His burden is heavy and his course is long.

"Perfect virtue is the burden which he considers it is his to sustain;-is it not heavy? Only with death does his course stop;-is it not long?

The Master said, "It is by the Odes that the mind is aroused.

"It is by the Rules of Propriety that the character is established.

"It is from Music that the finish is received." The Master said, "The people may be made to follow a path of action, but they may not be made to understand it."

The Master said, "The man who is fond of daring and is dissatisfied with poverty, will proceed to insubordination. So will the man who is not virtuous, when you carry your dislike of him to an extreme."

The Master said, "Though a man have abilities as admirable as those of the Duke of Zhou, yet if he be proud and niggardly, those other things are really not worth being looked at."

The Master said, "It is not easy to find a man who has learned for three years without coming to be good."

The Master said, "With sincere faith he unites the love of learning; holding firm to death, he is perfecting the excellence of his course.

"Such an one will not enter a tottering state, nor dwell in a disorganized one. When right principles of government prevail in the kingdom, he will show himself; when they are prostrated, he will keep concealed.

"When a country is well governed, poverty and a mean condition are things to be ashamed of. When a country is ill governed, riches and honor are things to be ashamed of."

The Master said, "He who is not in any particular office has nothing to do with plans for the administration of its duties."

The Master said, "When the music master Zhi first entered on his office, the finish of the Guan Ju was magnificent;-how it filled the ears!"

The Master said, "Ardent and yet not upright, stupid and yet not attentive; simple and yet not sincere:-such persons I do not understand."

The Master said, "Learn as if you could not reach your object, and were always fearing also lest you should lose it."

The Master said, "How majestic was the manner in which Shun and Yu held possession of the empire, as if it were nothing to them!"

The Master said, "Great indeed was Yao as a sovereign! How majestic was he! It is only Heaven that is grand, and only Yao corresponded to it. How vast was his virtue! The people could find no name for it."

"How majestic was he in the works which he accomplished! How glorious in the elegant regulations which he instituted!"

Shun had five ministers, and the empire was well governed.

King Wu said, "I have ten able ministers." Confucius said, "Is not the saying that talents are difficult to find, true? Only when the dynasties of Tang and Yu met, were they more abundant than in this of Zhou, yet there was a woman among them. The able ministers were no more than nine men.

"King Wen possessed two of the three parts of the empire, and with those he served the dynasty of Yin. The virtue of the house of Zhou may be said to have reached the highest point indeed."

The Master said, "I can find no flaw in the character of Yu. He used himself coarse food and drink, but displayed the utmost filial piety towards the spirits. His ordinary garments were poor, but he displayed the utmost elegance in his sacrificial cap and apron. He lived in a low, mean house, but expended all his strength on the ditches and water channels. I can find nothing like a flaw in Yu."

Think about it.

1. How does Confucius highlight the importance of virtue? Over what does it take precedence?
2. What is the "superior man" like?
3. What advice is given to rulers?

36. The Mozi

Translated by Yi-Pao Mei

The Mozi is a collection of the teachings of Mozi (old spelling Mo Tzu), a Chinese philosopher from around the 5th century BCE. The work was probably assembled within a century after Mozi's death. Although Mozi had a significant following in the Warring States Period (476–221 BCE), adherents to his teachings will disappear by the time of the first Chinese empire. Here are some selections from The Mozi concerning love and war.

BOOK IV

CHAPTER XIV

Universal Love (I)

1.   The wise man who has charge of governing the empire should know the cause of disorder before he can put it in order. Unless he knows its cause, he cannot regulate it. It is similar to the problem of a physician who is attending a patient. He has to know the cause of the ailment before he can cure it. Unless he knows its cause he cannot cure it. How is the situation different for him who is to regulate disorder? He too has to know the cause of the disorder before he can regulate it. Unless he knows its cause he cannot regulate it. The wise man who has charge of governing the empire must, then, investigate the cause of disorder.

2.   Suppose we try to locate the cause of disorder, we shall find it lies in the want of mutual love. What is called disorder is just the lack of filial piety on the part of the minister and the son towards the emperor and the father. As he loves himself and not his father the son benefits himself to the disadvantage of his father. As he loves himself and not his elder brother, the younger brother benefits himself to the disadvantage of his elder brother. As he loves himself and not his emperor, the minister benefits himself to the disadvantage of his emperor. And these are what is called disorder. When the father shows no affection to the son, when the elder brother shows no affection to the younger brother, and when the emperor shows no affection to the minister, on the other hand, it is also called disorder. When the father loves only himself and not the son, he benefits himself to the disadvantage of the son. When the elder brother loves only himself and not his younger brother, he benefits himself to the disadvantage of the younger brother. When the emperor loves only himself and not his minister, he benefits himself to the disadvantage of his minister, and the reason for all these is want of mutual love.

3.   This is true even among thieves and robbers. As he loves only his own family and not other families, the thief steals from other families to profit his own family. As he loves only his own person and not others, the robber does violence to others to profit himself. And the reason for all this is want

of love. This again is true in the mutual disturbance among the houses of the ministers and the mutual invasions among the states of the feudal lords. As he loves only his own house and not the others, the minister disturbs the other houses to profit his own. As he loves only his own state and not the others, the feudal lord attacks the other states to profit his own. These instances exhaust the confusion in the world. And when we look into the causes we find they all arise from want of mutual love.

4. Suppose everybody in the world loves universally, loving others as one's self. Will there yet be any unfilial individual? When every one regards his father, elder brother, and emperor as himself, whereto can he direct any unfilial feeling? Will there still be any unaffectionate individual? When every one regards his younger brother, son, and minister as himself, whereto can he direct any disaffection? Therefore there will not be any unfilial feeling or disaffection. Will there then be any thieves and robbers? When every one regards other families as his own family, who will steal? When every one regards other persons as his own person, who will rob? Therefore there will not be any thieves or robbers. Will there be mutual disturbance among the houses of the ministers and invasion among the states of the feudal lords? When every one regards the houses of others as one's own, who will be disturbing? When every one regards the states of others as one's own, who will invade? Therefore there will be neither disturbances among the houses of the ministers nor invasion among the states of the feudal lords.

5. If every one in the world will love universally; states not attacking one another; houses not disturbing one another; thieves and robbers becoming extinct; emperor and ministers, fathers and sons, all being affectionate and filial—if all this comes to pass the world will be orderly. Therefore, how can the wise man who has charge of governing the empire fail to restrain hate and encourage love? So, when there is universal love in the world it will be orderly, and when there is mutual hate in the world it will be disorderly. This is why Mozi insisted on persuading people to love others.

CHAPTER XVI

Universal Love (III)

1. Mozi said: The purpose of the magnanimous lies in procuring benefits for the world and eliminating its calamities. Now among all the current calamities, which are the most important? The attack on the small states by the large ones, disturbances of the small houses by the large ones, oppression of the weak by the strong, misuse of the few by the many, deception of the simple by the cunning, disdain towards the humble by the honoured—these are the misfortunes in the empire. Again, the lack of grace on the part of the ruler, the lack of loyalty on the part of the ruled, the lack of affection on the part of the father, the lack of filial piety on the part of the son—these are further calamities in the empire. Also, the mutual injury and harm which the unscrupulous do to one another with weapons, poison, water, and fire is still another calamity in the empire.

2. When we come to think about the cause of all these calamities, how have they arisen? Have they arisen out of love of others and benefiting others? Of course we should say no. We should say they have arisen out of hate of others and injuring others. If we should classify one by one all those who hate others and injure others, should we find them to be universal in love or partial? Of course we should say they are partial. Now, since partiality against one another is the cause of the major calamities in the empire, then partiality is wrong.

3. Mozi continued: Whoever criticizes others must have something to replace them. Criticism without suggestion is like trying to stop flood with flood and put out fire with fire. It will surely be without worth.

4. Mozi said: Partiality is to be replaced by universality. But how is it that partiality can be replaced

by universality? Now, when every one regards the states of others as he regards his own, who would attack the others' states? Others are regarded like self. When every one regards the capitals of others as he regards his own, who would seize the others' capitals? Others are regarded like self. When every one regards the houses of others as he regards his own, who would disturb the others' houses? Others are regarded like self. Now, when the states and cities do not attack and seize each other and when the clans and individuals do not disturb and harm one another—is this a calamity or a benefit to the world? Of course it is a benefit. When we come to think about the several benefits in regard to their cause, how have they arisen? Have they arisen out of hate of others and injuring others? Of course we should say no. We should say they have arisen out of love of others and benefiting others. If we should classify one by one all those who love others and benefit others, should we find them to be partial or universal? Of course we should say they are universal. Now, since universal love is the cause of the major benefits in the world, therefore Mozi proclaims universal love is right.

5.   And, as has already been said, the interest of the magnanimous lies in procuring benefits for the world and eliminating its calamities. Now that we have found out the consequences of universal love to be the major benefits of the world and the consequences of partiality to be the major calamities in the world; this is the reason why Mozi said partiality is wrong and universality is right. When we try to develop and procure benefits for the world with universal love as our standard, then attentive ears and keen eyes will respond in service to one another, then limbs will be strengthened to work for one another, and those who know the Tao will untiringly instruct others. Thus the old and those who have neither wife nor children will have the support and supply to spend their old age with, and the young and weak and orphans will have the care and admonition to grow up in. When universal love is adopted as the standard, then such are the

consequent benefits. It is incomprehensible, then, why people should object to universal love when they hear it.

BOOK V

CHAPTER XVII

Condemnation of Offensive War (I)

1.   Suppose a man enters the orchard of another and steals the other's peaches and plums. Hearing of it the public will condemn it; laying hold of him the authorities will punish him. Why? Because he injures others to profit himself. As to seizing dogs, pigs, chickens, and young pigs from another, it is even more unrighteous than to steal peaches and plums from his orchard. Why? Because it causes others to suffer more, and it is more inhumane and criminal. When it comes to entering another's stable and appropriating the other's horses and oxen, it is more inhumane than to seize the dogs, pigs, chickens, and young pigs of another. Why? Because others are caused to suffer more; when others are caused to suffer more, then the act is more inhumane and criminal. Finally, as to murdering the innocent, stripping him of his clothing, dispossessing him of his spear and sword, it is even more unrighteous than to enter another's stable and appropriate his horses and oxen. Why? Because it causes others to suffer more; when others are caused to suffer more, then the act is more inhumane and criminal.

2.   All the gentlemen of the world know that they should condemn these things, calling them unrighteous. But when it comes to the great attack of states, they do not know that they should condemn it. On the contrary, they applaud it, calling it righteous. Can this be said to be knowing the difference between righteousness and unrighteousness?

3.   The murder of one person is called unrighteous and incurs one death penalty. Following this argument, the murder of ten persons will be ten

times as unrighteous and there should be ten death penalties; the murder of a hundred persons will be a hundred times as unrighteous and there should be a hundred death penalties. All the gentlemen of the world know that they should condemn these things, calling them unrighteous. But when it comes to the great unrighteousness of attacking states, they do not know that they should condemn it. On the contrary, they applaud it, calling it righteous. And they are really ignorant of its being unrighteous. Hence they have recorded their judgment to bequeath to their posterity. If they did know that it is unrighteous, then why would they record their false judgment to bequeath to posterity?

4. Now, if there were a man who, upon seeing a little blackness, should say it is black, but, upon seeing much, should say it is white; then we should think he could not tell the difference between black and white. If, upon tasting a little bitterness one should say it is bitter, but, upon tasting much, should say it is sweet; then we should think he could not tell the difference between bitter and sweet. Now, when a little wrong is committed people know that they should condemn it, but when such a great wrong as attacking a state is committed people do not know that they should condemn it. On the contrary, it is applauded, called righteous. Can this be said to be knowing the difference between the righteous and the unrighteous? Hence we know the gentlemen of the world are confused about the difference between righteousness and unrighteousness.

5. Now, what does Heaven desire and what does it abominate? Heaven desires righteousness and abominates unrighteousness. Therefore, in leading the people in the world to engage in doing righteousness I should be doing what Heaven desires. When I do what Heaven desires, Heaven will also do what I desire. Now, what do I desire and what do I abominate? I desire blessings and emoluments, and abominate calamities and misfortunes. When I do not do what Heaven desires, neither will Heaven do what I desire. Then I should be leading the people into calamities and misfortunes. But how do we know Heaven desires righteousness and abominates unrighteousness? For, with righteousness the world lives and without it the world dies; with it the world becomes rich and without it the world becomes poor; with it the world becomes orderly and without it the world becomes chaotic. And Heaven likes to have the world live and dislikes to have it die, likes to have it rich and dislikes to have it poor, and likes to have it orderly and dislikes to have it disorderly. Therefore we know Heaven desires righteousness and abominates unrighteousness.

6. Moreover, righteousness is the standard. A standard is not to be given by the subordinates to the superior but by the superior to the subordinates. Therefore, while the common people should spare no pains at work they may not make the standard at will. There are the scholars to give them the standard. While the scholars should spare no pains at work, they may not make the standard at will. There are the ministers and secretaries to give them the standard.

7. While the ministers and secretaries should spare no pains at work, they may not make the standard at will. There are the high duke and feudal lords to give them the standard. While the high duke and the feudal lords should spare no pains at work, they may not make the standard at will. There is the emperor to give them the standard. The emperor may not make the standard at will (either). There is Heaven to give him the standard. That the emperor gives the standard to the high duke, to the feudal lords, to the scholars, and to the common people, the gentlemen in the world clearly understand. But that Heaven gives the standard to the emperor, the people do not know well. Therefore the ancient sage-kings of the Three Dynasties, Yu, T'ang, Wen, and Wu, desiring to make it clear to the people that Heaven gives the standard to the emperor, fed oxen and sheep with grass, and pigs and dogs with grain, and cleanly prepared the cakes and wine to do sacrifice to God on High and the

spirits, and invoked Heaven's blessing. But I have not yet heard of Heaven invoking the emperor for blessing. So I know Heaven gives the standard to the emperor.

8. The emperor is the most honourable of the world and the richest of the world. So, the honoured and the rich cannot but obey the will of Heaven. He who obeys the will of Heaven, loving universally and benefiting others, will obtain rewards. He who opposes the will of Heaven, by being partial and unfriendly and harming others, will incur punishment. Now, who were those that obeyed the will of Heaven and obtained rewards, and who were those that opposed the will of Heaven and incurred punishment?

9. Mozi said: The ancient sage-kings of the Three Dynasties, Yü, T'ang, Wen, and Wu, were those that obeyed the will of Heaven and obtained reward. And the wicked kings of the Three Dynasties, Jie, Zhou, Yu, and Li, were those that opposed the will of Heaven and incurred punishment. How did Yü, T'ang, Wen, and Wu obtain their reward?

10. Mozi said: In the highest sphere they revered Heaven, in the middle sphere they worshipped the spirits, and in the lower sphere they loved the people. Thereupon the will of Heaven proclaimed: "All those whom I love these love also, and all those whom I benefit these benefit also. Their love to men is all-embracing and their benefit to men is most substantial." And so, they were raised to the honour of Sons of Heaven and enriched with the heritage of the empire. They were succeeded by descendants for ten thousand generations to continue the spread of their righteousness all over the world. And people praise them unto this day, calling them righteous sage-kings.

11. How did Jie, Zhou, Yu, and Li incur their punishment?

12. Mozi said: In the highest sphere they blasphemed against Heaven, in the middle sphere they blasphemed against the spirits, and in the sphere below they oppressed the people. Thereupon the will of Heaven proclaimed: "From those whom I love those turn away and hate, and those whom I want to benefit they oppress. Their hate of men is without limit and their oppression of men the most severe." And, so, they were not permitted to finish out their lives, or to survive a single generation. And people condemn them unto this day, calling them wicked kings.

13. How do we know Heaven loves the people? Because it teaches them all. How do we know it teaches them all? Because it claims them all. How do we know it claims them all? Because it accepts sacrifices from them all. How do we know it accepts sacrifices from all? Because within the four seas all who live on grains feed oxen and sheep with grass, and dogs and pigs with grains, and prepare clean cakes and wine to do sacrifice to God on High and the spirits. Claiming all the people, why will Heaven not love them? Moreover, as I have said, for the murder of one innocent individual there will be one calamity. Who is it that murders the innocent? It is man. Who is it that sends down the calamity? It is Heaven. If Heaven should be thought of as not loving the people, why should it send down calamities for the murder of man by man? So, I know Heaven loves the people.

14. To obey the will of Heaven is to accept righteousness as the standard. To oppose the will of Heaven is to accept force as the standard. Now what will the standard of righteousness do?

15. Mozi said: He who rules a large state does not attack small states: he who rules a large house does not molest small houses. The strong does not plunder the weak. The honoured does not disdain the humble. The clever does not deceive the stupid. This is beneficial to Heaven above, beneficial to the spirits in the middle sphere, and beneficial to the people below. Being beneficial to these three it is beneficial to all. So the most excellent name is attributed to such a man and he is called sage-king.

16. The standard of force is different from this. It is contradictory to this in word and opposed to this in deed like galloping with back to back.

Leading a large state, he whose standard is force attacks small states; leading a large house he molests small houses. The strong plunders the weak. The honoured disdains the humble. The clever deceives the stupid. This is not beneficial to Heaven above, or to the spirits in the middle sphere, or to the people below. Not being beneficial to these three, it is beneficial to none. So, the most evil name in the world is attributed to him and he is called the wicked king.

17. Mozi said: The will of Heaven to me is like the compasses to the wheelwright and the square to the carpenter. The wheelwright and the carpenter measure all the square and circular objects with their square and compasses and accept those that fit as correct and reject those that do not fit as incorrect. The writings of the gentlemen of the world of the present day cannot be all loaded (in a cart), and their doctrines cannot be exhaustively enumerated. They endeavour to convince the feudal lords on the one-hand and the scholars on the other. But from magnanimity and righteousness they are far off. How do we know? Because I have the most competent standard in the world to measure them with.

Think about it.

1. According to Mozi, what is the cause of disorder in society?
2. What is the cure for disorder and calamity in society, and why?
3. How does Heaven operate in the world?

5th–4th centuries BCE

37. The Laozi

Translated by James Legge

The Laozi, named for its presumed author Laozi, and alternately known as the *Daodejing* ("Way and Power Classic"—old spelling *Tao Te Ching*), is the composition of several authors who lived in China during the 5th and 4th centuries BCE. This philosophical work will later achieve prominence as one of the foundational texts of Daoism. Here are a few excerpts giving advice to those in positions of power.

James Legge, *The Sacred Books of China: The Texts of Taoism, The Sacred Books of the East, Volume XXXIX*. Oxford University Press, 1891. Copyright in the Public Domain.

3 Not to value and employ men of superior ability is the way to keep the people from rivalry among themselves; not to prize articles which are difficult to procure is the way to keep them from becoming thieves; not to show them what is likely to excite their desires is the way to keep their minds from disorder.

Therefore the sage, in the exercise of his government, empties their minds, fills their bellies, weakens their wills, and strengthens their bones.

He constantly (tries to) keep them without knowledge and without desire, and where there are those who have knowledge, to keep them from presuming to act (on it). When there is this abstinence from action, good order is universal.

13 Favour and disgrace would seem equally to be feared; honour and great calamity, to be regarded as personal conditions (of the same kind).

What is meant by speaking thus of favour and disgrace? Disgrace is being in a low position (after the enjoyment of favour). The getting that (favour) leads to the apprehension (of losing it), and the losing it leads to the fear of (still greater calamity):—this is what is meant by saying that favour and disgrace would seem equally to be feared.

And what is meant by saying that honour and great calamity are to be (similarly) regarded as personal conditions? What makes me liable to great calamity is my having the body (which I call myself); if I had not the body, what great calamity could come to me?

Therefore he who would administer the kingdom, honouring it as he honours his own person, may be employed to govern it, and he who would administer it with the love which he bears to his own person may be entrusted with it.

17 In the highest antiquity, (the people) did not know that there were (their rulers). In the next age they loved them and praised them. In the next they feared them; in the next they despised them. Thus it was that when faith (in the Dao) was deficient (in the rulers) a want of faith in them ensued (in the people).

How irresolute did those (earliest rulers) appear, showing (by their reticence) the importance which they set upon their words! Their work was done and their undertakings were successful, while the people all said, 'We are as we are, of ourselves!'

18 When the Great Dao (Way or Method) ceased to be observed, benevolence and righteousness came into vogue. (Then) appeared wisdom and shrewdness, and there ensued great hypocrisy.

When harmony no longer prevailed throughout the six kinships, filial sons found their manifestation; when the states and clans fell into disorder, loyal ministers appeared.

19 If we could renounce our sageness and discard our wisdom, it would be better for the people a hundredfold. If we could renounce our benevolence and discard our righteousness, the people would again become filial and kindly. If we could renounce our artful contrivances and discard our (scheming for) gain, there would be no thieves nor robbers.

Those three methods (of government) Thought olden ways in elegance did fail And made these names their want of worth to veil; But simple views, and courses plain and true Would selfish ends and many lusts eschew.

26 Gravity is the root of lightness; stillness, the ruler of movement.

Therefore a wise prince, marching the whole day, does not go far from his baggage waggons. Although he may have brilliant prospects to look at, he quietly remains (in his proper place), indifferent to them. How should the lord of a myriad chariots carry himself lightly before the kingdom? If he do act lightly, he has lost his root (of gravity); if he proceed to active movement, he will lose his throne.

29 If any one should wish to get the kingdom for himself, and to effect this by what he does, I see that he will not succeed. The kingdom is a spirit-like thing, and cannot be got by active doing. He who would so win it destroys it; he who would hold it in his grasp loses it.

The course and nature of things is such that What was in front is now behind; What warmed anon we freezing find. Strength is of weakness oft the spoil; The store in ruins mocks our toil.

Hence the sage puts away excessive effort, extravagance, and easy indulgence.

30 He who would assist a lord of men in harmony with the Dao will not assert his mastery in the kingdom by force of arms. Such a course is sure to meet with its proper return.

Wherever a host is stationed, briars and thorns spring up. In the sequence of great armies there are sure to be bad years.

A skilful (commander) strikes a decisive blow, and stops. He does not dare (by continuing his operations) to assert and complete his mastery. He will strike the blow, but will be on his guard against being vain or boastful or arrogant in consequence of it. He strikes it as a matter of necessity; he strikes it, but not from a wish for mastery.

When things have attained their strong maturity they become old. This may be said to be not in accordance with the Dao: and what is not in accordance with it soon comes to an end.

31 Now arms, however beautiful, are instruments of evil omen, hateful, it may be said, to all creatures. Therefore they who have the Dao do not like to employ them.

The superior man ordinarily considers the left hand the most honourable place, but in time of war the right hand. Those sharp weapons are instruments of evil omen, and not the instruments of the superior man;—he uses them only on the compulsion of necessity. Calm and repose are what he prizes; victory (by force of arms) is to him undesirable. To consider this desirable would be to delight in the slaughter of men; and he who delights in the slaughter of men cannot get his will in the kingdom.

On occasions of festivity to be on the left hand is the prized position; on occasions of mourning, the right hand. The second in command of the army has his place on the left; the general commanding in chief has his on the right;—his place, that is, is assigned to him as in the rites of mourning. He who has killed multitudes of men should weep for them with the bitterest grief; and the victor in battle has his place (rightly) according to those rites.

57 A state may be ruled by (measures of) correction; weapons of war may be used with crafty dexterity; (but) the kingdom is made one's own (only) by freedom from action and purpose.

How do I know that it is so? By these facts:—In the kingdom the multiplication of prohibitive enactments increases the poverty of the people; the more implements to add to their profit that the people have, the greater disorder is there in the state and clan; the more acts of crafty dexterity that men possess, the more do strange contrivances appear; the more display there is of legislation, the more thieves and robbers there are.

Therefore a sage has said, 'I will do nothing (of purpose), and the people will be transformed of themselves; I will be fond of keeping still, and the people will of themselves become correct. I will take no trouble about it, and the people will of themselves become rich; I will manifest no ambition, and the people will of themselves attain to the primitive simplicity.'

58 The government that seems the most unwise, Oft goodness to the people best supplies; That which is meddling, touching everything, Will work but ill, and disappointment bring.

Misery!—happiness is to be found by its side! Happiness!—misery lurks beneath it! Who knows what either will come to in the end?

Shall we then dispense with correction? The (method of) correction shall by a turn become distortion, and the good in it shall by a turn become evil. The delusion of the people (on this point) has indeed subsisted for a long time.

Therefore the sage is (like) a square which cuts no one (with its angles); (like) a corner which injures no one (with its sharpness). He is straightforward, but allows himself no license; he is bright, but does not dazzle.

59 For regulating the human (in our constitution) and rendering the (proper) service to the heavenly, there is nothing like moderation.

It is only by this moderation that there is effected an early return (to man's normal state). That early return is what I call the repeated accumulation of the attributes (of the Dao). With that repeated accumulation of those attributes, there comes the subjugation (of every obstacle to such return). Of this subjugation we know not what shall be the limit; and when one knows not what the limit shall be, he may be the ruler of a state.

He who possesses the mother of the state may continue long. His case is like that (of the plant) of which we say that its roots are deep and its flower stalks firm:—this is the way to secure that its enduring life shall long be seen.

60 Governing a great state is like cooking small fish.

Let the kingdom be governed according to the Dao, and the manes of the departed will not manifest their spiritual energy. It is not that those manes have not that spiritual energy, but it will not be employed to hurt men. It is not that it could not hurt men, but neither does the ruling sage hurt them.

When these two do not injuriously affect each other, their good influences converge in the virtue (of the Dao).

61 What makes a great state is its being (like) a low-lying, down-flowing (stream);—it becomes the centre to which tend (all the small states) under heaven.

(To illustrate from) the case of all females:—the female always overcomes the male by her stillness. Stillness may be considered (a sort of) abasement.

Thus it is that a great state, by condescending to small states, gains them for itself; and that small states, by abasing themselves to a great state, win it over to them. In the one case the abasement leads to gaining adherents, in the other case to procuring favour.

The great state only wishes to unite men together and nourish them; a small state only wishes to be received by, and to serve, the other. Each gets what it desires, but the great state must learn to abase itself.

62 Dao has of all things the most honoured place. No treasures give good men so rich a grace; Bad men it guards, and doth their ill efface.

(Its) admirable words can purchase honour; (its) admirable deeds can raise their performer above others. Even men who are not good are not abandoned by it.

Therefore when the sovereign occupies his place as the Son of Heaven, and he has appointed his three ducal ministers, though (a prince) were to send in a round symbol-of-rank large enough to fill both the hands, and that as the precursor of the team of horses (in the court-yard), such an offering would not be equal to (a lesson of) this Dao, which one might present on his knees.

Why was it that the ancients prized this Dao so much? Was it not because it could be got by seeking for it, and the guilty could escape (from the stain of their guilt) by it? This is the reason why all under heaven consider it the most valuable thing.

65 The ancients who showed their skill in practising the Dao did so, not to enlighten the people, but rather to make them simple and ignorant.

The difficulty in governing the people arises from their having much knowledge. He who (tries to) govern a state by his wisdom is a scourge to it; while he who does not (try to) do so is a blessing.

He who knows these two things finds in them also his model and rule. Ability to know this model and rule constitutes what we call the mysterious excellence (of a governor). Deep and far-reaching is such mysterious excellence, showing indeed its possessor as opposite to others, but leading them to a great conformity to him.

66 That whereby the rivers and seas are able to receive the homage and tribute of all the valley streams, is their skill in being lower than they;—it is thus that they are the kings of them all. So it is that the sage (ruler), wishing to be above men, puts himself by his words below them, and, wishing to be before them, places his person behind them.

In this way though he has his place above them, men do not feel his weight, nor though he has his place before them, do they feel it an injury to them.

Therefore all in the world delight to exalt him and do not weary of him. Because he does not strive, no one finds it possible to strive with him.

74 The people do not fear death; to what purpose is it to (try to) frighten them with death? If the people were always in awe of death, and I could always seize those who do wrong, and put them to death, who would dare to do wrong?

There is always One who presides over the infliction death. He who would inflict death in the room of him who so presides over it may be described as hewing wood instead of a great carpenter. Seldom is it that he who undertakes the hewing, instead of the great carpenter, does not cut his own hands!

80 In a little state with a small population, I would so order it, that, though there were individuals with the abilities of ten or a hundred men, there should be no employment of them; I would make the people, while looking on death as a grievous thing, yet not remove elsewhere (to avoid it).

Though they had boats and carriages, they should have no occasion to ride in them; though they had buff coats and sharp weapons, they should have no occasion to don or use them.

I would make the people return to the use of knotted cords (instead of the written characters).

They should think their (coarse) food sweet; their (plain) clothes beautiful; their (poor) dwellings places of rest; and their common (simple) ways sources of enjoyment.

There should be a neighbouring state within sight, and the voices of the fowls and dogs should be heard all the way from it to us, but I would make the people to old age, even to death, not have any intercourse with it.

Think about it.

1. According to this text, how are rulers to rule? What should they not do?
2. What is the difference between a great state and a small one?
3. Compare and contrast the political views of Confucius, Mozi, and Laozi.

38. Khandhaka

Translated by Thomas W. Rhys Davids and Hermann Oldenberg

Scholars are generally of the opinion that the oldest scriptures of Buddhism are now to be found in the Pali Canon (also known as the *Tipitaka*), the standard collection of sacred writings for the Theravada Buddhist communities, which is preserved in the Pali language. Specifically, the section known as the Vinaya Pitaka and the first four *nikayas* of the Sutta Pitaka are believed to be the earliest. Here is a selection from a part of the Vinaya Pitaka called the "Khandaka," thought to have been composed within a century of the death of the Buddha (c. 563–483 BCE). It tells the story of how the Buddha formed the first monastic community of Bhikkus.

6.

1. Now the Blessed One[1] thought: 'To whom shall I preach the doctrine first? Who will understand this doctrine easily?' And the Blessed One thought: 'There is Âlâra Kâlâma; he is clever, wise, and learned; long since have the eye of his mind been darkened by scarcely any dust. What if I were to preach the doctrine first to Âlâra Kâlâma? He will easily understand this doctrine.'

2. Then an invisible deity said to the Blessed One: 'Âlâra Kâlâma has died, Lord, seven days ago.' And knowledge sprang up in the Blessed One's mind that Âlâra Kâlâma had died seven days ago. And the Blessed One thought: 'Highly noble was Alâra Kâlâma. If he had heard my doctrine, he would easily have understood it.'

3. Then the Blessed One thought: 'To whom shall I preach the doctrine first? Who will understand this doctrine easily?' And the Blessed One thought:

'There is Uddaka Râmaputta; he is clever, wise, and learned; long since have the eye or his mind been darkened by scarcely any dust. What if I were to preach the doctrine first to Uddaka Râmaputta? He will easily understand this doctrine.'

4. Then an invisible deity said to the Blessed One: 'Uddaka Râmaputta has died, Lord, yesterday evening.' And knowledge arose in the Blessed One's mind that Uddaka Râmaputta had died the previous evening. And the Blessed One thought: 'Highly noble was Uddaka Râmaputta. If he had heard my doctrine, he would easily have understood it.'

5. Then the Blessed One thought: 'To whom shall I preach the doctrine first? Who will understand this doctrine easily?' And the Blessed One thought: 'The five Bhikkhus have done many services to me; they attended on me during the time of my exertions (to attain sanctification by undergoing austerities). What if I were to preach the doctrine first to the five Bhikkhus?'

6. Now the Blessed One thought: 'Where do the five Bhikkhus dwell now?' And the Blessed One saw

---

1 The Buddha.

Thomas W. Rhys Davids and Hermann Oldenberg, *Vinaya Texts, Part I, The Sacred Books of the East, Volume XIII*. Oxford University Press, 1881. Copyright in the Public Domain.

by the power of his divine, clear vision, surpassing that of men, that the five Bhikkhus were living at Benares, in the deer park Isipatana. And the Blessed One, after having remained at Uruvelâ as long as he thought fit, went forth to Benares.

7. Now Upaka, a man belonging to the Âgîvaka sect,[2] saw the Blessed One travelling on the road, between Gayâ and the Bodhi tree; and when he saw him, he said to the Blessed One: 'Your countenance, friend, is serene; your complexion is pure and bright. In whose name, friend, have you retired from the world? Who is your teacher? Whose doctrine do you profess?'

8. When Upaka the Âgîvaka had spoken thus, the Blessed One addressed him in the following stanzas: 'I have overcome all foes; I am all-wise; I am free from stains in every way; I have left everything; and have obtained emancipation by the destruction of desire. Having myself gained knowledge, whom should I call my master? I have no teacher; no one is equal to me; in the world of men and of gods no being is like me. I am the holy One in this world, I am the highest teacher, I alone am the absolute Sambuddha; I have gained coolness (by the extinction of all passion) and have obtained Nirvâna. To found the Kingdom of Truth I go to the city of the Kâsis (Benares); I will beat the drum of the Immortal in the darkness of this world.'

9. (Upaka replied): 'You profess then, friend, to be the holy, absolute Gina.'

(Buddha said): ‹Like me are all Ginas who have reached extinction of the Âsavas[3]; I have overcome (gitâ me) all states of sinfulness; therefore, Upaka, am I the Gina.'

When he had spoken thus, Upaka the Âgîvaka replied: 'It may be so, friend;' shook his head, took another road, and went away.

10. And the Blessed One, wandering from place to place, came to Benares, to the deer park Isipatana,

to the place where the five Bhikkhus were. And he five Bhikkhus saw the Blessed One coming from afar; when they saw him, they concerted with each other, saying, 'Friends, there comes the samana Gotama, who lives in abundance, who has given up his exertions, and who has turned to an abundant life. Let us not salute him; nor rise from our seats when he approaches; nor take his bowl and his robe from his hands. But let us put there a seat; if he likes, let him sit down.'

11. But when the Blessed One gradually approached near unto those five Bhikkhus, the five Bhikkhus kept not their agreement. They went forth to meet the Blessed One; one took his bowl and his robe, another prepared a seat, a third one brought water for the washing of the feet, a foot-stool, and a towel. Then the Blessed One sat down on the seat they had prepared; and when he was seated, the Blessed One washed his feet. Now they addressed the Blessed One by his name, and with the appellation 'Friend.'

12. When they spoke to him thus, the Blessed One said to the five Bhikkhus: 'Do not address, O Bhikkhus, the Tathâgata[4] by his name, and with the appellation "Friend." The Tathâgata, O Bhikkhus, is the holy, absolute Sambuddha. Give ear, O Bhikkhus! The immortal (Amata) has been won (by me); I will teach you; to you I preach the doctrine. If you walk in the way I show you, you will, ere long, have penetrated to the truth, having yourselves known it and seen it face to face; and you will live in the possession of that highest goal of the holy life, for the sake of which noble youths fully give up the world and go forth into the houseless state.

13. When he had spoken thus, the five monks said to the Blessed One: 'By those observances, friend Gotama, by those practices, by those austerities, you have not been able to obtain power surpassing that of men, nor the superiority of full and holy knowledge and insight. How will you now, living in abundance, having given up your exertions, having

2   the sect of naked ascetics.
3   mental biases or cankers that keep a person bound to the cycle of reincarnation.

4   A term the Buddha uses to refer to himself.

turned to an abundant life, be able to obtain power surpassing that of men, and the superiority of full and holy knowledge and insight?'

14. When they had spoken thus, the Blessed One said to the five Bhikkhus: 'The Tathâgata, O Bhikkhus, does not live in abundance, he has not given up exertion, he has not turned to an abundant life. The Tathâgata, O Bhikkhus, is the holy, absolute Sambuddha. Give ear, O Bhikkhus; the immortal has been won (by me); I will teach you, to you I will preach the doctrine. If you walk in the way I show you, you will, ere long, have penetrated to the truth, having yourselves known it and seen it face to face; and you will live in the possession of that highest goal of the holy life, for the sake of which noble youths fully give up the world and go forth into the houseless state.'

15. And the five Bhikkhus said to the Blessed One a second time (as above). And the Blessed One said to the five Bhikkhus a second time (as above). And the five Bhikkhus said to the Blessed One a third time (as above).

16. When they had spoken thus, the Blessed One said to the five Bhikkhus: 'Do you admit, O Bhikkhus, that I have never spoken to you in this way before this day?'

'You have never spoken so, Lord.'

'The Tathâgata, O Bhikkhus, is the holy, absolute Sambuddha. Give ear, O Bhikkhus, etc. (as above).'

And the Blessed One was able to convince the five Bhikkhus; and the five Bhikkhus again listened willingly to the Blessed One; they gave ear, and fixed their mind on the knowledge (which the Buddha imparted to them).

17. And the Blessed One thus addressed the five Bhikkhus: 'There are two extremes, O Bhikkhus, which he who has given up the world, ought to avoid. What are these two extremes? A life given to pleasures, devoted to pleasures and lusts: this is degrading, sensual, vulgar, ignoble, and profitless; and a life given to mortifications: this is painful, ignoble, and profitless. By avoiding these two extremes, O Bhikkhus, the Tathâgata has gained the knowledge of the Middle Path which leads to insight, which leads to wisdom, which conduces to calm, to knowledge, to the Sambodhi, to Nirvâna.

18. 'Which, O Bhikkhus, is this Middle Path the knowledge of which the Tathâgata has gained, which leads to insight, which leads to wisdom, which conduces to calm, to knowledge, to the Sambodhi, to Nirvâna? It is the holy eightfold Path, namely, Right Belief, Right Aspiration, Right Speech, Right Conduct, Right Means of Livelihood, Right Endeavour, Right Mernory, Right Meditation. This, O Bhikkhus, is the Middle Path the knowledge of which the Tathâgata has gained, which leads to insight, which leads to wisdom, which conduces to calm, to knowledge, to the Sambodhi, to Nirvâna.

19. 'This, O Bhikkhus, is the Noble Truth of Suffering: Birth is suffering; decay is suffering; illness is suffering; death is suffering. Presence of objects we hate, is suffering; Separation from objects we love, is suffering; not to obtain what we desire, is suffering. Briefly, the fivefold clinging to existence is suffering.

20. 'This, O Bhikkhus, is the Noble Truth of the Cause of suffering: Thirst, that leads to re-birth, accornpanied by pleasure and lust, finding its delight here and there. (This thirst is threefold), namely, thirst for pleasure, thirst for existence, thirst for prosperity.

21. 'This, O Bhikkhus, is the Noble Truth of the Cessation of suffering: (It ceases with) the complete cessation of this thirst,—a cessation which consists in the absence of every passion,—with the abandoning of this thirst, with the doing away with it, with the deliverance from it, with the destruction of desire.

22. 'This, O Bhikkhus, is the Noble Truth of the Path which leads to the cessation of suffering: that holy eightfold Path, that is to say, Right Belief, Right Aspiration, Right Speech, Right Conduct, Right Means of Livelihood, Right Endeavour, Right Memory, Right Meditation.

23. '"This is the Noble Truth of Suffering;"—thus, O Bhikkhus, of this doctrine, which formerly had not been heard of, have I obtained insight, knowledge, understanding, wisdom, intuition. "This

Noble Truth of Suffering must be understood," thus, O Bhikkhus, of this doctrine, ... (etc., down to intuition). "This Noble Truth of Suffering I have understood," thus, O Bhikkhus, of this doctrine, ... (etc., down to intuition).

24. "'This is the Noble Truth of the Cause of suffering," thus, O Bhikkhus, (etc.) "This Noble Truth of the Cause of suffering must be abandoned has been abandoned by me," thus, O Bhikkhus, (etc.)

25. "'This is the Noble Truth of the Cessation of suffering," thus, O Bhikkhus, (etc.) "This Noble Truth of the Cessation of suffering must be seen face to face ... has been seen by me face to face," thus, O Bhikkhus, (etc.)

26. "'This is the Noble Truth of the Path which leads to the cessation of suffering," thus, O Bhikkhus, (etc.) "This Noble Truth of the Path which leads to the cessation of suffering, must be realised has been realised by me," thus, O Bhikkhus, (etc.)

27. 'As long, O Bhikkhus, as I did not possess with perfect purity this true knowledge and insight into these four Noble Truths, with its three modifications and its twelve constituent parts; so long, O Bhikkhus, I knew that I had not yet obtained the highest, absolute Sambodhi in the world of men and gods, in Mâra's and Brahma's world, among all beings, Samanas and Brâhmanas, gods and men.

28. 'But since I possessed, O Bhikkhus, with perfect purity this true knowledge and insight into these four Noble Truths, with its three modifications and its twelve constituent parts, then I knew, O Bhikkhus, that I had obtained the highest, universal Sambodhi in the world of men and gods, ... (etc., as in § 27).

29. 'And this knowledge and insight arose in my mind: "The emancipation of my mind cannot be lost; this is my last birth; hence I shall not be born again!"'

Thus the Blessed One spoke. The five Bhikkhus were delighted, and they rejoiced at the words of the Blessed One. And when this exposition was propounded, the venerable Kondañña obtained the pure and spotless Eye of the Truth (that is to say, the following knowledge): 'Whatsoever is subject to the condition of origination, is subject also to the condition of cessation.'

30. And as the Blessed One had founded the Kingdom of Truth (by propounding the four Noble Truths), the earth-inhabiting devas shouted: 'Truly the Blessed One has founded at Benares, in the deer park Isipatana, the highest kingdom of Truth, which may be opposed neither by a Samana nor by a Brâhmana, neither by a deva, nor by Mâra, nor by Brahma, nor by any being in the world.'

Hearing the shout of the earth-inhabiting devas, the kâtumahârâgika devas (gods belonging to the world of the four divine mahârâgas) shouted, ... (etc., as above). Hearing the shout of the kâtumahârâgika devas, the tâvatimsa devas, the yâma devas, the tusita devas, the nimmânarati devas, the paranimmitavasavatti devas, the brahmakâyika devas shouted: 'Truly the Blessed One, ... ' (etc., as above).

31. Thus in that moment, in that instant, in that second the shout reached the Brahma world; and this whole system of ten thousand worlds quaked, was shaken, and trembled; and an infinite, mighty light was seen through the world, which surpassed the light that can be produced by the divine power of the devas.

And the Blessed One pronounced this solemn utterance: 'Truly Kondañña has perceived it ("aññâsi"), truly Kondañña has perceived it!' Hence the venerable Kondañña received the name Aññâtakondañña (Kondañña who has perceived the doctrine).

32. And the venerable Aññâtakondañña, having seen the Truth, having mastered the Truth, having understood the Truth, having penetrated the Truth, having overcome uncertainty, having dispelled all doubts, having gained full knowledge, dependent on nobody else for knowledge of the doctrine of the Teacher, thus spoke to the Blessed One: 'Lord, let me receive the pabbaggâ and upasampadâ ordinations from the Blessed One.'

'Come, O Bhikkhu,' said the Blessed One, 'well taught is the doctrine; lead a holy life for the sake of the complete extinction of suffering.' Thus this venerable person received the upasampadâ ordination.

33. And the Blessed One administered to the other Bhikkhus exhortation and instruction by discourses relating to the Dhamma. And the venerable Vappa, and the venerable Bhaddiya, when they received from the Blessed One such exhortation and instruction by discourses relating to the Dhamma, obtained the pure and spotless Eye of the Truth (that is to say, the following knowledge): 'Whatsoever is subject to the condition of origination is subject also to the condition of cessation.'

34. And having seen the Truth, having mastered the Truth, ... (etc., as in § 32), they thus spoke to the Blessed One: 'Lord, let us receive the pabbaggâ and upasampadâ ordinations from the Blessed One.'

'Come, O Bhikkhus,' said the Blessed One, 'well taught is the doctrine; lead a holy life for the sake of the complete extinction of suffering.' Thus these venerable persons received the upasampadâ ordination.

35. And the Blessed One, living on what the Bhikkhus brought him, administered to the other Bhikkhus exhortation and instruction by discourse relating to the Dhamma; in this way the six persons lived on what the three Bhikkhus brought home from their alms pilgrimage.

36, 37. And the venerable Mahânâma and the venerable Assagi, when they received from the Blessed One, ... (etc., as in §§ 33, 34, down to:). Thus these venerable persons received the upasampadâ ordination.

38. And the Blessed One thus spoke to the five Bhikkhus: 'The body (Rûpa), O Bhikkhus, is not the self. If the body, O Bhikkhus, were the self, the body would not be subject to disease, and we should be able to say: "Let my body be such and such a one, let my body not be such and such a one." But since the body, O Bhikkhus, is not the self, therefore the body is subject to disease, and we are not able to say: "Let my body be such and such a one, let my body not be such and such a one."'

39–41. 'Sensation (Vedanâ), O Bhikkhus, is not the self, ... (etc.) Perception (Saññâ) is not the self, ... The Samkhâras are not the self, ... Consciousness (Viññâna) is not the self, ... (etc.)

42. 'Now what do you think, O Bhikkhus, is the body permanent or perishable?'

'It is perishable, Lord.'

'And that which is perishable, does that cause pain or joy?'

'It causes pain, Lord.'

'And that which is perishable, painful, subject to change, is it possible to regard that in this way: 'This is mine, this am I, this is my self?'

'That is impossible, Lord.'

43. 'Is sensation permanent or perishable?' ... (etc.)

44. 'Therefore, O Bhikkhus, whatever body has been, will be, and is now, belonging or not belonging to sentient beings, gross or subtle, inferior or superior, distant or near, all that body is not mine, is not me, is not my self: thus it should be considered by right knowledge according to the truth.

45. 'Whatever sensation, ... (etc.)

46. 'Considering this, O Bhikkhus, a learned, noble hearer of the word becomes weary of body, weary of sensation, weary of perception, weary of the Samkhâras, weary of consciousness. Becoming weary of all that, he divests himself of passion; by absence of passion he is made free; when he is free, he becomes aware that he is free; and he realises that re-birth is exhausted; that holiness is completed; that duty is fulfilled; and that there is no further return to this world.'

47. Thus the Blessed One spoke; the five Bhikkhus were delighted, and rejoiced at the words of the Blessed One. And when this exposition had been propounded, the minds of the five Bhikkhus became free from attachment to the world, and were released from the Âsavas.

At that time there were six Arahats[5] in the world.

End of the first Bhânavâra.

---

5   persons who had reached absolute holiness.

c. 380–360 BCE

39. The Republic, Phaedo

Translated by Benjamin Jowett

The Athenian philosopher Plato (c. 428–347 BCE) wrote these two Greek philosophical dialogues during what is often called the "middle period" of his literary activity (c. 380–360 BCE). The Republic (*Politeia*), the most famous and influential of Plato's works, tackles issues relating to justice. Phaedo concerns the afterlife. Socrates is the main character in both, but be careful not to assume these conversations actually took place. Here are excerpts from each work.

The Republic

336. Several times in the course of the discussion Thrasymachus had made an attempt to get the argument into his own hands, and had been put down by the rest of the company, who wanted to hear the end. But when Polemarchus and I had done speaking and there was a pause, he could no longer hold his peace; and, gathering himself up, he came at us like a wild beast, seeking to devour us. We were quite panic-stricken at the sight of him.

He roared out to the whole company: What folly, Socrates, has taken possession of you all? And why, sillybillies, do you knock under to one another? I say that if you want really to know what justice is, you should not only ask but answer, and you should not seek honour to yourself from the refutation of an opponent, but have your own answer; for there is many a one who can ask and cannot answer. And now I will not have you say that justice is duty or advantage or profit or gain or interest, for this sort of nonsense will not do for me; I must have clearness and accuracy.

I was panic-stricken at his words, and could not look at him without trembling. Indeed I believe that if I had not fixed my eye upon him, I should have been struck dumb: but when I saw his fury rising, I looked at him first, and was therefore able to reply to him.

Thrasymachus, I said, with a quiver, don't be hard upon us. Polemarchus and I may have been guilty of a little mistake in the argument, but I can assure you that the error was not intentional. If we were seeking for a piece of gold, you would not imagine that we were 'knocking under to one another,' and so losing our chance of finding it. And why, when we are seeking for justice, a thing more precious than many pieces of gold, do you say that we are weakly yielding to one another and not doing our utmost to get at the truth? Nay, my good friend, we are most willing and anxious to do so, but the fact is that we cannot. And if so, you people who know all things should pity us and not be angry with us.

337. How characteristic of Socrates! he replied, with a bitter laugh;—that's your ironical style! Did I not foresee—have I not already told you, that whatever he was asked he would refuse to answer, and try irony or any other shuffle, in order that he might avoid answering?

You are a philosopher, Thrasymachus, I replied, and well know that if you ask a person what numbers make up twelve, taking care to prohibit him whom you ask from answering twice six, or three times four, or six times two, or four times three, 'for this sort of nonsense will not do for me,'—then obviously, if that is your way of putting the question, no one can answer you. But suppose that he were to retort, 'Thrasymachus, what do you mean? If one of these numbers which you interdict be the true answer to the question, am I falsely to say some other number which is not the right one?—is that your meaning?'—How would you answer him?

Just as if the two cases were at all alike! he said.

Why should they not be? I replied; and even if they are not, but only appear to be so to the person who is asked, ought he not to say what he thinks, whether you and I forbid him or not?

I presume then that you are going to make one of the interdicted answers?

I dare say that I may, notwithstanding the danger, if upon reflection I approve of any of them.

But what if I give you an answer about justice other and better, he said, than any of these? What do you deserve to have done to you?

Done to me!—as becomes the ignorant, I must learn from the wise—that is what I deserve to have done to me.

What, and no payment! a pleasant notion!

I will pay when I have the money, I replied.

But you have, Socrates, said Glaucon: and you, Thrasymachus, need be under no anxiety about money, for we will all make a contribution for Socrates.

Yes, he replied, and then Socrates will do as he always does—refuse to answer himself, but take and pull to pieces the answer of some one else.

Why, my good friend, I said, how can any one answer who knows, and says that he knows, just nothing; and who, even if he has some faint notions of his own, is told by a man of authority not to utter them? The natural thing is, that the speaker should be some one like yourself who professes to know and can tell what he knows. Will you then kindly answer, for the edification of the company and of myself?

338. Glaucon and the rest of the company joined in my request, and Thrasymachus, as any one might see, was in reality eager to speak; for he thought that he had an excellent answer, and would distinguish himself. But at first he affected to insist on my answering; at length he consented to begin. Behold, he said, the wisdom of Socrates; he refuses to teach himself, and goes about learning of others, to whom he never even says Thank you.

That I learn of others, I replied, is quite true; but that I am ungrateful I wholly deny. Money I have none, and therefore I pay in praise, which is all I have; and how ready I am to praise any one who appears to me to speak well you will very soon find out when you answer; for I expect that you will answer well.

Listen, then, he said; I proclaim that justice is nothing else than the interest of the stronger. And now why do you not praise me? But of course you won't.

Let me first understand you, I replied. Justice, as you say, is the interest of the stronger. What, Thrasymachus, is the meaning of this? You cannot mean to say that because Polydamas, the pancratiast, is stronger than we are, and finds the eating of beef conducive to his bodily strength, that to eat beef is therefore equally for our good who are weaker than he is, and right and just for us?

That's abominable of you, Socrates; you take the words in the sense which is most damaging to the argument.

Not at all, my good sir, I said; I am trying to understand them; and I wish that you would be a little clearer.

Well, he said, have you never heard that forms of government differ; there are tyrannies, and there are democracies, and there are aristocracies?

Yes, I know.

And the government is the ruling power in each state?

Certainly.

And the different forms of government make laws democratical, aristocratical, tyrannical, with a view to their several interests; and these laws, which are made by them for their own interests, are the justice which they deliver to their subjects, and him who transgresses them they punish as a breaker of the law, and unjust. And that is what I mean when I say that in all states there is the same principle of justice, which is the interest of the government; and as the government must be supposed to have power, the only reasonable conclusion is, that everywhere there is one principle of justice, which is the interest of the stronger.

339. Now I understand you, I said; and whether you are right or not I will try to discover. But let me remark, that in defining justice you have yourself used the word 'interest' which you forbade me to use. It is true, however, that in your definition the words 'of the stronger' are added.

A small addition, you must allow, he said.

Great or small, never mind about that: we must first enquire whether what you are saying is the truth. Now we are both agreed that justice is interest of some sort, but you go on to say 'of the stronger'; about this addition I am not so sure, and must therefore consider further.

Proceed.

I will; and first tell me, Do you admit that it is just for subjects to obey their rulers?

I do.

But are the rulers of states absolutely infallible, or are they sometimes liable to err?

To be sure, he replied, they are liable to err.

Then in making their laws they may sometimes make them rightly, and sometimes not?

True.

When they make them rightly, they make them agreeably to their interest; when they are mistaken, contrary to their interest; you admit that?

Yes.

And the laws which they make must be obeyed by their subjects,—and that is what you call justice?

Doubtless.

Then justice, according to your argument, is not only obedience to the interest of the stronger but the reverse?

What is that you are saying? he asked.

I am only repeating what you are saying, I believe. But let us consider: Have we not admitted that the rulers may be mistaken about their own interest in what they command, and also that to obey them is justice? Has not that been admitted?

Yes.

Then you must also have acknowledged justice not to be for the interest of the stronger, when the rulers unintentionally command things to be done which are to their own injury. For if, as you say, justice is the obedience which the subject renders to their commands, in that case, O wisest of men, is there any escape from the conclusion that the weaker are commanded to do, not what is for the interest, but what is for the injury of the stronger?

340. Nothing can be clearer, Socrates, said Polemarchus.

Yes, said Cleitophon, interposing, if you are allowed to be his witness.

But there is no need of any witness, said Polemarchus, for Thrasymachus himself acknowledges that rulers may sometimes command what is not for their own interest, and that for subjects to obey them is justice.

Yes, Polemarchus,—Thrasymachus said that for subjects to do what was commanded by their rulers is just.

Yes, Cleitophon, but he also said that justice is the interest of the stronger, and, while admitting both these propositions, he further acknowledged that the stronger may command the weaker who are his subjects to do what is not for his own interest; whence follows that justice is the injury quite as much as the interest of the stronger.

But, said Cleitophon, he meant by the interest of the stronger what the stronger thought to be his interest,—this was what the weaker had to do; and this was affirmed by him to be justice.

Those were not his words, rejoined Polemarchus.

Never mind, I replied, if he now says that they are, let us accept his statement. Tell me, Thrasymachus, I said, did you mean by justice what the stronger thought to be his interest, whether really so or not?

Certainly not, he said. Do you suppose that I call him who is mistaken the stronger at the time when he is mistaken?

Yes, I said, my impression was that you did so, when you admitted that the ruler was not infallible but might be sometimes mistaken.

You argue like an informer, Socrates. Do you mean, for example, that he who is mistaken about the sick is a physician in that he is mistaken? or that he who errs in arithmetic or grammar is an arithmetician or grammarian at the time when he is making the mistake, in respect of the mistake? True, we say that the physician or arithmetician or grammarian has made a mistake, but this is only a way of speaking; for the fact is that neither the grammarian nor any other person of skill ever makes a mistake in so far as he is what his name implies; they none of them err unless their skill fails them, and then they cease to be skilled artists. No artist or sage or ruler errs at the time when he is what his name implies; though he is commonly said to err, and I adopted the common mode of speaking. But to be perfectly accurate, since you are such a lover of accuracy, we should say that the ruler, in so far as he is a ruler, is unerring, and, being unerring, always commands that which is for his own interest; and the subject is required to execute his commands; and therefore, as I said at first and now repeat, justice is the interest of the stronger.

341. Indeed, Thrasymachus, and do I really appear to you to argue like an informer?

Certainly, he replied.

And do you suppose that I ask these questions with any design of injuring you in the argument?

Nay, he replied, 'suppose' is not the word—I know it; but you will be found out, and by sheer force of argument you will never prevail.

I shall not make the attempt, my dear man; but to avoid any misunderstanding occurring between us in future, let me ask, in what sense do you speak of a ruler or stronger whose interest, as you were saying, he being the superior, it is just that the inferior should execute—is he a ruler in the popular or in the strict sense of the term?

In the strictest of all senses, he said. And now cheat and play the informer if you can; I ask no quarter at your hands. But you never will be able, never.

And do you imagine, I said, that I am such a madman as to try and cheat, Thrasymachus? I might as well shave a lion.

Why, he said, you made the attempt a minute ago, and you failed.

Enough, I said, of these civilities. It will be better that I should ask you a question: Is the physician, taken in that strict sense of which you are speaking, a healer of the sick or a maker of money? And remember that I am now speaking of the true physician.

A healer of the sick, he replied.

And the pilot—that is to say, the true pilot—is he a captain of sailors or a mere sailor?

A captain of sailors.

The circumstance that he sails in the ship is not to be taken into account; neither is he to be called a sailor; the name pilot by which he is distinguished has nothing to do with sailing, but is significant of his skill and of his authority over the sailors.

Very true, he said.

Now, I said, every art has an interest?

Certainly.

For which the art has to consider and provide?

Yes, that is the aim of art.

And the interest of any art is the perfection of it—this and nothing else?

What do you mean?

I mean what I may illustrate negatively by the example of the body. Suppose you were to ask me whether the body is self-sufficing or has wants, I should reply: Certainly the body has wants; for the body may be ill and require to be cured, and has therefore interests to which the art of medicine ministers; and this is the origin and intention of medicine, as you will acknowledge. Am I not right?

Quite right, he replied.

342. But is the art of medicine or any other art faulty or deficient in any quality in the same way that the eye may be deficient in sight or the ear fail of hearing, and therefore requires another art to provide for the interests of seeing and hearing—has art in itself, I say, any similar liability to fault or defect, and does every art require another supplementary art to provide for its interests, and that another and another without end? Or have the arts to look only after their own interests? Or have they no need either of themselves or of another?—having no faults or defects, they have no need to correct them, either by the exercise of their own art or of any other; they have only to consider the interest of their subject-matter. For every art remains pure and faultless while remaining true—that is to say, while perfect and unimpaired. Take the words in your precise sense, and tell me whether I am not right.

Yes, clearly.

Then medicine does not consider the interest of medicine, but the interest of the body?

True, he said.

Nor does the art of horsemanship consider the interests of the art of horsemanship, but the interests of the horse; neither do any other arts care for themselves, for they have no needs; they care only for that which is the subject of their art?

True, he said.

But surely, Thrasymachus, the arts are the superiors and rulers of their own subjects?

To this he assented with a good deal of reluctance.

Then, I said, no science or art considers or enjoins the interest of the stronger or superior, but only the interest of the subject and weaker?

He made an attempt to contest this proposition also, but finally acquiesced.

Then, I continued, no physician, in so far as he is a physician, considers his own good in what he prescribes, but the good of his patient; for the true physician is also a ruler having the human body as a subject, and is not a mere money-maker; that has been admitted?

Yes.

And the pilot likewise, in the strict sense of the term, is a ruler of sailors and not a mere sailor?

That has been admitted.

And such a pilot and ruler will provide and prescribe for the interest of the sailor who is under him, and not for his own or the ruler's interest?

He gave a reluctant 'Yes.'

Then, I said, Thrasymachus, there is no one in any rule who, in so far as he is a ruler, considers or enjoins what is for his own interest, but always what is for the interest of his subject or suitable to his art; to that he looks, and that alone he considers in everything which he says and does.

343. When we had got to this point in the argument, and every one saw that the definition of justice had been completely upset, Thrasymachus, instead of replying to me, said: Tell me, Socrates, have you got a nurse?

Why do you ask such a question, I said, when you ought rather to be answering?

Because she leaves you to snivel, and never wipes your nose: she has not even taught you to know the shepherd from the sheep.

What makes you say that? I replied.

Because you fancy that the shepherd or neatherd fattens or tends the sheep or oxen with a view to their own good and not to the good of himself or his master; and you further imagine that the rulers of states, if they are true rulers, never think of their subjects as sheep, and that they are not studying their own advantage day and night. Oh, no; and so entirely astray are you in your ideas about the just and unjust as not even to know that justice and the just are in reality another's good; that is to say, the interest of the ruler and stronger, and the loss of the subject and servant; and injustice the opposite; for the unjust is lord over the truly simple and just: he is the stronger, and his subjects do what is for his interest, and minister to his happiness, which is very far from being their own. Consider further, most foolish Socrates, that the just is always a loser in comparison with the unjust. First of all, in private contracts: wherever the unjust is the partner of the just you will find that, when the partnership is dissolved, the unjust man has always more and the just less. Secondly, in their dealings with the State: when there is an income-tax, the just man will pay more and the unjust less on the same amount of income; and when there is anything to be received the one gains nothing and the other much. Observe also what happens when they take an office; there is the just man neglecting his affairs and perhaps suffering other losses, and getting nothing out of the public, because he is just; moreover he is hated by his friends and acquaintance for refusing to serve them in unlawful ways. But all this is reversed in the case of the unjust man. I am speaking, as before, of injustice on a large scale in which the advantage of the unjust is most apparent; and my meaning will be most clearly seen if we turn to that highest form of injustice in which the criminal is the happiest of men,

and the sufferers or those who refuse to do injustice are the most miserable—that is to say tyranny, which by fraud and force takes away the property of others, not little by little but wholesale; comprehending in one, things sacred as well as profane, private and public; for which acts of wrong, if he were detected perpetrating any one of them singly, he would be punished and incur great disgrace—they who do such wrong in particular cases are called robbers of temples, and man-stealers and burglars and swindlers and thieves. But when a man besides taking away the money of the citizens has made slaves of them, then, instead of these names of reproach, he is termed happy and blessed, not only by the citizens but by all who hear of his having achieved the consummation of injustice. For mankind censure injustice, fearing that they may be the victims of it and not because they shrink from committing it. And thus, as I have shown, Socrates, injustice, when on a sufficient scale, has more strength and freedom and mastery than justice; and, as I said at first, justice is the interest of the stronger, whereas injustice is a man's own profit and interest.

344. Thrasymachus, when he had thus spoken, having, like a bath-man, deluged our ears with his words, had a mind to go away. But the company would not let him; they insisted that he should remain and defend his position; and I myself added my own humble request that he would not leave us. Thrasymachus, I said to him, excellent man, how suggestive are your remarks! And are you going to run away before you have fairly taught or learned whether they are true or not? Is the attempt to determine the way of man's life so small a matter in your eyes—to determine how life may be passed by each one of us to the greatest advantage?

And do I differ from you, he said, as to the importance of the enquiry?

You appear rather, I replied, to have no care or thought about us, Thrasymachus—whether we live better or worse from not knowing what you say you know, is to you a matter of indifference. Prithee, friend, do not keep your knowledge to yourself; we are a large party; and any benefit which you confer upon us will be amply rewarded. For my own part I openly declare that I am not convinced, and that I do not believe injustice to be more gainful than justice, even if uncontrolled and allowed to have free play. For, granting that there may be an unjust man who is able to commit injustice either by fraud or force, still this does not convince me of the superior advantage of injustice, and there may be others who are in the same predicament with myself. Perhaps we may be wrong; if so, you in your wisdom should convince us that we are mistaken in preferring justice to injustice.

345. And how am I to convince you, he said, if you are not already convinced by what I have just said; what more can I do for you? Would you have me put the proof bodily into your souls?

Heaven forbid! I said; I would only ask you to be consistent; or, if you change, change openly and let there be no deception. For I must remark, Thrasymachus, if you will recall what was previously said, that although you began by defining the true physician in an exact sense, you did not observe a like exactness when speaking of the shepherd; you thought that the shepherd as a shepherd tends the sheep not with a view to their own good, but like a mere diner or banquetter with a view to the pleasures of the table; or, again, as a trader for sale in the market, and not as a shepherd. Yet surely the art of the shepherd is concerned only with the good of his subjects; he has only to provide the best for them, since the perfection of the art is already ensured whenever all the requirements of it are satisfied. And that was what I was saying just now about the ruler. I conceived that the art of the ruler, considered as ruler, whether in a state or in private life, could only regard the good of his flock or subjects; whereas you seem to think that the rulers in states, that is to say, the true rulers, like being in authority.

Think! Nay, I am sure of it.

Then why in the case of lesser offices do men never take them willingly without payment, unless under the idea that they govern for the advantage not of themselves but of others?

346. Let me ask you a question: Are not the several arts different, by reason of their each having a separate function? And, my dear illustrious friend, do say what you think, that we may make a little progress.

Yes, that is the difference, he replied.

And each art gives us a particular good and not merely a general one—medicine, for example, gives us health; navigation, safety at sea, and so on?

Yes, he said.

And the art of payment has the special function of giving pay: but we do not confuse this with other arts, any more than the art of the pilot is to be confused with the art of medicine, because the health of the pilot may be improved by a sea voyage. You would not be inclined to say, would you, that navigation is the art of medicine, at least if we are to adopt your exact use of language?

Certainly not.

Or because a man is in good health when he receives pay you would not say that the art of payment is medicine?

I should not.

Nor would you say that medicine is the art of receiving pay because a man takes fees when he is engaged in healing?

Certainly not.

And we have admitted, I said, that the good of each art is specially confined to the art?

Yes.

Then, if there be any good which all artists have in common, that is to be attributed to something of which they all have the common use?

True, he replied.

And when the artist is benefited by receiving pay the advantage is gained by an additional use of the art of pay, which is not the art professed by him?

He gave a reluctant assent to this.

Then the pay is not derived by the several artists from their respective arts. But the truth is, that while the art of medicine gives health, and the art of the builder builds a house, another art attends them which is the art of pay. The various arts may be doing their own business and benefiting that over which they preside, but would the artist receive any benefit from his art unless he were paid as well?

I suppose not.

But does he therefore confer no benefit when he works for nothing?

Certainly, he confers a benefit.

Then now, Thrasymachus, there is no longer any doubt that neither arts nor governments provide for their own interests; but, as we were before saying, they rule and provide for the interests of their subjects who are the weaker and not the stronger—to their good they attend and not to the good of the superior. And this is the reason, my dear Thrasymachus, why, as I was just now saying, no one is willing to govern; because no one likes to take in hand the reformation of evils which are not his concern without remuneration. For, in the execution of his work, and in giving his orders to another, the true artist does not regard his own interest, but always that of his subjects; and therefore in order that rulers may be willing to rule, they must be paid in one of three modes of payment, money, or honour, or a penalty for refusing.

347. What do you mean, Socrates? said Glaucon. The first two modes of payment are intelligible enough, but what the penalty is I do not understand, or how a penalty can be a payment.

You mean that you do not understand the nature of this payment which to the best men is the great inducement to rule? Of course you know that ambition and avarice are held to be, as indeed they are, a disgrace?

Very true.

And for this reason, I said, money and honour have no attraction for them; good men do not wish to be openly demanding payment for governing and so to get the name of hirelings, nor by secretly helping themselves out of the public revenues to get the name of thieves. And not being ambitious they do not care about honour. Wherefore necessity must be laid upon them, and they must be induced to serve from the fear of punishment. And this, as I imagine, is the reason why the forwardness to take office, instead of waiting to be compelled, has been deemed dishonourable. Now the worst part of the punishment is that he who refuses to rule is liable to be ruled by one who is worse than himself. And the fear of this, as I conceive, induces the good to take office, not because they would, but because they cannot help—not under the idea that they are going to have any benefit or enjoyment themselves, but as a necessity, and because they are not able to commit the task of ruling to any one who is better than themselves, or indeed as good. For there is reason to think that if a city were composed entirely of good men, then to avoid office would be as much an object of contention as to obtain office is at present; then we should have plain proof that the true ruler is not meant by nature to regard his own interest, but that of his subjects; and every one who knew this would choose rather to receive a benefit from another than to have the trouble of conferring one. So far am I from agreeing with Thrasymachus that justice is the interest of the stronger. This latter question need not be further discussed at present; but when Thrasymachus says that the life of the unjust is more advantageous than that of the just, his new statement appears to me to be of a far more serious character. Which of us has spoken truly? And which sort of life, Glaucon, do you prefer?

I for my part deem the life of the just to be the more advantageous, he answered.

348. Did you hear all the advantages of the unjust which Thrasymachus was rehearsing?

Yes, I heard him, he replied, but he has not convinced me.

Then shall we try to find some way of convincing him, if we can, that he is saying what is not true?

Most certainly, he replied.

If, I said, he makes a set speech and we make another recounting all the advantages of being just, and he answers and we rejoin, there must be a numbering and measuring of the goods which are claimed on either side, and in the end we shall want judges to decide; but if we proceed in our enquiry as we lately did, by making admissions to one another, we shall unite the offices of judge and advocate in our own persons.

Very good, he said.

And which method do I understand you to prefer? I said.

That which you propose.

Well, then, Thrasymachus, I said, suppose you begin at the beginning and answer me. You say that perfect injustice is more gainful than perfect justice?

Yes, that is what I say, and I have given you my reasons.

And what is your view about them? Would you call one of them virtue and the other vice?

Certainly.

I suppose that you would call justice virtue and injustice vice?

What a charming notion! So likely too, seeing that I affirm injustice to be profitable and justice not.

What else then would you say?

The opposite, he replied.

And would you call justice vice?

No, I would rather say sublime simplicity.

Then would you call injustice malignity?

No; I would rather say discretion.

And do the unjust appear to you to be wise and good?

Yes, he said; at any rate those of them who are able to be perfectly unjust, and who have the power of subduing states and nations; but perhaps you imagine me to be talking of cutpurses. Even this profession if undetected has advantages, though they are not to be compared with those of which I was just now speaking.

I do not think that I misapprehend your meaning, Thrasymachus, I replied; but still I cannot hear without amazement that you class injustice with wisdom and virtue, and justice with the opposite.

Certainly I do so class them.

Now, I said, you are on more substantial and almost unanswerable ground; for if the injustice which you were maintaining to be profitable had been admitted by you as by others to be vice and deformity, an answer might have been given to you on received principles; but now I perceive that you will call injustice honourable and strong, and to the unjust you will attribute all the qualities which were attributed by us before to the just, seeing that you do not hesitate to rank injustice with wisdom and virtue.

You have guessed most infallibly, he replied.

349. Then I certainly ought not to shrink from going through with the argument so long as I have reason to think that you, Thrasymachus, are speaking your real mind; for I do believe that you are now in earnest and are not amusing yourself at our expense.

I may be in earnest or not, but what is that to you?—to refute the argument is your business.

Very true, I said; that is what I have to do: But will you be so good as answer yet one more question? Does the just man try to gain any advantage over the just?

Far otherwise; if he did he would not be the simple amusing creature which he is.

And would he try to go beyond just action?

He would not.

And how would he regard the attempt to gain an advantage over the unjust; would that be considered by him as just or unjust?

He would think it just, and would try to gain the advantage; but he would not be able.

Whether he would or would not be able, I said, is not to the point. My question is only whether the just man, while refusing to have more than another just man, would wish and claim to have more than the unjust?

Yes, he would.

And what of the unjust—does he claim to have more than the just man and to do more than is just?

Of course, he said, for he claims to have more than all men.

And the unjust man will strive and struggle to obtain more than the unjust man or action, in order that he may have more than all?

True.

We may put the matter thus, I said—the just does not desire more than his like but more than his unlike, whereas the unjust desires more than both his like and his unlike?

Nothing, he said, can be better than that statement.

And the unjust is good and wise, and the just is neither?

Good again, he said.

And is not the unjust like the wise and good and the just unlike them?

Of course, he said, he who is of a certain nature, is like those who are of a certain nature; he who is not, not.

Each of them, I said, is such as his like is?

Certainly, he replied.

Very good, Thrasymachus, I said; and now to take the case of the arts: you would admit that one man is a musician and another not a musician?

Yes.

And which is wise and which is foolish?

Clearly the musician is wise, and he who is not a musician is foolish.

And he is good in as far as he is wise, and bad in as far as he is foolish?

Yes.

And you would say the same sort of thing of the physician?

Yes.

And do you think, my excellent friend, that a musician when he adjusts the lyre would desire or claim to exceed or go beyond a musician in the tightening and loosening the strings?

I do not think that he would.

But he would claim to exceed the non-musician?

Of course.

And what would you say of the physician? In prescribing meats and drinks would he wish to go beyond another physician or beyond the practice of medicine?

He would not.

But he would wish to go beyond the non-physician?

Yes.

350. And about knowledge and ignorance in general; see whether you think that any man who has knowledge ever would wish to have the choice of saying or doing more than another man who has knowledge. Would he not rather say or do the same as his like in the same case?

That, I suppose, can hardly be denied.

And what of the ignorant? would he not desire to have more than either the knowing or the ignorant?

I dare say.

And the knowing is wise?

Yes.

And the wise is good?

True.

Then the wise and good will not desire to gain more than his like, but more than his unlike and opposite?

I suppose so.

Whereas the bad and ignorant will desire to gain more than both?

Yes.

But did we not say, Thrasymachus, that the unjust goes beyond both his like and unlike? Were not these your words?

They were.

And you also said that the just will not go beyond his like but his unlike?

Yes.

Then the just is like the wise and good, and the unjust like the evil and ignorant?

That is the inference.

And each of them is such as his like is?

That was admitted.

Then the just has turned out to be wise and good and the unjust evil and ignorant.

Thrasymachus made all these admissions, not fluently, as I repeat them, but with extreme reluctance; it was a hot summer's day, and the perspiration poured from him in torrents; and then I saw what I had never seen before, Thrasymachus blushing. As we were now agreed that justice was virtue and wisdom, and injustice vice and ignorance, I proceeded to another point:

Well, I said, Thrasymachus, that matter is now settled; but were we not also saying that injustice had strength; do you remember?

Yes, I remember, he said, but do not suppose that I approve of what you are saying or have no answer; if however I were to answer, you would be quite certain to accuse me of haranguing; therefore either permit me to have my say out, or if you would rather ask, do so, and I will answer 'Very good,' as they say to story-telling old women, and will nod 'Yes' and 'No.'

Certainly not, I said, if contrary to your real opinion.

Yes, he said, I will, to please you, since you will not let me speak. What else would you have?

Nothing in the world, I said; and if you are so disposed I will ask and you shall answer.

Proceed.

351. Then I will repeat the question which I asked before, in order that our examination of the relative nature of justice and injustice may be carried on regularly. A statement was made that injustice is stronger and more powerful than justice, but now justice, having been identified with wisdom and virtue, is easily shown to be stronger than injustice, if injustice is ignorance; this can no longer be questioned by any one. But I want to view the matter, Thrasymachus, in a different way: You would not deny that a state may be unjust and may be unjustly attempting to enslave other states, or may have already enslaved them, and may be holding many of them in subjection?

True, he replied; and I will add that the best and most perfectly unjust state will be most likely to do so.

I know, I said, that such was your position; but what I would further consider is, whether this power which is possessed by the superior state can exist or be exercised without justice or only with justice.

If you are right in your view, and justice is wisdom, then only with justice; but if I am right, then without justice.

I am delighted, Thrasymachus, to see you not only nodding assent and dissent, but making answers which are quite excellent.

That is out of civility to you, he replied.

You are very kind, I said; and would you have the goodness also to inform me, whether you think that a state, or an army, or a band of robbers and thieves, or any other gang of evil-doers could act at all if they injured one another?

No indeed, he said, they could not.

But if they abstained from injuring one another, then they might act together better?

Yes.

And this is because injustice creates divisions and hatreds and fighting, and justice imparts harmony and friendship; is not that true, Thrasymachus?

I agree, he said, because I do not wish to quarrel with you.

How good of you, I said; but I should like to know also whether injustice, having this tendency to arouse hatred, wherever existing, among slaves or among freemen, will not make them hate one another and set them at variance and render them incapable of common action?

Certainly.

And even if injustice be found in two only, will they not quarrel and fight, and become enemies to one another and to the just?

They will.

And suppose injustice abiding in a single person, would your wisdom say that she loses or that she retains her natural power?

Let us assume that she retains her power.

Yet is not the power which injustice exercises of such a nature that wherever she takes up her abode, whether in a city, in an army, in a family, or in any other body, that body is, to begin with, rendered incapable of united action by reason of sedition and distraction; and does it not become its own enemy and at variance with all that opposes it, and with the just? Is not this the case?

Yes, certainly.

352. And is not injustice equally fatal when existing in a single person; in the first place rendering him incapable of action because he is not at unity with himself, and in the second place making him an enemy to himself and the just? Is not that true, Thrasymachus?

Yes.

And O my friend, I said, surely the gods are just?

Granted that they are.

But if so, the unjust will be the enemy of the gods, and the just will be their friend?

Feast away in triumph, and take your fill of the argument; I will not oppose you, lest I should displease the company.

Well then, proceed with your answers, and let me have the remainder of my repast. For we have already shown that the just are clearly wiser and better and abler than the unjust, and that the unjust are incapable of common action; nay more, that to speak as we did of men who are evil acting at any time vigorously together, is not strictly true, for if they had been perfectly evil, they would have laid hands upon one another; but it is evident that there must have been some remnant of justice in them, which enabled them to combine; if there had not been they would have injured one another as well as their victims; they were but half-villains in their enterprises; for had they been whole villains, and utterly unjust, they would have been utterly incapable of action. That, as I believe, is the truth of the matter, and not what you said at first. But whether the just have a better and happier life than the unjust is a further question which we also proposed to consider. I think that they have, and for the reasons which I have given; but still I should like to examine further, for no light matter is at stake, nothing less than the rule of human life.

Proceed.

I will proceed by asking a question: Would you not say that a horse has some end?

I should.

And the end or use of a horse or of anything would be that which could not be accomplished, or not so well accomplished, by any other thing?

I do not understand, he said.

Let me explain: Can you see, except with the eye?

Certainly not.

Or hear, except with the ear?

No.

These then may be truly said to be the ends of these organs?

They may.

But you can cut off a vine-branch with a dagger or with a chisel, and in many other ways?

Of course.

And yet not so well as with a pruning-hook made for the purpose?

True.

May we not say that this is the end of a pruning-hook?

We may.

353. Then now I think you will have no difficulty in understanding my meaning when I asked the question whether the end of anything would be that which could not be accomplished, or not so well accomplished, by any other thing?

I understand your meaning, he said, and assent.

And that to which an end is appointed has also an excellence? Need I ask again whether the eye has an end?

It has.

And has not the eye an excellence?

Yes.

And the ear has an end and an excellence also?

True.

And the same is true of all other things; they have each of them an end and a special excellence?

That is so.

Well, and can the eyes fulfil their end if they are wanting in their own proper excellence and have a defect instead?

How can they, he said, if they are blind and cannot see?

You mean to say, if they have lost their proper excellence, which is sight; but I have not arrived at that point yet. I would rather ask the question more generally, and only enquire whether the things which fulfil their ends fulfil them by their own proper excellence, and fail of fulfilling them by their own defect?

Certainly, he replied.

I might say the same of the ears; when deprived of their own proper excellence they cannot fulfil their end?

True.

And the same observation will apply to all other things?

I agree.

Well; and has not the soul an end which nothing else can fulfil? for example, to superintend and command and deliberate and the like. Are not these functions proper to the soul, and can they rightly be assigned to any other?

To no other.

And is not life to be reckoned among the ends of the soul?

Assuredly, he said.

And has not the soul an excellence also?

Yes.

And can she or can she not fulfil her own ends when deprived of that excellence?

She cannot.

Then an evil soul must necessarily be an evil ruler and superintendent, and the good soul a good ruler?

Yes, necessarily.

And we have admitted that justice is the excellence of the soul, and injustice the defect of the soul?

That has been admitted.

Then the just soul and the just man will live well, and the unjust man will live ill?

That is what your argument proves.

And he who lives well is blessed and happy, and he who lives ill the reverse of happy?

Certainly.

Then the just is happy, and the unjust miserable?

So be it.

But happiness and not misery is profitable.

Of course.

Then, my blessed Thrasymachus, injustice can never be more profitable than justice.

Phaedo

78. Must we not, said Socrates, ask ourselves what that is which, as we imagine, is liable to be scattered, and about which we fear? and what again is that about which we have no fear? And then we may proceed further to enquire whether that which suffers dispersion is or is not of the nature of soul—our hopes and fears as to our own souls will turn upon the answers to these questions.

Very true, he said.

Now the compound or composite may be supposed to be naturally capable, as of being compounded, so also of being dissolved; but that which is uncompounded, and that only, must be, if anything is, indissoluble.

Yes; I should imagine so, said Cebes.

And the uncompounded may be assumed to be the same and unchanging, whereas the compound is always changing and never the same.

I agree, he said.

Then now let us return to the previous discussion. Is that idea or essence, which in the dialectical process we define as essence or true existence—whether essence of equality, beauty, or anything else—are these essences, I say, liable at times to some degree of change? or are they each of them always what they are, having the same simple self-existent and unchanging forms, not admitting of variation at all, or in any way, or at any time?

They must be always the same, Socrates, replied Cebes.

And what would you say of the many beautiful—whether men or horses or garments or any other things which are named by the same names and may be called equal or beautiful,—are they all unchanging and the same always, or quite the reverse? May they not rather be described as almost always changing and hardly ever the same, either with themselves or with one another?

The latter, replied Cebes; they are always in a state of change.

And these you can touch and see and perceive with the senses, but the unchanging things you can only perceive with the mind—they are invisible and are not seen?

That is very true, he said.

79. Well, then, added Socrates, let us suppose that there are two sorts of existences—one seen, the other unseen.

Let us suppose them.

The seen is the changing, and the unseen is the unchanging?

That may be also supposed.

And, further, is not one part of us body, another part soul?

To be sure.

And to which class is the body more alike and akin?

Clearly to the seen—no one can doubt that.

And is the soul seen or not seen?

Not by man, Socrates.

And what we mean by 'seen' and 'not seen' is that which is or is not visible to the eye of man?

Yes, to the eye of man.

And is the soul seen or not seen?

Not seen.

Unseen then?

Yes.

Then the soul is more like to the unseen, and the body to the seen?

That follows necessarily, Socrates.

And were we not saying long ago that the soul when using the body as an instrument of perception, that is to say, when using the sense of sight or hearing or some other sense (for the meaning of perceiving through the body is perceiving through the senses)—were we not saying that the soul too is then dragged by the body into the region of the changeable, and wanders and is confused; the world spins round her, and she is like a drunkard, when she touches change?

Very true.

But when returning into herself she reflects, then she passes into the other world, the region of purity, and eternity, and immortality, and unchangeableness, which are her kindred, and with them she ever lives, when she is by herself and is not let or hindered; then she ceases from her erring ways, and being in communion with the unchanging is unchanging. And this state of the soul is called wisdom?

That is well and truly said, Socrates, he replied.

And to which class is the soul more nearly alike and akin, as far as may be inferred from this argument, as well as from the preceding one?

I think, Socrates, that, in the opinion of every one who follows the argument, the soul will be infinitely more like the unchangeable—even the most stupid person will not deny that.

And the body is more like the changing?

Yes.

Yet once more consider the matter in another light: When the soul and the body are united, then nature orders the soul to rule and govern, and the body to obey and serve. Now which of these two functions is akin to the divine? and which to the mortal? Does not the divine appear to you to be that which naturally orders and rules, and the mortal to be that which is subject and servant?

True.

And which does the soul resemble?

The soul resembles the divine, and the body the mortal—there can be no doubt of that, Socrates.

80. Then reflect, Cebes: of all which has been said is not this the conclusion?—that the soul is in the very likeness of the divine, and immortal, and intellectual, and uniform, and indissoluble, and unchangeable; and that the body is in the very likeness of the human, and mortal, and unintellectual, and multiform, and dissoluble, and changeable. Can this, my dear Cebes, be denied?

It cannot.

But if it be true, then is not the body liable to speedy dissolution? and is not the soul almost or altogether indissoluble?

Think about it.

1. In the excerpt from The Republic, how does Socrates refute the idea that justice is relative to whoever happens to be in power?
2. In Phaedo, how does Socrates argue that the soul is indestructible?

---

c. 335–323 BCE

40. The Nicomachean Ethics

Translated by Drummond Percy Chase

The following is an excerpt from a treatise on ethics by the Athenian philosopher Aristotle (384–322 BCE). Sometimes simply called The Ethics, this Greek work was written c. 335–323 BCE and, like most of Aristotle's writings, was probably used as lecture notes and never meant for publication. It will go on, however, to be extremely influential, especially in the Postclassical Period.

[1.7.1] Let us again return to the good we are seeking, and ask what it can be. It seems different in different actions and arts; it is different in medicine, in strategy, and in the other arts likewise. What then is the good of each? Surely that for whose sake everything else is done. In medicine this is health, in strategy victory, in architecture a house, in any other sphere something else, and in every action and pursuit the end; for it is for the sake of this that all men do whatever else they do. Therefore, if there is an end for all that we do, this will be the good achievable by action, and if there are more than one, these will be the goods achievable by action.

[1.7.2-4] So the argument has by a different course reached the same point; but we must try to state this even more clearly. Since there are evidently more than one end, and we choose some of these (e.g. wealth, flutes, and in general instruments) for

Aristotle, "Book I, Part VII," *The Nicomachean Ethics of Aristotle*, trans. Drummond Percy Chase. Rivingtons, 1911. Copyright in the Public Domain.

the sake of something else, clearly not all ends are final ends; but the chief good is evidently something final. Therefore, if there is only one final end, this will be what we are seeking, and if there are more than one, the most final of these will be what we are seeking. Now we call that which is in itself worthy of pursuit more final than that which is worthy of pursuit for the sake of something else, and that which is never desirable for the sake of something else more final than the things that are desirable both in themselves and for the sake of that other thing, and therefore we call final without qualification that which is always desirable in itself and never for the sake of something else.

[1.7.5] Now such a thing happiness, above all else, is held to be; for this we choose always for self and never for the sake of something else, but honour, pleasure, reason, and every virtue we choose indeed for themselves (for if nothing resulted from them we should still choose each of them), but we choose them also for the sake of happiness, judging that by means of them we shall be happy. Happiness, on the other hand, no one chooses for the sake of these, nor, in general, for anything other than itself.

[1.7.6-8] From the point of view of self-sufficiency the same result seems to follow; for the final good is thought to be self-sufficient. Now by self-sufficient we do not mean that which is sufficient for a man by himself, for one who lives a solitary life, but also for parents, children, wife, and in general for his friends and fellow citizens, since man is born for citizenship. But some limit must be set to this; for if we extend our requirement to ancestors and descendants and friends' friends we are in for an infinite series. Let us examine this question, however, on another occasion; the self-sufficient we now define as that which when isolated makes life desirable and lacking in nothing; and such we think happiness to be; and further we think it most desirable of all things, without being counted as one good thing among others, if it were so counted it would clearly be made more desirable by the addition of even the least of goods; for that which is added becomes an excess

of goods, and of goods the greater is always more desirable. Happiness, then, is something final and self-sufficient, and is the end of action.

[1.7.9-15] Presumably, however, to say that happiness is the chief good seems a platitude, and a clearer account of what it is still desired. This might perhaps be given, if we could first ascertain the function of man. For just as for a flute-player, a sculptor, or an artist, and, in general, for all things that have a function or activity, the good and the 'well' is thought to reside in the function, so would it seem to be for man, if he has a function. Have the carpenter, then, and the tanner certain functions or activities, and has man none? Is he born without a function? Or as eye, hand, foot, and in general each of the parts evidently has a function, may one lay it down that man similarly has a function apart from all these? What then can this be? Life seems to be common even to plants, but we are seeking what is peculiar to man. Let us exclude, therefore, the life of nutrition and growth. Next there would be a life of perception, but it also seems to be common even to the horse, the ox, and every animal. There remains, then, an active life of the element that has a rational principle; of this, one part has such a principle in the sense of being obedient to one, the other in the sense of possessing one and exercising thought. And, as 'life of the rational element' also has two meanings, we must state that life in the sense of activity is what we mean; for this seems to be the more proper sense of the term. Now if the function of man is an activity of soul which follows or implies a rational principle, and if we say 'so-and-so' and 'a good so-and-so' have a function which is the same in kind, e.g. a lyre, and a good lyre-player, and so without qualification in all cases, eminence in respect of goodness being idded to the name of the function (for the function of a lyre-player is to play the lyre, and that of a good lyre-player is to do so well): if this is the case, and we state the function of man to be a certain kind of life, and this to be an activity or actions of the soul implying a rational principle, and the function of a good man to be the good and noble performance of these, and if any action is well performed when it is performed in accordance with the appropriate excellence: if this is the case, human good turns out to be activity of soul in accordance with virtue, and if there are more than one virtue, in accordance with the best and most complete.

[1.7.16] But we must add 'in a complete life.' For one swallow does not make a summer, nor does one day; and so too one day, or a short time, does not make a man blessed and happy.

[1.7.17-19] Let this serve as an outline of the good; for we must presumably first sketch it roughly, and then later fill in the details. But it would seem that any one is capable of carrying on and articulating what has once been well outlined, and that time is a good discoverer or partner in such a work; to which facts the advances of the arts are due; for any one can add what is lacking. And we must also remember what has been said before, and not look for precision in all things alike, but in each class of things such precision as accords with the subject-matter, and so much as is appropriate to the inquiry. For a carpenter and a geometer investigate the right angle in different ways; the former does so in so far as the right angle is useful for his work, while the latter inquires what it is or what sort of thing it is; for he is a spectator of the truth. We must act in the same way, then, in all other matters as well, that our main task may not be subordinated to minor questions. Nor must we demand the cause in all matters alike; it is enough in some cases that the fact be well established, as in the case of the first principles; the fact is the primary thing or first principle. Now of first principles we see some by induction, some by perception, some by a certain habituation, and others too in other ways. But each set of principles we must try to investigate in the natural way, and we must take pains to state them definitely, since they have a great influence on what follows. For the beginning is thought to be more than half of the whole, and many of the questions we ask are cleared up by it.

Think about it.

1.   According to Aristotle, what is the "chief good"?
2.   What does he say is the unique function of humans?

41. The Book of Lord Shang

Translated by Jan Julius L. Duyvendak

This selection comes from an early Chinese Legalist work attributed to Shang Yang (390–338 BCE), prime minister of the state of Qin under Duke Xiao. It is believed that his policies helped transform Qin from a backwater country to a militarily powerful kingdom with a strong central government.

Agriculture and War

1. The means, whereby a ruler of men encourages the people, are office and rank; the means, whereby a country is made prosperous, are agriculture and war. Now those, who seek office and rank, never do so by means of agriculture and war, but by artful words and empty doctrines. That is called "wearying the people." The country of those, who weary their people, will certainly have no strength, and the country of those, who have no strength, will certainly be dismembered. Those, who are capable in organizing a country, teach the people that office and rank can only be acquired through one opening, and thus, there being no rank without office, the state will do away with fine speaking, with the result that the people will be simple; being simple, they will not be licentious. The people, seeing that the highest benefit comes only through one opening, will strive for concentration, and having concentration, will not be negligent in their occupations. When the people are not negligent in their occupations, they will have much strength, and when they have much strength the state will be powerful.

2. But now the people within the territory all say that by avoiding agriculture and war, office and rank may be acquired, with the result that eminent men all change their occupations, to apply themselves to the study of the Odes and History and to follow improper standards; on the one hand, they obtain prominence, and on the other, they acquire office and rank. Insignificant individuals will occupy themselves with trade and will practise arts and crafts, all in order to avoid agriculture and war, thus preparing a dangerous condition for the state. Where the people are given to such teachings, it is certain that such a country will be dismembered.

3. The way to organize a country well is, even though the granaries are filled, not to be negligent in agriculture and even though the country is large and its population numerous, to have no licence of speech. (This being so) the people will be simple and have concentration; the people being simple and having concentration, then office and rank cannot be obtained by artfulness. If these cannot be obtained by artfulness, then wickedness will not originate, and if wickedness does not originate, the ruler will not be suspicious.

4. But now the people, within the territory, and those who hold office and rank, see that it is possible to obtain, from the court, office and rank by means of artful speech and sophistry. Therefore, there is no permanency in office and rank, with the result that, at court, they deceive their ruler and, retiring from court, they think of nothing but of how to realize their selfish interests and thus sell power to their inferiors. Now deceiving the ruler and being concerned for their own interests is not to the advantage of the state, but those who thus act, do so for the sake of rank and emolument; selling power to inferiors is not proper for a loyal minister, but those who thus act, do so for the sake of insignificant presents.

5. Consequently all the lower officials, who hope for promotion, say: "If we send many presents, we may obtain the higher office which we desire." They say too: "To strive for promotion, without serving superiors with presents, is like setting a cat as bait for a rat—it is absolutely hopeless. To strive for promotion by serving superiors with sincerity, is like wishing to climb a crooked tree by holding on to a broken rope—it is even more hopeless. If, to attain promotion, these two methods are out of the question, what else can we do, in striving for it, but to bring the masses below us into action and to obtain presents, for the purpose of serving our superiors?"

6. The people say: "We till diligently, first to fill the public granaries and then to keep the rest, for the nourishment of our parents; for the sake of our superiors we forget our love of life and fight for the honour of the ruler and for the peace of the country. But if the granaries are empty, the ruler debased and the family poor, then it is best to seek office. Let us then combine relatives and friends and think of other plans." Eminent men will apply themselves to the study of the Odes and History, and pursue these improper standards; insignificant individuals will occupy themselves with trade, and practise arts and crafts, all in order to avoid agriculture and war. Where the people are given to such teachings, how can the grain be anything but scarce, and the soldiers anything but weak?

7. The way to administer a country well, is for the law for the officials to be clear; therefore one does not rely on intelligent and thoughtful men. The ruler makes the people singleminded and therefore they will not scheme for selfish profit. Then the strength of the country will be consolidated. A country, where the strength has been consolidated, is powerful, but a country that loves talking is dismembered. Therefore is it said: "If there are a thousand people engaged in agriculture and war, and only one in the Odes and History, and clever sophistry, then those thousand will all be remiss in agriculture and war; if there are a hundred people engaged in agriculture and war and only one in the arts and crafts, then those hundred will all be remiss in agriculture and war.

8. The country depends on agriculture and war for its peace, and likewise the ruler, for his honour. Indeed, if the people are not engaged in agriculture and war, it means that the ruler loves words and that the officials have lost consistency of conduct. If there is consistency of conduct in officials, the country is well-governed, and if single-mindedness is striven after, the country is rich; to have the country both rich and well governed is the way to attain supremacy. Therefore is it said: "The way to supremacy is no other than by creating single-mindedness!"

9. However, nowadays, the ruler, in his appointments, takes into consideration talent and ability and cleverness and intelligence, and thus clever and intelligent men watch for the likes and dislikes of the ruler, so that officials are caused to transact their business in a way which is adapted to the ruler's mind. As a result there is no consistency of conduct in the officials, the state is in disorder and there is no concentration. Sophists (are honoured) and there is no law. Under such circumstances, how can the people's affairs be otherwise than many and how can the land be otherwise than fallow?

10. If, in a country, there are the following ten things: odes and history, rites and music, virtue and the cultivation thereof, benevolence and integrity, sophistry and intelligence, then the ruler has no one whom he can employ for defence and warfare. If a country is governed by means of these ten things, it will be dismembered, as soon as an enemy approaches, and, even if no enemy approaches, it will be poor. But if a country banishes these ten things, enemies will not dare to approach, and even if they should, they would be driven back. When it mobilizes its army and attacks, it will gain victories; when it holds the army in reserve, and does not attack, it will be rich. A country that loves strength makes assaults with what is difficult and thus it will be successful. A country that loves sophistry makes assaults with what is easy and thus it will be in danger.

11. Therefore sages and intelligent princes are what they are, not because they are able to go to the bottom of all things, but because they understand what is essential in all things. Therefore the secret of their administration of the country lies in nothing else than in their examination of what is essential. But now, those who run a state, for the most part, overlook what is essential, and the discussions at court, on government, are confused and efforts are made to displace each other in them; thus the prince is dazed by talk, officials confused by words, and the people become lazy and will not farm. The result is that all the people within the territory change and become fond of sophistry, take pleasure in study, pursue trade, practise arts and crafts, and shun agriculture and war and so in this manner (the ruin of the country) will not be far off. When the country has trouble, then, because studious people hate law, merchants are clever in bartering and artisans are useless, the state will be easily destroyed.

12. Indeed, if farmers are few, and those who live idly on others are many, then the state will be poor and in a dangerous condition. Now, for example, if various kinds of caterpillars, which are born in spring and die in autumn, appear only once, the result is that the people have no food for many years. Now, if one man tills and a hundred live on him, it means that they are like a great visitation of caterpillars. Though there may be a bundle of the Odes and History in every hamlet and a copy in every family, yet it is useless for good government, and it is not a method whereby this condition of things may be reversed. Therefore the ancient kings made people turn back to agriculture and war. For this reason is it said: "Where a hundred men farm and one is idle, the state will attain supremacy; where ten men farm and one is idle, the state will be strong; where half farms and half is idle, the state will be in peril." That is why those, who govern the country well, wish the people to take to agriculture. If the country does not take to agriculture, then, in its quarrels over authority with the various feudal lords, it will not be able to maintain itself, because the strength of the multitude will not be sufficient. Therefore the feudal lords vex its weakness and make use of its state of decadence; and if the territory is invaded and dismembered, without the country being stirred to action, it will be past saving.

13. A sage knows what is essential in administrating a country, and so he induces the people to devote their attention to agriculture. If their attention is devoted to agriculture, then they will be simple, and being simple, they may be made correct. Being perplexed it will be easy to direct them, being trustworthy, they may be used for defence and warfare. Being single-minded, opportunities of deceit will be few and they will attach importance to their homes. Being single-minded, their careers may be made dependent on rewards and penalties; being single-minded, they may be used abroad.

4th–3rd century BCE

42. The Mengzi

Translated by James Legge

Mencius (Mengzi in Chinese) was an itinerant Confucian philosopher who lived c. 372–289 BCE. The work that bears his name contains conversations that he had with various kings from the time. It will later attain high status as one of the "Four Books" among the Neo-Confucians of the Song Dynasty (960–1279 CE). The following excerpts reveal Mencius' views on the Mandate of Heaven.

Chapter 5.

1. Wan Zhang said, 'Was it the case that Yâo gave the throne to Shun?'[1] Mencius said, 'No. The sovereign cannot give the throne to another.'

2. 'Yes;—but Shun had the throne. Who gave it to him?' 'Heaven gave it to him,' was the answer.

3. '"Heaven gave it to him:"—did Heaven confer its appointment on him with specific injunctions?'

4. Mencius replied, 'No. Heaven does not speak. It simply showed its will by his personal conduct and his conduct of affairs.'

5. '"It showed its will by his personal conduct and his conduct of affairs:"—how was this?' Mencius's answer was, 'The sovereign can present a man to Heaven, but he cannot make Heaven give that man the throne. A prince can present a man to the sovereign, but he cannot cause the sovereign to make that man a prince. A great officer can present a man to his prince, but he cannot cause the prince to make that man a great officer. Yâo presented Shun to Heaven, and Heaven accepted him. He presented him to the people, and the people accepted him. Therefore I say, "Heaven does not speak. It simply indicated its will by his personal conduct and his conduct of affairs."'

6. Zhang said, 'I presume to ask how it was that Yâo presented Shun to Heaven, and Heaven accepted him; and that he exhibited him to the people, and the people accepted him.' Mencius replied, 'He caused him to preside over the sacrifices, and all the spirits were well pleased with them;—thus Heaven

---

1 Yao and Shun are legendary emperors who were thought to have ruled in the distant past. Shun was Yao's minister and successor.

accepted him. He caused him to preside over the conduct of affairs, and affairs were well administered, so that the people reposed under him;—thus the people accepted him. Heaven gave the throne to him. The people gave it to him. Therefore I said, "The sovereign cannot give the throne to another."

7. 'Shun assisted Yâo in the government for twenty and eight years;—this was more than man could have done, and was from Heaven. After the death of Yâo, when the three years' mourning was completed, Shun withdrew from the son of Yâo to the south of South river. The princes of the kingdom, however, repairing to court, went not to the son of Yâo, but they went to Shun. Litigants went not to the son of Yâo, but they went to Shun. Singers sang not the son of Yâo, but they sang Shun. Therefore I said, "Heaven gave him the throne." It was after these things that he went to the Middle Kingdom, and occupied the seat of the Son of Heaven. If he had, before these things, taken up his residence in the palace of Yâo, and had applied pressure to the son of Yâo, it would have been an act of usurpation, and not the gift of Heaven.

8. 'This sentiment is expressed in the words of The Great Declaration,—"Heaven sees according as my people see; Heaven hears according as my people hear."'

Chapter 6.

1. Wan Zhang asked Mencius, saying, 'People say, "When the disposal of the kingdom came to Yü,[2] his virtue was inferior to that of Yâo and Shun, and he transmitted it not to the worthiest but to his son." Was it so?' Mencius replied, 'No; it was not so. When Heaven gave the kingdom to the worthiest, it was given to the worthiest. When Heaven gave it to the son of the preceding sovereign, it was given to him. Shun presented Yü to Heaven. Seventeen years elapsed, and Shun died. When the three years' mourning was expired, Yü withdrew from the son of Shun to Yang Cheng. The people of the kingdom followed him just as after the death of Yâo, instead of following his son, they had followed Shun. Yü presented Yî[3] to Heaven. Seven years elapsed, and Yü died. When the three years' mourning was expired, Yî withdrew from the son of Yü to the north of mount Qi. The princes, repairing to court, went not to Yî, but they went to Qi[4]. Litigants did not go to Yî, but they went to Qi, saying, "He is the son of our sovereign;" the singers did not sing Yî, but they sang Qi, saying, "He is the son of our sovereign."

2. 'That Dan Zhu[5] was not equal to his father, and Shun's son not equal to his; that Shun assisted Yâo, and Yü assisted Shun, for many years, conferring benefits on the people for a long time; that thus the length of time during which Shun, Yü, and Yî assisted in the government was so different; that Qi was able, as a man of talents and virtue, reverently to pursue the same course as Yü; that Yî assisted Yü only for a few years, and had not long conferred benefits on the people; that the periods of service of the three were so different; and that the sons were one superior, and the other superior:—all this was from Heaven, and what could not be brought about by man. That which is done without man's doing is from Heaven. That which happens without man's causing is from the ordinance of Heaven.

3. 'In the case of a private individual obtaining the throne, there must be in him virtue equal to that of Shun or Yü; and moreover there must be the presenting of him to Heaven by the preceding sovereign. It was on this account that Confucius did not obtain the throne.

4. 'When the kingdom is possessed by natural succession, the sovereign who is displaced by Heaven must be like Jie[6] or Zhou.[7] It was on this ac-

---

2   According to Chinese tradition, Yü was the founder of the Xia Dynasty.

3   Yü's minister.
4   Yu's son.
5   Yao's son.
6   The last king of the Xia Dynasty.
7   The last king of the Shang Dynasty.

count that Yî, Yi Yin, and Zhou Gong[8] did not obtain the throne.

5. 'Yi Yin assisted T'ang so that he became sovereign over the kingdom. After the demise of T'ang, Tai Ding having died before he could be appointed sovereign, Wai Bing reigned two years, and Zhong Ren four. Tai Jia was then turning upside down the statutes of T'ang, when Yi Yin placed him in Tong for three years. There Tai Jia repented of his errors, was contrite, and reformed himself. In Tong be came to dwell in benevolence and walk in righteousness,

during those three years, listening to the lessons given to him by Yi Yin. Then Yi Yin again returned with him to Po.

6. 'Zhou Gong not getting the throne was like the case of Yî and the throne of Xia, or like that of Yi Yin and the throne of Yin.

7. 'Confucius said, "T'ang and Yü resigned the throne to their worthy ministers. The sovereign of Xia and those of Yin and Zhou transmitted it to their sons. The principle of righteousness was the same in all the cases."'

---

8   Honored officials under the founders of the first three dynasties, Yü, Tang, and Wu, respectively.

Think about it.

1. According to Mencius, how does Heaven reveal its will?
2. How does Mencius answer the objection that Chi, the son of Yu, was not as worthy to rule as the prime minister Yi? How might such reasoning support the idea that the practice of dynastic succession is in harmony with the Mandate of Heaven concept?

4th–3rd century BCE

43. The Zhuangzi

Translated by James Legge

The Zhuangzi is named after its credited author, Zhuangzi (old spelling Chuang Tzu), a Chinese philosopher who lived c. 369–286 BCE and was a minor official of the state of Song. A common view is that Zhuangzi wrote only the first seven chapters, that his disciples wrote the next 15 chapters, and that the final 11 chapters were written by others. It will later be considered one of the foundational texts of Daoism. The present edition is a product of the Neo-Daoist scholar Guo Xiang (c. 300 CE). The following excerpt, concerning government, is from Chapter 9.

James Legge, "Book IX, Part II, Section II," *The Sacred Books of China: The Texts of Taoism, The Sacred Books of the East, Volume XXXIX*. Oxford University Press, 1891. Copyright in the Public Domain.

PART II. SECTION II.

Horses' Hoofs.

1. Horses can with their hoofs tread on the hoarfrost and snow, and with their hair withstand the wind and cold; they feed on the grass and drink water; they prance with their legs and leap:—this is the true nature of horses. Though there were made for them grand towers and large dormitories, they would prefer not to use them. But when Bo-le (arose and) said, 'I know well how to manage horses,' (men proceeded) to singe and mark them, to clip their hair, to pare their hoofs, to halter their heads, to bridle them and hobble them, and to confine them in stables and corrals. (When subjected to this treatment), two or three in every ten of them died. (Men proceeded further) to subject them to hunger and thirst, to gallop them and race them, and to make them go together in regular order. In front were the evils of the bit and ornamented breast-bands, and behind were the terrors of the whip and switch. (When so treated), more than half of them died.

The (first) potter said, 'I know well how to deal with clay;' and (men proceeded) to mould it into circles as exact as if made by the compass, and into squares as exact as if formed by the measuring square. The (first) carpenter said, 'I know well how to deal with wood;' and (men proceeded) to make it bent as if by the application of the hook, and straight as if by the application of the plumb-line. But is it the nature of clay and wood to require the application of the compass and square, of the hook and line? And yet age after age men have praised Bo-le, saying, 'He knew well how to manage horses,' and also the (first) potter and carpenter, saying, 'They knew well how to deal with clay and wood.' This is just the error committed by the governors of the world.

2. According to my idea, those who knew well to govern mankind would not act so. The people had their regular and constant nature:—they wove and made themselves clothes; they tilled the ground and got food. This was their common faculty. They were all one in this, and did not form themselves into separate classes; so were they constituted and left to their natural tendencies. Therefore in the age of perfect virtue men walked along with slow and grave step, and with their looks steadily directed forwards. At that time, on the hills there were no foot-paths, nor excavated passages; on the lakes there were no boats nor dams; all creatures lived in companies; and the places of their settlement were made close to one another. Birds and beasts multiplied to flocks and herds; the grass and trees grew luxuriant and long. In this condition the birds and beasts might be led about without feeling the constraint; the nest of the magpie might be climbed to, and peeped into. Yes, in the age of perfect virtue, men lived in common with birds and beasts, and were on terms of equality with all creatures, as forming one family;—how could they know among themselves the distinctions of superior men and small men? Equally without knowledge, they did not leave (the path of) their natural virtue; equally free from desires, they were in the state of pure simplicity. In that state of pure simplicity, the nature of the people was what it ought to be. But when the sagely men appeared, limping and wheeling about in (the exercise of) benevolence, pressing along and standing on tiptoe in the doing of righteousness, then men universally began to be perplexed. (Those sages also) went to excess in their performances of music, and in their gesticulations in the practice of ceremonies, and then men began to be separated from one another. If the raw materials had not been cut and hacked, who could have made a sacrificial vase from them? If the natural jade had not been broken and injured, who could have made the handles for the libation-cups from it? If the attributes of the Dao had not been disallowed, how should they have preferred benevolence and righteousness? If the instincts of the nature had not been departed from, how should ceremonies and music have come into use? If the five colours had not been confused, how should the ornamental figures have been formed? If the five notes had not been confused, how should they have supplemented them by the musical accords? The cutting and

hacking of the raw materials to form vessels was the crime of the skilful workman; the injury done to the characteristics of the Dao in order to the practice of benevolence and righteousness was the error of the sagely men.

3. Horses, when living in the open country, eat the grass, and drink water; when pleased, they intertwine their necks and rub one another; when enraged, they turn back to back and kick one another;—this is all that they know to do. But if we put the yoke on their necks, with the moonlike frontlet displayed on all their foreheads, then they know to look slily askance, to curve their necks, to rush viciously, trying to get the bit out of their mouths, and to filch the reins (from their driver);—this knowledge of the horse and its ability thus to act the part of a thief is the crime of Bo-le. In the time of (the Di) He-xu, the people occupied their dwellings without knowing what they were doing, and walked out without knowing where they were going. They filled their mouths with food and were glad; they slapped their stomachs to express their satisfaction. This was all the ability which they possessed. But when the sagely men appeared, with their bendings and stoppings in ceremonies and music to adjust the persons of all, and hanging up their benevolence and righteousness to excite the endeavours of all to reach them, in order to comfort their minds, then the people began to stump and limp about in their love of knowledge, and strove with one another in their pursuit of gain, so that there was no stopping them:—this was the error of those sagely men.

Think about it.

1. How does the author use the illustration of horses, clay, and wood to show that humans were not intended to live in a class-based, urban society?
2. What, according to the author, is the true nature of human beings?

4th–3rd century BCE

44. The Liji

Translated by James Legge

The Liji, known in English as The Book of Rites, is a collection of ritual directions written by Confucians of the late Warring States Period and early Han Dynasty in China (c. 4th–3rd century BCE). It was edited by Dai Sheng in the early Han period and was one of the Five Classics taught at that time in the Imperial University. The following excerpt illustrates the importance of rules of propriety for Confucians of the time and how detailed such rules could be.

James Legge, *The Sacred Books of China, Volume IV: The Lî Kî (Book of Rites), Part I, The Sacred Books of the East, Volume XXVII.* Oxford University Press, 1885. Copyright in the Public Domain.

SUMMARY OF THE RULES OF PROPRIETY.

SECTION I. PART I.

Ch. 1. 1. The Summary of the Rules of Propriety says:—Always and in everything let there be reverence; with the deportment grave as when one is thinking (deeply), and with speech composed and definite. This will make the people tranquil.

2. 2. Pride should not be allowed to grow; the desires should not be indulged; the will should not be gratified to the full; pleasure should not be carried to excess.

3. 3. Men of talents and virtue can be familiar with others and yet respect them; can stand in awe of others and yet love them. They love others and yet acknowledge the evil that is in them. They accumulate (wealth) and yet are able to part with it (to help the needy); they rest in what gives them satisfaction and yet can seek satisfaction elsewhere (when it is desirable to do so). 4. When you find wealth within your reach, do not (try to) get it by improper means; when you meet with calamity, do not (try to) escape from it by improper means. Do not seek for victory in small contentions; do not seek for more than your proper share. 5. Do not positively affirm what you have doubts about; and (when you have no doubts), do not let what you say appear (simply) as your own view.

4. 6. If a man be sitting, let him do so as a personator of the deceased; if he be standing, let him do so (reverently), as in sacrificing. 7. In (observing) the rules of propriety, what is right (for the time and in the circumstances) should be followed. In discharging a mission (to another state), its customs are to be observed.

5. 8. They are the rules of propriety, that furnish the means of determining (the observances towards) relatives, as near and remote; of settling points which may cause suspicion or doubt; of distinguishing where there should be agreement, and where

difference; and of making clear what is right and what is wrong. 9. According to those rules, one should not (seek to) please others in an improper way, nor be lavish of his words, 10. According to them, one does not go beyond the definite measure, nor encroach on or despise others, nor is fond of (presuming) familiarities. 11. To cultivate one's person and fulfil one's words is called good conduct. When the conduct is (thus) ordered, and the words are accordant with the (right) course, we have the substance of the rules of propriety. 12. I have heard that it is in accordance with those rules that one should be chosen by others (as their model); I have not heard of his choosing them (to take him as such). I have heard in the same way of (scholars) coming to learn; I have not heard of (the master) going to teach. 13. The course (of duty), virtue, benevolence, and righteousness cannot be fully carried out without the rules of propriety; 14. nor are training and oral lessons for the rectification of manners complete; 15. nor can the clearing up of quarrels and discriminating in disputes be accomplished; 16. nor can (the duties between) ruler and minister, high and low, father and son, elder brother and younger, be determined; 17. nor can students for office and (other) learners, in serving their masters, have an attachment for them; 18. nor can majesty and dignity be shown in assigning the different places at court, in the government of the armies, and in discharging the duties of office so as to secure the operation of the laws; 19. nor can there be the (proper) sincerity and gravity in presenting the offerings to spiritual Beings on occasions of supplication, thanksgiving, and the various sacrifices. 20. Therefore the superior man is respectful and reverent, assiduous in his duties and not going beyond them, retiring and yielding;—thus illustrating (the principle of) propriety. 21. The parrot can speak, and yet is nothing more than a bird; the ape can speak, and yet is nothing more than a beast 22. Here now is a man who observes no rules of propriety; is not his heart that of a beast? But if (men were as) beasts, and without (the principle of) propriety, father and son might have the same mate.

22. Therefore, when the sages arose, they framed the rules of propriety in order to teach men, and cause them, by their possession of them, to make a distinction between themselves and brutes.

6. 23. In the highest antiquity they prized (simply conferring) good; in the time next to this, giving and repaying was the thing attended to. And what the rules of propriety value is that reciprocity. If I give a gift and nothing comes in return, that is contrary to propriety; if the thing comes to me, and I give nothing in return, that also is contrary to propriety. 24. If a man observe the rules of propriety, he is in a condition of security; if he do not, he is in one of danger. Hence there is the saying, 'The rules of propriety should by no means be left unlearned.' 25. Propriety is seen in humbling one's self and giving honour to others. Even porters and peddlers are sure to display this giving honour (in some cases); how much more should the rich and noble do so (in all)! 26. When the rich and noble know to love propriety, they do not become proud nor dissolute. When the poor and mean know to love propriety, their minds do not become cowardly.

7. 27. When one is ten years old, we call him a boy; he goes (out) to school. When he is twenty, we call him a youth; he is capped. When he is thirty, we say, 'He is at his maturity;' he has a wife. When he is forty, we say, 'He is in his vigour;' he is employed in office. When he is fifty, we say, 'He is getting grey;' he can discharge all the duties of an officer. When he is sixty, we say, 'He is getting old;' he gives directions and instructions. When he is seventy, we say, 'He is old;' he delegates his duties to others. At eighty or ninety, we say of him, 'He is very old.' When he is seven, we say that he is an object of pitying love. Such a child and one who is very old, though they may be chargeable with crime, are not subjected to punishment. At a hundred, he is called a centenarian, and has to be fed. 28. A great officer, when he is seventy, should resign (his charge of) affairs. 29. If he be not allowed to resign, there must be given him a stool and staff. When travelling on service, he must have the attendance of his wife; and when going to any other state, he will ride in an easy carriage. 30. (In another state) he will, style himself 'the old man;' in his own state, he will call himself by his name. 31. When from another they ask (about his state), he must tell them of its (old) institutions.

PART II

1. 1. In going to take counsel with an elder, one must carry a stool and a staff with him (for the elder's use). When the elder asks a question, to reply without acknowledging one's incompetency and (trying to) decline answering, is contrary to propriety.

2. 2. For all sons it is the rule:—In winter, to warm (the bed for their parents), and to cool it in summer; in the evening, to adjust everything (for their repose), and to inquire (about their health) in the morning; and, when with their companions, not to quarrel.

3. 3. Whenever a son, having received the three (first) gifts (of the ruler), declines (to use) the carriage and horses, the people of the hamlets and smaller districts, and of the larger districts and neighbourhoods, will proclaim him filial; his brothers and relatives, both by consanguinity and affinity, will proclaim him loving; his friends who are fellow-officers will proclaim him virtuous; and his friends who are his associates will proclaim him true.

4. 4. When he sees an intimate friend of his father, not to presume to go forward to him without being told to do so; nor to retire without being told; nor to address him without being questioned:—this is the conduct of a filial son, 5. A son, when he is going abroad, must inform (his parents where he is going); when he returns, he must present himself before them. Where he travels must be in some fixed (region); what he engages in must be some (reputable) occupation. 6. In ordinary conversation (with his parents), he does not use the term 'old' (with reference to them). 7. He should serve one twice as old as himself as he serves his father, one ten years older than himself as an elder brother; with one five years older he should walk shoulder to shoulder, but (a

little) behind him. 8. When five are sitting together, the eldest must have a different mat (by himself). 9. A son should not occupy the south-west corner of the apartment, nor sit in the middle of the mat (which he occupies alone), nor walk in the middle of the road, nor stand in the middle of the doorway. 10. He should not take the part of regulating the (quantity of) rice and other viands at an entertainment. 11. He should not act as personator of the dead at sacrifice. 12. He should be (as if he were) hearing (his parents) when there is no voice from them, and as seeing them when they are not actually there. 13. He should not ascend a height, nor approach the verge of a depth; he should not indulge in reckless reviling or derisive laughing. A filial son will not do things in the dark, nor attempt hazardous undertakings, fearing lest he disgrace his parents. 14. While his parents are alive, he will not promise a friend to die (with or for him), nor will he have wealth that he calls his own. 15. A son, while his parents are alive, will not wear a cap or (other) article of dress, with a white border. 16. An orphan son, taking his father's place, will not wear a cap or (other article of) dress with a variegated border.

5. 17. A boy should never be allowed to see an instance of deceit. 18. A lad should not wear a jacket of fur nor the skirt. He must stand straight and square, and not incline his head in hearing. 19. When an elder is holding him with the hand, he should hold the elder's hand with both his hands. When the elder has shifted his sword to his back and is speaking to him with the side of his face bent, down, he should cover his mouth with his hand in answering. 20. When he is following his teacher 4, he should not quit the road to speak with another person. When he meets his teacher on the road, he should hasten forward to him, and stand with his hands joined across his breast. If the teacher speak to him, he will answer; if he do not, he will retire with hasty steps. 21. When, following an elder, they ascend a level height, he must keep his face towards the quarter to which the elder is looking. 22. When one has ascended the wall

of a city, he should not point, nor call out. 23. When he intends to go to a lodging-house, let it not be with the feeling that he must get whatever he asks for. 24. When about to go up to the hall (of a house), he must raise his voice. When outside the door there are two (pairs of) shoes, if voices be heard, he enters; if voices be not heard, he will not enter. 25. When about to enter the door, he must keep his eyes cast down. As he enters, he should (keep his hands raised as high as if he were) bearing the bar of the door. In looking down or up, he should not turn (his head). If the door were open, he should leave it open; if it were shut, he should shut it again. If there be others (about) to enter after him, while he (turns to) shut the door, let him not do so hastily. 26. Let him not tread on the shoes (left outside the door), nor stride across the mat (in going to take his seat); but let him hold up his dress, and move hastily to his corner (of the mat). (When seated), he must be careful in answering or assenting.

6. 27. A great officer or (other) officer should go out or in at the ruler's doors, on the right of the middle post, without treading on the threshold.

7. 28. Whenever (a host has received and) is entering with a guest, at every door he should give place to him. When the guest arrives at the innermost door (or that leading to the feast-room), the host will ask to be allowed to enter first and arrange the mats. Having done this, he will come out to receive the guest, who will refuse firmly (to enter first). The host having made a low bow to him, they will enter (together). 29. When they have entered the door, the host moves to the right, and the guest to the left, the former going to the steps on the cast, and the latter to those on the west. If the guest be of the lower rank, he goes to the steps of the host (as if to follow him up them). The host firmly declines this, and he returns to the other steps on the west. 30. They then offer to each other the precedence in going up, but the host commences first, followed (immediately) by the other. They bring their feet together on every step, thus ascending by successive paces. He who ascends

by the steps on the cast should move his right foot first, and the other at the western steps his left foot. 31. Outside the curtain or screen (a visitor) should not walk with the formal hasty steps, nor above in the hall, nor when carrying the symbol of jade. Above, in the raised hall, the foot-prints should be alongside each other, but below it free and separate.

In the apartment the elbows should not be held out like wings in bowing. 32. When two (equals) are sitting side by side, they do not have their elbows extended crosswise. One should not kneel in handing anything to a (superior) standing, nor stand in handing it to him sitting.

Think about it.

1. According to this text, why are the rules of propriety so important?
2. Some might consider the rules of conduct in Part II to be excessive (and the rest of the book is the same way). Why do you think such complex rules arose among the Confucians in this society?

early 3rd century BCE

45. The Arthashastra

Translated by Rudrapatnam Shamasastry

This is a selection from The Arthashastra, a book on statecraft from ancient India. The author identifies himself as "Kautilya" and also as "Vishnugupta." The usual opinion is that these are other names for Chanakya (c. 370–283 BCE), the royal advisor to Chandragupta Maurya, founder of the Mauryan Empire in India. Chanakya was a teacher at Takshashila University and is thought to have been instrumental in Chandragupta Maurya's rise to power.

Book III

In virtue of his power to uphold the observance of the respective duties of the four castes and of the four divisions of religious life, and in virtue of his power to guard against the violation of the Dharmas, the king is the fountain of justice (dharmapravartaka).

Sacred law (Dharma), evidence (Vyavahára), history (Charitra), and edicts of kings (Rájasásana) are the four legs of Law. Of these four in order, the later is superior to the one previously named.

Dharma is eternal truth holding its sway over the world; Vyavahára, evidence, is in witnesses; Charitra, history, is to be found in the tradition (sangraha), of the people; and the order of kings is what is called sásana.

As the duty of a king consists in protecting his subjects with justice, its observance leads him to heaven. He who does not protect his people or upsets the social order wields his royal sceptre (danda) in vain.

It is power and power (danda) alone which, only when exercised by the king with impartiality and in proportion to guilt either over his son or his enemy, maintains both this world and the next.

The king who administers justice in accordance with sacred law (Dharma), evidence (vyavahára), history (samsthá) and edicts of kings (Nyáya) which is the fourth will be able to conquer the whole world bounded by the four quarters (Chaturantám mahím).

Whenever there is disagreement between history and sacred law or between evidence and sacred law, then the matter shall be settled in accordance with sacred law.

But whenever sacred law (sástra) is conflict with rational law (Dharmanyáya = kings' law), then reason shall be held authoritative; for there the original text (on which the sacred law has been based) is not available.

Self-assertion (svayamváda) on the part of either of the parties has often been found faulty. Examination (anuyoga), honesty (árjava), evidence (hetu) and asseveration by oath (sapatha)—these alone can enable a man to win his cause.

Whenever by means of the deposition of witnesses, the statements of either of the parties are found contradictory, and whenever the cause of either of the parties is found through the king's spies to be false, then the decree shall be passed against that party.

Think about it.

1. What were the "four legs of law," and what role did each of them play in the Mauryan legal system?

3rd century BCE

46. The Xunzi

Translated by Homer Dubs

Xunzi (old spelling Hsun Tzu) was a Confucian scholar of China c. 313–238 BCE. He was known not only for criticizing other philosophical views, like Daoism and Mohism, but also the views of other Confucians like Mencius. The teachings found in his book were a great influence in the formation of the policies of the Han empire.

BOOK XXIII

THE NATURE OF MAN IS EVIL

1. The nature of man is evil; his goodness is only acquired training. The original nature of man to-day is to seek for gain. If this desire is followed, strife and rapacity results, and courtesy[1] dies. Man originally is envious and naturally hates others. If these tendencies are followed, injury and destruction follows; loyalty and faithfulness are destroyed. Man originally possesses the desires of the ear and eye; he likes praise and is lustful. If these are followed, impurity and disorder results, and the rules of proper conduct (Li) and justice (Yi) and etiquette[2] are destroyed. Therefore to give rein to man's original nature, to follow man's feelings, inevitably results in strife and rapacity, together with violations of etiquette and confusion in the proper way of doing things, and reverts to a state of violence. Therefore the civilizing influence of teachers and laws, the guidance of the rules of proper conduct (Li) and justice (Yi) is absolutely necessary. Thereupon courtesy results; public and private etiquette is observed; and good government is the consequence. By this line of reasoning it is evident that the nature of man is evil and his goodness is acquired.

2. Crooked wood needs to undergo steaming and bending to conform to the carpenter's rule[3]; then only is it straight. Blunt metal needs to undergo grinding and whetting; then only is it sharp. The original nature of man to-day is evil, so he needs to undergo the instruction of teachers and laws, then only will he be upright. He needs the rules of proper conduct (Li) and justice (Yi), then only will there be good government. But man to-day

is without good teachers and laws so he is selfish, vicious, and unrighteous. He is without the rules of proper conduct (Li) and justice (Yi), so there is rebellion, disorder, and no good government. In ancient times the Sage-Kings knew that man's nature was evil, selfish, vicious, unrighteous, rebellious, and of itself did not bring about good government. For this reason they created the rules of proper conduct (Li) and justice (Yi); they established laws and ordinances to force and beautify the natural feelings of man, thus rectifying them. They trained to obedience and civilized men's natural feelings, thus guiding them. Then good government arose and men followed the right Way (Dao). Now the people who are influenced by good teachers and laws, who accumulate literature and knowledge, who are led by the rules of proper conduct (Li) and justice (Yi) become superior men. Those who give rein to their natural feelings, who take joy in haughtiness, and break the rules of proper conduct (Li) and justice (Yi), become small-minded men. By this line of reasoning it is evident that the original nature of man is evil, and his goodness is acquired.

3. Mencius says, "The fact that men are teachable shows that their original nature is good." I reply: This is not so. This is not understanding the nature of man, nor examining the original nature of man, nor the part played by acquired elements. Whatever belongs to original nature is the gift of Nature. It cannot be learned. It cannot be worked for. The Sage-Kings brought forth the rules of proper conduct (Li) and justice (Yi). Men learn them and gain ability; they work for them and obtain results in the development of character. What cannot be learned and cannot be worked for, what is in the power of Nature only is what is meant by original nature. That which can be learned and which gives men ability, which can be worked for and which brings results in the development of character, whatever is in the power of man is what is meant by acquired character. This is the distinction between original nature and acquired character. Now according to the nature of man, the eye has the power

---

1   Lit., "declining and yielding,"; if an honour is offered you, make a show of declining it; if you are asked to take the precedence make a show of yielding it to others—still the standard procedure in China.

2   Lit., "the beauty of private and public etiquette."

3   An instrument used to straighten crooked wood.

of seeing and the ear has the power of hearing. However, when a person sees a thing, his quickness of sight is not outside of his eye; when he hears, his quickness of hearing is not outside of his ear. It is evident that quickness of sight and quickness of hearing cannot be learned.[4] Mencius says: Now the original nature of man is good; all have lost and destroyed their original nature, hence it is evil. I reply: When he says this, he is greatly mistaken. Now considering the nature of man, as soon as he is born, he would already have grown away from his first estate, he would already have grown from his natural disposition. He would already have lost and destroyed it. By this line of reasoning it is evident that the original nature of man is evil and his goodness is acquired.

4.   The doctrine that man's original nature is good implies that without growing away from his first estate, he becomes admirable; without growing away from his natural disposition, he becomes beneficial. To say that man's original nature is admirable, his heart and thoughts are good, is the same as to say that the power of seeing is not apart from the eye and the power of hearing is not apart from the ear.[5] So we say, if there is an eye, there is the power of seeing; if there is an ear, there is the power of hearing. Now the nature of man is that when he is hungry, he desires repletion; when he is cold, he desires warmth; when he labours, he seeks rest. This is man's natural feeling. But now when a man is hungry and sees food, he dares not rush in ahead of others; instead the eater yields to others. When working, he dares not seek rest, instead he works for others. The son yielding precedence to his father, the younger brother yielding to his older brother; the son working for his father, the younger brother working for his older brother—these two kinds of actions are contrary to original nature and antagonistic to natural feeling. Nevertheless there

is the doctrine (Dao) of filial piety, the etiquette of the rules of proper conduct (Li) and justice (Yi). If a person follows his natural feelings, he has no courtesy; if he has courtesy, then it is antagonistic to his natural feelings. By this line of reasoning it is evident that man's original nature is evil and his goodness is acquired.

5.   A questioner may say: If man s original nature is evil, then whence come the rules of proper conduct (Li) and justice (Yi)? In answer I say: All rules of proper conduct (Li) and justice (Yi) come from the acquired training of the Sage, not from man's original nature. The potter[6] pounds and moulds the clay and makes the vessel—but the vessel comes from the potter's acquired skill, not from the potter's innate character. The workman hews a piece of wood and makes a vessel; but the vessel comes from the workman's acquired training, not from his innate character. The Sage gathers together ideas and thoughts, and becomes skilled by his acquired training, so as to bring forth the rules of proper conduct (Li) and justice (Yi), and originate laws and regulations. So the rules of proper conduct (Li), justice (Yi), laws and regulations come from the acquired knowledge of the Sage, not from man's original nature.

6.   The eye desires colour, the ear desires sound, the mouth desires flavours, the heart desires gain, the body desires pleasure and ease: these all come from man's original nature and feelings. Give man a stimulus and they come forth of their own accord; they do not need to be taught to man before they can come forth. But if a man is stimulated and the virtue we are seeking cannot of itself come forth, if it needs to wait to be taught and then only can come forth—this is what is meant by an acquired characteristic. This is the distinction between original nature and acquired characteristics,

---

4   i.e., that they are innate. Xunzi is struggling to express the concept of "innate".
5   It is to say that goodness is innate and natural.

6   This example and language is taken from the *Daodejing*, sect. 11.

the evidence of their dissimilarity.[7] So the Sages influenced men's nature and established acquired training. When acquired training had arisen, the rules of proper conduct *(Li)* and justice *(Yi)* were evolved, laws and regulations were made. Hence the rules of proper conduct *(Li)*, justice *(Yi)*, laws, and regulations were brought forth by the Sages. The Sage has his original nature in common with ordinary people; he is not different from ordinary people in this respect. He is different and superior to ordinary people in his acquired training.

7. It is the original nature and tendency of man to desire gain and to seek to obtain it. If brothers have property and are to divide it, if they follow their original nature and feelings of desiring gain and seeking to obtain it, thus they will mutually thwart each other and endeavour to seize the property. But reform them by the etiquette of the rules of proper conduct *(Li)* and justice *(Yi)*, and they will be willing to yield to outsiders. So by following the original nature and feelings, brothers will quarrel; influence them by the rules of proper conduct *(Li)* and justice *(Yi)*, and they will yield to strangers. Every man's desire to be good is because his nature is evil. So if he is mean, he wants to be generous; if he is in circumscribed circumstances he wants un-hampered circumstances; if he is poor, he wants to be rich; if he is in a low social position, he wishes to be in an honourable position; if he has it not within himself, he inevitably seeks it from without. For if he were rich, he would not desire wealth; if he were in a high position, he would not want more power. If he has it within his power, he would certainly not seek it from without. By this line of reasoning we

see that men's desire to be good comes from his original nature being evil.

8. Now the original nature of man is really without the rules of proper conduct *(Li)* and justice *(Yi)*, hence he strives to learn and seeks to have it. By his original nature he does not know the rules of proper conduct *(Li)* and justice *(Yi)*, hence he thinks and reflects, and seeks to learn these principles. Then only are they developed. So man is naturally without the rules of proper conduct *(Li)* and justice *(Yi)*, he does not know the rules of proper conduct *(Li) and* justice *(Yi)*. If man is without the rules of proper conduct *(Li)* and justice *(Yi)*, there is disorder; if he does not know the rules of proper conduct *(Li)* and justice *(Yi)*, there is rebellion. So these virtues are evolved. Then rebellion and disorder are within man himself. By this line of reasoning it is evident that the original nature of man is evil and his goodness is an acquired characteristic.

9. Mencius says, "The nature of man is good." I reply: This is not so. In whatever age or place on earth, in ancient times or in the present, men have meant by goodness true principles and just government. They have meant by evil partiality, a course bent on evil, rebellion, and disorder. This is the distinction between goodness and evil. Now if we sincerely consider the nature of man, is it firmly established in true principles and just government? If so, then what use are the Sage-Kings? What use are the rules of proper conduct *(Li)* and justice *(Yi)*? Although there were Sage-Kings, the rules of proper conduct *(Li)* and justice *(Yi)*, what could they add to true principles and just government?

10. Now that is not the situation. Man's nature is evil. Anciently the Sage-Kings knew that man's nature was evil, that it was partial, bent on evil, and corrupt, rebellious, disorderly, without good government, hence they established the authority of the prince to govern man; they set forth clearly the rules of proper conduct *(Li)* and justice *(Yi)* to reform him; they established laws and government to rule him; they made punishments severe to warn him; and so they caused the whole country to come

---

7   Cf. Laozi, *Daodejing*, sect. 18. "When the great Principle *(Dao)* is lost there is benevolence *(Jen)* and justice *(Yi)*; knowledge and wisdom appear, and there is great acquired training." Xunzi and Laozi differ in that Laozi supposes man was anciently perfect, but has deteriorated; hence we must return to the ancient practices and to its simplicity. Xunzi supposes man had always been innately evil, but under the influence of the ancient Sage-Kings, he was developed to a state of goodness now unrealized because of the lack of a Sage to influence the people.

to a state of good government and prosperity, and to accord with goodness. This is the government of the Sage-Kings, the reforming influence of the rules of proper conduct *(Li)* and justice *(Yi)*.

11. Now suppose we try to remove the authority of the prince, and be without the reforming influence of the rules of proper conduct *(Li)* and justice *(Yi)*; suppose we try to remove the beneficent control of the laws and the government, and be without the restraining influence of punishments. Let us stand and see how the people of the whole country would behave. If this were the situation, then the strong would injure the weak and rob him; the many would treat cruelly the few and rend them. The whole country would be in a state of rebellion and disorder. It would not take an instant to get into this condition. By this line of reasoning, it is evident that the nature of man is evil and that his goodness is acquired.

12. The man who is versed in the ancient times certainly sees its evidences in the present; he who is versed in the principles of Nature can certainly give evidence of their effect upon man. Every debater prizes distinctions and has evidence to support them. So he can sit down and discuss them; he can rise and establish them; he can act and exhibit them. Now Mencius says: Man's nature is good. This is without discrimination or evidence. A person can sit and discuss it, but he cannot rise and establish it; he cannot act and exhibit it. Isn't this extraordinarily erroneous? For if man's nature were good, then we could do away with the Sage-Kings; we would put an end to the rules of proper conduct *(Li)* and justice *(Yi)*. But if man's nature is evil, then we should follow the Sage-Kings and prize the rules of proper conduct *(Li)* and justice *(Yi)*. For the carpenter's square and rule are produced because there is crooked wood; the plumb-line arose because things were not straight; princes were established, the rules of proper conduct *(Li)* and justice *(Yi)* became evident because man's nature is evil. By this line of reasoning, it is evident that the nature of man is evil and his goodness is acquired.

13. Straight wood does not need to undergo the action of the carpenter's rule in order to be straight; its nature is straight, Crooked wood does need to undergo the action of the carpenter's rule; it needs to be steamed and then only will it be straight, because its nature is crooked. Now the nature of man is evil; he needs to undergo the government of the Sage-Kings, the reforming action of the rules of proper conduct *(Li)* and justice *(Yi)*, then good government and order will issue, and actions will accord with virtue. By this line of reasoning it is evident that the nature of man is evil and his goodness is acquired.

14. A questioner may say: Even if the rules of proper conduct *(Li)* and justice *(Yi)* are accumulated acquired training, they are from man's nature. For the Sage-Kings could bring them forth. In reply I say: This is not so. The potter pounds and moulds the clay and brings the piece of pottery into being; then from clay there comes to be pottery. Can it be that this is the potter's nature? The workman hews a piece of wood and brings a vessel into being; thus from wood there comes to be a vessel. Can it be that this is the workman's original nature? Now the relation of the Sage to the rules of proper conduct *(Li)* and justice *(Yi)* is the same as that of the potter and the clay; he brings them into being; thus the rules of proper conduct *(Li)* and justice *(Yi)* are accumulated acquired training. How can they be the original nature of man? The nature of all men, of Yao and Shun, of Jie and Zhi is the same. The nature of the superior man and of the little-minded man is the same. Now do we use the rules of proper conduct *(Li)* and justice *(Yi)* to make men's nature; do we accumulate acquired training for that purpose? Then why do we prize Yao and Yu? Why do we honour the superior man? What we prize in Yao, Yu, and the superior man is that they could reform their original nature and create acquired training. When their acquired training was created, they brought forth the rules of proper conduct *(Li)* and justice *(Yi)*. Thus the relation of the Sage to the rules of proper conduct *(Li)* and justice *(Yi)* and accumulated acquired

training is the same as that of the potter and the clay: he brings the pottery into being. By this line of reasoning how can the rules of proper conduct *(Li)* and justice *(Yi)* and accumulated acquired training be of man's nature? What was low about Jie, Zhi and the little-minded man was that they followed their nature and acted according to their inclinations: they took joy in haughtiness and the result was that they were avaricious for gain, striving and grasping. Hence it is evident that the nature of man is evil and his goodness is acquired.

15. Heaven was not partial to Zeng,[8] Qian,[9] and Xiao Yi,[10] nor did it neglect the common multitude. Then why are Zeng, Qian, and Xiao Yi alone truly and perfectly filial, and why do they alone have the name of special filiality? The reason is that they observed the rules of proper conduct *(Li)* and justice *(Yi)* to the utmost extent. Heaven was not partial to the people of Qi [11] and Lu,[12] nor did it neglect the people of Qin.[13] But the people of Qin are not as good in the righteous relation between father and son and in the proper reserve between husband and wife, as are the people of Qi and Lu in filial piety and reverential respect.[14] Why is this? The reason is that the people of Qin follow their feelings and original nature, take pleasure in haughtiness, and are remiss in observing the rules of proper conduct *(Li)* and justice *(Yi)*. How can it be that their nature could be different?

16. "The man on the street can become a Yu"[15]—how about that? What gave Yu the qualities of Yu was that he carried into practice benevolence *(Jen)*, justice *(Yi)*, obedience to laws, uprightness. If so, then there is the means of knowing and practising benevolence *(Jen)*, justice *(Yi)*, obedience to law, and uprightness. Moreover, every man on the street has the nascent ability of knowing the principles of benevolence *(Jen)*, justice *(Yi)*, obedience to law, and uprightness, and the means whereby he can carry out the principles of benevolence *(Jen)*, justice *(Yi)* to law, and uprightness. Thus it is evident that he can become a Yu.

17. Now are the qualities of benevolence *(Jen)*, justice *(Yi)*, obedience to law, and uprightness definitely without the possibility of being known or of being carried out? If so, then even Yu could not have known benevolence *(Jen)*, justice *(Yi)*, obedience to law and uprightness, nor could he have been able to be benevolent *(Jen)*, just *(Yi)*, law-abiding, or upright. Then is the man on the street definitely without the power of knowing benevolence *(Jen)*, justice *(Yi)*, obedience to law, and uprightness, and definitely without the ability to be benevolent (Jen), just *(Yi)*, law-abiding, and upright? Then the man on the street, on the one hand, could not know the righteous relation between father and son, nor on the other hand could he know the standard of correctness of prince and minister. Now that is not so. Every man on the street can on the one hand know the righteous relation between father and son, and on the other hand he can know the standard of uprightness of prince and minister. Thus it is evident that the man on the street possesses the power of knowing and the ability to practise these virtues. Now if the man on the street uses his power of knowledge and his ability of acting on the nascent ability of knowing benevolence *(Jen)* and justice *(Yi)* and the means of becoming so, then it is clear that he can become a Yu; if he concentrates his mind on one purpose, if he thinks and studies

---

8 Zeng Shun, the most important of the immediate disciples of Confucius. His teachings stress filial piety. With this saying compare Laozi: "Heaven treats men like straw dogs "—treats all alike.
9 Min Ziqian another famous disciple of Confucius.
10 Heir-apparent of one of the sovereigns of the Shang dynasty.
11 The cultivated feudal state which produced Duke Huan and Guan Zhong.
12 The cultivated state which produced Confucius; these were two centres of Chinese culture.
13 The more barbarous state which was later to conquer the whole of China; elsewhere it is criticized by Xunzi for its lack of refinement and scholarship.
14 Reverent respectfulness is the attitude which should exist between husband and wife.

---

15 A saying found in Mencius, VI, n, ii, 1.

and investigates thoroughly, daily adding to his knowledge and retaining it long, if he accumulates goodness and does not stop, then he will Become as wise as the gods, a third with Heaven and Earth. For the Sage is the man who has attained to that state by accumulative effort.

*****

18. Fanruo and Jüshu were famous bows of antiquity. But if they had not been put in frames for straightening, they could not have been straight of themselves. The Cong of Duke Huan, the Chue of Duke T'ai, the Lu of King Wen, the Fu of Prince Zhuang, Helü's Ganjiang, Moxie, Juchue, Pilu: these were renowned swords of ancient times. But if they had not been ground, they could not have become sharp; if somebody had not laboured on them, they could not have cut. Hua, Liu, Qi, Ji, Xianli, Luer: these were all famous horses of antiquity. But on the one hand they needed the control of a bit and reins, and on the other they needed the fear of the whip. Add to that the driving of Zao Fu,[16] and then they could do the thousand *li* in one day. Thus although a man has fine natural qualities and knows how to discuss, he needs to seek a virtuous teacher and serve him as a disciple; he needs to pick out good friends and attach himself to them. When he obtains a virtuous teacher and serves him as a disciple, then what he hears is the Way *(Dao)* of Yao, Shun, Yu, and T'ang. When he obtains good friends and attaches himself to them, then what he sees is conduct according to loyalty, faithfulness, reverence, and humility. His character daily advances in benevolence *(Jen)* and justice *(Yi)*, and unconsciously he grows like those people. Now if he should live with people who are not virtuous, then what he would hear would be cheating, maliciousness, falseness, and hypocrisy. What he would see would be impurity, boasting, excesses, erroneous doctrine, and conduct that is avaricious of gain., His character would advance towards deserving capital punishment, and unconsciously he would become like these people. It is said: If you do not know a person, look at his friends. If you do not know the prince of a state, look to the right and left. Follow that and it will be sufficient! Follow that and it will be sufficient!

---

16   A famous legendary driver.

Think about it.

1.   In Xunzi's view, how is human nature best controlled?
2.   What arguments does Xunzi bring against the ideas of Mencius?
3.   According to Xunzi, can anyone learn to be good?

47. Edicts of Ashoka

Translated by Vincent A. Smith

Ashoka was the ruler of Mauryan India from 269 to 232 BCE and was known for his conversion to Buddhism and implementation of non-violent policies (*ahimsa*) in the kingdom. All over his empire he inscribed edicts on pillars, boulders, and cave walls for his subjects to read or have read to them. His support for Buddhism is evident in these inscriptions. In the "Fourteen Rock Edicts" provided below, one can get a taste of his policies. He identifies himself as King Piyadasi, which means, "He who regards everyone with affection."

EDICT I

THE SACREDNESS OF LIFE

This scripture of the Law of Duty has been written by command of His Sacred and Gracious Majesty the King:

'Here no animal may be slaughtered for sacrifice, nor shall any merry-making be held. Because in merry-makings His Sacred and Gracious Majesty sees much offence, although certain merry-makings are excellent in the sight of His Sacred and Gracious Majesty the King. Formerly, in the kitchen of His Sacred and Gracious Majesty the King each day many hundred thousands of living creatures were slaughtered to make curries. But now, when this scripture of the Law is being written, only three living creatures are slaughtered for curry [daily], to wit, two peacocks and one antelope the antelope, however, not invariably. Even those three living creatures shall not be slaughtered in future.'

EDICT II

PROVISION OF COMFORTS FOR MEN AND ANIMALS

'Everywhere in the dominions of His Sacred and Gracious Majesty the King, as well as among his frontagers, the Cholas, Pt'indyas, the Satiyaputra, the Ketalaputra, as far as the Tainbaparni, Antiochos the Greek king, or even the kings the neighbours of that Antiochos everywhere have been made the healing arrangements of His Sacred and Gracious Majesty the King in two kinds, [namely], healing arrangements for men and healing arrangements for beasts. Medicinal herbs also, both medicinal herbs for men and medicinal herbs for beasts, wheresoever lacking, have been everywhere both imported and planted. Roots also and fruits, wheresoever lacking, have been everywhere imported and planted.

On the roads, too, wells have been dug and trees planted for the enjoyment of man and beast.'

Vincent A. Smith, *Asoka: The Buddhist Emperor of India*, pp. 158, 160–161, 163, 165–166, 168–169, 172–173, 175–176, 178–183, 185–187, 189–190. Clarendon Press, 1920. Copyright in the Public Domain.

EDICT III

THE SYSTEM OF QUINQUENNIAL OFFICIAL
TRANSFERS

Thus saith His Sacred and Gracious Majesty the
King:

'When I had been consecrated twelve years this
command was issued by me:

"Everywhere in my dominions the subordinate
officials, the Governor, and the District Officer must
every five years proceed in succession on transfer, as
well for their other business, as for this special purpose, the inculcation of the Law of Duty (or Piety),"
to wit:

"An excellent thing is the hearkening to father
and mother; an excellent thing is liberality to friends,
acquaintances, relatives, Brahmans, and ascetics;
excellent is abstention from the slaughter of living
creatures; excellent is small expense with small
accumulation."

The Council also will inculcate [the same] on the
officials in the Accounts Department, with regard
both to the principle and the text [of the order].'

EDICT IV

THE PRACTICE OF THE LAW OF PIETY
OR DUTY

'For a long period past, even for many hundred years,
have increased the sacrificial slaughter of living
creatures, the killing of animate beings, unseemly
behaviour (or "discourtesy ") to relatives, unseemly
behaviour to Brahmans and ascetics.

But now, by reason of the practice of piety by
His Sacred and Gracious Majesty the King, the
reverberation of the war-drums has become the reverberation of the law while he exhibits spectacles of
the dwellings of the gods, spectacles of elephants (or
"the elephant"), bonfires, and other representations
of a divine nature.

As for many hundred years before lias not
happened, now at this present, by reason of the

inculcation of the Law of Piety by His Sacred and
Gracious Majesty the King, have increased abstention from the sacrificial slaughter of living creatures,
abstention from the killing of animate beings,
seemly behaviour (or "courtesy") to relatives,seemly
behaviour to Brahmans and ascetics, hearkening to
father and mother, hearkening to elders.

Thus, and in many other ways the practice of the
Law has increased, and His Sacred and Gracious
Majesty the King will make such practice of the Law
increase further.

The sons, grandsons, and great-grandsons of his
Sacred and Gracious Majesty the King will cause
this practice of the Law to increase until the aeon of
universal destruction. Standing firm in the Law of
Piety and in morality they will inculcate the Law. For
this is the best of deeds even the inculcation of the
Law. Practice of the Law is not for the immoral man.
Both increase and non-diminution in this matter are
excellent.

For this purpose has this [document] been
caused to be written that they may strive for increase
and not give countenance to diminution.

EDICT V

THE CENSORS OR HIGH OFFICERS OF
THE LAW OF PIETY OR DUTY

Thus saith His Sacred and Gracious Majesty the
King:

'A good deed is a difficult thing. He who is the
author of a good deed does a difficult, thing. Now by
me many good deeds have been done.'

Should my sons, grandsons, and my descendants
after them until the end of the aeon follow in this
path, they will do well; but in this matter he who
shall neglect a part of his duty [or "the commandment"] will do ill, because sin easily develops.

Now in all the long time past, officers known
as Censors [or "High Officers"] of the Law of Piety

never had existed, whereas such Censors were created by me when I had been consecrated thirteen years.

Among people of all [non-Buddhist] sects they are employed for the establishment of the Law of Piety, for the increase of that Law, and for the welfare and happiness of the subordinates of the Law of Piety Department [or "the faithful of the true religion"], as well as of the Yavanas, Kambojas, Gandharas, Rashtrikas, Pitinikas, with other nations on my western frontier.

Among servants and masters, Brahmans and the wealthy, among the helpless and the aged, they are employed in freeing from worldly cares their subordinates [in the department] of the Law of Piety.

They are also employed on the revision of [sentences of] imprisonment or execution, in the reduction of penalties, or [the grant of] release, on the grounds of motive, having children, instigation, or advanced years.

Here, and in all provincial towns, in the female establishments of my brothers and sisters, as well as of other relatives, they are everywhere employed. These Censors of the Law of Piety are engaged everywhere in my dominions, among the subordinate officials of that Law with regard to the concerns of the Law, the establishment of the Law, and the business of almsgiving.

For that purpose has this scripture of the Law been written, that it may long endure, and that my subjects may act accordingly.'

EDICT VI

THE PROMPT DISPATCH OF BUSINESS

Thus saith His Sacred and Gracious Majesty the King:

'A long period has elapsed during which in the past business was not carried on or information brought in at all times. So by me the arrangement has been made that at all times, when I am eating, or in the ladies' apartments, or in my private room, or in the mews, or in my conveyance, or in the pleasure-grounds, everywhere the persons appointed to give information should keep me informed about the affairs of the people.

And in all places I attend to the affairs of the people. And, if, perchance, by word of mouth I personally command a donation or injunction; or, again, when a matter of urgency has been committed to the High Officers, and in that matter a division or adjournment takes place in the Council, then without delay information must be given to me in all places, at all times. Such is my command.

Because I never feel satisfaction in my exertions and dispatch of business. For work I must for the welfare of all the folk; and of that, again, the root is energy and the dispatch of business; for nothing is more essential than the welfare of all the folk. And whatsoever efforts I make they are made that I may attain release from my debt to animate beings, so that while in this world I make some persons happy, they may win heaven in the world beyond. For that purpose have I caused this scripture of the Law to be written in order that it may endure, while my sons, grandsons, and great-grandsons may take action for the welfare of all folk. That, however, is difficult save by the utmost exertion.'

EDICT VII

IMPERFECT FULFILMENT OF THE LAW

'His Sacred and Gracious Majesty the King desires that in all places men of every denomination (or "sect") may abide, for they all desire mastery over their senses and purity of mind. Man, however, is various in his wishes and various in his passions. They (the denominations) will perform either the whole or only a part of the commandments. Even for a person to whom lavish liberality is impossible, mastery over the senses, purity of mind, gratitude, and steady devotion are altogether indispensable.'

EDICT VIII

PIOUS TOURS

'In times past Their Sacred Majesties used to go out on so-called "tours of pleasure." In those tours hunting and other similar amusements used to be practised.

His Sacred and Gracious Majesty the present King, after he had been consecrated ten years went out to Bodh Gaya (or "towards supreme knowledge"). Thence arose "tours of piety." In them this is the practice visiting ascetics and Brahmans, with liberality to them; visiting elders, with largess of gold; visiting the people of the country, with instruction in the Law of Piety, and discussion of that Law.

Consequently, since that time a different portion constitutes the pleasuring of His Sacred and Gracious Majesty the King.'

EDICT IX

TRUE CEREMONIAL

Thus saith His Sacred and Gracious Majesty the King:

'People perform various ceremonies. In sickness, at the weddings of sons, the weddings of daughters, the birth of children, departure on journeys on those and other similar occasions people perform many ceremonies. Nay, the womankind perform many, manifold, trivial, and worthless ceremonies.

Ceremonies, however, have to be performed, although that kind bears little fruit. This sort, on the other hand, to wit, the ceremonial of piety, bears great fruit. In it are included proper treatment of slaves and servants, honour to teachers, gentleness towards living creatures, and liberality towards ascetics and Brahmans. These things and others of the same kind are called the Ceremonial of Piety.

Therefore ought a father, son, brother, master, friend, or comrade, or even a neighbour to say: "This is excellent, this is the ceremonial to be performed until the attainment of the desired end."

This I will perform, for the ceremonial of this world is of doubtful efficacy; perchance it may accomplish the desired end, perchance it may not, and it remains a thing of this world. This Ceremonial of Piety, on the contrary, is not temporal; because, even if it fails to attain the desired end in this world, it certainly produces endless merit in the world beyond. If it happens to attain the desired end here, then both gains are assured, namely, in this world the desired end, and in the world beyond endless merit is produced by that Ceremonial of Piety.'

EDICT X

TRUE GLORY

'His Sacred and Gracious Majesty the King does not believe that glory or renown brings much profit unless in both the present and the future my people obediently hearken to the Law of Piety and conform to its precepts. For that purpose only does His Sacred and Gracious Majesty the King desire glory or renown.

Whatsoever exertions His Sacred and Gracious Majesty the King makes, all are for the sake of the life hereafter, so that every one may be freed from peril, and that peril is vice.

Difficult, verily, it is to attain such freedom, whether by people of low or of high degree, save by the utmost exertion, giving up all other aims. That, however, for him of high degree is difficult.'

EDICT XI

TRUE ALMSGIVING

Thus saith His Sacred and Gracious Majesty the King:

'There is no such almsgiving as is the almsgiving of the Law of Piety, friendship in piety, liberality in piety, kinship in piety.

Herein does it consist in proper treatment of slaves and servants, in hearkening to father and mother, in giving to friends, comrades, relations, ascetics, and Brahmans, in abstaining from the sacrificial slaughter of living creatures.

This ought to be said by father, son, brother, master, friend, or comrade, nay, even by a neighbour. "This is excellent, this ought to be done."

Acting thus a man both gains this world and in the other world produces endless merit, by means of this almsgiving of piety.'

EDICT XII

TOLERATION

'His Sacred and Gracious Majesty the King does reverence to men of all sects, whether ascetics or householders, by gifts and various forms of reverence.

His Sacred Majesty, however, cares not so much for gifts or external reverence as that there should be a growth of the essence of the matter in all sects. The growth of the essence of the matter assumes various forms, but the root of it is restraint of speech, to wit, a man must not do reverence to his own sect or disparage that of another without reason. Depreciation should be for specific reasons only, because the sects of other people all deserve reverence for one reason or another.

By thus acting a man exalts his own sect, and at the same time does service to the sects of other people. By acting contrariwise a man hurts his own sect, and does disservice to the sects of other people. For he who does reverence to his own sect while disparaging the sects of others wholly from attachment to his own. with intent to enhance the splendour of his own sect, in reality by such conduct inflicts the severest injury on his own sect.

Concord, therefore, is meritorious, to wit, hearkening and hearkening willingly to the Law of Piety as accepted by other people. For this is the desire of His Sacred Majesty that all sects should hear much teaching and hold sound doctrine.

Wherefore the adherents of all sects, whatever they may be, must be informed that His Sacred Majesty does not care so much for gifts or external reverence as that there should be growth in the essence of the matter and respect for all sects.

For this very purpose are employed the Censors of the Law of Piety, the Censors of the Women, the Superintendents of pastures, and other [official] bodies. And this is the fruit thereof the growth of one's own sect and the enhancement of the splendour of the Law of Piety.'

EDICT XIII

TRUE CONQUEST

'Kalinga was (or "the Kalingas were") conquered by His Sacred and Gracious Majesty the King when he bad been consecrated eight years. One hundred and fifty thousand persons were thence carried away captive, one hundred thousand were there slain, and many times that number died.

Directly after the Kalingas had been annexed began His Sacred Majesty's zealous protection of the Law of Piety, his love of that Law, and his inculcation of that Law. Thence arises the remorse of His Sacred Majesty for having conquered the Kalingas, because the conquest of a country previously unconquered involves the slaughter, death, and carrying away captive of the people. That is a matter of profound sorrow and regret to His Sacred Majesty.

There is, however, another reason for His Sacred Majesty feeling still more regret, inasmuch as the Brahmans and ascetics, or men of other denominations, or householders who dwell there, and among whom these duties are practised, [to wit], hearkening to superiors, hearkening to father and mother, hearkening to teachers (or "elders"), and proper treatment (or "courtesy to") of friends, acquaintances, comrades, relatives, slaves, and servants, with steadfastness of devotion to these befalls violence (or "injury"), or slaughter, or separation from their loved ones. Or violence happens to the friends, acquaintances, comrades, and relatives of those who are themselves well protected, while their affection [for those injured] continues undiminished. Thus for them also that is a mode of violence, and the share of this distributed among all men is a matter of regret to His Sacred Majesty, because it never is the case that faith in some one denomination or another does not exist.

So that of all the people who were then slain, done to death, or carried away captive in Kalinga, if the hundredth part or the thousandth part were now to suffer the same fate, it would be matter of regret to His Sacred Majesty. Moreover, should any one do him wrong, that too must be borne with by His Sacred Majesty, so far as it can possibly be borne with. Even upon the forest folk in his dominions, His Sacred Majesty looks kindly, and he seeks to make them think, [aright], for [otherwise] repentance would come upon His Sacred Majesty. They are bidden to turn from their [evil] ways that they be not chastised. Because His Sacred Majesty desires for all animate beings security, self-control, peace of mind, and joyousness.

And this the chiefest conquest in the opinion of His Sacred Majesty, that conquest of the Law of Piety, which, again, has been won by His Sacred Majesty both here [in his own dominions] and among all his neighbours as far as six hundred leagues, where the king of the Greeks named Antiochos dwells, and to the north of that Antiochos [where dwell] the four kings named severally Ptolemy, Antigonos, Magas, and Alexander [likewise] in the south, the Cholas and Pandyas as far as the Tamraparni [river] and here, too, in the King's dominions among the Greeks, Kambojas, the Nabhapantis of Nabhaka; among the Bhojas, Pitinikas; -ndhras, and Pulindas everywhere they follow the instruction of His Sacred Majesty in the Law of Piety.

Even where the envoys of His Sacred Majesty do not penetrate, these people, too, hearing His Sacred Majesty's ordinance based upon the Law of Piety and his instruction in that Law, practise and will practise the Law.

And, again, the conquest thereby won everywhere is everywhere a conquest full of delight. Delight is won in the conquests of the Law. A small matter, however, is that delight. His Sacred Majesty regards as bearing much fruit only that which concerns the other world.

And for this purpose has this scripture of the Law been recorded, in order that my sons and grandsons, who may be, may not think it their duty to conquer a new conquest.

If, perchance, a conquest should please them (?) they should take heed only of patience and gentleness, and regard as a conquest only that which is effected by the Law of Piety. That avails for both this world and the next. Let all their joy be that which lies in effort; that avails for both this world and the next.'

EDICT XIV

EPILOGUE

'This scripture of the Law of Piety has been written by command of His Sacred Majesty the King, [in a form] sometimes condensed, sometimes of medium length, and sometimes expanded; and everything is not brought together everywhere. For great is my dominion, and much has been written, and much shall I cause to be written.

And certain phrases have been uttered again and again by reason of the honeyed sweetness of this topic or that, in the hope that the people may act accordingly. It may be that something may have been written incompletely by reason of mutilation of a passage, or of misunderstanding, or by a blunder of the writer.'

3rd century BCE

48. The Han Feizi

Translated by Wenkui Liao

The Han Feizi, named for its author, is a work of political philosophy of the Legalist tradition. Indeed, some consider it to be the definitive statement of Legalism. Han Feizi (281–233 BCE) successfully synthesized the ideas of Shang Yang (see reading #41), Shen Buhai, and Shen Dao into a single system, which was used successfully by Li Si, prime minister of the state of Qin under Shi Huang Di. Han Feizi was also greatly influenced by his former teacher, the Confucian philosopher Xunzi, who had a negative view of human nature.

Chapter XLIX

FIVE VERMIN
A PATHOLOGICAL ANALYSIS OF POLITICS
In the age of remote antiquity, human beings were few while birds and beasts were many. Mankind being unable to overcome birds, beasts, insects, and serpents, there appeared a sage who made nests by putting pieces of wood together to shelter people from harm. Thereat the people were so delighted that they made him ruler of All-under-Heaven and called him the Nest-Dweller. In those days the people lived on the fruits of trees and seeds of grass as well as mussels and clams, which smelt rank and fetid and hurt the digestive organs. As many of them were affected with diseases, there appeared a sage who twisted a drill to make fire which changed the fetid and musty smell. Thereat the people were so delighted that they made him ruler of All-under-Heaven.

In the age of middle antiquity, there was a great deluge in All-under-Heaven, wherefore Gun[1] and Yü opened channels for the water. In the age of recent

---

1 Yü 's father. He was appointed by Yao to control the Great Flood.

antiquity, Jie and Zhou were violent and turbulent, wherefore T'ang and Wu overthrew them.

Now, if somebody fastened the trees or turned a drill in the age of the Xiahou Clan, he would certainly be ridiculed by Gun and Yü. Again, if somebody opened channels for water in the age of the Yin and Zhou Dynasties, he would certainly be ridiculed by T'ang and Wu. That being so, if somebody in the present age praises the ways of Yao, Shun, Gun, Yü, T'ang, and Wu, he would, no doubt, be ridiculed by contemporary sages.

That is the reason why the sage neither seeks to follow the ways of the ancients nor establishes any fixed standard for all times but examines the things of his age and then prepares to deal with them.

There was in Song a man, who tilled a field in which there stood the trunk of a tree. Once a hare, while running fast, rushed against the trunk, broke its neck, and died. Thereupon the man cast his plough aside and watched that tree, hoping that he would get another hare. Yet he never caught another hare and was himself ridiculed by the people of Song. Now supposing somebody wanted to govern the people of the present age with the policies of the early kings, he would be doing exactly the same thing as that man who watched the tree.

In olden times, men did not need to till, for the seeds of grass and the fruits of trees were sufficient to feed them; nor did women have to weave, for the skins of birds and beasts were sufficient to clothe them. Thus, without working hard, they had an abundance of supply. As the people were few, their possessions were more than sufficient. Therefore the people never quarrelled. As a result, neither large rewards were bestowed nor were heavy punishments employed, but the people governed themselves. Nowadays, however, people do not regard five children as many. Each child may in his or her turn beget five offspring, so that before the death of the grandfather there may be twenty-five grand-children. As a result, people have become numerous and supplies scanty; toil has become hard and provisions meager. Therefore people quarrel so

much that, though rewards are doubled and punishments repeated, disorder is inevitable.

When Yao was ruling All-under-Heaven, his thatched roof was untrimmed and his beam unplanned. He ate unpolished grain and made soup of coarse greens and wore deerskin garments in winter and rough fibre-cloth in summer. Even the clothes and provisions of a gate-keeper were not more scanty than his. When Yü was ruling All-under-Heaven, he led the people with plough and spade in hands, till his thighs had no down and his shins grew no hair. Even the toil of a prisoner of war was not more distressful than his. Speaking from this viewpoint, indeed, he who abdicated the throne of the Son of Heaven in favour of others in olden times, was simply forsaking the living of a gate-keeper and the toil of a prisoner of war. Therefore the inheritance of All-under-Heaven in olden days was not very great. Yet the prefect of today, upon the day of his death, hands down luxurious chariots to his descendants from generation to generation. Accordingly people think much of his position.

Thus, in the matter of leaving office, men make light of resigning from the ancient dignity of the Son of Heaven and consider it hard to quit the present post of a prefect. Really it is the difference between meagerness and abundance.

Indeed, those who dwell in the mountains and draw water from the valleys, give water to each other on the occasion of festivals; those who live in swamps hire men to open channels for the water. Likewise, in the spring of famine years men do not even feed their infant brothers, while in the autumn of abundant years even strange visitors are always well fed. Not that men cut off their blood-relations and love passers-by, but that the feelings are different in abundance and in scarcity. For the same reason, men of yore made light of goods, not because they were benevolent, but because goods were abundant; while men of today quarrel and pillage, not because they are brutish, but because goods are scarce. Again, men of yore made light of resigning from the dignity of the Son of Heaven, not because their personalities were noble, but because the power of the Son of Heaven was scanty; while men of today make much of fighting for office in government, not because their personalities are mean, but because the powers of the posts are great. Therefore the sage, considering quantity and deliberating upon scarcity and abundance, governs accordingly. So it is no charity to inflict light punishments nor is it any cruelty to enforce severe penalties: the practice is simply in accordance with the custom of the age. Thus, circumstances change with the age and measures change according to circumstances.

Of old, King Wen, located between Feng and Hao, in a territory of one hundred square li, practised benevolence and righteousness and won the affection of the Western Barbarians, till he finally became ruler of All-under-Heaven. King Yan of Xu, located to the east of the Han River in a territory of five hundred square li, practised benevolence and righteousness, till the states that ceded their territories and paid tributary visits to his court numbered thirty-six. King Wen of Jing, fearing lest King Yan should do him harm, raised armies, attacked Xu, and finally destroyed it. Thus, King Wen practising benevolence and righteousness became ruler of All-under-Heaven, while King Yan practising benevolence and righteousness lost his state. Evidently benevolence and righteousness once serviceable in olden times are not so at present. Hence the saying: "There are as many situations as there are generations." In the time of Shun the Miao tribes disobeyed. When Yu moved to send an expedition against them, Shun said: "By no means. As our De is not great, any resort to arms is not in accord with the Dao." Thenceforth for three years he cultivated the ways of civic training and then he made a parade of shields and battle-axes, whereupon the Miao tribes submitted. In a subsequent age, during the war with the Gun-kung tribes men using short iron weapons hardly reached their enemies while those whose armour was not strong suffered bodily injuries. It means that mere parade with shields and battle-axes once effective m olden times is not so at present.

Hence the saying: "Situations differ, so measures change."

Men of remote antiquity strove to be known as moral and virtuous; those of the middle age struggled to be known as wise and resourceful; and now men fight for the reputation of being vigorous and powerful. When Qi was about to attack Lu, Lu sent Zigong to dissuade Qi. To the peace envoy the spokesman of Qi said: "Your speech is not ineloquent. But what we want is territory, and that is not what you are talking about."[2] In the end Qi raised armies, invaded Lu, and settled the inter-state boundary at ten li from the city-gate of the capital of Lu.

Thus, although King Yan was benevolent and righteous, Xu went to ruin; although Zigong was benevolent and righteous, Lu was dismembered. From such a viewpoint, indeed, benevolence, righteousness, eloquence, and intelligence, are not instruments to maintain the state. If the benevolence of King Yan were put aside and the intelligence of Zigong extinguished, and if the forces of Xu and Lu were exerted, they could resist the powers of ten thousand chariots. Then the ambitions of Qi and Jing could never be accomplished in those two states.

Thus, we see that ancients and moderns have different customs, new and old have different measures. To govern with generous and lenient regulations a people in imminent danger is the same as to drive wild horses without reins or slips. This is a calamity of ignorance.

In these days, the Literati[3] and the Mohists[4] all praise the early kings for practising impartial love for which the people revered them as parents. How do they know that was so? They say: "We know that was so because whenever the Minister of Punishment inflicted any penalty, the ruler would stop having music, and at the news of any capital punishment he

---

2   Zigong being a close follower of Confucius must have advanced moral arguments to dissuade Ch`i from attacking Lu.
3   the followers of Confucius.
4   the followers of Mozi.

would shed tears. This is the reason why we praise the early kings."

Indeed, from the proposition that if ruler and minister act, like father and son, there is always order, there can be inferred the judgment that there are no disorderly fathers and sons. It is human nature, however, that nobody is more affectionate than parents. If both parents reveal love to their children, and yet order is not always found in a family, then how could there be no disorder in a state even though the ruler deepens his love for the ministers? Since the early kings loved the people not more than parents love their children, and children do not always refrain from causing disturbance, how could the people so easily keep order?

Moreover, when a penalty was inflicted in accordance with the law, the ruler shed tears therefor. By so doing he intended to show his benevolence but not to do any good to political order. To shed bitter tears and to dislike penalties, is benevolence; to see the necessity of inflicting penalties, is law. Since the early kings held to the law and never listened to weeping, it is clear enough that benevolence cannot be applied to the attainment of political order.

Still further, the people are such as would be firmly obedient to authority, but are rarely able to appreciate righteousness. For illustration, Confucius, who was a sage of All-under-Heaven, cultivated virtuous conduct, exemplified the right way, and travelled about within the seas; but those within the seas who talked about his benevolence and praised his righteousness and avowed discipleship to him, were only seventy. For to honour benevolence was rare and to practise righteousness was hard. Notwithstanding the vastness of All-under-Heaven, those who could become his avowed disciples, were only seventy, and there was only one person really benevolent and righteous—Confucius himself! Contrary to this, Duke Ai of Lu, inferior ruler as he was, when he faced the south and ruled the state, found nobody among the people within the boundary daring disobedience. This was because the people are by nature obedient to authority. As by exercising authority it is easy to lord it over people, Confucius remained minister while Duke Ai continued on the throne. Not that Confucius appreciated the righteousness of Duke Ai but that he submitted to his authority. Therefore, on the basis of righteousness Confucius would not have yielded to Duke Ai, but by virtue of authority Duke Ai did lord it over Confucius! Now, the learned men of today, when they counsel the Lord of Men, assert that if His Majesty applied himself to the practice of benevolence and righteousness instead of making use of victory-ensuring authority, he would certainly become ruler of All-under-Heaven. This is simply to require every lord of men to come up to the level of Confucius and all the common people of the world to act like his disciples. It is surely an ineffectual measure.

Now suppose there is a boy who has a bad character. His parents are angry at him, but he never makes any change. The villagers in the neighbourhood reprove him, but he is never thereby moved. His masters teach him, but he never reforms. Thus with all the three excellent disciplines, the love of his parents, the conduct of the villagers, and the wisdom of the masters, applied to him, he makes no change, not even a hair on his shins is altered. It is, however, only after the district-magistrate sends out soldiers in accordance with the law to search for wicked men that he becomes afraid and changes his ways and alters his deeds. So the love of parents is not sufficient to educate children. But if it is necessary to have the severe penalties of the district-magistrate come at all, it is because people are naturally spoiled by love and obedient to authority.

Thus, over a city-wall forty feet[5] high, even Louji[6] could not pass, for it is steep; but on a mountain four thousand feet high even crippled she-goats can easily graze, for it is flat-topped.[7] For the same reason the intelligent king makes his laws strict and his punish-

---

5 One *jên* is about four feet long.

6 A younger brother of Marquis Wên of Wey, known to be a good athlete.

7 Thus, a good athlete can not pass over a steep wall, but crippled she-goats can easily graze on a flat-topped mountain.

ments severe. Again, where there is a piece of cloth eight[8] or sixteen[9] feet long, common people would not give it up, but where there is molten gold two thousand pounds in weight, even Robber Zhi would not pick it up. Thus, if no harm at all should come to them, people would not give up eight or sixteen feet of cloth; but if their hands would always be hurt, they would never dare to pick up even two hundred pounds of molten gold. Therefore, the intelligent ruler makes his punishments definite.

That being so, rewards should not be other than great and certain, thus making the people regard them as profitable; punishments should not be other than severe and definite, thus making the people comprehend them. Consequently, if the ruler in bestowing rewards makes no change and in carrying out punishments grants no pardon, but adds honour to rewards and disgrace to punishments, then both the worthy and the unworthy will exert their efforts.

That is not true at present. On the one hand, ranks are conferred for meritorious services; but on the other, official careers are scorned. Rewards are bestowed for diligent tillage, but hereditary occupations[10] are slighted. Whoever declines appointment to office is shunned, but his contempt for worldly affairs is esteemed. Whoever transgresses prohibitions is convicted, but his boldness is admired. Thus there are nowadays opposed to each other the objectives of honour and disgrace as well as of reward and punishment. Small wonder laws and interdicts are ruined and the people are becoming more and more violent.

Now, he who would always fall on the enemy when his brother is attacked, is called upright; he who would always resent an. insult to his good friend, is called pure. Yet once these deeds of uprightness and purity are done, the law of the ruler is violated. In case the lord of men esteems such deeds of uprightness and purity and forgets the crime violating his prohibitions, the people will be honoured according to their boldness and the magistrates will be unable to control them. Again, he who gets clothes and food without working hard, is called capable; he who gets honours without rendering any meritorious service in war, is called worthy. Yet once the deeds of capability and worthiness are done, the army will become weak and the land will be waste. If the Lord of Men is delighted at such deeds of worthiness and capability and forgets the calamities of the army in decline and the land in waste, then private advantage will prevail and public welfare will come to naught.

The literati by means of letters disturbed laws, the cavaliers by means of weapons transgressed prohibitions. Yet the lord of men respects them both. That is the reason why disorder prevails. Indeed, every departure from laws ought to be condemned, but all the professors are taken into office on account of their literary learning. Again, every transgression of prohibitions ought to be punished, but all cavaliers are accorded patronage because of their private swords.[11] Thus, what the law prohibits is what the ruler himself recognizes; what the magistrate punishes is what the sovereign himself maintains. Thus legal standard and personal inclination are in conflict. Without any fixed standard, however, even ten Yellow Emperors would not be able to rule. Therefore, those who practise benevolence and righteousness, should not be praised; for, if praised, they would damage meritorious achievements. Again, those who specialize in refinement and learning, should not be employed; for, if employed, they would confuse the law of the state.

Of old, there was in the Ch'u State a man named Qigong. Once his father stole a sheep, wherefore he reported to the authorities. Thereupon the prefect said, "Put him to death", as he thought the man was loyal to the ruler but undutiful to his father. So that

Likewise, great robbers dare not violate strict laws, but common people would dare to disregard laws that are lenient.

8 One *hsin* is about eight feet long.

9 One *ch'ang* re; is about sixteen feet long.

10 Such as farming and spinning, which were handed down from generation to generation.

11 The cavaliers were known for their courage in using their swords.

man was tried and executed. From this it can be seen that the honest subject of the ruler was an outrageous son of his father.

Again, there was a man of Lu, who followed the ruler to war, fought three battles, and ran away thrice. When Confucius asked him his reason, he replied: "I have an old father. Should I die, nobody would take care of him." So Confucius regarded him as a man of filial piety, praised him, and exalted him. From this it can be seen that the dutiful son of the father was a rebellious subject of the ruler. Naturally, following the punishment of the honest man by the prefect, no other culprit in Ch'u was ever reported to the authorities and after the reward of the runaway by Confucius, the people of Lu were apt to surrender and run away. The interests of superior and inferior are thus so different that it is certainly impossible to expect the Lord of Men both to praise the deed of the common man and to promote the welfare of the Altar of the Spirits of Land and Grain.

In olden times, when Cangjie invented the system of writing, he assigned the element "self-centered" to the character "private"; and combined the elements, "opposite to" and "private" to form the character "public". The contradiction between "public" and "private" was thus from the beginning well understood by Cangjie. To regard them both as having identical interest at the present time, is a calamity of thoughtlessness.

That being so, speaking of the common man, there comes first the cultivation of benevolence and righteousness and then the practice of refinement and learning. Having cultivated benevolence and righteousness, he will get office. Having practised refinement and learning, he will become an erudite teacher. Having become an erudite teacher, he will become celebrated for his honours. This is the ideal career of the common man. However, it may be that with no merit one gets office, with no rank one becomes celebrated for one's honours. If there be any government like this, the state will certainly be in chaos and the lord in peril.

Therefore, incompatible things do not coexist. For instance, to reward those who kill their enemies in battle, and at the same time to esteem deeds of mercy and generosity; to reward with ranks and bounties those who capture enemy cities, and at the same time to believe in the theory of impartial love; to improve armour and encourage warriors as provisions against emergencies, and at the same time to admire the ornaments of the robes and girdles of the civil gentry; to depend upon the farmers for enriching the state and upon the warriors for resisting the enemies, and at the same time to honour the men of letters; and to neglect the men who respect the superior and revere the law, and at the same time to maintain gangs of wandering cavaliers and self-seeking swordsmen: out of such incompatible acts, how can a state attain order and strength? When the state is at peace, literati and cavaliers are supported; once an emergency arises, armed officers are taken into service. Thus, the privileged are not used; the used are not privileged. For this reason, men who ought to attend to public affairs neglect their duties, while wandering scholars daily increase in numbers. This is the reason why the age is full of chaos.

Moreover, what the age calls "worthy" consists of merciful and faithful deeds; what it calls "wise" consists of subtle and mysterious words. Such subtle and mysterious words are hard even for the wisest men to understand. Now, if you set up laws for the masses in such terms as are hard for the wisest men to understand, then the people will find no way to comprehend them. Just as men who find not even coarse rice to fill them would not think of wine and meat, and just as those who have not even rags to wear would not think of silk and embroidered garments, in governing the world, if one is not able to settle affairs of the most urgent need, one should pay no attention to things short of great urgency. Now most of the affairs to be administered are ordinary civil cases. Yet not to use standards that ordinary men and women plainly understand, but to long for those theories which even the wisest do not comprehend; that certainly is the negation of government.

Therefore subtle and mysterious words are no business of the people.

Indeed, men who regard deeds of mercy and faithfulness as worthy will naturally honour gentlemen who are not deceitful, but those that honour gentlemen who are not deceitful might have no means to escape deception. The commoners, in cultivating friendships, have neither wealth to benefit each other nor influence to terrify each other. Naturally they seek for gentlemen who are not deceitful. Now the Lord of Men avails himself of his position to control men and possesses the wealth of a state. If he makes rewards large and punishments severe and thereby succeeds in holding his handles to improve points illuminated by his brilliant policies, then ministers like Tian Chang and Zihan, wicked as they were, would not dare to deceive him, not to mention gentlemen who are not deceitful. Now there are not more than ten truly merciful and faithful men in this country, whereas there are hundreds of official posts. So if only merciful and faithful men are selected for public service, the candidates will not be sufficient for filling all the official posts. In that case, those who maintain order would be few while disturbers would abound. Therefore, the way of the enlightened lord is to unify laws instead of seeking for wise men, to solidify policies instead of yearning after faithful persons. In consequence, as long as laws do not fail to function, the body of officials will practise neither villainy nor deception.

In these days, the lord of men, as regards speeches, is delighted at their eloquence but does not seek for their consequences,[12] and, as regards the utility of deeds, admires their fame but does not strictly check over their accomplishments. For this reason, the people of All-under-Heaven, when making speeches, strive for eloquence but do not care for actual usefulness. As a result, men who quote the early kings and preach benevolence and righteousness, fill up the court, wherefore the government can not be freed from disorder. Men who devote themselves to practical deeds struggle for eminence, but do not bring about any meritorious service. Small wonder wise men retire to dwell in rocky caves, decline all bounties, and refuse to accept any offer; while soldiers are not immune from degeneration and the government is not freed from chaos. What is the reason for this? It is this: in what the people revere and what the sovereign respects, lies the cause of disturbing the state.

Now the people within the boundary all talk about political order, and, though in every family there are men who preserve copies of the Laws of Shang Yang and Guan Zhong, yet the state is becoming poorer and poorer. This is because many talk about tillage but few take up the plough. Again, everybody within the boundary talks about strategy, and, though in every family there are men who preserve copies of the Books of Sun Wu and Wu Qi, yet the army is becoming weaker and weaker. This is because many talk about warfare but few put on armour.

Therefore, the enlightened sovereign uses his men's strength but does not listen to their words, rewards them for their meritorious services but always eliminates the useless. The people, accordingly, exert themselves to the point of death in obeying the sovereign.

Indeed, tillage requires physical force, and is toil. But the people who perform it say, "Through it we can become wealthy." Again, warfare, as a matter of fact, involves risks. But the people who wage it say, "Through it we can become noble." Now, if those who cultivate refinement and learning and practise persuasion and eloquence get the fruits of wealth without the toil of tillage, and gain the honour of nobility with no risk in warfare, then who will not do the same? Naturally, one hundred men will attend to "wisdom" while only one man will exert physical energy. If men who attend to "wisdom" are many,

---

12 Han Feizi's theory of truth is very similar to the modern pragmatic theory. A name is true only if the fact it connotes actually exists; a word is true only if the deed it purports is equivalent to it; and a task is true only if the result of its function comes up to its expected level and not beyond the level. The "consequence theory" of truth thus stands in sharp contrast with both the "coherence" and the "correspondence" theories.

the law will go for naught; if men who exert physical energy are few, the state will fall into poverty. That is the reason why the world is in chaos.

Therefore, in the state of the enlightened sovereign there is no literature written on bamboo slips, but the law is the only teaching; there are no quoted sayings of the early kings, but the magistrates are the only instructors; there is no valour through private swords, but slaughter of the enemy is the only courageous deed. As a result, the people, within the boundary, when practising persuasion and eloquence, always conform to the law; when up and doing, they always aim at meritorious services; and when pretending to valour, they always exert themselves in the army. Therefore, in time of peace the state is rich; in time of emergency the army is strong. Such is what they call the resources of the ruler. Having stored up the resources of the ruler, the sovereign waits for the enemy state to reach an unguarded moment. Those who have surpassed the Five Emperors and have rivalled the Three Kings, have always followed this method.

The same is not true in these days, however. Inside, the gentry and the commoners do as they please; outside, eloquent speakers create their own favourable circumstances. If both foreign and home affairs alike are bad, is it not dangerous for the ruler to confront strong enemies? It is so particularly because the ministers who speak on foreign affairs either side with the advocates of the Perpendicular Union or the Horizontal Alliance, or have personal hatred for foreign states and want to utilize the forces of the native state. Now, neither the Perpendicular Union aiming to attack a single strong state by uniting all the weak ones, nor the Horizontal Alliance aiming to attack the weak ones by serving a single strong state, is a policy to maintain the existence and prosperity of a state.

Now, ministers who speak about the Horizontal Alliance, all say: "If we do not serve a big power, we will have enemies and suffer disasters." To serve a big power, however, always requires material concessions. Wherefore they must entrust their whole territory to the strong state and put their own state seal in pawn for military help. If territorial concessions are offered, the land will be cut off; if the state seal is handed over, the prestige will be impaired. When the land is cut off, the state will be dismembered; when the prestige is impaired, the government will fall into chaos. Thus, before actualizing the benefit from serving a big power forming the Horizontal Alliance, the land is already dismembered and the government disordered.

Again, ministers who speak about the Perpendicular Union, all say: "If we do not save small states and attack big powers, we will lose the favour of All-under-Heaven. If we lose the favour of All-under-Heaven, our state will fall into peril. If our state falls into peril, our lord will fall into contempt." To save small states, however, always requires material sacrifices, wherefore you must mobilize armies and oppose big powers. Yet when you start to save a small state, you are not always able to preserve it; when you oppose a big power, you can not always be sure that there is no discord between you and your allies. If there is any such discord at all, you will be dominated by the big power. As soon as you send out reinforcements, the whole army will be defeated. Before you turn back to assume the defensive, the city will have fallen into the hands of the enemies. Thus, before you get the benefit of saving the small state and thereby form the Perpendicular Union, your land is already occupied and your troops defeated.

For this reason, he who insists on serving the strong state really means to hold his office through foreign influence; he who insists on saving the small state, really means to seek advantage abroad by virtue of his prestige at home. Before the state is benefited, the ministers have got estates and high emoluments. Thus, though the sovereign falls into contempt, the ministers are honoured; though the land of the state is cut off, their own families have become wealthy. If their projects succeed, they will become mighty in authority; if their projects fail, they will retire from active life with riches in their pockets.

However, such is the usual way the Lord of Men listens to tile proposals of his ministers that before their projects are successful, their ranks and bounties are already exalted. And, if they are not punished when their projects fail, who can be sure that the itinerant gentlemen are not going to display their irresponsible sophistries elsewhere and count on unexpected good fortune? Nevertheless, why is heed paid to such frivolous ideas of the persuasive politicians as would break the state and ruin the lord? That is because the Lord of Men never distinguishes between public and private benefits, never scrutinizes whether the ideas are true or false, and never definitely enforces censure and punishment.

The itinerants all say, "Success in foreign relations at its best can help the prince become ruler of All-under-Heaven or, at least, can make the state secure." Indeed, the ruler of All-under-Heaven must be able to attack others. If secure, he can not be attacked by others. If strong, he is able to attack others. If in order, he can not be attacked by others. Accordingly, order and strength should not be dependent upon external factors: both depend upon internal administration. Now, if the sovereign does not carry out his laws and policies at home but counts on the wise men's services abroad, order and strength will not be attained.

There is a common saying: "Wearers of long sleeves are skilful in dancing; possessors of much money are skilful in trading." It means that people who are resourceful acquire skill very easily. Accordingly, in the state that is orderly and strong it is easy to devise schemes, but in the state that is weak and chaotic it is hard to make any plan at all. For illustration, the schemes adopted by Qin, though changed ten times, rarely fail; whereas any plan adopted by Yan, once changed, rarely succeeds. Not that whatever Qin adopts is always clever and whatever Yan adopts is always stupid, but that the factors of order and chaos are different.

Thus, Zhou quit Qin and joined the Perpendicular Union only to be taken within a year; and Wei left Wey for the Horizontal Alliance only to be ruined in half a year. This means that Zhou was destroyed by the Perpendicular Union while Wei was ruined by the Horizontal Alliance. Supposing Zhou and Wei postponed their plans to join the Perpendicular Union and the Horizontal Alliance and strictly improved the political order within their boundaries, made their laws and interdicts clear, made their rewards and punishments definite, utilized their natural resources to increase provisions, and constrained their peoples even to the point of death in strengthening the defensive preparations of the city-walls; then All-under-Heaven would find little gain in occupying their lands and great harm in attacking their states, so that even a state of ten thousand chariots would not dare to come to camp beneath their well-fortified city-walls and expose its weaknesses to the attack of strong enemies. This is the way to escape destruction. To abandon this way of escaping destruction and to follow the road to inevitable ruin is the fault of the governor of the state. With wisdom exhausted abroad and politics disordered at home, no state can be saved from ruin.

The plan of the people for themselves is to seek only for security and profit and to avoid danger and poverty. Now, if you force them to attack and fight, they face death at the hands of enemies at the front, and death through official punishment at the rear. That is peril, indeed! Again, they have to abandon their own domestic affairs and undergo the toil of military service.[13] In the long run their households are reduced to poverty. Yet the ruler takes no notice of it. That is destitution, indeed! Wherever lie destitution and danger, how can the people do other than shun them? Naturally they would frequent the gates of the private residences of influential men so as to exempt themselves from military service. If exempted from military service, they keep aloof from warfare. If aloof from warfare, they can remain in safety. Again, if they can by virtue of bribes approach the authorities concerned, they get what they want. If they get what they want, they have profit and

---

13 literally means "such toil as would make the horse perspire".

security. Wherever lie security and profit, how can the people do other than crowd in? Hence, citizens in public service are few but private proteges are numerous.

Indeed, the enlightened king so administers his state as to diminish the number of tradesmen, craftsmen, and idlers, and to lower their names in order to incline their minds to primary callings and to lessen their interest in secondary occupations. In the present age, if the requests of the courtiers prevail at all, then office and rank can be purchased. If office and rank are purchasable, tradesmen and craftsmen, as they have money, will no longer be low in status. If forged money and faked articles can circulate at the market-place, traders will no longer fall short of demands and supplies. If the profits they make thereby are twice as much as by farming and the honours they get thereby surpass those of tillers and warriors, men of firm integrity and strong character will become few while merchants and tradesmen will increase in number.

For such reasons, it is a common trait of the disorderly state that its learned men adore the ways of the early kings by pretending to benevolence and righteousness and adorn their manners and clothes and gild their eloquent speeches so as to cast doubts on the law of the present age and thereby, beguile the mind of the lord of men; that its itinerant speakers advocate deceptive theories and utilize foreign influence to accomplish their self-seeking purposes at the expense of their Altar of the Spirits of Land and Grain; that wearers of private swords gather pupils and dependents and set up standards of self-discipline and fidelity with a view to cultivating their fame but thereby violate the interdicts of the Five Ministries[14]; that the courtiers assemble inside the gates of private residences, use all kinds of bribes, and rely on influential men's access to the sovereign in order to escape the burden of military service; and that the tradesmen and craftsmen disguise worthless, broken articles as proper goods, collect useless luxuries, accumulate riches, wait for good opportunities, and exploit the farmers. These five types of men are the vermin of the state. Should the Lord of Men fail to get rid of such people as the five vermin and should he not patronize men of firm integrity and strong character, it would be no wonder at all if within the seas there should be states breaking up in ruin and dynasties waning and perishing.

---

14 The Ministries of War, of Instruction, of Revenue, of Public Works, and of Justice.

Think about it.

1. Does Han Fei agree with those who believe that the teachings of past sages should apply to the present time? Why or why not?
2. According to Han Fei, how should a legal system be structured?
3. What similarities do you see between the teachings of Shang Yang and Han Fei?

The Middle Classical Period
(200 BCE–200 CE)

Cavalryman (Early Han Dynasty)

Middle Classical Period

B.C.E / C.E.	1000	1	100	200
Central America	Zapotec Civilization			
		Teotihuacan		
South America				Moche Culture
Mediterranean	Roman Republic		Roman Empire	
Northeast Africa	Kingdom of the Ptolemies			
East Africa	Meroë			Aksum
West Asia	Parthian Empire			
Central Asia	Indo-Greek Kingdoms		Kushan Empire	
South Asia	Satavahana Empire			
East Asia	Early Han Dynasty		Later Han Dynasty	

49. Luxuriant Dew of the Spring and Autumn Annals

Translated by Derk Bodde

Known in Chinese as *Chūnqiū Fánlù*, the Luxuriant Dew of the Spring and Autumn Annals is a commentary on a much older work, the Spring and Autumn Annals, which was an official chronicle of the Chinese state of Lu covering the years 722 to 479 BCE. In later times it was thought to have been written by Confucius (it wasn't) and so became one of the "Five Classics" of Confucianism studied at university in the early Han period (206 BCE–8 CE). The Luxuriant Dew was written at that time. It has traditionally been ascribed to Dong Zhongshu (old spelling, Tung Chung-shu), a Confucian scholar who lived c. 179–104 BCE and who was instrumental in making Confucianism the official ideology of the Han state. The work, however, appears to be the product of several hands, and whether one or not of these is Dong Zhongshu is not known for certain. Many ideas contained within it, however, appear to have been held by him. What follows are some excerpts.

"According to a rough classification, when things in Heaven and Earth undergo abnormal changes, these are called 'prodigies'; lesser ones are called Visitations.' Visitations always appear first and are then followed by prodigies. Visitations are the reprimands of Heaven; prodigies are its warnings. If (man), being thus reprimanded, still fails to understand, he is then made to feel awe through such warnings. When the *Odes* (IV, i, Ode 7) says: 'Stand in awe of Heaven's warnings,' it probably refers to this. The source of all such visitations and prodigies lies in faults that exist within the nation. Heaven sends forth fearful visitations in order to announce its reprimand. If, being thus reprimanded, (man) fails to understand (the reason for) these manifestations, strange prodigies then appear in order to strike him with terror. And if, being thus terrified, he still does not understand (the cause for) his fear, only then do misfortunes and calamities overtake him. From this may be seen the goodness of Heaven's purpose and its unwillingness to bring ruin upon man" (8. 24).

"If now water be poured on level ground, it will avoid the parts that are dry and move toward those that are wet. Whereas if (two) identical pieces of firewood are exposed to fire, the latter will avoid the one that is wet and catch to that which is dry. All things avoid that from which they differ and cleave to that to which they are similar. Thus forces that are similar meet each other, and tones that match respond to each other. Experience makes this evident. For suppose (two) lutes are played in alternation to each other. If the note of *kung* is struck on the one, that of *kung* will respond on the other, and if the note of *shang* is struck on the one, that of *shang* will respond on the other. Among the five notes, each one that matches sounds of itself. There is nothing supernatural in this. It is because of their numerical (harmonies). (Likewise) a thing that is beautiful will call to itself another beautiful thing the same in kind,

Fung Yu-lan, *A History of Chinese Philosophy, Volume II: The Period of Classical Learning (From the Second Century B.C. to the Twentieth Century A.D.)*, trans. Derk Bodde, pp. 55–58. Copyright © 1983 by Princeton University Press. Reprinted with permission.

whereas an ugly thing will call to itself another ugly thing the same in kind. For example, when a horse neighs, another horse will respond; when an ox lows, another ox will respond. In the same way, when an emperor or king is about to arise, auspicious omens first appear, whereas when he is about to be destroyed, evil auguries likewise first appear. Thus it is that things of the same kind call to one another. ...

"Heaven possesses the *yin* and *yang* and man also possesses the *yin* and *yang*. When the *yin* ether of the universe arises, man's *yin* ether likewise arises in response. And vice versa, when man's *yin* ether arises, the *yin* ether of the universe should arise in harmonious response. Their course is one. He who understands this, when he wishes to bring rain, activates the (human) *yin* in order to arouse the *yin* (of the universe); when he wishes to stop rain, activates the (human) *yang* in order to arouse the *yang* (of the universe). Therefore the bringing of rain is not a supernatural matter, though its principle, abstruse and wonderful, resembles the supernatural. It is not solely the *yin* and *yang* ethers which thus approach and withdraw according to their kind. The generation of inauspicious misfortune or of good fortune also proceeds in the same way. It is nothing but a case in which, when one begins something oneself, things act in response according to their kind" (13. 4-6).

"Man causes the myriad things to grow below, and equates himself with Heaven and Earth above. Therefore, as a result of his good or disorderly government, the forces of activity or of calm, of compliance or of contrariness, act either to diminish or increase the transformations of the *yin* and *yang* and to agitate all within the four seas. Even in the case of things difficult to understand, such as the supernatural, it may not be said to be otherwise. Thus then, if (something) is thrown onto (hard) ground, it is (itself) injured and destroyed and causes no movement in the latter; if thrown into soft mire, it causes movement within a limited distance; if thrown into water, it causes movement over a greater distance. Thus we may see that the softer a thing is, the more readily does it undergo movement and agitation. The transforming ether is much softer than water (or the other things here mentioned); yet the ruler of men ever acts upon all of them without surcease. This is why the influences of government are constantly becoming maladjusted in respect to the transforming influences of Heaven and Earth, with the result that there is no good government.

"Therefore when the human world is well governed and the people are at peace, or when the will (of the ruler) is equable and his character is correct, then the transforming influences of Heaven and Earth operate in a state of perfection and among the myriad things only the finest are produced. But when the human world is in disorder and the people become perverse, or when the (ruler's) will is depraved and his character is rebellious, then the transforming influences of Heaven and Earth suffer injury, so that their (*yin* and *yang*) ethers generate visitations and harm arises" (17. 7).

Think about it.

1. How, according to the author, does Heaven send warnings and why?
2. How does he try to show the reasonableness of his conclusions?

50. Records of the Grand Historian

Translated by Herbert J. Allen

Commonly called *Shiji* in Chinese ("Historical Records"), the Records of the Grand Historian is a groundbreaking work of Chinese narrative history. Written by Sima Qian (old spelling—Szu-ma Chien) (c. 135–86 BCE), who served the emperor Wu of the early Han dynasty as Prefect of the Grand Scribes, it is the first Chinese history that was written with the intention to be objective and to use primary source material. This is not to say it always succeeds in being objective (no history does), but it differs greatly from previous narratives, which show their biases proudly. The history begins in the mythical past (which Sima Qian takes to be historical) and ends in the author's own time. It was likely written between 109 and 91 BCE. The following excerpt concerns the fall of the Shang dynasty and the rise of the Zhou.

Emperor Yi died, and his son Xin sat on the throne. Emperor Xin was called by everybody in the empire Zhou (the tyrant). Emperor Zhou's discrimination was acute, his hearing and sight particularly good, his natural abilities extraordinary, and his physical strength equal to that of a wild beast. He had cunning enough to evade reproofs, and volubility enough to gloss over his faults. He boasted that he was above his ministers on the ground of ability, and that he surpassed the people of the empire on account of his reputation. He indulged in wine, women, and lusts of all sorts. His partiality for Daji[1] caused him to carry out whatever she desired, so that his ministers had to devise new forms of dissipation, the most depraved dances and extravagant music; he increased the taxation in order to fill the Stag tower with money, and to store the granary at 'Big bridge.' He made a collection of dogs, horses, and curiosities, with which he filled his palaces; and enlarging his parks and towers at Shaqiu procured numbers of wild beasts and birds and put them therein. He slighted the spirits, assembled a great number of play actors at Shaqiu, made a pond of wine, hung the trees with meat, made men and women chase each other about quite naked, and had drinking bouts the whole night long. The people murmured, and when the nobles rebelled Zhou Xin increased the severity of his punishments, instituting the punishment of roasting. He appointed Ch'ang[2] Chief of the West, the prince of Jiu, and the prince of Ou his three principal ministers. The prince of Jiu had a beloved daughter who was sent in to the emperor, and when she disapproved of his debaucheries the tyrant killed her in his rage, and made mincemeat of her father. The prince of Ou objected, and vehemently remonstrated with him, whereupon he was sliced to pieces. Ch'ang Chief of the West, hearing of all this, sighed furtively,

---

1   His wife.

2   Ji Chang, later known as Wen. He is the father of King Wu, founder of the Zhou Dynasty.

but 'Tiger' the prince of Zhong, being aware of it, informed the tyrant, who thereupon cast Chief of the West into prison at Youli. His servant Hongyao and others procured a pretty girl, rare curiosities, and fine horses, which they presented to the tyrant, who thereupon pardoned Chief of the West. The latter went forth and gave the country to the west of the Lo river to the tyrant, and begged that he would abolish the punishment of roasting. The emperor agreed to this, and gave him bows, arrows, axes, and halberds, with a commission to start on a warlike expedition. He was appointed Chief of the West, and Feizhong was employed in the government. Feizhong was fond of flattery and greedy of gain, so the men of Yin were not attached to him. The tyrant also gave Alai an appointment, but Alai was fond of vilifying persons, so the princes became more and more estranged from the court. Now Chief of the West, on returning from his expedition, secretly cultivated virtue, and was charitable; many of the princes revolted from the tyrant and gave their allegiance to Chief of the West, who from this time gained in influence, while the tyrant rather lost his authority. The monarch's son Bi Gan remonstrated with his father, but he was not listened to. Shangrong praised his worth, and the people loved him, but the tyrant set him aside. Chief of the West marched against and conquered the Ji State, and the tyrant's minister "Zuyi" heard of it, and "blaming [the house of] Zhou hurried off in alarm to report it to the tyrant." "He said: 'Heaven is bringing to an end the destiny of our dynasty of Yin; great men and the ancient tortoise do not venture to foretell good fortune. It is not that the former kings do not aid us men of this later time; but you, O king, by your dissoluteness and oppression are cutting yourself off. Heaven has therefore rejected us; we do not eat our meals in peace, we do not consider our heavenly nature, we do not follow and observe the statutes. Our people are now all longing for the destruction of the dynasty, saying, Why does not Heaven send down its awe-inspiring authority? Why is not its great decree manifested? What remedy is there against the present king?' The tyrant said: 'Is

not my life secured by the decree of Heaven?' Zuyi returned, and said, 'The tyrant cannot be remonstrated with.' Chief of the West having died, King Wu of Zhou in his march eastward arrived at the ford of Mêng. The princes revolted, and 800 princes of the house of Zhou having assembled declared that the tyrant ought to be attacked. King Wu said, 'You know nothing of Heaven's decree,' and retired. The tyrant abandoned himself all the more to lust and dissipation, and the viscount of Wei_remonstrated with him several times, but he would not heed, so having consulted with the senior and junior tutors the viscount of Wei withdrew from court. Bi Gan said, 'A minister cannot but argue to the death'; he accordingly remonstrated vehemently with the tyrant, who in a rage said, 'I have heard that the heart of a holy man has seven apertures,' and cut Bi Gan open to look at his heart. The viscount of Ji, in terror, then feigned himself mad, and "became a slave," and the tyrant again imprisoned him. The senior and junior tutors of Yin, accordingly, taking the sacrificial and musical implements, hastened to the Zhou State, and King Wu of Zhou upon this marched at the head of the princes to attack the tyrant, who also sent out an army to withstand him in the plain of Mu. On the day Jiazi the tyrant's troops were beaten, and he himself fled to the Stag tower, which he ascended, and, putting on his gorgeous robes and jewels, burnt himself to death. King Wu of Zhou then cut off the tyrant's head and exhibited it on a pole; he also slew Daji, "released the viscount of Ji from prison, raised a tumulus over the grave of Bi Gan, and made a eulogy to the memory of Shangrong." His sons, Wugeng and Lüfu, were appointed to continue the sacrifices to the Yins. He restored Pankêng's mode of administration, and the people of Yin were greatly rejoiced. Whereupon King Wu of Zhou became Son of Heaven (emperor). His descendants abolished the title of Di (divine emperor), and called themselves kings (Wang); and the descendants of the Yins were made princes subordinate to the house of Zhou.

After the death of King Wu of Zhou, Wugeng, Guanshu, and Caishu rebelled. King Ch'eng ordered

the duke of Zhou to execute them, and the viscount
of Wei was established in the Song State to continue
(the ancestral worship as) a descendant of the Yins.

Think about it.

1. Why, according to Sima Qian, did emperor Zhou Xin of the Shang Dynasty lose the Mandate of Heaven?
2. How was King Wu of the Zhou Dynasty made the Son of Heaven in Zhou Xin's place?

1st century BCE

51. Discourses on Salt and Iron

Translated by Esson M. Gale

During the reign of the Han dynasty emperor Wu (141–87 BCE), the laissez-faire economic policies of the past were abandoned and the government intervened in the economy in a number of ways. One way was to nationalize the salt and iron industries, which resulted in huge revenues for the government. After his death, there were discussions about reversing Wu's policies. In the year 81 BCE, during the reign of emperor Zhao (87–74 BCE), a group of scholars were called to the capital to debate the matter. On one side stood the Confucian literati, who were pushing for reform. On the other side stood the Lord Grand Secretary, Daifu, who held certain Legalist ideals and preferred the existing policies. The Confucian literati came out on the winning side in the end and the state monopolies were deliberately weakened. A short time later, a bureaucrat-scholar named Huan Kuan reconstructed the debate and published it as Discourses on Salt and Iron *(Yan tie lun)*. We believe the reconstruction is historically accurate, since Huan Kuan consulted people who were actually present at the debate and participated in it. Here is an excerpt from that work, in which the Lord Grand Secretary and the Literati argue over the circulation of goods. It provides an interesting glimpse into the political thinking of the time and a good example of the way disputes were handled.

Huan Kuan, "Chapter III," *Discourses on Salt and Iron: A Debate on State Control of Commerce and Industry in Ancient China*, trans. Esson M. Gale, pp. 18–24. Copyright © 1931 by Estate of Esson M. Gale. Reprinted with permission.

CHAPTER III
The Circulation of Goods

a. The Lord Grand Secretary: Zuo and Ji of Tan, Handan of Zhao, Wen and Zhi of Wei, Ying Yang of Han, Linzi of Qi, Wanqiu of Chu, Yangzhai of Zheng, the two Zhou of Sanchuan, in riches surpassing all within the seas, are famous municipalities of the world. They are so not because there has been someone who has helped them to cultivate their country side and till their fields, but because they are situated on the intersecting routes of the five feudal states and sit astride the network of highways. In other words, where products abound, the people multiply; when the house is near the market, the family will get rich. Getting rich depends on 'methods' and 'statistical calculation', not on hard manual labor; profits depend on 'circumstances', not on strenuous farming.

b. The Literati: In Qingyang, there is the fertile land of Guilin to the south, the facilities of the rivers and the lakes within its borders, the gold of Ling Yang to the left and the timber supply of Shu and Han to the right. Forests were cut down in order to raise grain, and brush was burnt to give room for the sowing of millet. Through clearing by fire for farming and water-weeding, arable land was extended and natural resources were abundant. Thereupon evil habits of idleness imperceptibly grew up. People wear fine clothes and eat delicate food. Even in humble cottages and straw-thatched huts, we hear ballad-singing and playing on stringed instruments; wanton for a day, in want for a month, carolling in the morning, mourning in the evening. Zhao and Zhongshan border the great River; they form the connecting center of the radiating roads and are situated on the highway of the world. Merchants throng the ways. Princes meet on the streets. But the people's trend is to the non-essential pursuits. They grow luxurious, disregarding the fundamentals. The fields are not cultivated, while the men and women vie with one another in dress. Without a peck of reserve in the house, the lute thrums in

the hall. This is why of the people of Chu and Zhao most are poor and few rich. On the other hand, the people in Song, Wei, Han and Liang adhere to the fundamental and till the soil. Among the common people and yeomanry every house prospers and every person is satisfied. Therefore profit comes from care for one's self, not from favorable location on the highways. Riches come from thrift and labor at the right season and not from having supervising officials throughout the year and in increasing the display in the ceremonies.

c. The Lord Grand Secretary: According to the theory of the Five Elements, the East pertains to Wood, but at Danzhang we have mountains containing gold and copper. The South pertains to Fire, but in Qiaozhi we have rivers as big as the ocean. The West pertains to Metal, but in Shu and Long we find forests of famous timber. The North pertains to Water, but in Yudu we find the land of heaped up sand. This is how Heaven and Earth compensate scarcity with abundance and facilitate the circulation of all goods. Now the supply of bamboo in Wu and Yue, and the timber in Sui and Tang is more than can be used while in Cao, Wei, Liang and Song they are forced to use coffins over again for the dead. The fish of the regions of the great River and the lakes and the globe fish of Lai and Huang are too many for local consumption, while in Zou, Lu, Zhou and Han they have only vegetable fare. The wealth of nature is not deficient, and the treasures of the mountains and the seas are indeed rich, and yet the people still remain necessitous and the available wealth is not adequate.

The reason is that surplus and scarcity have not been adjusted and the wealth of the world has not been circulated.

d. The Literati: In olden times, the rafters were not carved, and the hut-thatch was left untrimmed. People wore plain clothes and ate from earthenware. They cast metal into mattocks and shaped clay into containers. Craftsmen did not fashion novel, clever articles. The world did not value things that could not be worn or eaten. Each was satisfied with his own dwelling, enjoyed his own customs, found his own food and implements satisfactory. Hence, things from distant lands were not exchanged and the jade of Kunshan did not arrive. Nowadays manners have degenerated in a race of extravagance. Women go to the extreme in finery and the artisans aim at excessive cleverness. Unadorned raw materials are carved and strange objects prized. They bore into the rocks to get gold and silver. They dive into the watery deeps looking for pearls. Pitfalls are devised to trap rhinoceri and elephants. Nets are spread for the kingfisher. Barbarian products are sought out to dazzle the Middle Kingdom. The goods of Kong and Zuo are transported to the Eastern Sea at a cost of ten thousand miles. Time and labor are spent for nothing. This is why the common men and women, weary and heavy-laden, wear themselves out without getting enough to clothe and feed themselves. Hence the true King would prohibit excessive profits, and cut off unnecessary expenses. When undue gain is prohibited, people return to the fundamental. When unnecessary expenses are cut off, people have enough to spend. Hence people will not suffer from want while alive, nor from exposure of their corpses when dead.

e. The Lord Grand Secretary: In ancient times, reasonable limits were set to the style of palaces and houses, chariots and liveries. Plain rafters and straw thatch were not a part of the system of the Ancient Emperors. The true gentleman, while checking extravagance, would disapprove of parsimoniousness because over-thriftiness tends to narrowness. When Sunshu Ao was the prime minister of Chu and his wife did not wear silk nor his horses feed on grain, Confucius said: *One should not be too thrifty so as to be hard on one's inferiors.* This is how the poem *The Cricket* was written. Guanzi said: *If palaces and houses are not decorated, the timber supply will be over-abundant. If animals and fowls are not used in the kitchens, there will be no decrease in their numbers. Without the hankering for profit, the fundamental occupation will have no outlet. Without the embroidered ceremonial robes, the seamstresses will have no occupation.* Therefore, artisans, merchants,

carpenters and mechanics are all for the use of the state and to provide tools and implements. They have existed from ancient times and are not a unique feature of the present age. Xiangao fed cattle at Zhou. Wugu carried on a cart-renting business in order to enter Qin. Gongshuzi was an expert in the compass and square and Ou Ye in founding. Thus the saying goes: *The various craftsmen dwell in their booths that they may do their work effectively.* Farmers and merchants exchange their goods so that both the fundamental and the accessory pursuits may be benefited. People who live in the mountains and marshes, or on moors and sterile uplands, depend on the effective circulation of goods to satisfy their wants. Thus it would not be only those who have abundance that have a surplus and only those who have little that would starve. If everybody stays where he lives and consumes his own food, then oranges and pumaloes would not be sold, Qulu salt would not appear, rugs and carpets would not be marketed and the timber of Wu and Tang would not be used.

f. The Literati: Mencius says that *if the seasons of husbandry are not disturbed there will be more grain than can be eaten. If silk worms and hemp are raised according to the seasons, cloth and silk will be more than what is required for wear. If the axes and bills enter the forest according to season, the timber supply will be more than the demand. Hunting and fishing according to season, fish and game will be more than can be eaten.* If you do not do all these things according to the seasons, and on the other hand, you decorate the palaces and dwelling houses and raise terraces and arbors higher and higher, and if carpenters and mechanics carve the large into the small, the round into the square, so as to represent clouds and mists above and mountains and forests below, then there will not be enough timber for use. If the men folk abandon the fundamental in favor of the non-essential, carving and engraving in imitation of the forms of animals, exhausting the possibilities of manipulation of materials, then there will not be enough grain for consumption. If the women folk decorate the small things and work on the minute and form elaborate articles to the best of their skill and art, then there will not be enough silk and cloth for wear. If the cooks boil and slaughter the immature, fry and roast and mix and blend, exhausting all the varieties of the Five Flavors, then there will not be enough fish and meat for food. At present while there is no question of suffering from fowls and animals not declining in number, and of the timber supply being more than can be consumed, the trouble is that we are extravagant without limit; and while we do not suffer from the lack of rugs, carpets, oranges and pumeloes, the trouble is that we have no hovels and husks and chaff.

Think about it.

1. The Lord Grand Secretary and the Literati disagree as to why people are able to prosper. What are their positions?
2. According to the Literati, why is it bad for the people to get excessively rich?
3. How does each side feel about "artisans, merchants, carpenters and mechanics"?

---

c. 47 BCE

52. Commentaries on the Civil War

Translated by William A. McDevitte and W. S. Bohn

The Commentaries on the Civil War (*Commentarii de bello civile*) is a Latin work that gives an account of the Great Roman Civil War (49–45 BCE), which pitted the Roman generals Gaius Julius Caesar and Gnaeus Pompeius (Pompey, for short) against each other. The book was written by Caesar himself but is incomplete, as it covers only the years 49–48 BCE. It may be that the ending has been lost or that Caesar never completed it. In this passage from the beginning of the work, Caesar (speaking in the third person) describes how he reasoned it would be proper for him to turn against the established authorities in Rome.

Book 1

[1.0] When Caesar, after reducing all Transalpine Gaul, had passed into Cisalpine Gaul, he determined for many reasons to send embassadors to Rome to request for him the consulate, and a prolongation of the command of his province. Pompey, who was

Julius Caesar, *Caesar's Commentaries*, trans. William A. McDevitte and W. S. Bohn. Harper & Brothers, 1869. Copyright in the Public Domain.

estranged from Caesar, although he was not as yet at open enmity with him, determined neither to aid him by his influence nor openly oppose him on this occasion. But the consuls Lentulus and Marcellus, who had previously been on unfriendly terms with Caesar, resolved to use all means in their power to prevent him from gaining his object. Marcellus in particular did not hesitate to offer Caesar other insults. Caesar had lately planned the colony of Novumcomum in Gaul: Marcellus, not content with taking from it the right of citizenship, ordered the principal man of the colony to be arrested and scourged at Rome, and sent him to make his complaints to Caesar: an insult of this description had never before been offered to a Roman citizen. While these transactions are taking place, Caius Curio, tribune of the commons, comes to Caesar in his province. Curio had made many and energetic struggles, in behalf of the republic and Caesar's cause: at length when he perceived that all his efforts were vain, he fled through fear of his adversaries, and informed Caesar of all the transactions that had taken place, and of the efforts made by his enemies to crush him. Caesar received Curio with great kindness, as he was a man of the highest rank, and had great claims on himself and the republic, and thanked him warmly for his numerous personal favors. But Curio, as war was being openly prepared against Caesar, advised him to concentrate his troops, and rescue the republic now oppressed by a few daring men. Caesar, although he was not ignorant of the real state of affairs, was however of opinion that particular regard should be paid to the tranquillity of the republic, lest any one should suppose that he was the originator of the war. Therefore, through his friends, he made this one request, that two legions, and the province of Cisalpine Gaul, and Illyricum, should be left him. All these acts were performed by Caesar, with the hope that his enemies might be induced by the justice of his demands, to preserve the peace of the republic. Even Pompey himself did not dare to oppose them. But when Caesar could not obtain his request from the consuls, he wrote to the senate a letter, in which he briefly stated his exploits and public services, and entreated that he should not be deprived of the favor of the people, who had ordered, that he, although absent, should be considered a candidate at the next elections; and he stated also that he would disband his army, if the senate and people of Rome would pass a resolution to that effect, provided that Pompey would do the same. That, as long as the latter should retain the command of his army, no just reason could exist that he [Caesar] should disband his troops and expose himself to the insults of his enemies. He intrusts this letter to Curio to bear to its destination; the latter traveled one hundred and sixty miles with incredible dispatch, and reached the city in three days' time, before the beginning of January, and before the consuls could pass any decree concerning Caesar's command. Curio, after accomplishing his journey, kept the letter, and did not give it up, until there was a crowded meeting of the senate, and the tribunes of the commons were present; for he was afraid, lest, if he gave it up previously, the consuls should suppress it.

[1.1] When Caesar's letter was delivered to the consuls, they were with great difficulty, and a hard struggle of the tribunes, prevailed on to suffer it to be read in the senate; but the tribunes could not prevail, that any question should be put to the senate on the subject of the letter. The consuls put the question on the regulation of the state. Lucius Lentulus the consul promises that he will not fail the senate and republic, "if they declared their sentiments boldly and resolutely, but if they turned their regard to Caesar, and courted his favor, as they did on former occasions, he would adopt a plan for himself, and not submit to the authority of the senate: that he too had a means of regaining Caesar's favor and friendship." Scipio spoke to the same purport, "that it was Pompey's intention not to abandon the republic, if the senate would support him; but if they should hesitate and act without energy, they would in vain implore his aid, if they should require it hereafter."

[1.2] This speech of Scipio's, as the senate was convened in the city, and Pompey was near at hand, seemed to have fallen from the lips of Pompey himself. Some delivered their sentiments with more moderation, as Marcellus first, who in the beginning of his speech, said, "that the question ought not to be put to the senate on this matter, till levies were made throughout all Italy, and armies raised under whose protection the senate might freely and safely pass such resolutions as they thought proper;" as Marcus Calidius afterward, who was of opinion, "that Pompey should set out for his province, that there might be no cause for arms; that Caesar was naturally apprehensive as two legions were forced from him, that Pompey was retaining those troops, and keeping them near the city to do him injury:" as Marcus Rufus, who followed Calidius almost word for word. They were all harshly rebuked by Lentulus, who peremptorily refused to propose Calidius's motion. Marcellus, overawed by his reproofs, retracted his opinion. Thus most of the senate, intimidated by the expressions of the consul, by the fears of a present army, and the threats of Pompey's friends, unwillingly and reluctantly adopted Scipio's opinion, that Caesar should disband his army by a certain day, and should he not do so, he should he considered as acting against the state. Marcus Antonius, and Quintus Cassius, tribunes of the people, interposed. The question was immediately put on their interposition. Violent opinions were expressed; whoever spoke with the greatest acrimony and cruelty was most highly commended by Caesar's enemies.

[1.3] The senate having broken up in the evening, all who belonged to that order were summoned by Pompey. He applauded the forward, and secured their votes for the next day; the more moderate he reproved and excited against Caesar. Many veterans, from all parts, who had served in Pompey's armies, were invited to his standard by the hopes of rewards and promotions. Several officers belonging to the two legions, which had been delivered up by Caesar, were sent for. The city and the comitium were crowded with tribunes, centurions, and veterans. All the consul's friends, all Pompey's connections, all those who bore any ancient enmity to Caesar, were forced into the senate house. By their concourse and declarations the timid were awed, the irresolute confirmed, and the greater part deprived of the power of speaking their sentiments with freedom. Lucius Piso, the censor, offered to go to Caesar: as did likewise Lucius Roscius, the praetor, to inform him of these affairs, and require only six days' time to finish the business. Opinions were expressed by some to the effect that commissioners should be sent to Caesar to acquaint him with the senate's pleasure.

[1.4] All these proposals were rejected, and opposition made to them all, in the speeches of the consul, Scipio, and Cato. An old grudge against Caesar and chagrin at a defeat actuated Cato. Lentulus was wrought upon by the magnitude of his debts, and the hopes of having the government of an army and provinces, and by the presents which he expected from such princes as should receive the title of friends of the Roman people, and boasted among his friends, that he would be a second Sylla, to whom the supreme authority should return. Similar hopes of a province and armies, which he expected to share with Pompey on account of his connection with him, urged on Scipio; and moreover [he was influenced by] the fear of being called to trial, and the adulation and an ostentatious display of himself and his friends in power, who at that time had great influence in the republic, and courts of judicature. Pompey himself, incited by Caesar's enemies, because he was unwilling that any person should bear an equal degree of dignity, had wholly alienated himself from Caesar's friendship, and procured a reconciliation with their common enemies; the greatest part of whom he had himself brought upon Caesar during his affinity with him. At the same time, chagrined at the disgrace which he had incurred by converting the two legions from their expedition through Asia and Syria, to [augment] his own power and authority, he was anxious to bring matters to a war.

[1.5] For these reasons every thing was done in a hasty and disorderly manner, and neither was time given to Caesar's relations to inform him [of the state of affairs] nor liberty to the tribunes of the people to deprecate their own danger, nor even to retain the last privilege, which Sylla had left them, the interposing their authority; but on the seventh day they were obliged to think of their own safety, which the most turbulent tribunes of the people were not accustomed to attend to, nor to fear being called to an account for their actions, till the eighth month. Recourse is had to that extreme and final decree of the senate (which was never resorted to even by daring proposers except when the city was in danger of being set on fire, or when the public safety was despaired of). "That the consuls, praetors, tribunes of the people, and proconsuls in the city, should take care that the state received no injury." These decrees are dated the eighth day before the ides of January; therefore, in the first five days, on which the senate could meet, from the day on which Lentulus entered into his consulate, the two days of election excepted, the severest and most virulent decrees were passed against Caesar's government, and against those most illustrious characters, the tribunes of the people. The latter immediately made their escape from the city, and withdrew to Caesar, who was then at Ravenna, awaiting an answer to his moderate demands; [to see] if matters could be brought to a peaceful termination by any equitable act on the part of his enemies.

[1.6] During the succeeding days the senate is convened outside the city. Pompey repeated the same things which he had declared through Scipio. He applauded the courage and firmness of the senate, acquainted them with his force, and told them that he had ten legions ready; that he was moreover informed and assured that Caesar's soldiers were disaffected, and that he could not persuade them to defend or even follow him. Motions were made in the senate concerning other matters; that levies should be made through all Italy; that Faustus Sylla should be sent as propraetor into Mauritania; that money should be granted to Pompey from the public treasury. It was also put to the vote that king Juba should be [honored with the title of] friend and ally. But Marcellus said that he would not allow this

motion for the present. Philip, one of the tribunes, stopped [the appointment of] Sylla; the resolutions respecting the other matters passed. The provinces, two of which were consular, the remainder praetorian, were decreed to private persons; Scipio got Syria, Lucius Domitius Gaul: Philip and Marcellus were omitted, from a private motive, and their lots were not even admitted. To the other provinces praetors were sent, nor was time granted as in former years, to refer to the people on their appointment, nor to make them take the usual oath, and march out of the city in a public manner, robed in the military habit, after offering their vows: a circumstance which had never before happened. Both the consuls leave the city, and private men had lictors in the city and capital, contrary to all precedents of former times. Levies were made throughout Italy, arms demanded, and money exacted from the municipal towns, and violently taken from the temples. All distinctions between things human and divine, are confounded.

[1.7] These things being made known to Caesar, he harangued his soldiers; he reminded them "of the wrongs done to him at all times by his enemies, and complained that Pompey had been alienated from him and led astray by them through envy and a malicious opposition to his glory, though he had always favored and promoted Pompey's honor and dignity. He complained that an innovation had been introduced into the republic, that the intercession of the tribunes, which had been restored a few years before by Sylla, was branded as a crime, and suppressed by force of arms; that Sylla, who had stripped the tribunes of every other power, had, nevertheless, left the privilege of intercession unrestrained; that Pompey, who pretended to restore what they had lost, had taken away the privileges which they formerly had; that whenever the senate decreed, 'that the magistrates should take care that the republic sustained no injury' (by which words and decree the Roman people were obliged to repair to arms), it was only when pernicious laws were proposed; when the tribunes attempted violent measures; when the people seceded, and possessed themselves of the temples and eminences of the city; (and these instances of former times, he showed them were expiated by the fate of Saturninus and the Gracchi): that nothing of this kind was attempted now, nor even thought of: that no law was promulgated, no intrigue with the people going forward, no secession made; he exhorted them to defend from the malice of his enemies the reputation and honor of that general under whose command they had for nine years most successfully supported the state; fought many successful battles, and subdued all Gaul and Germany." The soldiers of the thirteenth legion, which was present (for in the beginning of the disturbances he had called it out, his other legions not having yet arrived), all cry out that they are ready to defend their general, and the tribunes of the commons, from all injuries.

Think about it.

1. What justifications are given for Caesar's march against Rome?
2. Does Caesar agree that the whole senate was opposed to him? To what does Caesar attribute the decree against him?
3. Do you think Caesar would have reasons to stretch the truth in this account? How might Pompey have described these events?

---

45 BCE

53. On the Nature of the Gods

Translated by Francis Brooks

The book On the Nature of the Gods (*De natura deorum*), written in 45 BCE by the Roman statesman Marcus Tullius Cicero (106–43 BCE), is a dialogue that presents the views of various Greco-Roman philosophies on the gods. The following selection is from Cicero's introduction, in which he presents the issue and its implications.

Marcus Tullius Cicero, "Book I, Part II," *De Natura Deorum (On the Nature of the Gods)*, trans. Francis Brooks. Methuen Publishing Ltd., 1896. Copyright in the Public Domain.

BOOK I.

II. For there are and have been philosophers who thought that the gods had absolutely no direction of human affairs, and if their opinion is true, what piety can there be, and what holiness, and what obligation of religion? It is right that these should be accorded, in purity and innocence of heart, to the divinity of the gods, but only if the offering is observed by them, and if something has been accorded by the immortal gods to humanity. But if they have neither the power nor the wish to aid us, if they have no care at all for us and take no notice of what we do, if there is nothing that can find its way from them to human life, what reason is there for our rendering to them any worship, or honour, or prayers? On the other hand, in an empty and artificial pretence of faith piety cannot find a place any more than the other virtues; with piety it is necessary that holiness and religious obligation should also disappear, and when these are gone a great confusion and disturbance of life ensues; indeed, when piety towards the gods is removed, I am not so sure that good faith, and human fraternity, and justice, the chief of all the virtues, are not also removed. But there is another school of philosophers, and a great and high-minded one it is, who hold that the entire universe is ordered and ruled by the mind and the intelligence of the gods, and, more than this, that the gods also take counsel and forethought for the life of men; for they think that the crops and other produce of the earth, the variations in the weather, the succession of the seasons, and the changing phenomena of the sky, by means of which everything that the earth bears is ripened and comes to maturity, are gifts bestowed by the immortal gods upon mankind, and they adduce many instances which will be mentioned in the course of these books, and which are of such a kind as to almost make it seem that the immortal gods manufactured these precise things for the benefit of man! Against this school Carneades advanced many arguments, with the result of rousing men of intelligence to a desire for investigating the truth; for there is no question on which there is such marked disagreement, not only amongst the unlearned, but the learned as well, and the fact of their opinions being so various and so mutually opposed makes it of course possible, upon the one hand, that not one of them is true, and certainly impossible, upon the other, that more than one should be true.

Think about it.

1. According to Cicero, what would happen if the gods had no interest in human affairs?

54. Books from the Founding of the City

Translated by John H. Freese, Alfred J. Church, and William J. Brodribb

Titus Livius Patavinus (Livy, for short) wrote a monumental history of Rome (called *Ab urbe condita libri* in Latin) and published it in pieces over many years. Ultimately it consisted of 142 short books (more like chapters), but today only about a quarter of it survives. The first five books were published c. 27–25 BCE, and the following is a passage from Book 1, which recounts the story of Lucretia, the wife of Lucius Tarquinius Collatinus, one of the leaders of the revolution that overthrew the Roman monarchy.

[56] Their wealth was itself the actual occasion of the war: for the Roman king, whose resources had been drained by the magnificence of his public works, was desirous of enriching himself, and also of soothing the minds of his subjects by a large present of booty, as they, independently of the other instances of his tyranny, were incensed against his government, because they felt indignant that they had been kept so long employed by the king as mechanics, and in labour only fit for slaves. An attempt was made, to see if Ardea could be taken at the first assault; when that proved unsuccessful, the enemy began to be distressed by a blockade, and by siege-works. In the standing camp, as usually happens when a war is tedious rather than severe, furloughs were easily obtained, more so by the officers, however, than the common soldiers. The young princes also sometimes spent their leisure hours in feasting and mutual entertainments. One day as they were drinking in the tent of Sextus Tarquinius, where Collatinus Tarquinius, the son of Egerius, was also at supper, they fell to talking about their wives. Every one commended his own extravagantly: a dispute thereupon arising, Collatinus said there was no occasion for words, that it might be known in a few hours how far his wife Lucretia excelled all the rest. "If, then," added he, "we have any youthful vigour, why should we not mount our horses and in person examine the behaviour of our wives? Let that be the surest proof to every one, which shall meet his eyes on the unexpected arrival of the husband." They were heated with wine. "Come on, then," cried all. They immediately galloped to Rome, where they arrived when darkness was beginning to fall. From thence they proceeded to Collatia, [57] where they found Lucretia, not after the manner of the king's daughters-in-law, whom they had seen spending their time in luxurious banqueting with their companions, but, although the night was far advanced, employed at her wool, sitting in the middle of the house in the midst of her maids who were working around her. The honour of the contest regarding the women rested with Lucretia. Her husband on his arrival, and the Tarquinii, were kindly received; the husband, proud of his victory, gave the young princes a polite invitation. There an evil desire of

violating Lucretia by force seized Sextus Tarquinius; both her beauty, and her proved chastity urged him on. Then, after this youthful frolic of the night, they returned to the camp.

After an interval of a few days, Sextus Tarquinius, without the knowledge of Collatinus, came to Collatia with one attendant only: there he was made welcome by them, as they had no suspicion of his design, and, having been conducted after supper into the guest chamber, burning with passion, when all around seemed sufficiently secure, and all fast asleep, he came to the bedside of Lucretia, as she lay asleep, with a drawn sword, and with his left hand pressing down the woman's breast, said: "Be silent, Lucretia; I am Sextus Tarquinius. I have a sword in my hand. You shall die if you utter a word." When the woman, awaking terrified from sleep, saw there was no help, and that impending death was nigh at hand, then Tarquin declared his passion, entreated, mixed threats with entreaties, tried all means to influence the woman's mind. When he saw she was resolved, and uninfluenced even by the fear of death, to the fear of death he added the fear of dishonour, declaring that he would lay a murdered slave naked by her side when dead, so that it should be said that she had been slain in base adultery. When by the terror of this disgrace his lust (as it were victorious) had overcome her inflexible chastity, and Tarquin had departed, exulting in having triumphed over a woman's honour by force, Lucretia, in melancholy distress at so dreadful a misfortune, despatched one and the same messenger both to her father at Rome, and to her husband at Ardea, bidding them come each with a trusty friend; that they must do so, and use despatch, for a monstrous deed had been wrought. Spurius Lucretius came accompanied by Publius Valerius, the son of Volesus, Collatinus with Lucius Junius Brutus, in company with whom, as he was returning to Rome, he happened to be met by his wife's messenger. They found Lucretia sitting in her chamber in sorrowful dejection. On the arrival of her friends the tears burst from her eyes; and on her husband inquiring, whether all was well, "By no means," she replied, "for how can it be well with a woman who has lost her honour? The traces of another man are on your bed, Collatinus. But the body only has been violated, the mind is guiltless; death shall be my witness. But give me your right hands, and your word of honour, that the adulterer shall not come off unpunished. It is Sextus Tarquinius, who, an enemy last night in the guise of a guest has borne hence by force of arms, a triumph destructive to me, and one that will prove so to himself also, if you be men." All gave their word in succession; they attempted to console her, grieved in heart as she was, by turning the guilt of the act from her, constrained as she had been by force, upon the perpetrator of the crime, declaring that it is the mind sins, not the body; and that where there is no intention, there is no guilt. "It is for you to see," said she, "what is due to him. As for me, though I acquit myself of guilt, I do not discharge myself from punishment; nor shall any woman survive her dishonour by pleading the example of Lucretia." She plunged a knife, which she kept concealed beneath her garment, into her heart, and falling forward on the wound, dropped down expiring. Her husband and father shrieked aloud.

While they were overwhelmed with grief, Brutus drew the knife out of the wound, and, holding it up before him reeking with blood, said: "By this blood, most pure before the outrage of a prince, I swear, and I call you, O gods, to witness my oath, that I will henceforth pursue Lucius Tarquinius Superbus, his wicked wife, and all their children, with fire, sword, and all other violent means in my power; nor will I ever suffer them or any other to reign at Rome." Then he gave the knife to Collatinus, and after him to Lucretius and Valerius, who were amazed at such an extraordinary occurrence, and could not understand the newly developed character of Brutus. However, they all took the oath as they were directed, and, their sorrow being completely changed to wrath, followed the lead of Brutus, who from that time ceased not to call upon them to abolish the regal power. They carried forth the body of Lucretia from her house, and conveyed it to the forum, where they caused a number of persons to assemble, as generally happens, by reason of the unheard-of and atrocious nature of an extraordinary occurrence. They complained, each for himself, of the royal villainy and violence. Both the grief of the father affected them, and also Brutus, who reproved their tears and unavailing complaints, and advised them to take up arms, as became men and Romans, against those who dared to treat them like enemies. All the most spirited youths voluntarily presented themselves in arms; the rest of the young men followed also. From thence, after an adequate garrison had been left at the gates at Collatia, and sentinels appointed, to prevent any one giving intelligence of the disturbance to the royal party, the rest set out for Rome in arms under the conduct of Brutus. When they arrived there, the armed multitude caused panic and confusion wherever they went. Again, when they saw the principal men of the state placing themselves at their head, they thought that, whatever it might be, it was not without good reason. Nor did the heinousness of the event excite less violent emotions at Rome than it had done at Collatia: accordingly, they ran from all parts of the city into the forum, and as soon as they came thither, the public crier summoned them to attend the tribune of the celeres [58], with which office Brutus happened to be at the time invested. There a harangue was delivered by him, by no means of the style and character which had been counterfeited by him up to that day, concerning the violence and lust of Sextus Tarquinius, the horrid violation of Lucretia and her lamentable death, the bereavement of Tricipitinus, [59], in whose eyes the cause of his daughter's death was more shameful and deplorable than that death itself. To this was added the haughty insolence of the king himself, and the sufferings and toils of the people, buried in the earth in the task of cleansing ditches and sewers: he declared that Romans, the conquerors of all the surrounding states, instead of warriors had become labourers and stone-cutters. The unnatural murder of King Servius Tullius was recalled, and the fact of his daughter

having driven over the body of her father in her impious chariot, and the gods who avenge parents were invoked by him. By stating these and, I believe, other facts still more shocking, which, though by no means easy to be detailed by writers, the then heinous state of things suggested, he so worked upon the already incensed multitude, that they deprived the king of his authority, and ordered the banishment of Lucius Tarquinius with his wife and children. He himself, having selected and armed some of the younger men, who gave in their names as volunteers, set out for the camp at Ardea to rouse the army against the king: the command in the city he left to Lucretius, who had been already appointed prefect of the city by the king. During this tumult Tullia fled from her house, both men and women cursing her wherever she went, and invoking upon her the wrath of the furies, the avengers of parents.

News of these transactions having reached the camp, when the king, alarmed at this sudden revolution, was proceeding to Rome to quell the disturbances, Brutus—for he had had notice of his approach—turned aside, to avoid meeting him; and much about the same time Brutus and Tarquinius arrived by different routes, the one at Ardea, the other at Rome. The gates were shut against Tarquin, and sentence of banishment declared against him; the camp welcomed with great joy the deliverer of the city, and the king's sons were expelled. Two of them followed their father, and went into exile to Caere, a city of Etruria. Sextus Tarquinius, who had gone to Gabii, as if to his own kingdom, was slain by the avengers of the old feuds, which he had stirred up against himself by his rapines and murders. Lucius Tarquinius Superbus reigned twenty-five years: the regal form of government lasted, from the building of the city to its deliverance, two hundred and forty-four years. Two consuls, Lucius Junius Brutus and Lucius Tarquinius Collatinus, were elected by the prefect of at the comitia of centuries, according to the commentaries of Servius Tullius.

---

19 BCE

55. The Aeneid

Translated by E. Fairfax Taylor

The Aeneid is a Latin epic written by Publius Vergilius Maro (Vergil, for short). Vergil died in 19 BCE before the work was completed, but the Roman emperor Augustus Caesar liked it so much that he published it anyway (probably with some slight editorial work). The Aeneid consists of 12 books and tells the story of the mythical figure Aeneas, a Trojan who was supposed to have survived the Trojan War and traveled to Italy to start a line of kings that would eventually lead to Romulus, the first king of Rome. In this excerpt from Book 4, the Carthaginian queen Dido is losing her mind, having just been jilted by Aeneas.

BOOK FOUR

I.
Long since a prey to passion's torturing pains,
The Queen was wasting with the secret flame,
The cruel wound was feeding on her veins.
Back to the fancy of the lovelorn dame
Came the chief's valour and his country's fame.
His looks, his words still lingered in her breast,
Deep-fixt. And now the dewy Dawn upcame,
And chased the shadows, when her love's unrest
Thus to her sister's soul responsive she confessed:

II.

"What dreams, dear Anna, fill me with alarms;
What stranger guest is this? like whom in face?
How proud in portance, how expert in arms!
In sooth I deem him of celestial race;
Fear argues souls degenerate and base;
But he—how oft by danger sore bestead,
What warlike exploits did his lips retrace.
Were not my purpose steadfast, ne'er to wed,
Since love first played me false, and mocked me with the dead,

III.

"Were I not sick of bridal torch and bower,
This once, perchance, I had been frail again.
Anna—for I will own it—since the hour
When, poor Sychaeus miserably slain,
A brother's murder rent a home in twain,
He, he alone my stubborn will could tame,
And stir the balance of my soul. Too plain
I know the traces of the long-quenched flame;
The sparks of love revive, rekindled, but the same.

IV.

"But O! gape Earth, or may the Sire of might
Hurl me with lightning to the Shades amain,
Pale shades of Erebus and abysmal Night,
Ere, wifely modesty, thy name I stain,
Or dare thy sacred precepts to profane.
Nay, he whose love first linked us long ago,
Took all my love, and he shall still retain
And guard it with him in the grave below."
She spake, and o'er her lap the gushing tears outflow.

V.

Then Anna: "Sister, dearer than the day,
Why thus in loneliness and endless woe
Wilt thou for ever wear thy youth away?
Nor care sweet sons, fair Venus' gifts to know?
Think'st thou such grief concerns the shades below?
What though no husband, Libyan or of Tyre,
Could bend a heart made desolate; what though
In vain Iarbas did thy love desire,
And Africa's proud chiefs, why quench a pleasing fire?

VI.

"Think too, whose lands surround thee: on this side,
Gaetulian cities, an unconquered race,
Numidians, reinless as the steeds they ride,
And cheerless Syrtis hold thee in embrace;
There fierce Barcaeans and a sandy space
Wasted by drought. Why tell of wars from Tyre,
A brother's threats? Well know I Juno's grace
And heaven's propitious auspices conspire
To find for Trojans here the home of their desire.

VII.

"Sister, how glorious even now these towers,
What realm shall rise, with such a wondrous pair
When Teucrian arms join fellowship with ours,
What glory shall the Punic state upbear!
Pray thou to heaven and, having gained thy prayer,
Indulge thy welcome, and thy guest entreat
To tarry. Bid him winter's storms beware;
Point to Orion's watery star, the fleet
Still shattered, and the skies for mariners unmeet."

VIII.

So fanned, her passion kindled into flame:
Hope scattered scruples, and her doubts gave way,
And loosed were all the lingering ties of shame.
First to the fane the sisters haste away,
And there for peace at every shrine they pray,
And chosen ewes, as ancient rites ordain,
To Sire Lyaeus, to the God of Day,
And Ceres, giver of the law, are slain,
And most to Juno's power, who guards the nuptial chain.

IX.

Herself, the lovely Dido, bowl in hand,
O'er a white heifer's forehead pours the wine,
Or by the Gods' rich altars takes her stand,
And piles the gifts, and o'er the slaughtered kine
Pores, from the quivering heartstrings to divine
The doom of Fate. Blind seers, alas! what art
To calm her frenzy, now hath vow or shrine?
Deep in her marrow feeds the tender smart,

Unseen, the silent wound is festering in her heart.

X.
Poor Dido burns, and roams from street to street,
Wild as a doe, whom heedless, far away,
Some swain hath pierced amid the woods of Crete,
And left, unware, the flying steel to stay,
While through the forests and the lawns his prey
Roams, with the death-bolt clinging to her side.
Now to Aeneas doth the queen display
Her walls and wealth, the dowry of his bride;
Oft she essays to speak, so oft the utterance died.

XI.
Again, when evening steals upon the light,
She seeks the feast, again would fain give ear
To Troy's sad tale and, ravished with delight,
Hangs on his lips; and when the hall is clear,
And the moon sinks, and drowsy stars appear,
Alone she mourns, clings to the couch he pressed,
Him absent sees, his absent voice doth hear,
Now, fain to cheat her utter love's unrest,
Clasps for his sire's sweet sake Ascanius to her breast.

XII.
No longer rise the growing towers, nor care
The youths in martial exercise to vie,
Nor ports nor bulwarks for defence prepare.
The frowning battlements neglected lie,
And lofty scaffolding that threats the sky.
Her, when Saturnian Juno saw possessed
With love so tameless, as would dare defy
The shame that whispers in a woman's breast,
Forthwith the queen of Jove fair Venus thus addressed:

XIII.
"Fine spoils, forsooth, proud triumph ye have won,
Thou and thy boy,—vast worship and renown!
Two gods by fraud one woman have undone.
But well I know ye fear the rising town,
The homes of Carthage offered for your own.
When shall this end? or why a feud so dire?
Let lasting peace and plighted wedlock crown

The compact. See, thou hast thy heart's desire,
Poor Dido burns with love, her blood is turned to fire.

XXXII.
Now, borne along, beneath him he espies
The sides precipitous and towering peak
Of rugged Atlas, who upholds the skies.
Round his pine-covered forehead, wild and bleak,
The dark clouds settle and the storm-winds shriek.
His shoulders glisten with the mantling snow,
Dark roll the torrents down his aged cheek,
Seamed with the wintry ravage, and below,
Stiff with the gathered ice his hoary beard doth show.

XXXIII.
Poised on his wings, here first Cyllenius stood,
Then downward shot, and in the salt sea spray
Dipped like a sea-gull, who, in quest of food,
Searches the teeming shore-cliffs for his prey,
And scours the rocks and skims along the bay.
So swiftly now, between the earth and skies,
Leaving his mother's sire, his airy way
Cyllene's god on cleaving pinions plies,
As o'er the Libyan sands along the wind he flies.

XXXIV.
Scarce now at Carthage had he stayed his feet,
Among the huts Aeneas he espied,
Planning new towers and many a stately street.
A sword-hilt, starred with jasper, graced his side,
A scarf, gold-broidered by the queen, and dyed
With Tyrian hues, was o'er his shoulders thrown.
"What, thou—wilt thou build Carthage?" Hermes cried,
"And stay to beautify thy lady's town,
And dote on Tyrian realms, and disregard thine own?

XXXV.
"Himself, the Sire, who rules the earth and skies,
Sends me from heaven his mandate to proclaim.
What scheme is thine? what hope allures thine eyes,
To loiter thus in Libya? If such fame
Nowise can move thee, nor thy soul inflame,
If loth to labour for thine own renown,

Think of thy young Ascanius; see with shame
His rising promise, scarce to manhood grown,
Hope of the Roman race, and heir of Latium's throne."

XXXVI.
He spake and, speaking, vanished into air.
Dumb stood Aeneas, by the sight unmann'd:
Fear stifled speech and stiffened all his hair.
Fain would he fly, and quit the tempting land,
Surprised and startled by the god's command.
Ah! what to do? what opening can he find
To break the news, the infuriate Queen withstand?
This way and that dividing his swift mind,
All means in turns he tries, and wavers like the wind.

XXXVII.
This plan prevails; he bids a chosen few
Collect the crews in silence, arm the fleet
And hide the purport of these counsels new,
Himself, since Dido dreams not of deceit,
Nor thinks such passion can be frail or fleet,
Some avenue of access will essay,
Some tender moment for soft speeches meet,
And wit shall find, and cunning smooth the way.
With joy the captains hear, and hasten to obey.

XXXVIII.
But Dido—who can cheat a lover's care?
Could guess the fraud, the coming change descry,
And in the midst of safety feared a snare.
Now wicked Fame hath bid the rumour fly
Of mustering crews. Poor Dido, crazed thereby,
Raves like a Thyiad, when the frenzied rout
With orgies hurry to Cithaeron high,
And "Bacchus! Bacchus" through the night they shout.
At length the chief she finds, and thus her wrath breaks out:

XXXIX.
"Thought'st thou to steal in silence from the land,
False wretch! and cloak such treason with a lie?
Can neither love, nor this my plighted hand,
Nor dying Dido keep thee? Must thou fly,
When North-winds howl, and wintry waves are high?

O cruel! what if home before thee lay,
Not lands unknown, beneath an alien sky,
If Troy were standing, as in ancient day,
Would'st thou for Troy's own sake this angry deep essay?

XL.
"_Me_ dost thou fly? O, by these tears, thy hand
Late pledged, since madness leaves me naught beside,
But lovers' vows and wedlock's sacred band,
Scarce knit and now too soon to be untied;
If aught were pleasing in a new-won bride,
 f sweet the memory of our marriage day,
O by these prayers—if place for prayer abide—
In mercy put that cruel mind away.
Pity a falling house, now hastening to decay.

XLI.
"For thee the Libyans and each Nomad lord
Hate me, and Tyrians would their queen disown.
My wifely honour is a name abhorred,
And that chaste fame has perished, which alone
Perchance had raised me to a starry throne.
O think with whom thou leav'st me to thy fate,
Dear guest, no longer as a husband known.
Why stay I? till Pygmalion waste my state,
Or on Iarbas' wheels, a captive queen, to wait?

XLII.
"Ah! if at least, ere thou had'st sailed away,
Some babe, the token of thy love, were born,
Some child Aeneas, in my halls to play,
Like thee at least in look, I should not mourn
As altogether captive and forlorn."
She paused, but he, at Jove's command, his eyes
Keeps still unmoved, and, though with anguish torn,
Strives with his love, nor suffers it to rise,
But checks his heaving heart, and thus at length replies:

XLIII.
"Never, dear Queen, will I disown the debt,
Thy love's deserts, too countless to repeat,
Nor ever fair Elissa's name forget,

While memory shall last, or pulses beat.
Few words are mine, for fewest words are meet.
Think not I meant—the very thought were shame—
Thief-like to veil my going with deceit.
I gave no promise of a husband's name,
Nor talked of ties like that, or wedlock's sacred flame.

XLIV.
"Did Fate but let me shape my life at will,
And rest at pleasure, Ilion, first of all,
And Troy's sweet relics would I cling to still,
And Pergama and Priam's stately hall
Once more should cheer the vanquished for their fall.
But now Grynoean Phoebus bids me fare
To great Italia; to Italia call
The Lycian lots, and so the Fates declare.
There lies the land I love, my destined home is there.

XLV.
"If thee, Tyre-born, a Libyan town detain,
What grudge to Troy Ausonia's land denies?
We too may seek a foreign realm to gain.
Me, oft as Night's damp shadows from the skies
Have shrouded Earth, and fiery stars arise,
My sire Anchises' troubled ghost in sleep
Upbraids and scares, and ever louder cries
The wrong, that on Ascanius' head I heap,
Whom from Hesperia's plains, his destined realms, I keep.

XLVI.
"Now, too, Jove's messenger himself comes down—
Bear witness both—I heard the voice divine,
I saw the God just entering the town.
Cease then to vex me, nor thyself repine.
Heaven's will to Latium summons me, not mine."
Him, speaking thus and pleading but in vain,
She viewed askance, rolling her restless eyne,
Then scanned him o'er, long silent, in disdain,
And thus at length broke out, and gave her wrath the rein.

c. 50–52 CE

56. Letter to the Galatians

Translated by David Miano

The letters of Paul the Apostle are the earliest writings now to be found in the New Testament. His Letter to the Galatians, written in his native language of Greek, is directed to the communities of Jesus' followers in the Roman province of Galatia in Anatolia. The precise date of the letter is a matter of debate among scholars, but it is generally agreed that it was written at some time between 49 and 57 CE. In the following excerpt, Paul expresses his views on whether or not the Jewish Torah has authority over the followers of Christ.

1:6I marvel that you are so quickly moving from the one who called you with the grace of Christ over to a different gospel—1:7not that there is another gospel, but there are some who are confusing you and who want to pervert the gospel of the Christ.[1] 1:8But even if we or an angel out of heaven should proclaim to you a gospel beyond what we proclaimed to you, let that one be accursed. 1:9As we have said before, so now I say again, if anyone proclaims to you a gospel beyond what you received, let him be accursed!

1:10Is it now humans I am trying to convince or God? Or am I seeking to please humans? If I were still pleasing humans, I would not be a servant of Christ. 1:11For I want you to know, brothers, that the gospel that was proclaimed by me is not of human origin, 1:12for I did not receive it from, nor was I taught it by, a human, but through a revelation of Jesus Christ.

1:13You have heard, of course, about my earlier conduct in Judaism, that I was excessively persecuting the congregation of God and was devastating it. 1:14And I was making greater progress in Judaism than many of my peers among my people, as I was

---

1   Paul is referring to the Judaizers of the church (the "circumcision party"), who were trying to compel non-Jewish converts to Christ to be circumcised and to follow the Jewish Torah.

far more zealous for the traditions of my forefathers. ¹ᐟ¹⁵However, when God, who set me apart when I was still in my mother's womb, called me through his grace ¹ᐟ¹⁶to reveal his Son in me, so that I might proclaim him as a gospel to the non-Jews, I did not immediately confer with flesh and blood, ¹ᐟ¹⁷nor did I go up to Jerusalem to those who were apostles before me, but I went off into Arabia, and then I returned to Damascus.

¹ᐟ¹⁸Then after three years I went up into Jerusalem to get acquainted with Cephas and stayed with him for fifteen days; ¹ᐟ¹⁹but I did not see any other apostle except James, the Lord's brother. ¹ᐟ²⁰In what I am writing to you, look—in God's sight I am not lying. ¹ᐟ²¹Then I went into the regions of Syria and Cilicia, ¹ᐟ²²and my face was still unknown to the congregations of Judea that are in Christ; ¹ᐟ²³they used to hear only that "the man who formerly persecuted us is now proclaiming as gospel the faith he once was devastating." ¹ᐟ²⁴And they were glorifying God because of me.

²ᐟ¹Then after fourteen years I went up again to Jerusalem with Barnabas, taking also Titus along with me, ²ᐟ²but I went up in response to a revelation. And I laid before them the gospel I am preaching among the non-Jews (but only in a private meeting with the ones who seemed to be important) for fear that somehow I was running or had run for nothing. ²ᐟ³However not even Titus, who was with me, though he was a Greek, was compelled to be circumcised ²ᐟ⁴on account of the fake brothers who were quietly brought in (and who sneaked in to spy on our freedom that we have in Christ that they might enslave us). ²ᐟ⁵To these we did not yield to submission, not even for an hour, in order that the truth of the gospel might remain with you. ²ᐟ⁶As for those who seemed to be important—what they really were makes no difference to me (God does not receive someone based on their appearance)—these ones contributed nothing to me. ²ᐟ⁷On the contrary, when they saw that I had been entrusted with the gospel for the uncircumcised, just as Peter had been for the circumcised ²ᐟ⁸(for he who worked through Peter to make an apostleship to the circumcised also worked through me to make one to the non-Jews), ²ᐟ⁹and when James, Cephas, and John, the ones who seemed to be pillars, recognized the grace that had been given to me, they offered me and Barnabas the right hand of fellowship in order that we should go to the non-Jews but they to the circumcised. ²ᐟ¹⁰They asked only that we keep the poor in mind, which I have earnestly endeavored to do.

²ᐟ¹¹However when Cephas came to Antioch, I opposed him to his face, because he condemned himself; ²ᐟ¹²for before the arrival of persons sent by James, he would eat with the non-Jews, but after they arrived he withdrew and kept himself separate out of fear of the circumcision party. ²ᐟ¹³And the rest of the Jews also joined him in this hypocrisy, so that even Barnabas was led astray with them in this hypocrisy. ²ᐟ¹⁴But when I saw they were not walking in accordance with the truth of the gospel, I said to Cephas in front of them all, "If you, though you are a Jew, act as a non-Jew and not as a Jew, how can you compel non-Jews to act like Jews? ²ᐟ¹⁵We are Jewish by birth and not sinners from among the non-Jews, ²ᐟ¹⁶yet we know that a person is justified not by works of law, but only through the faith of Christ Jesus, and we also have put our faith in Christ Jesus, that we might be justified by the faith of Christ and not by works of law, because by works of law no one will be justified. ²ᐟ¹⁷Now if we, in seeking to be justified in Christ, have ourselves also been found to be sinners, then Christ is really the servant of sin. But that could never happen. ²ᐟ¹⁸For if the very things I once tore down I build up again, I demonstrate myself to be a transgressor. ²ᐟ¹⁹As for me, through law I died to law, so that I might live to God. I have been crucified along with Christ, ²ᐟ²⁰so that it is no longer I that live, but it is Christ who lives in me. And the life I now live in the flesh I live by faith in the Son of God, who loved me and surrendered himself for me. ²ᐟ²¹I do not shove aside God's grace; for if righteousness is through law, Christ really died for nothing!"

Think about it.

1. Why do you think Paul is so insistent that he did not meet with the apostles as a group before he went on his missionary tours?
2. From what you can gather from the letter, what sort of friction existed among Jesus' followers at this time and why?

1st century CE

57. The Letter of James

Translated by David Miano

Because it contains a string of moral exhortations and precepts, the Letter of James is sometimes viewed as a work in the Wisdom Literature genre rather than as an actual letter. The author identifies himself as "James, a servant of God and of the Lord Jesus Christ," and this is usually assumed to mean James the Just, the brother of Jesus, a prominent figure in the first century CE Jerusalem church. Because of the author's cultured use of the Greek language, scholars are not convinced that it was written by James, who is presumed to have had no formal education. Whatever the case, the content of the letter reflects what we know of the sentiments of James the Just. Here is an excerpt in which the author weighs in on the issue of whether or not the Jewish Torah has authority over the followers of Christ.

2:1My brothers, do not hold the faith of our glorious
Lord Jesus Christ together with acts of favoritism.
2:2For if a man with gold rings and splendid clothing
enters your assembly, and also a poor man dressed
in filthy clothing, 2:3and you look favorably upon the
one wearing the splendid clothing and say to him,
"You sit here in a fine place," while you say to the poor
one, "You stand there," or "Sit below my footrest,"
2:4are you not conflicted within yourselves and have
you not become judges making wicked distinctions?

2:5Listen, my beloved brothers. Has not God chosen the poor in the world to be rich in faith and to be
heirs of the kingdom that he has promised to those
who love him? 2:6But you have dishonored the poor
one! Is it not the rich ones who oppress you, and are
they not the very ones who are dragging you into
courts? 2:7Are they not the very ones blaspheming
the noble name that has been invoked over you? 2:8If
you actually fulfill a kingly law, "You shall love your
neighbor as yourself," according to Scripture, you are
doing well; 2:9but if you are practicing favoritism, you

are committing a sin. You are convicted by the Law as transgressors, [2:10]because whoever undertakes to observe the entire Law, yet fails in one point, has become accountable for all of them. [2:11]For the One who said, "Do not commit adultery," also said, "Do not kill." So if you do not commit adultery but do kill, you have become a transgressor of the Law. [2:12]So speak and so act as people who are going to be judged by a law of freedom, [2:13]because judgment is merciless to the one who has not shown mercy. Mercy triumphs over judgment.

[2:14]Of what benefit is it, my brothers, if someone says he has faith but does not have works? That faith is not able to save him, is it? [2:15]If a brother or a sister is going naked and lacking daily nourishment, [2:16]and if one of you should say to them, "Go in peace! Be warm and well fed," but does not give to them what is necessary for the body, what is the benefit? [2:17]So also faith, if it does not have works, is by itself dead. [2:18]But someone will say that you have faith, and I have works. Show me your faith apart from works, and by my works I will show you my faith! [2:19]You believe that God is one? You do well, but even the demons believe, and they shudder. [2:20]Do you care to know, you empty fellow, that faith apart from works is useless? [2:21]Was not our father Abraham justified on the basis of works when he offered his son Isaac on the altar? [2:22]You see that faith was working together with his works, and by the works faith was brought to perfection, [2:23]and the Scripture was fulfilled that says, "And Abraham put faith in God, and it was reckoned to him as righteousness,"[1] and he was called a friend of God. [2:24]You see that a person is justified on the basis of works and not on the basis of faith only. [2:25]And likewise also Rahab the prostitute—was she not justified on the basis of works when she received the messengers and sent them out by another way? [2:26]Just as the body apart from spirit is dead, so also faith apart from works is dead.

---

1   The apostle Paul had used this scripture to demonstrate the opposite: that it was Abraham's faith alone that justified him (Romans 4:1-8).

Think about it.

1.   What is the author's view of the Jewish Torah?
2.   From what you read in Paul's Letter to the Galatians, what would be Paul's reaction to this passage?

58.   The Gospel of Mark

Translated by David Miano

A work in the Gospel genre presents the message of Christianity in a narrative about the life of Jesus. The Gospel of Mark is the earliest example we have from this genre. Originally published anonymously c. 65–69 CE, it was later attributed to a Christian named Mark, who is said to have obtained his stories from the apostle Peter. In the following passage, Jesus tells his disciples the future of the city of Jerusalem.

13:1As [Jesus] was leaving the temple, one of his disciples said to him, "Teacher, look! What amazing stones and what amazing buildings!" 13:2And Jesus said to him, "Are you looking at these great buildings? Not one stone will be left here sitting on another and not be toppled off."

13:3And when he was sitting on the Mount of Olives opposite the temple, Peter, James, and John asked him privately, 13:4"Tell us, when will these things be, and what will be the sign that all these things are about to be accomplished?"

13:5Then Jesus began to say to them, "Beware that no one misleads you. 13:6Many will come in my name saying, 'I am he,' and many they will mislead. 13:7But when you hear wars and news of wars, do not be scared; it is necessary for this to happen.

"But the end is not yet, 13:8for people will rise up against people and kingdom against kingdom. There will be earthquakes in various places. There will be famines. These things are the beginning of birth pains.

13:9"But you yourselves beware! They will hand you over to sanhedrins,[1] and you will be beaten in synagogues, and you will be stood in front of governors and kings because of me, as a testimony to them. 13:10And to all the non-Jews it is first necessary for the gospel to be preached. 13:11But when they lead you away and hand you over, do not worry beforehand about what you should say; whatever is given you in that hour, speak that, for you are not the ones speaking, but the holy spirit is. 13:12And brother will hand over brother to death, and a father a child, and children will rise up against parents and have them put to death. 13:13And you will be objects of hatred by all because of my name. But the one that has endured to the end will be saved.

13:14"But whenever you see the 'abomination of desolation' standing where it ought not"[2] (may the reader understand),[3] "then those in Judea should flee

---

1   Local Jewish councils.

2   A reference to a prophecy recorded in the Hebrew Bible (Daniel 11:31).

3   Mark does not identify what the 'abomination of desolation' is (and hence his remark). The Gospel of Luke, written several years later, interprets the meaning as: "Jerusalem surrounded by

to the mountains. ¹³:¹⁵The one upon the housetop should not come down or go inside to pick up anything out of his house, ¹³:¹⁶and the one in the field should not return to the things behind to pick up his outer garment. ¹³:¹⁷But woe to the pregnant and to those nursing infants in those days. ¹³:¹⁸Be praying that it does not happen in winter, ¹³:¹⁹for those days will be a tribulation such as has not occurred since the beginning of creation, which God created, until now and will not occur again. ¹³:²⁰And if the Lord had not cut short those days, no one would likely be saved; but for the sake of the chosen ones, whom he has chosen, he has cut short the days. ¹³:²¹And then if anyone says to you, 'Look! There is the Christ' or 'Look! There he is!' do not believe it, ¹³:²²because false Christs and false prophets will rise up and produce signs and wonders to mislead, if possible, the chosen ones. ¹³:²³You, then, beware! I have told you everything beforehand.

¹³:²⁴"But in those days after the tribulation, 'the sun will be darkened, and the moon will not shed its light,'[4] ¹³:²⁵and 'the stars will be falling from the heavens, and the powers in the heavens will be shaken.'[5] ¹³:²⁶And then they will see the 'Son of Man coming in the clouds'[6] with much power and glory. ¹³:²⁷And then he will send out the angels and will gather together his chosen ones from the four winds, from the extremity of earth to the extremity of heaven.

¹³:²⁸Now learn the parable from the fig tree: As soon as its young branch grows tender and puts forth its leaves, you know that summer is near. ¹³:²⁹So also when you see these things taking place, you know that he is near, at the doors. ¹³:³⁰Truly I am telling you that this generation will not pass away until all these things happen. ¹³:³¹The heavens and the earth will pass away, but my words will not pass away."

---

encamped armies" (Luke 21:20), connecting it to the Roman siege of Jerusalem in 70 CE.

4   A reference to Isaiah 13:10 in the Hebrew Bible.
5   Isaiah 34:4. References to the Hebrew Bible appear to be taken from the Greek translation (used widely by the Greek-speaking early Christians).
6   A reference to Daniel 7:13.

Think about it.

1.   According to what is written here, when is this prophecy supposed to be fulfilled?
2.   What is the ultimate fate for the loyal followers of Jesus?

59. The Laws of Manu

Translated by George Bühler

The Laws of Manu (also known as *Manusmriti*) is a Sanskrit work of the Smriti tradition, that is, scripture having to do with dharma (religious duty) and written in metrical verse, second in authority to Sruti (divinely revealed dharma) in the Hindu belief system. The Smritis began to be composed orally in India after 500 BCE and written down later. The *Manusmriti* dates approximately to the first century CE. The rules are presented as a discourse to a group of seers by the legendary figure Manu, who is said to have survived the Great Flood and who became the first king of the earth and progenitor of the human race.

147. By a girl, by a young woman, or even by an aged one, nothing must be done independently, even in her own house.

148. In childhood a female must be subject to her father, in youth to her husband, when her lord is dead to her sons a woman must never be independent.

149. She must not seek to separate herself from her father, husband, or sons; by leaving them she would make both (her own and her husband's) families contemptible.

150. She must always be cheerful, clever in (the management of her) household affairs, careful in cleaning her utensils, and economical in expenditure.

151. Him to whom her father may give her, or her brother with the father's permission, she shall obey as long as he lives, and when he is dead, she must not insult (his memory).

152. For the sake of procuring good fortune to (brides), the recitation of benedictory texts (svasty-ayana), and the sacrifice to the Lord of creatures (Pragâpati) are used at weddings; (but) the betrothal (by the father or guardian) is the cause of (the husband's) dominion (over his wife).

153. The husband who wedded her with sacred texts* always gives happiness to his wife, both in season and out of season, in this world and in the next.

154. Though destitute of virtue, or seeking I pleasure (elsewhere), or devoid of good qualities, (yet) a husband must be constantly worshipped as a god by a faithful wife.

155. No sacrifice, no vow, no fast must be performed by women apart (from their husbands); if a wife obeys her husband, she will for that (reason alone) be exalted in heaven.

156. A faithful wife, who desires to dwell (after death) with her husband, must never do anything that might displease him who took her hand, whether he be alive or dead.

157. At her pleasure let her emaciate her body by (living on) pure flowers, roots, and fruit; but she must never even mention the name of another man after her husband has died.

158. Until death let her be patient (of hardships), self-controlled, and chaste, and strive (to fulfil) that most excellent duty which (is prescribed) for wives who have one husband only.

The Laws of Manu, The Sacred Books of the East, Volume XXV, trans. George Bühler, pp. 195–198. Oxford University Press, 1886. Copyright in the Public Domain.

159. Many thousands of Brâhma*n*as who were chaste from their youth, have gone to heaven without continuing their race.

160. A virtuous wife who after the death of her husband constantly remains chaste, reaches heaven, though she have no son, just like those chaste men.

161. But a woman who from a desire to have offspring violates her duty towards her (deceased) husband, brings on herself disgrace in this world, and loses her place with her husband (in heaven).

162. Offspring begotten by another man is here not (considered lawful), nor (does offspring begotten) on another man's wife (belong to the begetter), nor is a second husband anywhere prescribed for virtuous women.

163. She who cohabits with a man of higher caste, forsaking her own husband who belongs to a lower one, will become contemptible in this world, and is called a remarried woman (paraptirva).

164. By violating her duty towards her husband, a wife is disgraced in this world, (after death) she enters the womb of a jackal, and is tormented by diseases (the punishment of) her sin.

165. She who, controlling her thoughts, words, and deeds, never slights her lord, resides (after death) with her husband (in heaven), and is called a virtuous (wife).

166. In reward of such conduct, a female who controls her thoughts, speech, and actions, gains in this (life) highest renown, and in the next (world) a place near her husband.

167. A twice-born man, versed in the sacred law, shall burn a wife of equal caste who conducts herself thus and dies before him, with (the sacred fires used for) the Agnihotra, and with the sacrificial implements.

168. Having thus, at the funeral, given the sacred fires to his wife who dies before him, he may marry again, and again kindle (the fires).

169. (Living) according to the (preceding) rules, he must never neglect the five (great) sacrifices, and, having taken a wife, he must dwell in (his own) house during the second period of his life.

Think about it.

1. What religious duties does a woman have?
2. What are the rules concerning widows? Why do you think a rule like this was made?

60. Critical Essays

Translated by Alfred Forke

Critical Essays (*Lùnhéng*) is a Chinese work by Wang Chong (27–c. 100 CE), a Han Dynasty Confucian philosopher who rejected what he believed to be the superstitious excesses of Confucianism made popular by Dong Zhongshu and others (see reading #49). His book, written c. 80 CE, provides secular, rational, mechanistic explanations of natural phenomena. In the following excerpt, he criticizes belief in an afterlife.

CHAPTER XV.

On Death.

1. People say that the dead become ghosts, are conscious, and can hurt men. Let us examine this by comparing men with other beings:—

2. The dead do not become ghosts, have no consciousness, and cannot injure others. How do we know this? We know it from other beings. Man is a being, and other creatures are likewise beings. When a creature dies, it does not become a ghost, for what reason then must man alone become a ghost, when he expires? In this world you can separate man from other creatures, but not on the ground that he becomes a ghost. The faculty to become a ghost cannot be a distinctive mark. If, on the other hand, there is no difference between man and other creatures, we have no reason either to suppose that man may become a ghost.

3. Man lives by the vital fluid. When he dies, this vital fluid is exhausted. It resides in the arteries. At death the pulse stops, and the vital fluid ceases to work: then the body decays, and turns into earth and clay. By what could it become a ghost?

4. Without ears or eyes men have no perceptions. In this respect the deaf and the blind resemble plants and trees. But are men, whose vital fluid is gone, merely as if they had no eyes, or no ears? No. Their decay means complete dissolution.

5. That which is diffuse and invisible, is called a ghost, or a spirit. When people perceive the shape of a ghost or a spirit, it cannot be the vital fluid of a dead man, because ghost and spirit are only designations for something diffuse and invisible. When a man dies, his spirit ascends to heaven, and his bones return to the earth, therefore they are called *Kwei* (ghost) which means "to return." A spirit *(Shên)* is something diffuse and shapeless.

6. Some say that ghost and spirit are names of activity and passivity. The passive principle opposes things and returns, hence its name *Kuei* (ghost). The active principle fosters and produces things, and therefore is called *Shên* (spirit), which means "to extend." This is re-iterated without end. When it finishes, it begins again.

7. Man lives by the spiritual fluid. When he dies, he again returns this spiritual fluid. Activity and passivity are spoken of as spirit and ghost.

When man dies, one speaks likewise of his spirit and his ghost.

8. The fluid becomes man, just as water turns into ice. The water crystallizes to ice, and the fluid coagulates, and forms man. The ice melting becomes water, and man dying becomes spirit again. It is called spirit, just as molten ice resumes the name water. When we have a man before us, we use another name. Hence there are no proofs for the assertion that the dead possess knowledge, or that they can take a form, and injure people.

9. When men see ghosts, they appear like living men. Just from the fact that they have the shape of living men we can infer that they cannot be the essence of the dead, as will be seen from the following:—

10. Fill a bag with rice, and a sack with millet. The rice in the bag is like the millet in the sack. Full, they look strong, stand upright, and can be seen. Looking at them from afar, people know that they are a bag of rice, and a sack of millet, because their forms correspond to their contents, and thus become perceptible. If the bag has a hole, the rice runs out, and if the sack is damaged, the millet is spilt. Then the bag and the sack collapse. and are no more visible, when looked at from afar.

11. Plan's vital fluid resides in the body, as the millet and the rice do in the bag and the sack. At death the body decays, and the vital fluid disperses, just as the millet and the rice escape from the pierced or damaged bag, or sack. When the millet or the rice are gone, the bag and the sack do not take a form again. How then could there be a visible body again, after the vital fluid has been scattered and lost?

12. When animals die, their flesh decomposes, but their skin and their hair still remain, and can be worked into a fur, which appears still to have, the shape of an animal. Therefore dog thieves will don dog skins. People then do not discover them, because disguised in a dog's fur-skin, they do not rouse any suspicion.

13. Now, when a man dies, his skin and hair are destroyed. Provided that his vital force did still exist, how could the spirit again enter the same body, and become visible? The dead cannot borrow the body of a living man to re-appear, neither can the living borrow the soul of the dead to disappear.

14. The Six Animals can only be transformed into a human shape as long as their bodies and their vital fluid are still unimpaired. When they die, their bodies putrefy, and even, if they possess the courage and the audacity of a tiger or a rhinoceros, they can more be metamorphosed. Niu Ai, duke of Lu during an illness could be transformed into a tiger, because he was not yet dead. It happens that a living body is transformed into another living body, but not that a dead body is changed into a living one.

15. From the time, when heaven and earth were set in order, and the reign of the "Human Emperors" downward people died at their allotted time. Of those, who expired in their middle age, or quite young, millions and millions might be counted. The number of the persons actually living would be less than that of those who died. If we suppose that after death a man becomes a ghost, there would be a ghost on every road, and at every step. Should men appear as ghosts after death, then tens of thousands of ghosts ought to be seen. They would fill the halls, throng the courts, and block the streets and alleys, instead of the one or two which are occasionally met with.

16. When a man has died on a battle-field, they say that his blood becomes a will-o'-the-wisp. The blood is the vital force of the living. The will-o'-the-wisp seen by people, while walking at night, has no human form, it is desultory and concentrated like a light. Though being the blood of a dead man, it does not resemble a human shape in form, how then could a man, whose vital force is gone, still appear with a human body?

17. If the ghosts seen all looked like dead men, there might be some doubt left that the dead

become ghosts, and sometimes even assume human form.

18. Sick people see ghosts, and say that So-and-So has come to them. At that time So-and-So was not yet dead, but the fluid perceived resembled him. If the dead become ghosts, how is it that sick people see the bodies of the living?

19. The nature of heaven and earth is such, that a new fire can be lighted, but an extinguished fire cannot be set ablaze again. A new man can be born, but a dead one cannot be resurrected. If burnt-out ashes could be kindled again into a blazing fire, I would be very much of opinion that the dead might take a bodily form again. Since, however, an extinguished fire cannot burn again, we are led to the conclusion that the dead cannot become ghosts.

20. Ghosts are considered to be the vital spirits of the dead. If this were really the case, people seeing ghosts ought to see their bodies naked only, but not wearing dresses, or covered with garments, because garments have no vital spirits. When men die, their clothes become decomposed together with their bodies, how could they be put on again?

21. The vital spirits have their original seat in the blood fluid, and this fluid always adheres to the body. If notwithstanding the decay of the body the vital spirits were still extant, they might become ghosts. Now garments are made of silk stuffs and other fabrics. During man's life-time his blood fluid does not permeate them, nor have they any blood of their own. When the body is destroyed, they share its fate, how could they of themselves re-assume the shape of garments. Consequently, if ghosts are seen which bear a resemblance to dresses, they must also be like bodies, and if they are, we know that they cannot be the vital spirits of the dead.

22. Since the, dead cannot become ghosts, they cannot have any consciousness either. We infer this from the fact that before their birth men have no consciousness. Before they are born, they form part of the, primogenial fluid, and when they die, they revert to it. This primogenial fluid is vague and diffuse, and the human fluid, a part of it. Anterior to his birth, man is devoid of consciousness, and at his death lie returns to this original state of unconsciousness, for how should he be conscious?

23. Man is intelligent and sagacious, because he has in himself the fluid of the Five Virtues, which is in him, because the Five Organs are in his body. As long as the five parts are uninjured, man is bright and clever, but when they become diseased, his intellect is dimmed and confused, which is tantamount to stupidity and dullness.

24. After death the five inward parts putrefy, and when they do so the five virtues lose their substratum. That which harbours intelligence is destroyed, and that which is called intelligence disappears. The body requires the fluid for its maintenance, and the fluid, the body to become conscious. There is no fire in the world burning quite of itself, how could there be an essence without a body, but conscious of itself?

25. Man's death is like sleep, and sleep comes next to a trance, which resembles death. If a man does not wake up again from a trance, he dies. If he awakes, he returns from death, as though he had been asleep. Thus sleep, a trance, and death are essentially the same. A sleeper cannot know what he did, when he was awake, as a dead man is unaware of his doings during his life-time. People may talk or do anything by the side of a sleeping man, he does not know, and so the dead man has no consciousness of till good or bad actions performed in front of his coffin. When a man is asleep, his vital fluid is still there, and his body intact, and yet he is unconscious. How much more must this be the case with a dead man whose vital spirit is scattered and gone, and whose body is in a state of decay?

26. When a man has been beaten and hurt by another, lie goes to the magistrate, and makes his complaint, because he can talk to people, and is conscious. But, when a person is slain by somebody, the murderer is unknown, his family perhaps not knowing, even the place, where his corpse is lying. If under such circumstances the murdered man was conscious, he would assuredly be tilled with the

greatest wrath against his murderer. He ought to be able to speak into the magistrate's ear, and give him the name of the miscreant, and, if he were able to go home, and speak to his people, he would inform them, where the body was. But all that he cannot do. That shows that he has no consciousness.

27. Now-a-days, living persons in a trance will sometimes as mediums speak for those who have died, and diviners, striking black chords, will call down the dead, whose souls then will talk through the diviner's mouth. All that is brag and wild talk. If it be not mere gossip, then we have a manifestation of the vital fluid of some being.

28. Some say that the spirit cannot speak. If it cannot speak, it cannot have any knowledge either. Knowledge requires a force, just as speech does.

29. Anterior to man's death, his mental faculties and vital spirit are all in order. When he falls sick, he becomes giddy, and his vital spirit is affected. Death is the climax of sickness. If even during a sickness, which is only a small beginning of death, a man feels confused and giddy, how will it be, when the climax is reached? When the vital spirit is seriously affected, it loses its consciousness, and when it is scattered altogether?

30. Human death is like the extinction of fire. When a fire is extinguished, its light does not shine any more, and when man dies, his intellect does not perceive any more. The nature of both is the same. If people nevertheless pretend that the dead have knowledge, they are mistaken. What is the difference between a sick man about to die and a light about to go out? When a light is extinguished, its radiation is dispersed, and only the candle remains. When man has died, his vital force is gone, and the body alone remains. To assert that a person after death is still conscious is like saying that an extinguished light shines again.

31. During the chilly winter months the cold air prevails, and water turns into ice. At the approach of spring, the air becomes warm, and the ice melts to water. Man is born in the universe, as ice is produced, so to say. The *Yang* and the *Yin* fluids

crystallise, and produce man. When his years are completed, and his span of life comes to its end, he dies, and reverts to those fluids. As spring water cannot freeze, again, so the soul of a dead man cannot become a body again.

32. Let us suppose that a jealous husband and a jealous wife are living together. The debauchery and the disreputable conduct of one party is the cause of constant outbursts of anger, fighting, and quarrelling. Now, if the husband dies, the wife will marry again, and if the wife dies, the husband will do the same. If the other knew of it, he would undoubtedly fly into a rage. But husband and wife, when dead, keep perfectly quiet, and give no sound. The other may marry again, they take no heed, and it has no evil consequences. That proves that they are unconscious.

33. Confucius buried his mother at Fang. Subsequently such heavy rain fell, that the tomb at *Fang* collapsed. When Confucius heard of it, he wept bitterly and said:—The ancients did not repair graves." Therefore he did not repair it. Provided the dead are conscious, they ought to be angry with those who do not keep their tombs in repair. Knowing this, Confucius would have repaired the grave to please the departed soul, but he did not do so. His intelligence as a Sage was of the highest order, but he knew that spirits are unconscious.

34. When dried bones are lying about in lonely places, it may happen that some mournful cries are heard there. If such a wail is heard at night-time, people believe that it is the voice of a dead man, but they are wrong. When a living man talks, he breathes. His breath is kept in his mouth and his throat. He moves his tongue, opens and shuts his mouth, and thus produces words. It is like playing a flute. When the flute is broken, the air escapes, and does not keep inside, and the hands have nothing to touch. Consequently no sound is produced. The tubes of the flute correspond to the human mouth and throat. The hands touch the holes in the tubes in the same manner, as man moves his tongue. When he is dead, his mouth and throat decay, and

the tongue moves no more. How should words be articulated then? If, while dried bones are lying about, wails and laments are heard, they come from men, for bones cannot produce them.

35. Others imagine that it is the autumn (which produces these sounds). This statement is not much different from the other that ghosts cry at night. If the autumn air causes these extraordinary moans and wails, it must have some substratum. Because this has happened near the bones of a dead man, people have presumed that these bones are still conscious, and utter these mournful cries in the wilderness. There are thousands and thousands of skeletons bleaching in the grass and in the swamps, therefore we ought to be haunted by their laments at every step.

36. It is possible to make somebody speak, who usually does not speak, but impossible that somebody who speaks, should be induced to speak again after death. Even he who spoke before, cannot be caused to speak again. Similarly, when a plant comes forth, its fluid is green, which is, as it were, given it. When the same plant dies, the green colour disappears, or is taken away. Endowed with the fluid, the plant is green, deprived of it, it loses the green colour. After the latter is gone, it cannot he added again, nor can the plant grow green again of its own accord. Sound and colour correspond to one another, and are both derived from Heaven. The brilliant green colour is like a lugubrious cry. The colour of a faded plant cannot become green again, it would, therefore, be a mistake to assume that a dead man's cry could still be produced of itself.

37. Man is able to talk, because he possesses vital energy. As long as he can eat and drink, the vital energy is well fed, but no sooner do eating and drinking cease, than the energy is destroyed. After this destruction there are no more sounds possible. When the person is worn out, and cannot eat any more, the mouth cannot speak any further. Death is exhaustion in the highest degree, how could man still speak then?

38. There are those who say that the dead smell the sacrificed meat, and eat the air, and that they are thus enabled to speak. The vital force of the dead is that of the living. Let a living being neither eat nor drink, and only inhale the smell of offerings, and feed upon air, and he will die of starvation after no more than three days.

39. Another opinion is that the vital force of the dead is more powerful than that of the living, and that for this reason it can smell the air, and produce sounds.

40. The vital force of the living is in their body, that of the dead, out of it. In what do the dead and the living after, and what difference does it make that the vital fluid is within the body, or outside of it? Take water, and fill it into a big jug. When the jug breaks, the water flows to the earth, but can the water on the floor be different from that in the jug? The water on the floor is not different from that in the jug, then why should the vital force outside the body be different from that within?

41. Since a man, when dead, does not become a, ghost, has no knowledge, and cannot speak, he cannot hurt others either for the following reason. In his anger, a, man uses breath, but in order to injure others, he requires strength. To make use of it, his sinews and bones must he strong, then he can hurt others. An angry man may breathe heavily so near to others, that his breath shoots forth against their faces, but though he possess the valour of *Mêng Pên*, it does them no harm. However, when he stretches out his hand, and strikes, or lifts the foot and kicks, he breaks whatever he hits. The bones of the dead decay, the strength of his muscles is lost, and he does not lift hand or foot. Although the vital fluid be still existant, it is as if it were, only breathing, and nothing else follows. How then should it do harm to anybody?

42. Men and other creatures hurt others by means of knives, which they grasp with their hands and arms, and with their strong and sharp nails or teeth. Now, when a man is dead, his hands and arms waste away, and cannot lift a blade any more, and

nails and teeth fall out, and cannot bite any more. How should they do harm to others then?

43. When a child is just born, his hands and feet are quite complete, yet the hands cannot grasp, and the feet cannot kick. The fluid has just concreted, but has no strength. Hence it is evident that the vital fluid possesses no strength. The fluid forms the body. As long as the body is still feeble and weak, it cannot do harm to any one, and how much less still, when through death the fluid becomes lost, and the vital spirit is dissolved. Something feeble and weak is uncapable of injuring people, and one asserts that cold bones can do it? Is the fluid of the dead not lost? How should it injure anybody?

44. Before a hen's egg is hatched, there is a formless mass in the egg-shell, which, on leaking out, looks like water. After a good hen has covered the egg, the body of the chicken is formed, and when it has been completed, the young bird can pick the shell, and kick. Human death resembles the time of the formless mass. How could a formless fluid hurt anybody?

45. A man becomes bold and fierce, so that lie can assault others, by eating and drinking. Eating and drinking his fill, lie grows stout and strong, Bold and fierce, and can do harm to others. While a man is sick, he can neither eat nor drink, and his body becomes worn out and weak. When this weariness and languor reach the highest degree, death ensues. During that time of sickness and languor his enemy may stand by his side, he cannot revile him, and a thief may take his things away, he has means to prevent him, all on account of his debility and lassitude. Death is the debility and languor in the extreme, how then could a man after death still injure any one?

46. If chickens or dogs, which somebody keeps, are stolen, he will, at all events, wax angry, though he be timid, and not very strong, and his anger may be so violent, that he tries conclusions with the robber, and is slain by him. During the time of great anarchy people will use one another as food. Now, provided that the spirit was conscious, it ought to

be able to destroy its enemies. A human body is worth more than a chicken or a dog, and one's own death is of greater consequence than a robbery. The fact that a man is excited over a chicken or a dog, but has no bad feeling against the individual who devoured him, shows that he has not the power to hurt any one.

47. Prior to its casting off its exuviae, a cicada is a chrysalis. When it casts them off, it leaves the pupa state, and is transformed into a cicada. The vital spirit of a dead man leaving the body may be compared to the cicada emerging from the chrysalis. As cicada it cannot hurt the chrysalides. Since it cannot do so, why should the vital spirit of a dead man hurt living bodies?

48. The real nature of dreams is very doubtful. Some say that, while people are dreaming, their vital spirits remain in their bodies, and produce lucky or unlucky visions. Others hold thatthe vital spirit, communicates with men and other creatures. Now, if it really remains in the body, the vital spirit of the dead must do the same. If however, the spirit mixes with men, people may dream that they have killed somebody. Haling killed somebody, they are perhaps themselves murdered by somebody else. But if, on the following day, they look at the body of that person, or examine their own, they will find no trace whatever of a wound inflicted by a sword. Dreams are caused by the vital spirit, and this spirit is identical with the vital spirit of the dead. The vital spirit of dreams cannot injure people, therefore the spirit of the dead cannot do so either.

49. When the fire burns, the caldron boils, and when the boiling stops, the steam ceases. All depends on the fire. When the vital spirit is incensed, it can do harm, not being angry, it, cannot injure people. The fire blazing in the stove, the kettle bubbles, and the steam rises. When the vital force is enraged in the bosom, there is an innervation of strength, and the body is hot. Now, when a man is about to die, his body is cold and chilly. The cold and chilliness increase, until at last he expires. At the time of death, the vital spirit is not irritated,

and air the death of the body it is like the hot water taken from the caldron, how should it hurt people?

50. Things have a certain relation to man. When a man becomes insane, and one knows the proper thing, his malady may be cured by applying this tiling as a remedy. As long as a thing is alive, its vital spirit adheres to its body, and consequently can change its form, and enter into close connection with man. After it has died, its body rots, and the vital spirit is dispersed. In default of a substratum it cannot undergo any more changes. The human vital spirit is like that of things. While they are alive, their spirit may become sick, when they die, it evaporates and disappears. Men are like things in this respect, when they die, their vital spirit also becomes extinguished, how could it still do any mischief?

51. Should anybody object by saying that men are much more precious than things, and that their vital spirit is different, we can reply that, as a matter of fact, things can be metamorphosed, but man cannot, and that so far his vital spirit is on the contrary inferior to that of things, whose essence surpasses that of man.

52. Water and fire drown and burn. All that can injure man must be a substance belonging to one of the five elements. Metal hurts man, wood beats him, earth crushes him, water drowns him, and fire burns him. Is the vital spirit of the dead a substance like the five elements? Does it injure people, or is it not a substance?—It cannot injure people. Not being a substance, it must be a fluid. Of the fluids which injure man that of the sun is the most virulent. Does the fluid of a man, when he dies, become virulent? Can it injure people or not?—It cannot injure people.

53. Thus we hold that the dead do not become ghosts, are not conscious, and cannot hurt people. Consequently, it is evident that the ghosts, which are seen, are not the vital force of dead men, and that, when men have been hurt, it cannot have been done through this vital force.

Think about it.

1. How does Wang Chong attempt to show that ghosts do not exist?
2. What do his arguments reveal about common beliefs of the time?

61. Lessons for Women

By Nancy Lee Swann

Ban Zhao (45–c. 116 CE) was a female scholar of the later Han dynasty in China. She served as imperial historian under the emperor He (r. 88–105 CE), during which time she completed writing the Book of Han, a history of the early Han dynasty begun by her brother. Late in her life, she wrote Lessons for Women (*Nü Jie*), which gave advice on proper feminine behavior. Here are a few samples from the book, which illustrate the expectations of the times.

I, the unworthy writer, am unsophisticated, unenlightened, and by nature unintelligent, but I am fortunate both to have received not a little favor from my scholarly Father, and to have had a cultured mother and instructresses upon whom to rely for a literary education as well as for training in good manners. More than forty years have passed since at the age of fourteen I took up the dustpan and the broom in the Cao family [*the family into which she married*]. During this time with trembling heart I feared constantly that I might disgrace my parents, and that I might multiply difficulties for both the women and the men of my husband's family. Day and night I was distressed in heart, but I labored without confessing weariness. Now and hereafter, however, I know how to escape from such fears.

Being careless, and by nature stupid, I taught and trained my children without system. Consequently I fear that my son Gu may bring disgrace upon the Imperial Dynasty by whose Holy Grace he has unprecedentedly received the extraordinary privilege of wearing the Gold and the Purple, a privilege for the attainment of which by my son, I a humble subject never even hoped. Nevertheless, now that he is a man and able to plan his own life, I need not again have concern for him. But I do grieve that you, my daughters, just now at the age for marriage, have not at this time had gradual training and advice; that you still have not learned the proper customs for married women. I fear that by failure in good manners in other families you will humiliate both your ancestors and your clan. I am now seriously ill, life is uncertain. As I have thought of you all in so untrained a state, I have been uneasy many a time for you. At hours of leisure I have composed ... these instructions under the title, "Lessons for Women." In order that you may have something wherewith to benefit your persons, I wish every one of you, my daughters each to write out a copy for yourself.

From this time on every one of you strive to practice these lessons.

HUMILITY

On the third day after the birth of a girl the ancients observed three customs: first to place the baby below the bed; second to give her a potsherd[1] with which to play; and third to announce her birth to her ancestors by an offering. Now to lay the baby below the bed plainly indicated that she is lowly and weak, and should regard it as her primary duty to humble herself before others. To give her potsherds with which to play indubitably signified that she should practice labor and consider it her primary duty to be industrious. To announce her birth before her ancestors clearly meant that she ought to esteem as her primary duty the continuation of the observance of worship in the home.

These three ancient customs epitomize woman's ordinary way of life and the teachings of the traditional ceremonial rites and regulations. Let a woman modestly yield to others; let her respect others; let her put others first, herself last. Should she do something good, let her not mention it; should she do something bad let her not deny it. Let her bear disgrace; let her even endure when others speak or do evil to her. Always let her seem to tremble and to fear. When a woman follows such maxims as these then she may be said to humble herself before others.

Let a woman retire late to bed, but rise early to duties; let her nor dread tasks by day or by night. Let her not refuse to perform domestic duties whether easy or difficult. That which must be done, let her finish completely, tidily, and systematically, When a woman follows such rules as these, then she may be said to be industrious.

Let a woman be correct in manner and upright in character in order to serve her husband. Let her live in purity and quietness of spirit, and attend to her own affairs. Let her love not gossip and silly laughter. Let her cleanse and purify and arrange in order the wine and the food for the offerings to the ancestors. When a woman observes such principles as these, then she may be said to continue ancestral worship.

No woman who observes these three fundamentals of life has ever had a bad reputation or has fallen into disgrace. If a woman fail to observe them, how can her name be honored; how can she but bring disgrace upon herself?

HUSBAND AND WIFE

The Way of husband and wife is intimately connected with Yin and Yang[2]. and relates the individual to gods and ancestors. Truly it is the great principle of Heaven and Earth, and the great basis of human relationships. Therefore the "Rites"[3] honor union of man and woman; and in the "Book of Poetry"[4] the "First Ode" manifests the principle of marriage. For these reasons the relationships cannot but be an important one.

If a husband be unworthy, then he possesses nothing by which to control his wife. If a wife be unworthy, then she possesses nothing with which to serve her husband. If a husband does not control his wife, then the rules of conduct manifesting his authority are abandoned and broken. If a wife does not serve her husband, when the proper relationship between men and women and the natural order of things are neglected and destroyed. As a matter of fact the purpose of these two [the controlling of women by men, and the serving of men by women] is the same.

Now examine the gentlemen of the present age. They only know that wives must be controlled, and that the husband's rules of conduct manifesting his authority must be established. They therefore teach their boys to read books and study histories. But they do not in the least understand that husbands and masters must also be served, and that the proper relationship and the rites should be maintained. Yet only to teach men and not to teach women—is that not ignoring the essential relation between them?

---

1 A piece of broken pottery.

2 These are the two basis elements of the Universe: Yin, the soft yielding feminine element, and Yang the hard aggressive male element. Every substance contains both elements in varying proportions.

3 The Liji.

4 The Shijing.

According to the "Rites," it is the rule to begin to teach children to read at the age of eight years, and by the age of fifteen years they ought then to be ready for cultural training. Only why should it not be that girls' education as well as boys' be according to this principle?

RESPECT AND CAUTION

As Yin and Yang are not of the same nature, so man and woman have different characteristics. The distinctive quality of the Yang is rigidity; the function of the Yin is yielding. Man is honored for strength; a woman is beautiful on account of her gentleness. Hence there arose the common saying: "A man though born like a wolf may, it is feared, become a weak monstrosity; a woman though born like a mouse may, it is feared, become a tiger."

Now For self-culture nothing equals respect for others. To counteract firmness nothing equals compliance. Consequently it can be said that the Way of respect and acquiescence is woman's most important principle of conduct. So respect may be defined as nothing other than holding on to that which is permanent; and acquiescence nothing other than being liberal and generous. Those who are steadfast in devotion know that they should stay in their proper places; those who are liberal and generous esteem others, and honor and serve them.

If husband and wife have the habit of staying together, never leaving one another, and following each other around within the limited space of their own rooms, then they will lust after and take liberties with one another. From such action improper language will arise between the two. This kind of discussion may lead co-licentiousness. But of licentiousness will be born a heart of disrespect to the husband. Such a result comes From not knowing that one should stay in one's proper place.

Furthermore, affairs may be either crooked or straight; words may be either right or wrong. Straightforwardness cannot but lead to quarreling; crookedness cannot but lead to accusation. If there are really accusations and quarrels, then undoubtedly there will be angry affairs. Such a result comes from not esteeming others, and not honoring and serving them.

If wives suppress not contempt for husbands, then it follows that such wives rebuke and scold their husbands. If husbands stop not short of anger, then they are certain to beat their wives. The correct relationship between husband and wife is based upon harmony and intimacy, and conjugal love is grounded in proper union. Should actual blows be dealt, how could matrimonial relationship be preserved? Should sharp words be spoken, how could conjugal love exist? If love and proper relationship both be destroyed, then husband and wife are divided.

WOMANLY QUALIFICATIONS

A woman ought to have four qualifications: (1) womanly virtue; (2) womanly words; (3) womanly bearing; and (4) womanly work. Now what is called womanly virtue need not be brilliant ability, exceptionally different from others. Womanly words need be neither clever in debate nor keen in conversation. Womanly appearance requires neither a pretty nor a perfect face and form. Womanly work need not be work done more skillfully than that of others.

To guard carefully her chastity; to control circumspectly her behavior; in every motion to exhibit modesty; and to model each act on the best usage, this is womanly virtue.

To choose her words with care; to avoid vulgar language; to speak at appropriate times; and nor to weary others with much conversation, may be called the characteristics of womanly words.

To wash and scrub filth away; to keep clothes and ornaments fresh and clean; to wash the head and bathe the body regularly, and to keep the person free from disgraceful filth, may be called the characteristics of womanly bearing.

With whole-hearted devotion to sew and to weave; to love not gossip and silly laughter; in cleanliness and order to prepare the wine and food for serving guests, may be called the characteristics of womanly work.

These four qualifications characterize the greatest virtue of a woman. No woman can afford to be without them. In fact they are very easy to possess if a woman only treasure them in her heart. The ancients had a saying: "Is love afar off? If I desire love, then love is at hand!" So can it be said of these qualifications.

IMPLICIT OBEDIENCE

Whenever the mother-in-law says, "Do not do that," and if what she says is right, unquestionably the daughter-in-law obeys. Whenever the mother-in-law says, "Do that," even if what she says is wrong, still the daughter-in-law submits unfailingly to the command. Let a woman not act contrary to the wishes and the opinions of parents-in-law about right and wrong; let her not dispute with the them what is straight and what is crooked. Such docility may be called obedience which sacrifices personal opinion. Therefore the ancient book, "A Pattern for Women," says: "If a daughter-in-law who follows the wishes of her parents-in-law is like and echo and shadow, how could she not be praised?

Think about it.

1. What do Ban Zhao's words reveal about the way women lived and were treated in her time?
2. How does Ban Zhao justify the customs of her people?
3. What similarities do you see between the Laws of Manu and Ban Zhao's Lessons for Women? What differences?

62. Buddhacarita

Translated by E. B. Cowell, F. Max Müller and J. Takakusu

Written in Classical Sanskrit by Ashvaghosha (c. 80–150 CE), an Indian philosopher-poet from the Kushan Empire, the Buddhacarita ("Acts of the Buddha") is an epic poem on the life of the Buddha, the earliest full biography of the Buddha we have. Unfortunately, it was written six hundred years after he died. In the following selection, the Crown Prince Siddhartha, even prior to his becoming the Buddha, resists the beauty of women.

BOOK IV.

1. Then from that city-garden, with their eyes restless in excitement, the women went out to meet the prince as a newly-arrived bridegroom;

2. And when they came up to him, their eyes wide open in wonder, they performed their due homage with hands folded like a lotus-calyx.

3. Then they stood surrounding him, their minds overpowered by passion, as if they were drinking him in with their eyes motionless and blossoming wide with love.

4. Some of the women verily thought that he was Kâma incarnate,—decorated as he was with his brilliant signs as with connate ornaments.

5. Others thought from his gentleness and majesty that it was the moon with its ambrosial beams as it were visibly come down to the earth.

6. Others, smitten by his beauty, yawned as if to swallow him, and fixing their eyes on each other, softly sighed.

7. Thus the women only looked upon him, simply gazing with their eyes,—they spoke not, nor did they smile, controlled by his power.

8. But having seen them thus listless, bewildered in their love, the wise son of the family priest, Udâyin, thus addressed them:

9. Ye are all skilled in all the graceful arts, proficients in understanding the language of amorous sentiments, possessed of beauty and gracefulness, thorough masters in your own styles.

10. With these graces of yours ye may embellish even the Northern Kurus, yea, even the dances of Kuvera, much more this little earth.

11. Ye are able to move even sages who have lost all their desires, and to ensnare even the gods who are charmed by heavenly nymphs.

12. By your skill in expressing the heart's feelings, by your coquetry, your grace, and your perfect beauty, ye are able to enrapture even women, how much more easily men.

13. You thus skilled as ye are, each set in her own proper sphere,—such as this is your power,—I am not satisfied with your simplicity [when you profess to find him beyond your reach].

14. This timid action of yours would be fit for new brides, their eyes closed through shame,—or it

"Book IV," *Buddhist Mahayana Texts, The Sacred Books of the East, Volume XLIX*, trans. E. B. Cowell, F. Max Müller, and J. Takakusu. Oxford University Press, 1894. Copyright in the Public Domain.

might be a blandishment worthy even of the wives of the cowherds.

15. What though this hero be great by his exalted glory, yet "great is the might of women," let this be your firm resolve.

16. In olden time a great seer, hard to be conquered even by the gods, was spurned by a harlot, the beauty of Kâsi, planting her feet upon him.

17. The Bhikshu Manthâlagautama was also formerly spurned by Bâlamukhyâ with her leg, and wishing to please her he carried out dead bodies for her sake to be buried.

18. And a woman low in standing and caste fascinated the great seer Gautama, though a master of long penances and old in years.

19. So Sântâ by her various wiles captivated and subdued the sage's son Rishyasringa, unskilled in women's ways.

20. And the great seer Visvâmitra, though plunged in a profound penance, was carried captive for ten years in the forests by the nymph Ghritâkî.

21. Many such seers as these have women brought to shame,—how much more then a delicate prince in the first flower of his age?

22. This being so, boldly put forth your efforts that the prosperity of the king's family may not be turned away from him.

23. Ordinary women captivate similar lovers; but they are truly women who subdue the natures of high and low.

24. Having heard these words of Udâyin these women as stung to the heart rose even above themselves for the conquest of the prince.

25. With their brows, their glances, their coquetries, their smiles, their delicate movements, they made all sorts of significant gestures like women utterly terrified.

26. But they soon regained their confidence through the command of the king and the gentle temperament of the prince, and through the power of intoxication and of love.

27. Then surrounded by troops of women the prince wandered in the wood like an elephant in the forests of Himavat accompanied by a herd of females.

28. Attended by the women he shone in that pleasant grove, as the sun surrounded by Apsarasas in his royal garden.

29. There some of them, urged by passion, pressed him with their full firm bosoms in gentle collisions.

30. Another violently embraced him after making a pretended stumble,—leaning on him with her shoulders drooping down, and with her gentle creeper-like arms dependent.

31. Another with her mouth smelling of spirituous liquor, her lower lip red like copper, whispered in his ear, 'Let my secret be heard.'

32. Another, all wet with unguents, as if giving him her command, clasped his hand eagerly and said, 'Perform thy rites of adoration here.'

33. Another, with her blue garments continually slipping down in pretended intoxication, stood conspicuous with her tongue visible like the night with its lightning flashing.

34. Others, with their golden zones tinkling, wandered about here and there, showing to him their hips veiled with thin cloth.

35. Others leaned, holding a mango-bough in full flower, displaying their bosoms like golden jars.

36. Another, coming from a lotus-bed, carrying lotuses and with eyes like lotuses, stood like the lotus-goddess Padmâ, by the side of that lotus-faced prince.

37. Another sang a sweet song easily understood and with the proper gesticulations, rousing him, self-subdued though he was, by her glances, as saying, 'O how thou art deluded.'

38. Another, having armed herself with her bright face, with its brow-bow drawn to its full, imitated his action, as playing the hero.

39. Another, with beautiful full bosoms, and having her earrings waving in the wind, laughed loudly at him, as if saying, 'Catch me, sir, if you can!'

40. Some, as he was going away, bound him with strings of garlands,—others punished him with

words like an elephant-driver's hook, gentle yet reproachful.

41. Another, wishing to argue with him, seizing a mango-spray, asked, all bewildered with passion, 'This flower, whose is it?'

42. Another, assuming a gait and attitude like those of a man, said to him, 'Thou who art conquered by women, go and conquer this earth!'

43. Then another with rolling eyes, smelling a blue lotus, thus addressed the prince with words slightly indistinct in her excitement,

44. See, my lord, this mango covered with its honey-scented flowers, where the kokila sings, as if imprisoned in a golden cage.

45. Come and see this asoka tree, which augments lovers' sorrows,—where the bees make a noise as if they were scorched by fire.

46. Come and see this tilaka tree, embraced by a slender mango-branch, like a man in a white garment by a woman decked with yellow unguents.

47. Behold this kuruvaka in flower, bright like fresh resin-juice, which bends down as if it felt reproached by the colour of women's nails.

48. Come and see this young asoka, covered all over with new shoots, which stands as it were ashamed at the beauty of our hands.

49. See this lake surrounded by the sinduvâra shrubs growing on its banks, like a fair woman reclining, clad in fine white cloth.

50. See the imperial power of females,—yonder ruddy-goose in the water goes behind his mate following her like a slave.

51. Come and listen to the notes of this intoxicated cuckoo as he sings, while another cuckoo sings as if consenting, wholly without care.

52. Would that thine was the intoxication of the birds which the spring produces,—and not the thought of a thinking man, ever pondering how wise he is!

53. Thus these young women, their souls carried away by love, assailed the prince with all kinds of stratagems.

54. But although thus attacked, he, having his senses guarded by self-control, neither rejoiced nor smiled, thinking anxiously, 'One must die.'

55. Having seen them in their real condition, that best of men pondered with an undisturbed and steadfast mind.

56. What is it that these women lack that they perceive not that youth is fickle? for this old age will destroy whatever has beauty.

57. Verily they do not see any one's plunge into disease, and so dismissing fear, they are joyous in a world which is all pain.

58. Evidently they know nothing of death which carries all away; and so at ease and without distress they can sport and laugh.

59. What rational being, who knows of old age, death and sickness, could stand or sit down at his ease or sleep, far less laugh?

60. But he verily is like one bereft of sense, who, beholding another aged or sick or dead, remains self-possessed and not afflicted.

61. (So) even when a tree is deprived of its flowers and fruits, or if it is cut down and falls, no other tree sorrows.

62. Seeing him thus absorbed in contemplation, with his desires estranged from all worldly objects, Udâyin, well skilled in the rules of policy, with kindly feelings addressed him:

63. Since I was appointed by the king as a fitting friend for thee, therefore I have a wish to speak to thee in this friendliness of my heart.

64. To hinder from what is disadvantageous,—to urge to what is advantageous,—and not to forsake in misfortune,—these are the three marks of a friend.

65. If I, after having promised my friendship, were not to heed when thou turnest away from the great end of man, there would be no friendship in me.

66. Therefore I speak as thy friend,—such rudeness as this to women is not befitting for one young in years and graceful in person.

67. It is right to woo a woman even by guile,—this is useful both for getting rid of shame and for one's own enjoyment.

68. Reverential behaviour and compliance with her wishes are what binds a woman's heart; good qualities truly are a cause of love, and women love respect.

69. Wilt thou not then, O large-eyed prince, even if thy heart is unwilling, seek to please them with a courtesy worthy of this beauty of thine?

70. Courtesy is the balm of women, courtesy is the best ornament; beauty without courtesy is like a grove without flowers.

71. But of what use is courtesy by itself? let it be assisted by the heart's feelings; surely, when worldly objects so hard to attain are in thy grasp, thou wilt not despise them.

72. Knowing that pleasure was the best of objects, even the god Puramdara (Indra) wooed in olden time Ahalyâ the wife of the saint Gautama.

73. So too Agastya wooed Rohinî, the wife of Soma; and therefore, as Sruti saith, a like thing befell Lopâmudrâ.

74. The great ascetic Vrihaspati begot Bharadvâga on Mamatâ the daughter of the Maruts, the wife of Autathya.

75. The Moon, the best of offerers, begat Buddha of divine nature on the spouse of Vrihaspati as she was offering a libation.

76. So too in old time Parâsara, overpowered by passion on the bank of the Yamunâ, lay with the maiden Kâlî who was the daughter of the son of the Water (Agni).

77. The sage Vasishtha through lust begot a son Kapiñgalâda on Akshamâlâ a despised low-caste woman.

78. And the seer-king Yayâti, even when the vigour of his prime was gone, sported in the Kaitraratha forest with the Apsaras Visvâkî.

79. And the Kaurava king Pându, though he knew that intercourse with his wife would end in death, yet overcome by the beauty and good qualities of Mâdrî yielded to the pleasures of love.

80. And so Karâlaganaka, when he carried off the Brâhman's daughter, incurred loss of caste thereby, but he would not give up his love.

81. Great heroes such as these pursued even contemptible desires for the sake of pleasure, how much more so when they are praiseworthy of their kind?

82. And yet thou, a young man, possessed of strength and beauty, despisest enjoyments which rightly belong to thee, and to which the whole world is devoted.'

83. Having heard these specious words of his, well-supported by sacred tradition, the prince made reply, in a voice like the thundering of a cloud:

84. This speech manifesting affection is well-befitting in thee; but I will convince thee as to where thou wrongly judgest me.

85. I do not despise worldly objects, I know that all mankind are bound up therein; but remembering that the world is transitory, my mind cannot find pleasure in them.

86. Old age, disease, and death—if these three things did not exist, I too should find my enjoyment in the objects that please the mind.

87. Yet even though this beauty of women were to remain perpetual, still delight in the pleasures of desire would not be worthy of the wise man.

88. But since their beauty will be drunk up by old age, to delight therein through infatuation cannot be a thing approved even by thyself.

89. He who himself subject to death, disease, and old age, can sport undisturbed with those whose very nature implies death, disease, and old age, such a man is on a level with birds and beasts.

90. And as for what thou sayest as to even those great men having become victims to desire, do not be bewildered by them, for destruction was also their lot.

91. Real greatness is not to be found there, where there is universally destruction, or where there is attachment to earthly objects, or a want of self-control.

92. And when thou sayest, "Let one deal with women even by guile," I know nought about guile, even if it be accompanied with courtesy.

93. That compliance too with a woman's wishes pleases me not, if truthfulness be not there; if there be not a union with one's whole soul and nature, then "out upon it" say I.

94. A soul overpowered by passion, believing in falsehood, carried away by attachment and blind to the faults of its objects,—what is there in it worth being deceived?

95. And if the victims of passion do deceive one another,—are not men unfit for women to look at and women for men?

96. Since then these things are so, thou surely wouldest not lead me astray into ignoble pleasures,— me afflicted by sorrow, and subject to old age and death?

97. Ah! thy mind must be very firm and strong, if thou canst find substance in the transitory pleasures of sense; even in the midst of violent alarm thou canst cling to worldly objects, when thou seest all created beings in the road of death.

98. But I am fearful and exceedingly bewildered, as I ponder the terrors of old age, death, and disease; I can find no peace, no self-command, much less can I find pleasure, while I see the world as it were ablaze with fire.

99. If desire arises in the heart of the man, who knows that death is certain,—I think that his soul must be made of iron, who restrains it in this great terror and does not weep.

100. Then the prince uttered a discourse full of resolve and abolishing the objects of desire; and the lord of day, whose orb is the worthy centre of human eyes, departed to the Western Mountain.

101. And the women, having worn their garlands and ornaments in vain, with their graceful arts and endearments all fruitless, concealing their love deep in their hearts, returned to the city with broken hopes.

102. Having thus seen the beauty of the troop of women who had gone out to the city-garden, now withdrawn in the evening,—the prince, pondering the transitoriness which envelopes all things, entered his dwelling.

103. Then the king, when he heard how his mind turned away from all objects of sense, could not lie down all that night, like an elephant with an arrow in its heart; but wearied in all sorts of consultation, he and his ministers could find no other means beside these (despised) pleasures to restrain his son's purpose.

Think about it.

1. What is the moral or message of this tale?
2. Do you think this story, or any part of it, is historically accurate? Why or why not?

63. The Lotus Sutra

Translated by Hendrik Kern

The most famous text of the Mahayana Buddhist tradition is the Lotus Sutra. Compiled by Buddhist monks over a period of years, it was completed in Sanskrit before the year 255 CE, when the first Chinese translation was made, but the oldest parts of the text (Chapters 1–9, 17) date to around the time of the Fourth Buddhist Council in Kashmir (c. 140 CE). The text exists in several versions, the most widely read being that of Kumarajiva, who translated it into Chinese in 406 CE. Its teachings are presented as a discourse of the Buddha, delivered near the end of his life. The following is a passage from Chapter 2.

Chapter II

Skillfulness

The Lord then rose with recollection and consciousness from his meditation, and forthwith addressed the venerable Sâriputra[1]: The Buddha knowledge, Sâriputra, is profound, difficult to understand, difficult to comprehend. It is difficult for all disciples and Pratyekabuddhas[2] to fathom the knowledge arrived at by the Tathâgatas,[3] and that, Sâriputra, because the Tathâgatas have worshipped many hundred thousand myriads of kotis[4] of Buddhas; because they have fulfilled their course for supreme, complete enlightenment, during many hundred thousand myriads of kotis of Æons; because they have wandered far, displaying energy and possessed of wonderful and marvellous properties; possessed of properties difficult to understand; because they have found out things difficult to understand.

The mystery of the Tathâgatas, is difficult to understand, Sâriputra, because when they explain the laws (or phenomena, things) that have their causes in themselves they do so by means of skilfulness, by the display of knowledge, by arguments, reasons, fundamental ideas, interpretations, and suggestions. By a variety of skilfulness they are able to release creatures that are attached to one point or another. The Tathâgatas, Sâriputra, have acquired the highest perfection in skilfulness and the display of knowledge; they are endowed with wonderful properties, such as the display of free and unchecked knowledge; the powers; the absence of hesitation; the independent conditions; the strength of the organs; the constituents of Bodhi[5]; the contemplations; emancipations; meditations; the degrees of concentration of mind. The Tathâgatas, Sâriputra, are able to expound various things and have something wonderful and marvellous. Enough,

---

1   One of the Buddha's most prominent disciples.
2   "Lone Buddhas," that is, those who achieve enlightenment on their own.
3   Those who are beyond all transitory phenomena.
4   A koti = 10 million.

---

5   Enlightenment.

Saddharma-Pundarîka or, *The Lotus Flower of the True Law, The Sacred Books of the East, Volume XXI*, trans. Hendrik Kern. Clarendon Press, 1884. Copyright in the Public Domain.

Sâriputra, let it suffice to say, that the Tathâgatas, have something extremely wonderful, Sâriputra. None but a Tathâgatha, Sâriputra, can impart to a Tathâgata those laws which the Tathâgata knows. And all laws, Sâriputra, are taught by the Tathâgata, and by him alone; no one but he knows all laws, what they are, how they are, like what they are, of what characteristics and of what nature they are.

[...]

The eminent disciples in the assembly headed by Âgñâta-Kaundinya, the twelve hundred Arhats[6] faultess and self-controlled, the other monks, nuns, male and femal lay devotees using the vehicle of disciples, and those who had entered the vehicle of Pratyeka-buddhas, all of them made this reflection: What may be the cause, what the reason of the Lord so extremely extolling the skilfulness of the Tathâgatas? of his extolling it by saying, 'Profound is the law by me discovered;' of his extolling it by saying, 'It is difficult for all disciples and Pratyekabuddhas to understand it.' But as yet the Lord has declared no more than one kind of emancipation, and therefore we also should acquire the Buddha-laws on reaching Nirvâna. We do not catch the meaning of this utterance of the Lord.

And the venerable Sâriputra, who apprehended the doubt and uncertainty of the four classes of the audience and guessed their thoughts from what was passing in his own mind, himself being in doubt about the law, then said to the Lord: What, O Lord, is the cause, what the reason of the Lord so repeatedly and extremely extolling the skilfulness, knowledge, and preaching of the Tathâgata? Why does he repeatedly extol it by saying, 'Profound is the law by me discovered; it is difficult to understand the mystery of the Tathâgatas.' Never before have I heard from the Lord such a discourse on the law. Those four classes of the audience, O Lord, are overcome with doubt and perplexity. Therefore may the Lord be pleased to explain what the Tathâgata is alluding

to, when repeatedly extolling the profound law of the Tathâgatas.

[...]

The venerable Sâriputra having spoken, the Lord said to him: Enough, Sâriputra; it is of no use explaining this matter. Why? Because, Sâriputra, the world, including the gods, would be frightened if this matter were expounded.

But the venerable Sâriputra entreated the Lord a second time, saying: Let the Lord expound, let the Sugata expound this matter, for in this assembly, O Lord, there are many hundreds, many thousands, many hundred thousands, many hundred thousand myriads of kotis of living beings who have seen former Buddhas, who are intelligent, and will believe, value, and accept the words of the Lord.

[...]

A third time the venerable Sâriputra entreated the Lord, saying, Let the Lord expound, let the Sugata expound this matter. In this assembly, O Lord, there are many hundreds of living beings my equals, and many hundreds, many thousands, many hundred thousands, many hundred thousand myriads of kotis of other living beings more, who in former births have been brought by the Lord to full ripeness. They will believe, value, and accept what the Lord declares, which shall tend to their advantage, weal, and happiness in length of time.

[...]

When the Lord for the third time heard the entreaty of the venerable Sâriputra, he spoke to him as follows: Now that thou entreatest the Tathâgata a third time, Sâriputra, I will answer thee. Listen then, Sâriputra, take well and duly to heart what I am saying; I am going to speak.

Now it happened that the five thousand proud monks, nuns and lay devotees of both sexes in the congregatino rose from their seats and, after saluting with their heads the Lord's feet, went to leave the assembly. Owing to the principle of good which there is in pride they imagined having attained what they had not, and having understood what they had not. Therefore, thinking themselves aggrieved, they

---

6 Perfected ones, i.e., those who have achieved nirvana.

went to leave the assembly, to which the Lord by his silence showed assent.

Thereupon the Lord addressed the venerable Sâriputra: My congregation, Sâriputra, has been cleared from the chaff, freed from the trash; it is firmly established in the strength of faith. It is good, Sâriputra, that those proud ones are gone away. Now I am going to expound the matter, Sâriputra. 'Very well, Lord,' replied the venerable Sâriputra. The Lord then began and said:

It is but now and then, Sâriputra, that the Tathâgata preaches such a discourse on the law as this. just as but now and then is seen the blossom of the glomerous fig-tree, Sâriputra, so does the Tathâgata but now and then preach such a discourse on the law. Believe me, Sâriputra; I speak what is real, I speak what is truthful, I speak what is right. It is difficult to understand the exposition of the mystery of the Tathâgata, Sâriputra; for in elucidating the law, Sâriputra, I use hundred thousands of various skilful means, such as different interpretations, indications, explanations, illustrations. It is not by reasoning, Sâriputra, that the law is to be found: it is beyond the pale of reasoning, and must be learnt from the Tathâgata. For, Sâriputra, it is for a sole object, a sole aim, verily a lofty object, a lofty aim that the Buddha, the Tathâgata, appears in the world. And what is that sole object, that sole aim, that lofty object, that lofty aim of the Buddha, the Tathâgata, appearing in the world? To show all creatures the sight of Tathâgata-knowledge does the Buddha, the Tathâgata, appear in the world; to open the eyes of creatures for the sight of Tathâgata-knowledge does the Buddha, the Tathâgata, appear in the world. This, O Sâriputra, is the sole object, the sole aim, the sole purpose of his appearance in the world. Such then, Sâriputra, is the sole object, the sole aim, the lofty object, the lofty aim of the Tathâgata. And it is achieved by the Tathâgata. For, Sâriputra, I do show all creatures the sight of Tathâgata-knowledge; I do open the eyes of creatures for the sight of Tathâgata-knowledge, Sâriputra; I do firmly establish the teaching of Tathâgata-knowledge, Sâriputra; I do lead the teaching of Tathâgata-knowledge on the right path, Sâriputra. By means of one sole vehicle, to wit, the Buddha-vehicle, Sâriputra, do I teach creatures the law; there is no second vehicle, nor a third. This is the nature of the law, Sâriputra, universally in the world, in all directions. For, Sariputra, all the Tathâgatas, who in times past existed in countless, innumerable spheres in all directions for the weal of many, the happiness of many, out of pity to the world, for the benefit, weal, and happiness of the great body of creatures, and who preached the law to gods and men with able means, such as several directions and indications, various arguments, reasons, illustrations, fundamental ideas, interpretations, paying regard to the dispositions of creatures whose inclinations and temperaments are so manifold, all those Buddhas and Lords, Sâriputra, have preached the law to creatures by means of only one vehicle, the Buddhavehicle, which finally leads to omniscience; it is identical with showing all creatures the sight of Tathâgata-knowledge; with opening the eyes of creatures for the sight of Tathâgata-knowledge; with the awakening (or admonishing) by the display (or sight) of Tathâgata -knowledge; with leading the teaching of Tathâgata-knowledge on the right path. Such is the law they have preached to creatures. And those creatures, Sâriputra, who have heard the law from the past Tathâgatas, have all of them reached supreme, perfect enlightenment.

[...]

1. According to this text, why is the wisdom of the buddhas beyond the understanding of individual disciples of the Buddha (monks and nuns)? How is this a comment on the way that Buddhism was formerly practiced? (Contrast with the reading from *Khandaka*.)
2. What is the relationship between buddhas and bodhisattvas?
3. How does this account explain the split between Mahayana and Theravada Buddhists? Would Theravada Buddhists accept the truth of this story?

---

c. 170–180 CE

64. Meditations

Translated by George Long

Not only one of Rome's greatest emperors but also a notable Stoic philosopher, Marcus Aurelius (r. 161–180 CE) wrote *Meditations* in Greek while on campaign between 170 and 180 CE. It reads more like a journal than a philosophical work and was probably used simply for personal guidance and self-improvement. Though it never was meant to be published, it was and has inspired many of its readers. Here is a selection in which he relates some of the lessons he learned from family and friends.

15. From Maximus[1] I learned self-government, and not to be led aside by anything; and cheerfulness in all circumstances, as well as in illness; and a just admixture in the moral character of sweetness and dignity, and to do what was set before me without complaining. I observed that everybody believed that he thought as he spoke, and that in all that he did he never had any bad intention; and he never showed amazement and surprise, and was never in a hurry, and never put off doing a thing, nor was perplexed nor dejected, nor did he ever laugh to disguise his vexation, nor, on the other hand, was he ever passionate or suspicious. He was accustomed to do acts of beneficence, and was ready to forgive, and was free from all falsehood; and he presented the appearance of a man who could not be diverted from right rather than of a man who had been improved. I observed, too, that no man could ever think that he was despised by Maximus, or ever venture to think himself a better man. He had also the art of being humorous in an agreeable way.

16. In my father I observed mildness of temper, and unchangeable resolution in the things which he

---

1 Claudius Maximus was a Stoic philosopher, who was highly-esteemed also by Antoninus Pius, Marcus' predecessor. The character of Maximus is that of a perfect man.

had determined after due deliberation; and no vain-glory in those things which men call honors; and a love of labor and perseverance; and a readiness to listen to those who had anything to propose for the common weal; and undeviating firmness in giving to every man according to his deserts; and a knowledge derived from experience of the occasions for vigorous action and for remission. And I observed that he had overcome all passion for joys; and he considered himself no more than any other citizen, and he released his friends from all obligation to sup with him or to attend him of necessity when lie went abroad, and those who had failed to accompany him, by reason of any urgent circumstances, always found him the same. I observed, too, his habit of careful inquiry in all matters of deliberation, and his persistency, and that he never stopped his investigation through being satisfied with appearances which first present themselves; and that his disposition was to keep his friends, and not to be soon tired of them, nor yet to be extravagant in his affection; and to be satisfied on all occasions, and cheerful; and to foresee things a long way off, and to provide for the smallest without display; and to check immediately popular applause and flattery; and to be ever watchful over the things that were necessary for the administration of the empire, and to be a good manager of the expenditure, and patiently to endure the blame which he got for such conduct; and he was neither superstitious with respect to the gods, nor did he court men by gifts or by trying to please them, or by flattering the populace; but he showed sobriety in all things and firmness, and never any mean thoughts or action, nor love of novelty. And the things which conduce in any way to the commodity of life, and of which fortune gives an abundant supply, he used without arrogance and without excusing himself; so that when he had them, he enjoyed them without affectation, and when he had them not he did not want them. No one could ever say of him that he was either a sophist or a [home-bred] flippant slave or a pedant; but every one acknowledged him to be a man ripe, perfect, above flattery, able to manage

his own and other men's affairs. Besides this, he honored those who were true philosophers, and he did not reproach those who pretended to be philosophers, nor yet was he easily led by them. He was also easy in conversation, and he made himself agreeable without any offensive affectation. He took a reasonable care of his body's health, not as one who was greatly attached to life, nor out of regard to personal appearance, nor yet in a careless way, but so that, through his own attention, he very seldom stood in need of the physician's art or of medicine or external applications. He was most ready to give way without envy to those who possessed any particular faculty, such as that of eloquence or knowledge of the law or of morals, or of anything else; and he gave them his help, that each might enjoy reputation according to his deserts; and he always acted conformably to the institutions of his country, without showing any affectation of doing so. Further, he was not fond of change, nor unsteady, but he loved to stay in the same places, and to employ himself about the same things; and after his paroxysms of headache he came immediately fresh and vigorous to his usual occupations. His secrets were not many, but very few and very rare, and these only about public matters; and he showed prudence and economy in the exhibition of the public spectacles and the construction of public buildings, his donations to the people, and in such things, for he was a man who looked to what ought to be done, not to the reputation which is got by a man's acts. He did not take the bath at unseasonable hours; he was not fond of building houses, nor curious about what he eat, nor about the texture and color of his clothes, nor about the beauty of his slaves. His dress came from Lorium, his villa on the coast, and from Lanuvium generally. We know how he behaved to the toll-collector at Tusculum who asked his pardon; and such was ail his behavior. There was in him nothing harsh, nor implacable, nor violent, nor, as one may say, anything carried to the sweating point: but he examined all things severally, as if he had abundance of time, and without confusion, in an orderly way, vigorously and consistently.

And that might be applied to him which is recorded of Socrates, that he was able both to abstain from, and to enjoy, those things which many are too weak to abstain from, and cannot enjoy without excess. But to be strong enough both to bear the one and to be sober in the other is the mark of a man who has a perfect and invincible soul, such as he showed in the illness of Maximus.

17. To the gods I am indebted for having good grandfathers, good parents, a good sister, good teachers, good associates, good kinsmen and friends, nearly everything good. Further, I owe it to the gods that I was not hurried into any offense against any of them, though I had a disposition which, if opportunity had offered, might have led me to do something of this kind; but, through their favor, there never was such a concurrence of circumstances as put me to the trial. Further, I am thankful to the gods that I was not longer brought up with my grandfather's concubine, and that I preserved the flower of my youth, and that I did not make proof of my virility before the proper season, but even deferred the time; that I was subjected to a ruler and a father who was able to take away all pride from me, and to bring me to the knowledge that it is possible for a man to live in a palace without wanting either guards or embroidered dresses, or torches and statues, and such-like show; but it is in such a man's power to bring himself very near to the fashion of a private person, without being for this reason either meaner in thought, or more remiss in action, with respect to the things which must be done for the public interest in a manner that befits a ruler. I thank the gods for giving me such a brother, who was able by his moral character to rouse me to vigilance over myself, and who, at the same time, pleased me by his respect and affection; that my children have not been stupid nor deformed in body; that I did not make more proficiency in rhetoric, poetry, and the other studies, in which I should perhaps have been completely engaged, if I had seen that I was making progress in them; that I made haste to place those who brought me up in the station of honor, which they seemed to desire, without putting them off with hope of my doing it some time after, because they were then still young; that I knew Apollonius, Rusticus, Maximus; that I received clear and frequent impressions about living according to nature, and what kind of a life that is, so that, so far as depended on the gods, and their gifts and help, and inspirations, nothing hindered me from forthwith living according to nature, though I still fall short of it through my own fault, and though not observing the admonitions of the gods, and, I may almost say, their direct instructions; that my body has held out so long in such a kind of life; that I never touched either Benedicta or Theodotus, and that, after having fallen into amatory passions, I was cured; and, though I was often out of humor with Rusticus, I never did anything of which I had occasion to repent; that, though it was my mother's fate to die young, she spent the last years of her life with me; that whenever I wished to help any man in his need, or on any other occasion, I was never told that I had not the means of doing it; and that to myself the same necessity never happened, to receive any thing from another; that I have such a wife,[2] so obedient, and so affectionate, and so simple; that I had abundance of good masters for my children; and that remedies have been shown to me by dreams, both others, and against blood-spitting and giddiness;[3] ... and that, when I had an inclination to philosophy I did not fall into the hands of any sophist, and that I did not waste my time on writers [of histories], or in the resolution of syllogisms, or occupy myself about the investigation of appearances in tne heavens; for all these things require the help of the gods and fortune.

---

2   See the Life of Antoninus.
3   This is corrupt.

The Late Classical Period
(200–600 CE)

Woman with child (Kushan Empire)

Late Classical Period

C.E	300	400	500	600
Central America	Zapotec Civilization			
	Teotihuacan			
	Maya Civilization			
South America	Moche Culture			
			Tiwanaku	
				Wari
Europe	Roman Empire		Western Roman Empire	Kingdom of the Franks
Eastern Mediterranean			Eastern Roman (Byzantine) Empire	
East Africa	Aksum			
West Asia	Sassanid Persian Empire			
Central Asia	Kushan Empire			
South Asia	Many Kingdoms	Gupta Empire		
East Asia	Six Dynasties			

65. Letter to the Palestinians

Translated by Ernest C. Richardson

The following is the full text of an imperial statute issued by the Roman emperor Constantine the Great (r. 306–337 CE) to his non-Christian subjects in the province of Palestine in the year 323 CE. The letter is preserved in Eusebius Pamphilus' (d. 339 CE) unfinished *Life of Constantine*.

Victor Constantinus, Maximus Augustus to the inhabitants of the province of Palestine.

1.   To all who entertain just and sound sentiments respecting the character of the Supreme Being, it has long been most clearly evident, and beyond the possibility of doubt, how vast a difference there has ever been between those who maintain a careful observance of the hallowed duties of the Christian religion, and those who treat this religion with hostility or contempt. But at this present time, we may see by stilt more manifest proofs, and still more decisive instances, both how unreasonable it were to question this truth, and how mighty is the power of the Supreme God: since it appears that they who faithfully observe His holy laws, and shrink from the transgression of His commandments, are rewarded with abundant blessings, and are endued with well-grounded hope as well as ample power for the accomplishment of their undertakings. On the other hand, they who have cherished impious sentiments have experienced results corresponding to their evil choice. For how is it to be expected that any blessing would be obtained by one who neither desired to acknowledge nor duly to worship that God who is the source of all blessing? Indeed, facts themselves are a confirmation of what I say.

2.   For certainly any one who will mentally retrace the course of events from the earliest period down to the present time, and will reflect on what has occurred in past ages, will find that all who have made justice and probity the basis of their conduct, have not only carried their undertakings to a successful issue, but have gathered, as it were, a store of sweet fruit as the produce of this pleasant root. Again, whoever observes the career of those who have been bold in the practice of oppression or injustice; who have either directed their senseless fury against God himself, or have conceived no kindly feelings towards their fellow-men, but have dared to afflict them with exile, disgrace, confiscation, massacre, or other miseries of the like kind, and all this without any sense of compunction, or wish to direct thoughts to a better course, will find that such men have received a recompense proportioned to their crimes. And these are results

Eusebius of Caesarea, Selection from: "The Life of the Blessed Emperor Constantine," *Nicene and Post-Nicene Fathers, Volume I, 2nd Series*, ed. Philip Schaff and Henry Wallace; trans. Ernest C. Richardson. William B. Eerdmans Publishing Co., 1890. Copyright in the Public Domain.

which might naturally and reasonably be expected to ensue?

3. For whoever have addressed themselves with integrity of purpose to any course of action, keeping the fear of God continually before their thoughts, and preserving an unwavering faith in him, without allowing present fears or dangers to outweigh their hope of future blessings--such persons, though for a season they may have experienced painful trials, have borne their afflictions lightly, being supported by the belief of greater rewards in store for them; and their character has acquired a brighter luster in proportion to the severity of their past suffer-rags. With regard, on the other hand, to those who have either dishonorably slighted the principles of justice, or refused to acknowledge the Supreme God themselves, and yet have dared to subject others who have faithfully maintained his worship to the most cruel insults and punishments; who have failed equally to recognize their own wretchedness in oppressing others on such grounds, and the happiness and blessing of those who preserved their devotion to God even in the midst of such sufferings: with regard, I say, to such men, many a time have their armies been slaughtered, many a time have they been put to flight; and their warlike preparations have ended in total ruin and defeat.

4. From the causes I have described, grievous wars arose, and destructive devastations. Hence followed a scarcity of the common necessaries of life, and a crowd of consequent miseries: hence, too, the authors of these impieties have either met a disastrous death of extreme suffering, or have dragged out an ignominious existence, and confessed it to be worse than death itself, thus receiving as it were a measure of punishment proportioned to the heinousness of their crimes. For each experienced a degree of calamity according to the blind fury with which he had been led to combat, and as he thought, defeat the Divine will: so that they not only felt the pressure of the ills of this present life,

but were tormented also by a most lively apprehension of punishment in the future world.

5. And now, with such a mass of impiety oppressing the human race, and the commonwealth in danger of being utterly destroyed, as if by the agency of some pestilential disease, and therefore needing powerful and effectual aid; what was the relief, and what the remedy which the Divinity devised for these evils? (And by Divinity is meant the one who is alone and truly God, the possessor of almighty and eternal power: and surely it cannot be deemed arrogance in one who has received benefits from God, to acknowledge them in the loftiest terms of praise.) I myself, then, was the instrument whose services He chose, and esteemed suited for the accomplishment of his will. Accordingly, beginning at the remote Britannic ocean, and the regions where, according to the law of nature, the sun sinks beneath the horizon, through the aid of divine power I banished and utterly removed every form of evil which prevailed, in the hope that the human race, enlightened through my instrumentality, might be recalled to a due observance of the holy laws of God, and at the same time our most blessed faith might prosper under the guidance of his almighty hand.

6. I said, under the guidance of his hand; for I would desire never to be forgetful of the gratitude due to his grace. Believing, therefore, that this most excellent service had been confided to me as a special gift, I proceeded as far as the regions of the East, which, being under the pressure of severer calamities, seemed to demand still more effectual remedies at my hands. At the same time I am most certainly persuaded that I myself owe my life, my every breath, in short, my very inmost and secret thoughts, entirely to the favor of the Supreme God. Now I am well aware that they who are sincere in the pursuit of the heavenly hope, and have fixed this hope in heaven itself as the peculiar and predominant principle of their lives, have no need to depend on human favor, but rather have enjoyed higher honors in proportion as they have separated

themselves from the inferior and evil things of this earthly existence. Nevertheless I deem it incumbent on me to remove at once and most completely from all such persons the hard necessities laid upon them for a season, and the unjust inflictions under which they have suffered, though free from any guilt or just liability. For it would be strange indeed, that the fortitude and constancy of soul displayed by such men should be fully apparent during the reign of those whose first object it was to persecute them on account of their devotion to God, and yet that the glory of their character should not be more bright and blessed, under the administration of a prince who is His servant.

7. Let all therefore who have exchanged their country for a foreign land, because they would not abandon that reverence and faith toward God to which they had devoted themselves with their whole hearts, and have in consequence at different times been subject to the cruel sentence of the courts; together with any who have been enrolled in the registers of the public courts though in time past exempt from such office let these, I say, now render thanks to God the Liberator of all, in that they are restored to their hereditary property, and their wonted tranquility. Let those also who have been despoiled of their goods, and have hitherto passed a wretched existence, mourning under the loss of all that they possessed, once more be restored to their former homes, their families, and estates, and receive with joy the bountiful kindness of God.

8. Furthermore, it is our command that all those who have been detained in the islands against their will should receive the benefit of this present provision; in order that they who rill now have been surrounded by rugged mountains and the encircling barrier of the ocean, being now set free from that gloomy and desolate solitude, may fulfill their fondest wish by revisiting their dearest friends. Those, too, who have prolonged a miserable life in the midst of abject and wretched squalor, welcoming their restoration as an unlooked-for gain, and

discarding henceforth all anxious thoughts, may pass their lives with us in freedom from all fear. For that any one could live in a state of fear under our government, when we boast and believe ourselves to be the servants of God, would surely be a thing most extraordinary even to hear of, and quite incredible; and our mission is to rectify the errors of the others.

9. Again, with regard to those who have been condemned either to the grievous labor of the mines, or to service in the public works, let them enjoy the sweets of leisure in place of these long-continued toils, and henceforth lead a far easier life, and more accordant with the wishes of their hearts, exchanging the incessant hardships of their tasks for quiet relaxation. And if any have forfeited the common privilege of liberty, or have unhappily suffered dishonor, let them hasten back every one to the country of his nativity, and resume with becoming joy their former positions in society, from which they have been as it were separated by long residence abroad.

10. Once more, with respect to those who had previously been preferred to any military distinction, of which they were afterwards deprived, for the cruel and unjust reason that they chose rather to acknowledge their allegiance to God than to retain the rank they held; we leave them perfect liberty of choice, either to occupy their former stations, should they be content again to engage in military service, or after an honorable discharge, to live in undisturbed tranquillity. For it is fair and consistent that men who have displayed such magnanimity and fortitude in meeting the perils to which they have been exposed, should be allowed the choice either of enjoying peaceful leisure, or resuming their former rank.

11. Lastly, if any have wrongfully been deprived of the privileges of noble lineage, and subjected to a judicial sentence which has consigned them to the women's apartments and to the linen making, there to undergo a cruel and miserable labor, or reduced them to servitude for the benefit of the public

treasury, without any exemption on the ground of superior birth; let such persons, resuming the honors they had previously enjoyed, and their proper dignities, henceforward exult in the blessings of liberty, and lead a glad life. Let the free man, too, by some injustice and inhumanity, or even madness, made a slave, who has felt the sudden transition from liberty to bondage, and ofttimes bewailed his unwonted labors, return to his family once more a free man in virtue of this our ordinance, and seek those employments which befit a state of freedom; and let him dismiss from his remembrance those services which he found so oppressive, and which so ill became his condition.

12. Nor must we omit to notice those estates of which individuals have been deprived on various pretenses. For if any of those who have engaged with dauntless and resolute determination in the noble and divine conflict of martyrdom have also been stripped of their fortunes; or if the same has been the lot of the confessors, who have won for themselves the hope of eternal treasures; or if the loss of property has befallen those who were driven from their native land because they would not yield to the persecutors, and betray their faith; lastly, if any who have escaped the sentence of death have yet been despoiled of their worldly goods; we ordain that the inheritances of all such persons be transferred to their nearest kindred. And whereas the laws expressly assign this right to those most nearly related, it will be easy to ascertain to whom these inheritances severally belong. And it is evidently reasonable that the succession in these cases should belong to those who would have stood in the place of nearest affinity, had the deceased experienced a natural death.

13. But should there be no surviving relation to succeed in due course to the property of those above-mentioned, I mean the martyrs, or confessors, or those who for some such cause have been banished from their native land; in such cases we ordain that the church locally nearest in each instance shall succeed to the inheritance. And surely it will be no wrong to the departed that that church should be their heir, for whose sake they have endured every extremity of suffering. We think it necessary to add this also, that in case any of the above-mentioned persons have donated any part of their property in the way of free gift, possession of such property shall be assured, as is reasonable, to those who have thus received it.

14. And that there may be no obscurity in this our ordinance, but every one may readily apprehend its requirements, let all men hereby know that if they are now maintaining themselves in possession of a piece of land, or a house, or garden, or anything else which had appertained to the before-mentioned persons, it will be good and advantageous for them to acknowledge the fact, and make restitution with the least possible delay. On the other hand, although it should appear that some individuals have reaped abundant profits from this unjust possession, we do not consider that justice demands the restitution of such profits. They must, however, declare explicitly what amount of benefit they have thus derived, and from what sources, and entreat our pardon for this offense; in order that their past covetousness may in some measure be atoned for, and that the Supreme God may accept this compensation as a token of contrition, and be pleased graciously to pardon the sin.

15. But it is possible that those who have become masters of such property (if it be right or possible to allow them such a title) will assure us by way of apology for their conduct, that it was not in their power to abstain from this appropriation at a time when a spectacle of misery in all its forms everywhere met the view; when men were cruelly driven from their homes, slaughtered without mercy, thrust forth without remorse: when the confiscation of the property of innocent persons was a common thing, and when persecutions and property seizures were unceasing. If any defend their conduct by such reasons as these, and still persist in their avaricious temper, they shall be made sensible that such a course will bring punishment on

themselves, and all the more because this correction of evil is the very characteristic of our service to the Supreme God. So that it will henceforth be dangerous to retain what dire necessity may in time past have compelled men to take; especially because it is in any case incumbent on us to discourage covetous desires, both by persuasion, and by warning exam-pies.

16. Nor shall the treasury itself, should it have any of the things we have spoken of, be permitted to keep them; but, without venturing as it were to raise its voice against the holy churches, it shall justly relinquish in their favor what it has for a time unjustly retained. We ordain, therefore, that all things whatsoever which shall appear righteously to belong to the churches, whether the property consist of houses or fields and gardens, or whatever the nature of it may be, shall be restored in their full value and integrity, and with undiminished right of possession.

17. The Tombs of Martyrs and the Cemeteries to be transferred to the Possession of the Churches.

18. Again, with respect to those places which are honored in being the depositories of the remains of martyrs, and continue to be memorials of their glorious departure; how can we doubt that they rightly belong to the churches, or refrain from issuing our injunction to that effect? For surely there can be no better liberality, no labor more pleasing or profitable, than to be thus employed under the guidance of the Divine Spirit, in order that those things which have been appropriated on false pretenses by unjust and wicked men, may be restored, as justice demands, and once more secured to the holy churches.

19. And since it would be wrong in a provision intended to include all cases, to pass over those who have either procured any such property by right of purchase from the treasury, or have retained it when conveyed to them in the form of a gift; let all who have thus rashly indulged their insatiable thirst of gain be assured that, although by daring to make such purchases they have done all in their power to alienate our clemency from themselves, they shall nevertheless not fail of obtaining it, so far as is possible and consistent with propriety in each case. So much then is determined.

20. And now, since it appears by the clearest and most convincing evidence, that the miseries which erewhile oppressed the entire human race are now banished from every part of the world, through the power of Almighty God, and at the same time the counsel and aid which he is pleased on many occasions to administer through our agency; it remains for all, both individually and unitedly, to observe and seriously consider how great this power and how efficacious this grace are, which have annihilated and utterly destroyed this generation, as I may call them, of most wicked and evil men; have restored joy to the good, and diffused it over all countries; and now guarantee the fullest authority both to honor the Divine law as it should be honored, with all reverence, and pay due observance to those who have dedicated themselves to the service of that law. These rising as from some dark abyss and, with an enlightened knowledge of the present course of events, will henceforward render to its precepts that becoming reverence and honor which are consistent with their pious character.

Let this ordinance be published in our Eastern provinces.

Think about it.

1. What is the purpose of this letter?
2. How does Constantine see himself in relationship to God?

66. Letter to Valentinian

Translated by Henry E. De Romestin

This letter was written by Aurelius Ambrosius (Ambrose, for short), who was the Christian bishop of Milan from 374 to 397 CE, to the Roman emperor Valentinian II (r. 375–392 CE). In 386 Ambrose had been ordered by the emperor to hand over a basilica to a group of Arian Christians led by a man named Auxentius. As a Nicene Christian, Ambrose refused. He and his supporters then barricaded themselves inside the basilica in opposition to the emperor's order. This was the occasion for the following letter, in which Ambrose justifies his actions.

LETTER XXI.

Ambrose, Bishop, to the most gracious Emperor and blessed Augustus, Valentinian.

1. Dalmatius, the tribune and notary, summoned me by the orders of your Clemency, as he asserted, demanding that I should also choose judges, as Auxentius had done. He did not mention the names of those who had been asked for, but he added that there was to be a discussion in the consistory, and that the judgment of your piety would give the decision.

2. To this I make, as I think, a suitable answer. No one ought to consider me contumacious when I affirm what your father of august memory not only replied by word of mouth, but also sanctioned by his laws, that, in a matter of faith, or any ecclesiastical ordinance, he should judge who was not unsuited by office, nor disqualified by equity, for these are the words of the rescript. That is, it was his desire that priests should judge concerning priests. Moreover, if a bishop were accused of other matters also, and a question of character was to be enquired into, it was also his will that this should be reserved for the judgment of bishops.

3. Who, then, has answered your Clemency contumaciously? He who desires that you should be like your father, or he that wishes you to be unlike him? Unless, perhaps, the judgment of so great an Emperor seems to any persons of small account, whose faith has been proved by the constancy of his profession, and his wisdom declared by the continual improvement of the State.

4. When have you heard, most gracious Emperor, that laymen gave judgment concerning a bishop in a matter of faith? Are we so prostrate through the flattery of some as to be unmindful of the rights of the priesthood, and do I think that I can entrust to others what God has given me? If a bishop is to be taught by a layman, what will follow? Let the layman argue, and the bishop listen, let the bishop learn of the layman. But undoubtedly, whether we go through the series of the holy Scriptures, or the times of old, who is there who can deny that, in a matter of faith,—in a matter I say of faith,—bishops are wont to judge of Christian emperors, not emperors of bishops.

5. You will, by the favour of God, attain to a riper age, and then you will judge what kind of bishop he is who subjects the rights of the priesthood to laymen. Your father, by the favour of God a man of riper age, used to say: It is not my business to judge between bishops. Your Clemency now says: I ought to judge. And he, though baptized in Christ, thought himself unequal to the burden of such a judgment, does your Clemency, who have yet to earn for yourself the sacrament of baptism, arrogate to yourself a judgment concerning the faith, though ignorant of the sacrament of that faith?

6. I can leave it to be imagined what sort of judges he will have chosen, since he is afraid to publish their names. Let them simply come to the Church, if there are any to come; let them listen with the people, not for every one to sit as judge, but that each may examine his own disposition, and choose whom to follow. The matter is concerning the bishop of that Church: if the people hear him and think that he has the best of the argument, let them follow him, I shall not be jealous.

7. I omit to mention that the people have themselves already given their judgment. I am silent as to the fact that they demanded of your father him whom they now have. I am silent as to the promise of your father that if he who was chosen would undertake the bishopric there should be tranquillity. I acted on the faith of these promises.

8. But if he boasts himself of the approval of some foreigners, let him be bishop there from whence they are who think that he ought to receive the name of bishop. For I neither recognize him as a bishop, nor know I whence he comes.

9. And how, O Emperor, are we to settle a matter on which you have already declared your judgment, and have even promulgated laws, so that it is not open to any one to judge otherwise? But when you laid down this law for others, you laid it down for yourself as well. For the Emperor is the first to keep the laws which he passes. Do you, then, wish me to try how those who are chosen as judges will either come, contrary to your decision, or at least excuse themselves, saying that they cannot act against so severe and so stringent a law of the Emperor?

10. But this would be the act of one contumacious, not of one who knew his position. See, O Emperor, you are already yourself partially rescinding your law, would that it were not partially but altogether! for I would not that your law should be set above the law of God. The law of God has taught us what to follow; human laws cannot teach us this. They usually extort a change from the fearful, but they cannot inspire faith.

11. Who, then, will there be, who when he reads that at one instant through so many provinces the order was given, that whoever acts against the Emperor shall be beheaded, that whoever does not give up the temple of God shall at once be put to death; who, say, is there who will be able either alone or with a few others to say to the Emperor: I do not approve of your law? Priests are not allowed to say this, are then laymen allowed? And shall he judge concerning the faith who either hopes for favour or is afraid of giving offence?

12. Lastly, shall I myself choose laymen for judges, who, if they upheld the truth of their faith, would be either proscribed or put to death, as that law passed concerning the faith decrees? Shall I then expose these men either to denial of the truth or to punishment?

13. Ambrose is not of sufficient importance to degrade the priesthood on his own account. The life of one is not of so much value as the dignity of all priests, by whose advice I gave those directions, when they intimated that there might perchance be some heathen or Jew chosen by Auxentius, to whom I should give a triumph over Christ, if I entrusted to him a judgment concerning Christ. What else pleases them but to hear of some insult to Christ? What else can please them unless (which God forbid) the Godhead of Christ should be denied? Plainly they agree well with the Arian who says that Christ is a creature, which also heathen and Jews most readily acknowledge.

14. This was decreed at the Synod of Ariminum, and rightly do I detest that council, following the rule of the Nicene Council, from which neither death nor the sword can detach me, which faith the father of your Clemency also, Theodosius, the most blessed Emperor, both approved and follows. The Gauls hold this faith, and Spain, and keep it with the pious confession of the Divine Spirit.

15. If anything has to be discussed I have learnt to discuss it in church as those before me did. If a conference is to be held concerning the faith, there ought to be a gathering of Bishops, as was done under Constantine, the Prince of august memory, who did not promulgate any laws beforehand, but left the decision to the Bishops. This was done also under Constantius, Emperor of august memory, the heir of his father's dignity. But what began well ended otherwise, for the Bishops had at first subscribed an unadulterated confession of faith, but since some were desirous of deciding concerning the faith inside the palace, they managed that those decisions of the Bishops should be altered by fraud. But they immediately recalled this perverted decision, and certainly the larger number at Ariminum approved the faith of the Nicene Council and condemned the Arian propositions.

16. If Auxentius appeals to a synod, in order to discuss points concerning the faith (although it is not necessary that so many Bishops should be troubled for the sake of one man, who, even if he were an angel from heaven, ought not to be preferred to the peace of the Church), when I hear that a synod is gathering, I, too, will not be wanting. Repeal, then, the law if you wish for a disputation.

17. I would have come, O Emperor, to your consistory, and have made these remarks in your presence, if either the Bishops or the people had allowed me, but they said that matters concerning the faith ought to be treated in the church, in presence of the people.

18. And I wish, O Emperor, that you had not given sentence that I should go into banishment whither I would. I went out daily. No one guarded me. You ought to have appointed me a place wherever you would, for I offered myself for anything. But now the clergy say to me, "There is not much difference whether you voluntarily leave the altar of Christ or betray it, for if you leave it you will betray it."

19. And I wish it were clearly certain to me that the Church would by no means be given over to the Arians. I would then willingly offer myself to the will of your piety. But if I only am guilty of disturbance, why is there a command to invade all other churches? I would it were established that no one should trouble the churches, and then I could wish that whatever sentence seems good should be pronounced concerning me.

20. Vouchsafe, then, O Emperor, to accept the reason for which I could not come to the consistory. I have never learned to appear in the consistory except on your behalf, and I am not able to dispute within the palace, who neither know nor wish to know the secrets of the palace.

21. I, Ambrose, Bishop, offer this memorial to the most gracious Emperor, and most blessed Augustus Valentinian.

Think about it.

1. What is Ambrose's view concerning the state's involvement in church affairs? Why does he hold this view?

2. What is Ambrose asking for? If his request were granted, how might this affect the outcome of the controversy?

67. The City of God

Translated by Marcus Dods

The City of God (*De Civitate Dei*) is a Christian philosophical work in Latin written by Aurelius Augustinus (better known as Augustine), the bishop of Hippo Regius in North Africa, soon after the Visigoths sacked Rome in 410 CE. He wrote it to explain Christianity's relationship to the government and to other religions. The following passages taken from the work deal with human nature and lay out Augustine's doctrine of Original Sin.

Book VIII

Chapter 13.—What Was the First Punishment of the Transgression of Our First Parents.

For, as soon as our first parents had transgressed the commandment, divine grace forsook them, and they were confounded at their own wickedness; and therefore they took fig-leaves (which were possibly the first that came to hand in their troubled state of mind), and covered their shame; for though their members remained the same, they had shame now where they had none before. They experienced a new motion of their flesh, which had become disobedient to them, in strict retribution of their own disobedience to God. For the soul, revelling in its own liberty, and scorning to serve God, was itself deprived of the command it had formerly maintained over the body. And because it had willfully deserted its superior Lord, it no longer held its own inferior servant; neither could it hold the flesh subject, as it would always have been able to do had it remained itself subject to God. Then began the flesh to lust against the Spirit,[1] in which strife we are born, deriving from the first transgression a seed of death, and bearing in our members, and in our vitiated nature, the contest or even victory of the flesh.

Chapter 14.—In What State Man Was Made by God, and into What Estate He Fell by the Choice of His Own Will.

For God, the author of natures, not of vices, created man upright; but man, being of his own will corrupted, and justly condemned, begot corrupted and condemned children. For we all were in that one man, since we all were that one man, who fell into sin by the woman who was made from him before the sin. For not yet was the particular form created and distributed to us, in which we as individuals were to live, but already the seminal nature was there from which we were to be propagated; and this being vitiated by sin, and bound by the chain of death, and justly condemned, man could not be born of man in any other state. And thus, from the bad use of

---

1 Gal. v. 17.

free will, there originated the whole train of evil, which, with its concatenation of miseries, convoys the human race from its depraved origin, as from a corrupt root, on to the destruction of the second death, which has no end, those only being excepted who are freed by the grace of God.

Book XIV

Chapter 11.—Of the Fall of the First Man, in Whom Nature Was Created Good, and Can Be Restored Only by Its Author.

But because God foresaw all things, and was therefore not ignorant that man also would fall, we ought to consider this holy city in connection with what God foresaw and ordained, and not according to our own ideas, which do not embrace God's ordination. For man, by his sin, could not disturb the divine counsel, nor compel God to change what He had decreed; for God's foreknowledge had anticipated both,—that is to say, both how evil the man whom He had created good should become, and what good He Himself should even thus derive from him. For though God is said to change His determinations (so that in a tropical sense the Holy Scripture says even that God repented[2], this is said with reference to man's expectation, or the order of natural causes, and not with reference to that which the Almighty had foreknown that He would do. Accordingly God, as it is written, made man upright,[3] and consequently with a good will. For if he had not had a good will, he could not have been upright. The good will, then, is the work of God; for God created him with it. But the first evil will, which preceded all man's evil acts, was rather a kind of falling away from the work of God to its own works than any positive work. And therefore the acts resulting were evil, not having God, but the will itself for their end; so that the will or the man himself, so far as his will is bad, was as it were the

evil tree bringing forth evil fruit. Moreover, the bad will, though it be not in harmony with, but opposed to nature, inasmuch as it is a vice or blemish, yet it is true of it as of all vice, that it cannot exist except in a nature, and only in a nature created out of nothing, and not in that which the Creator has begotten of Himself, as He begot the Word, by whom all things were made. For though God formed man of the dust of the earth, yet the earth itself, and every earthly material, is absolutely created out of nothing; and man's soul, too, God created out of nothing, and joined to the body, when He made man. But evils are so thoroughly overcome by good, that though they are permitted to exist, for the sake of demonstrating how the most righteous foresight of God can make a good use even of them, yet good can exist without evil, as in the true and supreme God Himself, and as in every invisible and visible celestial creature that exists above this murky atmosphere; but evil cannot exist without good, because the natures in which evil exists, in so far as they are natures, are good. And evil is removed, not by removing any nature, or part of a nature, which had been introduced by the evil, but by healing and correcting that which had been vitiated and depraved. The will, therefore, is then truly free, when it is not the slave of vices and sins. Such was it given us by God; and this being lost by its own fault, can only be restored by Him who was able at first to give it. And therefore the truth says, "If the Son shall make you free, ye shall be free indeed;"[4] which is equivalent to saying, If the Son shall save you, ye shall be saved indeed. For He is our Liberator, inasmuch as He is our Saviour. Man then lived with God for his rule in a paradise at once physical and spiritual. For neither was it a paradise only physical for the advantage of the body, and not also spiritual for the advantage of the mind; nor was it only spiritual to afford enjoyment to man by his internal sensations, and not also physical to afford him enjoyment through his external senses. But obviously it was both for both ends. But after that proud

---

2 Gen. vi. 6, and 1 Sam. xv. 11.
3 Eccles. vii. 29.

---

4 1 John viii. 36.

and therefore envious angel (of whose fall I have said as much as I was able in the eleventh and twelfth books of this work, as well as that of his fellows, who, from being God's angels, became his angels), preferring to rule with a kind of pomp of empire rather than to be another's subject, fell from the spiritual Paradise, and essaying to insinuate his persuasive guile into the mind of man, whose unfallen condition provoked him to envy now that himself was fallen, he chose the serpent as his mouthpiece in that bodily Paradise in which it and all the other earthly animals were living with those two human beings, the man and his wife, subject to them, and harmless; and he chose the serpent because, being slippery, and moving in tortuous windings, it was suitable for his purpose. And this animal being subdued to his wicked ends by the presence and superior force of his angelic nature, he abused as his instrument, and first tried his deceit upon the woman, making his assault upon the weaker part of that human alliance, that he might gradually gain the whole, and not supposing that the man would readily give ear to him, or be deceived, but that he might yield to the error of the woman. For as Aaron was not induced to agree with the people when they blindly wished him to make an idol, and yet yielded to constraint; and as it is not credible that Solomon was so blind as to suppose that idols should be worshipped, but was drawn over to such sacrilege by the blandishments of women; so we cannot believe that Adam was deceived, and supposed the devil's word to be truth, and therefore transgressed God's law, but that he by the drawings of kindred yielded to the woman, the husband to the wife, the one human being to the only other human being. For not without significance did the apostle say, "And Adam was not deceived, but the woman being deceived was in the transgression;"[5] but he speaks thus, because the woman accepted as true what the serpent told her, but the man could not bear to be severed from his only companion, even though this involved a partnership in sin. He was not on this account less culpable, but sinned with his eyes open. And so the apostle does not say, "He did not sin," but "He was not deceived." For he shows that he sinned when he says, "By one man sin entered into the world,"[6] and immediately after more distinctly, "In the likeness of Adam's transgression." But he meant that those are deceived who do not judge that which they do to be sin; but he knew. Otherwise how were it true "Adam was not deceived?" But having as yet no experience of the divine severity, he was possibly deceived in so far as he thought his sin venial. And consequently he was not deceived as the woman was deceived, but he was deceived as to the judgment which would be passed on his apology: "The woman whom thou gavest to be with me, she gave me, and I did eat."[7] What need of saying more? Although they were not both deceived by credulity, yet both were entangled in the snares of the devil, and taken by sin.

Chapter 12.—Of the Nature of Man's First Sin.

If any one finds a difficulty in understanding why other sins do not alter human nature as it was altered by the transgression of those first human beings, so that on account of it this nature is subject to the great corruption we feel and see, and to death, and is distracted and tossed with so many furious and contending emotions, and is certainly far different from what it was before sin, even though it were then lodged in an animal body,—if, I say, any one is moved by this, he ought not to think that that sin was a small and light one because it was committed about food, and that not bad nor noxious, except because it was forbidden; for in that spot of singular felicity God could not have created and planted any evil thing. But by the precept He gave, God commended obedience, which is, in a sort, the mother and guardian of all the virtues in the reasonable creature, which was so created that submission is advantageous to it, while the fulfillment of its own will in preference to

---

5   1 Tim. ii. 14.

6   Rom. v. 12.

7   Gen. iii. 12.

the Creator's is destruction. And as this commandment enjoining abstinence from one kind of food in the midst of great abundance of other kinds was so easy to keep,—so light a burden to the memory,—and, above all, found no resistance to its observance in lust, which only afterwards sprung up as the penal consequence of sin, the iniquity of violating it was all the greater in proportion to the ease with which it might have been kept.

Chapter 13.—That in Adam's Sin an Evil Will Preceded the Evil Act.

Our first parents fell into open disobedience because already they were secretly corrupted; for the evil act had never been done had not an evil will preceded it. And what is the origin of our evil will but pride? For "pride is the beginning of sin."[8] And what is pride but the craving for undue exaltation? And this is undue exaltation, when the soul abandons Him to whom it ought to cleave as its end, and becomes a kind of end to itself. This happens when it becomes its own satisfaction. And it does so when it falls away from that unchangeable good which ought to satisfy it more than itself. This falling away is spontaneous; for if the will had remained steadfast in the love of that higher and changeless good by which it was illumined to intelligence and kindled into love, it would not have turned away to find satisfaction in itself, and so become frigid and benighted; the woman would not have believed the serpent spoke the truth, nor would the man have preferred the request of his wife to the command of God, nor have supposed that it was a venial transgression to cleave to the partner of his life even in a partnership of sin. The wicked deed, then,—that is to say, the transgression of eating the forbidden fruit,—was committed by persons who were already wicked. That "evil fruit"[9] could be brought forth only by "a corrupt tree." But that the tree was evil was not the result of nature; for certainly it could become so only by the vice of the will,

and vice is contrary to nature. Now, nature could not have been depraved by vice had it not been made out of nothing. Consequently, that it is a nature, this is because it is made by God; but that it falls away from Him, this is because it is made out of nothing. But man did not so fall away[10] as to become absolutely nothing; but being turned towards himself, his being became more contracted than it was when he clave to Him who supremely is. Accordingly, to exist in himself, that is, to be his own satisfaction after abandoning God, is not quite to become a nonentity, but to approximate to that. And therefore the holy Scriptures designate the proud by another name, "self-pleasers." For it is good to have the heart lifted up, yet not to one's self, for this is proud, but to the Lord, for this is obedient, and can be the act only of the humble. There is, therefore, something in humility which, strangely enough, exalts the heart, and something in pride which debases it. This seems, indeed, to be contradictory, that loftiness should debase and lowliness exalt. But pious humility enables us to submit to what is above us; and nothing is more exalted above us than God; and therefore humility, by making us subject to God, exalts us. But pride, being a defect of nature, by the very act of refusing subjection and revolting from Him who is supreme, falls to a low condition; and then comes to pass what is written: "Thou castedst them down when they lifted up themselves."[11] For he does not say, "when they had been lifted up," as if first they were exalted, and then afterwards cast down; but "when they lifted up themselves" even then they were cast down,—that is to say, the very lifting up was already a fall. And therefore it is that humility is specially recommended to the city of God as it sojourns in this world, and is specially exhibited in the city of God, and in the person of Christ its King; while the contrary vice of pride, according to the testimony of the sacred writings, specially rules his adversary the devil. And certainly this is the great difference which

---

8   Ecclus. x. 13.
9   Matt. vii. 18.

10   Defecit.
11   Ps. lxxiii. 18.

distinguishes the two cities of which we speak, the one being the society of the godly men, the other of the ungodly, each associated with the angels that adhere to their party, and the one guided and fashioned by love of self, the other by love of God. The devil, then, would not have ensnared man in the open and manifest sin of doing what God had forbidden, had man not already begun to live for himself. It was this that made him listen with pleasure to the words, "Ye shall be as gods,"[12] which they would much more readily have accomplished by obediently adhering to their supreme and true end than by proudly living to themselves. For created gods are gods not by virtue of what is in themselves, but by a participation of the true God. By craving to be more, man becomes less; and by aspiring to be self-sufficing, he fell away from Him who truly suffices him. Accordingly, this wicked desire which prompts man to please himself as if he were himself light, and which thus turns him away from that light by which, had he followed it, he would himself have become light,—this wicked desire, I say, already secretly existed in him, and the open sin was but its consequence. For that is true which is written, "Pride goeth before destruction, and before honor is humility;"[13] that is to say, secret ruin precedes open ruin, while the former is not counted ruin. For who counts exaltation ruin, though no sooner is the Highest forsaken than a fall is begun? But who does not recognize it as ruin, when there occurs an evident and indubitable transgression of the commandment? And consequently, God's prohibition had reference to such an act as, when committed, could not be defended on any pretense of doing what was righteous.[14] And I make bold to say that it is useful for the proud to fall into an open and indisputable transgression, and so displease themselves, as already, by pleasing themselves, they had fallen. For Peter was in a healthier

condition when he wept and was dissatisfied with himself, than when he boldly presumed and satisfied himself. And this is averred by the sacred Psalmist when he says, "Fill their faces with shame, that they may seek Thy name, O Lord;"[15] that is, that they who have pleased themselves in seeking their own glory may be pleased and satisfied with Thee in seeking Thy glory.

Chapter 14.—Of the Pride in the Sin, Which Was Worse Than the Sin Itself.

But it is a worse and more damnable pride which casts about for the shelter of an excuse even in manifest sins, as these our first parents did, of whom the woman said, "The serpent beguiled me, and I did eat;" and the man said, "The woman whom Thou gavest to be with me, she gave me of the tree, and I did eat."[16] Here there is no word of begging pardon, no word of entreaty for healing. For though they do not, like Cain, deny that they have perpetrated the deed, yet their pride seeks to refer its wickedness to another,—the woman's pride to the serpent, the man's to the woman. But where there is a plain transgression of a divine commandment, this is rather to accuse than to excuse oneself. For the fact that the woman sinned on the serpent's persuasion, and the man at the woman's offer, did not make the transgression less, as if there were any one whom we ought rather to believe or yield to than God.

Chapter 15.—Of the Justice of the Punishment with Which Our First Parents Were Visited for Their Disobedience.

Therefore, because the sin was a despising of the authority of God,—who had created man; who had made him in His own image; who had set him above the other animals; who had placed him in Paradise; who had enriched him with abundance of every kind and of safety; who had laid upon him neither

---

12 Gen. iii. 5.
13 Prov. xviii. 12.
14 That is to say, it was an obvious and indisputable transgression.

---

15 Ps. lxxxiii. 16.
16 Gen. iii. 12, 13.

many, nor great, nor difficult commandments, but, in order to make a wholesome obedience easy to him, had given him a single very brief and very light precept by which He reminded that creature whose service was to be free that He was Lord,—it was just that condemnation followed, and condemnation such that man, who by keeping the commandments should have been spiritual even in his flesh, became fleshly even in his spirit; and as in his pride he had sought to be his own satisfaction, God in His justice abandoned him to himself, not to live in the absolute independence he affected, but instead of the liberty he desired, to live dissatisfied with himself in a hard and miserable bondage to him to whom by sinning he had yielded himself, doomed in spite of himself to die in body as he had willingly become dead in spirit, condemned even to eternal death (had not the grace of God delivered him) because he had forsaken eternal life. Whoever thinks such punishment either excessive or unjust shows his inability to measure the great iniquity of sinning where sin might so easily have been avoided. For as Abraham's obedience is with justice pronounced to be great, because the thing commanded, to kill his son, was very difficult, so in Paradise the disobedience was the greater, because the difficulty of that which was commanded was imperceptible. And as the obedience of the second Man was the more laudable because He became obedient even "unto death,"[17] so the disobedience of the first man was the more detestable because he became disobedient even unto death. For where the penalty annexed to disobedience is great, and the thing commanded by the Creator is easy, who can sufficiently estimate how great a wickedness it is, in a matter so easy, not to obey the authority of so great a power, even when that power deters with so terrible a penalty? In short, to say all in a word, what but disobedience was the punishment of disobedience in that sin? For what else is man's misery but his own disobedience to himself, so that in consequence of his not being willing to do what he could do, he

17   Phil. ii. 8.

now wills to do what he cannot? For though he could not do all things in Paradise before he sinned, yet he wished to do only what he could do, and therefore he could do all things he wished. But now, as we recognize in his offspring, and as divine Scripture testifies, "Man is like to vanity." For who can count how many things he wishes which he cannot do, so long as he is disobedient to himself, that is, so long as his mind and his flesh do not obey his will? For in spite of himself his mind is both frequently disturbed, and his flesh suffers, and grows old, and dies; and in spite of ourselves we suffer whatever else we suffer, and which we would not suffer if our nature absolutely and in all its parts obeyed our will. But is it not the infirmities of the flesh which hamper it in its service? Yet what does it matter how its service is hampered, so long as the fact remains, that by the just retribution of the sovereign God whom we refused to be subject to and serve, our flesh, which was subjected to us, now torments us by insubordination, although our disobedience brought trouble on ourselves, not upon God? For He is not in need of our service as we of our body's; and therefore what we did was no punishment to Him, but what we receive is so to us. And the pains which are called bodily are pains of the soul in and from the body. For what pain or desire can the flesh feel by itself and without the soul? But when the flesh is said to desire or to suffer, it is meant, as we have explained, that the man does so, or some part of the soul which is affected by the sensation of the flesh, whether a harsh sensation causing pain, or gentle, causing pleasure. But pain in the flesh is only a discomfort of the soul arising from the flesh, and a kind of shrinking from its suffering, as the pain of the soul which is called sadness is a shrinking from those things which have happened to us in spite of ourselves. But sadness is frequently preceded by fear, which is itself in the soul, not in the flesh; while bodily pain is not preceded by any kind of fear of the flesh, which can be felt in the flesh before the pain. But pleasure is preceded by a certain appetite which is felt in the flesh like a craving, as hunger and thirst and that generative appetite which is most commonly identified with the name" lust," though this is the generic word for all desires. For anger itself was defined by the ancients as nothing else than the lust of revenge;[18] although sometimes a man is angry even at inanimate objects which cannot feel his vengeance, as when one breaks a pen, or crushes a quill that writes badly. Yet even this, though less reasonable, is in its way a lust of revenge, and is, so to speak, a mysterious kind of shadow of [the great law of] retribution, that they who do evil should suffer evil. There is therefore a lust for revenge, which is called anger; there is a lust of money, which goes by the name of avarice; there is a lust of conquering, no matter by what means, which is called opinionativeness; there is a lust of applause, which is named boasting. There are many and various lusts, of which some have names of their own, while others have not. For who could readily give a name to the lust of ruling, which yet has a powerful influence in the soul of tyrants, as civil wars bear witness?

---

18   Cicero, Tusc. Quaest. iii. 6 and iv. 9. So Aristotle

Think about it.

1. According to Augustine, what happened to the natures of Adam and Eve after they sinned against God? What evil will preceded the evil act?
2. What was the result to the human race?

---

413 CE

68. Letter to Demetrias

Translated by Bryn R. Rees

In contrast to the views of Augustine on human nature are those of Pelagius (c. 354–420 CE), a British monk who took issue with the doctrine of Original Sin and blamed it for the moral laxity of Christians in his day. Pelagius wrote two major treatises called *On Nature* and *Defense of the Freedom of the Will*, neither of which has survived. We do, however, possess some of his letters, from which we can learn a bit of his views. One of these was a letter written in 413 to a fourteen-year-old girl named Demetrias, who had recently taken a vow of virginity. Her mother, a widow, wrote to Pelagius to ask him to write to Demetrias with advice concerning the requirements of Christian chastity. Pelagius sent a lengthy reply, and here are two excerpts from the letter that concern human nature.

2:2. First, then, you ought to measure the good of human nature by reference to its creator, I mean God, of course: if it is he who, as report goes, has made all the works of and within the world good, exceeding good, how much more excellent do you suppose that he has made man himself, on whose account he has clearly made everything else? And before actually making man, he determines to fashion him in his own image and likeness and shows what kind of creature he intends to make him. Next, since he has made all animals subject to man and set him as lord over creatures which have been made more powerful than men either by their bodily size and greater strength or by the weapons which they have in their teeth, he makes it abundantly clear how much more gloriously man himself has been fashioned and wants him to appreciate the dignity of his own nature by marvelling that strong animals have been made subject to him. For he did not leave man naked and defenceless nor did he expose him in his weakness to a variety of dangers; but, having made him seem unarmed outwardly, he provided him with a better armament inside, that is, with reason and wisdom, so that by means of his intelligence and mental vigour, in which he surpassed the other animals, man alone was able to recognize the maker of all things and to serve God by using those same faculties which enabled him to hold sway over the rest. Moreover, the Lord of Justice wished man to be free to act and not under compulsion; it was for this reason that 'he left him free to make his own decisions' (Sir.15.14) and set before him life and death, good and evil, and he shall be given whatever pleases him (ibid. 17). Hence we read in the Book Deuteronomy also: I have set before you life and death, blessing and curse; therefore choose life, that you may live (Dt.30.19).

3:1. That is why we must now take precautions to prevent you from being embarrassed by something in which the ignorant majority is at fault for lack of proper consideration, and so from supposing, with them, that man has not been created truly good simply because he is able to do evil and is not obliged by the overpowering inclination of his own nature to do good on compulsion and without any possibility of variation. If you reconsider this matter carefully and force your mind to apply a more acute understanding to it, it will be revealed to you that man's status is better and higher for the very reason for which it is thought to be inferior: it is on this choice between two ways, on this freedom to choose either alternative, that the glory of the rational mind is based, it is in this that the whole honour of our nature consists, it is from this that its dignity is derived and all good men win others' praise and their own reward. Nor would there be any virtue at all in the good done by the man who perseveres, if he could not at any time cross over to the path of evil.

3.2. It was because God wished to bestow on the rational creature the gift of doing good of his own free will and the capacity to exercise free choice, by implanting in man the possibility of choosing either alternative, that he made it his peculiar right to be what he wanted to be, so that with his capacity for good and evil he could do either quite naturally and then bend his will in the other direction too. He could not claim to possess the good of his own volition, unless he were the kind of creature that could also have possessed evil. Our most excellent creator wished us to be able to do either but actually to do only one, that is, good, which he also commanded, giving us the capacity to do evil only so that we might do his will by exercising our own. That being so, this very capacity to do evil is also good—good, I say, because it makes the good part better by making it voluntary and independent, not bound by necessity but free to decide for itself. We are certainly permitted to choose, oppose, approve, reject, and there is no ground for preferring the rational creature to the others except that, while all the others possess only the good derived from their own circumstances and necessity, it alone possesses the good of free will also.

3:3. But most of those who, from lack of faith as much as of knowledge, deplore the status of man, are—I am ashamed to admit it—criticising the Lord's work and asserting that man ought to have been so made that he could do no evil at all, and we are then in a position where what is moulded says to its moulder: Why have you made me thus (Rom.9.20)? And these most shameless of men, while hiding the fact that they ate managing quite well with what they have been made, would prefer to have been made otherwise; and so those who are unwilling to correct their own way of life appear to want to correct nature itself instead, the good of which has been so universally established in all that it sometimes reveals itself and brings itself to notice even in pagans who do not worship God. For how many of the pagan philosophers have we heard and read and even seen for ourselves to be chaste, tolerant, temperate, generous, abstinent and kindly, rejecters of the world's honours as well as its delights, lovers of justice no less than knowledge? Whence, I ask you, do these good qualities pleasing to God come to men who are strangers to him? Whence *can* these good qualities come to them, unless it be from the good of nature? And since we see the qualities of which I have spoken contained either all in one person or severally in several persons and since the nature of all is one and the same, by their example they show each other that all qualities which are found either all together in all or severally in each one are able to exist in all alike. But if even men without God can show what kind of creatures they were made by God, consider what Christians are able to do whose nature and life have been instructed for the better by Christ and who are assisted by the aid of divine grace as well.

4:1. Come now, let us approach the secret places of our soul, let everyone examine himself more attentively, let us ask what opinion our own personal thoughts have of this matter, let our conscience itself deliver its judgement on the good of nature, let us be instructed by the inner teaching of the mind, and let us learn about each of the good qualities of the mind from no other source but the mind itself. Why is it, I ask you, that we either blush or fear at every sin we commit, displaying our guilt for what we have done at one moment by the blush on our countenance, at another by its pallor, anxiously trying to avoid any witness even of our smallest offences and suffering pangs of conscience all the while? And why, on the other hand, are we happy, resolute, bold after every good deed we have done and, if this fact is hidden from sight, desire and wish it to be seen in broad daylight? Why else unless it is because nature itself is its own witness and discloses its own good by the very fact of its disapproval of evil and, by putting its trust only in a good deed, shows what alone benefits it? Hence it comes about that frequently, though a murderer's identity remains concealed, torments of conscience make furious attacks on the author of the crime, and the secret punishment of the mind takes vengeance on the guilty man in hiding; nor is there any room for escape from punishment after the crime has been committed, since guilt is itself the penalty. That is why the innocent man, contrariwise, enjoys the peace of mind that comes from a good conscience even while undergoing torture and, though he fears punishment, still glories in his innocence.

4:2. There is, I maintain, a sort of natural sanctity in our minds which, presiding as it were in the mind's citadel, administers judgement equally on the evil and the good and, just as it favours honourable and upright actions, so too condemns wrong deeds and, on the evidence of conscience, distinguishes the one side from the other by a kind of inner law; nor, in fine, does it seek to deceive by any display of cleverness or of counterfeit brilliance in argument but either denounces or defends us by our thoughts themselves, surely the most reliable and incorruptible of witnesses. This is the law which the apostle recalls when he writes to the Romans, testifying that it is implanted in all men and written as it were on the tablets of the heart: For when gentiles who have not the law do by nature what the law requires, they are a law to themselves, even though they do not have the law. They show that what the law requires is written in their hearts, while their conscience also bears them witness and their conflicting thoughts accuse or perhaps excuse them (Rom.2.15,16). It is this law that all have used whom scripture records as having lived in sanctity and having pleased God between the time of Adam and that of Moses: some of these must be set before you as examples, so that you may not find it difficult to understand how great is the good of nature, when once you have satisfied yourself that it has replaced the law in the task of teaching righteousness.

4:7. After the many things which we have said about nature we have also shown its good by the examples of holy men and have proved it And lest, on the other hand, it should be thought to be nature's fault that some have been unrighteous, I shall use the evidence of the scriptures, which everywhere lay upon sinners the heavy weight of the charge of having used their own will and do not excuse them for having acted only under constraint of nature. In Genesis we read: The brothers Simeon and Levi have carried out their wickedness of their own free will (Gen.49.5,6). To Jerusalem the Lord said: Because they themselves have forsaken my way which I set before them, and have not obeyed my voice, but have followed the will of their own evil hearts (Jer.9.13,14). And again the same prophet: And you sinned against the Lord and did not obey his voice and refused to walk in his commands and in his laws and in his testimonies (Jer.44.23). He spoke also through the prophet Isaiah: If you are willing and obedient, you shall eat the good of the land; but if you refuse and rebel, you shall be devoured by the sword (Is.1.19,20). And again: All of you shall bow down in the slaughter; because, when I called, you did not obey, when I spoke, you did not listen, but you did evil before my eyes and chose what I did not delight in (Is.65.12). The Lord also says in the gospel: O Jerusalem, Jerusalem, killing the prophets and stoning those who are sent to you! How often would I have gathered your children together as a hen gathers her brood under her wings, and you would not (Mt.23.37)! When we see 'willing' and 'not willing', 'choosing' and 'rejecting', it is not the force of nature

but the freedom of the will that is then understood to be at work. The books of both Testaments are full of evidence of this kind, wherein all good, as well as all evil, is described as voluntary, and we omit it now only for the sake of brevity, especially when we know that, dedicated as you are to sacred reading, you can drink more copious draughts direct from the fountain itself.

8:1. Yet we do not defend the good of nature to such an extent that we claim that it cannot do evil, since we undoubtedly declare also that it is capable of good and evil; we merely try to protect it from an unjust charge, so that we may not seem to be forced to do evil through a fault in our nature, when, in fact, we do neither good nor evil without the exercise of our will and always have the freedom to do one of the two, being always able to do either. For on what grounds are some to be judges, others to be judged, unless it is because the will works in different ways in one and the same nature and because, though all of us are able to do the same, we actually do different things? And so, in order that this essential fact may stand out more clearly, we must cite some examples. Adam is cast out of paradise, Enoch is snatched away from the world; in both the Lord shows freedom of choice at work, for, just as the one who sinned could have pleased the Lord, so the other, who did please him, could have sinned instead. Neither would the former have deserved to be punished nor the latter to be chosen by a just God, unless both had been able to choose either course of action. This is how we are to understand the matter of Cain and Abel and also of Jacob and Esau, the twin brothers, and we have to realize that, when merits differ in the same nature, it is will that is the sole cause of an action.

8:2. Noah in his righteousness rejected the world when it was destroyed by flood because of its sins, Lot in his holiness passed judgement on the crimes of the Sodomites; and the fact that those first men were without the rebukes of the law for the space of so many years gives us no small grounds for acknowledging the good of nature, not, assuredly, because God at any time did not care for his creatures but because he knew that he had made human nature such that it would suffice them in place of the law for the practice of righteousness. In a word, as long as a nature which was still comparatively fresh was in vigorous use and long habituation to sinning did not draw a dark veil, as it were, over human reason, nature was set free and left without law; but when it had now become buried beneath an excess of vices and as if tainted with the rust of ignorance, the Lord applied the file of the law to it, and so, thoroughly polished by its frequent admonishments, it was enabled to recover its former brilliance.

8:3. Nor is there any reason why it is made difficult for us to do good other than that long habit of doing wrong which has infected us from childhood and corrupted us little by little over many years and ever after holds us in bondage and slavery to itself, so that it seems somehow to have acquired the force of nature. We now find ourselves being resisted and opposed by all that long period in which we were carelessly instructed, that is, educated in evil, in which we even strove to be evil, since, to add to the other incentives to evil, innocence itself was held to be folly. That old habit now attacks our new-found freedom of will, and, as we languish in ignorance through our sloth and idleness, unaccustomed to doing good after having for so long learned to do only evil, we wonder why sanctity is also conferred on us as if from an outside source.

Think about it.

1. How does Pelagius differ from Augustine?
2. Why does Pelagius have a problem with the idea that humans have a corrupt nature?

---

438 CE

69. Codex Theodosianus

Translated by Oliver J. Thatcher

In 438 CE, the Eastern Roman Empire, and in 439, the Western Roman Empire, published a compilation of laws called the Codex Theodosianus, named for the Eastern emperor Theodosius II (r. 408–450 CE). Theodosius had appointed a commission in 429 to gather all the laws passed by Christian emperors since 312. After nine years of work, the end product contained 16 books with 2,500 laws. Here is a selection of some of those laws.

Oliver J. Thatcher, "The Codex Theodosianus: On Religion, 4th Century CE," *The Library of Original Sources, Volume IV: The Early Medieval World*, pp. 69–71. University Research Extension Co., 1907. Copyright in the Public Domain.

C.Th. XI.vii.13: Let the course of all law suits and all business cease on Sunday, which our fathers have rightly called the Lord's day, and let no one try to collect either a public or a private debt; and let there be no hearing of disputes by any judges either those required to serve by law or those voluntarily chosen by disputants. And he is to be held not only infamous but sacrilegious who has turned away from the service and observance of holy religion on that day. Gratian, Valentinian and Theodosius Augusti.

C.Th. XV.v.1: On the Lord's day, which is the first day of the week, on Christmas, and on the days of Epiphany, Easter, and Pentecost, inasmuch as then the [white] garments [of Christians] symbolizing the light of heavenly cleansing bear witness to the new light of holy baptism, at the time also of the suffering of the apostles, the example for all Christians, the pleasures of the theaters and games are to be kept from the people in all cities, and all the thoughts of Christians and believers are to be occupied with the worship of God. And if any are kept from that worship through the madness of Jewish impiety or the error and insanity of foolish paganism, let them know that there is one time for prayer and another for pleasure. And lest anyone should think he is compelled by the honor due to our person, as if by the greater necessity of his imperial office, or that unless he attempted to hold the games in contempt of the religious prohibition, he might offend our serenity in showing less than the usual devotion toward us; let no one doubt that our clemency is revered in the highest degree by humankind when the worship of the whole world is paid to the might and goodness of God. Theodosius Augustus and Caesar Valentinian.

C. Th. XV.xii.1: Bloody spectacles are not suitable for civil ease and domestic quiet. Wherefore since we have proscribed gladiators, those who have been accustomed to be sentenced to such work as punishment for their crimes, you should cause to serve in the mines, so that they may be punished without shedding their blood. Constantine Augustus.

C. Th.XVI.i.2: We desire that all the people under the rule of our clemency should live by that religion which divine Peter the apostle is said to have given to the Romans, and which it is evident that Pope Damasus and Peter, bishop of Alexandria, a man of apostolic sanctity, followed; that is that we should believe in the one deity of Father, Son, and Holy Spirit with equal majesty and in the Holy Trinity according to the apostolic teaching and the authority of the gospel. Gratian, Valentinian and Theodosius Augusti.

C. Th. XVI.v.1: It is necessary that the privileges which are bestowed for the cultivation of religion should be given only to followers of the Catholic faith. We desire that heretics and schismatics be not only kept from these privileges, but be subjected to various fines. Constantine Augustus.

C. Th. XVI.v.iii: Whenever there is found a meeting of a mob of Manichaeans, let the leaders be punished with a heavy fine and let those who attended be known as infamous and dishonored, and be shut out from association with men, and let the house and the dwellings where the profane doctrine was taught be seized by the officers of the city. Valentinian and Valens Augusti.

C. Th. XVI.vii.1: The ability and right of making wills shall be taken from those who turn from Christians to pagans, and the testament of such an one, if he made any, shall be abrogated after his death. Gratian, Valentinian, and Valens Augusti.

C. Th. XVI.x.4: It is decreed that in all places and all cities the temples should be closed at once, and after a general warning, the opportunity of sinning be taken from the wicked. We decree also that we shall cease from making sacrifices. And if anyone has committed such a crime, let him be stricken with the avenging sword. And we decree that the property of the one executed shall be claimed by the city, and that rulers of the provinces be punished in the same way, if they neglect to punish such crimes. Constantine and Constans Augusti.

Think about it.

1. How might these laws have changed Roman society?
2. If you were a non-Christian or an "unorthodox" Christian who lived at that time, what might your reaction have been to these laws?

c. 5ᵗʰ century CE

70. The Kama Sutra

Translated by the Hindu Kama Shastra Society

In Sanskrit, the word *kāma* means "affection, love, desire, sensual pleasure," etc. By Hindus it is considered one of the four goals of life. There were many *sutras* or manuals written about *kāma* in ancient India, but the one by Vatsyayana, a Hindu philosopher who probably lived during the Gupta period (320–550 CE), is the earliest to have survived and the most famous. Despite the book's reputation, only a portion of it gives practical advice in sexual practice. The rest concerns matters relating generally to relationships between men and women. The following passages from Book 4 give advice to wives.

CHAPTER I.

On the Manner of Living of a Virtuous Woman, and of Her Behavior During the Absence of Her Husband

A virtuous woman, who has affection for her husband, should act in conformity with his wishes as if he were a divine being, and with his consent should take upon herself the whole care of his family. She should keep the whole house well cleaned, and arrange flowers of various kinds in different parts of it, and make the floor smooth and polished so as to give the whole a neat and becoming appearance. She

should surround the house with a garden, and place ready in it all the materials required for the morning, noon, and evening sacrifices. Moreover she should herself revere the sanctuary of the Household Gods, for says Gonardiya, "nothing so much attracts the heart of an householder to his wife as a careful observance of the things mentioned above."

Towards the parents, relations, friends, sisters, and servants of her husband she should behave as they deserve. In the garden she should plant beds of green vegetables, bunches of the sugar cane, and clumps of the fig tree, the mustard plant, the parsley plant, the fennel plant, and the xanthochymus

The Kama Sutra of Vatsyayana, trans. Hindu Karma Shastra Society, pp. 91–99. Society of the Friends of India, 1883. Copyright in the Public Domain.

pictorius. Clusters of various flowers such as the trapa bispinosa, the jasmine, the gasminum grandiflorum, the yellow amaranth, the wild jasmine, the tabernamontana coronaria, the nadyaworta, the china rose and others, should likewise be planted, together with the fragrant grass andropogon, schasnanthus, and the fragrant root of the plant andropogon miricatus. She should also have seats and arbors made in the garden, in the middle of which a well, tank, or pool should be dug.

The wife should always avoid the company of female beggars, female buddhist mendicants, unchaste and rougish women, female fortune tellers and witches. As regards meals she should always consider what her husband likes and dislikes, and what things are good for him, and what are injurious to him When she hears the sounds of his footsteps coming home she should at once get up, and be ready to do whatever he may command her, and either order her female servant to wash his feet, or wash them herself. When going anywhere with her husband she should put on her ornaments, and without his consent she should not either give or accept invitations, or attend marriages and sacrifices, or sit in the company of female friends, or visit the temples of the Gods.

And if she wants to engage in any kind of games or sports, she should not do it against his will. In the same way she should always sit down after him, and get up before him, and should never awaken him when he is asleep. The kitchen should be situated in a quiet and retired place, so as not to be accessible to strangers, and should always look clean.

In the event of any misconduct on the part of her husband, she should not blame him excessively, though she be a little displeased. She should not use abusive language towards him, but rebuke him with conciliatory words, whether he be in the company of friends or alone. Moreover, she should not be a scold, for says Gonardiya "there is no cause of dislike on the part of a husband so great as this characteristic in a wife." Lastly she should avoid bad expressions, sulky looks, speaking aside, standing in the doorway, and looking at passers-by, conversing in pleasure groves, and remaining in a lonely place for a long time; and finally she should always keep her body, her teeth, her hair, and everything belonging to her tidy, sweet, and clean.

When the wife wants to approach her husband in private her dress should consist of many ornaments, various kinds of flowers, and a cloth decorated with different colors, and some sweet-smelling ointments or unguents. But her everyday dress should be composed of a thin, close-textured cloth, a few ornaments and flowers, and a little scent, not too much.

She should also observe the fasts and vows of her husband, and when he tries to prevent her doing this, she should persuade him to let her do it.

At appropriate times of the year, and when they happen to be cheap, she should buy earth, bamboos, firewood, skins, and iron pots, as also salt and oil. Fragrant substances, vessels made of the fruit of the plant wrightea antidysenterica, or oval leaved wrightea, medicines, and other things which are always wanted, should be obtained when required and kept in a secret place of the house. The seeds of the radish, the potato, the common beet, the Indian wormwood, the mangoe, the cucumber, the egg plant, the kushmanda, the pumpkin gourd, the surana, the bignonia indica, the sandal wood, the premna spinosa, the garlic plant, the onion, and other vegetables, should be bought and sown at the proper seasons.

The wife, moreover, should not tell to strangers the amount of her wealth, nor the secrets which her husband has confided to her. She should surpass all the women of her own rank in life in her cleverness, her appearance, her knowledge of cookery, her pride, and her manner of serving her husband. The expenditure of the year should be regulated by the profits. The milk that remains after the meals should be turned into ghee or clarified butter. Oil and sugar should be prepared at home; spinning and weaving should also be done there; and a store of ropes and cords, and barks of trees for twisting into ropes should be kept. She should also attend to the pounding and cleaning of rice, using its small grain and chaff in some way or other. She should pay the salaries of the servants, look after the tilling of the fields, the keeping of the flocks and herds, superintend the making of vehicles, and take care of the rams, cocks, quails, parrots, starlings, cuckoos, peacocks, monkeys, and deer; and finally adjust the income and expenditure of the day. The worn out clothes should be given to those servants who have done good work, in order to show them that their services have been appreciated, or they may be applied to some other use.

The vessels in which wine is prepared, as well as those in which it is kept, should be carefully looked after, and put away at the proper time. All sales and purchases should also be well attended to. The friends of her husband she should welcome by presenting them with flowers, ointment, incense, betel leaves, and betel nut. Her father-in-law and mother-in-law she should treat as they deserve, always remaining dependent on their will, never contradicting them, speaking to them in few and not harsh words, not laughing loudly in their presence, and acting with their friends and enemies as with her own. In addition to the above she should not be vain, or too much taken up with her enjoyments. She should be liberal towards her servants, and reward them on holidays and festivals; and not give away anything without first making it known to her husband.

Thus ends the manner of living of a virtuous woman.

During the absence of her husband on a journey the virtuous woman should wear only her auspicious ornaments, and observe the fasts in honor of the Gods. While anxious to hear the news of her husband, she should still look after her household affairs. She should sleep near the elder women of the house, and make herself agreeable to them. She should look after and keep in repair the things that are liked by her husband, and continue the works that have been begun by him. To the abode of her relations she should not go except on occasions of joy and sorrow, and then she should go in her usual travelling dress, accompanied by her husband's servants, and not remain there for a long time. The fasts and feasts should be observed with the consent of the elders of the house. The resources should be increased by making purchases and sales according to the practice of the merchants, and by means of honest servants, superintended by herself. The income should be increased, and the expenditure diminished as much as possible. And when her husband returns from his journey, she should receive him at first in her ordinary clothes, so that he may know in what way she has lived during his absence, and should bring to him some presents, as also materials for the worship of the Deity.

Thus ends the part relating to the behavior of a wife during the absence of her husband on a journey.

There are also some verses on the subject as follows:

"The wife, whether she be a woman of noble family, or a virgin widow[1] remarried, or a concubine, should lead a chaste life, devoted to her husband, and doing every thing for his welfare. Women acting thus, acquire Dharma, Artha, and Kama, obtain a high position, and generally keep their husbands devoted to them."

CHAPTER 11.

On the Conduct of the Elder Wife Towards the Other Wives of Her Husband, and on that of a Younger Wife towards the Elder Ones. Also on the Conduct of a Virgin Widow Re-married; of a Wife Disliked by Her Husband; of the Women in the King's Harem; and Lastly on the Conduct of a Husband Towards Many Wives.

The causes of re-marriage during the lifetime of the wife are as follows:

(1) The folly or ill temper of the wife.

(2) Her husband's dislike to her.

---

1 This probably refers to a girl married in her infancy, or when very young and whose husband had died before she arrived at the age of puberty. [...]

(3) The want of offspring.

(4) The continual birth of daughters.

(5) The incontinence of the husband.

From the very beginning a wife should endeavor to attract the heart of her husband by showing to him continually her devotion, her good temper, and her wisdom. If however, she bears him no children, she should herself tell her husband to marry another woman. And when the second wife is married, and brought to the house, the first wife should give her a position superior to her own, and look upon her as a sister. In the morning the elder wife should forcibly make the younger one decorate herself in the presence of their husband, and should not mind all the husband's favor being given to her. If the younger wife does anything to displease her husband the elder one should not neglect her, but should always be ready to give her the most careful advice, and should teach her to do various things in the presence of her husband. Her children she should treat as her own, her attendants she should look upon with more regard even than on her own servants, her friends she should cherish with love and kindness, and her relations with great honor.

When there are many other wives besides herself, the elder wife should associate with the one who is immediately next to her in rank and age, and should instigate the wife who has recently enjoyed her husband's favor to quarrel with the present favorite. After this she should sympathize with the former, and having collected all the other wives together, should get them to denounce the favorite as a scheming and wicked woman, without however committing herself in any way. If the favorite wife happens to quarrel with the husband, then the elder wife should take her part and give her false encouragement, and thus cause the quarrel to be increased. If there be only a little quarrel between the two, the elder wife should do all she can to work it up into a large quarrel. But if after all this she finds that her husband still continues to love his favorite wife, she should then change her tactics, and endeavor to

bring about a conciliation between them, so as to avoid her husband's displeasure.

Thus ends the conduct of the elder wife.

The younger wife should regard the elder wife of her husband as her mother, and should not give anything away, even to her own relations, without her knowledge. She should tell her everything about herself, and not approach her husband without her permission. Whatever is told to her by the elder wife she should not reveal to others, and she should take care of the children of the senior even more than of her own. When alone with her husband she should serve him well, but should not tell him of the pain she suffers from the existence of a rival wife. She may also obtain secretly from her husband some marks of his particular regard for her, and may tell him that she lives only for him, and for the regard that he has for her. She should never reveal her love for her husband, nor her husband's love for her to any person either in pride or in anger, for a wife that reveals the secrets of her husband is despised by him. As for seeking to obtain the regard of her husband, Gonardiya says, that it should always be done in private, for fear of the elder wife. If the elder wife be disliked by her husband, or be childless, she should sympathize with her, and should ask her husband to do the same, but should surpass her in leading the life of a chaste woman.

Thus ends the conduct of the younger wife towards the elder.

A widow in poor circumstances, or of a weak nature, and who allies herself again to a man, is called a widow re-married.

The followers of Babhravya say that a virgin widow should not marry a person whom she may be obliged to leave on account of his bad character, or of his being destitute of the excellent qualities of a man, she thus being obliged to have recourse to another person. Gonardya is of opinion that as the cause of a widow's marrying again is her desire for happiness, and as happiness is secured by the possession of excellent qualities in her husband, joined to a love of enjoyment, it is better therefore to secure a person endowed with such qualities in the first instance. Vatsyayana, however, thinks that a widow may marry any person that she likes, and that she thinks will suit her.

At the time of her marriage the widow should obtain from her husband the money to pay the cost of drinking parties, and picnics with her relations, and of giving them and her friends kindly gifts and presents; or she may do these things at her own cost if she likes. In the same way she may wear either her husband's ornaments or her own.

As to the presents of affection mutually exchanged between the husband and herself there is no fixed rule about them.

If she leaves her husband after marriage of her own accord, she should restore to him whatever he may have given her, with the exception of the mutual presents. If however, she is driven out of the house by her husband she should not return anything to him.

After her marriage she should live in the house of her husband like one of the chief members of the family, but should treat the other ladies of the family with kindness, the servants with generosity, and all the friends of the house with familiarity and good temper. She should show that she is better acquainted with the sixty-four arts than the other ladies of the house, and in any quarrels with her husband she should not rebuke him severely, but in private do everything that he wishes, and make use of the sixty-four ways of enjoyment. She should be obliging to the other wives of her husband, and to their children she should give presents, behave as their mistress, and make ornaments and play-things for their use. In the friends and servants of her husband she should confide more than in his other wives, and finally she should have a liking for drinking parties, going to picnics, attending fairs and festivals, and for carrying out all kinds of games and amusements.

Thus ends the conduct of a virgin widow re-married.

A woman who is disliked by her husband, and annoyed and distressed by his other wives, should associate with the wife who is liked most by her husband, and who serves him more than the others, and should teach her all the arts with which she is acquainted. She should act as the nurse of her husband's children, and having gained over his friends to her side, should through them make him acquainted of her devotion to him. In religious ceremonies she should be a leader, as also in vows and fasts, and should not hold too good an opinion of herself. When her husband is lying on his bed, she should only go near him when it is agreeable to him, and should never rebuke him, or show obstinacy in any way.

If her husband happens to quarrel with any of his other wives, she should reconcile them to each other, and if he desires to see any woman secretly, she should manage to bring about the meeting between them. She should moreover make herself acquainted with the weak points of her husband's character, but always keep them secret, and on the whole behave herself in such a way as may lead him to look upon her as a good and devoted wife.

Here ends the conduct of a wife disliked by her husband.

The above sections will show how all the women of the King's seraglio are to behave, and therefore we shall now speak separately only about the king.

The female attendants in the harem (called severally Kanchukiyas[2] Mahallarikas[3] and Mahauikas[4]) should bring flowers, ointments and clothes from the King's wives to the King, and he having received these things should give them as presents to the

---

2 A name given to the maid servants of the zenana of the King in ancient times, on account of their always keeping their breasts covered with a cloth called kanchuki. It was customary in the olden time for the maid servants to cover their breasts with a cloth, while the Queens kept their breasts un-covered. This custom is distinctly to be seen in the Ajunta cave paintings.
3 The meaning of this word is a superior woman, so it would seem that a Mahallarika must be a person in authority over the maid servants of the harem.
4 This was also appertaining to the rank of women employed in the harem.
In later times this place was given to eunuchs.

servants, along with the things worn by him the previous day. In the afternoon the King having dressed and put on his ornaments should interview the women of the harem, who should also be dressed and decorated with jewels. Then having given to each of them such a place and such respect as may suit the occasion and as they may deserve, he should carry on with them a cheerful conversation. After that he should see such of his wives as may be virgin widows re-married, and after them the concubines and dancing girls. All of these should be visited in their own private rooms.

The meaning of this word is a superior woman, so it would seem that a Mahallarika must be a person in authority over the maid servants of the harem.

This was also appertaining to the rank of women employed in the harem.

In later times this place was given to eunuchs.

When the King rises from his noonday sleep, the woman whose duty it is to inform the King regarding the wife who is to spend the night with him should come to him accompanied by the female attendants of that wife whose turn may have arrived in the regular course, and of her who may have been accidentally passed over as her turn arrived, and of her who may have been unwell at the time of her turn.

These attendants should place before the King the ointments and unguents sent by each of these wives, marked with the seal of her ring, and their names and their reasons for sending the ointments should be told to the King. After this the King accepts the ointment of one of them, who then is informed that her ointment has been accepted, and that her day has been settled.[5]

At festivals, singing parties and exhibitions all the wives of the King should be treated with respect and served with drinks.

But the women of the harem should not be allowed to go out alone, neither should any woman outside the harem be allowed to enter it except those whose character is well known. And lastly the work which the King's wives have to do should not be too fatiguing.

Thus ends the conduct of the King towards the women of the harem, and of their own conduct.

A man marrying many wives should act fairly towards them all. He should neither disregard nor pass over their faults, and should not reveal to one wife the love, passion, bodily blemishes, and confidential reproaches of the other. No opportunity should be given to any one of them of speaking to him about their rivals, and if one of them should begin to speak ill of another, he should chide her and tell her that she has exactly the same blemishes in her character. One of them he should please by secret confidence, another by secret respect, and another by secret flattery, and he should please them all by going to gardens, by amusements, by presents, by honoring their relations, by telling them secrets, and lastly by loving unions. A young woman who is of a good temper, and who conducts herself according to the precepts of the Holy Writ wins her husband's attachment, and obtains a superiority over her rivals.

Thus ends the conduct of a husband towards many wives.

---

5   As Kings generally had many wives, it was usual for them to enjoy their wives by turns. But as it happened sometimes that some of them lost their turns owing to the King's absence, or to their being unwell, then in such cases the women whose turns had been passed over, and those whose turns had come, used to have a sort of lottery, and the ointment of all the claimants were sent to the King, who accepted the ointment of one of them, and thus settled the question.

c. 507–511 CE

71. Lex Salica

Translated by Ernest F. Henderson

The Lex Salica, or Salic Law, was a body of law governing the Franks during the early Middle Ages in Europe. It was originally commissioned and published in Latin by Clovis I (r. 481–511 CE) at some time between 507 and 511. It was based on the traditional oral law of the Salian Franks, so the law reflects ancient practices. The law was regularly revised over the next three centuries to keep up with the times. Here are some excerpts.

Title I. Concerning Summonses.

1. If any one be summoned before the "Thing" by the king's law, and do not come, he shall be sentenced to 600 denars, which make 15 shillings (solidi).

2. But he who summons another, and does not come himself, shall, if a lawful impediment have not delayed him, be sentenced to 15 shillings, to be paid to him whom he summoned.

3. And he who summons another shall walk with witnesses to the home of that man, and, if he be not at home, shall bid the wife or any one of the family to make known to him that he has been summoned to court.

4. But if he be occupied in the king's service he can not summon him.

5. But if he shall be inside the hundred seeing about his own affairs, he can summon him in the manner explained above.

Title II. Concerning Thefts of Pigs, etc.

1. If any one steal a sucking pig, and it be proved against him, he shall be sentenced to 120 denars, which make three shillings.

Ernest F. Henderson, *Select Historical Documents of the Middle Ages*, pp. 176–189. George Bell and Sons, 1903. Copyright in the Public Domain.

2. If any one steal a pig that can live without its mother, and it be proved on him, he shall be sentenced to 40 denars that is, 1 shilling.

14. If any one steal 25 sheep where there were no more in that flock, and it be proved on him, he shall be sentenced to 2500 denars that is, 62 shillings.

Title III. Concerning Thefts of Cattle.

4. If any one steal that bull which rules the herd and never has been yoked, he shall be sentenced to 1800 denars, which make 45 shillings.

5. But if that bull is used for the cows of three villages in common, he who stole him shall be sentenced to three times 45 shillings.

6. If any one steal a bull belonging to the king he shall be sentenced to 3600 denars, which make 90 shillings.

Title IV. Concerning Damage done among Crops or in any Enclosure.

1. If any one finds cattle, or a horse, or flocks of any kind in his crops, he shall not at all mutilate them.

2. If he do this and confess it, he shall restore the worth of the animal in place of it, and shall himself keep the mutilated one.

3. But if he have not confessed it, and it have been proved on him, he shall be sentenced, besides the value of the animal and the fines for delay, to 600 denars, which make 15 shillings.

Title XI. Concerning Thefts or Housebreakings of Freemen.

1. If any freeman steal, outside of the house, something worth 2 denars, he shall be sentenced to 600 denars, which make 15 shillings.

2. But if he steal, outside of the house, something worth 40 denars, and it be proved on him, he shall be sentenced, besides the amount and the fines for delay, to 400 denars, which make 35 shillings.

3. If a freeman break into a house and steal something worth 2 denars, and it be proved on him, he shall be sentenced to 15 shillings.

4. But if he shall have stolen something worth more than 5 denars, and it have been proved on him, he shall be sentenced, besides the worth of the object and the fines for delay, to 1400 denars, which make 35 shillings.

5. But if he have broken, or tampered with, the lock, and thus have entered the house and stolen anything from it, he shall be sentenced, besides the worth of the object and the fines for delay, to 1800 denars, which make 45 shillings.

6. And if he have taken nothing, or have escaped by flight, he shall, for the housebreaking alone, be sentenced to 1200 denars, which make 30 shillings.

Title XII. Concerning Thefts or Housebreakings on the Part of Slaves.

1. If a slave steal, outside of the house, something worth two denars, he shall, besides paying the worth of the object and the fines for delay, be stretched out and receive 120 blows.

2. But if he steal something worth 40 denars, he shall either be castrated or pay 6 shillings. But the lord of the slave who committed the theft shall restore to the plaintiff the worth of the object and the fines for delay.

Title XIII. Concerning Rape Committed by Freemen.

1. If three men carry off a free born girl, they shall be compelled to pay 30 shillings.

2. If there are more than three, each one shall pay 5 shillings.

3. Those who shall have been present with boats shall be sentenced to three shillings.

4. But those who commit rape shall be compelled to pay 2500 denars, which make 63 shillings.

5. But if they have carried off that girl from behind lock and key, or from the spinning room, they shall be sentenced to the above price and penalty.

6. But if the girl who is carried off be under the king's protection, then the "frith" (peace-money) shall be 2500 denars, which make 63 shillings.

7. But if a bondsman of the king, or a leet, should carry off a free woman, he shall be sentenced to death.

8. But if a free woman have followed a slave of her own will, she shall lose her freedom.

9. If a freeborn man shall have taken an alien bonds-woman, he shall suffer similarly.

10. If any body take an alien spouse and join her to himself in matrimony, he shall be sentenced to 2500 denars, which make 63 shillings.

Title XIV. Concerning Assault and Robbery.

1. If any one have assaulted and plundered a free man, and it be proved on him, he shall be sentenced to 2500 denars, which make 63 shillings.

2. If a Roman have plundered a Salian Frank, the above law shall be observed.

3. But if a Frank have plundered a Roman, he shall be sentenced to 35 shillings.

4. If any man should wish to migrate, and has permission from the king, and shall have shown this in the public "Thing:" whoever, Contrary to the decree of the king, shall presume to oppose him, shall be sentenced to 8000 denars, which make 200 shillings.

Title XV. Concerning Arson.

1. If any one shall set fire to a house in which men were sleeping, as many freemen as were in it can make complaint before the "Thing;" and if any one shall have been burned in it, the incendiary shall be sentenced to 2500 denars, which make 63 shillings.

Title XVII. Concerning Wounds.

1. If any one have wished to kill another person, and the blow have missed, he on whom it was proved shall be sentenced to 2500 denars, which make 63 shillings.

2. If any person have wished to strike another with a poisoned arrow, and the arrow have glanced aside, and it shall be proved on him: he shall be sentenced to 2500 denars, which make 63 shillings.

3. If any person strike another on the head so that the brain appears, and the three bones which lie above the brain shall project, he shall be sentenced to 1200 denars, which make 30 shillings.

4. But if it shall have been between the ribs or in the stomach, so that the wound appears and reaches to the entrails, he shall be sentenced to 1200 denars which make 30 shillings besides five shillings for the physician's pay.

5. If any one shall have struck a man so that blood falls to the floor, and it be proved on him, he shall be sentenced to 600 denars, which make 15 shillings.

6. But if a freeman strike a freeman with his fist so that blood does not flow, he shall be sentenced for each blow up to 3 blows to 120 denars, which make 3 shillings.

Title XVIII. Concerning him who, before the King, accuses an innocent Man.

If any one, before the king, accuse an innocent man who is absent, he shall be sentenced to 2500 denars, which make 63 shillings.

Title XIX. Concerning Magicians.

1. If any one have given herbs to another so that he die, he shall be sentenced to 200 shillings (or shall surely be given over to fire).

2. If any person have bewitched another, and he who was thus treated shall escape, the author of the crime, who is proved to have committed it, shall be sentenced to 2500 denars, which make 63 shillings.

Title XXIV. Concerning the Killing of little children and women.

1. If anyone have slain a boy under 10 years up to the end of the tenth and it shall have been proved on

him, he shall be sentenced to 24000 denars, which make 600 shillings.

3. If any one have hit a free woman who is pregnant, and she dies, he shall be sentenced to 28000 denars, which make 700 shillings.

6. If any one have killed a free woman after she has begun bearing children, he shall be sentenced to 24000 denars, which make 600 shillings.

7. After she can have no more children, he who kills her shall be sentenced to 8000 denars, which make 200 shillings.

Title XXX. Concerning Insults.

3. If any one, man or woman, shall have called a woman harlot, and shall not have been able to prove it, he shall be sentenced to 1800 denars, which make 45 shillings.

4. If any person shall have called another "fox," he shall be sentenced to 3 shillings.

5. If any man shall have called another "hare," he shall be sentenced to 3 shillings.

6. If any man shall have brought it up against another that he have thrown away his shield, and shall not have been able to prove it, he shall be sentenced to 120 denars, which make 3 shillings.

7. If any man shall have called another "spy" or "perjurer," and shall not have been able to prove it, he shall be sentenced to 600 denars, which make 15 shillings.

Title XXXIII. Concerning the Theft of hunting animals.

2. If any one have stolen a tame marked stag (-hound?) trained to hunting, and it shall have been proved through witnesses that his master had him for hunting, or had killed with him two or three beasts, he shall be sentenced to 1800 denars, which make 45 shillings.

Title XXXIV. Concerning the Stealing of Fences.

1. If any man shall have cut 3 staves by which a fence is bound or held together, or have stolen or cut the heads of 3 stakes, he shall be sentenced to 600 denars, which make 15 shillings.

2. If any one shall have drawn a harrow through another's harvest after it has sprouted, or shall have gone through it with a waggon where there was no road, he shall be sentenced to 120 denars, which make 3 shillings.

3. If any one shall have gone, where there is no way or path, through another's harvest which has already become thick, he shall be sentenced to 600 denars, which make 15 shillings.

Title XLI. Concerning the Murder of Free Men.

1. If any one shall have killed a free Frank, or a barbarian living under the Salic law, and it have been proved on him, he shall be sentenced to 8000 denars.

2. But if he shall have thrown him into a well or into the water, or shall have covered him with branches or anything else, to conceal him, he shall be sentenced to 24000 denars, which make 600 shillings.

3. But if any one has slain a man who is in the service of the king, he shall be sentenced to 24000 denars, which make 600 shillings.

4. But if he have put him in the water or in a well, and covered him with anything to conceal him, he shall be sentenced to 72000 denars, which make 1800 shillings.

5. If any one have slain a Roman who eats in the king's palace, and it have been proved on him, he shall be sentenced to 12000 denars, which make 300 shillings.

6. But if the Roman shall not have been a landed proprietor and table companion of the king, he who killed him shall be sentenced to 4000 denars, which make 100 shillings.

7. But if he shall have killed a Roman who was obliged to pay tribute, he shall be sentenced to 63 shillings.

9. If any one have thrown a free man into a well, and he have escaped alive, he (the criminal) shall be sentenced to 4000 denars, which make 100 shillings.

Title XLV. Concerning Migrators.

1. If any one wish to migrate to another village and if one or more who live in that village do not wish to receive him, if there be only one who objects, he shall not have leave to move there.

2. But if he shall have presumed to settle in that village in spite of his rejection by one or two men, then some one shall give him warning. And if he be unwilling to go away, he who gives him warning shall give him warning, with witnesses, as follows: I warn thee that thou may'st remain here this next night as the Salic law demands, and I warn thee that within 10 nights thou shalt go forth from this village. After another 10 nights he shall again come to him and warn him again within 10 nights to go away. If he still refuse to go, again 10 nights shall be added to the command, that the number of 30 nights may be full. If he will not go away even then, then he shall summon him to the "Thing," and present his witnesses as to the separate commands to leave. If he who has been warned will not then move away, and no valid reason detains him, and all the above warnings which we have mentioned have been given according to law: then he who gave him warning shall take the matter into his own hands f and request the "comes" to go to that place and expel him. And because he would not listen to the law, that man shall relinquish all that he has earned there, and, besides, shall be sentenced to 1200 denars, which make 30 shillings.

3. But if anyone have moved there, and within 12 months no one have given him warning, he shall remain as secure as the other neighbours.

Title XLVI. Concerning Transfers of Property.

1. The observance shall be that the Thunginus or Centenarius shall call together a "Thing," and shall have his shield in the "Thing," and shall demand three men as witnesses for each of the three transactions. He (the owner of the land to be transferred) shall seek a man who has no connection with himself, and shall throw a stalk into his lap. And to him into whose lap he has thrown the stalk he shall tell, concerning his property, how much of it or whether the whole or a half he wishes to give. He in whose lap he threw the stalk shall remain in his (the owner's) house, and shall collect three or more guests, and shall have the property as much as is given him in his power. And, afterwards, he to whom that property is entrusted shall discuss all these things with the witnesses collected afterwards, either before the king or in the regular "Thing," he shall give the property up to him for whom it was intended. He shall take the stalk in the "Thing," and, before 12 months are over, shall throw it into the lap of him whom the owner has named heir; and he shall restore not more nor less, but exactly as much as was entrusted to him.

2. And if any one shall wish to say anything against this, three sworn witnesses shall say that they were in the "Thing" which the "Thunginus" or "Centenarius" called together, and that they saw that man who wished to give his property throw a stalk into the lap of him whom he had selected. They shall name by name him who threw his property into the lap of the other, and, likewise, shall name him whom he named his heir. And three other sworn witnesses shall say that he in whose lap the stalk was thrown had remained in the house of him who gave his property, and had there collected three or more guests, and that they had eaten porridge at table, and that he had collected those who were bearing witness, and that those guests had thanked him for their entertainment. All this those other sworn witnesses shall say, and that he who received that property in his lap in the "Thing" held before the king, or in the regular public "Thing," did publicly,

before the people, either in the presence of the king or in public "Thing" namely on the Mallberg, before the "Thunginus" throw the stalk into the lap of him whom the owner had named as heir. And thus 9 witnesses shall confirm all this.

Title L. Concerning Promises to Pay.

1. If any freeman or leet have made to another a promise to pay, then he to whom the promise was made shall, within 40 days or within such term as was agreed when he made the promise, go to the house of that man with witnesses, or with appraisers. And if he (the debtor) be unwilling to make the promised payment, he shall be sentenced to 15 shillings above the debt which he had promised.

2. If he then be unwilling to pay, he (the creditor) shall summon him before the "Thing" and thus accuse him: "I ask thee, ' Thunginus,' to bann my opponent who made me a promise to pay and owes me a debt." And he shall state how much he owes and promised to pay. Then the "Thunginus" shall say: "I bann thy opponent to what the Salic law decrees." Then he to whom the promise was made shall warn him (the debtor) to make no payment or pledge of payment to any body else until he have fulfilled his promise to him (the creditor). And straightway on that same day, before the sun sets, he shall go to the house of that man with witnesses, and shall ask if he will pay that debt. If he will not, he (the creditor) shall wait until after sunset; then, if he have waited until after sunset, 120 denars, which make 3 shillings shall be added on to the debt. And this shall be done up to 3 times in 3 weeks. And if at the third time he will not pay all this, it (the sum) shall increase to 360 denars, or 9 shillings: so, namely, that, after each admonition or waiting until after sunset, 3 shillings shall be added to the debt.

3. If any one be unwilling to fulfil his promise in the regular assembly, then he to whom the promise was made shall go the count of that place, in whose district he lives, and shall take the stalk and shall say: oh count, that man made me a promise to pay, and I have lawfully summoned him before the court according to the Salic law on this matter; I pledge thee myself and my fortune that thou may'st safely seize his property. And he shall state the case to him, and shall tell how much he (the debtor) had agreed to pay. Then the count shall collect 7 suitable bailiffs, and shall go with them to the house of him who made the promise and shall say: thou who art here present pay voluntarily to that man what thou didst promise, and choose any two of those bailiffs who shall appraise that from which thou shalt pay; and make good what thou dost owe, according to a just appraisal. But if he will not hear, or be absent, then the bailiffs shall take from his property the value of the debt which he owes. And, according to the law, the accuser shall take two thirds of that which the debtor owes, and the count shall collect for himself the other third as peace money; unless the peace money shall have been paid to him before in this same matter.

4. If the count have been appealed to, and no sufficient reason, and no duty of the king, have detained him and if he have put off going, and have sent no substitute to demand law and justice: he shall answer for it with his life, or shall redeem himself with his "wergeld."

Title LIV. Concerning the Slaying of a Count.

1. If any one slay a count, he shall be sentenced to 2400 denars, which make 600 shillings.

Title LV. Concerning the Plundering of Corpses.

2. If any one shall have dug up and plundered a corpse already buried, and it shall have been proved on him, he shall be outlawed until the day when he comes to an agreement with the relatives of the dead man, and they ask for him that he be allowed to come among men. And whoever, before he come to an arrangement with the relative, shall give him bread or shelter even if they are his relations or his

own wife shall be sentenced to 600 denars which make 15 shillings.

3. But he who is proved to have committed the crime shall be sentenced to 8000 denars, which make 200 shillings.

Title LVI. Concerning him who shall have scorned to come to Court.

1. If any man shall have scorned to come to court, and shall have put off fulfilling the injunction of the bailiffs, and shall not have been willing to consent to undergo the fine, or the kettle ordeal, or anything prescribed by law: then he (the plaintiff) shall summon him to the presence of the king. And there shall be 12 witnesses who 3 at a time being sworn shall testify that they were present when the bailiff enjoined him (the accused) either to go to the kettle ordeal, or to agree concerning the fine; and that he had scorned the injunction. Then 3 others shall swear that they were there on the day when the bailiffs enjoined that he should free himself by the kettle ordeal or by composition; and that 40 days after that, in the "mallberg," he (the accuser) had again waited until after sunset, and that he (the accused) would not obey the law. Then he (the accuser) shall summon him before the king for a fortnight thence; and three witnesses shall swear that they were there when he summoned him and when he waited for sunset. If he does not then come, those 9, being sworn, shall give testimony as we have above explained. On that day likewise, if he do not come, he (the accuser) shall let the sun go down on him, and shall have 3 witnesses who shall be there when he waits till sunset. But if the accuser shall have fulfilled all this, and the accused shall not have been willing to come to any court, then the king, before whom he has been summoned, shall withdraw his protection from him. Then he shall be guilty, and all his goods shall belong to the fisc, or to him to whom the fisc may wish to give them. And whoever shall have fed or housed him even if it were his own wife shall be sentenced to 600 denars, which make 15 shillings;

until he (the debtor) shall have made good all that has been laid to his charge.

Title LVII. Concerning the "Chrenecruda."

1. If any one have killed a man, and, having given up all his property, has not enough to comply with the full terms of the law, he shall present 12 sworn witnesses to the effect that, neither above the earth nor under it, has he any more property than he has already given. And he shall afterwards go into his house, and shall collect in his hand dust from the four corners of it, and shall afterwards stand upon the threshold, looking inwards into the house. And then, with his left hand, he shall throw over his shoulder some of that dust on the nearest relative that he has. But if his father and (his father's) brothers have already paid, he shall then throw that dust on their (the brothers') children that is, over three (relatives) who are nearest on the father's and three on the mother's side. And after that, in his shirt, without girdle and without shoes, a staff in his hand, he shall spring over the hedge. And then those three shall pay half of what is lacking of the compounding money or the legal fine; that is, those others who are descended in the paternal line shall do this.

2. But if there be one of those relatives who has not enough to pay his whole indebtedness, he, the poorer one, shall in turn throw the "chrenecruda" on him of them who has the most, so that he shall pay the whole fine.

3. But if he also have not enough to pay the whole, then he who has charge of the murderer shall bring him before the "Thing," and afterwards to 4 Things, in order that they (his friends) may take him under their protection. And if no one have taken him under his protection that is, so as to redeem him for what he can not pay then he shall have to atone with his life.

Title LIX. Concerning private Property.

1. If any man die and leave no sons, if the father and mother survive, they shall inherit.

3. If the father and mother do not survive, and he leave brothers or sisters, they shall inherit.

3. But if there are none, the sisters of the father shall inherit.

4. But if there are no sisters of the father, the sisters of the mother shall claim that inheritance.

5. If there are none of these, the nearest relatives on the father's side shall succeed to that inheritance.

6. But of Salic land no portion of the inheritance shall come to a woman: but the whole inheritance of the land shall come to the male sex.

Title LXII. Concerning Wergeld.

1. If any one's father have been killed, the sons shall have half the compounding money (wergeld); and the other half the nearest relatives, as well on the mother's as on the father's side, shall divide among themselves.

2. But if there are no relatives, paternal or maternal, that portion shall go to the fisc.

Think about it.

1. What do most penalties in this law code have in common? What effect on society would knowledge of such penalties have?
2. Based on the degree of the penalties, what crimes are considered the worst? Why do you think the severity of crimes is determined as it is?
3. What is the Frankish view of immigration?

---

c. 590–594 CE

72. History of the Franks

Translated by Earnest Brehaut

The *Decem Libri Historiarum* ("Ten Books of Histories"), better known as the *Historia Francorum* ("History of the Franks"), was written in Latin by the Christian bishop Gregory of Tours (c. 538–594 CE) and probably completed late in his life. Though designed primarily to promote Christianity, it is nevertheless a valuable source of information for events during the transition period from Roman to medieval society in Europe. The following passage tells the story of the conversion to Christianity of Clovis I, king of the Franks (r. 481–511 CE).

Gregory of Tours, *History of the Franks*, trans. Earnest Brehaut. Columbia University Press, 1916. Copyright in the Public Domain.

28. Now the king of the Burgundians was Gundevech, of the family of king Athanaric the persecutor, whom we have mentioned before. He had four sons; Gundobad, Godegisel, Chilperic and Godomar. Gundobad killed his brother Chilperic with the sword, and sank his wife in water with a stone tied to her neck. His two daughters he condemned to exile; the older of these, who became a nun, was called Chrona, and the younger Clotilda. And as Clovis often sent embassies to Burgundy, the maiden Clotilda was found by his envoys. And when they saw that she was of good bearing and wise, and learned that she was of the family of the king, they reported this to King Clovis, and he sent an embassy to Gundobad without delay asking her in marriage. And Gundobad was afraid to refuse, and surrendered her to the men, and they took the girl and brought her swiftly to the king. The king was very glad when he saw her, and married her, having already by a concubine a son named Theodoric.

29. He had a first-born son by queen Clotilda, and as his wife wished to consecrate him in baptism, she tried unceasingly to persuade her husband, saying: "The gods you worship are nothing, and they will be unable to help themselves or any one else. For they are graven out of stone or wood or some metal. And the names you have given them are names of men and not of gods, as Saturn, who is declared to have fled in fear of being banished from his kingdom by his son; as Jove himself, the foul perpetrator of all shameful crimes, committing incest with men, mocking at his kinswomen, not able to refrain from intercourse with his own sister as she herself says: *Jovisque et soror et conjunx.* What could Mars or Mercury do? They are endowed rather with the magic arts than with the power of the divine name. But he ought rather to be worshipped who created by his word heaven and earth, the sea and all that in them is out of a state of nothingness, who made the sun shine, and adorned the heavens with stars, who filled the waters with creeping things, the earth with living things and the air with creatures that fly, at whose nod the earth is decked with growing crops, the trees with fruit, the vines with grapes, by whose hand mankind was created, by whose generosity all that creation serves and helps man whom he created as his own." But though the queen said this the spirit of the king was by no means moved to belief, and he said: "It was at the command of our gods that all things were created and came forth, and it is plain that your God has no power and, what is more, he is proven not to belong to the family of the gods." Meantime the faithful queen made her son ready for baptism; she gave command to adorn the church with hangings and curtains, in order that he who could not moved by persuasion might be urged to belief by this mystery. The boy, whom they named Ingomer, died after being baptized, still wearing the white garments in which he became regenerate. At this the king was violently angry, and reproached the queen harshly, saying: " If the boy had been dedicated in the name of my gods he would certainly have lived; but as it is, since he was baptized in the name of your God, he could not live at all." To this the queen said: "I give thanks to the omnipotent God, creator of all, who has judged me not wholly unworthy, that he should deign to take to his kingdom one born from my womb. My soul is not stricken with grief for his sake, because I know that, summoned from this world as he was in his baptismal garments, he will be fed by the vision of God."

After this she bore another son, whom she named Chlodomer at baptism; and when he fell sick, the king said: "It is impossible that anything else should happen to him than happened to his brother, namely, that being baptized in the name of your Christ, should die at once." But through the prayers of his mother, and the Lord's command, he became well.

30. The queen did not cease to urge him to recognize the true God and cease worshipping idols. But he could not be influenced in any way to this belief, until at last a war arose with the Alamanni, in which he was driven by necessity to confess what before he had of his free will denied. It came about that as the two armies were fighting fiercely, there was much slaughter, and Clovis's army began to be in danger of destruction. He saw it and raised his eyes to heaven, and with remorse in his heart he burst into tears and cried: "Jesus Christ, whom Clotilda asserts to be the son of the living God, who art said to give aid to those in distress, and to bestow victory on those who hope in thee, I beseech the glory of thy aid, with the vow that if thou wilt grant me victory over these enemies, and I shall know that power which she says that people dedicated in thy name have had from thee, I will believe in thee and be baptized in thy name. For I have invoked my own gods but, as I find, they have withdrawn from aiding me; and therefore I believe that they possess no power, since they do not help those who obey them. I now call upon thee, I desire to believe thee only let me be rescued from my adversaries." And when he said thus, the Alamanni turned their backs, and began to disperse in flight. And when they saw that their king was killed, they submitted to the dominion of Clovis, saying: "Let not the people perish further, we pray; we are yours now." And he stopped the fighting, and after encouraging his men, retired in peace and told the queen how he had had merit to win the victory by calling on the name of Christ. This happened in the fifteenth year of his reign.

31. Then the queen asked saint Remi, bishop of Rheims, to summon Clovis secretly, urging him to introduce the king to the word of salvation. And the bishop sent for him secretly and began to urge him to believe in the true God, maker of heaven and earth, and to cease worshipping idols, which could help neither themselves nor any one else. But the king said: "I gladly hear you, most holy father; but there remains one thing: the people who follow me cannot endure to abandon their gods; but I shall go and speak to them according to your words." He met with his followers, but before he could speak the power of God anticipated him, and all the people cried out together: "O pious king, we reject our mortal gods, and we are ready to follow the immortal God whom Remi preaches." This was reported to the bishop, who was greatly rejoiced, and bade them get ready the baptismal font. The squares were shaded with tapestried canopies, the churches adorned with white curtains, the baptistery set in order, the aroma of incense spread, candles of fragrant odor burned brightly, and the whole shrine of the baptistery was filled with a divine fragrance: and the Lord gave such grace to those who stood by that they thought they were placed amid the odors of paradise. And the king was the first to ask to be baptized by the bishop. Another Constantine advanced to the baptismal font, to terminate the disease of ancient leprosy and wash away with fresh water the foul spots that had long been borne. And when he entered to be baptized, the saint of God began with ready speech: "Gently bend your neck, Sigamber; worship what you burned; burn what you worshipped." The holy bishop Remi was a man of excellent wisdom and especially trained in rhetorical studies, and of such surpassing holiness that he equalled the miracles of Silvester. For there is extant a book of his life which tells that he raised a dead man. And so the king confessed all-powerful God in the Trinity, and was baptized in the name of the Father, Son and holy Spirit, and was anointed with the holy ointment with the sign of the cross of Christ. And of his army more than 3000 were baptized. His sister also, Albofled, was baptized, who not long after passed to the Lord. And when the king was in mourning for her, the holy Remi sent a letter of consolation which began in this way: "The reason of your mourning pains me, and pains me greatly, that Albofled your sister, of good memory, has passed; away. But I can give you this comfort, that her departure from the world was such that she ought to be envied rather than be mourned." Another sister also was converted, Lanthechild by name, who had fallen into the heresy of the Arians, and she confessed that the Son and the holy Spirit were equal to the Father, and was anointed.

1. According to Gregory, how did Clovis come to be a Roman Catholic Christian?
2. Why do you think Clovis' conversion story has many similarities with the conversion experience of Constantine?

The Postclassical Period
(600–1300 CE)

Smoke Jaguar, ruler of Copán (Maya)

Postclassical Period

C.E.	700	800	900	1000	1100	1200	1300
Central America	Zapotec Civilization						
	Teotihuacan		Toltec Kingdom				
	Maya Civilization						
South America	Tiwanaku						
	Wari						
				Chimor			
Europe	Kingdom of the Franks	Medieval France, Germany, and England					
	Umayyad Caliphate		Abassid Caliphate		Islamic Emirates of Spain		
Eastern Mediteranean					Independent Islamic Emirates		
North Afirca					Independent Islamic Emirates		
West Asia							
East Africa	Aksum			Zagwe Dynazty			
Central Asia	Khazar Khaganate						
South Asia	Gurjar-Pratihara					Mamluk Dynasty	
			Pala Empire				
			Rashtrakuta Empire				
East Asia	Tang Dynasty			Five Dynaties & Ten Kingdoms	Song Dynasty		

73. The Quran

Translated by Maulvi Muhammad Ali

The Quran ("The Recitation") is a collection of messages that Muslims believe were revealed to the prophet Muhammad (c. 570–632) by God through the angel Jibril (Gabriel) in Arabic. The messages were originally memorized and transmitted orally, but after Muhammad's death, efforts were made to put them in written form. A volume was prepared by the caliph Abu Bakr (r. 632–634). According to Shias and Sufis, a volume was also prepared at this time by Muhammad's son-in-law Ali. The caliph Uthman (r. 644–656) produced a version, which became the standard text. The Quran consists of 114 *suras* or chapters, ordered from longest to shortest. Here is a selection of excerpts.

25. The Discrimination (Al-Furqan)

In the name of Allah, the Beneficent, the Merciful.I Blessed is He Who sent down the Discrimination upon His servant that he might be a warner to the nations—

² He, Whose is the kingdom of the heavens and the earth, and Who did not take to Himself a son, and Who has no associate in the kingdom, and Who created everything, then ordained for it a measure.

³ And they take besides Him gods who create naught, while they are themselves created, and they control for themselves no harm nor profit, and they control not death, nor life, nor raising to life.

⁴ And those who disbelieve say this is nothing but a lie, which he has forged, and other people have helped him at it. So indeed they have brought an iniquity and a falsehood.

⁵ And they say Stories of the ancients, which he has got written, so they are read out to him morning and evening!

⁶ Say: He has revealed it, Who knows the secret of the heavens and the earth. Surely He is ever Forgiving, Merciful.

⁷ And they say: What a Messenger is this? He eats food and goes about in the markets. Why has not an angel been sent down to him to be a warner with him?

⁸ Or a treasure given to him, or a garden from which to eat? And the evildoers say: You follow but a man bewitched!

⁹ See what parables they set forth for thee—they have gone astray, so they cannot find a way.

* * *

¹⁰ Blessed is He Who if He please, will give thee what is better than this: Gardens wherein flow rivers. And He will give thee palaces.

¹¹ But they deny the Hour, and We have prepared a burning Fire for him who denies the Hour.

¹² When it sees them from a faroff place, they will hear its raging and roaring.

¹³ And when they are cast into a narrow place thereof in chains, they will there pray for destruction.

The Holy Qur'an, trans. Maulvi Muhammad Ali. Ahmadiyya Anjuman-I-Ishaat-I-Islam, 1920. Copyright in the Public Domain.

¹⁴ Pray nor this day for destruction once but pray for destruction again and again.

¹⁵ Say: Is this better or the Garden of Perpetuity, which the dutiful are promised? That is a reward and a resort for them.

¹⁶ For them therein is what they desire, to abide. It is a promise to be prayed for from thy Lord.

¹⁷ And on the day when He will gather them, and that which they serve besides Allah, He will say: Was it you who led astray these My servants, or did they themselves stray from the path?

¹⁸ They will say: Glory be to Thee! it was not beseeming for us that we should take for protectors others besides Thee, but Thou didst make them and their fathers to enjoy until they forgot the Reminder, and they became a lost people.

¹⁹ So they will give you the lie in what you say, then you can neither ward off (evil), nor (obtain) help. And whoever among you does wrong, We shall make him taste a great chastisement.

²⁰ And We did not send before thee any messengers but they surely ate food and went about in the markets. And We make some of you a trial for others. Will you bear patiently? And thy Lord is ever Seeing.

* * *

²¹ And those who look not for meeting with Us, say: Why have not angels been sent down to us, or (why) do we not see our Lord? Indeed they are too proud of themselves and revolt in great revolt.

²² On the day when they will see the angels, there will be no good news for the guilty, and they will say: Let there be a strong barrier!

²³ And We shall turn to the work they have done, so We shall render it as scattered motes.

²⁴ The owners of the Garden will on that day be in a better abiding-place and a fairer resting-place.

²⁵ And on the day when the heaven bursts asunder with clouds, and the angels are sent down, as they are sent.

²⁶ The kingdom on that day rightly belongs to the Beneficent, and it will be a hard day for the disbelievers.

²⁷ And on the day when the wrongdoer will bite his hands, saying: Would that I had taken a way with the Messenger!

²⁸ O woe is me! would that I had not taken such a one for a friend!

²⁹ Certainly he led me astray from the Reminder after it had come to me. And the devil ever deserts man.

³⁰ And the Messenger will say My Lord, surely my people treat this Qur'an as a forsaken thing.

³¹ And thus have We made for every prophet an enemy from among the guilty, and sufficient is thy Lord as a Guide and a Helper.

³² And those who disbelieve say: Why has not the Qur'an been revealed to him all at once? Thus, that We may strengthen thy heart thereby and We have arranged it well in arranging.

³³ And they cannot bring thee a question, but We have brought thee the truth and the best explanation.

³⁴ Those who will be gathered to hell on their faces they are in an evil plight and straying farther away from the path.

* * *

³⁵ And certainly We gave Moses the Book and We appointed with him his brother Aaron, an aider.

³⁶ Then We said: Go you both to the people who reject Our messages. So We destroyed them with utter destruction.

³⁷ And the people of Noah, when they rejected the messengers, We drowned them, and made them a sign for men. And We have prepared a painful chastisement for the wrongdoers—

³⁸ And 'Ad and Thamud and the dwellers of Rass and many generations in between.

³⁹ And to each We gave examples and each did We destroy with utter destruction.

⁴⁰ And indeed they pass by the town wherein was rained an evil rain. Do they not see it? Nay, they hope not to be raised again.

⁴¹ And when they see thee, they take thee for naught but a jest Is this he whom Allah has raised to be a messenger?

⁴²He had well-nigh led us astray from our gods had we not adhered to them patiently! And they will know, when they see the chastisement, who is mote astray from the path.

⁴³Hast thou seen him who takes his low desires for his god? Wilt thou be a guardian over him?

⁴⁴Or thinkest thou that most of them hear or understand? They are but as the cattle; nay, they are farther astray from the path.

2. The Cow (Al-Baqarah)

In the name of God, the Beneficent, the Merciful.

¹I, God, am the best knower.

²This Book, there is no doubt in it, is a guide to those who keep their duty.

³Who believe in the Unseen and keep up prayer and spend out of what We have given them.

⁴And who believe in that which has been revealed to thee and that which was revealed before thee, and of the Hereafter they are sure.

⁵These are on a right course from their Lord and these it is that are successful.

⁶Those who disbelieve—it being alike to them whether thou warn them or warn them not—they will not believe.

⁷God has sealed their hearts and their hearing; and there is a covering on their eyes, and for them is a grievous chastisement.

* * *

⁸And there are some people who say: We believe in God and the Last Day and they are not believers.

⁹They seek to deceive God and those who believe, and they deceive only themselves and they perceive not.

¹⁰In their hearts is a disease, so God increased their disease, and for them is a painful chastisement because they lie.

¹¹And when it is said to them, Make not mischief in the land, they say: We are but peacemakers.

¹²Now surely they are the mischief-makers, but they perceive not.

¹³And when it is said to them, Believe as the people believe, they say: Shall we believe as the fools believe? Now surely they are the fools, but they know not.

¹⁴And when they meet those who believe, they say, We believe; and when they are alone with their devils, they say: Surely we are with you, we were only mocking.

¹⁵God will pay them back their mockery, and He leaves them alone in their inordinacy, blindly wandering on.

¹⁶These are they who buy error for guidance, so their bargain brings no gain, nor are they guided.

¹⁷Their parable is as the parable of one who kindles a fire but when it illumines all around him, God takes away their light, and leaves them in darkness—they cannot see.

¹⁸Deaf dumb, (and) blind, so they return not:

¹⁹Or like abundant rain from the clouds in which is darkness, and thunder and lightning; they put their fingers into their ears because of the thunderpeal, for fear of death. And God encompasses the disbelievers.

²⁰The lightning almost takes away their sight. Whenever it shines on them they walk in it, and when it becomes dark to them they stand still. And if God had pleased, He would have taken away their hearing and their sight. Surely God is Possessor of power over all things.

* * *

³⁰And when thy Lord said to the angels, I am going to place a ruler in the earth, they said: Wilt Thou place in it such as make mischief in it and shed blood? And we celebrate Thy praise and extol Thy holiness. He said: Surely I know what you know not.

³¹And He taught Adam all the names, then presented them to the angels; He said: Tell Me the names of those if you are right.

³²They said: Glory be to Thee We have no knowledge but that which Thou hast taught us. Surely Thou art the Knowing, the Wise.

³³He said: O Adam, inform them of their names. So when he informed them of their names, He said:

Did I not say to you that I know what is unseen in the heavens and the earth? And I know what you manifest and what you hide.

³⁴ And when We said to the angels, Be submissive to Adam, they submitted, but Iblis (did not). He refused and was proud, and he was one of the disbelievers.

³⁵ And We said: O Adam, dwell thou and thy wife in the garden, and eat from it a plenteous (food) wherever you wish, and approach not this tree, lest you be of the unjust.

³⁶ But the devil made them slip from it, and caused them to depart from the state in which they were. And We said: Go forth, some of you are the enemies of others. And there is for you in the earth an abode and a provision for a time.

³⁷ Then Adam received (revealed) words from his Lord, and He turned to him (mercifully). Surely He is Oft-returning (to mercy), the Merciful.

³⁸ We said: Go forth from this state all. Surely there will come to you guidance from Me, then whoever follows My guidance, no fear shall come upon them, nor shall they grieve.

³⁹ And (as to) those who disbelieve in and reject Our messages, they are the companions of the Fire in it they will abide.

* * *

⁴⁰ O Children of Israel, call to mind My favour which I bestowed on you and be faithful to (your) covenant with Me, I shall fulfil (My) covenant with you; and Me, Me alone, should you fear.

⁴¹ And believe in that which I have revealed, verifying that which is with you, and be not the first to deny it; neither take a mean price for My messages; and keep your duty to Me, Me alone.

⁴² And mix not up truth with falsehood, nor hide the truth while you know.

⁴³ And keep up prayer and pay the poor-rate and bow down with those who bow down.

⁴⁴ Do you enjoin men to be good and neglect your own souls while you read the Book? Have you then no sense?

⁴⁵ And seek assistance through patience and prayer, and this is hard except for the humble ones,

⁴⁶ Who know that they will meet their Lord and that to Him they will return.

* * *

⁴⁷ O Children of Israel, call to mind My favour which I bestowed on you and that I made you excel the nations.

⁴⁸ And guard yourselves against a day when no soul will avail another in the least, neither will intercession be accepted on its behalf, nor will compensation be taken from it, nor will they be helped.

⁴⁹ And when We delivered you from Pharaoh's people, who subjected you to severe torment, killing your sons and sparing your women, and in this there was a great trial from your Lord.

⁵⁰ And when We parted the sea for you, so We saved you and drowned the people of Pharaoh while you saw.

⁵¹ And when We appointed a time of forty nights with Moses, then you took the calf (for a god) after him, and you were unjust.

⁵² Then We pardoned you after that so that you might give thanks.

⁵³ And when We gave Moses the Book and the Discrimination that you might walk aright.

⁵⁴ And when Moses said to his people: O my people, you have surely wronged yourselves by taking the calf (for a god), so turn to your Creator (penitently), and kill your passions. That is best for you with your Creator. So He turned to you (mercifully). Surely He is the Oft-returning (to mercy), the Merciful.

⁵⁵ And when you said: O Moses, we will not believe in thee till we see God manifestly, so the punishment overtook you while you looked on.

⁵⁶ Then We raised you up after your stupor that you might give thanks.

⁵⁷ And We made the clouds to give shade over you and We sent to you manna and quails. Eat of the good things that We have given you. And they did not do Us any harm, but they wronged their own souls.

⁵⁸ And when We said: Enter this city, then eat from it a plenteous (food) whence you wish, and enter the gate submissively, and make petition for forgiveness. We will forgive you your wrongs and increase the reward of those who do good (to others).

⁵⁹ But those who were unjust changed the word which had been spoken to them, for another saying, so We sent upon the wrongdoers a pestilence from heaven, because they transgressed.

* * *

⁶⁰ And when Moses prayed for water for his people, We said: March on to the rock with thy staff. So there flowed from it twelve springs. Each tribe knew their drinking-place. Eat and drink of the provisions of God, and act not corruptly, making mischief in the land.

⁶¹ And when you said: O Moses, we cannot endure one food, so pray thy Lord on our behalf to bring forth for us out of what the earth grows, of its herbs and its cucumbers and its garlic and its lentils and its onions. He said: Would you exchange that which is better for that which is worse? Enter a city, so you will have what you ask for. And abasement and humiliation were stamped upon them, and they incurred God's wrath. That was so because they disbelieved in the messages of God and would kill the prophets unjustly. That was so because they disobeyed and exceeded the limits.

* * *

⁶² Surely those who believe, and those who are Jews, and the Christians, and the Sabians, whoever believes in God and the Last Day and does good, they have their reward with their Lord, and there is no fear for them, nor shall they grieve.

⁶³ And when We made a covenant with you and raised the mountain above you: Hold fast that which We have given you, and bear in mind what is in it, so that you may guard against evil.

⁶⁴ Then after that you turned back; and had it not been for the grace of God and His mercy on you, you had certainly been among the losers.

⁶⁵ And indeed you know those among you who violated the Sabbath, so We said to them: Be (as) apes, despised and hated.

⁶⁶ So We made them an example to those who witnessed it and those who came after it and an admonition to those who guard against evil.

⁶⁷ And when Moses said to his people: Surely God commands you to sacrifice a cow. They said: Dost thou ridicule us? He said: I seek refuge with God from being one of the ignorant.

⁶⁸ They said: Call on thy Lord for our sake to make it plain to us what she is. (Moses) said: He says, Surely she is a cow neither advanced in age nor too young, of middle age between these (two); so do what you are commanded.

⁶⁹ They said: Call on thy Lord for our sake to make it clear to us what her colour is. (Moses) said: He says, She is a yellow cow; her colour is intensely yellow delighting the beholders.

⁷⁰ They said: Call on thy Lord for our sake to make it dear to us what she is, for surely to us the cows are all alike, and if God please we shall surely he guided aright.

⁷¹ (Moses) said: He says: She is a cow not made submissive to plough the land, nor does she water the tilth, sound, without a blemish in her. They said: Now thou hast brought the truth. So they slaughtered her, though they had not the mind to do (it).

* * *

⁷² And when you (almost) killed a man, then you disagreed about it. And God was to bring forth that which you were going to hide.

⁷³ So We said: Smite him with it partially. Thus God brings the dead to life, and He shows you His signs that you may understand.

⁷⁴ Then your hearts hardened after that, so that they were like rocks, rather worse in hardness. And surely there are some rocks from which streams burst forth; and there are some of them which split asunder so water flows from them; and there are some of them which fall down for the fear of God. And God is not heedless of what you do.

75 Do you then hope that they would believe in you, and a party from among them indeed used to hear the word of God, then altered it after they had understood it, and they know (this).

76 And when they meet those who believe they say, We believe, and when they are apart one with another they say: Do you talk to them of what God has disclosed to you that they may contend with you by this before your Lord? Do you not understand?

77 Do they not know that God knows what they keep secret and what they make known?

78 And some of them are illiterate; they know not the Book but only (from) hearsay, and they do but conjecture.

79 Woe! then to those who write the Book with their hands then say, This is from God; so that they may take for it a small price. So woe! to them for what their hands write and woe! to them for what they earn.

80 And they say: Fire will not touch us but for a few days. Say Have you received a promise from God? Then God will not fail to perform His promise. Or do you speak against God what you know not?

81 Yea, whoever earns evil and his sins beset him on every side, those are the companions of the Fire therein they abide."

82 And those who believe and do good deeds, these are the owners of the Garden; therein they abide.

* * *

83 And when We made a covenant with the Children of Israel. You shall serve none but God. And do good to (your) parents, and to the near of kin and to orphans and the needy, and speak good (words) to (all) men, and keep up prayer and pay the poor-rate. Then you turned back except a few of you, and you are averse.

84 And when We made a covenant with you: You shall not shed your blood, nor turn your people out of your cities; then you promised and you bear witness.

85 Yet you it is who would slay your people and turn a party from among you out of their homes, backing each other up against them unlawfully and exceeding the limits. And if they should come to you as captives you would ransom them, whereas their turning out itself was unlawful for you. Do you then believe in a part of the Book and disbelieve in the other? What then is the reward of such among you as do this but disgrace in the life of this world, and on the day of Resurrection they shall be sent back to the most grievous chastisement. And God is not heedless of what you do.

86 These are they who buy the life of this world for the Hereafter, so their chastisement shall not be lightened, nor shall they be helped.

* * *

87 And We indeed gave Moses the Book and We sent messengers after him one after another and We gave Jesus, son of Mary, clear arguments and strengthened him with the Holy Spirit. Is it then that whenever there came to you a messenger with what your souls desired not, you were arrogant? And some you gave the lie to and others you would slay.

88 And they say: Our hearts are repositories. Nay, God has cursed them on account of their unbelief so little it is that they believe.

89 And when there came to them a Book from God verifying that which they have, and aforetime they used to pray for victory against those who disbelieved—but when there came to them that which they recognized, they disbelieved in it; so God's curse is on the disbelievers.

90 Evil is that for which they sell their souls—that they should deny that which God has revealed, out of envy that God should send down of His grace on whomsoever of His servants He pleases; so they incur wrath upon wrath. And there is an abasing chastisement for the disbelievers.

91 And when it is said to them, Believe in that which God has revealed, they say: We believe in that which was revealed to us. And they deny what is besides that, while it is the Truth verifying that which they have. Say: Why then did you kill God's prophets before (this) if you were believers?

⁹² And Moses indeed came to you with clear arguments, then you took the calf (for a god) in his absence and you were wrongdoers.

⁹³ And when We made a covenant with you and raised the mountain above you: Take hold of that which We have given you with firmness and obey. They said: We hear and disobey. And they were made to imbibe (the love of) the calf into their hearts on account of their disbelief. Say: Evil is that which your faith bids you if you are believers.

⁹⁴ Say: If the abode of the Here-after with God is specially for you to the exclusion of the people, then invoke death if you are truthful.

⁹⁵ And they will never invoke it on account of what their hands have sent on before, and God knows the wrongdoers.

⁹⁶ And thou wilt certainly find them the greediest of men for life (greedier) even than those who set gods (with God). One of them love to be granted a life of a thousand years, and his being granted a long life will in no way remove him further off from the chastisement. And God is Seer of what they do.

* * *

⁹⁷ Say: Whoever is an enemy to Gabriel for surely he revealed it to thy heart by God's command, verifying the which is before it and a guidance and glad tidings for the believers.

⁹⁸ Whoever is an enemy to God and His angels and His messengers and Gabriel and Michael, then surely God is an enemy to disbelievers.

⁹⁹ And We indeed have revealed to thee clear messages, and none disbelieve in them except the transgressors.

¹⁰⁰ Is it that whenever they make a covenant, a party of them cast it aside? Nay, most of them have no faith.

¹⁰¹ And when there came to them a messenger from God verifying that which they have, a party of those who were given the Book threw the Book of God behind their backs as if they knew nothing.

¹⁰² And they follow what the devils fabricated against the kingdom of Solomon. And Solomon disbelieved not, but the devils disbelieved, teaching men enchantment. And it was not revealed to the two angels in Babel, Harut and Marut. Nor did they teach (it to) anyone, so that they should have said, We are only a trial, so disbelieve not. But they learn from these two (sources) that by which they make a distinction between a man and his wife. And they cannot hurt with it anyone except with God's permission. And they learn that which harms them and profits them nor. And certainly they know that he who buys it has no share of good in the Hereafter. And surely evil is the price for which they have sold their souls, did they but know!

¹⁰³ And if they had believed and kept their duty, reward from God would certainly have been better; did they but know!

* * *

¹¹³ And the Jews say, The Christians follow nothing (good), and the Christians say, The Jews follow nothing (good), while they recite the (same) Book. Even thus say those who have no knowledge, like what they say. So God will judge between them on the day of Resurrection in that wherein they differ.

¹¹⁴ And who is more unjust than he who prevents (men) from the mosques of God, from His name being remembered therein, and strives to ruin them? (As for) these, it was not proper for them to enter them except in fear. For them is disgrace in this world, and theirs is a grievous chastisement in the Hereafter.

¹¹⁵ And God's is the East and the West, so whither you turn thither is God's purpose. Surely God is Ample-giving, Knowing.

¹¹⁶ And they say: God has taken to Himself a son— glory be to Him! Rather, whatever is in the heavens and the earth is His. All are obedient to Him.

¹¹⁷ Wonderful Originator of the heavens and the earth! And when He decrees an affair, He says to it only, Be, and it is.

¹¹⁸ And those who have no knowledge say: Why does not God speak to us or a sign come to us? Even thus said those before them, the like of what they say. Their hearts are all alike. Indeed We have made the messages clear for a people who are sure.

¹¹⁹ Surely We have sent thee with the Truth as a bearer of good news and as a warner, and thou wilt not be called upon to answer for the companions of the flaming Fire.

¹²⁰ And the Jews will not be pleased with thee, nor the Christians, unless thou follow their religion. Say Surely God's guidance, that is the (perfect) guidance. And if thou follow their desires after the knowledge that has come to thee thou shalt have from God no friend, nor helper.

¹²¹ Those to whom We have given the Book follow it as it ought to be followed. These believe in it. And whoever disbelieves in it, these it is that are the losers.

* * *

¹²² O Children of Israel, call to mind My favour which I bestowed on you and that I made you excel the nations.

¹²³ And be on your guard against a day when no soul will avail another in the least, neither will any compensation be accepted from it, nor will intercession profit it, nor will they be helped.

¹²⁴ And when his Lord tried Abraham with certain commands he fulfilled them. He said: Surely I will make thee a leader of men. (Abraham) said: And of my offspring? My covenant does not include the wrongdoers, said He.

¹²⁵ And when We made The House a resort for men and a (place of) security. And: Take ye the place of Abraham for a place of prayer. And We enjoined Abraham and Ishmael, saying: Purify My House for those who visit (it) and those who abide (in it) for devotion and those who bow down (and) those who prostrate themselves.

¹²⁶ And when Abraham said: My Lord, make this a secure town and provide its people with fruits, such of them as believe in God and the Last Day. He said: And whoever disbelieves, I shall grant him enjoyment for a short while, then I shall drive him to the chastisement of the Fire. And it is an evil destination.

¹²⁷ And when Abraham and Ishmael raised the foundations of the House: Our Lord, accept from us surely Thou art the Hearing, the Knowing.

¹²⁸ Our Lord, and make us both submissive to Thee, and (raise) from out offspring, a nation submissive to Thee, and show us our ways of devotion and turn to us (mercifully); surely Thou art the Oft-returning (to mercy), the Merciful.

¹²⁹ Our Lord, and raise up in them a Messenger from among them who shall recite to them Thy messages and teach them the Book and the Wisdom, and purify them Surely Thou art the Mighty, the Wise.

¹³⁰ And who forsakes the religion of Abraham but he who makes a fool of himself. And certainly We made him pure in this world and in the Hereafter he is surely among the righteous.

¹³¹ When his Lord said to him, Submit, he said: I submit myself to the Lord of the worlds.

¹³² And the same did Abraham enjoin on his sons, and (so did) Jacob: O my sons, surely God has chosen for you (this) religion, so die not unless you are submitting ones.

¹³³ Or were you witnesses when death visited Jacob, when he said to his sons: What will you serve after me? They said: We shall serve thy God and the God of thy fathers, Abraham and Ishmael and Isaac, one God only, and to Him do we submit.

¹³⁴ Those are a people that have passed away; for them is what they earned and for you what you earn and you will not be asked of what they did.

¹³⁵ And they say: Be Jews or Christians, you will be on the right course. Say: Nay, (we follow) the religion of Abraham, the upright one, and he was not one of the polytheists.

¹³⁶ Say: We believe in God and (in) that which has been revealed to us, and (in) that which was revealed to Abraham, and Ishmael and Isaac and Jacob and the tribes, and (in) that which was given to Moses and Jesus, and (in) that which was given to the prophets from their Lord, we do not make any distinction between any of them and to Him do we submit.

¹³⁷ So if they believe as you believe, they are indeed on the right course; and if they turn back, then they are only in opposition. But God will suffice thee against them and He is the Hearing, the Knowing.

¹³⁸ (We take) God's colour, and who is better than God at colouring, and we are His worshippers.

¹³⁹ Say: Do you dispute with us about God, and He is our Lord and your Lord, and for us are our deeds and for you your deeds; and we are sincere to Him?

¹⁴⁰ Or do you say that Abraham and Ishmael and Isaac and Jacob and the tribes were Jews or Christians? Say: Do you know better or God? And who is more unjust than he who conceals a testimony that he has from God? And God is not heedless of what you do.

¹⁴¹ Those are a people that have passed away; and for them is what they earned and for You what you earn and you will not be asked of what they did.

* * *

¹⁷⁷ It is not righteousness that you turn your faces towards the East and the West, but righteous is the one who believes in God, and the Last Day, and the angels and the Book and the prophets, and gives away wealth out of love for Him to the near of kin and the orphans and the needy and the wayfarer and to those who ask and to set slaves free and keeps up prayer and pays the poor-rate and the performers of their promise when they make a promise, and the patient in distress and affliction and in the time of conflict. These are they who are truthful; and these are they who keep their duty.

¹⁷⁸ O you who believe, retaliation is prescribed for you in the matter of the slain the free for the free, and the slave for the slave, and the female for the female. But if remission is made to one by his (aggrieved) brother, prosecution (for blood-wit) should be according to usage, and payment to him in a good manner. This is an alleviation from your Lord and a mercy. Whoever exceeds the limit after this, will have a painful chastisement. And there is life for you in retaliation, O men of understanding, that you may guard yourselves.

¹⁸⁰ It is prescribed for you, when death approaches one of you, if he leaves behind wealth for parents and near relatives, to make a bequest in a kindly manner; it is incumbent upon the dutiful.

¹⁸¹ Then whoever changes it after he has heard it, the sin of it is only upon those who change it. Surely God is Hearing, Knowing.

¹⁸² But if one fears a wrong or a sinful course on the part of the testator, and effects an agreement between the parties, there is no blame on him. Surely God is Forgiving, Merciful.

* * *

¹⁸³ O you who believe, fasting is prescribed for you, as it was prescribed for those before you, so that you may guard against evil.

¹⁸⁴ For a certain number of days. But whoever among you is sick or on a journey, (he shall fast) a (like) number of other days And those who find it extremely hard may effect redemption by feeding a poor man. So whoever does good spontaneously, it is better for him; and that you fast is better for you if you know.

¹⁸⁵ The month of Ramadan is that in which the Qur'an was revealed, a guidance to men and clear proofs of the guidance and the Criterion. So whoever of you is present in the month, he shall fast therein, and whoever is sick or on a journey, (he shall fast) a (like) number of other days. God desires ease for you, and He desires not hardship for you, and (He desires) that you should complete the number and that you should exalt the greatness of God for having guided you and that you may give thanks.

¹⁸⁶ And when My servants ask thee concerning Me, surely I am nigh. I answer the prayer of the suppliant when he calls on Me, so they should hear My call and believe in Me that they may walk in the right way.

¹⁸⁷ It is made lawful for you to go in to your wives on the night of the fast. They are an apparel for you and you are an apparel for them. God knows that you acted unjustly to yourselves, so He turned to you in mercy and removed (the burden) from you. So now be in contact with them and seek what God has

ordained for you, and eat and drink until the whiteness of the day becomes distinct from the blackness of the night at dawn, then complete the fast till nightfall, and touch them not while you keep to the mosques. These are the limits of God, so go not near them. Thus does God make clear His messages for men that they may keep their duty.

188 And swallow not up your property among yourselves by false means, nor seek to gain access thereby to the judges, so that you may swallow up a part of the property of men wrongfully while you know.

* * *

189 They ask thee of the new moons. Say: They are times appointed for men, and (for) the pilgrimage. And it is not righteousness that you enter the houses by their backs, but he is righteous who keeps his duty. And go into the houses by their doors; and keep your duty to God, that you may be successful.

190 And fight in the way of God against those who fight against you but be not aggressive. Surely God loves not the aggressors.

191 And kill them wherever you find them, and drive them out from where they drove you out, and persecution is worse than slaughter. And fight not with them at the Sacred Mosque until they fight with you in so if they fight you (in it), slay them. Such is the recompense of the disbelievers.

192 But if they desist, then surely God is Forgiving, Merciful.

193 And fight them until there is no persecution, and religion is only for Allah. But if they desist, then there should be no hostility except against the oppressors.

194 The sacred month for the sacred month, and retaliation (is allowed) in sacred things. Whoever then acts aggressively against you, inflict injury on him according to the injury he has inflicted on you and keep your duty to God, and know that God is with those who keep their duty.

195 And spend in the way of God and cast not yourselves to perdition with your own hands and do good (to others). Surely God loves the doers of good.

196 And accomplish the pilgrimage and the visit for God. But if you are prevented, (send) whatever offering is easy to obtain; and shave not your heads until the offering reaches its destination. Then whoever among you is sick or has an ailment of the head, he (may effect) a compensation by fasting or alms or sacrificing. And when you are secure, whoever profits by combining the visit with the pilgrimage (should take) whatever offering is easy to obtain. But he who cannot find (an offering) should fast for three days during the pilgrimage and for seven days when you return. These are ten (days) complete. This is for him whose family is not present in the Sacred Mosque. And keep your duty to God, and know that God is severe in requiting (evil).

* * *

197 The months of the pilgrimage are well known; so whoever determines to perform pilgrimage therein there shall be no immodest speech, nor abusing, nor altercation in the pilgrimage. And whatever good you do, God knows it. And make provision for yourselves, the best provision being to keep one's duty. And keep your duty to Me, O men of understanding.

198 It is no sin for you that you seek the bounty of your Lord. So when you press on from Arafat, remember God near the Holy Monument, and remember Him as He has guided you, though before that you were certainly of the erring ones.

199 Then hasten on from where the people hasten on, and ask the forgiveness of God. Surely God is Forgiving, Merciful.

200 And when you have performed your devotions, laud God as you lauded your fathers, rather a more hearty lauding. But there are some people who say, Our Lord, give us in the world. And for such there is no portion in the Hereafter.

201 And there are some among them who say: Our Lord, grant us good in this world and good in the Hereafter, and save us from the chastisement of the Fire.

202 For those there is a portion on account of what they have earned. And God is Swift in reckoning.

²⁰³ And remember God during the appointed days. Then whoever hastens off in two days, it is no sin for him and whoever stays behind, it is no sin for him, for one who keeps his duty. And keep your duty to God, and know that you will be gathered together to Him.

²⁰⁴ And of men is he whose speech about the life of this world pleases thee, and he calls God to witness as to that which is in his heart, yet he is the most violent of adversaries.

²⁰⁵ And when he holds authority, he makes effort in the land to cause mischief in it and destroy tilth and offspring; and God loves not mischief.

²⁰⁶ And when it is said to him, Be careful of thy duty to God, pride carries him off to sin—so hell is sufficient for him. And certainly evil is the resting-place.

²⁰⁷ And of men is he who sells himself to seek the pleasure of God. And God is Compassionate to the servants.

²⁰⁸ O you who believe, enter into complete peace and follow not the footsteps of the devil. Surely he is your open enemy.

²⁰⁹ But if you slip after clear arguments have come to you, then know that God is Mighty, Wise.

²¹⁰ They wait for naught but that God should come to them in the shadows of the clouds with angels, and the matter has (already) been decided. And to God are (all) matters returned.

* * *

²¹¹ Ask of the Children of Israel how many a clear sign We gave them! And whoever changes the favour of God after it has come to him, then surely God is Severe in requiting (evil).

²¹² The life of this world is made to seem fair to those who disbelieve, and they mock those who believe. And those who keep their duty will be above them on the Day of Resurrection. And God gives to whom He pleases without measure.

²¹³ Mankind is a single nation. So God raised prophets as bearers of good news and as warners, and He revealed with them the Book with truth, that it might judge between people concerning that in which they differed. And none but the very people who were given it differed of about it after clear arguments had come to them, envying one another. So God has guided by His will those who believe to the truth about which they differed. And God guides whom He pleases to the right path.

²¹⁴ Or do you think that you will enter the Garden, while there has not yet befallen you the like of what befell those who have passed away before you. Distress and affliction befell them and they were shaken violently, so that the Messenger and those who believed with him said: When will the help of God come? Now surely the help of God is nigh!

²¹⁵ They ask thee as to what they should spend. Say: Whatever wealth you spend, it is for the parents and the near of kin and the orphans and the needy and the wayfarer. And whatever good you do, God surely is Knower of it.

²¹⁶ Fighting is enjoined on you, though it is disliked by you and it may be that you dislike a thing while it is good for you, and it may be that you love a thing while it is evil for you; and God knows while you know not.

* * *

²¹⁷ They ask thee about fighting in the sacred month. Say: Fighting in it is a grave (offence). And hindering (men) from God's way and denying Him and the Sacred Mosque and turning its people out of it, are still graver with God and persecution is graver than slaughter And they will not cease fighting you until they turn you back from your religion, if they can. And whoever of you turns back from his religion, then he dies while an unbeliever—these it is whose works go for nothing in this world and the Hereafter. And they are the companions of the Fire: therein they will abide.

²¹⁸ Those who believed and those who fled (their homes) and strove hard in God's way—these surely hope for the mercy of God. And God is Forgiving, Merciful.

²¹⁹ They ask thee about intoxicants and games of chance. Say: In both of them is a great sin and (some) advantage for men, and their sin is greater than their

advantage. And they ask thee as to what they should spend. Say: What you can spare. Thus does God make clear to you the messages that you may ponder.

²²⁰ On this world and the Hereafter. And they ask thee concerning the orphans. Say: To set right their (affairs) is good; and if you mix with them, they are your brethren. And God knows him who makes mischief from him who sets right. And if God pleased, He would have made matters difficult for you. Surely God is Mighty, Wise.

²²¹ And marry not the idolatresses until they believe; and certainly a believing maid is better than an idolatress even though she please you. Nor give (believing women) in marriage to idolaters until they believe, and certainly a believing slave is better than an idolater, even though he please you. These invite to the Fire and God invites to the Garden and to forgiveness by His will and He makes clear His messages to men that they may be mindful.

* * *

²²² And they ask thee about menstruation. Say: It is harmful, so keep aloof from women during menstrual discharge and go not near them until they are clean. But when they have cleansed themselves, go in to them as God has commanded you. Surely God loves those who turn much (to Him), and He loves those who purify themselves.

²²³ Your wives are a tilth for you, so go in to your tilth when you like, and send (good) beforehand for yourselves. And keep your duty to God, and know that you will meet Him. And give good news to the believers.

²²⁴ And make not God by your oaths a hindrance to your doing good and keeping your duty and making peace between men. And God is Hearing, Knowing.

²²⁵ God will not call you to account for what is vain in your oaths, but He will call you to account for what your hearts have earned. And God is Forgiving, Forbearing.

²²⁶ Those who swear that they will not go in to their wives should wait four months; then if they go back, God is surely Forgiving, Merciful.

²²⁷ And if they resolve on a divorce, God is surely Hearing, Knowing.

²²⁸ And the divorced women should keep themselves in waiting for three courses. And it is not lawful for them to conceal that which God has created in their wombs, if they believe in God and the Last Day. And their husbands have a better right to take them back in the meanwhile if they wish for reconciliation. And women have rights similar to those against them in a just manner, and men are a degree above them. And God is Mighty, Wise.

* * *

²²⁹ Divorce may be (pronounced) twice; then keep (them) in good fellowship or let (them) go with kindness. And it is not lawful for you to take any part of what you have given them, unless both fear that they cannot keep within the limits of God. Then if you fear that they cannot keep within the limits of God there is no blame on them for what she gives up to become free thereby. These are the limits of God, so exceed them not and whoever exceeds the limits of God, these are the wrongdoers.

²³⁰ So if he divorces her (the third time), she shall not be lawful to him afterwards until she marries another husband. If he divorces her, there is no blame on them both if they return to each other (by marriage), if they think that they can keep within the limits of God. And these are the limits of God which He makes clear for a people who know.

²³¹ And when you divorce women and they reach their prescribed time, then retain them in kindness or set them free with kindness and retain them not for injury so that you exceed the limits. And whoever does this, he indeed wrongs his own soul. And take not God's messages for a mockery, and remember God's favour to you, and that which He has revealed to you of the Book and the Wisdom, admonishing you thereby. And keep your duty to God, and know that God is the Knower of all things.

* * *

²³² And when you divorce women and they end their term, prevent them not from marrying their husbands if they agree among themselves in a lawful

manner. With this is admonished he among you who believes in God and the Last Day. This is more profitable for you and purer. And God knows while you know not.

²³³ And mothers shall suckle their children for two whole years, for him who desires to complete the time of suckling. And their maintenance and their clothing must be borne by the father according to usage. No soul shall be burdened beyond its capacity. Neither shall a mother be made to suffer harm on account of her child, nor a father on account of his child and a similar duty (devolves) on the (father's) heir. But if both desire weaning by mutual consent and counsel, there is no blame on them. And if you wish to engage a wet-nurse for your children, there is no blame on you so long as you pay what you promised according to usage. And keep your duty to God and know that God is Seer of what you do.

²³⁴ And (as for) those of you who die and leave wives behind, such women should keep themselves in waiting for four months and ten days; when they reach their term, there is no blame on you for what they do for themselves in a lawful manner. And God is Aware of what you do.

²³⁵ And there is no blame on you respecting that which you speak indirectly in the asking of (such) women in marriage or keep (the proposal) concealed within your minds. God knows that you will have them in your minds, but give them not a promise in secret unless you speak in a lawful manner. And confirm not the marriage tie until the prescribed period reaches its end. And know that God knows what is in your minds, so beware of Him; and know that God is Forgiving, Forbearing.

* * *

²³⁶ There is no blame on you if you divorce women while yet you have not touched them, nor appointed for them a portion. And provide for them, the wealthy according to his means and the strained according to his means, a provision according to usage. (This is) a duty on the doers of good.

²³⁷ And if you divorce them before you have touched them and you have appointed for them a portion, (pay) half of what you have appointed unless they forgo or he forgoes in whose hand is the marriage tie. And it is nearer to dutifulness that you forgo. Nor neglect the giving of free gifts between you. Surely God is Seer of what you do.

²³⁸ Guard the prayers and the most excellent prayer, and stand up truly obedient to God.

²³⁹ But if you are in danger (say your prayers) on foot or on horseback. And when you are secure, remember God as He has taught you what you knew not.

²⁴⁰ And those of you who die and leave wives behind, should make a bequest in favour of their wives of maintenance for a year without turning (them) out Then if they themselves go away, there is no blame on you for what they do of lawful deeds concerning themselves. And God is Mighty, Wise.

²⁴¹ And for the divorced women, provision (must be made) in kindness, This is incumbent on those who have regard for duty.

²⁴² God thus makes clear to you His messages that you may understand.

47. Muhammad

In the name of Allah, the Beneficent, the Merciful.

¹ Those who disbelieve and turn (men) from Allah's way, He will destroy their works.

² And those who believe and do good, and believe in that which has been revealed to Muhammad—and it is the Truth from their Lord—He will remove their evil from them and improve their condition.

³ That is because those who disbelieve follow falsehood, and those who believe follow the Truth from their Lord. Thus does Allah set forth their descriptions for men.

⁴ So when you meet in battle those who disbelieve, smite the necks; then, when you have overcome them, make (them) prisoners, and afterwards (set them free) as a favour or for ransom till the war lay down its burdens. That (shall be so). And if Allah please, He would certainly exact retribution from

them, but that He may try some of you by means of others. And those who are slain in the way of Allah, He will never allow their deeds to perish.

⁵ He will guide them and improve their condition.

⁶ And make them enter the Garden, which He has made known to them.

⁷ O you who believe, if you help Allah, He will help you and make firm your feet.

⁸ And those who disbelieve, for them is destruction, and He will destroy their works.

⁹ That is because they hate that which Allah reveals, so He has rendered their deeds fruitless.

¹⁰ Have they not travelled in the land and seen what was the end of those before them? Allah destroyed them. And for the disbelievers is the like thereof.

¹¹ That is because Allah is the patron of those who believe, and because the disbelievers have no patron.

* * *

¹² Surely Allah will make those who believe and do good enter Gardens wherein flow rivers. And those who disbelieve enjoy themselves and eat as the cattle eat, and the Fire is their abode.

¹³ And how many a town, more powerful than thy town which has driven thee out—We destroyed them, so there was no helper for them.

¹⁴ Is then he who has a clear argument from his Lord like him to whom his evil conduct is made fair-seeming; and they follow their low desires.

¹⁵ A parable of the Garden which the dutiful are promised: Therein are rivers of water not altering for the worse, and rivers of milk whereof the taste changes not, and rivers of wine delicious to the drinkers, and rivers of honey clarified; and for them therein are all fruits and protection from their Lord. (Are these) like those who abide in the Fire and who are made to drink boiling water, so it tends their bowels asunder?

¹⁶ And there are those of them who seek to listen to thee, till, when they go forth from thee, they say to those who have been given knowledge: What was it that he said just now? These are they whose hearts Allah has sealed and they follow their low desires.

¹⁷ And those who follow guidance, He increases them in guidance and grants them their observance of duty.

¹⁸ Wait they for aught but the Hour that it should come upon them of a sudden? Now tokens thereof have already come. Fur how will they have their reminder, when it comes on them?

¹⁹ So know that there is no God but Allah and ask protection for thy sin and for the believing men and the believing women. And Allah knows your moving about and your staying (in a place).

* * *

²⁰ And those who believe say: Why is not a chapter revealed? But when a decisive chapter is revealed, and fighting is mentioned therein, thou seest those in whose hearts is a disease look to thee with the look of one fainting at death So woe to them!

²¹ Obedience and a gentle word (was proper). Then when the affair is settled, it is better for them if they remain true to Allah.

²² But if you turn away, you are sure to make mischief in the land and cut off the ties of kinship!

²³ Those it is whom Allah has cursed, so He has made them deaf and blinded their eyes.

²⁴ Do they not reflect on the Qur'an? Or, are there locks on the hearts?

²⁵ Surely those who turn back after guidance is manifest to them, the devil embellishes it for them and lengthens false hopes for them.

²⁶ That is because they say to those who hate what Allah has revealed We will obey you in some matters. And Allah knows their secrets.

²⁷ But how will it be when the angels cause them to die, smiting their faces and their hacks?

²⁸ That is because they follow that which displeases Allah and are averse to His pleasure, so He makes their deeds fruitless.

* * *

²⁹ Or do those in whose hearts is a disease think that Allah will nor bring forth their spite?

³⁰ And if We please, We could show them to thee so that thou shouldst know them by their marks.

And certainly thou canst recognize them by the tone of (their) speech. And Allah knows your deeds.

³¹ And certainly We shall try you, till We know those among you who strive hard, and the steadfast, and manifest your news.

³² Surely those who disbelieve and hinder (men) from Allah's way and oppose the Messenger after guidance is quite clear to them, cannot harm Allah in any way, and He will make their deeds fruitless.

³³ O you who believe, obey Allah and obey the Messenger and make not your deeds vain.

³⁴ Surely those who disbelieve and hinder (men) from Allah's way, then die disbelievers, Allah will not forgive them.

³⁵ And be nor slack so as to cry for peace—and you are the uppermost—and Allah is with you, and He will not bring your deeds to naught.

³⁶ The life of this world is but idle sport and play, and, if you believe and keep your duty, He will give you your reward, and He does not ask of you your wealth.

³⁷ If He should ask you for it and press you, you will be niggardly, and He will bring forth your malice.

³⁸ Behold! you are those who are called to spend in Allah's way, but among you are those who are niggardly; and whoever is niggardly, is niggardly against his own soul. And Allah is Self-Sufficient and you are needy. And if you turn back He will bring in your place another people, then they will not be like you.

98. The Clear Evidence (Al-Bayyinah)

In the name of Allah, the Beneficent, the Merciful.

¹ Those who disbelieve from among the People of the Book and the idolaters could not have been freed till clear evidence came to them—

² A Messenger from Allah, reciting pure pages,

³ Wherein are (all) right books.

⁴ Nor did those to whom the Book was given become divided till clear evidence came to them.

⁵ And they are enjoined naught but to serve Allah, being sincere to Him in obedience, upright, and to keep up prayer and pay the poor-rate, and that is the right religion.

⁶ Those who disbelieve from among the People of the Book and the idolaters will be in the Fire of hell, abiding therein. They are the worst of creatures.

⁷ Those who believe and do good, they are the best of creatures.

⁸ Their reward is with their Lord Gardens of perpetuity wherein flow rivers, abiding therein for ever. Allah is well pleased with them and they are well pleased with Him. That is for him who fears his Lord.

Think about it.

1. What is the Quran's view of the Bible? How are Jews and Christians presented in this text? What distinction is made between Jews and Christians, on the one hand, and true followers of God, on the other?
2. According to the Quran, is belief a part of being righteous? Why or why not?
3. What passages here might have been used to justify military expansion?
4. What regulations are given concerning women? Are these generally intended to help the men or protect the women, would you say?

74. The Pact of Ibn Muslamah

Translated by Philip K. Hitti

This is an example of the type of treaties made with Christians, Zoroastrians, and Jews who were conquered by Muslim forces during the campaigns of Umar (r. 634–644). Between 639 and 645, the Arab forces invaded Armenia. The commander Habîb ibn Maslamah al-Fihrî took the city of Taflis (Tbilisi, now in the country of Georgia) and made this pact with the inhabitants.

In the name of Allah, the compassionate, the merciful. This is a statement from Habib ibn-Maslamah to the inhabitants of Taflis which lies in Manjalis at Jurzan al-Hurmuz, securing them safety for their lives, churches, convents, religious services and faith, provided they acknowledge their humiliation and pay tax to the amount of one dinar on every household. Ye are not to combine more than one household into one in order to reduce the tax, nor are we to divide the same household into more than one in order to increase it. Ye owe us counsel and support against the enemies of Allah and his Prophet to the utmost of your ability, and are bound to entertain the needy Moslem for one night and provide him with that food used by 'the people of the Book' and which it is legal for us to partake of.

If a Moslem is cut off from his companions and falls into your hands, ye are bound to deliver him to the nearest body of the 'Believers', unless something stands in the way. If ye return to the obedience of Allah and observe prayer, ye are our brethren in faith, otherwise poll-tax is incumbent on you. In case an enemy of yours attacks and subjugates you while the Moslems are too busy to come to your aid, the Moslems are not held responsible, nor is it a violation of the covenant with you. The above are your rights and obligations to which Allah and his angels are witness and it is sufficient to have Allah for witness.

Think about it.

1. What does Ibn Muslamah require of the Christians in Taflis and what do they receive in return?
2. What effect do you think such a law was intended to have?

Al-Baladhuri, Kitab Futah al-Buldan (The Origins of the Islamic State), trans. Philip K. Hitti, pp. 316–317. Longmans, Green and Co., 1916. Copyright in the Public Domain.

75. The Tang Code

Translated by Wallace Johnson

The Tang Code is the earliest complete surviving law code from China. Originally a penal code, which was published in 624 under the emperor Gaozu, it was supplemented by civil statutes in 627 and 637. Commentary was added in a final edition of 653. Below is an extract from Article 6 of the code concerning the worst possible crimes.

Article 6

The Ten Abominations

[15] SUBCOMMENTARY: The ten abominations (*shih-o*) are the most serious of those offenses that come within the five punishments. They injure morality and destroy ceremony. They are specially placed near the head of this chapter [14b] in order to serve as a clear warning. The number of extreme abominations being classified as ten is the reason why they are called the ten abominations.

ARTICLE: The first is called plotting rebellion (*mou-fan*).

SUBCOMMENTARY: The *Kung-yang Commentary* states: "The ruler or parent has no harborers [of plots]. If he does have such harborers, he must put them to death." This means that if there are those who harbor rebellious hearts which would harm the ruler or father, he must then put them to death. The *Tso Commentary* states: "When the seasons of heaven are reversed, we have calamities, ... when the virtues of men are reversed, we have disorders."

The king occupies the most honorable position and receives heaven's precious decrees. Like heaven and earth, he acts to shelter and support, thus serving as the father and mother of the masses. As his children, as his subjects, they must be loyal and filial. However, should they dare to cherish wickedness and have rebellious hearts, they will run counter to heaven's constancy and violate human principle. Therefore this is called plotting rebellion.

COMMENTARY: Plotting rebellion means to plot to endanger the Altars of Soil and Grain (*she chi* that is, the ruler and the state which he rules).

[15a] SUBCOMMENTARY: *She* is the spirit of the five colors of soil. *Chi* is the regulator of the fields, which uses the spirits' earthly virtue to control the harvest. The ruler is the lord of these spirits of agriculture. The food which they ensure is as heaven to the people. When their lord is in peace, these spirits are at rest. When the spirits are in repose, the seasons give a plentiful harvest.

However, ministers and subjects may plot and scheme to rebel against morality and have minds which would discard their ruler. If the ruler's position is endangered, what will the spirits rely upon? Not daring to make direct allusion to the honored name of the ruler, we therefore use the phrase, "Altars of Soil and Grain" to designate him. The *Rites of Chou*

The T'ang Code, Volume I, trans. Wallace Johnson, pp. 61–66, 68–83. Princeton University Press, 1979. Copyright in the Public Domain.

states: "On the left the Temple of the Ancestors, on the right the Altar of the Soil." These are what the ruler honors.

ARTICLE: The second is called plotting great sedition (mou ta-ni).

SUBCOMMENTARY: This type of person breaks laws and destroys order, is against morality, and goes contrary to virtue. There can be no greater sedition. Therefore it is called great sedition.

COMMENTARY: Plotting great sedition means to plot to destroy the ancestral temples, tombs, or palaces of the reigning house.

SUBCOMMENTARY: There are persons who "offend against heaven," "who do not know where to stop," and who secretly think of letting loose their hatred. Planning recklessness, they conceive evil thoughts and plot destruction of the ancestral temples, tombs, or palaces of the reigning house.

ARTICLE: The third is called plotting treason (mou-p'an).

COMMENTARY: Plotting treason means to plot to betray the country or to serve rebels.

SUBCOMMENTARY: There are persons who would betray the reigning house or go over to a foreign country, or who would betray a city and serve rebels, or who would want to flee the country.

ARTICLE: The fourth is called contumacy (o-ni).

SUBCOMMENTARY: The kindness of father and mother is like "great heaven, illimitable." "Entering into the inheritance of our ancestors," we may not be frivolous. Let one's heart be like the hsiao bird or the ching beast, and then love and respect both cease.

Those whose relationship is within the five degrees of mourning are of the closest kin. For them to kill each other is the extreme abomination and the utmost in rebellion, destroying and casting aside human principles. Therefore this is called contumacy.

COMMENTARY: Contumacy means to beat or plot to kill (without actually killing) one's paternal grandparents or parents; or to kill one's paternal uncles or their wives, or one's elder brothers or sisters, or one's maternal grandparents, or one's husband, or one's husband's paternal grandparents, or his parents.

SUBCOMMENTARY: Beat (ou) means to beat or strike. Plot (mow) means to form a plan. When the relationship is that of paternal uncle through to husband's parents [on the list above], if the person has already been killed [the offense then comes under this section on contumacy]. But if there is only a plan to kill, [16a] which has not yet been carried out, the offense comes under the section on discord.

Cases of contumacy are not exempted from punishment under ordinary amnesties (ch'ang-she) and sentences are not delayed. Cases of discord, however, are eligible for pardon under amnesties, and such criminals if officials are only disenrolled (ch'u-ming). This distinguishes the two, and therefore the rules established for the two categories of cases differ.

ARTICLE: The fifth is called depravity (pu-tao).

SUBCOMMENTARY: This article describes those who are cruel and malicious and who turn their backs on morality. Therefore it is called depravity.

COMMENTARY: Depravity means to kill three members of a single household (chia) who have not committed a capital crime, or to dismember someone.

SUBCOMMENTARY: This means that of the three persons from a single household that are killed none has committed a capital crime. If of the three persons, one has been condemned to death, or if in each of several households two persons are killed, this only provides for the death penalty and the crime does not come under the ten abominations. Or if one kills three members of one household and the specific article does not provide for death, this again does not come under the ten abominations. To dismember someone means to kill him and to dismember the body. This comes under the same article as killing three members of one household and also deserves death.

COMMENTARY: The offense also includes the making or keeping of ku poison, or sorcery.

[17a] SUBCOMMENTARY: This means to prepare the poison oneself, or to keep it, or to give it to others in order to harm people. But if the preparation of the poison has not yet been completed, this offense

does not come under the ten abominations. As to sorcery, there are a great many methods not all of which can be described. All, however, comprise evil customs and secret practices which are illegal and whose intent is to cause the victim pain and death.

ARTICLE: The sixth is called great irreverence (*ta pu-ching*).

[18] SUBCOMMENTARY: Ritual is the basis of respect; respect is the vehicle of ritual. Therefore "The Changes in Ritual" chapter of the *Book of Rites* states: "Ritual is the instrument of the ruler whereby he can clear up doubts, cast light on what is difficult to perceive, … test the institutions and regulations and specify benevolence and right conduct." The responsibility of those who offend against ritual is great and their hearts lack reverence and respect. Therefore it is called great irreverence.

COMMENTARY: Great irreverence means to steal the objects of the great sacrifices to the spirits, or the carriage or possessions of the emperor.

SUBCOMMENTARY: As to the great sacrifices, the statute on sacrifices [states: "The country has great sacrifices, medium sacrifices, and small sacrifices. These are] to the Lord on High of Great Heaven, the Lord on High of the Five Directions, the Spirit of Sovereign Earth, the Spiritual Continent, and the Ancestral Temple. [These comprise the great sacrifices.]" Further, the Articles on Administrative Regulations state: "In all references to sacrifice, *chi* and *hsiang* are equally applicable." Thus the great *chi* and great *hsiang* sacrifices are both considered to be great sacrifices.

As to the objects of the spirits, this means the objects which have been presented to the spirits. The commentary on the specific article states: "This means the things presented to the spirits [17b] such as hangings, tables, and staffs." If the objects have been made but are stolen before they have been presented, this also is considered to be great irreverence. If liquor, food containers, and *pien-tou* a and *fu-kuei* sacrificial vessels are in front of the spirits and are stolen, this also is considered to be great

irreverence. But if they are not in the place where the spirits are, it is not so considered.

The imperial possessions mean the things used by the emperor. The ruler's home is the empire and in his chariot he makes tours. We do not dare refer to the honored name of the ruler and therefore rely on the term "chariot" to designate him. The commentary on the specific article states: "Possessions include such things as quilts and cushions, things which are actually worn, and supplementary things, all of which must be submitted to the inspecting officials. Those things which have been selected for presentation to the emperor are also imperial objects."

COMMENTARY: The offense also includes stealing or forging the imperial seals.

COMMENTARY: This section also includes failure to follow the correct prescription when preparing medicine for the emperor, or making a mistake in attaching the label.

SUBCOMMENTARY: When mixing medicine for the emperor, to commit an error despite reliance on the correct prescription is to violate the correct prescription by mistake. Making a mistake in attaching the label means [18a] to follow the prescription in compounding but then to make a mistake in the label such as to designate pills as powder, or to speak of the medicine as being hot in nature when it is cold.

COMMENTARY: This section also includes making a mistake in preparing the emperor's food by violating the dietary proscriptions.

[19] SUBCOMMENTARY: The *Rites of Chou* states: "The food-doctors are in charge of the eight flavors of the king's [food]." They must be especially careful and reverent in managing the imperial food and must follow the standard cookbook. If they mistakenly do not follow the cookbook, this comes under irreverence.

COMMENTARY: This section also includes making mistakes in constructing boats for imperial use so that they are not sturdy.

SUBCOMMENTARY: Everywhere the emperor goes there is happiness and rejoicing. Boats that are offered to the emperor are called imperial. The workmen who make them must use their minds and strength to the utmost. If by mistake the boats are not sturdy, then the crime comes under this section.

Now crimes involving the imperial boats and the preceeding three clauses are all crimes committed by mistake. Even if these items have not yet been presented to the emperor, the crime still comes under the ten abominations. If such crimes are intentional, then the sentence is for plotting rebellion. The inspecting officials [who fail to note the mistake], however, according to the law have their sentences reduced and are not accounted as irreverent.

COMMENTARY: This section further includes criticizing the emperor where the circumstances are completely reprehensible (ch'ieh-hai).

SUBCOMMENTARY: This refers to being disappointed in some circumstance and to issue slanders, thereby criticizing the emperor, and the circumstances are completely reprehensible. If it is not a matter of complaining against the emperor [literally, "heaven"], but only of someone wishing falsely to accuse others of crime, then the case is decided according to the law on reciprocal punishment [for false accusation] ([wu-kao] fan-tso), and does not come under the section on the ten abominations [18b]. ... The reason for this is that the emperor desires to seek out the basic circumstances, spread wide his mercy, and to be cautious in punishing.

COMMENTARY: This section finally includes resisting or driving away messengers carrying imperial decrees (chih), or lacking the proper behavior that a subject owes to his emperor.

SUBCOMMENTARY: Messengers receive the imperial decrees and are sent out to announce them to the four corners of the empire. If there are those who resist or drive them away and do not respect the imperial decrees, such persons lack the proper behavior that a subject owes to his emperor. A messenger who carries the imperial decree means one who receives the imperial decree and is ordered to carry it to the provinces.

ARTICLE: The seventh is called lack of filial piety (pu-hsiao).

SUBCOMMENTARY: Serving one's parents well is called filial piety. Disobeying them is called lack of filial piety.

COMMENTARY: This has reference to accusing to the court, or cursing one's paternal grandparents or parents.

SUBCOMMENTARY: The specific article simply speaks of kao "accusing" one's paternal grandparents or parents, whereas the present commentary speaks in an extended manner of kao-yen accusingly speaking." Though the texts are different, the meaning is the same. Tsu is like chu [and means to curse by spells]. Li is like ma [and means to curse with bad language].

According to the specific article, [20] those who use spells desiring to cause death or illness are sentenced for plotting to kill, which is considered to be contumacy. Only if the spell was made to gain the doting love of the parents does it come under the present article.

COMMENTARY: This section further includes having a separate household register (pieh-chi) or separate goods (yi-ts'ai) while the paternal grandparents or parents are still living.

SUBCOMMENTARY: While the paternal grandparents or parents are alive, the sons and grandsons must put no limit on supporting them. When going out, sons and grandsons state where they are going, and when returning report to their parents[158] without following their own wishes.

However, if they have separate goods or have a separate household register, then the circumstance is one in which they lack hearts of utmost filial piety. Reputation and honor are thereby both lost, and parental affection and appropriateness are both thrown aside. If we search through the canons of morality, this crime is the most difficult to forgive. These two crimes [that is, separate goods and separate household registers] need not be combined. Cases of violation of either are considered to be one of the ten abominations.

COMMENTARY: This section also includes being deficient in support of one's elders.

SUBCOMMENTARY: The *Book of Rites* states: "A filial son in taking care of his parents, seeks to please them. He does not oppose their desires … and loyally supports them with food and drink." In cases where the sons have the ability to support their elders and yet are deficient, if the paternal grandparents or parents accuse them to the courts, then they will be prosecuted.

[19b] COMMENTARY: Further offenses under this section are during the period of mourning for one's parents to arrange for one's own marriage, to make music, or to take off mourning garments and put on ordinary clothing [suitable for happy occasions].

SUBCOMMENTARY: To arrange for one's own marriage during the period of mourning for one's parents means that everyone, principal and accessories alike, is guilty of breaking the law. If, however, it is only the master of the marriage (*chu-hun*) who is prosecuted, then the bridegroom and bride are not deemed unfilial. The reason given here, referring to arranging for one's own marriage, is in order to make clear that the law regarding the master of the marriage is not the same as this one, which is included in the ten abominations.

If a man during mourning for his wife takes a concubine [rather than another wife], he may be permitted to resign from one occupied office [in place of other punishment]. If a woman during mourning for her husband becomes a concubine, her punishment is three degrees less than that for becoming a wife. In neither case does the offense come under lack of filial piety.

As to making music, this includes both the mourner himself or herself making music, and having others to do so for him or her. Music means beating bells or drums; playing stringed instruments, gourds, or chimes; blowing wind instruments; singing, dancing; variety shows; and so on.

Taking off mourning garments and putting on ordinary clothing means that when the mourning period is not yet over, that is, within twenty-seven months, one takes off the mourning garments and puts on ordinary clothing.

[21] COMMENTARY: Still other offenses under this section are on hearing of the death of one's paternal grandparents or parents to conceal and not mourn their death; also to state falsely that one's paternal grandparents or parents have died.

SUBCOMMENTARY: According to the *Book of Rites*, "Hearing of the death of a parent, one responds to the messenger with crying, giving oneself over to sorrow. One asks the cause …" The death of a parent is the greatest of all pain. On hearing that news, one should collapse utterly, beat the breast, stamp the floor, and cry to heaven. However, if one conceals and does not mourn their death, or selects a particular day to begin mourning, both are considered to be lack of filial piety.

Falsely to state that one's paternal grandparents or parents have died means that while they are still alive one falsely states that they are dead. If, however, when they have previously died, and one falsely states that they have only just died, this is not accounted as lack of filial piety.

[20a] ARTICLE: The eighth is called discord *(pu-mu)*.

COMMENTARY: Discord means to plot to kill or also to sell relatives who are of the fifth or closer degree of mourning.

SUBCOMMENTARY: All the cases of plotting to kill or of selling relatives who are of the fifth or closer degree of mourning, irrespective of whether they are of a higher or lower generation or are older or younger than oneself, come under this section. If one plots to kill a relative of a higher generation, or of the same generation but older than oneself within the second degree of mourning, and actually carries out the murder, this comes under the section on contumacy.

Here, plot to kill is stated, not intentional killing or killing in an affray. But killing which is intentional or done in an affray also comes under this section on discord. Plotting to kill but failing to wound is brought up as being a lighter offense in order to make clear that the crime of killing by intent or in an affray which results in death is punished more heavily. In this way the lighter and the heavier are mutually made clear, so that it is reasonable that they both are considered among the ten abominations.

As to selling a relative of the fifth or closer degree of mourning, it comes under this section on discord, whether it is done by force or by consent. This is not so, however, if the sale has not yet been completed.

COMMENTARY: This section further includes beating or accusing to the court one's husband or relatives, whether of a higher generation or of the same generation but older than oneself, of the third (*ta-kung*) or closer degree of mourning, or relatives of an older generation of the fourth *(hsiao-kung)* degree of mourning.

ARTICLE: The ninth is called unrighteousness *(pu-yi)*.

[22] SUBCOMMENTARY: *Li* [that is, morality, rules of propriety, good manners] honors righteousness. This section originally did not include blood relatives because, basically, righteousness is exercised only toward associates. It is concerned with turning one's back on righteousness and violating benevolence. Therefore it is called unrighteousness.

COMMENTARY: Unrighteousness means to kill one's department head, prefect, or magistrate, or the teacher from whom one has received one's education.

COMMENTARY: This section also includes an employee or a soldier who

COMMENTARY: This section also includes concealing and not mourning the death of one's husband, or making music, or taking off mourning and putting on ordinary clothing, or remarrying during the period of mourning.

SUBCOMMENTARY: The husband is the wife's heaven. Having changed from mourning for her father, she mourns her husband. Mourning for the husband is the first degree of mourning (*chan-ts'ui*). This tie of love and righteousness being the highest, the wife on hearing of the death of her husband must cry out and grieve.

If, however, she conceals and does not mourn his death, or if during the period of mourning she makes music or takes off mourning and puts on ordinary clothing, or if again she forgets her sorrow and remarries, all these acts mean turning one's back on morality and violating righteousness. Therefore all come under the ten abominations. If, however, the wife remarries as a concubine, it is not considered to be one of the ten abominations.

ARTICLE: The tenth is called incest (*nei-luan).*

SUBCOMMENTARY: The *Tso Commentary* states: "The woman has her husband's house; the man has his wife's chamber; and there must be no defilement on either side." If this is changed, then there is incest. If one behaves like the birds and beasts, and introduces licentious associates into one's family, the rules of morality are confused. Therefore this is called incest.

[21b] COMMENTARY: This section includes having illicit sexual intercourse (*chien*) with relatives who are of the fourth degree of mourning or closer.

SUBCOMMENTARY: To have illicit sexual intercourse with relatives who are of the fourth degree of mourning or closer means for a man to have illicit sexual intercourse with a woman for whom, according to the *Book of Ceremonies and Rites*, he must wear the fourth degree of mourning. If the woman must wear the fourth degree of mourning for the man, but the man [23] only fifth degree of mourning for the woman in return, then illicit sexual intercourse is not accounted incest. This has reference to such relationships as that of a daughter's daughter with one's maternal grandfather, or a sister's daughter with one's maternal uncle.

COMMENTARY: This section also includes illicit sexual intercourse with one's father's or paternal grandfather's concubines, including those who give their consent.

SUBCOMMENTARY: As to the father's or paternal grandfather's *ch'ieh* concubines, the case is the same regardless of whether they have had children. To have intercourse with *ying* concubines is also considered to be incest. Including those who give their consent means that if the woman consents to have illicit sexual intercourse with the man, then both are guilty of incest. If she is forced but later gives her consent, this is also incest.

Think about it.

1. Why do you think these particular offenses were considered the most heinous?
2. Where do you see Confucian influence in these laws?

7th–16th centuries CE

76. The Popol Vuh

Translated by Delia Goetz and Sylvanus G. Morley

The Popol Vuh ("Book of the People") is a book containing the sacred stories of the Maya people from the Ki'che' kingdom of Q'umarkaj (13th century–1524) in present-day Guatemala. The text was produced by a Dominican friar named Francisco Ximénez in the early 18th century, but his source was apparently a phonetic text made in the 16th century. It is believed that many of the stories of the Popol Vuh have their origin in the Classic period of Maya civilization (c. 250–900 CE). The following excerpt is part of the myth of the creation of humankind.

Chapter 1

First the earth was formed, the mountains and the valleys; the currents of water were divided, the rivulets were running freely between the hills, and the water was separated when the high mountains appeared.

Thus was the earth created, when it was formed by the Heart of Heaven, the Heart of Earth, as they are called who first made it fruitful, when the sky was in suspense, and the earth was submerged in the water.

So it was that they made perfect the work, when they did it after thinking and meditating upon it.

Popol Vuh: The Sacred Book of the Ancient Quiché Maya, trans. Delia Goetz and Sylvanus G. Morley, pp. 84–93. Copyright © 1950 by University of Oklahoma Press. Reprinted with permission.

CHAPTER 2

Then they made the small wild animals, the guardians of the woods, the spirits of the mountains,[1] the deer, the birds, pumas, jaguars, serpents, snakes, vipers, guardians of the thickets.

And the Forefathers asked: "Shall there be only silence and calm under the trees, under the vines? It is well that hereafter there be someone to guard them."

So they said when they meditated and talked. Promptly the deer and the birds were created. Immediately they gave homes to the deer and the birds. "You, deer, shall sleep in the fields by the river bank and in the ravines. Here you shall be amongst the thicket, amongst the pasture; in the woods you shall multiply, you shall walk on four feet and they will support you. Thus be it done!" So it was they spoke.

Then they also assigned homes to the birds big and small. "You shall live in the trees and in the vines. There you shall make your nests; there you shall multiply; there you shall increase in the branches of the trees and in the vines." Thus the deer and the birds were told; they did their duty at once, and all sought their homes and their nests.

And the creation of all the four-footed animals and the birds being finished, they were told by the Creator and the Maker and the Forefathers: "Speak, cry, warble, call, speak each one according to your variety, each, according to your kind." So was it said to the deer, the birds, pumas, jaguars, and serpents.

"Speak, then, our names, praise us, your mother, your father. Invoke then, Huracán, Chipi-Caculhá, Raxa-Caculhá, the Heart of Heaven, the Heart of Earth, the Creator, the Maker, the Forefathers; speak, invoke us, adore us," they were told.

But they could not make them speak like men; they only hissed and screamed and cackled; they were unable to make words, and each screamed in a different way.

When the Creator and the Maker saw that it was impossible for them to talk to each other, they said: "It is impossible for them to say our names, the names of us, their Creators and Makers. This is not well," said the Forefathers to each other.

Then they said to them: "Because it has not been possible for you to talk, you shall be changed. We have changed our minds: Your food, your pasture, your homes, and your nests you shall have; they shall be the ravines and the woods, because it has not been possible for you to adore us or invoke us. There shall be those who adore us, we shall make other [beings] who shall be obedient. Accept your destiny: your flesh shall be torn to pieces. So shall it be. This shall be your lot." So they said, when they made known their will to the large and small animals which are on the face of the earth.

They wished to give them another trial; they wished to make another attempt; they wished to make [all living things] adore them.

But they could not understand each other's speech; they could succeed in nothing, and could do nothing. For this reason they were sacrificed, and the animals which were on earth were condemned to be killed and eaten.

For this reason another attempt had to be made to create and make men by the Creator, the Maker, and the Forefathers.

"Let us try again! Already dawn draws near: Let us make him who shall nourish and sustain us! What shall we do to be invoked, in order to be remembered on earth? We have already tried with our first creations, our first creatures; but we could not make them praise and venerate us. So, then, let us try to make obedient, respectful beings who will nourish and sustain us." Thus they spoke.

---

1 *U vinaquil huyub*, literally, "the little man of the forest." The Indians in ancient times believed that the forests were peopled with these little beings, guardians, spirits of the forests, a species of hobgoblin similar to the *alux* of the Maya. The *Memorial Cakchiquel* calls them *ru vinakil chee*, from *che* "tree," which Father Coto translates as "the hobgoblin which walks in the mountains," and by another name, the Zakikoxol. According to the *Memorial*, the ancient Cakchiquel used to speak with these little men who were the spirits of the volcano of Fuego, *ru cux huyu chi Gag*, called Zakikoxol.

Then was the creation and the formation. Of earth, of mud, they made [man's] flesh. But they saw that it was not good. It melted away, it was soft, did not move, had no strength, it fell down, it was limp, it could not move its head, its face fell to one side, its sight was blurred, it could not look behind. At first it spoke, but had no mind. Quickly it soaked in the water and could not stand.

And the Creator and the Maker said: "Let us try again because our creatures will not be able to walk nor multiply. Let us consider this," they said.

Then they broke up and destroyed their work and their creation. And they said: "What shall we do to perfect it, in order that our worshipers, our invokers, will be successful?"

Thus they spoke when they conferred again: "Let us say again to Xpiyacoc, Xmucané, Hunahpú-Vuch, Hunahpú-Utiú: 'Cast your lot again. Try to create again.'" In this manner the Creator and the Maker spoke to Xpiyacoc and Xmucané.

Then they spoke to those soothsayers, the Grandmother of the day, the Grandmother of the Dawn, as they were called by the Creator and the Maker, and whose names were Xpiyacoc and Xmucané.

And said Huracán, Tepeu, and Gucumatz when they spoke to the soothsayer, to the Maker, who are the diviners: "You must work together and find the means so that man, whom we shall make, man, whom we are going to make, will nourish and sustain us, invoke and remember us."

"Enter, then, into council, grandmother, grandfather, our grandmother, our grandfather, Xpiyacoc, Xmucané, make light, make dawn, have us invoked, have us adored, have us remembered by created man, by made man, by mortal man. Thus be it done.

"Let your nature be known, Hunahpú-Vuch, Hunahpú-Utiú, twice mother, twice father,[2]

Nim-Ac,[3] Nima-Tziís,[4] the master of emeralds, the worker in jewels, the sculptor, the carver, the maker of beautiful plates, the maker of green gourds, the master of resin, the master Toltecat,[5] grandmother of the sun, grandmother of dawn, as you will be called by our works and our creatures.

"Cast the lot with your grains of corn and the *tzité*[6] Do it thus,[7] and we shall know if we are to make, or carve his mouth and eyes out of wood." Thus the diviners were told.

They went down at once to make their divination, and cast their lots with the corn and the *tzité*. "Fate! Creature!" said an old woman and an old man. And this old man was the one who cast the lots with Tzité, the one called Xpiyacoc. And the old woman was the diviner, the maker, called Chiracán Xmucané.

Beginning the divination, they said: "Get together, grasp each other! Speak, that we may hear." They

---

2 *Camul Alom, camul Qaholom.* The author calls Hunahpu-Vuch, "two times mother," and Hunahpu-Utiu, "two times father," thus giving the sex of each of the two members of the Creator-couple.

3 Large wild boar, or wild pig. *Nim-Ac* is the father.

4 *Nimá-Tziís*, the mother, large *pisote* or *coati mundi (Nasua nasica)*. It might also be interpreted as large tapir (*Tix* in Poconchf, *tzimin* in Jacalteca). The tapir was the sacred animal of the Tzeltal Indians of Chiapas, and Bishop Nunez de la Vega says that, according to legend, Votan took a tapir to Huehuetlan, and that it multiplied in the waters of the river which runs through Soconusco, a district in the present state of Chiapas, Mexico.

5 Here the text seems to enumerate the usual occupations of the men of that time. The author calls upon *ahqual*, who is evidently the one who carves emeralds or green stones; *ahyamanic*, the jeweler or silversmith; *ahchut*, engraver or sculptor; *ahtzalam*, carver or cabinetmaker; *ahraxalac*, he who fashions green or beautiful plates; *ahraxazel*, he who makes the beautiful green vases or gourds (called *Xicalli* in Náhuatl,)—the word *raxá* has both meanings; *ahgol*, he who makes the resin or copal; and, finally, *ahtoltecat*, he who, without doubt, was the silversmith. The Tolteca were in fact, skilled silversmiths who, according to the legend, were taught the art by Quetzalcoatl himself.

6 *Erythrina corallodendron. Tzité, arbol de pito* in Guatemala; *Tzompanquahuitl* in the Mexican language. It is used in both countries to make fences. Its fruit is a pod which contains red grains resembling a bean which the Indians used, as they still do, together with grains of corn, in their fortunetelling and witchcraft. In his *Informe contra Idolorum Cultores*, Sánchez de Aguilar says that the Maya Indians "cast lots with a large handful of corn." As is seen, the practice which is still observed by the Maya-Quiché is of respectable antiquity.

7 *Chi banatahic xa pu ch'el apon-oc*, literally: "Do it so and it will be done."

said, "Say if it is well i that the wood be got together and that it be carved by the Creator and the Maker, and if this [man of wood] is he who must nourish and sustain us when there is light when it is day!

"Thou, corn; thou, *tzité;* thou, fate; thou, creature; get together, take each other," they said to the corn, to the *tzité,* to fate, to the creature. "Come to sacrifice here, Heart of Heaven; do not punish Tepeu and Gucumatz!"[8]

Then they talked and spoke the truth: "Your figures of wood shall come out well; they shall speak and talk on earth."

"So may it be," they answered when they spoke.

And instantly the figures were made of wood. They looked like men, talked like men, and populated the surface of the earth."

They existed and multiplied; they had daughters, they had sons, these wooden figures; but they did not have souls, nor minds, they did not remember their Creator, their Maker; they walked on all fours, aimlessly.

They no longer remembered the Heart of Heaven and therefore they fell out of favor. It was merely a trial, an attempt at man. At first they spoke, but their face was without expression; their feet and hands had no strength; they had no blood, nor substance, nor moisture, nor flesh; their cheeks were dry, their feet and hands were dry, and their flesh was yellow.

Therefore, they no longer thought of their Creator nor their Maker, nor of those who made them and cared for them.

These were the first men who existed in great numbers on the face of the earth.

CHAPTER 3

Immediately the wooden figures were annihilated, destroyed, broken up, and killed.

A flood was brought about by the Heart of Heaven; a great flood was formed which fell on the heads of the wooden creatures.

Of *tzité,* the flesh of man was made, but when woman was fashioned by the Creator and the Maker, her flesh was made of rushes.[9] These were the materials the Creator and the Maker wanted to use in making them.

But those that they had made, that they had created, did not think, did not speak with their Creator, their Maker. And for this reason they were killed, they were deluged. A heavy resin fell from the sky. The one called Xecotcovach came and gouged out their eyes; Camalotz came and cut off their heads; Cotzbalam came and devoured their flesh. Tucumbalam[10] came, too, and broke and mangled their bones and their nerves, and ground and crumbled their bones.

This was to punish them because they had not thought of their mother, nor their father, the Heart of Heaven, called Huracán. And for this reason the face of the earth was darkened and a black rain began to fall, by day and by night.

---

8 *C'at quix la uloc, at u Qux cab, m'a cahizah u chi, u vach Tepeu, Gucumatz.* Here other translators have rendered the verb *quix* as "to shame." Brasseur de Bourbourg observes that it may also signify "to sting" or "take out blood" with a thorn. This was a common form of sacrifice among the Indians, and seems to indicate the real meaning of the sentence as used by the author. *Qahizan vach* is "to punish," according to the *Vocabulario de los Padres Franciscanos.* The entire passage is an invitation to the Heart of Heaven to come and take part in casting lots and not let the diviners fail.

9 The Quiché name *zibaque* is commonly used in Guatemala to designate this plant of the Typhaceae family, which is much used in making the mats called *petates tules* in that country. Basseta says it is the part of a reed with which mats are made.

10 It is difficult to interpret the names of these enemies of man. Ximénez says that *Xecotcovach* was a bird, probably an eagle *(cot)* or sparrow hawk. The *Camalotz* which cut off men's heads was evidently the large vampire *(nimá chicop) Camazotz,* bat of death, which decapitated the young hero Hunahpú in Part II of the manuscript. *Cotzbalam* may be interpreted as the jaguar who lies in wait for his prey. *Tucumbalam* is another name for the danta or tapir. Seler *(Der Fledermausgott der Maya-Stämme,* Vol. II of *Gesammelte Abhandlungen)* argues that these "wild animal demons of the *Popol Vuh*" are equivalent to the four monstrous figures which are seen in folio 44 of the *Codex Borgiano.* According to Seler, Tucumbalam is represented in that *Códice* as a species of shark or crocodile. The bat of the East had torn off the head of his neighbor in front of him, and the shark or crocodile of the West had torn off his foot.

Then came the small animals and the large animals, and sticks and stones struck their faces. And all began to speak: their earthen jars,[11] their griddles,[12] their plates, their pots, their grinding stones,[13] all rose up and struck their faces.

"You have done us much harm; you ate us, and now we shall kill you," said their dogs and birds of the barnyard.[14]

And the grinding stones said: "We were tormented by you; every day, every day, at night, at dawn, all the time our faces went *holt, holi, huqui, huqui,* because of you.[15] This was the tribute we paid you. But now that you are no longer men, you shall feel our strength. We shall grind and tear your flesh to pieces," said their grinding stones.

And then their dogs spoke and said: "Why did you give us nothing to eat? You scarcely looked at us, but you chased us and threw us out. You always had a stick[16] ready to strike us while you were eating.

"Thus it was that you treated us. You did not speak to us. Perhaps we shall not kill you now; but why did you not look ahead, why did you not think about yourselves? Now we shall destroy you, now you shall feel the teeth of our mouths; we shall devour you," said the dogs, and then, they destroyed their faces.

And at the same time, their griddles and pots spoke: "Pain and suffering you have caused us. Our mouths and our faces were blackened with soot;

we were always put on the fire and you burned us as though we felt no pain. Now you shall feel it, we shall burn you," said their pots, and they all destroyed their [the wooden men's] faces. The stones of the hearth,[17] which were heaped together, hurled themselves straight from the fire against their heads causing them pain.[18]

The desperate ones [the men of wood] ran as quickly as they could; they wanted to climb to the tops of the houses, and the houses fell down and threw them to the ground; they wanted to climb to the treetops, and the trees cast them far away; they wanted to enter the caverns, and the caverns repelled them.[19]

So was the ruin of the men who had been created and formed, the men made to be destroyed and annihilated; the mouths and "[faces of all of them were mangled.

And it is said that their descendants are the monkeys which now live in the forests;[20] these are all that remain of them because their flesh was made only of wood by the Creator and the Maker.

---

11   *Quebal*, which Ximénez translates "grinding stones," is a water jug or pitcher here. Brasseur de Bourbourg translates it incorrectly as *tout ce qui leur avait servi*.

12   *Comalli* in the Mexican language, *xot* in Quiché, a large plate or the disk of clay upon which the corn tortillas are baked.

13   *Qui caa*, in the original, grinding stone, *metate* in Mexico. Brasseur de Bourbourg read it incorrectly as *qui aq y* and translated the passage "their hens."

14   The dogs which the wooden men ate were not like those which are now in America, but a species which the Spanish chroniclers called "silent dogs," because they did not bark. The barnyard fowls were the turkey, the pheasant, and the wild hen.

15   These words are merely an imitation of the noise made when the corn is being ground by the grinding stone.

16   *Yacal u bi*, "leaning against the wall," or "lying on the ground," according to the *Diccionario Cakchiquel*.

---

17   They are the three hearthstones of the Indians on which the *comal*, or the cooking pots, rested.

18   The idea of a flood in olden times and the belief in another which would be the end of the world, and would have had characters similar to those described here in the *Popol Vuh*, still existed among the Indians of Guatemala in the years following the Spanish conquest, according to the *Apologética Historia* (Chap. CCXXXV, p. 620). Bishop Las Casas says in this work that "They had, among them, information of the flood and of the end of the world, and called it *Butic*, which is the word which means flood of many waters and means [the final] judgment, and so they believe fhat another *Butic* is about to come, which is another flood and judgment, not of water, but of fire, which they say would be the end of the world, in which all the creatures would have to quarrel, especially those which serve man, like the stones on which they grind their corn and wheat, the pots, the pitchers, giving to understand that they will turn against man."

19   *Xa chi yuch hul chi qui vach*, literally, the caverns covered their faces, scorned them.

20   According to the *Anales de Cuauhtitlán*, in the fourth age of the earth, "many people were drowned and others hurled into the mountains and were changed into monkeys."

And therefore the monkey looks like man, and is an example of a generation of men which were created and made but were only wooden figures.

Think about it.

1. According to this text, why were humans created?
2. What message or moral can be found in the account of each mistake that the gods make in creation?

---

686 CE

77. The Kota Kapur Inscription

Translated by George Coedès

Kota Kapur is a site on the island of Bangka off the coast of Sumatra, Indonesia. In 1892 an obelisk-shaped stone was found there, which contained an inscription of ten lines, written by the king of Srivijaya, a powerful maritime empire centered on Sumatra that flourished from the 7th to the 13th centuries. The inscription is dated to February 28, 686 and is therefore from very early in that period. Written in Old Malay, it is one of the earliest representations of Indonesian writing. There are three other inscriptions (from Kedukan Bukit, Talang Tuwo, and Karang Brahi), which may have been composed by the very same king. If so, we can identify the name of the king as Jayanasa. He seems to have been the founder of the empire.

Translation

Success! [there follows an untelligible curse formula]. O you, all the powerful divinities who are assembled, and who protect [this] province [*kadatuan*] of Śrīwijaya; you too, *Tandrun luah* and all the divinities with whom all curse formulas begin!

When, within all the lands [*bhūmi*] [dependent on this province (*kadatuan*)], people revolt [...]

conspire with the rebels, speak to the rebels, listen to the rebels, know the rebels, are not respectful, are not obedient, are not faithful to me and those invested by me with the power of *dātu*, let the authors of these actions be killed by a curse; let an expedition [against them] be sent into the field under the command of the *dātu* (or *dātu's*) of Śrīwijaya, and may they be punished, with their clans and their families. And also, may all their evil deeds, [such as] troubling the minds of others, making them ill, making them mad, using formulas and poisons, using the *upas* and *tuba* poisons, hemp, *sarāmwat*, or philtres, imposing their will on others, etc., [may these actions] fail and fall upon those who are guilty of these evil deeds, and also may they be killed by the curse. And what is more, those who incite others to damage, or themselves damage the stone placed here, may they also be killed by the curse and immediately punished. May the murderers' the rebels, those who are not devoted or faithful to me, may the authors of these actions be killed by the curse. But if people are obedient, are faithful to me and to those invested by me with the power of *dātu*, may their undertakings be blessed, as well as their clans and families: success, ease, lack of disasters, abundance for all their countries!

Śaka 608, on the first day of the light fortnight of the month of Waiśākha, it was at this time that this curse was pronounced; it was carved at the time when the army of Śrīwijaya had just set out on an expedition against the land [*bhūmi*] of Java which was not obedient to Śrīwijaya.

Think about it.

1. What is the king's aim in publishing this inscription?
2. What actions does the king pronounce to be evil? Why?
3. What is the purpose of the curse?

---

720 CE

78. The Nihon Shoki

Translated by William G. Aston

The Nihon Shoki (also known as the Nihongi) is the second oldest chronicle of Japan. It was compiled by officials at the imperial court and published in 720, under the supervision of Prince Toneri, son of the emperor Temmu, during the reign of the Empress Gensho (715–724). It is far more detailed and more secular than the early Kojiki and makes use of many earlier sources. The following excerpts concern the introduction of Buddhism into Japan.

Selections from: "Nihongi: Chronicles of Japan from Earliest Times to A.D. 697," *Supplement to The Transactions and Proceedings of the Japan Society*, trans. William G. Aston. Kegan Paul, Trench, Trübner & Company, 1896. Copyright in the Public Domain.

[552 CE] xix. 33. Winter, 10th month. King Syöng-myöng of Pèkché [also called King Syong] sent Kwi-si of the Western Division, and the Tal-sol, Nu-ri Sa-chhi-hyé, with a present to the Emperor of an image of Shaka[1] Butsu in gold and copper,[2] several flags and umbrellas, and a number of volumes of "Sutras."

xix. 34. Separately he presented a memorial in which he lauded the merit of diffusing abroad religious worship, saying:—"This doctrine is amongst all doctrines the most excellent. But it is hard to explain, and hard to comprehend. Even the Duke of Zhou and Confucius had not attained to a knowledge of it This doctrine can create religious merit and retribution[3] without measure and without bounds, and so lead on to a full appreciation of the highest wisdom.[4] Imagine a man in possession of treasures to his heart's content, so that he might satisfy all his wishes in proportion as he used them. Thus it is with the treasure of this wonderful doctrine. Every prayer is fulfilled and naught is wanting. Moreover, from distant India it has extended hither to the three Han,[5] where there are none who do not receive it with reverence as it is preached to them.

xix. 35. Thy servant, therefore, Myöng, King of Pèkché, has humbly despatched his retainer,[6] Nu-ri Sa-chhi, to transmit it to the Imperial Country, and to diffuse it abroad throughout the home provinces, so as to fulfil the recorded saying of Buddha: 'My law shall spread to the East.'"

This day the Emperor, having heard to the end, leaped for joy, and gave command to the Envoys, saying:—"Never from former days until now have we had the opportunity of listening to so wonderful a doctrine. We are unable, however, to decide of ourselves." Accordingly he inquired of his Ministers

one after another, saying:—"The countenance of this Buddha which has been presented by the Western frontier State is of a severe dignity, such as we have never at all seen before. Ought it to be worshipped or not?" Soga no Oho-omi, Iname no Sukune, addressed the Emperor, saying:—"All the Western frontier lands without exception do it worship. Shall Akitsu Yamato alone refuse to do so? " Okoshi, Mononobe no Oho-muraji, and Kamako, Nakatomi no Muraji, addressed the Emperor jointly, saying:— "Those who have ruled the Empire in this our State have always made it their care to worship in Spring, Summer, Autumn and Winter the 180 Gods of Heaven and Earth, and the Gods of the Land and of Grain. If just at this time we were to worship in their stead foreign Deities, it may be feared that we should incur the wrath of our National Gods."

xix. 36. The Emperor said:—"Let it be given to Iname no Sukune, who has shown his willingness to take it, and, as an experiment, make him to worship it."

The Oho-omi knelt down and received it with joy. HE enthroned it in his house at Oharida, where he diligently CARRIED out the rites of retirement from the world, and on that SCORE purified his house at Muku-hara and made it a Temple. After this a pestilence was rife in the Land, from which the PEOPLE died prematurely. As time went on it became worse and worse, and there was no remedy. Okoshi, Mononobe no Ohomuraji, and Kamako, Nakatomi no Muraji, addressed the Emperor jointly, saying:—"It was because thy servants' advice on a former day was not approved that the people are dying thus of disease. If thou dost now retrace thy steps before matters have gone too far, joy will surely be the result! It will be well promptly to fling it away, and diligently to seek happiness in the future."

The Emperor said:—"Let it be done as you advise." Accordingly officials took the image of Buddha and abandoned it to the current of the Canal of Naniha. They also set fire to the Temple, and burnt it so that nothing was left. Hereupon, there being in the Heavens neither clouds nor wind,

---

1 Sakyamuni.
2 Copper with a small admixture of gold.
3 Either good or bad. Here in a good sense.
4 Bôdhi.
5 Buddhism had been introduced into Koryö A.D. 372, from the Chin country in Western China. It penetrated to Pèkché in 384.
6 The character used means the vassal of a vassal, and implies an acknowledgment of Japan's suzerainty.

a sudden conflagration consumed the Great Hall (of the Palace).

[577 CE] xx. 8. Winter, 11th month, 1st day. The King of the Land of Pèkché presented to the Emperor, through the returning Envoys Prince Ohowake and his companions, a number of volumes of religious books, with an ascetic, a meditative monk, a nun, a reciter of mantras, a maker of Buddhist images, and a temple architect, six persons in all. Eventually there was founded the Temple of Prince Ohowake of Naniha.

[584 CE] xx. 14. Autumn, 9th month. Kafuka no Omi [the personal name is wanting], who had come from Pèkché, had a stone image of Miroku,[7] and Saheki no Muraji [the personal name is wanting] an image of Buddha. This year Soga no Mŭmako no Sukune, having asked for these two Buddhist images, sent Shiba Tattō, Kurabe no Sukuri, and Hida, Ikenobe no Atahe, in all directions to search out persons who practised (Buddhism). Upon this he only found in the province of Harima a man named Hyéphyon of Koryö who from a Buddhist priest had become a layman again. So the Oho-omi made him teacher, and caused him to receive Shima, the daughter of Shiba Tattō, into religion. She took the name of Nun Zen-shin [twelve years of age]. Moreover he received into religion two pupils of the Nun Zen-shin. One was Toyome, the daughter of Ayabito[8] no Yaho. She took the name of Nun Sen-zō. The other was Ishime, daughter of Nishikori Tsubu. She took the name of Nun Kei-zen. Mŭmako no Sukune, still in accordance with the Law of Buddha, reverenced the three nuns, and gave them to Hida no Atahe and Tattō, with orders to provide them with food and clothing. He erected a Buddhist Temple on the east side of his dwelling, in which he enshrined the stone image of Miroku. He insisted on the three nuns holding a general meeting to partake of maigre fare. At this time Tattō found a Buddhist relic on the food of abstinence, and presented it to Mŭmako no Sukune. Mŭmako no Sukune, by way of experiment, took the relic, and placing it on the middle of a block of iron, beat it with an iron sledge-hammer, which he flourished aloft. The block and the sledge-hammer were shattered to atoms, but the. relic could not be crushed. Then the relic was cast into water when it floated on the water or sank as one desired. In consequence of this, Mŭmako no Sukune, Ikenobe no Hida, and Shiba Tattō held faith in Buddhism and practised it unremittingly. Mŭmako no Sukune built another Buddhist Temple at his house in Ishikaha. From this arose the beginning of Buddhism.

[585 CE] xx. 15. 14th year, Spring, 2nd month, 15th day. Soga no Oho-omi, Mŭmako no Sukune, erected a pagoda north of the Hill of Ohono, and having held a general meeting to partake of maigre food, deposited the relic obtained by Tattō on the top of the pillar.[9]

24th day. Soga no Oho-omi took ill. Having made inquiry of a diviner,[10] the diviner answered and said:—"It is a curse sent by will of the Buddha[11] worshipped in thy father's time." Soga no Oho-omi accordingly sent a young man of his family to report to the Emperor the nature of the divination. The Emperor gave orders, saying:—"In accordance with the words of the diviner, let thy father's Gods be worshipped." The Oho-omi, in obedience to the Emperor's commands, worshipped the stone image, and prayed that his life might be prolonged. At this time there was a pestilence rife in the land, and many of the people died.

3rd month, 1st day. Mononobe no Yugehi no Moriya no Ohomuraji and Nakatomi no Katsumi no Daibu addressed the Emperor, saying:—"Why hast thou not consented to follow thy servants' counsel? Is not the prevalence of pestilence from the reign of the late Emperor thy father down to thine, so that the nation is in danger of extinction, owing absolutely

---

7 In Sanskrit Maitréya, the expected Messiah of the Buddhists.
8 Ayabito is written i.e. a man of Han (China). Here it is a proper name, though no doubt indicating a Chinese ancestry.

9 i.e. the central pillar round which a pagoda is built.
10 Urabe, or native augurs.
11 The word for Buddha is Buddha-Kami.

to the establishment of the exercise of the Buddhist religion by Soga no Omi?" The Emperor gave command, saying:—"Manifestly so: let Buddhism be discontinued."

xx. 16. 30th day. Mononobe no Yugehi no Moriya no Ohomuraji went himself to the Temple, and sitting on a chair, cut down the pagoda,[12] which he then set fire to and burnt. He likewise burnt the image of Buddha and the Temple of Buddha. Having done so, he took the remains of the image of Buddha which were left from the burning and had them flung into the Naniha canal. On this day there was wind and rain without any clouds, and the Ohomuraji had on his rain-coat. He upbraided Mŭmako no Sukune and those who followed him in the exercise of religion, and made them feel shame and contrition of heart. Moreover he sent Mimoro [also called Oruke], Saheki no Miyakko, to summon Zen-shin and the other nuns provided for by Mŭmako no Sukune. So Mŭmako no Sukune did not dare to disobey this command, but with grief and lamentation called forth the nuns and delivered them to Mimoro. The officials accordingly took away from the nuns their three garments,[13] imprisoned them and flogged them at the road-station of Tsubaki no ichi.

The Emperor, with the view of establishing Imna, appointed as his Envoy Prince Mimiko of Sakata. Just at this time the Emperor and the Ohomuraji were suddenly afflicted with sores, and he was therefore after all not sent. The Emperor gave command to the Imperial Prince Tachibana no Toyohi, saying:—"The injunctions of the late Emperor my father must not be disregarded: the Government of Imna must be diligently put in order."

Again the Land was filled with those who were attacked with sores and died thereof. The persons thus afflicted with sores said:—"Our bodies are as if they were burnt, as if they were beaten, as if they were broken," and so lamenting, they died. Old and young said privately to one another, " Is this a punishment for the burning of the Image of Buddha?"

xx. 17. Summer, 6th month. Mŭmako no Sukune addressed the Emperor, saying:—"Thy servant's disease has not yet been healed; nor is it possible for succour to be afforded me unless by the power of the three precious things."[1] Hereupon the Emperor commanded Mŭmako no Sukune, saying:—"Thou mayest practise the Buddhist religion alone, but discontinue it in so far as others are concerned." So the three nuns were given back to Mŭmako no Sukune, who received them with rejoicing, lamenting their unexampled misfortunes, and bowing down his head in their honour. He built them a Temple anew, into which he welcomed them, and provided them with sustenance.

One book says:—"Mononobe no Yugehi no Moriya no Ohomuraji, Oho-miwa no Sakahe no Kimi and Nakatomi no Ihare no Muraji conspired together to destroy the Buddhist religion. They wanted to burn the Temple and pagoda, and also to throw away the Buddhist images. Mŭmako no Sukune opposed this project, and would not agree to it."

---

12 The meaning may be that he sat on a chair to superintend the workmen who were employed for this purpose.

13 The three priestly garments, viz. the Samghâti, reaching from the shoulders to the knees, the Uttara Samghâti, a sort of overcoat, and the Kachâya (*Kesa* in Japanese), a coloured mantle. *Vide* Eitel, *sub vocibus*.

Think about it.

1. From what you can gather from this reading, what factors contributed to the spread of Buddhism in Japan?

2. How are the pestilences and illnesses interpreted by the Emperor and his advisors?

79. Poems of Li Bai

Translated by Shigeyoshi Obata

Li Bai (Li Po in the old spelling) was a Chinese poet (701–762) who worked under the emperor Xuanzong (712–756) of the Tang dynasty, first as a translator and then as a poet. His works were very influential, and today he is considered one of China's greatest poets. Two of his poems are presented here.

THE NEFARIOUS WAR

Last year we fought by the head-stream of the Sanggan,
This year we are fighting on the Zhonghe road.
We have washed our armor in the waves of the Chaoji lake,
We have pastured our horses on Tian Shan's snowy slopes.
The long, long war goes on ten thousand miles from home,
Our three armies are worn and grown old.

The barbarian does man-slaughter for plowing;
On his yellow sand-plains nothing has been seen but blanched skulls and bones.
Where the Qin emperor built the walls against the Tartars,
There the defenders of Han are burning beacon fires.
The beacon fires burn and never go out,
There is no end to war!—

In the battlefield men grapple each other and die;
The horses of the vanquished utter lamentable cries to heaven,
While ravens and kites peck at human entrails,
Carry them up in their flight, and hang them on the branches of dead trees.
So, men are scattered and smeared over the desert grass,
And the generals have accomplished nothing.
Oh, nefarious war! I see why arms
Were so seldom used by the benign sovereigns.

The Works of Li Po: The Chinese Poet, trans. Shigeyoshi Obata. J.M. Dent & Sons Limited, 1922. Copyright in the Public Domain.

LETTER FROM CHANG'AN I

(A river-merchant's wife writes)
I would play, plucking flowers by the gate;
My hair scarcely covered my forehead, then.
You would come, riding on your bamboo horse,
And loiter about the bench with green plums for toys.
So we both dwelt in Chang'an town,
We were two children, suspecting nothing.

At fourteen I became your wife,
And so bashful that I could never bare my face,
But hung my head, and turned to the dark wall;
You would call me a thousand times,
But I could not look back even once.

At fifteen I was able to compose my eyebrows,
And beg you to love me till we were dust and ashes.
You always kept the faith of Wei-sheng,
Who waited under the bridge, unafraid of death,
I never knew I was to climb the Hill of Wang-fu
And watch for you these many days.

I was sixteen when you went on a long journey,
Traveling beyond the Qu Tang Gorge,
Where the giant rocks heap up the swift river,
And the rapids are not passable in May.
Did you hear the monkeys wailing
Up on the skyey height of the crags?
Do you know your foot-marks by our gate are old,
And each and every one is filled up with green moss?

The mosses are too deep for me to sweep away;
And already in the autumn wind the leaves are falling.
The yellow butterflies of October
Flutter in pairs over the grass of the west garden.
My heart aches at seeing them. ...
I sit sorrowing alone, and alas!
The vermilion of my face is fading.
Some day when you return down the river,
If you will write me a letter beforehand,
I will come to meet you—the way is not long—
I will come as far as the Long Wind Beach instantly.

Think about it.

1. What are Li Bai's views of warfare?
2. From the second poem, what can be learned about the life of merchant's wives in this period?

— late 8th century CE —

80. Introduction to the Law of Nations

Translated by Majid Khadduri

Muhammad al-Shaybani (750–805) was a Sunni Muslim jurist of the Hanafi school, sometimes referred to as the father of Islamic international law. He was primarily a teacher, but he did serve as a judge of the Abbassid capital city of Ar-Raqqah from 796 to 803 under the Caliph Harun al-Rashid (r. 786–809). Earlier he had written several works, including *Introduction to the Law of Nations*, a book that provided detailed guidelines for the conduct of *jihad* against unbelievers and for the treatment of non-Muslims under Muslim rule. Here are a few selections from the work.

Chapter I

[TRADITIONS RELATING TO THE CONDUCT OF WAR]

In the Name of God, the Merciful, the Compassionate. Praise Be to God, the One, the Just.

1. Abū Sulaymān [al-Juzjānī] from Muhammad b. al-Hasan [al-Shāybanī] from Abū Hanīfa from 'Alqama b. Marthad from 'Abd-Allāh b. Burayda from his father [Burayda b. al-Husayb al-Aslamī], who said:

Whenever the Apostle of God sent forth an army or a detachment, he charged its commander personally to fear God, the Most High, and he enjoined the Muslims who were with him to do good [i.e., to conduct themselves properly].

And [the Apostle] said:

Fight in the name of God and in the "path of God" [i.e., truth]. Combat [only] those who disbelieve in God. Do not cheat or commit treachery, nor should you mutilate anyone or kill children. Whenever you meet your polytheist enemies, invite them [first] to adopt Islam. If they do so, accept it, and let them alone. You should then invite them to move from their territory to the territory of the *émigrés* [Madīna]. If they do so, accept it and let them alone. Otherwise, they should be informed that they would be [treated] like the Muslim nomads (Bedouins) [who take no part in the war] in that they are subject to God's orders as [other] Muslims, but that they will receive no share in either the ghanima (spoil of war) or in the fay'. If they refuse [to accept Islam], then call upon them to pay the jizya (poll tax); if they do, accept it and leave them alone. If you besiege the inhabitants of a fortress or a town and they try to get you to let them surrender on the basis of God's judgment, do not do so, since you do not know what God's judgment is, but make them surrender to your judgment and then decide their case according to your own views. But if the besieged inhabitants of a fortress or a town asked you to give them a pledge [of security] in God's name or in the name of His Apostle, you should not do so, but give the pledge in your names or in the names of your fathers; for, if you should ever break it, it would be an easier matter if it were in the names of you or your fathers.

2. Muhammad [b. al-Hasan] from Abū Yūsuf from [Muhammad b. al-Sā'ib] al-Kalbī from Abū Sālih [al-Sammān] from ['Abd-Allāh] b. 'Abbās [who said]:

The one-fifth [share of the spoil] was divided in the time of the Apostle of God into five parts: one for God and the Apostle, one for the near of kin, one for the poor, one for the orphans, and one for the wayfarer.

He [Ibn 'Abbās] said that [the Caliphs] Abū Bakr, 'Umar, 'Uthmān, and 'Alī divided [the one-fifth share] into three

Chapter II

ON THE CONDUCT OF THE ARMY IN ENEMY TERRITORY

[*General Rules*]

55. If the army [of Islam] attacks the territory of war and it is a territory that has received an invitation to accept Islam, it is commendable if the army renews the invitation, but if it fails to do so it is not wrong. The army may launch the attack [on the enemy] by night or by day and it is permissible to burn [the enemy] fortifications with fire or to inundate them with water. If [the army] captures any spoil of war, it should not be divided up in enemy territory

until [the Muslims] have brought it to a place of security and removed it to the territory of Islam.56.

Abū Yūsuf said: I asked Abū Hanīfa [his opinion] concerning the food and fodder that may be found in the spoil and whether a warrior in need may take from that spoil [before division] any of the food for himself and fodder for his mount.

57. He [Abū Hanīfa] replied: There is no harm in all that.

58. I asked: If there were weapons among the spoil, [do you hold that it would be permissible] for a Muslim [warrior] who needed a weapon with which to fight to take one without the permission of the Imām?

59. He replied: There is no harm in it, but he should return the weapon to the spoil after the battle is over.

60. I asked: Why have you held that it is permissible [for the warrior] to take food and fodder [from the spoil]?

61. He replied: Because a narrative from the Apostle of God has come to my knowledge to the effect that in [the campaign of] Khaybar the believers captured some food and ate from it before it was divided. Fodder falls in the same category as food, for both provide the strength necessary for the warrior [while fighting against the enemy].

62. I asked: Why do you hold that it is permissible [for the warrior] to take a weapon with which to fight?

63. He replied: Do you think that it would be objectionable if the unbelievers shot an arrow at one of the believers and the latter shot it back at the enemy, or if one of the unbelievers attacked a believer with a sword and the latter snatched it from him and struck him with it?

64. I said: No.

65. He said: The latter situation is similar to the former.

66. I asked: Do you think that it is objectionable for a person to take clothings and goods from the spoil for his own use before it is divided?

67. He replied: I disapprove of that for him.

68. I asked: If the believers were in need of clothing, animals, and goods, would it be incumbent on the Imām to divide the spoil among them before they returned to the territory of Islam (dār al-Islām)?

69. He replied: If they were [really] in need, it would be all right to divide it among them, but if they were not in need I should disapprove of dividing it.

70. I asked: Why?

71. He replied: Because [the believers] had not yet taken [the spoil] to a secure place so long as they remained in the territory of war (dār al-harb). Besides, do you not think that if another [Muslim] army entered the territory of war [and took part in the fighting] it would be entitled to participate in that spoil?

72. I asked: Do you think that the Imām should divide up the captives before the believers returned to the territory of Islam, if the believers need them?

73. He replied: No.

74. I asked: What should the Imām do with the captives, if the believers do not need them? Should he sell them?

75. He replied: If I held that it would be permissible for the Imām to sell them [before the believers returned to the territory of Islam], I should hold that it would be permissible for him to divide them up [there].

76. I asked: What should [the Imām] do about transporting them?

77. He replied: If [the Imām] possesses surplus means of transport he should use it to carry [the captives]; if there is none he should see if there is any surplus means among the Muslims. If he finds such means he should get them to carry it with them of their own free will.

78. I asked: If neither the Imām nor the Muslims possess surplus means of transport but some [private] individuals among them [have their own means], should the Imām cause the spoil to be transported on the animals belonging to those particular persons?

79. He replied: Yes, provided those persons are willing to do so. Otherwise, the Imām should hire means of transport rather than force the owners of private means to carry the spoil. As to the captives, the Imām should oblige them to go on foot if they are able to do so.

80. I asked: And if they are unable to walk?

81. He replied: He [the Imām] should kill the men and spare the women and children, for whom he should hire means for carrying them.

Muhammad [b. al-Hasan] held that it would be permissible to the Imām [in these circumstances] to divide the spoil in the territory of war, since the jurists have disagreed on the matter.

82. I asked: If the believers in the territory of war capture spoil in which there are [animals such as] sheep, riding animals, and cows which resist them and they are unable to drive them to the territory of Islam, or weapons which they are unable to carry away, what should they do [with them]?

83. He replied: As to weapons and goods, they should be burned, but riding animals and sheep should be slaughtered and then burned.

84. I asked: Why should not [the animals] be hamstrung?

85. He replied: Because that is mutilation, which they should not do because it was prohibited by the Apostle of God. However, they should not leave anything that the inhabitants of the territory of war could make use of.

86. I asked: Do you think that they should do the same with whatever [other] animals refuse to be driven away or with whatever weapons and goods are too heavy to carry?

87. He replied: Yes.

88. I asked: Do you think that it is objectionable for the believers to destroy whatever towns of the territory of war that they may encounter?

89. He replied: No. Rather do I hold that this would be commendable. For do you not think that it is in accordance with God's saying, in His Book: "Whatever palm trees you have cut down or left standing upon their roots, has been by God's permission, in order that the ungodly ones might be

humiliated." So, I am in favor of whatever they did to deceive and anger the enemy.

90. I asked: If the Imām attacked an enemy territory and took possession of it, do you think that he should divide the land [among the warriors] as he divides the spoil of war?

91. He replied: The Imām is free either to divide the land into five shares, distributing the four-fifths among the warriors who participated in conquering it, or not to divide it up [i.e., hold it as state-owned land] as [the Caliph] 'Umar did in [the case of] the land of al-Sawād [of southern 'Irāq].

92. I asked: Should [the Imām] leave it [immobilized] while its inhabitants paid the kharāj?

93. He replied: Yes. So it was related to us that 'Umar b. al-Khaṭṭāb did. But God knows best!

The Killing of Captives and the Destruction of Enemy Fortifications

94. I asked: If male captives of war were taken from the territory of war, do you think that the Imām should kill them all or divide them as slaves among the Muslims?

95. He replied: The Imām is entitled to a choice between taking them to the territory of Islam to be divided [among the warriors] and killing them [while in the territory of war].

96. I asked: Which is preferable?

97. He replied: [The Imām] should examine the situation and decide whatever he deems to be advantageous to the Muslims.

98. I asked: If killing them were advantageous to the Muslims, [do you think that the Imām] should order their killing?

99. He replied: Yes.

100. I asked: If all of them became Muslims, would he be entitled to kill them?

101. He replied: He should not kill them if they became Muslims; they should be regarded as booty to be divided among the Muslims.

102. I asked: If they did not become Muslims, but they claimed that they had been given a safe-conduct

and a few Muslims declared that they had given such a pledge to them, would such a claim be accepted?

103. He replied: No.

104. I asked: Why?

105. He replied: Because both [merely] stated their own claim.

106. I asked: If a group of Muslims known to be of just character testified that a safe-conduct had been given by a party of warriors to the prisoners of war who were still capable of resistance [in a fortification before their surrender], would that testimony be valid?

107. He replied: Yes.

108. I asked: Would the prisoners of war be set free?

109. He replied: Yes.

110. I asked: Do you think that the blind, the crippled, the helpless insane, if taken as prisoners of war or captured by the warriors in a surprise attack, would be killed?

111. He replied: [No], they should not be killed.

112. I asked: Would it be permissible to inundate a city in the territory of war with water, to burn it with fire, or to attack [its people] with mangonels even though there may be slaves, women, old men, and children in it?

113. He applied: Yes, I would approve of doing all of that to them.

114. I asked: Would the same be true if those people have among them Muslim prisoners of war or Muslim merchants?

115. He replied: Yes, even if they had among them [Muslims], there would be no harm to do all of that to them.[34]

116. I asked: Why?

117. He replied: If the Muslims stopped attacking the inhabitants of the territory of war for any of the reasons that you have stated, they would be unable to go to war at all, for there is no city in the territory of war in which there is no one at all of these you have mentioned.

118. I asked: If the Muslims besieged a city, and its people [in their defense] from behind the walls

shielded themselves with Muslim children, would it be permissible for the Muslim [warriors] to attack them with arrows and mangonels?

119. He replied: Yes, but the warriors should aim at the inhabitants of the territory of war and not the Muslim children.[35]

120. I asked: Would it be permissible for the Muslims to attack them with swords and lances if the children were not intentionally aimed at?

121. He replied: Yes.

122. I asked: If the Muslim [warriors] attack [a place] with mangonels and arrows, flood it with water, and burn it with fire, thereby killing or wounding Muslim children or men, or enemy women, old men, blind, crippled, or lunatic persons, would the [Muslim warriors] be liable for the diya (blood money) or the kaffāra (expiation or atonement)?

123. He replied: They would be liable neither for the diya nor for the kaffāra.

Penalties in the Territory of War and the Shortening of Prayer

124. I asked: If a [Muslim] army entered the territory of war led by a commander, do you think he would be [competent] to enforce the religious penalties (hudūd) in his army camp?

125. He replied: No.

126. I asked: If the governor of a city or a province, such as al-Shām or 'Irāq, entered the territory of war at the head of an army, would he be [competent] to impose religious penalties or retaliation in his army camp?

127. He replied: Yes.

128. I asked: Would he be [competent] to order the cutting off of the hand for theft and enforce the penalty for false accusation (qadhf)?

129. He replied: Yes.

130. I asked: And [also] to enforce the penalties for zina (adultery or fornication) and [the drinking of] wine?

131. He replied. Yes.

132. I asked: If there was at the head of the army a commander—not the governor of al-Shām or 'Irāq—and [the army] was four or five thousand

strong, would he be [competent] to enforce any of the [religious penalties] stated above?

133. He replied: No.

134. I asked: Would the same be true for the commanders of detachments, that they are [incompetent] to enforce penalties?

135. He replied: Yes [that is right].

136. I asked: If the governor of al-Shām or 'Irāq were at the head of a large army laying siege to a city for over a month, should he celebrate [the conquest] in the Friday prayer or perform them in their complete form?

137. He replied: He is [under obligation] neither to celebrate Friday prayer nor to perform them completely, because he is on travel status.

138. I asked: If a group of Muslims desired to attack the territory of war but did not have the [sufficient] force or the finances to do so, do you not think that it would be lawful for them to help each other and the ones who would not go forth to battle to contribute [supplies] to those who take the field?

139. He replied: It would be lawful to do so in such a situation; but if the Imām had the wherewithal and the Muslim had the forces, I would neither approve of it nor should I permit it. However, if the Imām lacked the means, it would be lawful [for some to contribute to others who take the field].

140. I asked: Which [act] is more commendable to you: guarding [i.e., to act as sentinel] or performing a supererogatory prayer?

141. He replied: If sentineling were sufficiently provided for, performance of the [supererogatory] prayer would be the more commendable to me; but if those who act as sentinels were not sufficient, then the performance of guarding would be the more commendable.

142. I asked: If a [Muslim] warrior is run through by a lance, would you disapprove if he advances—though the lance be piercing him—in order to kill his adversary with the sword?

143. He replied: No.

144. I asked: Do you not think that he helped against his own life by so doing [i.e., that he committed suicide, which is forbidden]?

145. He replied: No.

146. I asked: If a group were on board a ship that was set on fire, do you think that it would be more commendable if they resigned themselves to being burned to death or if they threw themselves into the sea?

147. He replied: Either one of the two [courses] would be permissible.

Think about it.

1. How does al-Shaybani present rules of conduct? Why doesn't he simply express his own opinion directly?
2. What restrictions are placed on the Muslim army in their treatment of non-Muslims?
3. What are the Muslim soldiers permitted to do?

---

c. 9ᵗʰ–10ᵗʰ century CE

81. One Thousand and One Nights

Translated by Richard F. Burton

Also known as the *Arabian Nights*, *The One Thousand and One Nights* is a collection of folk tales from Western and Southern Asia in an Islamic cultural setting. The work has a long evolutionary history. The oldest stories come from Persia and India, and they were translated into Arabic in the 8th century under the title *The Thousand Nights*. Then, in the 9th and 10th centuries, Arabic tales were added, and the work was called *The Book of the Tale of the Thousand Nights*. By the 12th century, it was called *The One Thousand and One Nights*. Syrian and Egyptian stories were brought in during and after the 13th century until the early modern period, when the number of tales did indeed reach 1,001. Several versions of the text exist, and not all contain the same stories. The first European version was in French and was published in the early 18th century. It contained many stories that were not in any of the earlier versions. Reproduced here is one of the early Arabic tales (9th–10th centuries) featuring a historical figure, the Caliph Harun al-Rashid, who ruled the Abassid Caliphate from 786 to 809. The story, however, is not historical.

THE LOVERS OF BASSORAH.

The Caliph Harun al-Rashid was sleepless one night; so he sent for Al-Asma'i and Husayn al-Khalí'a and said to them, "Tell me a story you two, and do begin, O Husayn." He said, "'Tis well, O Commander of the Faithful;" and thus began: Some years ago, I dropped down stream to Bassorah, to present to Mohammed bin Sulayman al-Rabí'ía Kasidah or elegy I had composed in his praise; and he accepted it and bade me abide with him. One day, I went out to Al-Mirbad, by way of Al-Muháliyah; and, being oppressed by the excessive heat, went up to a great door, to ask for drink, when I was suddenly aware of a damsel, as she were a branch swaying, with eyes languishing, eye brows arched and finely pencilled and smooth cheeks rounded clad in a shift the colour of a pomegranate flower, and a mantilla of Sana'á work; but the perfect whiteness of her body overcame the redness of her shift, through which glittered two breasts like twin granadoes and a waist, as it were a roll of fine Coptic linen, with creases like scrolls of pure white paper stuffed with musk Moreover, O Prince of True Believers, round her neck was slung an amulet of red gold that fell down between her breasts, and on the plain of her forehead were browlocks like jet. Her eyebrows joined and her eyes were like lakes; she had an aquiline nose and thereunder shell-like lips showing teeth like pearls. Pleasantness prevailed in every part of her; but she seemed dejected, disturbed, distracted and in the vestibule came and went, walking upon the hearts of her lovers, while her legs made mute the voices of their ankle rings; and indeed she was as says the poet, "Each portion of her charms we see / Seems of the whole a simile."

I was overawed by her, O Commander of the Faithful, and drew near her to greet her, and behold, the house and vestibule and highways breathed fragrant with musk. So I saluted her and she returned my salaam with a voice dejected and heart depressed and with the ardour of passion consumed. Then said I to her, "O my lady, I am an old man and a stranger and sore troubled by thirst. Will you order me a draught of water, and win reward in heaven?" She cried, "Away, O Shaykh, from me! I am distracted from all thought of meat and drink." … Said I, "By what ailment, O my lady?" and said she, "I love one who deals not justly by me, and I desire one who of me will have none. Wherefore I am afflicted with the wakefulness of those who wake star gazing." I asked, "O my lady, is there on the wide expanse of earth one to whom you have a mind and who to you has no mind?" Answered she, "Yes; and this for the perfection of beauty and loveliness and goodliness wherewith he is endowed." "And why do you stand in this porch?" inquired I. "This is his road," replied she, "and the hour of his passing by." I said, "O my lady, have you ever foregathered and had such commerce and converse as might cause this passion?" At this she heaved a deep sigh; the tears rained down her cheeks, as they were dew falling upon roses, and she versified with these couplets,

> "We were like willow boughs in garden shining / And scented joys in happiest life combining;
> When as one bough from other self would rend / And oh! thou seest this for that repining!"

Said I, "O maid, and what betides you of your love for this man?"; and said she, "I see the sun upon the walls of his folk, and I think the sun is he; or haply I catch sight of him unexpectedly and am confounded, and the blood and the life fly my body, and I abide in unreasoning plight a week or even week more." Said I, "Excuse me, for I also have suffered that which is upon you of love longing and distraction of soul and wasting of frame and loss of strength; and I see in you pallor of complexion and emaciation, such as testify of the fever fits of desire. But how should you be unsmitten of passion and a sojourner in the land of Bassorah?" Said she, "By Allah, before I fell in love of this youth, I was perfect in beauty and loveliness and amorous grace which ravished all the Princes of Bassorah, till he fell in love with me." I asked, "O maid, and who parted you?"; and she answered, "The vicissitudes of fortune, but the manner of our separation was strange; and 'twas on this wise. One New Year's day I had invited the damsels of Bassorah and amongst them a girl belonging to Siran, who had bought her out of Oman for four score thousand dirhams. She loved me and loved me to madness and when she entered she threw herself upon me and well nigh tore me in pieces with bites and pinches. Then we withdrew apart, to drink wine at our ease, till our meat was ready and our delight was complete, and she toyed with me and I with her, and now I was upon her and now she was upon me. Presently, the fumes of the wine moved her to strike her hand on the inkle of my petticoat trousers, whereby it became loosed, unknown of either of us, and my trousers fell down in our play. At this moment he came in unobserved and, seeing me thus, was angry at the sight and made off, as the Arab filly hearing the tinkle of her bridle. …And 'tis now, O Shaykh, three years ago, and since then I have never ceased to excuse myself to him and coax him and crave his indulgence, but he will neither cast a look at me from the corner of his eye, nor write me a word nor speak to me by messenger nor hear from me aught."

Said I, "Listen maid, is he an Arab or an Ajam?[1]"; and said she, "Out on you! He is of the Princes of Bassorah." "Is he old or young?" asked I; and she looked at me laughingly and answered, "You are certainly a simpleton! He is like the moon on the night of its full, smooth checked and beardless, nor is there any defect in him except his aversion to me." Then I put the question, "What is his name?" and she replied, "What will you do with him?" I rejoined, "I will do my best to come at him, that I may bring about a reunion between you." Said she, "I will tell you on condition that you carry him a note;" and I said "I have no objection to that." Then said she, "His name is Zamrah bin al-Mughayrah, hight Abú al-Sakhá, and his palace is in the Mirbad." Therewith

she called to those within for inkcase and paper and tucking up her sleeves, showed two wrists like broad rings of silver. She then wrote after the Basmalah as follows:

"My lord, the omission of blessings at the head of this letter shows my insufficiency, and know that had my prayer been answered, you would had never left me; for how often have I prayed that you should not leave me, and yet you did leave me! Were it not for the fact that distress with me exceeds the bounds of restraint, that which your servant has forced herself to do in writing this writ were an aidance to her, despite her despair of you, because of her knowledge of you that you will fail to answer. Do fulfill her desire, my lord, of a sight of you from the porch, as you pass in the street, wherewith you will preserve the dead soul in her. Or, far better for her still than this, write her a letter with your own hand (Allah endow it with all excellence!), and appoint it in requital of the intimacy that was between us in the nights of time past, whereof you must preserve the memory. My lord, was I not to you a lover sick with passion? And if you answer my prayer, I will give to you thanks and to Allah praise; and so The Peace!"

Then she gave me the letter and I went away. Next morning I repaired to the door of the Viceroy Mohammed bin Sulayman, where I found an assembly of the notables of Bassorah, and amongst them a youth who adorned the gathering and surpassed in beauty and brightness all who were there; and indeed the Emir Mohammed set him above himself. I asked who he was and behold, it was Zamrah himself: so I said in my mind, "Truly there has befallen yonder unhappy one that which has befallen her." Then I betook myself to the Mirbad and stood waiting at the door of his house, till he came riding up in state, when I accosted him and invoking more than usual blessings on him, handed him the missive. When he read it and understood it, he said to me, "O Shaykh, we have taken another in her stead. Say, will you see the substitute?" I answered, "Yes." Whereupon he called out a woman's name, and there came forth a damsel who shamed the two greater lights; swelling

---

1   Non-Arab.

breasted, walking the gait of one who hastens without fear, to whom he gave the note, saying, "Answer it." When she read it, she turned pale at the contents and said to me, "O old man, crave pardon of Allah for this that you have brought."

So I went out, O Commander of the Faithful, dragging my feet and returning to her asked leave to enter. When she saw me, she asked, "What is behind you?"; and I answered, "Evil and despair." Said she, "Have no concern of him. Where are Allah and His power?" Then she ordered me five hundred dinars, and I took them and went away.

Some days after I passed by the place and saw there horsemen and footmen. So I went in and lo! these were the companions of Zamrah, who were begging her to return to him; but she said, "No, by Allah, I will not look him in the face!" And she prostrated herself in gratitude to Allah and exultation over Zamrah's defeat. Then I drew near her, and she pulled out to me a letter, wherein was written, after the Bismillah, "My lady, but for my forbearance towards you (whose life Allah lengthen!) I would relate somewhat of what betided from you and set out my excuse, in that you transgressed against me, when as you were manifestly a sinner against yourself and me in breach of vows and lack of constancy and preference of another over us; for, by Allah, on whom we call for help against that which was of your free will, you did transgress against the love of me; and so The Peace!" Then she showed me the presents and rarities he had sent her, which were of the value of thirty thousand dinars. I saw her again after this, and Zamrah had married her. Said Al-Rashid, "Had not Zamrah been beforehand with us, I should certainly have had to do with her myself."

Think about it.

1. What did the damsel do that upset her love interest?
2. From the storyteller's point of view, what is commendable about the damsel?

82. The Life of Charlemagne

Translated by Samuel E. Turner

The Life of Charlemagne (*Vita Karoli Magni*), which recounts the life of Frankish king Charlemagne (r. 774–814), is generally considered the first European biography. It was written by Einhard (c. 775–840) at some time between 817 and 833. Einhard had worked under Charlemagne as a minister of public works, so he was intimately familiar with the king. The biography was written in Latin in the Roman style. The following selections provide an interesting view of Charlemagne as a man.

18. Private Life

Thus did Charles defend and increase as well, as beautify his, kingdom, as is well known; and here let me express my admiration of his great qualities and his extraordinary constancy alike in good and evil fortune. I will now forthwith proceed to give the details of his private and family life.

After his father's death, while sharing the kingdom with his brother, he bore his unfriendliness and jealousy most patiently, and, to the wonder of all, could not be provoked to be angry with him. Later he married a daughter of Desiderius, King of the Lombards, at the instance of his mother; but he repudiated her at the end of a year for some reason unknown, and married Hildegard, a woman of high birth, of Suabian origin. He had three sons by her—Charles, Pepin and Louis—and as many daughters—Hruodrud, Bertha, and Gisela. He had three other daughters besides these—Theoderada, Hiltrud, and Ruodhaid—two by his third wife, Fastrada, a woman of East Frankish (that is to say, of German) origin, and the third by a concubine, whose name for the moment escapes me. At the death of Fastrada [794], he married Liutgard, an Alemannic woman, who bore him no children. After her death [Jun 4, 800] he had three concubines—Gersuinda, a Saxon by whom he had Adaltrud; Regina, who was the mother of Drogo and Hugh; and Ethelind, by whom he lead Theodoric. Charles' mother, Berthrada, passed her old age with him in great honor; he entertained the greatest veneration for her; and there was never any disagreement between them except when he divorced the daughter of King Desiderius, whom he had married to please her. She died soon after Hildegard, after living to three grandsons and as many granddaughters in her son's house, and he buried her with great pomp in the Basilica of St. Denis, where his father lay. He had an only sister, Gisela, who had consecrated herself to a religious life from girlhood, and he cherished as much affection for her as for his mother. She also died a few years before him in the nunnery where she passed her life.

19. Private Life (continued) [Charles and the Education of His Children]

The plan that he adopted for his children's education was, first of all, to have both boys and girls

Einhard, *The Life of Charlemagne*, trans. Samuel E. Turner. Harper & Brothers, 1880. Copyright in the Public Domain.

instructed in the liberal arts, to which he also turned his own attention. As soon as their years admitted, in accordance with the custom of the Franks, the boys had to learn horsemanship, and to practise war and the chase, and the girls to familiarize themselves with cloth-making, and to handle distaff and spindle, that they might not grow indolent through idleness, and he fostered in them every virtuous sentiment. He only lost three of all his children before his death, two sons and one daughter, Charles, who was the eldest, Pepin, whom he had made King of Italy, and Hruodrud, his oldest daughter, whom he had betrothed to Constantine [VI, 780–802], Emperor of the Greeks. Pepin left one son, named Bernard, and five daughters, Adelaide, Atula, Guntrada, Berthaid and Theoderada. The King gave a striking proof of his fatherly affection at the time of Pepin's death [810]: he appointed the grandson to succeed Pepin, and had the granddaughters brought up with his own daughters. When his sons and his daughter died, he was not so calm as might have been expected from his remarkably strong mind, for his affections were no less strong, and moved him to tears. Again, when he was told of the death of Hadrian [796], the Roman Pontiff, whom he had loved most of all his friends, he wept as much as if he had lost a brother, or a very dear son. He was by nature most ready to contract friendships, and not only made friends easily, but clung to them persistently, and cherished most fondly those with whom he had formed such ties. He was so careful of the training of his sons and daughters that he never took his meals without them when he was at home, and never made a journey without them; his sons would ride at his side, and his daughters follow him, while a number of his body-guard, detailed for their protection, brought up the rear. Strange to say, although they were very handsome women, and he loved them very dearly, he was never willing to marry any of them to a man of their own nation or to a foreigner, but kept them all at home until his death, saying that he could not dispense with their society. Hence, though otherwise happy, he experienced the malignity of fortune as far as they were concerned; yet he concealed his knowledge of the rumors current in regard to them, and of the suspicions entertained of their honor.

20. Conspiracies Against Charlemagne

By one of his concubines he had a son, handsome in face, but hunchbacked, named Pepin, whom I omitted to mention in the list of his children. When Charles was at war with the Huns, and was wintering in Bavaria [792], this Pepin shammed sickness, and plotted against his father in company with some of the leading Franks, who seduced him with vain promises of the royal authority. When his deceit was discovered, and the conspirators were punished, his head was shaved, and he was suffered, in accordance with his wishes, to devote himself to a religious life in the monastery of Prüm. A formidable conspiracy against Charles had previously been set on foot in Germany, but all the traitors were banished, some of them without mutilation, others after their eyes had been put out. Three of them only lost their lives; they drew their swords and resisted arrest, and, after killing several men, were cut down, because they could not be otherwise overpowered. It is supposed that the cruelty of Queen Fastrada was the primary cause of these plots, and they were both due to Charles' apparent acquiescence in his wife's cruel conduct, and deviation from the usual kindness and gentleness of his disposition. All the rest of his life he was regarded by everyone with the utmost love and affection, so much so that not the least accusation of unjust rigor was ever made against him.

21. Charlemagne's Treatment of Foreigners

He liked foreigners, and was at great pains to take them under his protection. There were often so many of them, both in the palace and the kingdom, that they might reasonably have been considered a nuisance; but he, with his broad humanity, was very little disturbed by such annoyances, because he felt himself compensated for these great inconveniences by the praises of his generosity and the reward of high renown.

22. Personal Appearance

Charles was large and strong, and of lofty stature, though not disproportionately tall (his height is well known to have been seven times the length of his foot); the upper part of his head was round, his eyes very large and animated, nose a little long, hair fair, and face laughing and merry. Thus his appearance was always stately and dignified, whether he was standing or sitting; although his neck was thick and somewhat short, and his belly rather prominent; but the symmetry of the rest of his body concealed these defects. His gait was firm, his whole carriage manly, and his voice clear, but not so strong as his size led one to expect. His health was excellent, except during the four years preceding his death, when he was subject to frequent fevers; at the last he even limped a little with one foot. Even in those years he consulted rather his own inclinations than the advice of physicians, who were almost hateful to him, because they wanted him to give up roasts, to which he was accustomed, and to eat boiled meat instead. In accordance with the national custom, he took frequent exercise on horseback and in the chase, accomplishments in which scarcely any people in the world can equal the Franks. He enjoyed the exhalations from natural warm springs, and often practised swimming, in which he was such an adept that none could surpass him; and hence it was that he built his palace at Aix-la-Chapelle, and lived there constantly during his latter years until his death. He used not only to invite his sons to his bath, but his nobles and friends, and now and then a troop of his retinue or body guard, so that a hundred or more persons sometimes bathed with him.

23. Dress

He used to wear the national, that is to say, the Frank, dress next his skin a linen shirt and linen breeches, and above these a tunic fringed with silk; while hose fastened by bands covered his lower limbs, and shoes his feet, and he protected his shoulders and chest in winter by a close-fitting coat of otter or marten skins. Over all he flung a blue cloak, and he always had a sword girt about him, usually one with a gold or silver hilt and belt; he sometimes carried a jewelled sword, but only on great feast-days or at the reception of ambassadors from foreign nations. He despised foreign costumes, however handsome, and never allowed himself to be robed in them, except twice in Rome, when he donned the Roman tunic, chlamys, and shoes; the first time at the request of Pope Hadrian, the second to gratify Leo, Hadrian's successor. On great feast-days he made use of embroidered clothes, and shoes bedecked with precious stones; his cloak was fastened by a golden buckle, and he appeared crowned with a diadem of gold and gems: but on other days his dress varied little from the common dress of the people.

24. Habits

Charles was temperate in eating, and particularly so in drinking, for he abominated drunkenness in anybody, much more in himself and those of his household; but he could not easily abstain from food, and often complained that fasts injured his health. He very rarely gave entertainments, only on great feast-days, and then to large numbers of people. His meals ordinarily consisted of four courses, not counting the roast, which his huntsmen used to bring in on the spit; he was more fond of this than of any other dish. While at table, he listened to reading or music. The subjects of the readings were the stories and deeds of olden time: he was fond, too, of St. Augustine's books, and especially of the one entitled "The City of God."

He was so moderate in the use of wine and all sorts of drink that he rarely allowed himself more than three cups in the course of a meal. In summer after the midday meal, he would eat some fruit, drain a single cup, put off his clothes and shoes, just as he did for the night, and rest for two or three hours. He was in the habit of awaking and rising from bed four or five times during the night. While he was dressing and putting on his shoes, he not only gave audience to his friends, but if the Count of the Palace told him of any suit in which his judgment was necessary, he had the parties brought before him forthwith, took cognizance of the case, and gave his decision, just as if he were sitting on the Judgment-seat. This was not the only business that he transacted at this time, but he performed any duty of the day whatever, whether he had to attend to the matter himself, or to give commands concerning it to his officers.

25. Studies

Charles had the gift of ready and fluent speech, and could express whatever he had to say with the utmost clearness. He was not satisfied with command of his native language merely, but gave attention to the study of foreign ones, and in particular was such a master of Latin that he could speak it as well as his native tongue; but he could understand Greek better than he could speak it. He was so eloquent, indeed, that he might have passed for a teacher of eloquence. He most zealously cultivated the liberal arts, held those who taught them in great esteem, and conferred great honors upon them. He took lessons in grammar of the deacon Peter of Pisa, at that time an aged man. Another deacon, Albin of Britain, surnamed Alcuin, a man of Saxon extraction, who was the greatest scholar of the day, was his teacher in other branches of learning. The King spent much time and labour with him studying rhetoric, dialectics, and especially astronomy; he learned to reckon, and used to investigate the motions of the heavenly bodies most curiously, with an intelligent scrutiny. He also tried to write, and used to keep tablets and blanks in bed under his pillow, that at leisure hours he might accustom his hand to form the letters; however, as he did not begin his efforts in due season, but late in life, they met with ill success.

26. Piety

He cherished with the greatest fervor and devotion the principles of the Christian religion, which had been instilled into him from infancy. Hence it was that he built the beautiful basilica at Aix-la-Chapelle, which he adorned with gold and silver and lamps, and with rails and doors of solid brass. He had the columns and marbles for this structure brought from Rome and Ravenna, for he could not find such as were suitable elsewhere. He was a constant worshipper at this church as long as his health permitted, going morning and evening, even after nightfall, besides attending mass; and he took care that all the services there conducted should be administered with the utmost possible propriety, very often warning the sextons not to let any improper or unclean thing be brought into the building or remain in it. He provided it with a great number of sacred vessels of gold and silver and with such a quantity of clerical robes that not even the doorkeepers who fill the humblest office in the church were obliged to wear their everyday clothes when in the exercise of their duties. He was at great pains to improve the church reading and psalmody, for he was well skilled in both although he neither read in public nor sang, except in a low tone and with others.

27. Generosity [Charles and the Roman Church]

He was very forward in succoring the poor, and in that gratuitous generosity which the Greeks call alms, so much so that he not only made a point of giving in his own country and his own kingdom, but when he discovered that there were Christians living in poverty in Syria, Egypt, and Africa, at Jerusalem, Alexandria, and Carthage, he had compassion on their wants, and used to send money over the seas to them. The reason that he zealously strove to make friends with the kings beyond seas was that he might get help and relief to the Christians living under their rule.

He cherished the Church of St. Peter the Apostle at Rome above all other holy and sacred places, and heaped its treasury with a vast wealth of gold, silver, and precious stones. He sent great and countless gifts to the popes; and throughout his whole reign the wish that he had nearest at heart was to re-establish the ancient authority of the city of Rome under his care and by his influence, and to defend and protect the Church of St. Peter, and to beautify and enrich it out of his own store above all other churches. Although he held it in such veneration, he only repaired to Rome to pay his vows and make his supplications four times during the whole forty-seven years that he reigned.

28. Charlemagne Crowned Emperor

When he made his last journey thither, he also had other ends in view. The Romans had inflicted many injuries upon the Pontiff Leo, tearing out his eyes and cutting out his tongue, so that he had been complied to call upon the King for help [Nov 24, 800]. Charles accordingly went to Rome, to set in order the affairs of the Church, which were in great confusion, and passed the whole winter there. It was then that he received the titles of Emperor and Augustus [Dec 25, 800], to which he at first had such an aversion that he declared that he would not have set foot in the Church the day that they were conferred, although it was a great feast-day, if he could have foreseen the design of the Pope. He bore very patiently with the jealousy which the Roman emperors showed upon his assuming these titles, for they took this step very ill; and by dint of frequent embassies and letters, in which he addressed them as brothers, he made their haughtiness yield to his magnanimity, a quality in which he was unquestionably much their superior.

29. Reforms

It was after he had received the imperial name that, finding the laws of his people very defective (the Franks have two sets of laws, very different in many particulars), he determined to add what was wanting, to reconcile the discrepancies, and to correct what was vicious and wrongly cited in them. However, he went no further in this matter than to supplement the laws by a few capitularies, and those imperfect ones; but he caused the unwritten laws of all the tribes that came under his rule to be compiled and reduced to writing. He also had the old rude songs that celebrate the deeds and wars of the ancient kings written out for transmission to posterity. He began a grammar of his native language. He gave the months names in his own tongue, in place of the Latin and barbarous names by which they were formerly known among the Franks. He likewise designated the winds by twelve appropriate names; there were hardly more than four distinctive ones in use before. He called January, Wintarmanoth; February, Hornung; March, Lentzinmanoth; April, Ostarmanoth; May, Winnemanoth; June, Brachmanoth; July, Heuvimanoth; August, Aranmanoth; September, Witumanoth; October, Windumemanoth; November, Herbistmanoth; December, Heilagmanoth. He styled the winds as follows; Subsolanus, Ostroniwint; Eurus, Ostsundroni; Euroauster, Sundostroni; Auster, Sundroni; Austro-Africus, Sundwestroni; Africus, Westsundroni; Zephyrus, Westroni; Caurus, Westnordroni; Circius, Nordwestroni; Septentrio, Nordroni; Aquilo, Nordostroni; Vulturnus, Ostnordroni.

Think about it.

1. What aspects of Charlemagne's personality and customs does Einhard find praiseworthy?
2. Do you see evidence of bias in the writing? Where?

83. Hávamál

Translated by Olive Bray

Hávamál is an Old Norse poem providing practical wisdom for daily living. The poem, which actually is a combination of verses from various sources dating between the 10th and 13th centuries, was traditionally attributed to the Norse god Odin. It was found in the collection known as the Poetic Edda preserved in an Icelandic manuscript written in the 1270s. Here are some excerpts.

61. Fed and washed should one ride to court though in garments none too new; thou shalt not shame thee for shoes or breeks, nor yet for a sorry steed.

62.   Like an eagle swooping over old ocean, snatching after his prey, so comes a man into court who finds there are few to defend his cause.

63. Each man who is wise and would wise be called must ask and answer aright. Let one know thy secret, but never a second,—if three a thousand shall know.

64. A wise counselled man will be mild in bearing and use his might in measure, lest when he come his fierce foes among he find others fiercer than he.

65. Each man should be watchful and wary in speech, and slow to put faith in a friend, for the words which one to another speaks he may win reward of ill.

66. At many a feast I was far too late, and much too soon at some; drunk was the ale or yet unserved: never hits he the joint who is hated.

67. Here and there to a home I had haply been asked had I needed no meat at my meals, or were two hams left hanging in the house of that friend where I had partaken of one.

68. Most dear is fire to the sons of men, most sweet the sight of the sun; good is health if one can but keep it, and to live a life without shame.

69. Not reft of all is he who is ill, for some are blest in their bairns, some in their kin and some in their wealth, and some in working well.

70. More blest are the living than the lifeless, 'tis the living who come by the cow; I saw the hearth-fire burn in the rich man's hall and himself lying dead at the door.

71. The lame can ride horse, the handless drive cattle, the deaf one can fight and prevail, 'tis happier for the blind than for him on the bale-fire, but no man hath care for a corpse.

72. Best have a son though he be late born and before him the father be dead: seldom are stones on the wayside raised save by kinsmen to kinsmen.

73. Two are hosts against one, the tongue is the head's bane, 'neath a rough hide a hand may be hid; he is glad at nightfall who knows of his lodging, short is the ship's berth, and changeful the autumn

Selection from: "Hávamál: The Words of Odin the High One," *The Elder or Poetic Edda, Part I: The Mythological Poems*, trans. Olive Bray. AMS Press, Inc., 1908. Copyright in the Public Domain.

night, much veers the wind ere the fifth day and blows round yet more in a month.

74. He that learns nought will never know how one is the fool of another, for if one be rich another is poor and for that should bear no blame.

75. Cattle die and kinsmen die, thyself too soon must die, but one thing never, I ween, will die,— fair fame of one who has earned.

76. Cattle die and kinsmen die, thyself too soon must die, but one thing never, I ween, will die,— the doom on each one dead.

77. Full-stocked folds had the Fatling's sons, who bear now a beggar's staff: brief is wealth, as the winking of an eye, most faithless ever of friends.

78. If haply a fool should find for himself wealth or a woman's love, pride waxes in him but wisdom never and onward he fares in his folly.

79. All will prove true that thou askest of runes— those that are come from the gods, which the high Powers wrought, and which Odin painted: then silence is surely best.

Maxims for All Men

80. Praise day at even, a wife when dead, a weapon when tried, a maid when married, ice when 'tis crossed, and ale when 'tis drunk.

81. Hew wood in wind, sail the seas in a breeze, woo a maid in the dark,—for day's eyes are many,—work a ship for its gliding, a shield for its shelter, a sword for its striking, a maid for her kiss;

82. Drink ale by the fire, but slide on the ice; buy a steed when 'tis lanky, a sword when 'tis rusty; feed thy horse neath a roof, and thy hound in the yard.

83. The speech of a maiden should no man trust nor the words which a woman says; for their hearts were shaped on a whirling wheel and falsehood fixed in their breasts.

84. Breaking bow, or flaring flame, ravening wolf, or croaking raven, routing swine, or rootless tree, waxing wave, or seething cauldron,

85. flying arrows, or falling billow, ice of a night-time, coiling adder, woman's bed-talk, or broken blade, play of bears or a prince's child,

86. sickly calf or self-willed thrall, witch's flattery, new-slain foe, brother's slayer, though seen on the highway, half burned house, or horse too swift—be never so trustful as these to trust.

87. Let none put faith in the first sown fruit nor yet in his son too soon; whim rules the child, and weather the field, each is open to chance.

88. Like the love of women whose thoughts are lies is the driving un-roughshod o'er slippery ice of a two year old, ill-tamed and gay; or in a wild wind steering a helmless ship, or the lame catching reindeer in the rime-thawed fell.

Lessons for Lovers

89. Now plainly I speak, since both I have seen; unfaithful is man to maid; we speak them fairest when thoughts are falsest and wile the wisest of hearts.

90. —Let him speak soft words and offer wealth who longs for a woman's love, praise the shape of the shining maid—he wins who thus doth woo.

91. —Never a whit should one blame another whom love hath brought into bonds: oft a witching form will fetch the wise which holds not the heart of fools.

92. Never a whit should one blame another for a folly which many befalls; the might of love makes sons of men into fools who once were wise.

93. The mind knows alone what is nearest the heart and sees where the soul is turned: no sickness seems to the wise so sore as in nought to know content.

1058 CE

84. Memorial of a Myriad Words

Translated by Henry R. Williamson

The "Memorial of a Myriad Words" is a lengthy letter (not quite 10,000 words) written to the Chinese emperor Renzong (r. 1022–1063) of the Song Dynasty by Wang Anshi (1021–1086). At the time of the writing of the letter in 1058, Wang had been serving as a regional official for some time. He saw problems in the way the government was run and in the letter urges the emperor to make some changes. Some years later, Wang will be appointed chancellor to the emperor Shenzong (r. 1067–1085) and will have the opportunity to realize his ideas of reform. The letter, an extract of which is provided below, gives a preview of some of the things Wang had in mind.

I implore your Majesty to note the reason for the fall of Han and T'ang and the confusion and decadence of the Five Dynasties, and to take warning from the calamity which overtook Jin Wu Di for his negligence and *laissez-faire* policy.

I trust too that you will make it quite clear to your ministers that they should take steps to ensure the production of capable men, and that they may make such plans for this object as may be gradually carried into effect, seeking to adapt them to present circumstances, without doing violence to the principles of the ancient rulers. If such plans are made

and rendered effective, the capable men will be more numerous than can be employed; you will have no desire which cannot be fulfilled, and there will be nothing that you cannot accomplish.

When I first began to study Mencius, and read that he said 'It is easy to carry out the government of the ancient rulers,' I thought that that was really so. But later on when I came to the place where Mencius was discussing with Shenzi[1] about the territory of Qi and Lu, I realized that the area governed by the ancient rulers was generally speaking only about

---

1   a.k.a. Shen Buhai.

100 li square. Then I began to see that if a new ruler were to arise he must induce the princes who were controlling territory of 1,000 li or 500 li in extent to reduce their area to some tens of li square. I began to doubt whether Mencius, worthy and wise though he was, with wisdom and love so great that he could unify the whole empire, could without military force speedily reduce the territory of these princes by 80 or 90 per cent so that they should revert to the conditions which obtained in the days of the ancient rulers.

Later on again I began to take thought about the policy of Zhufu Yan of which Han Wu Di availed himself. His plan was to order the princes of states and rulers of territories to apportion as gifts of grace parts of their territory to their sons. At the same time the emperor fixed the titles and designations of these, bringing them all under the direct control of the ruler. In this way the territory got split up into smaller regions, the sons and brothers of the princes each getting their own share. But the plan ultimately resulted in the powerful and great princes being deprived of much of their influence, their large domains being split up into many smaller and weaker ones.

Thus I came to see that by careful planning and estimating, and making the changes gradually, the large could be made small, and the strong weak, without revolts or rebellions, or the confusion and distress of war. The words of Mencius were seen after all not to be either extravagant or unreasonable. So to my mind it became clear that the difficulties in the way of one wishing to introduce such changes were not so formidable as might at first sight appear. So I repeat we should plan carefully for the changes that need to be made, estimate everything, and gradually introduce the changes. Then it will be comparatively easy to carry them out.

But under the regime of the ancient rulers they were not so much concerned at what men left undone, as that they lacked the ability to do any particular thing. Again they were more concerned about their own inability to do things, or to get the people to do things, than they were about the people's inability to do them.

What man naturally desires is to live well, earn a good reputation, gain honourable rank, and get good pay. The success which attended the efforts of the ancient rulers in training the people to become their officers, and in gaining the loyal obedience of their officials so that good government was made to prevail, was entirely due to their giving them what they desired. When an officer found himself incapable of discharging the duties of any post, he gave it up. But granted that he had the ability, he exerted himself to make himself still more capable, and naturally would not resign the chance of getting what he really desired. That is the implication of my first point above.

By the second I mean that it was the practice of the ancient rulers to treat their officers handsomely, so that all who had any intelligence and ability at all, were enabled to make good progress. But it was considered vital that the emperor himself should give them an example of sincerity, and care, and devotion. This was with the idea that all might be stimulated to respond in a similar manner. So I say that their first concern was to rouse themselves to the task, rather than to be distressed at the inability of others.

If your Majesty is sincerely desirous of securing a body of capable officials to help you, and I believe you possess this desire, all that is necessary is that you should devote yourself to the task.

I have, however, observed that on former occasions whenever the Court has been desirous of introducing some reforms, that the pros and cons are most carefully considered at the beginning. But should some compromising and opportunist sort of fellow criticize the measure and evince some displeasure with it, the Court immediately desists and dare not go on with the matter.

The laws are not set up for the advantage of any one special class. Under the regime of the ancient rulers, their laws were administered for the whole empire and its benefit. But we must bear in mind that their regime was instituted after a time of corruption and decay, when it was considered most fortunate that such laws could be instituted at all. If after setting up their laws, all the opportunists had been pleased to agree to their promulgation and there had been no opposition, then of course the laws of the ancient rulers would still have been extant.

However, not only were the times most difficult for the setting up of the laws, but the opportunist officials were all unwilling to carry them out, so whenever the ancient rulers desired to carry anything of importance into effect, they had to have recourse to punishments. Only then could they carry out their original ideas.

So we read in the Ode 'Huang I'

> 'By punishments and extermination,
> We eliminate opposition.'

The reference here is to the way in which Wen Wang carried out his ideas in the stabilizing of the empire. We find therefore that the ancient rulers, in their attempt to reform corrupt customs, and to create a body of capable officials, made their laws and regulations with firmness, and nerved themselves to the task even though they had to mete out strict punishments. They saw that there was no other way of carrying their plans through.

Think for a moment of Confucius, who though a commoner by birth, travelled to all the states, giving advice to the princes, causing them to relinquish old practices; to oppose what they had once approved; and succeeded in rousing them to attempt tasks which they had formerly despised. Yet with all his energy and devotion, he was greatly hampered ultimately by their opposition. That, however, in no sense dissuaded him from his purpose, as he knew perseverence was the only way to ensure success. In his determination he may be classed with Wen Wang.

Wen Wang is the greatest of all rulers, and Confucius the greatest of all sages. It is reasonable to suggest that all who are desirous of introducing reforms should act after their fashion. You exercise the power of regal sway, and occupy the throne of the ancient rulers. You have not the difficulty that they had in regard to this matter of punishment. There are some opportunists who show their displeasure by criticizing and opposing anything in the nature of reform, but they are nothing like so numerous as those who will be delighted with and approve of such a policy.

You will therefore be at fault if you refrain from your purpose because of the displeasure or opposition of this conventional and opportunist body of opinion. If your Majesty is sincere in your desire to create a body of capable officials, I beseech you to tie yourself down to it absolutely. If in addition to having a policy of reform, you have the mind and will to carry out the same, gradually it may be, but nevertheless determinedly, you will be assured of success in your object, as far as I can see.

Unfortunately, it has to be admitted that these matters which I present to your notice are not the subjects which these conventionalists discuss. Those who are regarded as critics of current events either regard them as impracticable, or so commonplace as to be beneath their notice. I know that there are amongst your great officers those who are exerting themselves to the limit of their power and intelligence to assist you. But in the main their ideas are confined to the detailed discussion of any proposal that is made, and it is this power of discussion which is held in esteem as a practical gift. The great officials regard such a gift as of the most estimable and rare variety, and so naturally enough, the Court is guided by such considerations in the selection of their officials.

But they rarely or never touch upon those greater matters affecting human relationships, the laws of the land, the greater ceremonies and duties, the very things to which the ancient rulers devoted themselves so earnestly to understand and preserve. The moment anyone should raise discussion on any of these matters, the crowd begins to mock him as an unpractical idealist.

Nowadays the Court goes into all the details and minutiae of every proposal with the greatest deliberation and care. The officers of law and the laws themselves have been functioning for a prolonged period of time, but what of the visible results? It is my earnest hope that your Majesty will give some consideration to these matters which are termed 'impracticable and commonplace'.

Think about it.

1. Is Wang Anshi a big government or small government proponent? Why do you so answer?
2. What does Wang Anshi suggest that the emperor do about any who oppose reform?

---

late 11th century CE

85. The Song of Roland

Translated by Charles K. Moncrieff

Our oldest surviving major work from France is the heroic poem *The Song of Roland* (*Le Chanson de Roland*). It belongs to the genre *chansons de geste* ("songs of heroic deeds") and is our earliest example of such. Written in the mid- to late 11th century in Old French, it contains about 4,000 lines of verse. There are several surviving manuscripts, dating between the 12th and 14th centuries, with some variations between them. The story is based on an actual battle that took place between Charlemagne's forces and the Basques at the Battle of Roncevaux Pass in 778. In the poem, however, the account has been highly romanticized, and the Basques have been replaced by Muslims. The following scenes from the poem concern the trial of the traitor Ganelon (Guenelun in this translation), a knight who betrayed Charlemagne's army under Roland (Rollant) to the Muslims.

CCLXXII

"Lords and barons," Charles the King doth speak,
"Of Guenelun judge what the right may be!
He was in th'host, even in Spain with me;
There of my Franks a thousand score did steal,
And my nephew,[1] whom never more you'll see,
And Oliver,[2] in's pride and courtesy,
And, wealth to gain, betrayed the dozen peers."
"Felon be I," said Guenes,[3] "aught to conceal!
He did from me much gold and wealth forfeit,
Whence to destroy and slay him did I seek;
But treason, no; I vow there's not the least."
Answer the Franks: "Take counsel now must we."

CCLXXIII

So Guenelun, before the King there, stood;
Lusty his limbs, his face of gentle hue;
Were he loyal, right baron-like he'd looked.
He saw those Franks, and all who'ld judge his doom,
And by his side his thirty kinsmen knew.
After, he cried aloud; his voice was full:
"For th' Love of God, listen to me, baruns!
I was in th' host, beside our Emperour,
Service I did him there in faith and truth.
Hatred of me had Rollant, his nephew;
So he decreed death for me and dolour.
Message I bare to king Marsiliun;
By my cunning I held myself secure.
To that fighter Rollant my challenge threw,
To Oliver, and all their comrades too;
Charles heard that, and his noble baruns.
Vengeance I gat, but there's no treason proved."
Answered the Franks: "Now go we to the moot.

CCLXXIV

When Guenes sees, his great cause is beginning,
Thirty he has around him of his kinsmen,

There's one of them to whom the others listen,
'Tis Pinabel, who in Sorence castle liveth;
Well can he speak, soundly his reasons giving,
A good vassal, whose arm to fight is stiffened.
Says to him Guenes: "In you my faith is fixed.
Save me this day from death, also from prison."
Says Pinabel: "Straightway you'll be delivered.
Is there one Frank, that you to hang committeth?
Let the Emperour but once together bring us,
With my steel brand he shall be smartly chidden."
Guenes the count kneels at his feet to kiss them.

CCLXXV

To th' counsel go those of Bavier and Saxe,
Normans also, with Poitevins and Franks;
Enough there are of Tudese and Germans.
Those of Alverne the greatest court'sy have,
From Pinabel most quietly draw back.
Says each to each: "'Twere well to let it stand.
Leave we this cause, and of the King demand
That he cry quits with Guenes for this act;
With love and faith he'll serve him after that.
Since he is dead, no more ye'll see Rollanz,
Nor any wealth nor gold may win him back.
Most foolish then is he, would do combat."
There is but one agrees not to their plan;
Tierri, brother to Don Geifreit, 's that man.

AOI.

CCLXXVI

Then his barons, returning to Carlun,
Say to their King: "Sire, we beseech of you
That you cry quits with county Guenelun,
So he may serve you still in love and truth;
Nay let him live, so noble a man 's he proved.
Rollant is dead, no longer in our view,
Nor for no wealth may we his life renew."
Then says the King: "You're felons all of you!"

AOI.

---

1 Roland (Rollant).
2 Rollant's best friend.
3 Another name for Guenelun.

CCLXXVII

When Charles saw that all of them did fail,
Deep down he bowed his head and all his face
For th' grief he had, caitiff himself proclaimed.
One of his knights, Tierris, before him came,
Gefrei's brother, that Duke of Anjou famed;
Lean were his limbs, and lengthy and delicate,
Black was his hair and somewhat brown his face;
Was not too small, and yet was hardly great;
And courteously to the Emperour he spake:
"Fair' Lord and King, do not yourself dismay!
You know that I have served you many ways:
By my ancestors should I this cause maintain.
And if Rollant was forfeited to Guenes
Still your service to him full warrant gave.
Felon is Guene, since th' hour that he betrayed,
And, towards you, is perjured and ashamed:
Wherefore I judge that he be hanged and slain,
His carcass flung to th' dogs beside the way,
As a felon who felony did make.
But, has he a friend that would dispute my claim
With this my sword which I have girt in place
My judgement will I warrant every way."
Answer the Franks: "Now very well you spake."

CCLXXVIII

Before the King is come now Pinabel;
Great is he, strong, vassalous and nimble;
Who bears his blow has no more time to dwell:
Says to him: "Sire, on you this cause depends;
Command therefore this noise be made an end.
See Tierri here, who hath his judgment dealt;
I cry him false, and will the cause contest."
His deer-hide glove in the King's hand he's left.
Says the Emperour: "Good pledges must I get."
Thirty kinsmen offer their loyal pledge.
"I'll do the same for you," the King has said;
Until the right be shewn, bids guard them well.
                                                    AOI.

CCLXXIX

When Tierri sees that battle shall come after,

His right hand glove he offereth to Chares.
That Emperour by way of hostage guards it;
Four benches then upon the place he marshals
Where sit them down champions of either party.
They're chos'n aright, as the others' judgement
cast them;
Oger the Dane between them made the parley.
Next they demand their horses and their armour.
                                                    AOI.

CCLXXX

For battle, now, ready you might them see,
They're well confessed, absolved, from sin set
free;
Masses they've heard, Communion received,
Rich offerings to those minsters they leave.
Before Carlun now both the two appear:
They have their spurs, are fastened on their feet,
And, light and strong, their hauberks brightly
gleam;
Upon their heads they've laced their helmets
clear,
And girt on swords, with pure gold hilted each;
And from their necks hang down their quartered
shields;
In their right hands they grasp their trenchant
spears.
At last they mount on their swift coursing steeds.
Five score thousand chevaliers therefor weep,
For Rollant's sake pity for Tierri feel.
God knows full well which way the end shall be.

CCLXXXI

Down under Aix there is a pasture large
Which for the fight of th' two barons is marked.
Proof men are these, and of great vassalage,
And their horses, unwearied, gallop fast;
They spur them well, the reins aside they cast,
With virtue great, to strike each other, dart;
All of their shields shatter and rend apart.
Their hauberks tear; the girths asunder start,
The saddles slip, and fall upon the grass.

Five score thousand weep, who that sight regard.

AOI.

CCLXXXII

Upon the ground are fallen both the knights;
Nimbly enough upon their feet they rise.
Nimble and strong is Pinabels, and light.
Each the other seeks; horses are out of mind,
But with those swords whose hilts with gold are lined
Upon those helms of steel they beat and strike:
Great are the blows, those helmets to divide.
The chevaliers of France do much repine.
"O God!" says Charles, "Make plain to us the right!"

CCLXXXIII

Says Pinabel "Tierri, I pray thee, yield:
I'll be thy man, in love and fealty;
For the pleasure my wealth I'll give to thee;
But make the King with Guenelun agree."
Answers Tierri: "Such counsel's not for me.

Pure felon I, if e'er I that concede!
God shall this day the right shew, us between!"

AOI.

CCLXXXIV

Then said Tierri "Bold art thou, Pinabel,
Thou'rt great and strong, with body finely bred;
For vassalage thy peers esteem thee well:
Of this battle let us now make an end!
With Charlemagne I soon will have thee friends;
To Guenelun such justice shall be dealt
Day shall not dawn but men of it will tell."
"Please the Lord God, not so!" said Pinabel.
"I would sustain the cause of my kindred
No mortal man is there from whom I've fled;
Rather I'ld die than hear reproaches said."
Then with their swords began to strike again
Upon those helms that were with gold begemmed
Into the sky the bright sparks rained and fell.
It cannot be that they be sundered,
Nor make an end, without one man be dead.

AOI.

Think about it.

1. How is Guenelun's guilt determined, and what punishments are meted out?
2. What does the story of Guenelun's trial tell you about conceptions of justice in Europe in those days?

86. Revival of the Religious Sciences

Translated by Syed Nawab Ali

The *Revival of the Religious Sciences* (*Ihyā' 'ulūm al-dīn*) is an Arabic philosophical work by Abū Hāmed Muhammad al-Ghazālī (1058–1111). Al-Ghazali was Persian Muslim Sufi (mystic), known as Algazel in Europe, who reacted against the use of Plato, Aristotle, and other Classical authors by earlier Muslim philosophers like Ibn Sina (Avicenna). In *Revival of the Religious Sciences*, which was written at some time between 1099 and 1106, al-Ghazali expounds on theology and ethics from a moderate Sufi standpoint. With its constructive point of view, it became very influential in the Muslim world and to this very day is widely read. The following extract is from Part 4, Book 35 of the work.

Human Freedom and Responsibility

Actions are either voluntary or involuntary. The difference between them is not of kind but of degree. Analyse the process of an involuntary action and you will find that if, for example, a man intends to thrust a needle in your eye or draws a sword to strike on your head, your eye in the former case will at once close and in the latter your hand will suddenly be raised up to shield your head. This prompt action on the part of your eye and hand is due to your consciousness of the evil to be evaded, and this gives rise to volition which moves the eye and the hand without the least delay. There are, however, cases the desirability or rejection of which needs meditation, but the moment mind decides, the decision is carried out as promptly as in the above example. This meditation translated into choice or rejection constitutes will. Now will makes its choice between two alternatives and takes its cue either from imagination or reason. For example, a man may be unable to cut his own throat, not because his hand is weak or a knife is not available, but because will is lacking which would give the stimulus to suicide. For man loves his own life. But suppose he gets tired of his life, owing to having harrowing pains and unbearable mental sufferings. He has now to choose between two alternatives which are both undesirable A struggle commences and he hangs between life and death. If he thinks that death which will put an end to his sufferings quickly is preferable to life with its lingering intolerable pains, he will choose death although he loves his life. This choice gives rise to will, the command to which, communicated through proper channels, would then be faithfully executed by his hand in the manner of suicide. Thus, though the process from the commencement of mental struggle for the choice between too alternatives down to the stimulus to physical action is uniformly determinate there is at any rate a sort of freedom tracable in the will.

Man holds the balance between determinism and freedom. The uniform succession of events is on the lines of determination but his choice which is an essential element of will is his own. Our Ulamas have therefore coined a separate phrase: Kasb (acquisition), distinguishing it from Jabr (necessity) and Ikhtiyar (freedom) They say that fire burns of necessity (Jabr) but man may acquire fire through the appropriate methods, while in Almighty God is the ultimate cause of fire (Ikhtiyar). But it must be noted that when we use the word Ikhtiyar for God, we must exclude the notion of choice, which is an essential element of will in man. Let it be here recognised once for all as a general principle that all the words of man's vocabulary when used for God's attributes are similarly metaphorical.

The question may be asked: If God is the ultimate cause why should there be a causal connection in the orderly succession of events? The answer to this lies in the correct understanding of the nature of causation. Nothing causes anything. Antecedents have consequents. God alone is the efficient cause, but the ignorant have misunderstood and misapplied the word power. As to the orderly succession of events, let it be understood that the two events are conjoined like the relation between the condition and the conditioned. Now certain conditions are very apparent and can be known easily by people of little understanding, but there are conditions which are understood only by those who see through the light of intuition: hence the common error of miscalculating the uniformity of events. There is a divine purpose linking the antecedents to the consequents and manifesting itself in the existing orderly succession of events, without the least break or irregularity. "Verily", says the Quran. "We did not create the heavens and the earth and what is between them in sport. We did not create them both but with truth, but most of them do not know".

Surely, there is a set purpose pervading the universe. The uniform succession of events is not at random. There is no such thing as chance. Here again it may be asked: If God is the efficient cause, how will you account for actions attributed to man in the scriptures? Are we to believe that there are two causes for one effect? My answer to this will be

that the word cause is vaguely understood. It can be used in two different senses. Just as we say that the death of A was caused by (1) B. the executioner, and (2) C the king's order. Both these statements are correct. Similarly God is the cause of actions as He has creative power and efficiency. At the same time man is the cause of actions as he is the source of the manifestation of uniform succession of events. In the former case we have a real causal connection, while in the latter a relation of the antecedent to the consequent after the manner of the connection between the condition and the conditioned. There are passages in the Quran where the word cause is used in different senses.

"The angel of death who is given charge of you shall cause you to die: then to your Lord you shall be brought back". "Allah takes the souls at the time of their death".

"Have you considered what you sow?"[7] "We pour down the water, pouring it down in abundance. Then we cleave the earth; cleaving it asunder. Then we cause to grow therein the grain".

"Fight them: Allah will chastise them by your hands and bring them to disgrace"."So you did not slay them, but it was Allah who slew them, and thou didst not smite when thou didst smite, but it was Allah who smote, that he might confer upon the believers a good gift from himself".

These passages show that the word, cause, signifies creative power, and must be applied to God alone. But as man's power is the image of God's power the word was applied to him figuratively. Yet, just as the death of a culprit is caused by the actual killing by the hand of the executioner and not the king's order, so the word cause actually applied to man is contrary to fact. God alone is the real efficient cause, and the word must be applied to him in its root sense of power.

It may be asked then, why man should be rewarded for his good actions and punished for his misdeeds. Let us consider first the nature of reward and punishment. Experience tells us that things have natural properties and that physical laws operate in a uniform manner. Take, for example, the science of medicine. Certain drugs are found to possess certain qualities. If a man swallows poison of his own accord he has no right to ask why poison kills him. Its natural property has simply operated in his system and caused his death. Similarly actions make an impression on mind. Good and bad actions are invariably followed by pleasure and pain respectively. A good action is its own reward of pleasure and a bad one of pain. The former works like an elixir; the latter like poison. The properties of actions have been discovered, like discoveries in medicine, but by the physicians of the heart, the saints and the prophets. If you will not listen to them you must suffer the consequence. Now hear a parable:

A certain king sent a horse, a robe of honour, and travelling expenses to one of his suzerains in a distant land. Although the king had no need of his services, the royal gift was a favour shown to his suzerain, so that he might come to the king's court and be happy in his presence. If the suzerain understands the king's intention from the nature of the gift and utilizes it properly with a grateful heart, he will wait on the king and live happily, but if he misuses the gift or takes no heed of it, he will prove an ungrateful wretch.

It is thus that the boundless mercy of the omnipotent and omniscient God bestowed on us the gift of life, providing us with bodily organs, mental and moral faculties, so that we uplift ourselves by utilizing them properly, and be worthy of being admitted into his holy presence. If we misuse them or pay no regard to them, surely we shall be (Kafirs) (literally "ungrateful") for his blessings bestowed on us for our good, and thus be doomed.

"Verily," says the Quran, "we created man in the best make. Then we render him the lowest of the low. Except those who believe and do good, so they shall have a reward never to be cut off".

Think about it.

1. How does al-Ghazali argue that the universe has a purpose?
2. How does he harmonize the idea that humans have free will with the idea that God causes everything?

87. The Alexiad

Translated by Elizabeth A. Dawes

The Alexiad is a biography of the Byzantine emperor Alexius I (r. 1081–1118) written in Greek by his daughter, Anna Komnene (1083–1153). It is one of very few works of political history written by women in this period. In the following passage from Book 6, Anna relates the account of an exchange that took place during the First Crusade (1096–1099) between the emperor Alexius and Bohemund, Prince of Taranto, one of the leaders of the Crusade. Bohemund had promised to hand over to Alexius any lands that he took from the Muslims, but he reneged on that promise.

BOOK XI

[290] Soon the Emperor learnt of the seizure of Laodicea by Tancred, and therefore sent a letter to Bohemund which ran as follows: "You know the oaths and promises which not only you but all the Counts took to the Roman Empire. Now you were the first to break them, by retaining possession of Antioch, and then taking more fortresses and even Laodicea itself. Therefore withdraw from Antioch and all the other cities and do what is just and right, and do not provoke more wars and troubles for yourself." Now Bohemund after reading the Emperor's letter could not reply by a falsehood, as he usually did, for the facts openly declared the truth, so outwardly he assented to it, but put the blame for all the wrong he had done upon the Emperor and wrote to him thus, "It is not I, but you, who are the cause of all this. For you promised you would follow us with a large army, but you never thought of making good your promise by deeds. When we reached Antioch we fought for three months under great difficulty both against the enemy and against famine, which was more severe

than had ever been experienced before, with the result that most of us ate of the very foods which are forbidden by law. We endured for a long time and while [291] we were in this danger even Taticius, your Majesty's most loyal servant, whom you had appointed to help us, went away and left us to our danger. Yet we captured Antioch unexpectedly and utterly routed the troops which had come from Chorosan to succour Antioch. In what way would it be just for us to deprive ourselves willingly of what we gained by our own sweat and toil?" When the envoys returned from him the Emperor recognized from the reading of his letter that he was still the same Bohemund and in no wise changed for the better, and therefore decided that he must protect the boundaries of the Roman Empire, and as far as possible, check his impetuous advance. Accordingly he sent Butumites into Cilicia with numerous forces and the pick of the military roll, all very warlike men and devotees of Ares, amongst them too Bardas and the chief cup-bearer Michael, both in the flower of youth with beards newly-grown. These two the Emperor had taken to himself from childhood and trained thoroughly in military science; he now gave them to Butumites as being more loyal than the rest besides another thousand men of noble birth, Franks and Romans, mixed, who were to accompany him and obey him in everything and also acquaint him himself by secret letters of the hourly happenings. His desire was to subdue the whole province of Cilicia and thus more easily carry out his designs upon Antioch. Butumites started with all his forces and reached the city of Attalus; there he noticed that Bardas and the chief cup-bearer, Michael, would not comply with his wishes and to prevent the whole army perhaps mutinying, and all his labour being in vain, and his being obliged to return from Cilicia without accomplishing anything, he at once wrote to the Emperor full details about these men, and asked to be relieved of their company. The Emperor vividly aware of the harm that is wont to result from such beginnings, turned them and the others he suspected into another direction by writing to them to go to Cyprus with all speed and join Constantine Euphorbenus, who held the position of Duke of Cyprus at the time, and obey him in everything. On receiving the letters they gladly embarked for Cyprus. But after they had been a short time with the Duke of Cyprus, they began their usual impudence with him, in consequence of which he looked upon them askance. But the young men mindful of the Emperor's affection for them wrote to the Emperor and ran down Euphorbenus, and asked to be recalled to Constantinople. After perusing their letters the Emperor, [292] who had sent several of the richer men (of whom he was suspicious) with these two to Cyprus, was afraid lest these might from annoyance join the two in rebellion, and straight-way enjoined Cantacuzenus to go and bring them back with him. Directly Cantacuzenus arrived in Cyrenea he sent for them and took them back. This is what happened to those two, I mean Bardas and the chief cup-bearer Michael.

Butumites meanwhile with Monastras and the picked officers who remained with him, reached Cilicia and found that the Armenians had already concluded a truce with Tancred. So he passed them by and seized Marasin and all the neighbouring villages and forts; then he left the semibarbarian Monastras (who has often been mentioned in this history) as governor with sufficient troops to protect the whole country, and himself returned to the capital.

Think about it.

1. Why, according the Anna Komnene, did Bohemund not keep his word and give the lands he conquered to Alexius?
2. To what does Anna Komene attribute Alexius' military failures?

88. A History of Deeds Done Beyond the Sea

By Emily A. Babcock and August C. Krey

A History of Deeds Done Beyond the Sea (*Historia rerum in partibus transmarinis gestarum*), also known as the History of Jerusalem (*Historia Ierosolimitana*), is a Latin chronicle that covers the history of the Christian kingdom of Jerusalem from the First Crusade (1096–1099) until 1184. It was written by a Christian archbishop William of Tyre (c. 1130–1186), between 1170 and 1184. The following extract concerns the discovery of a holy relic in the city of Antioch during the First Crusade, when the city was surrounded by Muslim forces.

While the people of God were suffering affliction in this way, the Lord looked upon them and heard their groans and sent them consolation from the seat of His majesty. A certain cleric named Peter, as it is said, from the land called Provence, came to the bishop of Puy and the count of Toulouse. He claimed that the blessed apostle Andrew had appeared to him in dreams three or four times and had commanded him most urgently to tell the leaders that the Lance which pierced the side of our Lord Jesus Christ lay hidden in the church of the Prince of the Apostles. They were to seek it there with all diligence in the spot which the apostle had indicated by definite signs. Accordingly Peter went to those beloved servants of God and made known to them in full detail the command which he swore had been laid upon him. He declared that he had been forced by the apostle to do this under threats of many terrors. Again and again he had refused to undertake the mission because he was a poor and unlearned man, yet at last he could no longer evade the urgent command of the apostle, even though it be at the risk of his life.

This communication was confided in all secrecy to the other leaders, and Peter was brought before them that they might learn from him the exact mode and form of the command. After listening to his words, they put faith in his story and assembled at the place which he had named, within the precincts of the church mentioned above. The earth in that spot was dug up to some depth, and there they found the Lance just as Peter had said.

When the people heard the news, they ran to the church as one man, for they felt that consolation had been sent them from on high. Gifts and offerings were brought to honor the discovery of that precious token. Freed from their anxiety, they began to breathe once more and felt renewed strength to carry out the divine commands. There were some, also, who claimed to have had visions of angels and the holy apostles, which, as corroborating evidence, tended to strengthen faith in Peter's dream. The despondent spirits of the people rose marvelously. Then, at the suggestion of venerable and God-fearing men, all the chiefs renewed their vows and took an oath of fidelity to one another. They promised that, if the

Lord would mercifully rescue them from their present critical situation and grant them the longed-for victory over their enemies, they would not separate until, by the help of God, they had restored the Holy City and His glorious sepulchre to the Christian faith and its own former state of liberty.

Think about it.

1. What evidence does William give that God was on the side of the Crusaders at Antioch?
2. What does this story reveal about the beliefs of the Crusaders?

---

c. 1160 CE

89. On the Harmony of Religion and Philosophy

Translated by Mohammed Jamil-ur-Rehman

The following is an English translation of the treatise *On the Harmony of Religion and Philosophy* (*Kitab fasl al-maqal* in Arabic), published c. 1160 by Ibn Rushd (known as Averroes in Europe), a Muslim polymath from Andalusia in Spain. Ibn Rushd (1126–1198) sparked controversy among Muslims by defending the reconciliation of classical philosophy (particularly that of Aristotle) with Islam (and religion in general). His writings greatly influenced scholarship in Christian Europe.

And after: Praise be to God for all His praiseworthy acts, and blessings on Mohammad, His slave, the Pure, the Chosen One and His Apostle. The purpose of the following treatise is to inquire through sacred Law whether the learning of philosophy and other sciences appertaining thereto is permitted, or called dangerous, or commended by the Law, and if commended, is it only approved or made obligatory.

We maintain that the business of philosophy is nothing other than to look into creation and to ponder over it in order to be guided to the Creator,—in other words, to look into the meaning of existence. For the knowledge of creation leads to the cognisance of the Creator, through the knowledge of the created. The more perfect becomes the knowledge of creation, the more perfect becomes the knowledge of the Creator. The Law encourages and exhorts us

Ibn Rushd, "A Decisive Discourse on the Delineation of the Relation Between Religion and Philosophy," *The Philosophy and Theology of Averroes*, trans. Mohammed Jamil-ur-Rehman. A. G. Withery, 1921. Copyright in the Public Domain.

to observe creation. Thus, it is clear that this is to be taken either as a religious injunction or as something approved by the Law. But the Law urges us to observe creation by means of reason and demands the knowledge thereof through reason. This is evident from different verses of the Quran. For example the Quran says: "Wherefore take example *from them,* ye who have eyes." That is a clear indication of the necessity of using the reasoning faculty, or rather both reason and religion, in the interpretation of things. Again it says: "Or do they not contemplate the kingdom of heaven and earth and the things which God hath created." This is a plain exhortation to encourage the use of observation of creation. And remember that one whom God especially distinguishes in this respect, Abraham, the prophet. For He says: "And this did we show unto Abraham: the kingdom of heaven and earth." Further He says: "Do they not consider the camels, how they are created; and the heaven, how it is raised." Or still again: "And (who) meditate on the creation of heaven and earth, saying, O Lord thou hast not created this in vain." There are many other verses on this subject: too numerous to be enumerated.

Now, it being established that the Law makes the observation and consideration of creation by reason obligatory—and consideration is nothing but to make explicit the implicit—this can only be done through reason. Thus we must look into creation with the reason. Moreover, it is obvious that the observation which the Law approves and encourage must be of the most perfect type, performed with the most perfect kind of reasoning. As the Law emphasises the knowledge of God and His creation by inference, it is incumbent on any who wish to know God and His whole creation by inference, to learn the kinds of inference, their conditions and that which distinguishes philosophy from dialectic and exhortation from syllogism. This is impossible unless one possesses knowledge beforehand of the various kinds of reasoning and learns to distinguish between reasoning and what is not reasoning. This

cannot be done except one knows its different parts, that is, the different kinds of premises.

Hence, for a believer in the Law and a follower of it, it is necessary to know these things before he begins to look into creation, for they are like instruments for observation. For, just as a student discovers by the study of the law, the necessity of knowledge of legal reasoning with all its kinds and distinctions, a student will find out by observing the creation the necessity of metaphysical reasoning. Indeed, he has a greater claim on it than the jurist. For if a jurist argues the necessity of legal reasoning from the saying of God: "Wherefore take example *from them* O ye who have eyes," a student of divinity has a better right to establish the same from it on behalf of metaphysical reasoning.

One cannot maintain that this kind of reasoning is an innovation in religion because it did not exist in the early days of Islam. For legal reasoning and its kinds are things which were invented also in later ages, and no one thinks they are innovations. Such should also be our attitude towards philosophical reasoning. There is another reason why it should be so, but this is not the proper place to mention it. A large number of the followers of this religion confirm philosophical reasoning, all except a small worthless minority, who argue from religious ordinances. Now, as it is established that the Law makes the consideration of philosophical reasoning and its kinds as necessary as legal reasoning, if none of our predecessors has made an effort to enquire into it, we should begin to do it, and so help them, until the knowledge is complete. For if it is difficult or rather impossible for one person to acquaint himself single-handed with all things which it is necessary to know in legal matters, it is still more difficult in the case of philosophical reasoning. And, if before us, somebody has enquired into it, we should derive help from what he has said. It is quite immaterial whether that man is our co-religionist or not; for the instrument by which purification is perfected is not made uncertain in its usefulness, by its being in the hands of one of our own party, or of a foreigner, if it possesses the attributes of truth. By these latter we mean those Ancients who investigated these things before the advent of Islam.

Now, such is the case. All that is wanted in an enquiry into philosophical reasoning has already been perfectly examined by the Ancients. All that is required of us is that we should go back to their books and see what they have said in this connection. If all that they say be true, we should accept it and if there be something wrong, we should be warned by it. Thus, when we have finished this kind of research we shall have acquired instruments by which we can observe the universe, and consider its general character. For so long as one does not know its general character one cannot know the created, and so long as he does not know the created, he can have no knowledge of the Creator. Thus we must begin an inquiry into the universe systematically, such as we have learned from the trend of rational inference. It is also evident that this aim is to be attained by the investigation of one part of the universe after another, and that help must be derived from predecessors, as is the case in other sciences. Imagine that the science of geometry and astronomy had become extinct in our day, and a single individual desired to find out by himself the magnitude of the heavenly bodies, their forms, and their distances from one another. Even though he were the most sagacious of men, it would be as impossible for him as to ascertain the proportion of the sun and the earth and the magnitude of the other stars. It would only be attainable by aid of divine revelation, or something like it. If it be said to him that the sun is a hundred and fifty or sixty times as big as the earth, he would take it to be sheer madness on the part of the speaker, though it is an established fact in the science of astronomy, so that no one learned in that science will have any doubt about it.

The science which needs most examples from other sciences is that of Law. For the study of jurisprudence cannot be completed except in a very long time. If a man today would himself learn of all the arguments discovered by the different disputants of diverse sects, in problems which have always excited contentions in all the big cities, except those of Al-Maghrib, he would be a proper object to be laughed at on account of the impossibility of the task, in spite of the existence of every favourable circumstance. This is similar not only in the sciences but also in the arts. For no one is capable of discovering by himself alone everything which is required. And if this is so in other sciences and arts, how is it possible in the art of arts-philosophy?

This being so, it becomes us to go back to the Ancients, and to see what observations and considerations they have made into the universe, according to the tests of inference. We should consider what they have said in this connection and proved in their books, so that whatever may be true in them we may accept and, while thanking them, be glad to know it, and whatever be wrong, we should be warned by it, be cautioned, and hold them excused for their mistake.

From what has been said, it may be taken that a search into the books of the Ancients is enjoined by the Law, when their meaning and purpose be the same as that to which the Law exhorts us. Anyone who prevents a man from pondering over these things, that is, a man who has the double quality of natural sagacity and rectitude in the Law, with the merit of learning and disposition, turns away the people from the door by which the Law invites them to enter into the knowledge of God, and that is the door of observation which leads to the perfect knowledge of God. Such an action is the extreme limit of ignorance and of remoteness from God.

If, by studying these books, a man has been led astray and gone wrong on account of some natural defect, bad training of the mind, inordinate passion, or the want of a teacher who might explain to him the true significance of things, by all or some of these causes, we ought not on this account to prevent one fit to study these things from doing so. For such harm is not innate in man, but is only an accident of training.

It is not right that a drug which is medically useful by its nature should be discarded because it may prove harmful by accident. The Prophet told a man whose brother was suffering with diarrhea to treat him with honey. But this only increased the ailment. On his complaining, the Prophet said: "God was right and thy brother's stomach was wrong." We would even say that a man who prevents another fit for it, from studying the books of philosophy, because certain worthless people have been misled by them, is like a man who refused a thirsty man cold and sweet water, till he died, because some people under the same circumstances have been suffocated by it and have died. For death by suffocation through drinking cold water is accidental, while by thirst it is natural and inevitable.

This state of things is not peculiar to this science only, but is common to all. How many jurists there are in whom jurisprudence has become the cause of worldliness and lack of piety? We should say that a large majority of jurists are of this kind, although their science should result in better action than other sciences which only lead to better knowledge.

So far, then, the position is established. Now, we Muslims firmly believe that our Law is divine and true. This very Law urges us and brings us to that blessing which is known as the knowledge of God, and His creation. This is a fact to which every Muslim will bear testimony by his very nature and temperament. We say this, because temperaments differ in believing: one will believe through philosophy; while another will believe through dogmatic discourse, just as firmly as the former, as no other method appeals to his nature. There are others who believe by exhortation alone, just as others believe through inferences. For this reason our divine Law invites people by all the three methods, which every man has to satisfy, except those who stubbornly refuse to believe, or those, according to whom these divine methods have not been established on account of the waywardness of their hearts. This is why the mission of the Prophet has been declared common to the whole world, for his Law comprises all the three methods leading men towards God. What we say is quite clear from the following saying of God: "Invite men unto the way of the Lord, by wisdom and mild exhortation, and dispute with them in the most condescending manner."

As this Law is true and leads to the consideration of the knowledge of God, we Muslims should believe that rational investigation is not contrary to Law, for truth cannot contradict truth, but verifies it and bears testimony to it. And if that is so, and rational observation is directed to the knowledge of any existent objects, then the Law may be found to be silent about it, or concerned with it. In the former case no dispute arises, as it would be equivalent to the absence of its mention in the Law as injunctory, and hence the jurist derives it from legal conjecture. But if the Law speaks of it, either it will agree with that which has been proved by inference, or else it will disagree with it. If it is in agreement it needs no comment, and if it is opposed to the Law, an interpretation is to be sought. Interpretation means to carry the meaning of a word from its original sense to a metaphorical one. But this should be done in such a manner as will not conflict with the custom of the Arabian tongue. It is to avoid the naming of an object, by simply mentioning its like, its cause, its attribute, or associate, etc. which are commonly quoted in the definition of the different kinds of metaphorical utterances. And if the jurist does so in many of the legal injunctions, how very befitting would it be for a learned man to do the same with his arguments. For the jurist has only his fanciful conjectures to depend upon, while a learned man possesses positive ones.

We hold it to be an established truth that if the Law is apparently opposed to a truth proved by philosophy it admits of an interpretation according to the canons of the Arabic language. This is a proposition which a Muslim cannot doubt and a believer cannot mistrust. One who is accustomed to these things divine can experience for himself what we have said. The aim of this discourse is to bring together intellectual and traditional science. Indeed, we would even say that no logical conclusion will be found to be opposed to the Law, which when sifted and investigated in its different parts will be found in accordance, or almost so, with it.

> ### *Think about it.*
>
> 1. According to Ibn Rushd, why is the study of philosophy not only approved of God, but obligatory?
> 2. Why is the study of ancient pagan texts necessary in this enterprise?

12th century CE

90. Writings of Zhu Xi

Translated by J. Percy Bruce

Zhu Xi (1130–1200), or Chu Hsi in the old spelling, was a Neo-Confucian scholar from the Song Dynasty in China. He wrote extensive commentaries on *The Analects* (see reading #35), *The Mencius* (see reading #42), *The Great Learning* (a chapter from the Liji), and *The Doctrine of the Mean* (another chapter from the Liji) and was instrumental in making the study of "The Four Books," as they came to be called, the core curriculum among scholar officials. The following extracts from his writings illustrate his conception of human nature.

From *The Conversations.*

13. The Nature is that which precedes activity, the Feelings follow activity; and the Mind includes both the pre-activo and the post-active states. For the Mind's pre-active state is the Nature, and its post-active state is Feeling, as is expressed in the saying: "The Mind unites the Nature and the Feelings." Desire is Feeling in its manifestation. The Mind is like water, the Nature is the stillness of water at rest, Feeling, the flow of water, and Desires are the waves. But waves are good and bad. So with desires: there are good desires, as when "I desire virtue"; and there are evil desires which rush out precipitately like wild and boisterous waves. For the most part, evil desires destroy the Divine Law, as when a dam bursts and carries with it universal destruction. When Mencius speaks of the Feelings as constituted for the practice

of what is good, he refers to the Feelings as they ought to be. As they flow from the Nature they are infallibly good.

14. The Mind must be thought of as ruler. In activity and repose alike it is ruler. It is not that in repose the Mind is unemployed, and only rules when there is activity. When I say "ruler" I mean that an all-comprehensive supreme ruler dwells within. The Mind unites and controls the Nature and Feelings; but it is not united with the Nature and Feelings in such a way as to form one entity, without any distinction.

19. The meaning of the statement that the Mind unites the Nature and the Feelings is this: When the Mind is still and as jet without movement, the principles of Love, Righteousness, Reverence, and Wisdom are present; when it is active we have Feeling. Some assert that the state of repose is the Nature, the activity the Mind, but this is dividing the Mind into two separate compartments, the Mind and the Nature. It is not to be accounted for in terms of activity and repose. Everything has Mind, and within, it is hollow like the heart of a, chicken or pig which you have in your food, and which when you carve it you see to be hollow. Man's Mind is like that: it consists of such hollow places in which numerous principles are stored. If we take into consideration the whole universe with eternal time, and apply this reasoning, we shall recognize that in the whole heaven and in the whole earth there is nothing which does not have its origin here; and that this is what constitutes the mystery of Man's Mind. Law inherent in man's Mind is what we call the Nature. The Nature is like the soil of the Mind: that which fills the Mind is simply Law. The Mind is the seat of the spiritual intelligence, the ruler of the entire personality. The Nature consists of numerous principles received from Heaven and contained in the Mind, the manifestations of which in knowledge and thought are all Feelings. Hence the statement: "The Mind unites the Nature and Feelings."

20. *Question.* You have discussed the Mind from the point of view of man's personality. Can you take what we learn from man's personality and apply it to the universe?

Answer. The Decree of Heaven pervades all things; the agent by which these principles are controlled is the Mind of Heaven; that which possesses these principles is the Nature of Heaven, as, for example, the law which produces the four seasons; and those influences which are put forth and nourish all things are the Feelings of Heaven.

From *The Collected Writings.*

6. The possession of form implies the possession of Mind; the principles received by the Mind from Heaven are termed the Nature, and the movements of the Nature when affected by the external world are termed the Feelings. These three all men have. The distinction between the sage and the rest of men is not that the sage has them and that others have not. But in the case of the sage the Ether is clear and the Mind true, therefore the Nature is complete and the Feelings are without confusion. The-student should preserve his Mind so as to nourish the Nature and control the Feelings. You, say that in the sage the Mind is non-existent, and go on to maintain that we ought not to keep anything in our Mind for a single moment. But among all those benefits which Heaven has given to us how comes it that there is just this one thing that is a useless drag upon us? (Reply to Hsü Ching Kuang.)

7. *Question.* The Nature in its beginning is only good; there is no evil originally which can be attributed to it. It is the Principle of Origin, the first of the Four Attributes, Love the parent of the Five Cardinal Virtues. This is what is implied in Menchis' dictum, "The Nature of man is good," what Ming Tao means when, quoting the statement "The law of their succession is goodness", he says it refers to the manifested operations of the Nature, the Mind of the Four Terminals. How then can you describe it as one with Feeling?

Answer. The Nature from beginning to end is wholly good: you must not say that it is at the beginning that the Nature is wholly good. Could you, in line with what your statement suggests, say that the Nature in the end is evil? If the manifested operations of the Nature are not Feelings, what are they? What you may say is that the Feeling's in their beginning are wholly good and without any evil. In the phrase, "If we look at the feeling's which flow from the Nature," I do not think that the word *jo* (if we look at) means "to accord with", (Reply to Wang Tzǔ Ho.)

8. *Question.* Mencius said, "If we look at the Feelings which flow from the Nature we may know that they are constituted for the practice of what is good"; and Chou Tzǔ said, "When tho five nature-principles act in response to affection by the external world there comes the distinction between good and evil." This again connects both good and evil with activity. Can it be that Mencius is speaking from the standpoint of the condition prior to the activity of the Feelings, and Chou Tzǔ from the standpoint of their post-active condition?

Answer. The Feelings are not necessarily wholly good, but in their origin they are constituted for doing good, and not for doing evil; it is when they are perverted, that they issue in the practice of evil. Mencius spoke of them in their original perfection; Chou Tzǔ spoke of them both in their original perfection and as they are when perverted. Chuang Tzǔ has the same idea when he speaks of forsaking Heaven and violating the Feelings. (Reply to Chang Ching Chih.)

10. "Before there are any stirrings of pleasure, anger, sorrow, or joy, the Mind may be said to be in a state of equilibrium." This is the Nature. "After they have been stirred, and they act in their due degree, there ensues what may be called a state of harmony." This is Feeling. Tzǔ Ssǔ in writing this desired the student to recognize what he said as referring to Mind. The Mind! How wonderfully it "moulds the virtues of the Nature and Feelings"! (Reply to Chang Ching Fu.)

Think about it.

1. According to Zhu Xi, is human Nature good or evil? What about human Feelings?
2. How does he differ from Xunzi on this point? How does he differ from Augustine? Pelagius?

91. The Guide for the Perplexed

Translated by Michael Friedländer

The Guide for the Perplexed is a philosophical work by Moshe ben Maimon (1135–1204), a Jewish scholar known also as Maimonides or as the Rambam (an acronym for Rabbi Moshe ben Maimon) who lived under Almoravid rule in Cordoba, Spain. Originally published in Arabic in the late 12th century, it was written as a letter (in three volumes) to the Rabbi Joseph ben Judah of Ceuta. Though directed to a Jewish audience, the book's philosophical concepts were found to be relevant by Christians and Muslims and proved to be very influential. In the following excerpt from the first volume, ben Maimon explains why the Bible's descriptions of God don't seem to harmonize with the current philosophical views of God.

CHAPTER XXXI

Know that for the human mind there are certain objects of perception which are within the scope of its nature and capacity; on the other hand, there are, amongst things which actually exist, certain objects which the mind can in no way and by no means grasp: the gates of perception are dosed against it. Further, there are things of which the mind understands one part, but remains ignorant of the other; and when man is able to comprehend certain things, it does not follow that he must be able to comprehend everything. This also applies to the senses: they are able to perceive things, but not at every distance: and all other power; of the body are limited in a similar way. A man can, e.g., carry two kikkar, but he cannot carry ten kikkar. How individuals of the same species surpass each other in these sensations and in other bodily faculties is universally known, but there is a limit to them, and their power cannot extend to every distance or to every degree.

All this is applicable to the intellectual faculties of man. There is a considerable difference between one person and another as regards these faculties, as is well known to philosophers. While one man can discover a certain thing by himself, another is never able to understand it, even if taught by means of all possible expressions and metaphors, and during a long period; his mind can in no way grasp it, his capacity is insufficient for it. This distinction is not unlimited. A boundary is undoubtedly set to the human mind which it cannot pass. There are things (beyond that boundary) which are acknowledged to be inaccessible to human understanding, and man does not show any desire to comprehend them, being aware that such knowledge is impossible, and that there are no means of overcoming the difficulty: e.g., we do not know the number of stars in heaven, whether the number is even or odd; we do not know the number of animals, minerals, or plants, and the like. There are other things, however, which man very much desires to know, and strenuous efforts to examine and to investigate them have been made by thinkers of all classes, and at all times. They differ and disagree, and constantly raise new doubts with regard to them, because their minds are bent on comprehending such things, that is to say, they are moved by desire and every one of them believes that he has discovered the way leading to a true knowledge of the thing, although human reason is entirely unable to demonstrate the fact by convincing evidence. For a proposition which can be proved by evidence is not subject to dispute, denial, or rejection: none but the ignorant would contradict it, and such contradiction is called "denial of a demonstrated proof." Thus you find men who deny the spherical form of the earth, or the circular form of the line in which the stars move, and the like: such men are not considered in this treatise. This confusion prevails mostly in metaphysical subjects, less in problems relating to physics, and is entirely absent from the exact sciences. Alexander Aphrodisius said that there are three causes which prevent men from discovering the exact truth: first, arrogance and vainglory; secondly, the subtlety, depth, and difficulty of any subject which is being examined; thirdly, ignorance and want of capacity to comprehend what might be comprehended. These causes are enumerated by Alexander. At the present time there is a fourth cause not mentioned by him, because it did not then prevail, namely, habit and training. We naturally like what we have been accustomed to, and are attracted towards it. This may be observed amongst villagers; though they rarely enjoy the benefit of a douche or bath, and have few enjoyments, and pass a life of privation, they dislike town life and do not desire its pleasures, preferring the inferior things to which they are accustomed, to the better things to which they are strangers; it would give them no satisfaction to live in palaces, to be clothed in silk, and to indulge in baths, ointments, and perfumes.

The same is the case with those opinions of man to which he has been accustomed from his youth; he likes them, defends them, and shuns the opposite views. This is likewise one of the causes which prevent men from finding truth, and which make them cling to their habitual opinions. Such is, e.g., the case with the vulgar notions with respect to the corporeality of God, and many other metaphysical questions, as we shall explain. It is the result of long familiarity with passages of the Bible, which they are accustomed to respect and to receive as true, and the literal sense of which implies the corporeality of God and other false notions; in truth, however, these words were employed as figures and metaphors for reasons to be mentioned below. Do not imagine that what we have said of the insufficiency of our understanding and of its limited extent is an assertion founded only on the Bible: for philosophers likewise assert the same, and perfectly understand it, without having regard to any religion or opinion. It is a fact which is only doubted by those who ignore things fully proved. This chapter is intended as an introduction to the next.

CHAPTER XXXII

You must consider, when reading this treatise, that mental perception, because connected with matter, is subject to conditions similar to those to which physical perception is subject. That is to say, if your eye looks around, you can perceive all that is within the range of your vision: if, however, you overstrain your eye, exerting it too much by attempting to see an object which is too distant for your eye, or to examine writings or engravings too small for your sight, and forcing it to obtain a correct perception of them, you will not only weaken your sight with regard to that special object, but also for those things which you otherwise are able to perceive: your eye will have become too weak to perceive what you were able to see before you exerted yourself and exceeded the limits of your vision.

The same is the case with the speculative faculties of one who devotes himself to the study of any science. If a person studies too much and exhausts his reflective powers, he will be confused, and will not be able to apprehend even that which had been within the power of his apprehension. For the powers of the body are all alike in this respect.

The mental perceptions are not exempt from a similar condition. If you admit the doubt, and do not persuade yourself to believe that there is a proof for things which cannot be demonstrated, or to try at once to reject and positively to deny an assertion the opposite of which has never been proved, or attempt to perceive things which are beyond your perception, then you have attained the highest degree of human perfection, then you are like R. Akibha, who "in peace entered [the study of these theological problems], and came out in peace." If, on the other hand, you attempt to exceed the limit of your intellectual power, or at once to reject things as impossible which have never been proved to be impossible, or which are in fact possible, though their possibility be very remote, then you will be like Elisha Aher; you will not only fail to become perfect, but you will become exceedingly imperfect. Ideas founded on mere imagination will prevail over you, you will incline toward defects, and toward base and degraded habits, on account of the confusion which troubles the mind, and of the dimness of its light, just as weakness of sight causes invalids to see many kinds of unreal images, especially when they have looked for a long time at dazzling or at very minute objects.

Respecting this it has been said, "Hast thou found honey? eat so much as is sufficient for thee, lest thou be filled therewith, and vomit it" (Prov. xxv. 16). Our Sages also applied this verse to Elisha Aher.

How excellent is this simile! In comparing knowledge to food (as we observed in chap. xxx.), the author of Proverbs mentions the sweetest food, namely, honey, which has the further property of irritating the stomach, and of causing sickness. He thus fully describes the nature of knowledge. Though great, excellent, noble and perfect, it is injurious if not kept within bounds or not guarded properly; it is like honey which gives nourishment and is pleasant, when eaten in moderation, but is totally thrown

away when eaten immoderately. Therefore, it is not said "lest thou be filled and loathe it," but "lest thou vomit it." The same idea is expressed in the words, "It is not good to eat much honey" (Prov. xxv. 27); and in the words, "Neither make thyself over-wise: why shouldst thou destroy thyself?" (Eccles. vii. 16); comp. "Keep thy foot when thou goest to the house of God" (ibid. v. 1). The same subject is alluded to in the words of David, "Neither do I exercise myself in great matters, or in things too high for me" (Ps. cxxxi. 2), and in the sayings of our Sages: "Do not inquire into things which are too difficult for thee, do not search what is hidden from thee: study what you are allowed to study, and do not occupy thyself with mysteries." They meant to say, Let thy mind only attempt things which are within human perception; for the study of things which lie beyond man's comprehension is extremely injurious, as has been already stated. This lesson is also contained in the Talmudical passage, which begins, "He who considers four things," etc., and concludes, "He who does not regard the honour of his Creator"; here also is given the advice which we have already mentioned, viz., that man should not rashly engage in speculation with false conceptions, and when he is in doubt about anything, or unable to find a proof for the object of his inquiry, he must not at once abandon, reject and deny it; he must modestly keep back, and from regard to the honour of his Creator, hesitate [from uttering an opinion) and pause. This has already been explained.

It was not the object of the Prophets and our Sages in these utterances to close the gate of investigation entirely, and to prevent the mind from comprehending what is within its reach, as is imagined by simple and idle people, whom it suits better to put forth their ignorance and incapacity as wisdom and perfection, and to regard the distinction and wisdom of others as irreligion and imperfection, thus taking darkness for light and light for darkness. The whole object of the Prophets and the Sages was to declare that a limit is set to human reason where it must halt. Do not criticise the words used in this chapter and in others in reference to the mind, for we only intended to give some idea of the subject in view, not to describe the essence of the intellect: for other chapters have been dedicated to this subject.

CHAPTER XXXIII

You must know that it is very injurious to begin with this branch of philosophy, viz., Metaphysics: or to explain [at first] the sense of the similes occurring in prophecies, and interpret the metaphors which are employed in historical accounts and which abound in the writings of the Prophets. On the contrary, it is necessary to initiate the young and to instruct the less intelligent according to their comprehension: those who appear to be talented and to have capacity for the higher method of study, i.e., that based on proof and on true logical argument, should be gradually advanced towards perfection, either by tuition or by self-instruction. He, however, who begins with Metaphysics, will not only become confused in matters of religion, but will fall into complete infidelity. I compare such a person to an infant fed with wheaten bread, meat and wine; it will undoubtedly die, not because such food is naturally unfit for the human body, but because of the weakness of the child, who is unable to digest the food, and cannot derive benefit from it. The same is the case with the true principles of science. They were presented in enigmas, clad in riddles, and taught by an wise men in the most mysterious way that could be devised, not because they contain some secret evil, or are contrary to the fundamental principles of the Law (as fools think who are only philosophers in their own eyes), but because of the incapacity of man to comprehend them at the beginning of his studies: only slight allusions have been made to them to serve for the guidance of those who are capable of understanding them. These sciences were, therefore, called Mysteries (*sodoth*), and Secrets of the Law (*sitre torah*), as we shall explain.

This also is the reason why "the Torah speaks the language of man," as we have explained, for it is the object of the Torah to serve as a guide for the instruction of the young, of women, and of the common people; and as all of them are incapable to comprehend the true sense of the words, tradition was considered sufficient to convey all truths which were to be established; and as regards ideals, only such remarks were made as would lead towards a knowledge of their existence, though not to a comprehension of their true essence. When a man attains to perfection, and arrives at a knowledge of the "Secrets of the Law," either through the assistance of a teacher or by self-instruction, being led by the understanding of one part to the study of the other, he will belong to those who faithfully believe in the true principles, either because of conclusive proof, where proof is possible, or by forcible arguments, where argument is admissible; he will have a true notion of those things which he previously received in similes and metaphors, and he will fully understand their sense. We have frequently mentioned in this treatise the principle of our Sages "not to discuss the *Ma'aseh Mercabah* even in the presence of one pupil, except he be wise and intelligent; and then only the headings of the chapters are to be given to him." We must, therefore, begin with teaching these subjects according to the capacity of the pupil, and on two conditions, first, that he be wise, i.e., that he should have successfully gone through the preliminary studies, and secondly that he be intelligent, talented, clear-headed, and of quick perception, that is, "have a mind of his own" (*mebin midda'ato*), as our Sages termed it.

CHAPTER XXXV

Do not think that what we have laid down in the preceding chapters on the importance, obscurity, and difficulty of the subject, and its unsuitableness for communication to ordinary persons, includes the doctrine of God's incorporeality and His exemption from all affections (πάθη). This is not the case. For in the same way as all people must be informed, and even children must be trained in the belief that God is One, and that none besides Him is to be worshipped, so must all be taught by simple authority that God is incorporeal; that there is no similarity in any way whatsoever between Him and His creatures: that His existence is not like the existence of His creatures, His life not like that of any living being, His wisdom not like the wisdom of the wisest of men; and that the difference between Him and His creatures is not merely quantitative, but absolute [as between two individuals of two different classes]: I mean to say that all must understand that our wisdom and His, or our power and His do not differ quantitatively or qualitatively, or in a similar manner; for two things, of which the one is strong and the other weak, are necessarily similar, belong to the same class, and can be included in one definition. The same is the case with an other comparisons: they can only be made between two things belonging to the same class, as has been shown in works on Natural Science. Anything predicated of God is totally different from our attributes; no definition can comprehend both; therefore His existence and that of any other being totally differ from each other, and the term existence is applied to both homonymously, as I shall explain.

This suffices for the guidance of children and of ordinary persons who must believe that there is a Being existing, perfect, incorporeal, not inherent in a body as a force in it—God, who is above all kinds of deficiency, above A affections. But the question concerning the attributes of God, their inadmissibility, and the meaning of those attributes which are ascribed to Him; concerning the Creation, His Providence, in providing for everything; concerning His will, His perception, His knowledge of everything; concerning prophecy and its various degrees: concerning the meaning of His names which imply the idea of unity, though they are more than one; all these things are very difficult problems, the true "Secrets of the Law" the [paragraph continues] "secrets" mentioned so frequently in the books of the Prophets, and in the words of our Teachers, the subjects of which we should only mention the headings of the chapters, as we have already stated, and only in the presence of a person satisfying the above-named conditions.

That God is incorporeal, that He cannot be compared with His creatures, that He is not subject to external influence; these are things which must be explained to every one according to his capacity, and they must be taught by way of tradition to children and women, to the stupid and ignorant, as they are taught that God is One, that He is eternal, and that He alone is to be worshipped. Without incorporeality there is no unity, for a corporeal thing is in the first case not simple, but composed of matter and form which are two separate things by definition, and secondly, as it has extension it is also divisible. When persons have received this doctrine, and have been trained in this belief, and are in consequence at a loss to reconcile it with the writings of the Prophets, the meaning of the latter must be made clear and explained to them by pointing out the homonymity and the figurative application of certain terms discussed in this part of the work. Their belief in the unity of God and in the words of the Prophets will then be a true and perfect belief.

Those who are not sufficiently intelligent to comprehend the true interpretation of these passages in the Bible, or to understand that the same term admits of two different interpretations, may simply be told that the scriptural passage is clearly understood by the wise, but that they should content themselves with knowing that God is incorporeal, that He is never subject to external influence, as passivity implies a change, while God is entirely free from all change, that He cannot be compared to anything besides Himself, that no definition includes Him together with any other being, that the words of the Prophets are true, and that difficulties met with may be explained on this principle. This may suffice for that class of persons, and it is not proper to leave them in the belief that God is corporeal, or that He has any of the properties of material objects, just as there is no need to leave them in the belief that God does not exist, that there are more Gods than one, or that any other being may be worshipped.

Think about it.

1. What, according to Maimonides, prevents persons from discovering truth?
2. Why does he say the Torah was written in such simple language?
3. What ideas of God does he consider fundamental, and how can the words of the Bible be harmonized with such ideas?

1202 CE

92. Venerabilem fratrem nostrum

Translated by Ken Pennington

The "Venerabilem fratrem nostrum" is a decretal letter by Pope Innocent III (r. 1198–1216), written in 1202, to Berthold, the Duke of Zähringen, one of the princes of the Holy Roman Empire (r. 1186–1218). Berthold and other princes of the Ghibelline political faction had lodged complaints against the Pope for refusing to ratify their election of Philip of Swabia as Holy Roman Emperor and instead to support Otto IV of Brunswick, who had been elected by the Guelphs. The letter, part of which is reproduced here, is Innocent's response.

To Berthold, Noble Man and Duke of Zähringen

We have received with kindness our venerable brother, Eberhard, the archbishop of Salzburg, and Eberhard, abbot of Salmansweiler, together with the Marchese of the Eastern March, who were sent to us as nuncios by certain princes. We granted them a gracious audience. We had the letter carefully read that certain princes had sent to us, and we have noted all the contents in them. Among other things, these princes have noted in this letter to us that they objected principally that our venerable brother, the bishop of Palestrina, legate of the Apostolic See, exercised the office of an elector or of judge in the election of the emperor. They assert that if he acted as an elector, he inserted his sickle into the field of another. If he participated in the election he took away dignity from the princes. If he acted as a judge of the election, he proceeded illegally since the other party was absent. The opposing party had not been summoned and could not, therefore, be judged contumacious.

Truly we owe justice to every person because of our obligation to exercise our apostolic office. Just as we do not want our justice to be usurped by others, we do not wish to take away the right of the princes. We recognize, as we must, the princes' right and power to elect the king and afterward to raise him to emperor, which is known to belong to them by law and ancient custom. This is especially true since the Apostolic See bestowed this right and power on them when the pope translated Roman imperium in the person of the great Charles from the Greeks to the Germans.

The princes should recognize as they do (and have in our presence) that the right and authority of examining the person elected king and of promoting him to the imperial office pertains to us, since we anoint, consecrate and crown him. It is regularly and generally observed that the person who places his hands upon a candidate may examine him. There if the princes would elect a sacrilegious, excommunicated, tyrannical, fatuous, and heretical, even a pagan, person not in discord but unanimously, ought we anoint, consecrate and crown a man of this sort? Of course not.

Therefore, we respond to the objection of the princes by stating that our legate, the bishop of Palestrina, by approving our most beloved son in Christ, Otto, to be king and by reproving Phillip the duke of Swabia, did not exercise the office of elector as alleged by some of the princes in their letters to us, since he did not elect anyone or have anyone elected, and, consequently, did not participate in the election in any way. He did not usurp or infringe upon the rights of the princes. The bishop was not a judge of the person, since he was led to confirm or to deny the election of both. He was, in fact, an

officer of the papal court[1] who declared that the person of the duke was unworthy and the person of the king suitable for receiving the imperial office. He did not make his decision based on the worthiness of the electors but on the suitability of the elected. Many of those who had the power of electing the king and elevating him to emperor by right and by custom consented to Otto. The supporters of Phillip presumed to elect him with the other electors having been absent and having ignored their rights. It is clear that they unlawfully held their election, since it is a principle of law that an election can be held invalid more on account of the rights of one having been ignored than because of the opposition of many.[2] Whence, because they deserve to lose their privilege who abuse their power, it does not seem to be without merit that an injury of this sort not withstanding the others could exercise their rights.

Since Phillip ought not accept the crown and the anointing at that place and from that person and since Otto received the crown and anointing at Aachen from our venerable brother the archbishop of Cologne, we consider and name Otto not Phillip king, as justice demands. In reproving Duke Phillip of Swabia because of manifest defects of person, we did not accuse him with manifest proofs but we condemned him with manifest proofs, since condemnations, not accusations, require manifest proofs.

Furthermore, when the wishes of the princes are divided, we can favor one of the parties after admonishing them and waiting for the results, especially when both parties ask us for unction, consecration, and coronation. We have this authority by law and example. If the princes do not or will not reach a decision after warning them and waiting for their decision, should the Apostolic See suffer the consequences of not having an advocate and a defender because of their fault?

The princes know and your highness is not unmindful that when Lothair and Conrad were elected in discord, the Roman pontiff crowned Lothair. Conrad then returned to the pope's grace.[3] ...

The manifest defects of the duke of Swabia are his public excommunication, open perjury, and widely known persecution that his forebearers and he himself inflicted on the Apostolic See and other churches. Pope Celestine III of blessed memory, our predecessor, publically and solemnly excommunicated him while he was in Tuscany because of his invasion and destruction of the Patrimony of St Peter, even though Phillip had been often admonished to desist. ...

Since, therefore, we cannot be moved from our course, but rather we shall firmly persist in our decision, and since you have often stated in your letters that we ought nevertheless to favor the Duke, we warn your highness and exhort the Lord through Apostolic letters that, just as you are confident of our grace and we hope for your devotion, you should withdraw your loyalty from Duke Phillip, not withstanding your oath to him, which, if you have sworn it to him for reason of the kingdom, since he has been found unworthy of obtaining the imperial office, an oath of this sort should not be observed.

Written at the Lateran ca. 26 March, 1202

Think about it.

1. How does the Pope answer the claim that, when it comes to politics, the church should abide by decisions made by the princes?

1228 CE

93. The Secret History of the Mongols

Translated by Igor de Rachewiltz

There is still debate over who actually wrote *The Secret History of the Mongols*, but it is clear that is the oldest surviving work in the Mongolian language. It is an account of the life and deeds of Chinggis Qa'an (Ghengis Khan) and was likely completed in 1228, a year after his death, but it underwent editorial revisions until the early 15th century. The following is an excerpt that tells the tale of how a man named Jebe became one of the Khan's generals. The year of the events described is 1201.

The Secret History of the Mongols: A Mongolian Epic Chronicle of the Thirteenth Century, Volume I, trans. Igor de Rachewiltz, pp. 65–69. Copyright © 2006 by Brill Academic Publishers. Reprinted with permission.

As soon as A'uču Ba'atur reached his own people, he had them moved along with him in haste. The Tayiči'ut A'uču Ba'atur and Qodun Örčeng arrayed their troops at Ülengüt Turas on the other side of the Onan, and stood in battle order ready to fight.

Činggis Qa'an came up and fought with the Tayiči'ut. They battled to and fro incessantly until evening came; then, in the same place where they had been fighting, they passed the night right next to each other. When people arrived, fleeing in disarray, they set up a circular camp and also passed the night in the same spot, alongside their troops.

In that battle Činggis Qa'an was wounded in a vein of the neck. He could not stop the bleeding and was in a great plight. He waited till sundown, then he pitched camp just there where the two armies had encamped right next to each other.

Jelme sucked and sucked the blood which clogged Činggis Qa'an's wound and his mouth was all smeared with blood. Still, Jelme, not trusting other people, stayed there and looked after him. Until the middle of the night he swallowed down or spat out mouthfuls of the clogging blood.

When midnight had passed Činggis Qa'an revived and said, 'The blood has dried up completely; I am thirsty.' Then Jelme took off his hat, boots and clothes—everything—and stark naked but for his pants, he ran into the midst of the enemy who had settled right next to them. He jumped on to a cart of the people who had set up a circular camp over there. He searched for kumis, but was unable to find any because those people had fled in disarray and had turned the mares loose without milking them.

As he could not find kumis, he took from one of their carts a large covered bucket of curds and carried it back. In the time between his going and coming back he was not seen by anyone. Heaven indeed protected him!

Having brought the covered bucket of curds, the same Jelme, all by himself, searched for water, brought it back, and having mixed it with the curds got the Qa'an to drink it.

Three times, resting in between, the Qa'an drank, then he spoke: 'The eyes within me have cleared up.' He spoke and sat up: it was daybreak and growing light. He looked and saw that, all about the place where he was sitting, the wound-clogging blood that Jelme had kept on sucking and had spat about had formed small puddles. When he saw it, Činggis Qa'an said, 'What is this? Couldn't you have spat farther away?' Jelme then said, 'When you were in a great plight, had I gone farther away I would have feared being separated from you. As I was in haste, I swallowed what I could swallow and spat out what I could spit out; I was in a plight myself and quite a lot went also into my stomach!'

Činggis Qa'an again spoke: 'When I was in this state, lying down, why did you run naked into their camp? Had you been caught, wouldn't you have revealed that I was like this?' Jelme said, 'My thought, as I went naked, was that if somehow I got caught, I would have said, "I wanted to submit to you, but they found out and, seizing me, decided to kill me. They removed my clothes—everything—only my pants had not yet been removed when I suddenly managed to escape and have just come in haste to join you."

They would have regarded me as sincere, they would have given me clothes and looked after me. Then, I would have jumped on a horse and while they were astonished watching me flee, in that brief moment I would have surely got back! So thinking, and because I wished to get back in time to satisfy the Qa'an's craving for drink caused by his parching thirst, thinking this and without so much as blinking an eye I went there.'

Činggis Qa'an said, 'What can I say now? In former days, when the Three Merkit came and thrice circled Mount Burqan, you saved my life for the first time. Now, once more, you restored me to life when, with your mouth, you sucked the clotting blood from my wound. And, yet again, when I was in a great plight with a parching thirst, disregarding your life, you went amidst the enemy without so much as blinking an eye; you quenched my thirst and restored life to me. These three services of yours will stay in my heart!' Thus the Qa'an spoke.

When it had grown light, it turned out that the enemy troops who were bivouacking right next to us had dispersed during the night; only the people who had set up the circular camp had not moved from the place where they had encamped because they would not have been able to get away.

Činggis Qa'an moved from the place where he had spent the night in order to bring back the people who had fled. As he was bringing back the fugitives, Činggis Qa'an himself heard a woman in a red coat who, standing on top of a ridge, was wailing loudly, crying 'Temüjin!' He sent a man to enquire whose wife was the woman who was crying like that. The man went and, having asked her, that woman said, 'I am the daughter of Sorqan Šira and my name is Qada'an. The soldiers here captured my husband and were going to kill him. As my husband was being killed, I cried and wailed and called on Temüjin to save my husband.' So she said, and the man returned and reported these words to Činggis Qa'an.

Hearing these words, Činggis Qa'an rode at a trot and reached her; he dismounted near Qada'an and they embraced each other, but her husband had already been killed by our soldiers.

After Činggis Qa'an had brought back those people, he camped on the spot for the night with his great army. He invited Qada'an to come to him and had her sit by his side.

The following day, Sorqan Šira and Jebe, who had been retainers of Tödöge of the Tayiči'ut, also arrived—the two of them. Činggis Qa'an said to Sorqan Šira, 'It was indeed a good service of you, father and sons,

To throw to the ground
The heavy wood on my neck,
To remove the wooden cangue
That was on my collar.

Why, then, did you delay coming to me?"

Sorqan Šira said, 'At heart I felt full confidence in you, but how could I make haste? Had I hurried and come to you earlier, my Tayiči'ut masters would have blown to the winds, like hearth-ashes, my wife and children, and the cattle and provisions I had left behind. Because of this I did not hurry, but now that the Tayiči'ut have been defeated we came in haste to join our Qa'an.' When he had finished speaking, Činggis Qa'an said, 'You did right!'

Again Činggis Qa'an spoke, saying 'When we fought at Köyiten and, pressing on each other, were reforming our ranks, from the top of those ridges an arrow came. Who, from the top of the mountain, shot an arrow so as to sever the neckbone of my tawny war horse with the white mouth?'

To these words Jebe said, 'I shot the arrow from the top of the mountain. If now I am put to death by the Qa'an, I shall be left to rot on a piece of earth the size of the palm of a hand, but if I be favoured,

For the Qa'an I will charge forward
So as to rend the deep water,
So as to crumble the shining stone.
For him I will charge forward
So as to split the blue stone
In the place which I am told to reach,
So as to crush the black stone
At the time when I am told to attack.'

Činggis Qa'an said, 'A man who used to be an enemy, when it comes to his former killings and hostile actions "conceals his person and hides his tongue"—he is afraid. As for this one, however, he does not hide his killings and hostile actions; on the contrary, he makes them known. He is a man to have as a companion. He is named Jirqo'adai, but because he shot an arrow at the neckbone of my tawny war horse with the white mouth, I shall call him Jebe and I will use him as my *jebe* arrow.' He named him Jebe and said, 'Keep by my side!'

This is the way in which Jebe came from the Tayiči'ut and became a companion of Činggis Qa'an.

1233 CE

94. The Complete History

Translated by Donald S. Richards

The Complete History (*al-Kamil fi'l ta'rikh in Arabic*), often referred to as The Chronicle of Ibn al-Athir, is a lengthy work of Islamic narrative history, written in annalistic fashion, which begins with Creation and extends to the year 1230. Its author, Ali Ibn al-Athir (1160–1233), a Kurdish Muslim, died before completing it. In the following passage from the work, Ibn al-Athir writes of the rise of the Almohads under Abu Abd Allah Muhammad Ibn Tumart beginning in 1120.

[569] In this year the career of the Mahdi Abū 'Abd Allāh Muhammad ibn 'Abd Allāh ibn Tūmart al-'Alawl al-Hasanī began. His tribe, part of the Masmūda, was known as the Hargha in the Sūs Mountains of the Maghrib. They settled there when the Muslims with Mūsā ibn Nusayr conquered it. Under this year we shall give an account of the Mahdi and of⁴ Abd al-Mu'min up to the completion of the conquest of the Maghrib to give a continuous narrative.

In his youth Ibn Tūmart travelled to the lands of the East in search of learning. He was a lawyer, a man of culture, well versed in the Sharia and a student of Hadīth. He was knowledgeable in the fundamentals of religion and canon law and had a solid learning in the Arabic language. He was pious and an ascetic. On his journeys he came to Iraq and met with al-Ghazālī and al-Kiyā. In Alexandria he associated with Abū Bakr al-Tartūshī. It is reported that he had a conversation with al-Ghazālī concerning the power that he had achieved in the Maghrib. Al-Ghazālī said to him, 'This is not feasible in these lands. It is impossible for that to happen for the likes of us.' A certain historian of the Maghrib gave this account, but the truth is that he never met him.

He went on pilgrimage from there [570] and returned to the Maghrib. When he took ship from Alexandria to go west, he changed the wicked conduct on board and obliged the crew to observe the prayer times and to recite the Koran, until eventually he arrived in the year 505 [1111–12] at Mahdiyya, where the ruler at that time was Yaḥyā ibn Tamīm. He settled in a mosque to the south of the Saturday Mosque. He possessed nothing but a coffee pot and a staff. The townsfolk heard reports of him and sought him out to study various branches of learning under him. Whenever he was aware of something reprehensible, he reformed or abolished it. After many examples of this the Emir Yaḥyā summoned him along with a group of ulema and, when he saw his character and heard his words, he paid him honour and respect and asked him for his prayers.

He left the city and resided at Monastir with a group of pious men for a while. He then went to Bougie, where he acted as before. He was expelled from there to a village nearby, called Mallāla. There he met 'Abd al-Mu'min ibn 'Alī. In him he saw such nobility and enterprise as he interpreted to indicate leadership and an ability to succeed. He asked him his name and his tribe and was told that he was from Qays 'Aylan, and then from the Banū Sulaym. Ibn Tūmart said to him, This is what the Prophet (God bless him and give him peace) foretold, when he said, "God will give victory to this religion at the end of time through a man from Qays." He was asked, "From which branch of Qays?" and he replied, "From the Banū Sulaym." He was delighted with 'Abd al-Mu'min and rejoiced at meeting him. 'Abd al-Mu'min was born in the city of Tājara in the district of Tlemcen. He was from the 'Ā'idh, a branch of Kumara, who settled in this region in the year 180 [796–7].

The Mahdi continued zealously to order what is good and forbid what is evil on his travels until he arrived at Marrakech, the capital of the Emir of the Muslims, Yūsuf ibn 'Alī ibn Tāshfin. There he witnessed more reprehensible behaviour than he had

observed on his travels. He increased his ordering of the good and forbidding of evil, so his following became extensive and the people held a high opinion of him. One day on his travels he saw the sister of the Emir of the Muslims in her ceremonial procession, accompanied by her maid-servants, [571] beautiful, numerous and unveiled. This was the custom of the Veiled Ones, whose women uncovered their faces while the men veiled theirs. When he saw the women like this he expressed his disapproval, ordered them to cover their faces, and he and his followers struck out at their mounts. The sister of the Emir of the Muslims fell from her horse, which incident was reported to the Emir of the Muslims, 'Alī ibn Yūsuf who summoned him and summoned the lawyers to debate with him. The Mahdi began to preach and put the fear of God into the Emir who was reduced to tears. He ordered the lawyers to dispute with him but there was amongst them no one who could stand against him because of the power of his arguments in support of what he had done.

In the service of the Emir of the Muslims was a certain vizier called Mālik ibn Wuhayb. He said, 'O Emir of the Muslims, this man, by God, does not wish to order what is good and forbid what is evil. His only aim is to foment discord and to seize control of some region. Execute him and place the responsibility for his blood on me.' When the Emir refused, he said, 'If you will not kill him, then imprison him and shut him away, for otherwise he will provoke trouble which cannot be mended.' He then ordered his imprisonment but one of the leaders of the Veiled Ones, called Bayān ibn 'Uthmān, prevented this, so the Emir ordered his expulsion from Marrakech. He went to Aghmāt and stayed in the mountain, where he travelled until he came in the year 514 [1120–21] to Sus, where the Hargha tribe was and other members of the Masmūda, who came to him and flocked to join him.

The inhabitants of these regions exchanged reports about him and came to pay him visits. Their notables attended on him and he began to preach to them, reminding them of 'the days of God', and expound to them the ordinances of Islam, what had been corrupted and what new tyranny and wickedness had been introduced and also that obedience to any of these regimes was not binding because they followed what was false but rather it was obligatory to fight them and stop them doing what they were doing. He continued thus for about a year and the Hargha, his tribe, followed him. He called his followers the Almohads and taught them that the Prophet (God bless him and give him peace) had promised a Mahdi who would fill the earth with justice and that the place where he would appear was the Furthest Maghrib. Ten men arose to support him, one of whom was 'Abd al-Mu'min. They said, 'All this applies only to you. You are the Mahdi', and they swore allegiance to him on this basis.

[572] Reports about him reached the Emir of the Muslims, who prepared a force of his followers and sent them against the Mahdi. When they drew near the mountain where he was, the Mahdi said to his men, 'These people seek me but I fear what they may do to you. The best course is for me to leave these lands so that you may remain secure.' Ibn Tūfiyān, one of the shaykhs of the Hargha, said to him, 'Are you fearful of anything from the heavens?' 'No,' was the reply, 'rather from the heavens will your victory come.' So Ibn Tūfiyān said, 'Then let the whole world come against us.' All the tribe agreed with him, so the Mahdi said, 'Rest assured that with this little band will come victory and triumph. After a little while you will extirpate their regime and inherit their land.' They therefore descended from the mountain. So strong was their belief that the Mahdi spoke the truth that they were victorious as he had told them.

Tribes came to him in droves from the settlements around, both to east and west, and pledged him their loyalty. The tribe of Hintāta, one of the strongest of the tribes, offered him their allegiance. He welcomed them and placed much reliance on them. Envoys of the people of Tīnmāl came to him to tell of their submission and to request him to come to them. He set out for the mountain of Tīnmāl and

settled there. He composed a book on the oneness of God for them and also a treatise on the creed. He laid down for them how they should behave one to another, that they should limit themselves to short, inexpensive clothing, and urged them to fight their enemies and to expel any evil men from their midst.

He dwelt in Tīnmāl and built himself a mosque outside the city. There he would perform the daily prayers, he and a group of those around him. After the last prayer of the day he would enter the city. When he saw how numerous were the inhabitants of the mountain and how strong the city, he feared they would turn against him, so he ordered them to present themselves without weapons. They did this for several days, then he ordered his followers to kill them. They attacked [573] them, taking them by surprise, and killed them in that mosque. He then entered the city, where he carried out a massacre, enslaved the women and plundered property. The number of the slain was 15,000. He divided their houses and land amongst his followers and built a wall around the city and a citadel on the summit of a high hill.

In the Tīnmāl mountain there are running rivers, trees and fields of crops. Access is difficult. There is no mountain more impregnable. It is said that, when he feared the inhabitants of Tīnmāl, he looked about him and saw that many of their offspring were fair-haired and blue-eyed, while brown colouring was dominant for their fathers. The Emir of the Muslims had a large number of Frankish and [other] Christian mamlukes, whose colouring was predominantly fair. Once every year they used to go up into the mountain to take the money assigned them by the sultan. They would reside in the houses of the inhabitants, expelling their owners from them. When the Mahdi saw their offspring, he questioned them, 'Why is it that I see you brown in colouring, and I see your children to be fair and blue-eyed?' They told him their story in connection with the mamlukes of the Emir of the Muslims. He censured their toleration of that and expressed his scorn for them and his horror at their situation. They replied, 'What is to be done to get rid of them? We do not have the power to deal with them.' He said, 'When they come to you at the customary time and disperse to their lodgings, let each one of you rise up against his lodger and kill him. Then guard your mountain, for it is very defensible and not easily taken.' They waited patiently until those mamlukes arrived, then they killed them as the Mahdi had prescribed. Having done this, they feared what the Emir might do to them, so they fortified themselves in the mountain and closed off any passable route. This strengthened the Mahdi's spirit.

Later the Emir of the Muslims sent a powerful force against them, which besieged them in the mountain, imposing a tight blockade and preventing the passage of provisions. Food became scarce for the Mahdi's followers, [574] until bread was unobtainable. Each day just enough broth was cooked. To feed themselves, each person dipped his hand in the broth and then withdrew it. For that day he had to make do with whatever stuck to it. The notables of the Tīnmāl population met together and desired to repair their relations with the Emir of the Muslims. News of this came to the Mahdi Ibn Tūmart. There was with him a man called Abū 'Abd Allāh al-Wansharīshī, who appeared to be simple-minded and lacking in any knowledge of the Koran and religious studies. Spittle would drop on to his chest and it was as though he was out of his wits. Nevertheless the Mahdi showed him favour and honour and used to say, 'God has a mysterious purpose for this man which will be revealed.'

In fact al-Wansharīshī was assiduous in studying the Koran and religious learning in secret so that nobody should know about it. When it was the year 519 [1125–6] and the Mahdi was fearful of the inhabitants of the mountain, he went out one day to pray the morning prayer and alongside the *mihrāb* he saw a man, handsomely dressed and nicely perfumed. He pretended not to know him and said, 'Who is this?' 'I am Abū 'Abd Allāh al-Wansharīshī,' was the reply. The Mahdi said to him, 'How amazing this is!' He began his prayers and when he had finished, he called the people to gather together and said, 'This

man claims that he is al-Wansharīshī. Examine him and establish his identity.' When daylight had fully broken, they knew him. The Mahdi asked him, 'What has happened to you?' He replied, 'Last night an angel came to me from the heavens and washed my heart. God taught me the Koran and *al-Muwatta'* and other religious knowledge and hadlths.' In the presence of the people the Mahdi wept and said, 'We shall test you.' 'Do so,' was the answer.

He began to recite the Koran most excellently, starting from whatever point was requested, and likewise with *al-Muwatta'* and other books of law and jurisprudence. This astonished the people and they were awestruck. He said to them, 'God Almighty has given me a light by which I may tell the people of Paradise from the people of [575] Hellfire. I command you to kill the people of Hellfire and not to touch the people of Paradise. God has sent down angels to the well which is in such-and-such a place who will bear witness to my truthfulness.'

The Mahdi along with the people, all in tears, went to that well. At its mouth the Mahdi prayed and said, 'O angels of God, Abū 'Abd Allāh al-Wansharīshī has asserted such-and-such.' The reply from within was 'He has spoken the truth.' The Mahdi had placed some men there to give that testimony. When that reply came from the well, the Mahdi said, 'This is a purified and hallowed place into which the angels have descended. The right course is to fill it in lest any pollution or something unacceptable fall into it.' They threw in stones and earth sufficient to fill it. Then the Mahdi summoned the people of the mountain to gather at that spot and they assembled for 'the discrimination.' Al-Wansharīshī would pick out a man whose attitude was threatening and say, 'This man is one of the people of Hellfire,' and he would be cast down dead from the mountain. He would also pick out an inexperienced youth or someone not to be feared and say, 'This man is one of the people of Paradise,' and so he would be left on the right hand. The number of those slain was 70,000. When this was completed, the Mahdi felt secure for himself and his followers and his cause prospered.

This is what I have heard several learned men of the Maghrib say about 'the discrimination.' I have heard others say, 'When Ibn Tūmart saw the many wicked and corrupt people among the inhabitants of the mountain, he summoned the shaykhs of the tribes and said to them, "You have no true religion and it will only become strong by ordering what is good and forbidding what is evil and by expelling the corrupt from your midst. Seek out all those wicked and corrupt people among you. Tell them to desist and if they do not, write down their names and report them to me that I may look into their case." They did so and wrote down for him their names in every tribe. He ordered them to do this a second and a third time. Then he gathered all the lists and took from them the names that were repeated and made a record of them. He gathered all the people together, produced the names that he had written down and handed them to al-Wansharīshī, known as the Bringer of Good News (al-Bashīr). He commanded him to review the tribes and put the evildoers on the left side and the rest on the right. [576] He carried this out and it was ordered that those on al-Wansharīshī's left should have their hands tied, which was done. He then said, "These are wretched people who must be put to death." He ordered each tribe to kill those wretches in their ranks. They were killed to the last man. This was the day of discrimination.'

After Ibn Tūmart had completed 'the discrimination', he saw his surviving followers to be truly well-disposed with hearts united in obedience. He equipped an army of them and sent them to the mountains of Aghmāt, where was a force of the Almoravids. There was a battle and the followers of Ibn Tūmart, whose commander was Abū 'Abd Allāh al-Wansharishi, were defeated. Many of them were killed and 'Umar al-Hintati, one of his greatest men, was wounded. His senses were gone and his pulse had ceased. 'He is dead,' they said, but al-Wanshar-ish! said, 'Truly he is not dead. He will not die until he conquers the land.' After a while he opened his eyes and his strength returned to him. The people

were deceived and led astray by this. They returned defeated to Ibn Tūmart who preached to them and thanked them for their steadfastness.

After this he continued to send out squadrons into the far reaches of Muslim lands. If they saw an army, they clung close to their mountain and so were safe. The Mahdi had organised his followers in grades. The first was called *Ayt 'Ashara*, meaning 'the People of Ten'. Of these the first was 'Abd al-Mu'min, followed by Abū Hafs ['Umar] al-Hintati and then the others. These are the noblest of his followers and his close confidants, the first to follow him. The second grade was *Ayt Khamsīn*, meaning 'the People of Fifty', lower in rank but consisting of a number of the leaders of the tribes. The third was *Ayt Sab'īn*, meaning 'the People of Seventy', lower than the preceding ranks. The generality of his followers and those who entered into his allegiance were called 'Almohads' (*Muwahhidūn*). If the Almohads are mentioned in their histories, the Mahdi's followers and those of 'Abd al-Mu'min after him are intended.

Ibn Tūmart's position continued to grow until the year 524 [1130]. He fitted out [577] a mighty army, amounting to 40,000, most of whom were infantry, and put al-Wansharīshī in charge. He sent 'Abd al-Mu'min with them. They marched down to Marrakech and put it under siege, pressing hard on it. The Emir of the Muslims 'All ibn Yūsuf was there. The siege continued for twenty days. The Emir of the Muslims sent to the governor of Sijilmasa ordering him to come with his troops. The latter assembled a large force and set out. When he drew near the Mahdi's army, the people of Marrakech made a sortie from the opposite direction. Battle was joined and became fierce. Many of the Mahdi's followers were killed, including their commander al-Wansharīshī. They rallied around 'Abd al-Mu'min and appointed him commander.

The fighting continued most of the day. 'Abd al-Mu'min performed the prayer as in time of danger at both the noon and afternoon prayer times while the battle was in progress. It had not been performed previously in the Maghrib. When the Masmūda tribes saw how numerous the Almoravids were and how strong, they placed their backs up against a large orchard there. The orchard was called by them 'the Lake' (*al-Buhayra*) and thus one speaks of 'the battle of the Lake' and 'the year of the Lake.' They were now fighting on one front until they were overtaken by nightfall. Most of the Masmūda had been killed. When al-Wansharīshī was killed, 'Abd al-Mu'min buried him. The Masmūda looked for his body but could not find it amongst the slain. They said, 'The angels have lifted him up.' When night fell, 'Abd al-Mu'min and the survivors set out for the mountain.

Think about it.

1. What do you think made ibn Tumart's so popular?
2. What does this account reveal about the differences of opinion among Muslims of the time?
3. What does this account reveal about the way ibn Tumart's group believed God operates in the world?

---

c. 1240 CE

95. The Tale of the Heike

Translated by Arthur L. Sadler

The Genpei War (1180–1185), an epic Japanese conflict between the Taira (Heike) clan, led by Kiyomori, and the Minamoto (Genji) clan, led by Yoritomo, is immortalized in *The Tale of the Heike* (*Heike Monogatari*), a collection of oral stories by blind biwa-playing bards. Yukinaga, the former governor of Shinano, is thought to be the original compiler, who put it together around 1240, but it was enhanced over the next century by others. The standard version was produced around 1370 by a singer named Akashi Kakuichi. The following excerpt from the work recounts the death of the Taira samurai Atsumori at the Battle of Ichi-no-Tani.

CHAPTER XVI.

Now when the Heike were routed at Ichi-no-tani, and their Nobles and Courtiers were fleeing to the shore to escape in their ships, Kumagai Jirō Naozane came riding along a narrow path on to the beach, with the intention of intercepting one of their great captain's. Just then his eye fell on a single horseman who was attempting to reach one of the ships in the offing, and had swum his horse out some twenty yards from the water's edge.

Selection from: "The Heike Monogatari," *Transactions of the Asiatic Society of Japan, Volume XLVI, Part II*, trans. Arthur L. Sadler, pp. 156–158. Trübner & Company, 1918. Copyright in the Public Domain.

He was richly attired in a silk hitatare embroidered with storks, and the lacing of his armour was shaded green; his helmet was surmounted by lofty horns, and the sword he wore was gay with gold. His twenty four arrows had black and white feathers, and he carried a black-lacquered bow bound with rattan. The horse he rode was dappled grey, and its saddle glittered with gold mounting, Not doubting that he was one of the chief captains, Kumagai beckoned to him with his war fan,, crying out: "Shameful! to show an enemy your back. Return! Return!" Then the warrior turned his horse and rode him back to the beach, where Kumagai at once engaged him in mortal combat. Quickly hurling him to the ground, he sprang upon him and tore off his helmet to cut off his head, when he beheld the face of a youth of sixteen or seventeen, delicately powdered and with blackened teeth, just about the age of his own son, and with features of great beauty.

"Who are you?" he enquired; "Tell me your name, for I would spare your life." "Nay, first say who you are"; replied the young man. "I am Kumagai Jirō Naozane of Musashi, a person of no particular importance." "Then you have made a good capture"; said the youth. "Take my head and show it to some of my side and they will tell you who I am." "Though he is one of their leaders", mused Kumagai, "if I slay him it will not turn defeat into victory, and if I spare him, it will not turn victory into defeat. When my son Kojiro was but slightly wounded at Ichi-no-tani, did it not make my heart bleed? How pitiful then to put this youth to death." And so he was about to set him free, when, looking behind him, he saw Doi and Kajiwara coming up with fifty horsemen. "Alas! look there", he exclaimed, the tears running down his face, "though I would spare your life, the whole country side swarms with our men,and you cannot escape them. If you must die, let it be by my hand, and I will see that prayers are said for your re-birth in bliss."

"Indeed it must be so", said the young warrior, "so take off my head at once." Then Kumagai, weeping bitterly, and so overcome by his compassion for the fair youth that his eyes swam and his hand trembled so that he could scarcely wield his blade, hardly knowing what he did, at last cut off his head. "Alas!" he cried, "what life is so hard as that of a soldier? Only because I was born of a warrior family must I suffer this affliction! How lamentable it is to do such cruel deeds!" And he pressed his face to the sleeve of his armour and wept bitterly. Then, wrapping up the head, he was stripping off the young man's armour, when he discovered a flute in a brocade bag that he was carrying in his girdle. "Ah", he exclaimed, "it was this youth and his friends who were amusing themselves with music within the walls this morning. Among all our men of the Eastern Provinces I doubt if there is any who has brought a flute with him. What esthetes are these Courtiers of the Heike!" And when he brought them and showed them to the Commander, all who saw them were moved to tears; and he then discovered that the youth was Taiyū Atsumori, the youngest son of Shūri-no-taiyū Tsunemori, aged seventeen years. From this time the mind of Kumagai was turned toward the religious life and he eventually became a recluse.

The flute of Atsumori was one which his grandfather Tadamori, who was a famous player, had received as a present from the Emperor Toba, and had handed down to his father Tsunemori, who has given it to Atsumori because of his skill on the instrument. It was called, 'Saeda.' Concerning this story of Kumagai we may quote the saying that "even in the most droll and flippant farce there is the germ of a Buddhist Psalm."

Think about it.

1. The author clearly is painting Kumagai in a positive light. What makes him admirable?
2. What message is being conveyed here?

1273 CE

96. The Masnavi

Translated by Edward H. Whinfield

The Masnavi-I Ma'navi ("Rhyming Couplets of Profound Spiritual Meaning"), or *The Masnavi* for short, is a collection of six books of poetry by the Persian Sufi mystic Jalāl ad-Dīn Muhammad Balkhī (1207–1273), known more commonly as Rumi. He worked on the project between 1258 and 1273. *The Masnavi* contains stories and anecdotes designed to illustrate points of morality and spirituality. It is one of the most influential works of Persian literature. Here are a few passages.

All religions are in substance one and the same.

> In the adorations and benedictions of righteous men
> The praises of all the prophets are kneaded together.
> All their praises are mingled into one stream,
> All the vessels are emptied into one ewer.
> Because He that is praised is, in fact, only One,
> In this respect all religions are only one religion.
> Because all praises are directed towards God's light,
> Their various forms and figures are borrowed from it.
> Men never address praises but to One deemed worthy,
> They err only through mistaken opinions of Him.
> So, when a light falls upon a wall,
> That wall is a connecting-link between all its beams;
> Yet when it casts that reflection back to its source,
> It wrongly shows great as small, and halts in its praises.

Or if the moon be reflected in a well,
And one looks down the well, and mistakenly praises it,
In reality he is intending to praise the moon,
Although, through ignorance, he is looking down the well.
The object of his praises is the moon, not its reflection;
His infidelity arises from mistake of the circumstances.
That well-meaning man goes wrong through his mistake;
The moon is in heaven, and he fancies it in the well.
By these false idols mankind are perplexed,
And driven by vain lusts to their sorrow.

Satan's snares for mankind.

Thus spake cursed Iblis to the Almighty,
"I want a mighty trap to catch human game withal."
God gave him gold and silver and troops of horses,
Saying, "You can catch my creatures with these."
Iblis said, "Bravo!" but at the same time hung his lip,
And frowned sourly like a bitter orange.
Then God offered gold and jewels from precious mines
To that laggard in the faith,
Saying, "Take these other traps, O cursed one."
But Iblis said, "Give me more, O blessed Defender."
God gave him succulent and sweet and costly wines,
And also store of silken garments.
But Iblis said, "O Lord, I want more aids than these,
In order to bind men in my twisted rope
So firmly that Thy adorers, who are valiant men,
May not, man-like, break my bonds asunder."
When at last God showed him the beauty of women,
Which bereaves men of reason and self-control,
Then Iblis clapped his hands and began to dance,
Saying, "Give me these; I shall quickly prevail with these!"

This is followed by comments on the text, "Of goodliest fabric we created man, and then brought him down to the lowest of the low, saving those who believe and do the things that are right;" and on the verses,—

"If thou goest the road, they will show thee the road;
If thou becomest naught, they will turn thee to being."

Lofty philosophical speculation does not lead to the knowledge of God.

The Musulraan said, "O my friends,
My lord, the Prophet Muhammad, appeared to me,
And said, ' The Jew has hurried to the top of Sinai,

And plays a game of love with God's interlocutor;
The Christian has been carried by 'Isa, Lord of bliss
Up to the summit of the fourth heaven;
Thou who art left behind and hast endured anguish,
Arise quickly and eat the sweetmeats and confections!
Those two clever and learned men have ascended,
And read their titles of dignity and exaltation;
Those two exalted ones have found exalted science,
And rivalled the very angels in intellect;
O humble and simple and despised one,
Arise and eat of the banquet of the divine sweets!"
They said to him, "Then you have been gluttonous;
Well indeed! you have eaten all the sweets!
He answered, "When my sovereign lord commanded me,
Who am I that I should abstain from obeying?
Would you, O Jew, resist the commands of Moses
If he bade you do something, either pleasant or not?
Would you, O Christian, rebel against 'Isa's commands,
Whether those commands were agreeable or the reverse?
How could I rebel against the 'Glory of the prophets'?
Nay, I ate the sweets, and am now happy."
They replied, "By Allah, you have seen a true vision;
Your vision is better than a hundred like ours.
Your dream was seen by you when awake, O happy one,
For it was seen to be real by your being awake."
        Quit excessive speculation and inordinate science,
'Tis service of God and good conduct that gains its end.
'Tis for this that God created us,
"We created not mankind save to worship us."
What profit did his science bring to Samiri?
His science excluded him from God's portals.
Consider what Qarun gained by his alchemy;
He was swallowed up in the depths of the earth.
Abu-l Jahl, again, what gained he from his wit
Save to be hurled head-foremost into hell for infidelity?
Know real science is seeing the fire directly,
Not mere talk, inferring the fire from the smoke.
Your scientific proofs are more offensive to the wise
Than the urine and breath whence a physician infers.
If these be your only proofs, O son,
Smell foul breath and inspect urine like physicians.
Such proofs are as the staff of a blind man,
Which prove only the blindness of the holder.

All your outcry and pompous claims and bustle
Only say, "I cannot see, hold me excused!"

This is illustrated be an anecdote of a peasant who, hearing a proclamation issued by the Prince of Tirmid, to the effect that a large reward would be given to him who should take a message to Samarcaud in the space of four days, hurried to Tirmid by relays of post-horses in the utmost haste, and threw the whole city into alarm, as the people thought that his extreme haste and bustle must portend the approach of an enemy or some other calamity. But when he was admitted to the presence of the prince, all he had to say was, that he had hurried to inform him that he could not go to Samarcand so quickly. The prince was very angry with him for making all this disturbance about nothing, and threatened to punish him.

Think about it.

1. In the first poem, why does Rumi believe that all religions are only one religion?
2. What is Rumi's view of women?
3. According to Rumi, why is the study of science and philosophy unhealthy for a person?

1274 CE

97. Summa Theologica

Translated by the Fathers of the English Dominican Province

The *Summa Theologica*, also known as the *Summa Theologiae*, is a manual designed for beginners in Christian theology. It was written in Latin by the Italian Dominican priest Thomas Aquinas (c. 1225–1274) between 1265 and 1274. Although he never finished it, the work nevertheless became one of the most influential works of Christian philosophy ever made. The following section from the beginning of the work discusses the significance of theology in general.

Thomas Aquinas, *Summa Theologica*, trans. Fathers of the English Dominican Province. Benziger Bros., 1917. Copyright in the Public Domain.

Treatise on Sacred Doctrine

Question 1 — THE NATURE AND EXTENT OF SACRED DOCTRINE

Art. 1 —Whether, besides philosophy, any further doctrine is required?

Objection 1: It seems that, besides philosophical science, we have no need of any further knowledge. For man should not seek to know what is above reason: "Seek not the things that are too high for thee" (Ecclus. 3:22). But whatever is not above reason is fully treated of in philosophical science. Therefore any other knowledge besides philosophical science is superfluous.

Objection 2: Further, knowledge can be concerned only with being, for nothing can be known, save what is true; and all that is, is true. But everything that is, is treated of in philosophical science—even God Himself; so that there is a part of philosophy called theology, or the divine science, as Aristotle has proved (Metaph. vi). Therefore, besides philosophical science, there is no need of any further knowledge.

On the contrary, It is written (2 Tim. 3:16): "All Scripture, inspired of God is profitable to teach, to reprove, to correct, to instruct in justice." Now Scripture, inspired of God, is no part of philosophical science, which has been built up by human reason. Therefore it is useful that besides philosophical science, there should be other knowledge, i.e. inspired of God.

I answer that, It was necessary for man's salvation that there should be a knowledge revealed by God besides philosophical science built up by human reason. Firstly, indeed, because man is directed to God, as to an end that surpasses the grasp of his reason: "The eye hath not seen, O God, besides Thee, what things Thou hast prepared for them that wait for Thee" (Is. 64:4). But the end must first be known by men who are to direct their thoughts and actions to the end. Hence it was necessary for the salvation of man that certain truths which exceed human reason should be made known to him by divine revelation. Even as regards those truths about God which human reason could have discovered, it was necessary that man should be taught by a divine revelation; because the truth about God such as reason could discover, would only be known by a few, and that after a long time, and with the admixture of many errors. Whereas man's whole salvation, which is in God, depends upon the knowledge of this truth. Therefore, in order that the salvation of men might be brought about more fitly and more surely, it was necessary that they should be taught divine truths by divine revelation. It was therefore necessary that besides philosophical science built up by reason, there should be a sacred science learned through revelation.

Reply to Objection 1: Although those things which are beyond man's knowledge may not be sought for by man through his reason, nevertheless, once they are revealed by God, they must be accepted by faith. Hence the sacred text continues, "For many things are shown to thee above the understanding of man" (Ecclus. 3:25). And in this, the sacred science consists.

Reply to Objection 2: Sciences are differentiated according to the various means through which knowledge is obtained. For the astronomer and the physicist both may prove the same conclusion: that the earth, for instance, is round: the astronomer by means of mathematics (i.e. abstracting from matter), but the physicist by means of matter itself. Hence there is no reason why those things which may be learned from philosophical science, so far as they can be known by natural reason, may not also be taught us by another science so far as they fall within revelation. Hence theology included in sacred doctrine differs in kind from that theology which is part of philosophy.

Art. 2 —Whether sacred doctrine is a science?

Objection 1: It seems that sacred doctrine is not a science. For every science proceeds from self-evident principles. But sacred doctrine proceeds from articles of faith which are not self-evident, since their truth is not admitted by all: "For all men have not faith" (2 Thess. 3:2). Therefore sacred doctrine is not a science.

Objection 2: Further, no science deals with individual facts. But this sacred science treats of individual facts, such as the deeds of Abraham, Isaac and Jacob and such like. Therefore sacred doctrine is not a science.

On the contrary, Augustine says (De Trin. xiv, 1) "to this science alone belongs that whereby saving faith is begotten, nourished, protected and strengthened." But this can be said of no science except sacred doctrine. Therefore sacred doctrine is a science.

I answer that, Sacred doctrine is a science. We must bear in mind that there are two kinds of sciences. There are some which proceed from a principle known by the natural light of intelligence, such as arithmetic and geometry and the like. There are some which proceed from principles known by the light of a higher science: thus the science of perspective proceeds from principles established by geometry, and music from principles established by arithmetic. So it is that sacred doctrine is a science because it proceeds from principles established by the light of a higher science, namely, the science of God and the blessed. Hence, just as the musician accepts on authority the principles taught him by the mathematician, so sacred science is established on principles revealed by God.

Reply to Objection 1: The principles of any science are either in themselves self-evident, or reducible to the conclusions of a higher science; and such, as we have said, are the principles of sacred doctrine.

Reply to Objection 2: Individual facts are treated of in sacred doctrine, not because it is concerned with them principally, but they are introduced rather both as examples to be followed in our lives (as in moral sciences) and in order to establish the authority of those men through whom the divine revelation, on which this sacred scripture or doctrine is based, has come down to us.

Art. 3 —Whether sacred doctrine is one science?

Objection 1: It seems that sacred doctrine is not one science; for according to the Philosopher (Poster. i) "that science is one which treats only of one class of subjects." But the creator and the creature, both of whom are treated of in sacred doctrine, cannot be grouped together under one class of subjects. Therefore sacred doctrine is not one science.

Objection 2: Further, in sacred doctrine we treat of angels, corporeal creatures and human morality. But these belong to separate philosophical sciences. Therefore sacred doctrine cannot be one science.

On the contrary, Holy Scripture speaks of it as one science: "Wisdom gave him the knowledge [scientiam] of holy things" (Wis. 10:10).

I answer that, Sacred doctrine is one science. The unity of a faculty or habit is to be gauged by its object, not indeed, in its material aspect, but as regards the precise formality under which it is an object. For example, man, ass, stone agree in the one precise formality of being colored; and color is the formal object of sight. Therefore, because Sacred Scripture considers things precisely under the formality of being divinely revealed, whatever has been divinely revealed possesses the one precise formality of the object of this science; and therefore is included under sacred doctrine as under one science.

Reply to Objection 1: Sacred doctrine does not treat of God and creatures equally, but of God primarily, and of creatures only so far as they are referable to God as their beginning or end. Hence the unity of this science is not impaired.

Reply to Objection 2: Nothing prevents inferior faculties or habits from being differentiated by something which falls under a higher faculty or habit as well; because the higher faculty or habit regards the object in its more universal formality, as the object of the "common sense" is whatever affects the senses, including, therefore, whatever is visible or audible. Hence the "common sense," although one faculty, extends to all the objects of the five senses. Similarly, objects which are the subject-matter of different philosophical sciences can yet be treated of by this one single sacred science under one aspect precisely so far as they can be included in revelation. So that in this way, sacred doctrine bears, as it were, the stamp of the divine science which is one and simple, yet extends to everything.

Art. 4 —Whether sacred doctrine is a practical science?

Objection 1: It seems that sacred doctrine is a practical science; for a practical science is that which ends in action according to the Philosopher (Metaph. ii). But sacred doctrine is ordained to action: "Be ye doers of the word, and not hearers only" (James 1:22). Therefore sacred doctrine is a practical science.

Objection 2: Further, sacred doctrine is divided into the Old and the New Law. But law implies a moral science which is a practical science. Therefore sacred doctrine is a practical science.

On the contrary, Every practical science is concerned with human operations; as moral science is concerned with human acts, and architecture with buildings. But sacred doctrine is chiefly concerned with God, whose handiwork is especially man. Therefore it is not a practical but a speculative science.

I answer that, Sacred doctrine, being one, extends to things which belong to different philosophical sciences because it considers in each the same formal aspect, namely, so far as they can be known through divine revelation. Hence, although among the philosophical sciences one is speculative and another practical, nevertheless sacred doctrine includes both; as God, by one and the same science, knows both Himself and His works. Still, it is speculative rather than practical because it is more concerned with divine things than with human acts; though it does treat even of these latter, inasmuch as man is ordained by them to the perfect knowledge of God in which consists eternal bliss. This is a sufficient answer to the Objections.

Art. 5 —Whether sacred doctrine is nobler than other sciences?

Objection 1: It seems that sacred doctrine is not nobler than other sciences; for the nobility of a science depends on the certitude it establishes. But other sciences, the principles of which cannot be doubted, seem to be more certain than sacred doctrine; for its principles—namely, articles of faith—can be doubted. Therefore other sciences seem to be nobler.

Objection 2: Further, it is the sign of a lower science to depend upon a higher; as music depends on arithmetic. But sacred doctrine does in a sense depend upon philosophical sciences; for Jerome observes, in his Epistle to Magnus, that "the ancient doctors so enriched their books with the ideas and phrases of the philosophers, that thou knowest not what more to admire in them, their profane erudition or their scriptural learning." Therefore sacred doctrine is inferior to other sciences.

On the contrary, Other sciences are called the handmaidens of this one: "Wisdom sent her maids to invite to the tower" (Prov. 9:3).

I answer that, Since this science is partly speculative and partly practical, it transcends all others speculative and practical. Now one speculative science is said to be nobler than another, either by reason of its greater certitude, or by reason of the higher worth of its subject-matter. In both these respects this science surpasses other speculative sciences; in point of greater certitude, because other sciences derive their certitude from the natural light of human reason, which can err; whereas this derives its certitude from the light of divine knowledge, which cannot be misled: in point of the higher worth of its subject-matter because this science treats chiefly of those things which by their sublimity transcend human reason; while other sciences consider only those things which are within reason's grasp. Of the practical sciences, that one is nobler which is ordained to a further purpose, as political science is nobler than military science; for the good of the army is directed to the good of the State. But the purpose of this science, in so far as it is practical, is eternal bliss; to which as to an ultimate end the purposes of every practical science are directed. Hence it is clear that from every standpoint, it is nobler than other sciences.

Reply to Objection 1: It may well happen that what is in itself the more certain may seem to us the less certain on account of the weakness of our intelligence, "which is dazzled by the clearest objects of nature; as the owl is dazzled by the light of the sun" (Metaph. ii, lect. i). Hence the fact that some happen to doubt about articles of faith is not due to the uncertain nature of the truths, but to the weakness of human intelligence; yet the slenderest knowledge that may be obtained of the highest things is more desirable than the most certain knowledge obtained of lesser things, as is said in de Animalibus xi.

Reply to Objection 2: This science can in a sense depend upon the philosophical sciences, not as though it stood in need of them, but only in order to make its teaching clearer. For it accepts its principles not from other sciences, but immediately from God, by revelation. Therefore it does not depend upon other sciences as upon the higher, but makes use of them as of the lesser, and as handmaidens: even so the master sciences make use of the sciences that supply their materials, as political of military science. That it thus uses them is not due to its own defect or insufficiency, but to the defect of our intelligence, which is more easily led by what is known through natural reason (from which proceed the other sciences) to that which is above reason, such as are the teachings of this science.

Art. 6 —Whether this doctrine is the same as wisdom?

Objection 1: It seems that this doctrine is not the same as wisdom. For no doctrine which borrows its principles is worthy of the name of wisdom; seeing that the wise man directs, and is not directed (Metaph. i). But this doctrine borrows its principles. Therefore this science is not wisdom.

Objection 2: Further, it is a part of wisdom to prove the principles of other sciences. Hence it is called the chief of sciences, as is clear in Ethic. vi. But this doctrine does not prove the principles of other sciences. Therefore it is not the same as wisdom.

Objection 3: Further, this doctrine is acquired by study, whereas wisdom is acquired by God's inspiration; so that it is numbered among the gifts of the Holy Spirit (Is. 11:2). Therefore this doctrine is not the same as wisdom.

On the contrary, It is written (Dt. 4:6): "This is your wisdom and understanding in the sight of nations."

I answer that, This doctrine is wisdom above all human wisdom; not merely in any one order, but absolutely. For since it is the part of a wise man to arrange and to judge, and since lesser matters should be judged in the light of some higher principle, he is said to be wise in any one order who considers the highest principle in that order: thus in the order of building, he who plans the form of the house is called wise and architect, in opposition to the inferior laborers who trim the wood and make ready the stones: "As a wise architect, I have laid the foundation" (1 Cor. 3:10). Again, in the order of all human life, the prudent man is called wise, inasmuch as he directs his acts to a fitting end: "Wisdom is prudence to a man" (Prov. 10: 23). Therefore he who considers absolutely the highest cause of the whole universe, namely God, is most of all called wise. Hence wisdom is said to be the knowledge of divine things, as Augustine says (De Trin. xii, 14). But sacred doctrine essentially treats of God viewed as the highest cause—not only so far as He can be known through creatures just as philosophers knew Him—"That which is known of God is manifest in them" (Rm. 1:19)—but also as far as He is known to Himself alone and revealed to others. Hence sacred doctrine is especially called wisdom. **Reply to Objection 1:** Sacred doctrine derives its principles not from any human knowledge, but from the divine knowledge, through which, as through the highest wisdom, all our knowledge is set in order.

Reply to Objection 2: The principles of other sciences either are evident and cannot be proved, or are proved by natural reason through some other science. But the knowledge proper to this science comes through revelation and not through natural reason. Therefore it has no concern to prove the principles of other sciences, but only to judge of them. Whatsoever is found in other sciences contrary to any truth of this science must be condemned as false: "Destroying counsels and every height that exalteth itself against the knowledge of God" (2 Cor. 10:4,5).

Reply to Objection 3: Since judgment appertains to wisdom, the twofold manner of judging produces a twofold wisdom. A man may judge in one way by inclination, as whoever has the habit of a virtue judges rightly of what concerns that virtue by his very inclination towards it. Hence it is the virtuous man, as we read, who is the measure and rule of human acts. In another way, by knowledge, just as a man learned in moral science might be able to judge rightly about virtuous acts, though he had not the virtue. The first manner of judging divine things belongs to that wisdom which is set down among the gifts of the Holy Ghost: "The spiritual man judgeth all things" (1 Cor. 2:15). And Dionysius says (Div. Nom. ii): "Hierotheus is taught not by mere learning, but by experience of divine things." The second manner of judging belongs to this doctrine which is acquired by study, though its principles are obtained by revelation.

Art. 7 —Whether God is the object of this science?

Objection 1: It seems that God is not the object of this science. For in every science, the nature of its object is presupposed. But this science cannot presuppose the essence of God, for Damascene says (De Fide Orth. i, iv): "It is impossible to define the essence of God." Therefore God is not the object of this science.

Objection 2: Further, whatever conclusions are reached in any science must be comprehended under the object of the science. But in Holy Writ we reach conclusions not only concerning God, but concerning many other things, such as creatures and human morality. Therefore God is not the object of this science.

On the contrary, The object of the science is that of which it principally treats. But in this science, the treatment is mainly about God; for it is called theology, as treating of God. Therefore God is the object of this science.

I answer that, God is the object of this science. The relation between a science and its object is the same as that between a habit or faculty and its object. Now properly speaking, the object of a faculty or habit is the thing under the aspect of which all things are referred to that faculty or habit, as man and stone are referred to the faculty of sight in that they are colored. Hence colored things are the proper objects of sight. But in sacred science, all things are treated of under the aspect of God: either because they are God Himself or because they refer to God as their beginning and end. Hence it follows that God is in very truth the object of this science. This is clear also from the principles of this science, namely, the articles of faith, for faith is about God. The object of the principles and of the whole science must be the same, since the whole science is contained virtually in its principles. Some, however, looking to what is treated of in this science, and not to the aspect under which it is treated, have asserted the object of this science to be something other than God—that is, either things and signs; or the works of salvation; or the whole Christ, as the head and members. Of all these things, in truth, we treat in this science, but so far as they have reference to God.

Reply to Objection 1: Although we cannot know in what consists the essence of God, nevertheless in this science we make use of His effects, either of nature or of grace, in place of a definition, in regard to whatever is treated of in this science concerning God; even as in some philosophical sciences we demonstrate something about a cause from its effect, by taking the effect in place of a definition of the cause.

Reply to Objection 2: Whatever other conclusions are reached in this sacred science are comprehended under God, not as parts or species or accidents but as in some way related to Him.

Art. 8 —Whether sacred doctrine is a matter of argument?

Objection 1: It seems this doctrine is not a matter of argument. For Ambrose says (De Fide 1): "Put arguments aside where faith is sought." But in this doctrine, faith especially is sought: "But these things are written that you may believe" (Jn. 20:31). Therefore sacred doctrine is not a matter of argument.

Objection 2: Further, if it is a matter of argument, the argument is either from authority or from reason. If it is from authority, it seems unbefitting its dignity, for the proof from authority is the weakest form of proof. But if it is from reason, this is unbefitting its end, because, according to Gregory (Hom. 26), "faith has no merit in those things of which human reason brings its own experience." Therefore sacred doctrine is not a matter of argument.

On the contrary, The Scripture says that a bishop should "embrace that faithful word which is according to doctrine, that he may be able to exhort in sound doctrine and to convince the gainsayers" (Titus 1:9).

I answer that, As other sciences do not argue in proof of their principles, but argue from their principles to demonstrate other truths in these sciences: so this doctrine does not argue in proof of its principles, which are the articles of faith, but from them it goes on to prove something else; as the Apostle from the resurrection of Christ argues in proof of the general resurrection (1 Cor. 15). However, it is to be borne in mind, in regard to the philosophical sciences, that the inferior sciences neither prove their principles nor dispute with those who deny them, but leave this to a higher science; whereas the highest of them, viz. metaphysics, can dispute with one who denies its principles, if only the opponent will make some concession; but if he concede nothing, it can have no dispute with him, though it can answer his objections. Hence Sacred Scripture, since it has no science above itself, can dispute with one who denies its principles only if the opponent admits some at least of the truths obtained through divine revelation; thus we can argue with heretics from texts in Holy Writ, and against those who deny one article of faith, we can argue from another. If our opponent believes nothing of divine revelation, there is no longer any means of proving the articles of faith by reasoning, but only of answering his objections— if he has any—against faith. Since faith rests upon infallible truth, and since the contrary of a truth can never be demonstrated, it is clear that the arguments brought against faith cannot be demonstrations, but are difficulties that can be answered.

Reply to Objection 1: Although arguments from human reason cannot avail to prove what must be received on faith, nevertheless, this doctrine argues from articles of faith to other truths.

Reply to Objection 2: This doctrine is especially based upon arguments from authority, inasmuch as its principles are obtained by revelation: thus we ought to believe on the authority of those to whom the revelation has been made. Nor does this take away from the dignity of this doctrine, for although the argument from authority based on human reason is the weakest, yet the argument from authority based on divine revelation is the strongest. But sacred doctrine makes use even of human reason, not, indeed, to prove faith (for thereby the merit of faith would come to an end), but to make clear other things that are put forward in this doctrine. Since therefore grace does not destroy nature but perfects it, natural reason should minister to faith as the natural bent of the will ministers to charity. Hence the Apostle says: "Bringing into captivity every understanding unto the obedience of Christ" (2 Cor. 10:5). Hence sacred doctrine makes use also of the authority of philosophers in those questions in which they were able to know the truth by natural reason, as Paul quotes a saying of Aratus: "As some also of your own poets said: For we are also His offspring" (Acts 17:28). Nevertheless, sacred doctrine makes use of these authorities as extrinsic and probable arguments; but properly uses the authority of the canonical Scriptures as an incontrovertible proof, and the authority of the doctors of the Church as one that may properly be used, yet merely as probable. For our faith rests upon the revelation made to the apostles and prophets who wrote the canonical books, and not on the revelations (if any such there are) made to other doctors. Hence Augustine says (Epis. ad Hieron. xix, 1): "Only those books of Scripture which are called canonical have I learned to hold in such honor as to believe their authors have not erred in any way in writing them. But other authors I so read as not to deem everything in their works to be true, merely on account of their having so thought and written, whatever may have been their holiness and learning."

Think about it.

1. According to Aquinas, why is human reason insufficient to learn the whole truth?
2. How does Aquinas answer the objection that an argument from authority (that is, using scripture to prove a point) is not necessarily a weak form of argument?

late 13ᵗʰ century CE

98. Travels of Marco Polo

Translated by Henry Yule

The Travels of Marco Polo, known alternately as *Books of the Marvels of the World* or *Il Milione* ("The Million") is an account of the journeys of the Italian explorer Marco Polo through Persia, Central Asia, China, and Indonesia between 1271 and 1291. Marco Polo's stories were written down by the Italian writer Rustichello of Pisa, who found himself sharing a prison cell with Polo in 1298. The book was read widely in the 14th century and afterward. Here follow three excerpts.

The Travels of Marco Polo, ed. Henri Cordier, trans. Henry Yule. John Murray Publishers Limited, 1920. Copyright in the Public Domain.

How the Great Kaan Causes Stores of Corn to be Made, to Help his People Withal in Time of Dearth

You must know that when the Emperor sees that corn is cheap and abundant, he buys up large quantities, and has it stored in all his provinces in great granaries, where it is so well looked after that it will keep for three or four years.

And this applies, let me tell you, to all kinds of corn, whether wheat, barley, millet, rice, panic, or what not, and when there is any scarcity of a particular kind of corn, he causes that to be issued. And if the price of the corn is at one bezant the measure, he lets them have it at a bezant for four measures, or at whatever price will produce general cheapness; and every one can have food in this way. And by this providence of the Emperor's, his people can never suffer from dearth. He does the same over his whole Empire; causing these supplies to be stored everywhere, according to calculation of the wants and necessities of the people.

Of the Charity of the Emperor to the Poor

I have told you how the Great Kaan provides for the distribution of necessaries to his people in time of dearth, by making store in time of cheapness. Now I will tell you of his alms and great charity to the poor of his city of Cambaluc.

You see he causes selection to be made of a number of families in the city which are in a state of indigence, and of such families some may consist of six in the house, some of eight, some of ten, more or fewer in each as it may hap, but the whole number being very great. And each family he causes annually to be supplied with wheat and other corn sufficient for the whole year. And this he never fails to do every year. Moreover, all those who choose to go to the daily dole at the Court receive a great loaf apiece, hot from the baking, and nobody is denied; for so

the Lord hath ordered. And so some 30,000 people go for it every day from year's end to year's end. Now this is a great goodness in the Emperor to take pity of his poor people thus! And they benefit so much by it that they worship him as he were God.

[He also provides the poor with clothes. For he lays a tithe upon all wool, silk, hemp, and the like, from which clothing can be made; and he has these woven and laid up in a building set apart for the purpose; and as all artizans are bound to give a day's labour weekly, in this way the Kaan has these stuffs made into clothing for those poor families, suitable for summer or winter, according to the time of year. He also provides the clothing for his troops, and has woollens woven for them in every city, the material for which is furnished by the tithe aforesaid. You should know that the Tartars, before they were converted to the religion of the Idolaters, never practised almsgiving. Indeed, when any poor man begged of them they would tell him, "Go with God's curse, for if He loved you as He loves me, He would have provided for you." But the sages of the Idolaters, and especially the *Bacsis* mentioned before, told the Great Kaan that it was a good work to provide for the poor, and that his idols would be greatly pleased if he did so. And since then he has taken to do for the poor so much as you have heard.]

Concerning the Province of Tebet

After those five days' march that I spoke of, you enter a province which has been sorely ravaged; and this was done in the wars of Mongu Kaan. There are indeed towns and villages and hamlets, but all harried and destroyed.

In this region you find quantities of canes, full three palms in girth and fifteen paces in length, with some three palms' interval between the joints. And let me tell you that merchants and other travellers through that country are wont at nightfall to gather these canes and make fires of them; for as they burn they make such loud reports that the lions and bears and other wild beasts are greatly frightened, and make off as fast as possible; in fact nothing will induce them to come nigh a fire of that sort. So you see the travellers make those fires to protect themselves and their cattle from the wild beasts which have so greatly multiplied since the devastation of the country. And 'tis this great multiplication of the wild beasts that prevents the country from being reoccupied. In fact but for the help of these canes, which make such a noise in burning that the beasts are terrified and kept at a distance, no one would be able even to travel through the land.

I will tell you how it is that the canes make such a noise. The people cut the green canes, of which there are vast numbers, and set fire to a heap of them at once. After they have been awhile burning they burst asunder, and this makes such a loud report that you might hear it ten miles off. In fact, any one unused to this noise, who should hear it unexpectedly, might easily go into a wound or die of fright. But those who are used to it care nothing about it. Hence those who are not used to it stuff their ears well with cotton, and wrap up their heads and faces with all the clothes they can muster; and so they get along until they have become used to the sound. 'Tis just the same with horses. Those which are unused to these noises are so alarmed by them that they break away from their halters and heel-ropes, and many a man has lost his beasts in this way. So those who would avoid losing their horses take care to tie all four legs and peg the ropes down strongly, and to wrap the heads and eyes and ears of the animals closely, and so they save them. But horses also, when they have heard the noise several times, cease to mind it. I tell you the truth, however, when I say that the first time you hear it nothing can be more alarming. And yet, in spite of all, the lions and bears and other wild beasts will sometimes come and do much mischief; for their numbers are great in those tracts.

You ride for 20 days without finding any inhabited spot, so that travellers are obliged to carry all their provisions with them, and are constantly falling in with those wild beasts which are so numerous and so dangerous. After that you come at length to a tract where there are towns and villages in considerable numbers. The people of those towns have a strange custom in regard to marriage which I will now relate.

No man of that country would on any consideration take to wife a girl who was a maid; for they say a wife is nothing worth unless she has been used to consort with men. And their custom is this, that when travellers come that way, the old women of the place get ready, and take their unmarried daughters or other girls related to them, and go to the strangers who are passing, and make over the young women to whomsoever will accept them; and the travellers take them accordingly and do their pleasure; after which the girls are restored to the old women who brought them, for they are not allowed to follow the strangers away from their home. In this manner people travelling that way, when they reach a village or hamlet or other inhabited place, shall find perhaps 20 or 30 girls at their disposal. And if the travellers lodge with those people they shall have as many young women as they could wish coming to court them! You must know too that the traveller is expected to give the girl who has been with him a ring or some other trifle, something in fact that she can show as a lover's token when she comes to be married. And it is for this in truth and for this alone that they follow that custom; for every girl is expected to obtain at least 20 such tokens in the way I have described before she can be married. And those who have most tokens, and so can show they have been most run after, are in the highest esteem, and most sought in marriage, because they say the charms of such an one are greatest. But after marriage these people hold their wives very dear, and would consider it a great villainy for a man to meddle with another's wife; and thus though the wives have before marriage acted as you have heard, they are kept with great care from light conduct afterwards.

Now I have related to you this marriage custom as a good story to tell, and to show what a fine country that is for young fellows to go to!

The people are Idolaters and an evil generation, holding it no sin to rob and maltreat: in fact, they are the greatest brigands on earth. They live by the chase, as well as on their cattle and the fruits of the earth.

I should tell you also that in this country there are many of the animals that produce musk, which are called in the Tartar language *Gudderi*. Those rascals have great numbers of large and fine dogs, which are of great service in catching the musk-beasts, and so they procure great abundance of musk. They have none of the Great Kaan's paper money, but use salt instead of money. They are very poorly clad, for their clothes are only of the skins of beasts, and of canvas, and of buckram. They have a language of their own, and they are called Tebet. And this country of TEBET forms a very great province, of which I will give you a brief account.

Treating of the Great Province of Abash, Which is Middle India, and is on the Mainland

Abash is a very great Province, and you must know that it constitutes the MIDDLE INDIA; and it is on the mainland. There are in it six great Kings with six great Kingdoms; and of these six Kings there are three that are Christians and three that are Saracens; but the greatest of all the six is a Christian, and all the others are subject to him.

The Christians in this country bear three marks on the face; one from the forehead to the middle of the nose, and one on either cheek. These marks are made with a hot iron, and form part of their baptism; for after that they have been baptised with water, these three marks are made, partly as a token of gentility, and partly as the completion of their baptism. There are also Jews in the country, and these bear two marks, one on either cheek; and the Saracens have but one, to wit, on the forehead extending halfway down the nose.

The Great King lives in the middle of the country, the Saracens towards Aden. St. Thomas the Apostle preached in this region, and after he had converted the people he went away to the province of Maabar, where he died; and there his body lies, as I have told you in a former place.

The people here are excellent soldiers, and they go on horseback, for they have horses in plenty. Well they may; for they are in daily war with the Soldan of ADEN, and with the Nubians, and a variety of other nations. I will tell you a famous story of what befel in the year of Christ, 1288.

You must know that this Christian King, who is the Lord of the Province of Abash, declared his intention to go on pilgrimage to Jerusalem to adore the Holy Sepulchre of Our Lord God Jesus Christ the Saviour. But his Barons said that for him to go in person would be to run too great a risk; and they recommended him to send some bishop or prelate in his stead. So the King assented to the counsel which his Barons gave, and despatched a certain Bishop of his, a man of very holy life. The Bishop then departed and travelled by land and by sea till he arrived at the Holy Sepulchre, and there he paid it such honour as Christian man is bound to do, and presented a great offering on the part of his King who had sent him in his own stead.

And when he had done all that behoved him, he set out again and travelled day by day till he got to Aden. Now that is a Kingdom wherein Christians are held in great detestation, for the people are all Saracens, and their enemies unto the death. So when the Soldan of Aden heard that this man was a Christian and a Bishop, and an envoy of the Great King of Abash, he had him seized and demanded of him if he were a Christian? To this the Bishop replied that he was a Christian indeed. The Soldan then told him that unless he would turn to the Law of Mahommet he should work him great shame and dishonour. The Bishop answered that they might kill him ere he would deny his Creator.

When the Soldan heard that he waxed wroth, and ordered that the Bishop should be circumcised.

So they took and circumcised him after the manner of the Saracens. And then the Soldan told him that he had been thus put to shame in despite to the King his master. And so they let him go.

The Bishop was sorely cut to the heart for the shame that had been wrought him, but he took comfort because it had befallen him in holding fast by the Law of Our Lord Jesus Christ; and the Lord God would recompense his soul in the world to come.

So when he was healed he set out and travelled by land and by sea till he reached the King his Lord in the Kingdom of Abash. And when the King beheld him, he welcomed him with great joy and gladness. And he asked him all about the Holy Sepulchre; and the Bishop related all about it truly, the King listening the while as to a most holy matter in all faith. But when the Bishop had told all about Jerusalem, he then related the outrage done on him by the Soldan of Aden in the King's despite. Great was the King's wrath and grief when he heard that; and it so disturbed him that he was like to die of vexation. And at length his words waxed so loud that all those round about could hear what he was saying. He vowed that he would never wear crown or hold kingdom if he took not such condign vengeance on the Soldan of Aden that all the world should ring therewithal, even until the insult had been well and thoroughly redressed.

And what shall I say of it? He straightway caused the array of his horse and foot to be mustered, and great numbers of elephants with castles to be prepared to accompany them; and when all was ready he set out with his army and advanced till he entered the Kingdom of Aden in great force. The Kings of this province of Aden were well aware of the King's advance against them, and went to encounter him at the strongest pass on their frontier, with a great force of armed men, in order to bar the enemy from entering their territory. When the King arrived at this strong pass where the Saracens had taken post, a battle began, fierce and fell on both sides, for they were very bitter against each other. But it came to pass, as it pleased our Lord God Jesus Christ, that

the Kings of the Saracens, who were three in number, could not stand against the Christians, for they are not such good soldiers as the Christians are. So the Saracens were defeated, and a marvellous number of them slain, and the King of Abash entered the Kingdom of Aden with all his host. The Saracens made various sallies on them in the narrow defiles, but it availed nothing; they were always beaten and slain. And when the King had greatly wasted and destroyed the kingdom of his enemy, and had remained in it more than a month with all his host, continually slaying the Saracens, and ravaging their lands (so that great numbers of them perished), he thought it time to return to his own kingdom, which he could now do with great honour. Indeed he could tarry no longer, nor could he, as he was aware, do more injury to the enemy; for he would have had to force a way by still stronger passes, where, in the narrow defiles, a handful of men might cause him heavy loss. So he quitted the enemy's Kingdom of Aden and began to retire. And he with his host got back to their own country of Abash in great triumph and rejoicing; for he had well avenged the shame cast on him and on his Bishop for his sake. For they had slain so many Saracens, and so wasted and harried the land, that 'twas something to be astonished at. And in sooth 'twas a deed well done! For it is not to be borne that the dogs of Saracens should lord it over good Christian people! Now you have heard the story.

I have still some particulars to tell you of the same province. It abounds greatly in all kinds of victual; and the people live on flesh and rice and milk and sesame. They have plenty of elephants, not that they are bred in the country, but they are brought from the Islands of the other India. They have however many giraffes, which are produced in the country; besides bears, leopards, lions in abundance, and many other passing strange beasts. They have also numerous wild asses; and cocks and hens the most beautiful that exist, and many other kind of birds. For instance, they have ostriches that are nearly as big as asses; and plenty of beautiful parrots, with apes of sundry kinds, and baboons and other monkeys that have countenances all but human.

There are numerous cities and villages in this province of Abash, and many merchants; for there is much trade to be done there. The people also manufacture very fine buckrams and other cloths of cotton.

There is no more to say on the subject; so now let us go forward and tell you of the province of Aden.

Think about it.

1. According to this account, what did Kubilai Khan do for the poor people in his empire?
2. Why does the author consider Tibet an excellent place for young men to visit?
3. What is the moral or message of the tale about the Christian bishop who was dishonored by the Sultan of Aden?

---

late 13ᵗʰ century CE

99. The Customs of Cambodia

Translated by Peter Harris

A Chinese diplomat serving Temür Khan (Emperor Chengzong of the Yuan Dynasty) by the name of Zhou Daguan (1266–1346) wrote *The Customs of Cambodia* (*Zhenla feng tu ji*) after visiting the Khmer Empire in Cambodia in 1296 and 1297. The book is an important source of information on the customs of the people of Khmer, as the following extracts illustrate.

According to the *Treatise on the Various Foreigners*, Cambodia is seven thousand li in breadth. Going north from the capital, it is fifteen days by road to Champa, and to the southwest it is fifteen days' journey to Siam. In the south it is ten days' journey to Fanyu, and to the east there is the ocean.

It has long been a trading country.

The great Mandate of Heaven that the sacred dynasty has received includes everywhere within the four seas. Marshal Sodu set up a province in Champa, and sent out a general and a senior commander, who went there together. In the end they were seized and did not return. In the sixth month of the year *youwei* in the Yuanzhen reign period (1295), the sacred Son of Heaven dispatched an envoy with

Zhou Daguan, *A Record of Cambodia: The Land and Its People*, trans. Peter Harris, pp. 46, 54–58, 64–65, 80–81. Copyright © 2007 by Silkworm Books. Reprinted with permission.

an imperial edict, and ordered me to accompany him.

In the second month of the following year, the year *bingshen* in the Yuanzhen reign period (1296), we left Mingzhou, and on the twentieth day of that month we set sail from the harbor at Wenzhou. On the fifteenth day of the third month we reached Champa, having been set back by adverse winds mid-journey. We arrived in Cambodia in the autumn, at the beginning of the seventh month.

We duly secured the submission of local officials. In the sixth month of the year *dingyou* in the Dade reign period (1297) we turned our boat around, and by the twelfth day of the eighth month we were back at Mingzhou, anchored off the coast.

Although I could not get to know the land, customs, and affairs of state of Cambodia in every particular, I could see enough to get a general sense of them.

THE PEOPLE

The one thing people know about southern barbarians is that they are coarse, ugly, and very black. I know nothing at all about those living on islands in the sea or in remote villages, but this is certainly true of those in the ordinary localities. When it comes to the women of the palace and women from the *nanpeng*—that is, the great houses—there are many who are as white as jade, but that is because they do not see the light of the sun.

Generally, men and women alike wrap a cloth around their waist, but apart from that they leave their smooth chests and breasts uncovered. They wear their hair in a topknot and go barefoot. This is the case even with the wives of the king.

The king has five wives, one principal wife and one for each of the four cardinal points. Below them, I have heard, there are four or five thousand concubines and other women of the palace. They also divide themselves up by rank. They only go out of the palace on rare occasions.

Every time I went inside the palace to see the king, he always came out with his principal wife, and sat at the gold window in the main room. The palace women lined up by rank in two galleries below the window. They moved to and fro to steal looks at us, and I got a very full view of them. Any family with a female beauty is bound to have her summoned into the palace.

At the lower level there are also the so-called *chenjialan*, servant women who come and go providing services inside the palace and number at least a thousand or two. In their case they all have husbands and live mixed in among ordinary people. They shave back the hair on the top of their head, which gives them the look of northerners with their "open canal" partings. They paint the area with vermilion, which they also paint on to either side of their temples. In this way they mark themselves out as being *chenjialan*. They are the only women who can go into the palace; no one else below them gets to go in. There is a continuous stream of them on the roads in front of and behind the inner palace.

Apart from wearing their hair in a topknot, ordinary women do not have ornaments in their hair like pins or combs. They just wear gold bracelets on their arms and gold rings on their fingers. The *chenjialan* and the women in the palace all wear them too. Men and women usually perfume themselves with scents made up of a mixture of sandalwood, musk, and other fragrances.

Every family practices Buddhism.

There are a lot of effeminate men in the country who go round the markets every day in groups of a dozen or so. They frequently solicit the attentions of Chinese in return for generous gifts. It is shameful and wicked.

CHILDBIRTH

As soon as they give birth the local women prepare some hot rice, mix it with salt, and put it into the entrance of the vagina. They usually take it out after a day and a night. Because of this, women do not fall sick when they are giving birth, and usually contract so as to be like young girls again.

When I first heard this I was surprised by it, and seriously doubted whether it was true. Then a girl in the family I was staying with gave birth to a child, and I got a full picture of what happened to her. The day after the birth, she took up the baby right away and went to bathe in the river with it. It was a truly amazing thing to see.

Then again, I have often heard people say that the local women are very lascivious, so that a day or two after giving birth they are immediately coupling with their husbands. If a husband doesn't meet his wife's wishes he will be abandoned right away, as Zhu Maichen was. If the husband happens to have work to do far away, if it is only for a few nights that is all right, but if it is for more than ten nights or so the wife will say, "I'm not a ghost—why am I sleeping alone?" This is how strong their sexual feelings are. That said, I have heard that there are some who exercise self-restraint.

The women age very quickly indeed, the reason being that they marry and have children young. A twenty- or thirty-year-old woman is like a Chinese woman of forty or fifty.

YOUNG GIRLS

When a family is bringing up a daughter, her father and mother are sure to wish her well by saying, "May you have what really matters—in future may you marry thousands and thousands of husbands!"

When they are seven to nine years old—if they are girls from wealthy homes—or only when they are eleven—if they come from the poorest families—girls have to get a Buddhist monk or a Daoist to take away their virginity, in what is called *zhentan*.

So every year, in the fourth month of the Chinese calendar, the authorities select a day and announce it countrywide. The families whose daughters should be ready for *zhentan* let the authorities know

in advance. The authorities first give them a huge candle. They make a mark on it, and arrange for it to be lit at dusk on the day in question. When the mark is reached the time for *zhentan* has come.

A month, fifteen days, or ten days beforehand, the parents have to choose a Buddhist monk or a Daoist. This depends on where the Buddhist and Daoist temples are. The temples often also have their own clients. Officials' families and wealthy homes all get the good, saintly Buddhist monks in advance, while the poor do not have the leisure to choose.

Wealthy and noble families give the monks wine, rice, silk and other cloth, betel nuts, silverware, and the like, goods weighing as much as a hundred piculs and worth two or three hundred ounces of Chinese silver. The smallest amount a family gives weighs ten to forty piculs, depending on how thrifty the family is.

The reason poor families only start dealing with the matter when their girls reach eleven is simply that it is hard for them to manage these things. Some wealthy families do also give money for poor girls' *zhentan*, which they call doing good work. Moreover in any one year a monk can only take charge of one girl, and once he has agreed to and accepted the benefits, he cannot make another commitment.

On the night in question a big banquet with drums and music is laid on for relatives and neighbors. A tall canopy is put up outside the entrance to the house, and various clay figurines of people and animals are laid out on top of it. There can be ten or more of these, or just three or four—or none at all in the case of poor families. They all have to do with events long ago, and they usually stay up for seven days before people start taking them down.

At dusk the monk is met with palanquin, parasol, drums, and music and brought back to the house. Two pavilions are put up, made of colorful silk. The girl sits inside one, and the monk inside the other. You can't understand what he's saying because the drums and music are making so much noise—on that night the night curfew is lifted. I have heard that when the time comes the monk goes into a room with the girl and takes away her virginity with his hand, which he then puts into some wine. Some say the parents, relatives and neighbors mark their foreheads with it, others say they all taste it. Some say the monk and the girl have sex together, others say they don't. They don't let Chinese see this, though, so I don't really know.

Toward dawn the monk is seen off again with palanquin, parasol, drums, and music. Afterward silk, cloth, and the like have to be given to the monk to redeem the body of the girl. If this is not done the girl will be the property of the monk for her whole life and won't be able to marry anyone else.

The instance of this that I saw took place early on the sixth night of the fourth month of the year *dingyou* in the Dade reign period (1297).

Before this happens, the parents always sleep together with their daughter; afterward, she is excluded from the room and goes wherever she wants without restraint or precaution. When it comes to marriage, there is a ceremony with the giving of gifts, but it is just a simple, easygoing affair. There are many who get married only after leading a dissolute life, something local custom regards as neither shameful nor odd.

On a *zhentan* night up to ten or more families from a single alley may be involved. On the city streets people are out meeting Buddhist monks and Daoists, going this way and that, and the sounds of drums and music are everywhere.

SETTLING DISPUTES

If there is a dispute among the ordinary people, it must be referred up to the king, even if it is a small matter. There are never any whippings or floggings as punishment, only fines as I have heard. Nor do they hang or behead anyone guilty of a serious crime. Instead they just dig a ditch in the ground outside the west gate of the city, put the criminal inside it, fill it up solid with earth and stones, and leave it at that. Otherwise people have their fingers or toes amputated, or their nose cut off.

There is, however, no prohibition against adultery or gambling. If a husband finds out that his wife has committed adultery, he has her lover's feet squeezed between two pieces of wood. When he is unable to bear the pain the lover gives the husband everything he owns, and only then can he get his release. Given this practice, sometimes things are set up so as to defraud people.

If a person finds a dead body by his doorway, he himself drags it with a rope to wasteland outside the city. There is never anything that could be called an inquest or official inspection.

When a family catches a thief, they can also impose their own punishment, whether it is detention, torture, or beating. There is however one standard process for the use of, say, a family that has lost something and suspects it has been stolen by someone who won't own up. They heat some oil in a cauldron until it is extremely hot, and make the person concerned put their hand in it. If they are the thief, their hand turns putrid; if they are not, their skin and flesh stay the same as before. Such are the strange laws of foreigners.

Then again, if two families have a dispute to resolve and cannot agree on right and wrong, there are twelve small stone towers [Prasat Suor Prat] on a bank opposite the palace, and the two people concerned are sent to sit in two of them. Outside, members of each family keep guard against the other. They may sit in the towers for a day or two, or for three or four days. Then for sure the one who is in the wrong becomes visibly ill, and leaves. He may have sores, or a cough or fever or something of the kind. The one who is in the right is absolutely fine. Thus right and wrong are assessed and decided on, in what is known as the judgment of heaven. Such is the spiritual power of the local gods.

A STRANGE AFFAIR

Inside the east gate there was a barbarian who had sex with his younger sister. Their skin and flesh stuck together and would not come apart. After three days without eating they both died. My fellow country-man Mr. Xue has lived in this place for thirty-five years, and says he has seen this same thing happen twice. Such then is the spiritual power of the holy Buddha in this country.

BATHING

The place is unbearably hot, and no one can go on without bathing several times a day. Even at night you have to bathe once or twice. They may never have had bathrooms, buckets, or the like, but every family is sure to have a pool, or at least a pool to share among two or three families.

Everyone, male and female, goes naked into the pool. The only exceptions are when there are parents or elderly people in the pool, in which case children and youngsters do not venture in, or when there are young people in the pool, in which case elderly people have to stay away too. For people from the same generation there are no constraints, though women do cover their vagina with their left hand when they go into the water.

Every three or four days, or every four or five days, women in the capital get together in groups of three to five and go out of the city to bathe in the river. When they get to the riverside they take off the cloth they are wrapped in and go into the water. Those gathering together in the river often number in thousands. Even the women from the great houses join in, without the slightest embarrassment. You get to see everything, from head to toe.

In the big river outside the city not a day passes without this happening. On their leisure days Chinese regard it as quite a pleasant thing to go along and watch; and I have heard that there are those who go into the water for a surreptitious encounter.

The river is always warm, like heated water. Only in the fifth watch does it get a little cooler. But as soon as the sun appears it warms up again.

Think about it.

1. What customs does Zhou Daguan find unusual?

Timeline of Significant Events

Stone Age

2.3 million years ago	First humans appear
12,500 BCE	Beginning of Natufian culture, world's earliest known settlements
6000 BCE	Çatalhöyük built
5300 BCE	Tărtăria tablets, earliest example of proto-writing, inscribed

Bronze Age

3100-2900 BCE	The rise of Sumer; development of cuneiform, first writing system.
3000 BCE	Zhuangqiao tomb relics; first evidence of Chinese proto-writing
2950 BCE	Norte Chico, oldest civilization in the Americas, rises in the Supe Valley
2900 BCE	Narmer unites Egypt
2700 BCE	Gilgamesh reigns in Uruk
2500 BCE	Oldest cities built in Indus River valley (Harappan civilization)
2350 BCE	Sargon of Akkad creates Akkadian Empire
2070 BCE	Xia dynasty founded in China
2000 BCE	Minoan civilization appears on Crete
1772 BCE	Hammurabi publishes law code
1700-1100 BCE	Aryans move into northern India; Rig Veda composed
1628 BCE	Volcano erupts at Santorini (Thera)
1600 BCE	Shang dynasty founded in China
1600 BCE	Rise of Mycenaeans in Greece
1500 BCE	First Central American civilization appears (Olmecs)
1482 BCE	Thutmose III defeats Canaanites in Battle of Megiddo
1250 BCE	Earliest examples of Chinese writing (oracle bones)
1207 BCE	Merneptah composes Merneptah Stela (first mention of Israel)

Iron Age

1200 BCE	Trojan War
1175 BCE	Philistines settle in Gaza Strip
1045 BCE	King Wu establishes Zhou dynasty in China
1000 BCE	Zarathustra composes the Gathas
980 BCE	Solomon builds Temple in Jerusalem
934 BCE	Israel splits into two kingdoms—Israel and Judah
750 BCE	City of Rome built
720 BCE	Assyrians conquer kingdom of Israel
622 BCE	Josiah of Judah begins religious reforms
586 BCE	Babylonians conquer kingdom of Judah
563 BCE	Siddhartha Gautama born (the Buddha)
551 BCE	Birth of Confucius
539 BCE	Cyrus the Great conquers Babylon, frees Jewish exiles
515 BCE	Second Temple built in Jerusalem

Early Classical Period

509 BCE	Founding of the Roman Republic
490 BCE	Athenians win Battle of Marathon against the Persians
450 BCE	First evidence of writing in India since the fall of the Harappan civilization
400 BCE	Early versions of the Ramayana and Mahabharata completed in India
399 BCE	Trial and execution of Socrates
387 BCE	Plato founds Academy in Athens
331 BCE	Alexander defeats Persians at Battle of Gaugamela
300 BCE	Laozi (Daodejing) completed in China
268-232 BCE	Reign of Ashoka of the Mauryan Empire in India
250 BCE	First translation of the Hebrew Bible into another language (Greek)
221 BCE	Qin Shi Huang establishes first Chinese empire

Middle Classical Period

166-160 BCE	Maccabean Revolt against Seleucids
141-87 BCE	Reign of Wu Di of the Han dynasty in China
44 BCE	Assassination of Julius Caesar
27 BCE	Octavian made Augustus Caesar, first emperor of Rome
6 CE	Birth of Jesus
35-36 CE	Ministry of Jesus
50-120 CE	Earliest Christian texts written, including the New Testament

| 70 CE | Romans destroy Jerusalem and its Temple |
| 140 CE | Kanishka convenes Fourth Buddhist Council |

Late Classical Period

250 CE	The Classic period of Maya civilization begins
313 CE	Edict of Milan; Christianity made legal under Constantine
325 CE	Council of Nicea
350 CE	Ezana of Aksum embraces Christianity
381 CE	Christianity made official religion of Roman Empire
395 CE	Roman Empire splits into Eastern and Western empires
486 CE	Clovis defeats Syagrius, last surviving official of the Western Roman Empire
527-565 CE	Reign of Byzantine Emperor Justinian the Great
570 CE	Birth of Muhammad

Postclassical Period

622 CE	Date of the *Hijra* (Muhammad's flight to Medina)
645 CE	Taika Reform instituted in Japan
656-661 CE	First Islamic Civil War (First Fitna); creation of Sunni and Shia factions
710 CE	Muslims invade Spain
713-756 CE	Reign of Xuanzong; cultural high point of Tang dynasty in China
800 CE	Charlemagne crowned Holy Roman Emperor
993-1059 CE	Hu Yüan revives Confucianism in China
1037 CE	Tughril Beg founds the Seljuq Empire of the Turks
1066 CE	William the Conqueror wins Battle of Hastings
1095 CE	First Crusade begins
1180-1185 CE	Genpei War in Japan; Minamoto clan victorious
1206-1227 CE	Reign of Genghis Khan of the Mongols
1215 CE	John of England signs Magna Carta
1271 CE	Marco Polo embarks on a journey to Asia

Readings Arranged According to Subject Matter

The selections in this volume may be used to develop prompts for longer essays. It is hoped this arrangement will assist instructors in coming up with some ideas.

Legal Codes

3. The Code of Ur-Namma
6. The Code of Hammurabi
9. Old Hittite Laws
12. Middle Assyrian Laws
21. The Yahwist Legend (Ten Commandments)
23. The Josianic Code
47. Edicts of Ashoka
69. Codex Theodosianus
71. Lex Salica
75. The Tang Code

Ethics

1. The Instructions of Shuruppak
2. The Precepts of Ptahhotep
29. The Deuteronomic History (additions) (Ten Commandments)
35. The Analects
40. The Nicomachean Ethics
47. Edicts of Ashoka
59. The Laws of Manu
75. The Tang Code
83. Havamal
86. Revival of the Religious Sciences

The Nature of the Gods

4. The Cursing of Akkade
7. The Epic of Gilgamesh
8. The Enuma Elish
10. The Kirta Epic
11. Great Hymn to the Aten
13. The Rig Veda
14. The Legend of the Destruction of Mankind
15. Early Israelite Victory Hymns
16. The Gathas
22. The Brihadaranyaka Upanishad
28. Second Isaiah
49. Luxuriant Dew of the Spring and Autumn Annals
53. On the Nature of the Gods
72. History of the Franks
73. The Quran
88. A History of Deeds Done Beyond the Sea
91. The Guide for the Perplexed
96. The Masnavi

Service of the Gods

4. The Cursing of Akkade
21. The Yahwist Legend (Ten Commandments)
72. History of the Franks
76. The Popol Vuh

Authority and Government

8. The Enuma Elish
10. The Kirta Epic
17. The Shijing
18. The Shujing
24. The Deuteronomic History
30. Enquiries

31. Antigone
33. The Ramayana
35. The Analects (Part 8)
37. The Laozi
41. The Book of Lord Shang
42. The Mengzi
45. The Arthashastra
48. The Han Feizi
49. Luxuriant Dew of the Spring and Autumn Annals
50. Records of the Grand Historian
51. Discourses on Salt and Iron
65. Letter to the Palestinians
66. Letter to Valentinian
69. Codex Theodosianus
74. The Pact of Ibn Muslamah
77. The Kota Kapur Inscription
78. The Nihon Shoki
82. The Life of Charlemagne
84. Memorial of a Myriad Words
87. The Alexiad
92. Venerabilim fratrem nostrum
93. The Secret History of the Mongols
98. Travels of Marco Polo

Women

12. Middle Assyrian Laws
20. Theogony, Works and Days
23. The Josianic Code
26. The Zadokite History (Jealousies)
54. Books from the Founding of the City
59. The Laws of Manu
61. Lessons for Women
62. Buddhacarita
70. The Kama Sutra
73. The Quran
79. Poems of Li Bai (Letter from Chang'an)
81. One Thousand and One Nights
83. Havamal
96. The Masnavi (Satan's snares)
99. The Customs of Cambodia

Human Nature

20. Theogony, Works and Days
21. The Yahwist Legend (Garden of Eden, Flood)
43. The Zhuangzi
46. The Xunzi
67. The City of God
68. Letter to Demetrias
90. Writings of Zhu Xi

Good and Evil

16. The Gathas
46. The Xunzi
67. The City of God

Life and Death

5. The Man Who Was Tired of Life
19. The Iliad
22. The Brihadaranyaka Upanishad
34. The Mahabharata
39. Phaedo
58. The Gospel of Mark
60. Critical Essays

War

15. Early Israelite Victory Hymns
19. The Iliad
34. The Mahabharata
36. The Mozi
41. The Book of Lord Shang
52. Commentaries on the Civil War
73. The Quran
79. Poems of Li Bai (Nefarious War)
80. Introduction to the Law of Nations
94. The Complete History
95. The Tale of the Heike

Justice

3. The Code of Ur-Namma
6. The Code of Hammurabi
9. Old Hittite Laws

12. Middle Assyrian Laws

20. Theogony

21. The Yahwist Legend (Garden of Eden, Flood)

23. The Josianic Code

25. The King of Justice

26. The Zadokite History (Flood

27. Poems of Solon

29. The Deuteronomic History (additions) (Why Jerusalem Fell)

31. Antigone

39. The Republic

67. The City of God

85. The Song of Roland

34. The Mahabharata

38. Khandaka

44. The Liji

55. The Aeneid

56. Letter to the Galatians

57. The Letter of James

62. Buddhacarita

63. The Lotus Sutra

64. Meditations

89. On the Harmony of Religion and Philosophy

97. Summa Theologica

History Writing

32. History of the Peloponnesian War

Personal/Inner Development

22. The Brihadaranyaka Upanishad